Footprint Goa

Annie Dare
4th edition

"Goa is a state of mind. It is life lived without feeling conscribed
by geography or by time. We do not measure out our life in
coffee spoons...We are surrounded by rivers and
oceans whose stillness itself contributes to this
peaceful state of mind."

Maria Aurora Couto, *Goa, A Daughter's Story*.

Goa Highlights

See colour maps at back of book

1 Morjim beach
Share the sand with some Olive Ridley turtles

2 Goan trance
Go day-glo at a trance party in Vagator, or rubberneck the leftovers the next day on the beach

3 Anjuna flea market
Pick your way through one of the world's biggest bring-and-buy sales

4 Ommm…
Limber up with some downward dog poses at the Purple Valley Yoga Centre, Assagao

5 Ingo's night bazaar
Graze through the foodstalls in this night bazaar held in Arpora on a Saturday night

6 Party hard
Head for the state's biggest and most original nightclub, Tito's in Baga

7 Ayurvedic bliss in Saligao
Refresh and replenish with a session at the Ayurveda centre in Saligao

8 Neck some *feni*
Quaff the lethal cashewbrew, *feni*, in one of Panjim's many dives

9 Rome of the east
Take a turn about the relics at Old Goa

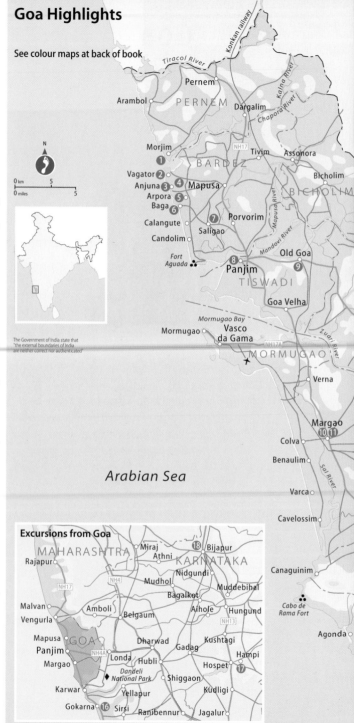

MAHARASHTRA

Vanati River

Sanguelim
Onda
SATARI
Iverm
Curdo
Valpoi

Savoi
Verem
PONDA
Pascoal
Ponda **15**
NH4A
Darbandora
Surla
Molem
GOA
SANGUEM
Dudhsagar
Falls
14

SALCETE
Calem

13 Chandor

Sanguem
Quepem
Curdi

KARNATAKA

Western Ghats

NH17
Kushavati River

QUEPEM

Jaqui

Palolem
12
Canacona
CANACONA

Talpona River

Mashen

10 Local football matches
Goa's top sport, so check out a game at Jawaharlal Nehru Fatorda Stadium in Margao

11 Margao
Tuck into a plate of fish-curry-rice in downtown Margao

12 Take it easy
Hang about in a hammock or charter a yacht in Palolem

13 Menezes-Braganza House
Scrub up for a tour round this elegant house

14 Dudhsagar waterfalls
Take a dip in the natural pools

15 Spice plantations
Spice things up with a trip to a plantation in Ponda

16 Beach life
See an Om-shaped beach in Gokarna

17 Ancient remains
Brave broader India with an excursion to the remains of the Hindu empire at Hampi

18 Bijapur
Visit a playground of the Deccani sultans on this excursion from Goa

Architectural treasures
The immense 16th-century Church of the Immaculate Conception in Panjim is one of many buildings to exhibit the Portuguese influence on the state.

A foot in the door

The bite-size chunk of lush land hemmed in by mountains on India's left haunch is a place wholly apart. Goa is India's smallest state and its only real Latin Quarter, an anomalous little pocket of coconut, paddy, fishing and fruit, where the living is easy and life is cheap and where you don't have to pay too much heed to what's happening out there over the Ghats. Goans themselves call the rest 'India' as if somehow Goa wasn't. Hell, even the beggars dress well here.

Although there are rococo and baroque marvels, its sights are no match for the giant landmarks of broader India. You'll find a humbler beauty here, in the homes of the old elite that stand crumbling in the shade of stately jackfruit trees, in the architectural hybrid temples built by the Hindus who fled Portuguese missionary zeal, and in the gentle-paced easy-living of a people with a shared flair for food, wine and song.

Goa ticks all the right boxes in terms of seaside hedonism – and then some. There are beautiful wide-sweeping bays with rocky headlands; small bays with giant boulders and craggy cliffs, topped off with Portuguese and Maratha forts. The sea bobs with bright-coloured fishing junks, their nets jumping with silvery mackerel, squid and sardines or kingfish, tiger prawns and pomfret. The fresh haul comes stewed to your table in the idiosyncratic flavours that are the hallmark of Goan cooking – the bastard culinary child of Portugal and India's kitchens. Come evening you can choose from the samba-inflected folk ballads of the *fado* to the infamous Freak-inspired Goa Trance, nurse cashew moonshine in any number of pokey bars or knock back international brand spirits on floating casinos.

1   Fort Aguada Lighthouse, part of the fort and prison complex built on the Calangute headland in the 17th century to protect Goa from attacks by the Dutch Navy. ▸▸ See page 99.

2   Sé Cathedral is the largest church in Old Goa, with a beautiful Tuscan exterior. ▸▸ See page 78.

3   Panjim is one of the friendliest and most laid-back state capitals in India. ▸▸ See page 58.

4   From Goa you can easily reach Karnataka, a state with astounding colour and culture. ▸▸ See page 220.

5   Palolem beach in the south of Goa has a calmer pace of life than the beaches in the north. ▸▸ See page 155.

6   Markets sell everything from locally-grown spices to day-glo hippy wear. ▸▸ See page 41.

7   Fish curry and rice, using the catch of the day, is the most common Goan meal. ▸▸ See page 37.

8   Religious offerings are one of the many things to add a dash of colour to Colva beach, including trinket stands, beach vendors and parachutes. ▸▸ See page 139.

9   Goa's Hindu temples are the centre of pilgrimages and special festivals. ▸▸ See page 246.

10 Watermelons, mangoes, papaya and jackfruit are the most common popular fruits. ▸▸ See page 38.

11 The Menezes Braganza House in Chandor is a fine old Portuguese mansion which remembers the state's former opulence with a treasure-trove of luxury items. ▸▸ See page 175.

12 Quiet backwaters are ringed with fertile paddy fields, especially in lush South Goa. ▸▸ See page 133.

Rainbow coloured state

The churches gleam lime-white in seas of lush parakeet-green paddy against skies of unbroken bright blue. Hamlets full of old, walled bungalows with terracotta-tiled roofs unfurl under age-old mango trees, their branches hanging low with fat, sweet fruit. Much of Goa's gold coast is divided between three long, blinding belts of sand that run from Arambol to Morjim, Baga to Sinquerim and Velsao to Mobor. Then there are tucked-away pockets and coves: tiny casuarina-backed Keri beach, lorded over by Tiracol Fort; the moonscape of Vagator's Spaghetti beach; the windswept Agonda bay and furthermost, Kindlebaga. And colour seeps inland too: for Carnaval whole families descend on the gentle city of Panjim and pack out the piazza in front of the capital's Club Nacionale in a human tide of crimson and black.

Daily life

In the purple dawn light, Goan women in sheeny three-quarter-length dresses pad along their village's sole street bidding their neighbours 'good morning' as they have done every day of their lives. Despite the very visible Catholic community, Goa is still predominantly Hindu. Shrines and temples are tucked away from the main tourist drags. Driving into interior Goa takes you to 12th-century Mahadeva in Tambdi Surla or the fusion architecture of the 18th-century temples in Ponda.

Where the 60s live on...

Most people have heard high tales of the American and European Freak scene that swarmed down from Kathmandu to descend on Baga, Calangute and, latterly, Anjuna from the 60s. There's still the odd old-timer weaving their customized Enfield motorbike through the sand-tracks behind south Anjuna, and there's plenty of neon waistcoats stitched with day-glo 'Om' embroidery, ample acid trance parties throbbing through the coconut thickets and plenty of new shipments of youngsters to build a throng. These days, though, they are more likely to be Israelis fresh out of their military service uniform, English gap year lovelies, upper middle-class Russians and Mumbai and Delhi high society than drop-out hippies.

East meets west

Don't imagine Goa's history of dissolute living began with the 1960s. St Francis Xavier suggested the Inquisition after he found a ragbag bunch of Portuguese stationed at 16th-century Old Goa, a city that was once the wonder of the east but has today all but crumbled leaving a World Heritage ghost town of churches and cathedrals with amazingly elaborate ornate baroque interiors.

Contents

Introducing
Highlights 2
A foot in the door 4

Essentials
Planning your trip 12
When to go 13
Tours and tour operators 13
Finding out more 15
Language 15
Disabled travellers 15
Gay and lesbian
travellers 15
Student travellers 16
Travelling with children 16
Women travellers 16
Before you travel 17
Visas and immigration 17
What to take 18
Insurance 19
Money 20
Getting there 22
Air 22
Rail 24
Road 24
Sea 24
Touching down 24
Airport information 24
Tourist information 25
Local customs and laws 26
Responsible tourism 27
Safety 28
Getting around 29
Air 29
Rail 30
Road 31
Sleeping 35
Eating 37
Entertainment 39
Festivals and events 39
Shopping 41
Sport and activities 43
Health 42
Before you go 45
An A-Z of health risks 46
Keeping in touch 51
Communications 51
Media 52

Panjim and Old Goa

**Mormugao
(Marmagao)** 56
Vasco da Gama and
Dabolim airport 56
Listings 57
Panjim (Panaji) 58
The Waterfront 60
West Panjim and the
Campal 63
City centre 64
Sao Thome and
Fontainhas 64
Around Panjim 66
Goa Velha 68
Listings 70
Old Goa and around 77
Ribandar, Divar and ex-
cursions from Old Goa 85
Listings 85

North Goa

**Mapusa and the Bardez
beaches** 90
Mapusa 90
Listings 92

**Calangute and the
beaches** 94
Calangute 95
Baga 97
Arpora 99
Candolim and
Sinquerim 99
Saligao 99
Reis Magos and
around 101
Listings 102
The party beaches 112
Anjuna 114
Vagator 116
Chapora 117
Listings 119
Coastal Pernem 122
Arambol 123
Morjim to Asvem 124
Mandrem 125
The Chapora river 125
Keri (Querim) and
Tiracol fort 126
Pernem and the
Tiracol river 128
Listings 129

South Goa

**Margao and coastal
Salcete** 136
Margao (Madgaon) 137
Colva (Colwa)
and around 139
South of Colva 142
Listings 144
**Cabo de Rama and
further south** 153

Cabo de Rama (Cape
Rama)   153
Agonda   154
Palolem and around 155
Partagali and around 158
Listings   159

Ponda, inland Salcete and the eastern border

Ponda   166
Temples around
Ponda   167
North of Ponda   171
Listings   175
**West of the Zuari
river**   **175**
Chandor   175
Rachol   178
Loutolim (Lutolim)   179
Listings   179
To the Ghats   **180**
Bicholim and around 181
Sanquelim and
around   182
Satari taluka   182
Listings   182
**The central and
southern interior**   **184**
The Bhagwan Mahaveer
Sanctuary   184

Southwest Sanguem 186
Listings   187

Beyond Goa

Mumbai (Bombay)   192
Gateway of India and
Colaba   195
Central Mumbai   197
Around CST or VT   199
Marine Drive, Malabar Hill
and around   200
Listings   202
Coastal excursions 215
The Maharashtran
border villages   215
Karnataka's coast   216
Gokarna   217
Listings   218
Interior Karnataka 220
Hospet   220
Hampi   221
Bijapur   224
Hindu temples around
Bijapur   226
Hospet to Bidar   229
Listings   231

Background

History   238
Early Goa   238

Contact with the
Muslim world   238
The Portuguese   239
Independence   240
Recent political
history   240
Culture   241
People   241
Language   241
Music and dance   242
Cinema   243
Architecture   243
Religion   245
Hinduism   246
Hindu society   248
Christianity   250
Islam   251
Buddhism   252
**Land and
environment   252**
Climate   253
Wildlife   253
Vegetation   256
Books   256

Footnotes

Glossary   260
**Useful words and
phrases   266**
Konkani   266
Hindi   267
Eating out   269
Index   272
Map index   275
Map symbols   277
Credits   278
About the author   279
Acknowledgements 279
**Complete title
listing   280**
Colour maps   297

Essentials

Planning your trip	**12**
Where to go	12
When to go	13
Tours and tour operators	13
Finding out more	15
Language	15
Disabled travellers	15
Gay and lesbian travellers	15
Student travellers	16
Travelling with children	16
Women travellers	16
Before you travel	**17**
Visas and immigration	17
What to take	18
Insurance	19
Money	**20**
Getting there	**22**
Air	22
Rail	24
Road	24
Sea	24
Touching down	**24**
Airport information	24
Tourist information	25
Local customs and laws	26
Responsible tourism	27
Safety	28
Getting around	**29**
Air	29
Rail	30
Road	31
Maps	34
Sleeping	**35**
Eating	**37**
Entertainment	**39**

Festivals and events	**39**
Shopping	**41**
Sport and activities	**43**
Health	**44**
Before you go	45
An A-Z of health risks	46
Keeping in touch	**51**
Communications	51
Media	52

⁞ Footprint features

Discount flight agents	23
Touching down	24
How big is your footprint?	28
Hotels with the most character	36
Best shopping in Goa	42

Planning your trip

One of the best things about Goa is just how little planning you need to do. Goa is splendidly tiny with enormous diversity packed into its lush range. Sunshine is a given for three quarters of the year, which, for many, means that the days are pretty much taken care of. Roads are good, motorcycles easy to hire or buy, buses are frequent, and English is spoken widely for when you lose your way. It's a place for wanton spontaneity: you can wake up in the morning and decide to go to the opposite end of the state and arrive in time for a late lunch. Equally, you can set aside a couple of days and make forays into the remainders of some of India's great empires and kingdoms in Goa's neighbouring states of Karnataka, Maharashtra and even Andhra Pradesh.

You don't necessarily need to hurry out of Goa's borders for culture. Although years of charter flights have created a strong tourist infrastructure that can make life amazingly easy, years of travel by unimaginative charter tours means there's much of Goa that is fairly untouched by foreigners. But you'll have to go looking: culture in Goa won't steal up on you while you're sipping a beer on the beach.

And what of those beaches? Each beach in Goa has its own dedicated fan-base who will repeat to anyone who'll listen that this, literally, is their idea of paradise. Palolem in the south bears the closest physical resemblance to the picture postcard ideal, but your favourite will probably have more to do with the types of travellers the beach attracts, the soundtrack in the bars (or the lack of it), the type of grub you can buy and the price of a bed.

The best advice is to plant your stuff at the beach that most closely resembles your notion of paradise, then pack a day-sack or overnight bag, and explore – whether that's inland for culture and nature or up and down the coast for new patches of sand. Or just pack ultra-light and keep moving in little bunny-hops from one bay to the next.

However you decide to divide up your time, set aside at least a day to visit the baroque riches of Old Goa's religious relics and give yourself an afternoon in the charmingly ramshackle, candy-coloured state capital of Panjim.

Where to go

Two weeks is the standard all-in period allotted to Goa by most charter companies, but life drifts by easily here, and two weeks becomes three, turns into four and, before you've blinked, your visa's up and you haven't even been to Hampi. The way into Goa is unusual in that it's very unlikely you'll arrive in **Panjim**, the capital – a shame because it's a charming city – so try to come here after you've been to **Old Goa**. Don't beat yourself up about it though. After a long-haul flight, or even longer train or bus journey from **Mumbai**, most people quite rightly want to feel the sand between their toes. This can mean heading for happening **Anjuna** and **Vagator**, through hippy **Arambol** or deluxe **Candolim** and **Mobor**. Make a virtue of your time on the beach and clamber up onto the rocky headlands to walk the remains of Maratha and Portuguese forts with their unrivalled views. **Cabo de Rama** in the south, **Chapora** near Anjuna, **Fort Tiracol** in the very north and, just beyond Goa's northern border into Maharashtra, **Fort Redi**, are all stunning and different enough to warrant their own visits. For an idea of Goa's Portuguese cultural heritage – rather than military legacy – there's more than Old Goa. The fine Menezes Braganza House in **Chandor** is a real eye-opener and the Rachol Seminary, just nearby, is worth a trip. Even if you don't want to shop, all tourist roads lead to the **Anjuna flea market** on a Wednesday, grown so huge that it's a sight in itself. Its more sanitized, and pricier version, Ingo's Saturday night bazaar in Arpora, is also photographers wanting some 'local colour'.

With two weeks in hand you could start at one end of Goa, head for the centre at Old Goa and Panjim then set off inland for a couple of days to take in a spice plantation (near Savoi Verem or Keri near Ponda), see something of Goa's Hindu majority in the temples of Ponda and look into the wealthy houses of the elite in Chandor. The arc of your journey could bring you out at a beach the other end. With three weeks or more it's worth considering leaving the state, which gives you enough time to see the riches of neighbouring Karnataka's past: seething pilgrims at Gokarna, ruins of a homegrown vanquished empire at Hampi, stone-masonry cut like lace at Badami and Aihole and the onion tombs of the Deccan's Islamic rulers at Bijapur.

If Mumbai is your entry point, you will find that this flourishing Indian regional capital contrasts sharply with the much smaller state capital of Goa. The road journey along the NH17 allows a night halt at the hill station of Mahabaleshwar; you can also stop at Chiplun, which enjoys picturesque river views, before continuing to Goa.

Essentials Planning your trip

When to go

Goa is warm throughout the year but its position on the coast means that it never suffers the unbearable heat of India's northern plains. The beautiful, warm, clear and dry weather of Goa's tropical winter, from mid-October to March, makes this the best time for foreign visitors. It is the period when charter flights operate direct to Goa and tourist facilities are in full swing. The peak season – Christmas and New Year – is perfect weather-wise, but is also when Goa rakes in the bulk of its tourist cash. Be prepared for prices to soar correspondingly and book accommodation in advance. Outside this main tourist season many restaurants, especially on the beach, are closed.

From mid-April until the beginning of the monsoon in early June, both the temperature and the humidity rise sharply, making the middle of the day steamy hot and the beach sand almost untouchable – this is when the foreign long-stayers start wilting away, making for the mountains, and when Goa becomes the seaside resort to bus-loads of domestic tourists who dunk themselves deep in the water wearing full sarees and salwaar kameez. The monsoon itself makes June and July very wet. On the coast, the heavy rain often comes as torrential storms accompanied by lashing winds, while up in the cooler Ghats, if it is not raining, the hill tops are often obscured by swirling cloud and mist. Heavy showers can persist in August and September and humidity can remain unpleasantly high, but by October rainfall drops significantly.

Tours and tour operators

There's nothing daunting in making your own independent travel plans in Goa, but you may still choose to try an inclusive package holiday or let a specialist operator quote for a tailor-made tour. Out of season these can be worth exploring. The lowest prices quoted for 2004 from the UK vary from about US$500 (£275) for a week (flights, three-star hotel and breakfast) in the low season, to over US$3,000 (£1,645) for three weeks during the peak season.

: Check websites like www.lastminute.com, www.expedia.co.uk and www.bargainholidays.com for cheap package deals.

Tour companies

GoAway, 111 Bell St, London NW1 6TL, T020-72587800, www.goaway.co.uk. Guesthouses to 5-stars and charter flight deals.

Greaves Tours, 53 Welbeck St, London, T020-74879111, www.greavesindia.com. Luxury, tailor-made tours only using schedule, non-charter, flights.

Jewel In The Crown Holidays, 3 Charlwood Ct, County Oak Way, Crawley T01293-533338, www.jewelholidays.com. One of the oldest independent tour operators with broad choice of hotel options.

Kuoni, Kuoni House, Dorking, Surrey, RH5 4AZ, T01306-744441, www.kuoni.co.uk. and subsidiary brand **Voyage Jules Vernes** run week-long culture and relaxation tours plus has information on birdwatching programmes.

On the Go Tours, T020-73711113, www.onthegotours.com. Call for an 'India on the menu' brochure.

Somak, Harrovian Village, Harrow on the Hill, Middlesex HA1 3EX, T020-84233000, www.somak.co.uk. Beach holidays with 2 to 5 star accommodation plus cultural programmes throughout South India using Goa as entry and exit point.

Trans Indus, Northumberland House ,11 The Pavement, Popes La, Ealing, London W5 4NG, T020-85662729, www.transindus.co.uk. Upmarket India travel specialists: scheduled flights and cultural tours.

TravelPack, 73-77 Lowlands Rd, Harrow, Middlesex, HA1 3AW, T0870-1212040, www.travelpack.co.uk. Charter flights and accommodation deals from guesthouses to 5-stars.

Western & Oriental, 18-24 Westbourne Grove, London W2 5RH, T0870-4991111, www.westernoriental.com. Tailor-made luxury tours, one-on-one guides, featuring spas, wildlife and classic tours.

North America

Greaves Tours, 304 Randolph St, Chicago, T1800-3187801, www.greavesindia.com. Luxury, tailor-made tours only using schedule, non-charter, flights.

Finding out more

India is fully online, and Goans are a well-travelled bunch, so there's plenty on the web to read up on about the state.

www.fco.gov.uk Foreign Office advice.
www.goacom.com/goatoday Fairly lively monthly magazine with news and comment.
www.goacom.com/goatourism A government undertaking, with information on a variety of topics.
www.goagovt.nic.in Demography, statistics of the state, plus practical information.
www.goanews.com For Goa-specific news, current affairs,and information.

www.incredibleindia.org The official website of the India Tourist Office.
www.indev.org British Council site devoted to development issues in India.
www.konkanrailway.com Indian Railways' interactive timetable and booking, where you can reserve and buy seats by credit card.
www.responsibletravel.com for green tourism and conservation issues.

Language → *See the glossary, page 260, for a list of useful words and phrases.*

There are few reminders of the Portuguese language once spoken by Goa's elite. Konkani and Marathi are now the most common languages, while English is widely understood in towns. Hindi is India's official language and is commonly understood. The use of English is also enshrined in the constitution for a wide range of official purposes, notably communication between Hindi and non-Hindi speaking states.

Disabled travellers

India isn't geared up towards the physically handicapped or wheelchair-bound traveller. Access to buildings, toilets (sometimes 'squat' type), pavements and kerbs and public transport can all prove frustrating, although it is easy to find people to give a hand with lifting and carrying. Provided there is an able-bodied companion to scout around and arrange help, and as long as you are prepared to spend on at least mid-price hotels or guesthouses, private car hire and taxis, Goa should be rewarding, even if on a somewhat limited scale.

Some travel companies are beginning to specialize in exciting holidays that are tailor-made for individuals depending on their level of disability. If you have access to the internet, look at www.geocities.com/Paris/1502 which is dedicated to providing travel information for disabled adventurers and includes a number of reviews and tips from members of the public. You might also want to read *Nothing Ventured*, edited by Alison Walsh (Harper Collins), which gives personal accounts of worldwide journeys by disabled travellers, plus advice and listings.

Gay and lesbian travellers

Indian law forbids homosexual acts for men (but not women) and carries a maximum sentence of life imprisonment. Although it is common to see young males holding hands in public, it doesn't necessarily indicate a gay relationship and is usually an expression of friendship. Overt displays of affection between both homosexuals and heterosexuals give offence and should be avoided.

Student travellers

Full-time students qualify for an **ISIC** (International Student Identity Card) which is issued by student travel and specialist agencies (eg STA Travel) at home and allows certain travel benefits, eg reduced prices.

Travelling with children

Children of all ages are widely welcomed, and the warmth with which they are greeted is often extended to those accompanying them. However, care should be taken when travelling to remote areas where health services are primitive as children tend to become ill more rapidly than adults.

It is best to visit Goa in the cooler months to protect children from the sun, heat, dehydration and mosquito bites. Cool showers or baths help, as does avoiding the hottest part of the day. Diarrhoea and vomiting are the most common problems, so take the usual precautions. In the big resorts you can get safe baby foods and formula milk. It doesn't harm a baby to eat an unvaried and limited diet of familiar food carried in packets for a few weeks if the local dishes are not acceptable, but it may be an idea to give vitamin and mineral supplements. See also under Health on page 42. Wet wipes are always useful and sometimes difficult to find in India, as are disposable nappies. The biggest hotels provide babysitting.

Women travellers

Independent travel is still largely unheard of for Indian women: if you travel alone outside Goa expect plenty of questions. The state itself is easy enough on solitary female travellers and friends are easy to meet along the way. Measures that some think necessary out of state – dying blonde hair black, wearing wedding rings and so on – are not necessary here. Privacy is rarely respected, but if you dress appropriately (a salwaar kameez, say, for outside Goa) you should avoid outright harassment. By and large, Goans dress less conservatively than the rest of India, but foreign women dressed too provocatively outside the tourist beach strips will still provoke unwanted attention – whole gaggles of Indian men continue to travel to Goa from other states to stalk the beaches of Baga and gawp at western women in bikinis. Modest dress for women is always advisable: loose-fitting, non-see-through clothes attract less attention and it is best to cover up when walking to or from the beach. Topless bathing is not permitted.

While being measured for clothing in tailors' shops or when having an ayurvedic massage, it is best to be accompanied by a friend to avoid any chance of being molested. Walk in large groups at night, especially when attending late-opening nightclubs and parties, and don't take taxis or rickshaws alone.

Take advantage of the gender segregation on public transport, both to duck hassle and talk with local women. Seats for women are set aside in buses, while separate compartments are intended to discourage 'eve teasing', a euphemism for physical harassment. One way of dealing with people who hassle you on the street is simply to say 'thank you' and smile and walk away. If you show annoyance, it may result in more pestering or abusive language. Although incidents of rape are rare compared with Europe and America it is sensible to take the same precautions as you would at home. Be 'beachwise' in Goa as you would be streetwise at home.

Before you travel

Visas and immigration → *Visa fees vary according to nationality.*

Virtually all foreign nationals require a visa to enter India. The rules for visas change frequently and arrangements for application and collection also vary from town to town so check details and costs with the relevant office. These are closed on Indian national holidays. In London, applications are processed in an hour or two (0800-1200). Your passport should be valid for at least six months beyond the period of the visit.

In 2004 the following visa rules applied: **Transit visas,** for passengers en route to another country (valid for three to five days); **Tourist visas,** valid for six months from the date of issue with multiple entry (most visitors require this type); **Business visas,** for up to one year from the date of issue (a letter from company giving the nature of business is required); **Five year visas,** for those of Indian origin only who have held Indian passports, and their spouses; **Student visas** are valid up to one year from the date of issue and you need to attach a letter of acceptance from Indian institution, and an AIDS test certificate. Allow up to three months for approval.

Visa extensions Applications should be made to the **Foreigners' Regional Registration Offices** at New Delhi, Mumbai, Kolkata or Chennai, or an office of the **Superintendent of Police** in the District Headquarters. After six months, you must leave India and apply for a new visa.

Registration Foreigners do not need to register within the 180-day period of their tourist visa. All foreign visitors who stay in India for more than 180 days are required to register at the nearest **Foreigners' Registration Office** and get an income tax clearance exemption certificate from the Foreign Section of the **Income Tax Department** in Delhi, Mumbai, Kolkata or Chennai. In Goa, contact **Directorate of Employment** (Enforcement, Foreign Exchange Regulation Act) ① *Shanta Building, 2nd flr, St Inez, Panjim.*

Embassies and consulates

Austria Kärntner Ring 2, A-1015 Vienna, T50-58666.
Australia 3-5 Moonah Pl, Yarralumla, Canberra T6273-3999; Sydney T9223-9500 Melbourne T9384-0141.
Bangladesh House 129, Rd 2, Dhanmondi RA, Dhaka-2, T503606, Chittagong T654021.
Belgium 217 Chaussée de Vleurgat, 1050 Brussels, T6409802. Consulates: Ghent T091-263423, Antwerp T03-2341122.
Canada 10 Springfield Rd, Ottawa, Ontario K1M 1C9, T613-7443751. Consulates: Toronto T416-9600751, Vancouver T604-6628811.
Denmark Vangehusvej 15, 2100 Copenhagen, T3918-2888.
France 15 Rue Alfred Dehodencq, Paris, T01-40507070. Visas from office in next street, 20 Rue Albéric Magnard, 75016, T01-40507171 (deposit passport 0930-1030, collect same day 1600-1700).

Germany Pohlstrasse 20, 10785 Berlin, T030-4853002 (visas), embassy in Tiergarten- strasse. Consulates: Willy-Brandt Allee 16, 53113 Bonn, T0228-540132; Friedrich Ebert An lage 26, 60325 Frankfurt, T069-1530050; Raboisen 6, 20095 Hamburg, T040-338036; Munich T089-92562067; Stuttgart T0711-297078.
Ireland 6 Lesson Park, Dublin 6, T01-4970843.
Israel 4 Kaufmann St, Sharbat, Tel Aviv 68012, T03-5101431.
Italy Via XX Settembre 5, 00187 Rome, T46-4884642. Consulates: Milan T02-8690314, Genoa T010-54891.
Japan 2-11, Kudan Minami 2-Chome, Chiyoda-ku, Tokyo 102, T03-32622391. Consulate: Kobe T078-2418116.
Nepal Lainchour, PO Box No 292, Kathmandu, T0891-410900.
Netherlands Buitenrustweg 2, The Hague (2517KD), T070-3469771.

New Zealand 10th Flr, Princess Tower, 180 Molesworth St (PO Box 4045), Wellington, T04-4736390.
Norway 30 Niels Jules Gate, 0272 Oslo-2, T22443194.
Pakistan G5 Diplomatic Enclave, Islamabad, T050-814371; Karachi T021-522275.
Spain Av Pio XII 30-32, 28016 Madrid, T091-4570209. Consulate: Barcelona T093-2120422.
Sri Lanka 36-38 Galle Rd, Colombo 3, T01-421605, Kandy T08-446430.
Sweden Adolf Fredriks Kyrkogata 12, Box 1340, 11183 Stockholm, T08-107008.
UK India House, Aldwych, London WC2B 4NA, T020-78368484, www.hcilondon.org

(0930-1300, 1400-1730). Consulates: 20 Augusta St, Hockley, Birmingham, B18 6DS, T0121-2122782; Rutland Sq, Edinburgh EH1 2BB, T0131-2292144; 6th Flr, 134 Renfrew St, Glasgow G3 7ST, T0141-331 0777. (Send SAE or print off from on website for postal applications.)
USA 2107 Massachusetts Av, Washington DC 20008, T202-9397000. Consulates: New Orleans T504-5828105, New York T212-8797800, San Francisco T415-6680662, Chicago T312-5950405.

Customs, duty free, export restrictions

Tourists are allowed to bring in all personal effects 'which may reasonably be required', without charge. The official customs allowance includes 200 cigarettes or 50 cigars, 0.95 litres of alcohol, a camera with five rolls of film and a pair of binoculars. You may be asked to register valuable personal effects or professional equipment on a **Tourist Baggage Re-Export Form** (TBRE), including jewellery, special camera equipment and lenses, laptops, sound- and video-recorders. These forms require the serial numbers of such equipment. It saves considerable frustration if you know the numbers in advance and are ready to show them on the equipment. In addition to the forms, details of imported equipment may be entered into your passport. Save time by completing the formalities while waiting for your baggage. It is essential to keep these forms for showing to the customs when leaving India, otherwise considerable delays are very likely at the time of departure.

❖ Duty free shops in Goa and Mumbai are extremely limited.

Currency regulations There are no restrictions on the amount of foreign currency or travellers' cheques a tourist may bring into India. If you are carrying more than US$2,500 or its equivalent in cash or US$10,000 in cash and travellers' cheques you will need to fill in a currency declaration form.

Prohibited and restricted items The import of dangerous drugs, live plants, gold coins, gold and silver bullion and silver coins not in current use, ivory, skins of all animals, toosh wool, snake skin and articles made from them, are either banned or subject to strict regulation. Similarly, the export of antiquities and art objects over 100 years old, and gold jewellery purchased in India costing over Rs 2,000 and other jewellery (including settings with precious stones) costing over Rs 10,000, is either banned or subject to strict regulation. It is illegal to import firearms into India without special permission.

Vaccinations

Yellow fever is not acquired in India, but you may be asked to show a certificate as proof of a **Yellow Fever** vaccination if you have travelled in from Africa or South America. For a full list of recommended vaccinations, see the Health section, page 44.

What to take → see page 45 for health information.

Keep luggage to the very barest minimum: Goa has played host to tourists for so many years that it's possible to get just about any supplies you might need, and probably for cheaper than at your local chemists: that goes for tampons, toiletries including brand name suntan lotion and contraceptives. It's also a great place to buy clothes: pack light (you need a jumper or fleece over Christmas as it gets chilly in the evening) and load up at the markets for the return journey. For feet, you probably only need flip-flops, but it's worth bringing a pair of lightweight, washable canvas shoes in case you want to do some walking. One thing almost impossible to buy is film stock outside the 100 to 400 ASA range. If you are serious about your photography, bring it from home.

Checklist: International driving licence; photocopies of essential documents; short wave radio; spare passport photographs; student card (ISIC); sun hat and sunglasses; sun protection cream (factor 15 plus); Swiss army knife; torch; wet wipes; zip-lock bags.

Budget travellers may also want to take the following: Cotton sheet sleeping bag (it's cheap to have one made at a tailor's in Goa); earplugs; eyeshades (given away by some airlines); mosquito net (impregnated, ideally); padlock, preferably with a secret combination number (for room and baggage), and a chain; soap; string (washing line); towel; washbasin plug.

Insurance

You can bungee-jump, scuba dive, jet-ski and sail in Goa, but probably the most dangerous thing you'll do is ride a motorbike. And nine times out of 10 you'll be doing so without a helmet. India has one of the worst road safety records in the world, but somehow this seems a terribly ordinary kind of risk to run once you're in the state. It is classed as a hazardous sport by most insurance companies, rendering your policy immune to any subsequent injuries or medical expenses incurred. Ask at the outset and read the fine print to know where you stand.

Always take out travel insurance before you set off and read the small print carefully. Check that the policy covers the activities you intend or may end up doing.

Also check exactly what your medical cover includes, ie ambulance, helicopter rescue or emergency flights back home, and check the payment protocol. You may have to cough up first before the insurance company reimburses you. It is always best to dig out all the receipts for expensive personal effects like jewellery or cameras. Take photos of these items and note down all serial numbers. If you are carrying specialist equipment, you will probably need to get separate cover for these items.,

‼ Remember that it is risky to buy medicinal tablets abroad because the doses may differ and India has a huge trade in false drugs.

You are advised to shop around. **STA Travel** and other reputable student travel organisations offer good value policies; in the UK, **Direct Line Travel** ① To845-2468744, www.directline.com, offer annual, single trip and backpacker cover. Young travellers from North America can try the **International Student Insurance Service** (ISIS), which is available through STA Travel, T1-800-7770112, www.sta-travel.com. Other recommended travel insurance companies in North America include: **Travel Guard** ① T1-800-8261300, www.noelgroup.com; **Access America** ① T1-800-2848300; **Travel Insurance Services** ① T1-800-9371387; **Travel Assistance International** ① T1-800-8212828. Older travellers should note that some companies will not cover people over 65 years old, or may charge higher premiums. The best policies for older travellers (UK) are offered by **Age Concern** ① To1883-346964 and **Saga** ① To800-0565464, www.saga.co.uk/travel.

Money

Currency

The Indian currency is the Rupee. It is not possible to purchase this currency overseas. The Rupee is divided into 100 Paise. New notes are printed in denominations of Rs 1,000 (though these are scarce), 500, 100, 50, 20 and 10. Coins are minted in denominations of Rs 5, 2, 1 and paise 50, 25, 20, 10, 5, 2 and 1 (although coins below 50 paise are rarely seen). NB It can be difficult to use torn or very worn notes; check notes carefully when you are given them and refuse any that are damaged. The Rs 500 and Rs 100 notes are easy to confuse. Always double check. NB Carry money, mostly as TCs, in a money belt worn under clothing.

‼ Both for hard currency and travellers' cheques, US dollars and Pounds sterling are the easiest currencies to convert. Euros are still a bit of a gamble.

Exchange → *A list of banks can be found in each town's individual directory.*

On arrival at the airport you should change money while waiting for your luggage since you will need some Rupees to pay for transport to the hotel. This is generally easy and fairly quick. If you are booked into a large resort hotel and have free transfer arranged, you can usually change money (often 24 hours) at their desk. In the major resort areas, banks, hotels and private dealers all offer exchange services. NB If you cash sterling, make certain you are given Rupees at the sterling and not at the dollar rate. The Rs 500 note is difficult to change outside the big cities, and there are many convincing forged copies. Avoid changing money with unlicensed dealers.

Travellers' cheques It is best to take travellers' cheques (TCs) into India, rather than cash, since the latter can't be replaced if lost or stolen. **American Express** and **Thomas Cook** travellers' cheques are widely accepted in the major resorts in Goa. Many private dealers (often doubling up as travel agents) offer competitive exchange rates and are generally much quicker than banks. They usually have long opening hours; some banks in Goa have also extended their opening times. Exchange desks in the large hotels may be open 24 hours but they often offer a poorer rate of exchange. To save time, it is worth changing enough to last for some days. You have to show your passport when exchanging TCs. In a large number of shops and travel agents, TCs are accepted for direct purchases. It is best to carry some US$ TCs, though Euro TCs and notes are likely to be accepted in major centres before long.

Take care to follow the advice given about keeping proof of purchase slips and make a note of TC numbers separately from the cheques. In the case of loss, you will need to get a police report and inform the travellers' cheque company. Replacement cheques may only be given by authorized agents and can sometimes take weeks. For example in Panjim, Thomas Cook deals with claims efficiently whereas the Amex agent in town is not authorized to issue cheques.

Unscrupulous dealers may offer a premium of 40-50% on the face value of your travellers' cheques in order to cash them with false signatures, and ask you to get replacements. Do not be tempted.

Credit cards Major credit cards are increasingly acceptable in the main centres. Payment by card for purchases can sometimes be more expensive than payment by cash. **Mastercard** and **Visa** are widely accepted, though not consistently and not by all. Railway reservation centres in some major cities are now accepting Visa cards. Remember that it often takes a long time to check authorization and you may be charged for the international call.

ATMs You can find automatic telling machines that accept major foreign credit cards in the main towns making it possible to travel wholly without travellers' cheques. ATM signs at many banks are for local account holders only, however. You should be fine with **Mastercard, Visa** and **Amex** cards. The minimum withdrawal is Rs 100, maximum Rs 10,000 per day (3 x Rs 3,000 plus 1 x Rs 1,000). It's best to take some hard currency with you just in case: after all what happens if there is a power cut while your card is in the machine? Some ATMs only process transactions from Indian bank accounts, so ask first. The **Bank of Baroda** and **Standard Chartered** both issue Rupees against Visa cards.

Encashment certificates These are given free whenever you exchange foreign currency (cash, travellers' cheques, etc) and let you change Rupees back to your own currency so you should retain enough certificates (valid for three months) to reconvert on leaving (note that the Dabolim airport bank gives a poor rate). The certificates also mean you can use Rupees to buy airline tickets or Foreign Tourist Quota rail tickets (although not Margao), and to pay bills in some of the swisher hotels where tourists have to pay in foreign currency. NB When receiving cash through a bank draft or transfer, insist on a certificate – you can't buy travellers' cheques without them. ATM machines don't give these certificates.

> ⦂ *Exchange rates*
> *Autumn 2004:*
> *£ = Rs 83.3*
> *US$ =Rs 46.4*
> *€ =Rs 55.9*
> *See also www.oanda.com.*

Black market There is virtually no black market in Goa now, since premiums are small. However, it is worth carrying one or two foreign currency notes of small denomination (eg £10 or US$10 notes) for emergencies, since it is usually easy to find someone to change them. NB Be aware that changing money through unauthorized dealers is illegal.

Transferring money Thomas Cook, American Express and Standard Chartered Grindlays can make instant transfers to their offices in India but charge a high fee (about 15%). **State Bank of India** branches abroad charge less but can take two to three days. A bank draft (up to US $1,000) that may be posted (three to five days by Speedpost) is the cheapest option. **Western Union** has a growing number of agents throughout the state, check www.westernunion.com, while Thomas Cook operates through international **Moneygram**, www.moneygram.com. See also under Panjim, Anjuna, Chapora, Margao and Palolem directories.

Cost of living

The Indian cost of living remains well below that in the industrialized world. Government employees earn about Rs 12,000 (US 240) per month on average, according to official statistics – manual workers and unskilled labourers earn as little as Rs 30 (US 70 cents) per day in parts of rural India. Most food, accommodation and public transport, especially rail and bus, are exceptionally cheap. There is a vast range of moderately priced but clean hotels and guesthouses and good, inexpensive beach restaurants, so your money can stretch further than elastic. Budget travellers sharing a room and taking public transport, avoiding tourist souvenir stalls and eating nothing but rice and daal can get away with a budget of Rs 350-400 (about US$8) a day to cover accommodation, food and travel. This sum leaps if you drink booze (about £1 or Rs 80 a pint) or want to have your own wheels (you can expect to spend Rs 100 to hire a Honda Kinetic per day). Those planning to stay in fairly comfortable hotels and use taxis sightseeing should budget at US$50 a day. Be prepared to spend a fair whack more in Mumbai when it's worth coughing up extra for a half-decent room: penny-pinch by the beach when you'll be spending precious little time indoors anyway. A newspaper costs Rs 5 and breakfast for two with coffee can come to as little as Rs 15 in a South Indian 'hotel', but if you intend to eat along the beach areas, you won't get much change from Rs 100 per person, still just over £1 sterling.

According to Thomas Cook, Goa is the cheapest place to buy a meal in the world. You really can live like a king with a pauper's price tag here.

If you're heading for the beach, carry only enough to cover your daily budget in a purse. Keep larger amounts of money in a belt worn under clothing, or use the hotel safe. Try to avoid taking large amounts of money out of your money belt or bag in public as this may attract unwelcome attention. Keep a supply of small denomination notes which are especially useful for tipping.

Getting there

Air

From the UK and Europe → *See also Tours and tour operators, page 13.*

Charter companies fly direct from the UK, Holland, Switzerland and Russia to Goa between October and April. Government rules protect Air India's monopoly on flight-only deals to Goa, but you can side-step these by searching for holiday deals, which work out cheaper than flight-onlys. Including accommodation these can cost as little as £199 for a week (including basic dormitory or one or two star accommodation which you can forfeit on arrival – you're under no obligation to stay), whereas flight-only deals cost £279. You will need to book through a tour operator (see Tour Operators above). During high season it's sometimes cheaper to book a scheduled flight (most often Mumbai, but worth looking at Hyderabad and Bangalore as less hectic entry points). **British Airways** and **Air India** run direct daily flights; **Emirates**, **Gulf Air**, **Kuwait Airways** and **Royal Jordanian** stop over in the Middle East, and **Virgin** has just begun flights to Delhi. **KLM**, **Air France**, **Lufthansa** and **Swiss Air** run scheduled flights to Mumbai from the rest of Europe.

www.cheapflights.com provides additional useful information.

Direct flights between the UK and Mumbai start at £360, while flights-only between the UK and Goa can be almost double that at £700. There are a number of low-cost domestic airlines within India: **Jet**, **Sahara** and **Indian Airlines** all fly between Mumbai's Santa Cruz and Goa's Dabolim airports for under US$100 in around an hour; there are also connections with Bangalore, Calicut, Cochin, Delhi and Trivandrum.

If you don't want to take a connecting flight down to Goa, the Konkan railway makes a pretty, and increasingly speedy, alternative. Do not be tempted to take the

⦂ Discount flight agents

UK and Ireland
STA Travel, 86 Old Brompton Rd, London, SW7 3LH, T020-74376262, www.statravel.co.uk. They have other branches in London, as well as in Brighton, Bristol, Cambridge, Leeds, Manchester, Newcastle-Upon-Tyne and Oxford and on many university campuses. Specialists in low-cost student/youth flights and tours, also good for student IDs and insurance.
Trailfinders, 194 Kensington High St, London, W8 7RG, T020-79383939.

North America
Air Brokers International, 323 Geary St, Suite 411, San Francisco, CA94102, T1-800-8833273, www.airbrokers.com. Consolidator and specialist on RTW and Circle Pacific tickets.
STA Travel, 5900 Wilshire Blvd, Suite 2110, Los Angeles, CA 90036, T1-800-7770112, www.sta-travel. com. Also branches in New York, San Francisco, Boston, Miami, Chicago, Seattle and Washington DC.

Travel CUTS, 187 College St, Toronto, ON, M5T 1P7, T1-800-667 2887, www.travelcuts.com. Specialist in student discount fares, IDs and other travel services. There are also branches in other Canadian cities.
Hari World Travels, 1 Adelaide St. East, Toronto, Ontario, T416-366 2000, www.hariworld.com, also have offices in New York, Toronto, Atlanta, Chicago and San Francisco.

Australia and New Zealand
Flight Centres, 82 Elizabeth St, Sydney, T133-133; 205 Queen St, Auckland, T09-309 6171. There are also branches in other towns and cities. www.flightcentre.com.au.
STA Travel, 702 Harris St, Ultimo, Sydney, and 256 Flinders St, Melbourne, T1300-360960, www.sta travelaus.com.au; In NZ: 10 High St, Auckland, T09-366 6673. There are also branches in major towns and university campuses.
Travel.com.au, 80 Clarence St, Sydney, T02-929 01500.

bus. The catamaran service, which was the favoured freak mode of the 1970s, was briefly resuscitated in 2003-4 but offered too erratic a service to be considered a viable alternative. ⏵ *See page 56 for Dabolim airport in Goa; see page 192 for Chhatrapati Sivaji International Airport in Mumbai.*

From North America and Canada
There are no direct flights between Goa and North America and Australasia. Flights to Mumbai, Delhi and Chennai are your best bets: **Air India** has the only direct flights from New York (18 hours to Mumbai) while the American west coast route is run by **Cathay Pacific, Singapore Airlines** or **Malaysia Airlines**. Some west coast old-hands recommend booking a cheap flight to Bangkok then getting a connecting ticket, which can work out cheaper, although more fraught. **Air Canada** operates between Vancouver and Delhi.

From Australasia via the Far East
Qantas, Singapore Airlines, Thai Airways, Malaysian Airlines, Cathay Pacific and **Air India** are the principal airlines connecting the continents, flying to one of the Indian regional capitals. From there you will need to get onward flights or rail connections to Goa. At present, there are no direct charter flights to Goa from this part of the world.

Rail → *Schedules change so check timings locally.*

Trains are often an excellent alternative way of getting to and from Goa. There are four trains a day on the Konkan Railway between Mumbai and Goa; it also runs to Goa from Mangalore. You can book tickets in advance via local agents or within seven days via the website, www.konkanrailway.com. Prices range from Rs 259 for sleeper (ie non airconditioned) class to Rs 1165 for airconditioned two-tier for the seven-hour (ish) journey. It stops at three main stations in Goa: get off at Tivim for the northern beaches (for everywhere from Arambol to Candolim); at Karmali near Old Goa for the capital Panjim; and Canacona for Palolem and around. There's a **broad-gauge service** from Vasco and Margao to Londa to give Goa easy connections to the Indian interior.

Road

The 18 hour **bus** marathon from Mumbai to Goa is only just cheaper than the train. These are run by state bus companies as well as private companies such as **Paulo Tours and Travel**. It takes 10 hours to reach Panjim by **taxi** and costs Rs 6,000 return.

Sea

The catamaran from Mumbai to Goa is operated by **Frank Shipping** ① *T25033146*, and costs around Rs 2,000. Reported as less than reliable, it only operates between October and May.

Touching down

Airport information

Goa's Dabolim airport is south of Panjim, across the Mormugao Bay. There are counters at the airport for car hire, foreign exchange and tourist information, all of which are normally open to meet flights, usually 1230-1530.

Transport to town Package tour companies and luxury hotels usually arrange courtesy buses for hotel transfer. Other options are to take a taxi, bus or hire a car. The **pre-paid taxi counter** immediately outside the international arrivals hall has rates clearly displayed (eg Panjim Rs 384, which takes 40 mins; Calangute Rs 516; Anjuna Rs 600; Colva Rs 288). State your destination at the counter, pay and take the receipt which will give the registration number of your taxi. Keep hold of this receipt until you reach your destination. There is no need to tip the driver since the pre-paid rate is already generous by local standards. Indian Airlines sometimes have a bus for transfer to Panjim to meet their incoming flights (Rs 30). The public bus stop on the far side of the roundabout outside the airport gates (left after leaving the arrivals hall), has regular buses to Vasco da Gama (Rs 3), from where there are connections to all major places in Goa. If you want to go straight to the nearest beach, go to the right of the roundabout, cross the road, and you will find a stop for buses to Bogmalo (Rs 3). NB The new Hotel Airport, 1 km away, is listed under Sleeping on page 57.

⁂ Immigration formalities in Mumbai can be particularly slow.

Security International airlines vary in their arrangements and requirements, in particular the carrying of equipment such as radios, tape recorders, laptops and

▪ Touching down

Emergency services Police 100, Fire 101, Ambulance 102.
IDD code 91. A double ring repeated regularly means it is ringing. Equal tones with equal pauses means engaged.
Telephone directory 197.
Official time GMT+5½ hours.
Offical language Konkani, Hindi English, Marathi and Portuguese sometimes spoken.
Business hours **Banks** Mon-Fri 1030-1430, Sat 1030-1230. Top hotels sometimes have a 24-hr service. **Post offices** Mon-Fri 1000-1700, some Sat mornings. **Government offices** Mon-Fri 0930-1700, Sat 0930-1300 (some only alternate Sats). **Shops** Mon-Sat 0930-1800. Bazaars keep longer hours.
Voltage and plugs 220-240 volts AC. Some top hotels have transformers. There may be pronounced variations in voltage and power cuts are common. Socket sizes vary so you are advised to take a universal adapter.
Weights and measures Metric, although some remote rural areas use local measures.

batteries. It is advisable to ring the airline in advance to confirm what their current regulations are. NB Internal airlines often have different rules from the international carriers. You are strongly advised not to pack valuables in your luggage (there have been several reports of vandalism and theft from luggage, particularly on **Air India**).

Documentation Despite recent improvements, 'Arrival' can be a slow process. Disembarkation cards, with an attached customs declaration, are handed out to passengers during the inward flight. The customs slip should be handed over when leaving the baggage collection hall.

Airport tax Rs 500 for all international departures but this is usually included in the price of the international air ticket; check this when buying (look for FT in the tax column of your ticket). A domestic departure tax must be paid in cash if tickets are bought in Rupees.

Tourist information

There are **Government of India** and **State Government** tourist offices in Panjim. The **Goa Tourism Development Council,** which has its own office, runs modest hotels and dormitories in over a dozen locations. NB Don't take advice from unofficial 'tourist offices' at airports or railway stations. Consult the official Indiatourism website **www.incredibleindia.org** for more information.

Indian tourist offices abroad

Australia Level 2 Picadilly, 210 Pitt St, Sydney, NSW 2000, T02-92644855.
Austria Opernring 1, 1010 Vienna, T1-5871462.
Canada 60 Bloor St, West Suite No 1003, Toronto, Ontario, T416-9623787.
France 8 Blvd de la Madeleine, 75009 Paris, T01-45233045.
Germany Baserler Str 48, 60329 Frankfurt 1, T069-2429490.
Italy Via Albricci 9, Milan 20122, T02-8053506.
Japan Pearl Building, 9-18 Chome Ginza, Chuo Ku, Tokyo 104, T03-5715196.
The Netherlands Rokin 9-15, 1012 Amsterdam, T020-608991.
Singapore 20 Kramat Lane, 01-01A United House, Singapore 0922. T2353800.
Sweden Sveavagen 9-11 1st Flr, S-III 57 Stockholm 11157, T468-215081.
Switzerland 1-3 rue de Chantepoulet, 1201 Geneva, T022-7321813.

Thailand 3rd Flr, 62/5 Thaniya Rd, Bangkok, T02-2352585.
UK Indiatourism, 7 Cork St, London, T020-74373677, 08700-102183.

USA 3550 Wiltshire Blvd, Room 204, Los Angeles, California 90010, T213-3808855; 1270 Av of the Americas, Suite 1808, New York, NY 10020, T212-5864901/3.

Local customs and laws

Begging

Beggars are often found on busy street corners as well as at bus and train stations, where they often target foreigners for special attention. Visitors usually find this very distressing, especially the sight of severely undernourished children or those displaying physical deformity. Some find market day in Anjuna particularly harrowing. You may be particularly affected when some persist on making physical contact. You might find a firm *jaao* ('go away') works. To avoid shaking hands, use the Indian greeting and say *namaste*. Those seeking alms near religious sites are another matter, and you may see Indian worshippers giving freely to those less fortunate than themselves since this is tied up with the religious concept of gaining 'merit'. How you deal with begging is a matter of personal choice but it is perhaps better to give to a recognized charity (see below) than to make largely ineffectual handouts to individuals. It is not helpful to hand out sweets, pens and money indiscriminately to open-palmed children who tag on to any foreigner.

Charitable giving

Some visitors like to support local self-help co-operatives, orphanages, schools, disabled or disadvantaged groups; Chapora, for example, has an orphanage. Others prefer international charities such as **Oxfam**, **Save the Children** or **Christian Aid** which work with local partners. **Oxfam** ① *Sushil Bhawan, 210 Shahpur Jat, New Delhi 110049, T011-6491774 or at 274 Banbury Rd, Oxford OX2 7D2, UK (400 grassroots projects)*. **SOS Children's Villages** ① *A-7 Nizamuddin (W), New Delhi 110013, T011-4647835*, has over 30 poor and orphaned children's projects in India.

Clothing/conduct

Dress sensibly: modest clothes and a smile go a long way. Scanty, tight clothing draws unwanted attention. Nudity is not permitted on beaches in India. Public displays of intimacy are inappropriate. The greeting when meeting or parting used universally among the Hindus across India is the palms joined together as in prayer, sometimes accompanied with the word *namaste*. 'Thank you' is often expressed by a smile and *abrigaad* in Goa, or with the somewhat formal *dhanyabad*.

You may at times be frustrated by delays, bureaucracy and inefficiency, but displays of anger and rudeness will not achieve anything positive, and often make things worse. The concept of time and punctuality is also rather vague so be prepared to be kept waiting.

Customs

Most travellers experience great warmth and hospitality. With it comes an open curiosity about personal matters. You should not be surprised if total strangers ask for details of your job, income and family circumstances, or discuss politics and religion.

● **Warning** *Anyone charged with the illegal possession of drugs faces a fine of Rs 100,000 and 10 years' imprisonment.*

Drugs

These tend to be available in areas where westerners have chosen to stay for long periods (eg Anjuna, Chapora, Palolem). All-night beach 'parties' are usually associated with drug-taking and 'stop and search' tactics are sometimes carried out by police at the entrance and exit roads to the parties. Police are also known to search cheap accommodation, particularly in the Anjuna to Chapora area. See also the Foreign Office website, www.fco.gov.uk/drugsinformation, for advice to travellers about drugs.

Hands and eating

Traditionally, Indians use the right hand for eating, cutlery being alien at the table except for serving spoons. In Goa however, most restaurants and beach shacks catering for tourists provide cutlery. Use your right hand for giving, receiving, eating or shaking hands as the left is considered to be unclean since it is associated with washing after using the toilet.

Photography

Many sites now charge a camera fee ranging from Rs 10 to Rs 50 for still cameras, to as much as Rs 500 for video cameras, and much more for professionals. When photographing people, it is polite to ask – they will usually respond warmly with smiles, although the 'moment' may be lost as they line up, military style! NB Photography of airports, military installations, bridges, and in tribal and 'sensitive border areas' is not permitted.

Tipping

A tip of Rs 10 to a bell boy carrying luggage in a modest hotel (Rs 20 in a higher category) would be appropriate. In upmarket restaurants, a 10% tip is acceptable (when service is not already included), while in places serving very cheap meals, round off the bill with small change. Indians don't normally tip taxi drivers but a small extra amount over the fare is welcomed. Porters at airports and railway stations often have a fixed rate displayed but will usually press for more. Ask fellow passengers what the fair rate is; usually Rs 10-20 per piece is adequate.

Tour companies sometimes make recommendations for tips for coach drivers and guides. The figures may seem modest by western standards but are very inflated compared with normal Indian earnings. A tip of Rs 50 per day from each member of a coach group (or Rs 100 per person in a car) can safely be regarded as generous.

Visiting religious sites

Visitors to all religious places should be dressed in clean, modest clothes; shorts and vests are inappropriate. Always remove shoes before entering a temple or mosque. Take thick socks for walking on sun-baked stone floors. Walk clockwise around the shrine. Non-Hindus are sometimes excluded from the inner sanctum of Hindu temples and occasionally from the temple itself. Look for signs or ask. In certain temples, and on special occasions, you may only enter if you wear unstitched clothing such as a *dhoti*. Menstruating women are considered 'unclean' and should not enter places of worship. Sitting with your back to a shrine is discourteous. Some temples have a register or a receipt book for donations; elsewhere you may use a donation box.

Responsible tourism

Use your money wisely. Stay in bed and breakfasts and spend your rupees in locally-owned shops and restaurants to be of most support to the local community. Buy local rather than international brands. The biggest environmental issue is certainly water. Purify water rather than buying endless plastic bottles-full. Buy bottled soft

Essentials Touching down

❢ How big is your footprint?

→ Where possible choose a destination, tour operator or hotel with a proven ethical and environmental commitment, and if in doubt ask.

→ Spend money on locally produced (rather than imported) goods and services and use common sense when bargaining – your few dollars saved may be a week's salary to others.

→ Consider staying in local, rather than foreign-owned, accommodation – the economic benefits for host communities are far greater – and there are far greater opportunities to learn about local culture.

→ Use water and electricity carefully – travellers may receive preferential supply while the needs of local communities are overlooked.

→ Don't give money or sweets to children – it encourages begging – instead give to a recognized project, charity or school.

→ Learn about local etiquette and culture – consider local norms and behaviour – and dress appropriately for local cultures and situations.

→ Protect wildlife and other natural resources – don't buy souvenirs or goods made from wildlife unless they are clearly sustainably produced and are not protected under CITES legislation.

→ Always ask before taking photographs or videos of people.

drinks that are recycled rather than plastic. Walk, bicycle or take public transport over fuel-guzzling cars and motorbikes. Air conditioning on the beach is normally totally superfluous, look instead for properties that are made of lime – that breathes and actively cools a building – rather than toxin-emitting concrete, with fan and through-breezes. Take non-biodegradable litter away with you. Environmental concern is very young in India: but don't be afraid to apply pressure on businesses by asking about their policies. A couple of organizations that are really serious about minimising the impact of tourism are **Bakti Kutir** in Palolem and **YogaMagic** near Anjuna.

Safety → See also Women travellers, page 16 and Health, page 42.

Compared with western holiday resorts, Goa has a very good record when it comes to personal safety, although, with more tourists coming into the state, the temptation for opportunistic thieves is growing. Theft is becoming more common especially in budget accommodation, and even upmarket hotels are not immune. Budget travellers should use their own strong padlock. Don't leave anything of value close to windows; better to keep them hidden when leaving your room. It is a good idea to take photocopies of all your important documents and keep them apart from the originals. Make sure you get a detailed receipt when leaving valuables in hotel safes. Better hotels have room safes. 'Safety deposit packets' are available at the **Bank of Baroda** in Calangute and Anjuna. Money belts worn under clothing are good for deterring pickpockets – keep small amounts of cash easily accessible in a purse. After changing money, put it in a safe place before leaving the bank. Thieves on motorbikes have been known to snatch bags from travellers. If you have items stolen, report it to the police as soon as possible. Your hotel may be able to assist in contacting and dealing with the police.

There have been incidents of sexual assault in and around the main tourist beach centres, particularly after full moon parties: avoid wandering alone outdoors late at night. During daylight hours be careful in out of the way places, especially when acquaintances, as it may be drugged.

Roads in the main tourist areas are usually quite narrow, with no pavements to speak of, so walking along them can be hazardous. At night carry a bright torch and wear light-coloured clothing. Motorcycles do not come fitted with helmets and accidents are common, so exercise caution, the horn and the brake. Horns carry their own code: pip to make pedestrians, stray dogs and other bikers aware you're about to overtake or hold a screaming continuous note to communicate urgent alarm to anything fast bearing down on you – even then be prepared to dive from the tarmac.

Trains First class compartments are self-contained and normally completely secure, although nothing of value should be left close to open train windows. Two-tier air-conditioned compartments are larger, allowing more movement of passengers and are therefore not so secure. Attendants may take little notice of what is going on, and thefts – particularly on the Goa to Hampi train route – are on the rise, so luggage should be chained to a seat for security overnight and care taken in daylight. Locks and chains are easily available at main stations and bazaars. Travelling bags and cases should be made of tough material, and external pockets (both on bags and on clothing) should never be used for carrying either money or important documents. Strong locks for travelling cases are invaluable. Use a leather strap around a case for extra security. Some travellers prefer to reserve upper berths, which offer some added protection against theft and also have the benefit of allowing daytime sleeping. Pickpockets and other thieves operate in crowded areas.

Goa has introduced a number of **Tourist Police** (easily identifiable in their blue and white uniforms), who are seen patrolling the major beaches. However, they mainly tend to hassle the beach vendors during the day, except on Wednesdays when they descend on Anjuna hoping to collect baksheesh from foreign motorcyclists who are not carrying the correct documents. It is rare to be stopped by the police for traffic violations except at Anjuna and Chapora, and on the roads leading to and from parties and popular night spots.

Dealings with the **police** can be very difficult. The paperwork involved in reporting losses can be time-consuming and irritating, and your own documentation (eg passport and visas) may be demanded. It is essential to ensure that you have a valid international driving licence, and insurance documents and ownership papers with you when driving a car or motorbike. If a fine is demanded from you, insist on a receipt. If you have to go to a police station, try to take someone with you. If you face really serious problems, for example in connection with a driving accident, you should contact your consular office as quickly as possible. However difficult it may seem, if you are faced with unlawful detention by the police, the best policy is to keep calm and be patient. Insist on seeing the senior officer and on reporting the matter to the Chief of Police.

Confidence tricksters are particularly common where people are on the move, notably around railway and bus stations or places where budget tourists gather. A common plea is some sudden and desperate calamity; sometimes a letter will be produced in English to back up the claim. The demands are likely to increase sharply if sympathy is shown.

Getting around

Air

In addition to **Indian Airlines** (the nationalized carrier) which connects Goa with Bangalore, Chennai, Delhi, Mumbai, Pune and Tiruchirapalli, private airlines, eg, **Jet**

Airways, **Sahara,** also operate on some of these routes. It is essential to book as early as possible, especially in the peak season. Since buying tickets on **Indian Airlines** can often be time-consuming, it is best to use a reputable travel agent and pay them a commission. You can also book internal flights from home on the internet. Details of flights are given under Dabolim and Mumbai.

Some travel agents will make reservations for internal flights abroad if the international ticket is booked through them on a major carrier. Alternatively, try a GSA of **Indian Airlines** (eg **SD Enterprises** ① *103 Wembley Park Drive, Wembley, Middlesex HA9 8HG, T020-89033411,* they are also agents for **Jet Airways.**

Non-resident foreigners buying air tickets in India must use foreign exchange and pay the 'dollar rate' (higher than the published Rupee rate). Competing airlines charge virtually the same price. Major credit cards, travellers' cheques and cash (with encashment certificate) are accepted. **Indian Airlines** ① *www.indian-airlines.nic.in,* and **Jet Airways** ① *www.jetairways.com,* offer special seven-, 15- and 21-day deals for between US$300 and 800, and a 25% discount for passengers under 30 years of age.

If you do not have a confirmed booking arrive early at the airport and to be persistent in enquiring about your position in the queue. NB **Indian Airlines** does not let passengers carry batteries in hand luggage and will confiscate them.

Discount internal flights can be bought from **Welcome Travels** ① *58 Wells St, London W1P 3RA, T020-74363011, www.welcometravel.com,* for Air India, and **Jet Airways** ① *188 Hammersmith Rd, London W6 7DJ, T020-89701555,* for Gulf Air, Kuwait Airways etc.

Rail → *Schedules change so check timings locally.*

Trains offer a unique experience, and are often an excellent alternative way of getting to and from Goa. **The Konkan Railway** allows you to reach Goa from either Mumbai or Mangalore on a comfortable modern train although the journey times are still slow. Those intending to get to a northern beach (eg Baga, Calangute) should get off at **Tivim** station. **Karmali** station, near Old Goa, is nearest to the capital, Panjim, while **Cancona** to the south is the nearest to Palolem. Equally, the broad-gauge service from Vasco and Margao to Londa allows easy connections to the Indian interior. Since it is such a small state, it is rarely worth taking rail journeys within Goa.

For those planning to travel outside Goa, regional timetables are available cheaply from station bookstalls; the monthly 'Indian Bradshaw' is sold in principal stations, while the handy *Trains at a Glance* (Rs 25) lists popular trains likely to be used by most foreign travellers. Indian railways are divided into regions, and, despite a computerized booking system, it can often prove difficult to book train tickets across the country. It is worth asking a travel agent to book your tickets for a small fee (about Rs 50). Tourists have special quotas on many trains. When tickets are not available over the general sales counter, it may still be possible to travel on a tourist quota ticket. **Indian Railways** also offer discounts on Indrail passes, for foreign tourists, which can mean a considerable saving. Payment must be in foreign exchange or in Rupees with a foreign currency encashment certificate.

Air-conditioned First Class, available only on main routes and cheaper than flying, is very comfortable (bedding provided). Air-conditioned Sleeper, two, and three-tier, are clean and comfortable and good value. Air-conditioned Executive Class, with wide reclining seats, is available on many Shatabdi trains at double the price of the ordinary air-conditioned Chair Car, which is equally comfortable. Second Class (non-air-conditioned) two and three-tier, provides exceptionally cheap travel but can be crowded and uncomfortable, and toilet facilities can be unpleasant. It is nearly always better to use the Indian-style toilets as they are better maintained.

Indrail passes

These allow travel across the network without having to pay extra reservation fees and sleeper charges, but you do need to spend a high proportion of your time on the train to make it worthwhile. The advantages of having an Indrail pass mean pre-arranged reservations and automatic access to 'tourist quotas', which can make them a good idea.

Tourists may buy these passes for periods ranging from seven to 90 days from the tourist sections of principal railway booking offices, and pay in foreign currency or equivalent. They can also be bought abroad from special agents. For most people contemplating a single long journey soon after arriving in India, a half-day pass with a confirmed reservation (eg US$ 30 for Mumbai to Margao) is well worth the peace of mind. The GSA in the UK: **SD Enterprises Ltd** ① *103 Wembley Park Drive, Wembley, Middx HA9 8HG*, *T020-89033411, dandpani@dircon.co.uk*, make all necessary reservations and offer excellent advice. They can also book **Indian Airlines** and **Jet Airways** internal flights. Other agencies include France: **Le Monde de L'Inde et de L'Asie** ① *15 Rue des Ecoles, Paris 75005*, *T01-53103100*. Germany: **Asra-Orient** ① *Kaiserstr 50, D-6000 Frankfurt/M*, *T069-253098*. USA: **Hari World Travels** ① *25W 45th St, 1003, New York, NY 10036, T212-9973300*.

Road

Roads offer the only way of reaching many sites of interest within Goa and the neighbouring states. For the uninitiated, travel by road can be a worrying experience, since drivers appear to follow few of the traffic rules that apply in the west.

Auto-rickshaw
Auto-rickshaws – *autos* – are cheap and convenient for getting about. Short journeys will usually cost a minimum Rs 10, Rs 4 per km thereafter. In some areas younger drivers often speak some English and know their local area well. You can hire them by the hour (about Rs 40), half-day, or full-day (about Rs 250). You pay a surcharge for a single journey outside the city. NB Rickshaw and taxi drivers often earn commissions from hotels, restaurants and gift shops, so their advice is not always impartial.

Bus → *Avoid the back half of the bus if possible – the ride is often very uncomfortable.*
Although the buses in Goa are not up to western standards they are a fascinating way of getting around and experiencing some of the local colour. They are also extremely cheap. Special tourist 'luxury' coaches, which may be air-conditioned, are the most comfortable. Overnight sleepers on limited routes (eg Goa-Mumbai, Goa-Hampi) have bunks but, since two often have to share, they are far from ideal even if you are travelling with a companion. 'Video coaches' can be unbearably noisy and so are best avoided – or take earplugs! Road speeds are very slow and express buses rarely average more than 40 km per hour. Despite advertised timetables, the fastest bus from Mumbai to Goa takes at least 16 hours.

Government-run and private buses connect with virtually all of Goa and it is rare for more than one change to be required to reach any particular destination unless travelling from north to south or vice versa. It is usually possible to get a seat, but if the bus is full just wait for the next one. On local routes they are generally quite frequent. There are now regular non-stop minibuses plying between the major towns. Buy tickets before boarding the bus at the nearby booths – prices and destinations are usually clearly stated. Bear in mind that some towns have different bus stations for different destinations. If your destination is only served by a local bus it may be wise to take the express bus and 'persuade' the driver/conductor in advance to stop at the place you want to get off with a tip. You have to pay the full fare to the first scheduled stop after your intended destination, but you will get there faster and more comfortably. Booking on major routes, particularly for travelling to other states is now computerized, and it is worth booking in advance for longer journeys where possible. When an unreserved bus pulls into a bus station, there is usually an unholy scramble for seats. An unwritten 'rule of reservation' using handkerchiefs or bags thrust through the windows operates so do as local people do and be prepared with a handkerchief or 'sarong'. As soon as it touches the seat, it's yours!

A car provides a chance to travel off the beaten track, and gives an unrivalled opportunity to see something of Goa's interior villages and small towns. However, the roads are often in poor condition. Furthermore, the most widely used hire car, the Hindustan Ambassador, can be unreliable; newer models are more trustworthy.

Car hire

A two- or three-day trip around Goa can give an excellent opportunity for sightseeing in reasonable comfort and very economically (especially when shared), but prices rise dramatically in the high season, especially Christmas/New Year. Check beforehand if fuel and inter-state taxes (if you are taking the car out of Goa) are included in the hire charge. Amex, Mastercard and Visa credit cards are accepted. Rates vary according to whether the car is hired for a city trip or an out-of-town trip.

Chauffeur-driven cars from GTDC start at a rate of Rs 7 per km. Sai Service rates are similar, although they work out cheaper over a longer period. A chauffeur-driven car (including fuel) may be hired for varying numbers of hours with a specified kilometre allowance, eg four hours or 50 km, eight hours or 80 km, 12 hours or 120 km. Drivers may be helpful in being able to communicate with local people and also make a journey more interesting by telling you about the places and local customs. If you hire the services of a driver for more than a day they are responsible for all their expenses, including their accommodation and meals. A tip at the end of the whole tour of Rs 100 per day (if you wish), in addition to their inclusive daily allowance, is adequate. NB Be sure to check carefully the mileage at the beginning and end of the trip.

Self-drive car hire is still in its infancy but the rates are attractive when compared to chauffeur-driven rates, especially for out-of-town travel. Drivers must have third party insurance. This may have to be with an Indian insurer, or with a foreign insurer who has a national guarantor. You must also carry an **International Driving Permit** issued by a recognized driving authority in your home country (eg **the AA** in the UK); you may need to apply at least six weeks before leaving.

When reserving the car, emphasize the importance of good tyres, brakes, headlamps and general roadworthiness. Check the car for scratches, dents, etc, before driving away. On main roads across India, petrol stations are reasonably frequent, but parts of Goa are poorly served. Some service stations only have diesel pumps though they may have small reserves of petrol, so always carry a spare can. When buying petrol at a petrol station, make sure that the meter is set at zero before filling up. Carry adequate food and drink, correct documentation (especially for inter-state travel) and a basic tool set in the car. Accidents can produce large and angry crowds very quickly. It is best to leave the scene of the accident and report it to the police as quickly as possible.

Automobile Association office ① *at the Tourist Hostel in Panjim and Lalji Narainji Memorial Building, 76, Veer Nariman Rd, Mumbai.*

Cycling

Cycling is an excellent way of seeing the quiet byways of Goa. Indian cycles are heavy and have no gears, but on the flat they offer a good way of exploring comparatively short distances outside towns. All cyclists should take bungy cords (to strap down a backpack) and good lights from home, but take care not to leave your bike parked anywhere with your belongings attached. It is possible to cover 50 to 80 km a day. Repair shops are universal and charges are nominal.

Cycle hire is widely available and costs around Rs 3-5 per hour or Rs 25-50 per day, depending on the town/resort, season and age of the cycle. It is possible to tour more extensively and you may then want to buy a cycle. There are shops in the larger towns and the local Raleighs are considered the best, with Atlas and BSA as good alternatives. Expect to pay around Rs 1,200-1,500 for a second-hand Indian one but remember to bargain. At the end of your trip you can usually sell it quite easily at half that price. Imported bicycles have the advantage of lighter weight and gears, but are more difficult to get repaired, and carry the much greater risk of being stolen.

Be sure to take all essential spares and a pump. Should you wish to take your bike on the train, allow plenty of time for booking it in and filling in forms. It is best to start any journey early in the morning, stop at midday and resume cycling in the late afternoon. Riding at night can be hazardous because of lack of lighting and poor road surfaces. Try to avoid the major highways as far as possible.

Motorbikes and scooters

One of the most popular and convenient ways of exploring Goa is to hire a motorbike or scooter. These are easily available at all the major resorts although a number of hazards accompany this seemingly carefree form of transport. Many small guest houses have one or two bikes for hire, or can arrange one. A few enterprising locals have built up small fleets of old (and often beaten-up) vehicles.

Motorcycle hire rates are generally consistent across Goa. Scooters (eg Kinetic Honda, TVS Scooty) are about Rs 150-200 per day; larger, 125cc motorbikes (eg Honda, Yamaha) cost between Rs 200-300 per day; the popular 350cc Enfield Bullet comes in the Rs 300-400 price range. Discounts are given for long-term rental so it pays to bargain. Some require a large deposit or passport for security against damages to the bike and to ensure that the bike is returned (some lazy travellers have hired a bike in Colva and abandoned it in Palolem!). Others are more relaxed and allow you to take a bike with no deposit and to pay upon return. Bikes rarely come with crash helmets since these are not compulsory in Goa. It may be worth asking if you can borrow one to increase your chances of avoiding serious injury.

When hiring a motorbike, check it carefully to see that everything is in working order, especially brakes, tyres, lights and the horn (usually your first line of defence against accidents). If there is any damage to the bodywork of the bike, point it out to the hirer and agree that it already exists. Otherwise you may face a repair bill. Except when the bike is covered by fully comprehensive insurance (rare) and that you are legally allowed to ride the bike (even rarer), any damages are expected to be paid for. It may be better to get damages repaired yourself rather than pay an inflated estimate, or at least insist that you accompany the owner to the garage to ensure a fair price is agreed for repairs. Hired bikes come with very little petrol in the tank. This is because the owners sell off unused petrol when the bike is returned. Estimate the amount of petrol you will need and ignore advice by owners to fill the tank up if you have any problem with the vehicle. Petrol is available at pumps in Panjim, Calangute, Mapusa, Arambol, Margao and Chaudi. Elsewhere, fuel sold in bottles may be adulterated.

www.indax.com has useful information on motorbike touring hazards.

Essentials Getting around

Motorcycle tour companies

Aventuremoto, www.aventuremoto.com. Offers tours further afield to Rajasthan and Garhwal Himalaya.
Blazing Trails, T01293-533338, jewel@ jewelholidays.com. Similar touring with good back-up to Peter and Friends below.

Peter & Friends Classic Adventures Casa Tres Amigos, Socol Vado, H No 425, Assagao (east of Anjuna), T0832-2268241, www.classic-bike-india.de. Indo-German company who run motorbike tours of Goa and South India with good backup.
Royal Enfield, www.royalenfield.com. Has information on pilgrim tours by motorbike and how to buy a new Bullet.

Taxis are readily available at major resorts usually waiting outside the larger hotels or at recognized taxi stands. Bargaining is required although they don't reduce the asking rate much in the tourist areas. In some areas they have a list of agreed prices, whilst larger hotels usually have a taxi desk with listed fares. Before travelling in an unmetered taxi, ask at the hotel desk for an estimated price. Whatever fare you agree, you are paying a very good rate by local standards so it is unnecessary to tip. Try to insist on the taxi meter being 'flagged' in your presence. In some cities taxis refuse to use the meter – the official advice is to call the police! At railway stations, and at Mumbai and Dabolim airports, it is often possible to share a taxi to a central point. It is worth looking for fellow passengers who may be travelling in your direction. When travelling from Mumbai airport at night always have a clear idea of where you want to go and insist on being taken there. Many Mumbai taxi drivers will do everything possible to convince you that the hotel you have named was 'closed three years ago' or is 'completely full'. It may be necessary to insist that you have an advance reservation.

Motorcycle taxis are peculiar to Goa and offer the cheapest means of covering short distances, although they are also the least safe and can be quite tiring if you have a heavy rucksack. Official motorcycle taxis are black and yellow. Agree a price in advance before getting on. Minimum fare is Rs 6, Rs 4 per km thereafter. NB Your insurance policy may not cover you if you are involved in an accident.

Maps

For anyone interested in the geography of India, or even simply getting around, trying to buy good maps is a depressing experience. For security reasons it is illegal to sell large-scale maps of any area within 80 km of the coast or national borders.

In Goa Goa tourist offices hand out a reasonable state map (updated with the Konkan railway) in colour. **Findoll Publications** have brought out an updated **Goa Yellow Pages** accompanied by two sheets of colour maps (Rs 60 each) aimed at the tourist market. Goa Map 1: State and towns (Panjim, Old Goa, Mapusa, Margao, Vasco, Dona Paula, Porvorim etc). Goa Map 2: Beaches covering all popular ones from Arambol in the north to Palolem in the south. Fairly detailed, including hotels, restaurants, tourist services (banks, travel agents, tailors, beach parties, etc) but not quite up to date and not wholly reliable in detail. **Lascelle's** 1995 Goa (1:200,000) is fairly accurate while www.geocities.com/johnmap2001/goa has very detailed maps of several beach sites. For most visitors the maps in this guide will give adequate coverage. The **Bartholomew** 1:4m map sheet of the country is the most authoritative, detailed and easy to use map of India available. This map is available to buy worldwide.

Map shops outside Goa

Blackwells, 53 Broad St, Oxford, T01645-792792, www.bookshop.blackwell.co.uk.
Stanfords, 12-14 Long Acre, London WC2E 9LP, T020-72242295, www.stanfords.co.uk.
Zumsteins Landkartenhaus, Leibkerrstr 5, 8 München 22, Germany.

Mapworld, 173 Gloucester St, Christchurch, NZ, T03-3745399, www.mapworld.co.nz.
Michael Chessler, PO Box 2436, Evergreen, CO 80439, USA T800-6548502.
Rand McNally, across the USA, T0800- 3330136 extn 2111, www.randmcnally.com.

Sleeping → *See inside front cover for a quick guide to hotel price codes.*

Like the rest of India, Goa has a wide range of accommodation and visitors can stay safely (and very cheaply by western standards) in resorts, towns and villages. There are also high-quality hotels, offering a full range of facilities. Prices at the top luxury resorts are sometimes comparable with prices in the west.

Prices and categories

The prices given are for a standard double room in high season. Prices over Christmas and New Year rise dramatically, in some cases almost doubling. However, generous reductions are offered during the monsoon off-season. At other times, many hotels are prepared to discount their listed price by at least 10% to independent travellers who ask for it, since the hotel saves the commission to an agency. Taxes can add considerably to the basic price (see below). The price categories are not star ratings, and individual facilities vary widely. Normally the following facilities will be found as standard in the given classes.

Most LL, L, AL and some A category hotels charge foreigners, except those working in India, and NRIs (non-resident Indians), a 'dollar price', about 50% more than the 'Rupee price'. All hotels in category C and above, and some below, accept payment by credit card. There are some excellent-value hotels and guest houses in the E and F categories, which, though very basic, can be clean and adequate; occasionally 'dormitories' have only four beds, making them very good value. Long-stay visitors often rent cheap rooms on a monthly basis. An extra bed or mattress in a room is usually available at an attractive rate.

> ✆ *www.i-escape.com is a useful online hotel resource with pictures of accommodation options available.*

For people travelling off the beaten track outside Goa there are several cheap options. Railway stations often have retiring rooms or 'rest rooms'. These may be hired for periods of between one and 24 hours by anyone holding an onward train ticket. They are cheap and usually provide a bed and a fan. Some stations have a couple of air-conditioned rooms, but they are often very heavily booked. They can be very convenient for short stops if travelling extensively by train, although some can be very noisy. In Mumbai, the domestic airport and CST railway station have similar facilities.

Taxes and bills

In Goa, a range of taxes applies to different categories of hotels. In the cheapest hotels no extra tax is chargeable. When a luxury tax applies in the higher category hotels, these are added to the bill presented at the end of your stay, which usually includes meals. To avoid the extra charge, if you eat in the hotel restaurant, it is worth paying the meals bill separately to ensure that tax is not added to food as well as room charges.

Some visitors have complained of miscalculations, even in the most expensive hotels. The problem particularly afflicts those that are part of a group, with last-minute extras sometimes appearing on some bills. Check at the desk the evening before departure, and keep all receipts. Check carefully again when paying your bill.

Facilities

You have to be prepared for difficulties that are uncommon in the west. It is best to inspect the room and check that all equipment (air conditioning, TV, water heater, flush) works before checking in at a modest hotel.

Air conditioning is usually only available in category B and above. Elsewhere, air-conditioned rooms are cooled by individual units and occasionally by large air-coolers which can be noisy and unreliable. When they fail to operate tell the

⁝ Hotels with the most character

→ **Fort Tiracol Heritage Hotel** The ferries stop running from Tiracol to the rest of Goa at dusk, leaving you alone with the views and church, see page 130.

→ **Home Guesthouse**, Patnem. Impromptu jazz sessions and artists dropping by for coffee, see page 160.

→ **Villa Riva Cat**, Mandrem. A commune of a house that overspills with colour and energy, see page 130.

→ **Bhakti Kutir**. Drumming, yoga and environmentalism, see page 159.

→ **Yogamagic**. Canvas hotel for all things yoga, reiki and vedic, see page 119.

→ **Kerkar Retreat**. For canvas-and-oil-paint creativity, see page 102.

→ **Ciaran's Camp**, Palolem. Good enough for Neil Morrissey, overrun with pedigree dogs, see page 159.

→ **Nilaya Hermitage**. Kate Moss's choice when she's in state, see page 104.

→ **Siolim House**. Huge rooms in grand old-style palatial villa, see page 119.

→ **Panjim Inn**. The first heritage hotel in Goa, see page 71.

management, as it is often possible to get a rapid repair done, or to transfer to a room where the unit is working. Fans are provided in all but the cheapest of hotels.

Where staff training is lacking, the person who brings up your cases may proceed to show you light switches, room facilities, TV tuning, and hang around waiting for a tip. Room boys may enter your room without knocking or without waiting for a response to a knock. Both for security and privacy, it is a good idea to lock your door when you are in the room. It is worth noting any incidents in the comments book when leaving as the management may then take action.

Apart from the AL and A categories, 'baths' do not necessarily refer to **bathrooms** with western-style bathtubs. Other hotels may provide a bathroom with a toilet, basin and a shower. Power cuts mean hot water may be restricted to certain times of day. The largest hotels have their own generators but it is best to carry a good torch. In the lower-priced hotels and outside large towns, a bucket and tap may replace the shower, and there may be an Indian 'squat' toilet instead of a western-style WC. Even medium-priced hotels that are clean and pleasant do not always provide towels, soap and toilet paper. In some Goan village homes, the toilet raised off the ground is not connected to a sewer, but is cleaned out by pigs which are allowed to roam underneath. Water supply is rationed periodically (especially in the dry season), occasionally even in the better hotels. Keep a bucket filled to use for flushing the toilet during water cuts. Occasionally, tap water may be discoloured, simply due to rusty tanks. Electric water heaters may provide enough for a shower but not enough to fill a bathtub! NB For advice on drinking water see page 38.

At some times of the year and in some places mosquitoes can be a real problem. In cheap hotels you need to be prepared for a wider range of **insect life**, including flies, cockroaches and ants. Poisonous insects are extremely rare in towns. Hotel management are nearly always prepared with insecticide sprays. Many small hotels in mosquito-prone areas supply nets. Remember to shut windows and doors at dusk. Electrical devices are now widely available, as are mosquito coils, which burn slowly. At night, fans can be very effective in discouraging mosquitoes. As well as common insects, expect to find spiders that are larger and hairier than those you see at home; they are mostly harmless. You will be lucky to come across a scorpion in rural areas (always check shoes/boots before putting them on). You are more likely to have a resident gecko (a harmless house lizard) in your room. Treat them as your friends, as they keep the number of mosquitoes down.

Hotels close to temples can be very noisy, especially during festivals. Music blares from loudspeakers late at night and from very early in the morning, often making sleep impossible. Mosques call the faithful to prayers at dawn. Some find earplugs helpful.

Laundry can be arranged very cheaply (eg a shirt washed and pressed for Rs 15-20 in C-D category, Rs 50 or more in luxury hotels) and quickly in 12-24 hours. It is best not to risk delicate fibres, though luxury hotels can usually handle these and can also dry-clean items.

Checkout time in most places is 1200. You may usually ask to leave your bags at the reception for some time after that if you wish. Some hotels expect you to vacate your room by 0900 (ask at the time of checking in).

Seasons → *Some hotels and restaurants close between Jun and Sep.*

Many hotels in Goa charge their highest room-rate over Christmas and New Year (between mid-December and mid-January), but also offer large discounts from mid-June to mid-September.

In the peak season (November to March) bookings can be extremely heavy so it is best to reserve accommodation well in advance. Double-check reconfirmation details, and always try to arrive as early as possible, or your reservation may be cancelled. If you travel out from the major centres (eg spending a night away from your booked hotel, when touring), be prepared to accept much more modest accommodation.

In the low season (May to Mid-September), when foreign package tours cease, some of the larger resort hotels turn their attention to attracting domestic tourists and Indian business conventions. During these periods they may take on quite a different character with restaurants offering a different menu with more spicy dishes to suit the change in clientele.

Eating → *See inside front cover for restaurant price codes.*

Most visitors are surprised – and often delighted – at the enormous variety of delicious food on offer, some bearing little relation to the various curries available outside India. There is a remarkable range of delicious savoury snacks and sweets. Restaurants and beach cafés in the main tourist centres offer Goan food as well as a good range of dishes from other parts of India. To suit the unaccustomed palate, they also have some western and Chinese options.

Although Goan food has similarities with that in the rest of India – rice, vegetable curries and daal, for example – there are many Goan specialities, which are usually served with local bread. Common ingredients in Goan cooking include coconut and cashew (*kaju*) nuts, pork and a wide variety of seafood. Not surprisingly, the food in this region is hot, making full use of the small bird's-eye chillies that are grown locally. Chilli was only introduced to Goa by the Portuguese, adding just one more ingredient to an already richly-flavoured, and highly-spiced diet. Goa's Christians have no qualms about using pork (not eaten by Muslims and most Hindus). A state dominated by its coastline, Goa freely uses the harvest from its seas. The standard 'fish curry and rice', the common Goan meal, has become a catchphrase. Most beach shacks offer a good choice (depending on the day's catch), and will usually include preparations of kingfish, tuna, mackerel, pomfret, tiger prawns and shark. You will find fried mussels, squid, lobsters, baked oysters, boiled clams and stuffed crabs as specialities.

> One recipe for the popular Goan dish sorpotel suggests that in addition to other spices you should use 20 dry chillies for 1 kg pork plus liver and heart, with four green chillies thrown in for good measure!

Vegetarians are well provided for in Goa. South Indian **Brahmin** food, for example, is wholly distinctive, with tamarind and coconut being typical ingredients. Three of its snacks – *dosai*, *idli* and *wada* (*vadai*) – are good vegetarian options.

North Indian cooking is often called **Mughlai**. Cream and ghee are favourite cooking mediums, and spices, herbs, nuts and fruit are all ingredients added to dishes, which usually have meat as the main focus of the meal. Several different kinds of kebab, meatballs and minced meat preparations are served alongside biriyani or pulao. **Tandoori** dishes, marinated meat cooked in a special earthenware oven, come from the far northwest, but are widely popular.

A **thali** is a complete meal served on a plate or stainless steel tray. Several preparations, placed in small bowls, surround the central serving of wholewheat *puris* and rice. A vegetarian *thali* basically includes chapati, rice, daal, two vegetable curries and poppadum, although there are regional variations. Fish, mutton or chicken curries are popular non-vegetarian dishes, which can be quite hot and spicy. A variety of sweet and hot pickles are offered – mango and lime are two of the most popular. These can be exceptionally hot, and are designed to be taken in minute quantities alongside the main dishes. Plain *dahi* (yoghurt) is usually included, which acts as a bland cooling dish to accompany highly spiced food. You may wish to order a sweet to end the meal.

Many hotel restaurants and beach cafés offer European options.

Fruit and nuts

Home of one of India's most famous mangoes, the alfonso, Goa has a wide range of fruit. Some are highly seasonal – mangoes in the hot season, for example – while others (eg bananas) are available throughout the year. The extremely rich jackfruit is common, as are papaya and watermelons. Cashew nuts and pineapples (brought from South America) and papaya (brought from the Philippines) were introduced to Goa by the Portuguese.

Water

Drinking water used to be regarded as one of India's biggest hazards. It is still true that water from taps or wells should never be regarded as safe to drink. Public water supplies are nearly always polluted and unsafe. However bottled purified water is now widely available (not all bottled water is mineral water; some is simply purified water from an urban supply). Check the seal carefully (some are now double sealed) and avoid street hawkers; crush the bottles when disposing of them. Water sterilization tablets can be bought from many chemists in Goa. This method reduces the amount of plastic bottles used throughout your trip and is a 'greener' option. Always carry plenty with you when travelling. NB It is important to use pure water for cleaning teeth.

Drinks

Tea and coffee are safe and widely available. If you wish to order it black say 'no sugar', 'no milk' when ordering. At a roadside stall, however, *chai* or *chaa* is milky and sweet. Nescafe, espresso and capuccino coffee are sometimes on offer but may not turn out as you would expect in the west. UHT milk in litre packs is sold widely.

Don't add ice cubes to any drink – the water used may be contaminated

There is a huge variety of bottled **soft drinks**, including well known international brands, which are perfectly safe. Popular and safe Indian brands include **Limca** or **Teem** (lime and lemon), **Thums Up** (cola) and **Mirinda** (lemon), but some find them too sweet. Fruit juice, including mango, pineapple and apple is available in cartons. Prices of pre-packed drinks range from Rs 8-15.

Fresh **fruit juice** (prepared hygienically) is a good option as is fresh lime-soda (plain, sweet or salty). Cool and refreshing fruit-flavoured milk-shakes and yoghurt-based *lassis* cost around Rs 35. Plain *lassi* is cheaper at about Rs 20.

Alcohol

A wide range of alcoholic drinks is available in Goa including some foreign brands in the major centres. Drinks in Goa remain relatively cheap compared with elsewhere in India. The increase in alcoholism (especially among Goan men) has led certain groups to call for prohibition.

The fermented juice of cashew apples, distilled for the local brew *kaju feni* (fen, froth), is strong and potent. Coconut or palm feni is made from the sap of the coconut palm. *Feni* is an acquired taste so it is often mixed with soda. It can also be taken on the rocks, as a cocktail mixed with fruit juice (bottle, about Rs 25) or pre-flavoured (eg with ginger). Don't drink this on an empty stomach. Sip slowly and avoid taking more than a couple of 'tots' when you are new to it.

Beer is usually available in several popular brands— **Kingfisher, Fosters, Kings, Pilsner** (brewed with imported German hops) and the stronger **Arlem** (brewed on the outskirts of Margao). All come in large bottles (650 ml) and cost Rs 30-40; the latter two also come in half-size bottles and cost Rs 25.

Goan **wines** tend to be of the fortified variety and are sweet. **Port** (a legacy of Portuguese rule) is a very sweet red wine, around 14% alcohol. A good bottle sells for Rs 50-60 in a wine shop, though beach shacks will charge Rs 40-80 depending on the quality of the bottle, or Rs 60 for a large peg, and quarter bottles for Rs 20-25. **Dark rum** is cheap (eg Old Monk, Rs 80 a bottle) and Honey Bee **brandy** is popular.

Entertainment

In Goa, beach raves and parties (associated with Goa Trance and the drug scene) taking place in makeshift venues continue to attract large groups of young foreigners to the state, particularly during Christmas and the New Year (see Festivals and events, below). More traditional, popular village entertainment takes the form of folk drama, dance and music. You will not escape the local Konkani pop, which blends East and West with a distinct flavour of the Caribbean. It is played aloud in all public places. To sample the more authentic sounds of folk and classical music (and dance), find out the programme at the **Kala Academy**, Panjim, and **Kerkar Gallery**, Candolim. The hugely popular Hindi film industry comes largely out of this tradition. It's always easy to find a cinema, but prepare for a lengthy showing with a standard story line and set of characters and lots of action. See page 243 for further details.

Festivals and events

In addition to the widespread celebration of Hindu festivals, with Goa's significant Christian population and the small minority of Muslims, the corresponding religious festivals are also widely observed. Hindu and Muslim festivals fall on different dates each year, depending on the lunar calendar so check dates with the tourist office.

National holidays

Jan 26 Republic Day
Aug 15 Independence Day
Oct 2 Mahatma Gandhi's Birthday
Dec 25 Christmas Day
These all count as full public holidays throughout Goa.

Religious festivals

Jan 6 Feast of the Three Kings Celebrated in Cansaulim (Cuelim), Chandor and Reis Magos, where a big fair is also held.
Jan 14 Makarashankranti A kite-flying festival when Hindus distribute sweets among friends and relatives.

Feb Mahasivaratri or Sivaratri A Hindu festival that marks the night when Siva danced his celestial dance of destruction (Tandava) celebrated with feasting and fairs at Siva temples, and preceded by a night of devotional readings and hymn singing. Special ceremonies are held at some temples, including, Arvalem, Fatorpa, Mangesh, Nagesh, Queula, Shiroda.

Feb The Carnival A non-religious festival celebrated all over Goa in February or March. On the first day (Fat Saturday), 'King Momo' leads a colourful procession of floats with competing 'teams' dressed in flamboyant costumes as they wind through the towns' main streets. Dances are held in clubs and hotels through the 3 days and traffic comes to a halt on some streets from time to time.

Mar Shigmotsav A Hindu spring festival (Holi) held at full moon in the month of Phalgun and celebrated all over Goa but particularly in Panjim, Mapusa, Vasco da Gama and Margao on successive days starting at around 1600. The festivities are accompanied by percussive music on drums and cymbals and the usual throwing of colourful powder and water at each other. The 'fun' can sometimes get out of hand.

Mar Procession of All Saints In Goa Velha, on the Mon of Holy Week. See page 69.

Apr Muharram Anniversary of the killing of the Prophet's grandson Hussain, is commemorated with Ashoura procession of Shi'a Muslims beating their chests to express their grief. Shi'as fast for 10 days.

Apr Ramnavami Celebrated by Hindus. It is the birthday of Lord Rama (the seventh incarnation of Vishnu), hero of the epic Ramayana.

Apr Feast of Our Lady of Miracles On the nearest Sunday, 16 days after Easter.

May Music Festival Pop, beat and jazz at the Kala Academy, Panjim.

May 30 Goa Statehood Day An official holiday when all government offices and many shops are closed.

Jun 13 Feast of St Anthony Songs in honour of the saint, requesting the gift of rain.

Jun 24 Feast of St John the Baptist (Sao Joao) A thanksgiving for the arrival of the monsoon.

Jun 29 Festival of St Peter Held at Fort Aguada. A pageant on a floating raft.

Jul-Aug Nagpanchami The Naga (Cobra) is worshipped in the form of the thousand headed Shesha and Ananta, on which Vishnu reclined.

Aug-Sep Raksha Bandhan (literally 'protection bond') A Hindu festival commemorating the wars between Indra, the King of the Heavens, and the demons when his wife tied a silk amulet (rakhi) around his wrist to protect him from harm. The festival symbolizes the bond between brother and sister, and is celebrated at full moon. A sister says special prayers and ties a rakhi around her brother's wrist to remind him of the special bond.

Aug-Sep Janmashtami (birth of Lord Krishna) A Hindu festival with mass bathing in the Mandovi River off Divar Island. Hymns are sung and night-long prayers are held.

Sep 21 and 24 Harvest Festival of Novidade The first sheaves of rice are offered to the priests, the Governor and Archbishop, and placed in the cathedral on the 24th. The festival includes a re-enactment on the lawns of the Lieutenant Governor's Palace of one of the battles between Albuquerque and the Adil Shah.

Sep Ganesh Chaturthi The elephant-headed deity, the God of good omen, is shown special reverence. The five-day Hindu festival follows the harvest. On the last day, clay images of Ganesh (Ganpati) are taken in procession, with dancers and musicians playing drums and cymbals and are then immersed in the sea, river or pond. The skies light up with fireworks displays and the air turns smoky from firecrackers.

Oct Dasara (Dussera) A Hindu festival celebrated in honour of minor deities. The celebrations continue for nine nights (Navaratri) with various episodes of the Ramayana story being enacted and recited, with particular reference to the battle between the forces of good and evil.

Oct 14 Fama of Menino Jesus Commemorates the miraculous figure in Colva. See page 140.

Oct Narkasur On the eve of Diwali, Goan Hindus remember the victory of Lord Krishna over the demon Narkasur. In Panjim there are processions and competitions.

Oct Diwali (Deepavali) The Hindu festival of lights when homes are decorated with lines of earthenware lamps, candles or tiny electric bulbs. Fireworks have become an integral part of the celebration, and are often set off days before Diwali.

Nov Ramadan The month of fasting, when all Muslims (except young children, the very elderly, the sick, pregnant women and travellers) must abstain from food and drink from sunrise to sunset.

Dec 17 Liberation Day A public holiday commemorating the end of Portuguese colonial rule and is marked by military parades.

Dec 25 Christmas Observed with Midnight Mass in churches across the state and family get-togethers, and involving every community. Special Goan sweets made with ground rice and sugar are prepared.

Dec Id-ul-Fitr (the 'small feast') The 3-day festival to mark the end of Ramadan determined by the sighting of the new moon Id-ul-Azha /Bakr-Id (the 'great feast'). Muslims commemorate Ibrahim's sacrifice of his son according to God's commandment. The main time of pilgrimage to Mecca (the Hajj). It is marked by the sacrifice of a goat, feasting and alms giving.

Shopping

Handicrafts

Handicrafts from all over India make their way to the streets and beaches of Goa to satisfy the hunger of the foreign travellers ready to indulge in exotic purchases. Shopping can be fun and rewarding, since you pay a fraction of the price charged for similar gifts and goods at home. Goa itself produces little to appeal to the foreigner, other than excellent cashew nuts and attractive packets of spices, some of which are grown locally.

Bargaining

Bargaining can be fun and a pastime in its own right here. It is best to get an idea of prices being asked by different stalls for items that interest before taking the plunge. Some beach hawkers and stall holders will happily quote twice the actual price to a foreigner showing interest, so you might well start by halving the asking price. On the other hand it would be inappropriate to do the same in an established shop with price-tags, though a plea for the 'best price' or a special discount might reap results even here. Remain good-humoured throughout. Walk away slowly to test to whether your custom is sought – you will probably be called back!

Crafts from the rest of India

Kashmiri salesmen are renowned for their success in spreading across the country to find outlets for their excellent products. They range from small items of hand-crafted papier maché lacquerware, 'silver' bangles and necklaces, walnut wood bowls, tables and trays, to much more pricey embroidered wool shawls and scarves (remember, trade in toosh wool is banned) and exquisite hand-knotted rugs using old Persian designs in wool or silk. Colourful crewel-work cushion covers and floor coverings are also attractive and more affordable.

Traders from the Himalaya – often Ladakhis or exiled Tibetans – sell chunky 'silver' jewellery often set with semi-precious stones, religious metalwork, thick-pile Tibetan-style wool carpets, wood carvings, rustic jackets and shoulder bags.

You are also likely to find craft items from Gujarat and neighbouring Karnataka fashioned out of tribal embroidery, as well as inlaid marble pieces from Agra inspired by the Taj Mahal. 'Mughal' miniatures, sometimes using natural pigments on old paper and new silk, and traditional string puppets, make their way from Rajasthan, while attractive wood and metal figures of Hindu deities from South India also make good souvenirs. Whatever the claim, the latter are not always carved out of

⁞ Best shopping in Goa

Many of the best brand labels – Levi's, Nike et al – have boutiques in Panjim where you can pick up jeans for a relative song.

→ **Oxford Arcade**, Anjuna. Has unimaginable luxuries stashed away: smoked salmon, homemade yogurts, posh toiletries as well as basics like muesli, see page 121.

→ **Mapusa bazaar**, Mapusa. For government fixed-rate rice, daal and spices, see page 93.

→ **The flea market**, Anjuna. Still best for sheer mad tripped-out threads, see page 115.

→ **Ingo's**, in Arpora. Saturday night bazaar with live music and a festival party vibe and a snazzier choice of clothes, see page 99.

→ **The Tibetan handicrafts market**, Calangute. Silver and turquoise from Rajasthan and Bhutan sold by the weight, see page 109.

→ **Sankars**, Candolim. Sells everything from Goan literature to self-help books, see page 109.

sandalwood or cast in bronze and are very unlikely to be genuine antiques (which are banned from export in any case).

Textiles

Goa offers a window for India's treasure house of textiles. Handlooms produce rich shot silk from Kanchipuram, skilfully crafted ikat from Gujarat, Orissa and Andhra, silk brocades with gold zari work from Varanasi, and printed silks and batiks from Bengal. Sober handspun *khadi*, colourful Rajasthani block-printed cottons using vegetable dyes, and tie-dye Gujarati *bandhani* are easier on the pocket.

Clothing

It is worth looking out for ready-made clothing (Indian and western styles) and leather sandals. International labels and quality local designer wear are now sold in smart boutiques. Fabrics are exceptional value so, if you don't find what you want, you can get an expert tailor to copy your own garment.

Markets

The hyped-up Wednesday flea market at Anjuna or one of the Saturday night markets north of Baga, though atmospheric, can be disappointing since some goods are shoddy and poor value. Identical items can be bought for less at a stall nearby during the rest of the week. You would do better to look around the shops near where you are staying or in the larger stores in Panjim or Margao. The government handicrafts emporia are generally the safest bet for guaranteed quality at fixed prices, but you will be expected to bargain elsewhere. The bazaars (as at Mapusa) are full of colour and, because they are for the local population, are competitively priced. They are often a great experience. For upmarket purchases, trendy studios (mostly in Panjim) and shops in luxury resort hotels sell fine household items.

Pitfalls

Taxi/rickshaw drivers and tour guides tend to recommend certain shops where they get a commission, but prices there are invariably inflated. Some shops offer to pack and post your purchases but can't always be trusted. Only make such arrangements in government emporia or in a large store. **Warning** Don't enter into any arrangement to help 'export' marble items, jewellery etc, no matter how tempting your 'cut'. Travellers have been cheated through misuse of their credit card accounts, and have been left with unwanted purchases. Make sure that credit cards are run off just the once. Traders sometimes pass off fake marble, ivory, silver, semi- precious stones, coral etc, as real. Watch out for artificial silk (as fabric and in carpets). Export of certain items such as antiquities, ivory, furs and skins is controlled or banned, so you need to get a certificate of legitimate sale and permission for export.

Sport and activities

Ayurveda, yoga and meditation

Ayurveda ('science of life/health') is the ancient Hindu system of medicine, a naturalistic system depending on diagnosis of the body's 'humours' (wind, mucus, gall and sometimes, blood) to achieve a balance. In its early form, gods and demons were associated with cures and ailments; treatment was carried out by using herbs, minerals, formic acid (from ant hills) and water, and hence was limited in scope. Ayurveda classified substances and chemical compounds in the theory of panchabhutas or five 'elements'. It also noted the action of food and drugs on the human body. Ayurvedic massage, using aromatic and medicinal oils to tone up the nervous system, has been practised in Kerala for centuries. Interest has been revived in this form of medicine and there are a growing number of centres which include a 'rejuvenation programme'.

Ancient ayurvedic therapy, yoga and meditation have been made accessible to foreign visitors at some of the upmarket resorts and specialist yoga centres. At a more down-to-earth level, you can sample simple living at **Bhakti Kutir** in Palolem or **Shanti Nature Resort** at distant Tambdi Surla. **Purple Valley Yoga Center** ① *Assagao, www.yogagoa.net*, offer one or two week retreats and drop-in yoga classes with peerless international ashtanga yoga teachers like John and Lucy Scott.

Birdwatching

Even a short visit can be very rewarding with ample opportunity for a keen visitor to spot 150 to 200 species in a fortnight's stay. The varied terrain, from the sea shore to the hill slopes of the Western Ghats rising to about 1000 m, provide diverse habitats ranging from wetland and grassland to scrub and forest cover. The **Bondla**, **Cotigao** and **Bhagwan Mahaveer Sanctuaries**, **Salim Ali Bird Sanctuary** (Chorao Island), **Mayem** and **Carambolim Lakes** are well worth visiting. Nearer the beach resorts, Baga river, Nerul estuary, the area around Aguada and Morjim/ Siolim are all rich in birdlife.

Harvey & Neil ① *T0832-2401814, birdwing@hotmail.com*, can organize tailor made birding trips and crocodile watching on the Cambarjua Canal. Further reading: Kazmierczak, K, and Singh, R, *A Birdwatchers' Guide to India* (UK, 1998). Excellent coverage with helpful practical information and maps.

Cricket

Reinforced by satellite TV and radio, and a national side that enjoys high world rankings and much outstanding individual talent, cricket is a national obsession. Stars have cult status, and you will see children trying to model themselves on their game on any and every open space.

Football

Sport has become India's greatest popular entertainment. Soccer is played from professional level to kickabout in any open space. Professional matches are played in Panjim and Margao in large stadiums attracting very big crowds; the latter holds

34,000 spectators. The season is from October to March and details of matches are published in the local papers. The top-class game tickets are Rs 25, but they are sold for much more on the black market. The crowds generate tremendous fervour for the big matches, and standards are improving. African and Brazilian players are now featuring more frequently with Indian teams and monthly salaries have risen to over Rs 40,000 per month, a very good wage by Indian standards.

Watersports

The watersports industry is still a fledgling enterprise. Agents offer a number of options (parasailing, windsurfing, waterskiing, etc) within easy reach of the major resorts, including a choice of boat trips. Popular trips to view dolphins are available from most areas. Some guarantee sighting of two species, usually bottle-nosed and humpbacked dolphins. Fishing trips usually set off in the early morning or late evening returning with a catch of kingfish, snappers, Goa fish or catfish. Watersports facilities on the beaches are generally limited to those offered by random westerners at various locations with no guarantee that they will be there the following year. There is a good chance of finding a choice on Bogmalo, Candolim and Colva beaches, while the Taj at Aguada near Panjim, and the resort hotels at Mobor in the south, offer several options – at a price.

Watersports are quite widely available but PADI-certificated scuba diving is only available at **Barracuda**, at the Goa Marriott, **Miramar**, and at **Goa Diving**, Bogmalo. The best time is after the monsoons, from October to April; the water temperature varies from 25 to 30 °c . The local dive sites are relatively shallow (usually between eight and 15 m) allowing underwater visibility of between two to 20 m. The dive sites on coral or rock beds off several islands are usually between 15 and 30 minutes' boat ride away and marine life-rich and varied, including damsels, groupers, sergeant-majors, puffers, surgeon, barracuda, wrasse, parrotfish, angles, moray eels, snappers and jacks among many others. It is also possible to see sharks, rays, tuna and turtles. See also diving websites in Goa: www.barracudadiving.com and www.goa.indiantravelportal.com/watersports.

It is dangerous to dive within 48 hours of flying. Also, check your insurance.

You can check for PADI-recognized courses in Goa before arriving, by contacting **PADI International Head Office** ① *Unit 6, Unicorn Park, Whitby Road, Bristol, BS4 4EX. T0117-9711717, www.padi.co.uk.*

Health

Local populations in Goa are exposed to a range of health risks not encountered in the western world. Many of the diseases are major problems for the local poor and destitute and, although the risk to travellers is more remote, they cannot be ignored. Obviously five-star travel is going to carry less risk than backpacking on a budget.

The health care in the region is varied. There are many excellent private and government clinics/hospitals. As with all medical care, first impressions count. If a facility is grubby then be wary of the general standard of medicine and hygiene. It's worth contacting your embassy or consulate on arrival and asking where the recommended (ie those used by diplomats) clinics are. Providing embassies with information of your whereabouts can be also useful if a friend/relative gets ill at home and there is a desperate search for you around the globe. You can also ask them about locally recommended medical do's and don'ts. If you do get ill, and you have the opportunity, you should also ask your medical insurer whether they are satisfied that the medical centre or hospital that you have been referred to is of a suitable standard.

Before you go

Ideally, you should see your GP or travel clinic at least six weeks before your departure for general advice on travel risks, malaria and vaccinations. Make sure you have travel insurance, get a dental check (especially if you are going to be away for more than a month), know your own blood group and if you suffer a long-term condition such as diabetes or epilepsy make sure someone knows or that you have a Medic Alert bracelet/necklace with this information on it. Remember that it is risky to buy medicinal tablets abroad because the doses may differ and India has a huge trade in false drugs.

Basic vaccinations recommended include **Polio** if none in last 10 years; **Tetanus** again if you haven't had one last 10 years (after five doses you have had enough for life); **Diptheria** if none in last 10 years; **Typhoid** if nil in last three years; **Hepatitis A** as the disease can be caught easily from food/water.

Special vaccines for Goa include **rabies**, possibly **BCG** and in some cases **Meningitis ACWY. Yellow Fever** is not acquired in India but you may be asked to show a certificate if you have travelled in from Africa or South America. **Japanese Encephalitis** may be required for rural travel at certain times of the year (mainly rainy seasons). A new and effective oral **cholera** vaccine (Dukoral) is now available as two doses (one week apart) providing three months protection.

Malaria does have some seasonality but it is too unpredictable to not take malaria prophylaxis. In the UK we still believe that Chloroquine and Paludrine are sufficient for most parts of India, but the US disagree and recommend either Malarone, Mefloquine or Doxycycline.

Mosquito repellents. Remember that DEET (Di-ethyltoluamide) is the gold standard. Apply the repellent every four to six hours but more often if you are sweating heavily. If a non-DEET product is used check who tested it. Validated products (tested at the London School of Hygiene and Tropical Medicine) include Mosiguard, Non-DEET Jungle formula and non-DEET Autan. If you want to use citronella remember that it must be applied very frequently (hourly) to be effective. If you are a target for insect bites or develop lumps quite soon after being bitten, carry an Aspivenin kit. This syringe suction device is available from many chemists and draws out some of the allergic materials and provides quick relief.

The Australians have a great campaign, which has reduced skin cancer. It is called Slip, Slap, Slop. Slip on a shirt, Slap on a hat, Slop on **sun screen.**

Pain killers. Paracetamol or a suitable painkiller can have multiple uses for symptoms but remember that taking more than eight paracetamol a day can lead to liver failure.

Ciproxin (Ciprofloaxcin). Can be a useful antibiotic for some forms of travellers' diarrhoea.

Immodium. A great standby for those diarrhoeas that occur at awkward times (ie before a long coach/train journey or on a trek). It helps stop the flow of diarrhoea and in my view is of more benefit than harm. (It was believed that letting the bacteria or viruses flow out had to be more beneficial. However, with Immodium they still come out, just in a more solid form.)

Pepto-Bismol. Used a lot by Americans for diarrhoea. It certainly relieves symptoms but like Immodium it is not a cure for underlying disease. Be aware that it turns the stool black as well as making it more solid.

MedicAlert. These simple bracelets, or an equivalent, should be carried or worn by anyone with a significant medical condition.

For longer trips involving jungle treks taking a clean needle pack, clean dental pack and water filtration devices are common-sense measures.

Essentials Health

An A-Z of health risks

Altitude sickness

Symptoms Acute mountain sickness can strike from about 3,000 m upwards and in general is more likely to affect those who ascend rapidly (for example by plane) and those who over-exert themselves. Teenagers are particularly prone. On reaching heights above 3,000 m, heart pounding and shortness of breath, especially on exertion, are almost universal and a normal response to the lack of oxygen in the air. Acute mountain sickness takes a few hours or days to come on and presents with heachache, lassitude, dizziness, loss of appetite, nausea and vomiting. Insomnia is common and often associated with a suffocating feeling when lying down in bed. You may notice that your breathing tends to wax and wane at night and your face is puffy in the mornings – this is all part of the syndrome.

Cures If the symptoms are mild, the treatment is rest, painkillers (preferably not aspirin-based) for the headaches and anti-sickness pills for vomiting. Should the symptoms be severe and prolonged it is best to descend to a lower altitude immediately and reascend, if necessary, slowly and in stages. The symptoms disappear very quickly with even a few 100 m of descent.

Prevention The best way of preventing acute mountain sickness is a relatively slow ascent. When trekking to high altitude, some time spent walking at medium altitude, getting fit and getting adapted, is beneficial. On arrival at places over 3,000 m a few hours rest and the avoidance of alcohol, cigarettes and heavy food will go a long way towards preventing acute mountain sickness.

Other problems experienced at high altitude are sunburn, excessively dry air causing skin cracking, sore eyes (it may be wise to leave your contact lenses out) and sore nostrils. Treat the latter with Vaseline. Do not ascend to high altitude if you are suffering from a bad cold or chest infection and certainly not within 24 hours following scuba diving.

Avian flu/SARS

Each year there is the possibilty that avian flu or SARS might rear its head. Check the news reports. If there is a problem in an area you are due to visit you may be advised to have an ordinary flu shot or to seek expert advice.

Bites and stings

It is a very rare event indeed for travellers, but if you are unlucky (or careless) enough to be bitten by a venomous snake, spider, scorpion or sea creature, try to identify the creature, without putting yourself in further danger (do not try to catch a live snake). Snake bites in particular are very frightening, but in fact rarely poisonous – even venomous snakes bite without injecting venom. Victims should be taken to a hospital or a doctor without delay. Commercial snake bite and scorpion kits are available, but are usually only useful for the specific types of snake or scorpion. Most serum has to be given intravenously so it is not much good equipping yourself with it unless you are used to making injections into veins. It is best to rely on local practice in these cases, because the particular creatures will be known about locally and appropriate treatment can be given.

Certain tropical sea fish when trodden upon inject venom into bathers' feet. This can be exceptionally painful. Wear plastic shoes if such creatures are reported. The pain can be relieved by immersing the foot in hot water (as hot as you can bear) for as long as the pain persists. Citric acid juices in fruits such as lemon are reported as being useful.

Symptoms Fright, swelling, pain and bruising around the bite and soreness of the regional lymph glands, perhaps accompanied by nausea, vomiting and a fever.

Symptoms of serious poisoning would be: numbness and tingling of the face, muscular spasms, convulsions, shortness of breath or a failure of the blood to clot, causing generalized bleeding.

Treatment of snake bite Reassure and comfort the victim frequently. Immobilize the limb with a bandage or a splint and get the person to lie still. Do not slash the bite area and try to suck out the poison because this sort of heroism does more harm than good. If you know how to use a tourniquet in these circumstances, you will not need this advice. If you are not experienced, do not apply a tourniquet.

Precautions Do not walk in snake territory in bare feet or sandals – wear proper shoes or boots. If you encounter a snake stay put until it slithers away and do not investigate a wounded snake. Spiders and scorpions may be found in the more basic hotels, especially in the Andean countries. If stung, rest and take plenty of fluids and call a doctor. The best precaution is to keep beds away from the walls and look inside your shoes and under the toilet seat every morning.

Dengue fever
Unfortunately there is no vaccine against this and the mosquitoes that carry it bite during the day. You will feel like a mule has kicked you for two to three days, you will then get better for a few days and then feel that the mule has kicked you again. It should all be over in seven to 10 days. Heed all the anti-mosquito measures that you can.

Diarrhoea and intestinal upset → *One study showed that up to 70% of all travellers may suffer during their trip.*

Symptoms Diarrhoea can refer either to loose stools or an increased frequency; both of these can be a nuisance. It should be short lasting but persistence beyond two weeks, with blood or pain, require specialist medical attention.

Cures Ciproxin (Ciprofloaxcin) is a useful antibiotic for bacterial traveller's diarrhoea. It can be obtained by private prescription in the UK. You need to take one 500 mg tablet when the diarrhoea starts and if you do not feel better in 24 hours, the diarrhoea is likely to have a non-bacterial cause and may be viral (in which case there is little you can do apart from keep yourself rehydrated and wait for it to settle on its own). The key treatment with all diarrhoeas is rehydration. Try to keep hydrated by taking the right mixture of salt and water. This is available as Oral Rehydration Salts (ORS) in ready-made sachets or can be made up by adding a teaspoon of sugar and a half teaspoon of salt to a litre of clean water. Drink at least one large cup of this drink for each loose stool. You can also use flat carbonated drinks as an alternative. Immodium and Pepto-Bismol provide symptomatic relief.

Prevention The standard advice is to be careful with water and ice for drinking. Ask yourself where the water came from. If you have any doubts then boil it or filter and treat it. There are many filter/treatment devices now available on the market. Food can also transmit disease. Be wary of salads (what were they washed in, who handled them), re-heated foods or food that has been left out in the sun having been cooked earlier in the day. There is a simple adage that says wash it, peel it, boil it or forget it. Also be wary of unpasteurised dairy products, these can transmit a range of diseases from brucellosis (fevers and constipation), to listeria (meningitis) and tuberculosis of the gut (obstruction, constipation, fevers and weight loss).

Hepatitis
Symptoms Hepatitis means inflammation of the liver. Viral causes of the disease can be acquired anywhere in the world. The most obvious symptom is a yellowing of your skin or the whites of your eyes. However, prior to this all that you may notice is itching and tiredness.

Cures Early on, depending on the type of hepatitis, a vaccine or immunoglobulin may reduce the duration of the illness.

Prevention Pre-travel hepatitis A vaccine is the best bet. Hepatitis B (for which there is a vaccine) is spread through blood and unprotected sexual intercourse, both of these can be avoided. Unfortunately there is no vaccine for hepatitis C or the increasing alphabetical list of other Hepatitis viruses.

Leishmaniasis

Symptoms If infected, you may notice a raised lump, which leads to a purplish discoloration on white skin and a possible ulcer. The parasite is transmitted by the bite of a sandfly. Sandflies do not fly very far and the greatest risk is at ground levels, so if you can avoid sleeping on the jungle floor do so. Seek advice for any persistent skin lesion or nasal symptom.

Cures Several weeks treatment is required under specialist supervision. The drugs themselves are toxic but if not taken in sufficient amounts recurrence of the disease is more likely.

Prevention Sleep above ground, under a permethrin treated net, use insect repellent and get a specialist opinion on any unusual skin lesions soon after return.

Leptospirosis

Various forms of leptospirosis occur throughout the world, transmitted by a bacterium which is excreted in rodent urine. Fresh water and moist soil harbour the organisms, which enter the body through cuts and scratches. If you suffer from any form of prolonged fever consult a doctor.

Prickly heat

A very common intensely itchy rash is avoided by frequent washing and by wearing loose clothing. It is cured by allowing skin to dry off (through use of powder and spending two nights in an air-conditioned hotel!).

Rabies

Remember that rabies is endemic throughout certain parts of the world, so avoid dogs that are behaving strangely and cover your toes at night from the vampire bats, which also carry the disease. If you are bitten by a domestic or wild animal, do not leave things to chance: scrub the wound with soap and water and/or disinfectant, try to at least determine the animal's ownership, where possible, and seek medical assistance at once. The course of treatment depends on whether you have already been satisfactorily vaccinated against rabies. If you have (this is worthwhile if you are spending lengths of time in developing countries) then some further doses of vaccine are all that is required. If you are not already vaccinated then anti-rabies serum (immunoglobulin) may be required in addition. It is important to finish the course of treatment.

Sexual health

The range of visible and invisible diseases is awesome. Unprotected sex can spread HIV, Hepatitis B and C, Gonorrhea (green discharge), chlamydia (nothing to see but may cause painful urination and later female infertility), painful recurrent herpes, syphilis and warts, just to name a few. You can cut down the risk by using condoms, a femidom or avoiding sex altogether.

Sun protection

Symptoms White Britons are notorious for becoming red in hot countries because they like to stay out longer than everyone else and do not use adequate sun protection. This can lead to sunburn, which is painful and followed by flaking of skin. Aloe vera gel is a good pain reliever for sunburn. Long-term sun damage leads to a loss of elasticity of skin and the development of pre-cancerous lesions. Years later a mild or a very malignant form of cancer may develop. The milder basal cell

carcinoma, if detected early, can be treated by cutting it out or freezing it. The much
nastier malignant melanoma may have already spread to bone and brain at the time
that it is first noticed.

Prevention Sun screen. SPF stands for Sun Protection Factor. It is measured by
determining how long a given person takes to 'burn' with and without the sunscreen
product on. So, if it takes 10 times longer to burn with the sunscreen product
applied, then that product has an SPF of 10. If it only takes twice as long then the SPF
is 2. The higher the SPF the greater the protection. However, do not just use higher
factors just to stay out in the sun longer. 'Flash frying' (desperate bursts of excessive
exposure), as it is called, is known to increase the risks of skin cancer. Follow the
Australians' with their Slip, Slap, Slop campaign referred to earlier.

Ticks and fly larvae

Ticks usually attach themselves to the lower parts of the body often after walking in
areas where cattle have grazed. They take a while to attach themselves strongly, but
swell up as they start to suck blood. The important thing is to remove them gently,
so that they do not leave their head parts in your skin, because this can cause a
nasty allergic reaction some days later. Do not use petrol, vaseline, lighted
cigarettes etc to remove the tick, but, with a pair of tweezers remove the beast
gently by gripping it at the attached (head) end and rock it out in very much the
same way that a tooth is extracted. Certain tropical flies which lay their eggs under
the skin of sheep and cattle also occasionally do the same thing to humans with the
unpleasant result that a maggot grows under the skin and pops up as a boil or
pimple. The best way to remove these is to cover the boil with oil, vaseline or nail
varnish to stop the maggot breathing, then to squeeze it out gently the next day.

Underwater health

Symptoms If you go diving make sure
that you are fit to do so. The **British
Sub-Aqua Club** (BSAC), Telford's Quay,
South Pier Rd, Ellesmere Port, Cheshire
CH65 4FL, UK, T01513-506200,
www.bsac.com, can put you in touch
with doctors who do medical
examinations. Protect your feet from
cuts, beach dog parasites (larva
migrans) and sea urchins. The latter are
almost impossible to remove but can be
dissolved with lime or vinegar. Keep an
eye out for secondary infection.

Cures Antibiotics for secondary
infections. Serious diving injuries may
need time in a decompression chamber.

Prevention Check that the dive
company know what they are doing,
have appropriate certification from
BSAC or **Professional Association of
Diving Instructors** (PADI), Unit 7, St
Philips Central, Albert Rd, St Philips,
Bristol, BS2 0TD, T0117-3007234,
www.padi.com, and that the equipment
is well maintained.

There are a number of ways of purifying water. Dirty water should first be strained through a filter bag and then boiled or treated. Bringing water to a rolling boil at sea level is sufficient to make the water safe for drinking, but at higher altitudes you have to boil the water for a few minutes longer to ensure all microbes are killed. There are sterilising methods that can be used and there are proprietary preparations containing chlorine (eg Puritabs) or iodine (eg Pota Aqua) compounds. Chlorine compounds generally do not kill protozoa (eg Giardia). There are now a number of water filters on the market available in personal and expedition size. They work either on mechanical or chemical principles, or may do both. Make sure you take the spare parts or spare chemicals with you and do not believe everything the manufacturers say.

Further information

Websites

Blood Care Foundation (UK), www.bloodcare.org.uk The Blood Care Foundation is a Kent-based charity 'dedicated to the provision of screened blood and resuscitation fluids in countries where these are not readily available'. They will dispatch certified non-infected blood of the right type to your hospital/clinic. The blood is flown in from various centres around the world.

British Travel Health Association (UK), www.btha.org This is the official website of an organization of travel health professionals.

Department of Health Travel Advice (UK), www.doh.gov.uk/traveladvice This excellent site is also available as a free booklet, the T6, from post offices. It lists vaccine requirements for each country.

Fit for Travel, www.fitfortravel.scot.nhs.uk This site from Scotland provides a quick A-Z of vaccine and travel health advice requirements for each country.

Foreign and Commonwealth Office (FCO) (UK), www.fco.gov.uk This is a key travel advice site, with useful information on the country, people, climate and lists the UK embassies/ consulates. The site also promotes the concept of 'Know Before You Go', and encourages travel insurance and appropriate travel health advice. It has links to the Department of Health travel advice site, see above.

The Health Protection Agency www.hpa.org.uk This site has up to date malaria advice guidelines for travel around the world. It gives specific advice about the right drugs for each location. It also has useful information for those who are pregnant, suffering from epilepsy or planning to travel with children.

Medic Alert (UK), www.medicalalert.co.uk This is the website of the foundation that produces bracelets and necklaces for those with existing medical problems. Once you have ordered your bracelet/necklace you write your key medical details on paper inside it, so that if you collapse, a medical person can identify you as someone with epilepsy or allergy to peanuts etc.

Travel Screening Services (UK), www.travelscreening.co.uk A private clinic dedicated to integrated travel health. The clinic gives vaccine, travel health advice, email and SMS text vaccine reminders and screens returned travellers for tropical diseases.

World Health Organisation, www.who.int The WHO site has links to the WHO Blue Book on travel advice. This lists the diseases in different regions of the world. It describes vaccination schedules and makes clear which countries have Yellow Fever Vaccination certificate requirements and malarial risk.

Books

International Travel and Health World Health Organisation Geneva ISBN 92 4 158026 7.

Lankester, T, *The Travellers Good Health Guide*, ISBN 0-85969-827-0.

Warrell, D and Anderson, A (eds), *Expedition Medicine (The Royal Geographic Society)* ISBN 1 86197 040-4.

Young Pelton, R, Aral, C and Dulles, W, *The World's Most Dangerous Places* ISBN 1-566952-140-9.

Keeping in touch

Communications

Internet

India has raced to embrace the internet and you're never far from an internet cafe, but Goa, unlike many of the more software-sector-savvy states like Karnataka and Andhra Pradesh, was at time of writing yet to get broadband links for truly high-speed connections. This means the usual precautions should apply when using their less reliable machines: write lengthy emails in word, save frequently, then paste them into your web-based email server rather than risking losing long emails by refreshing a page or crashing connections from power-cuts or surges. Browsing costs vary dramatically depending on the location: these can be anything from Rs 20 to Rs 100, with most charging somewhere in between. As a general rule, avoid emailing from upmarket hotels as, as a general rule, their prices tend towards the exorbitant.

Post offices → *Local post offices are listed under individual towns.*

The post in Goa is frequently unreliable and delays are common. It is best to use a post office to hand over mail across the counter for franking. Valuable items should be sent by registered post. Government emporia or shops in the larger hotels will send purchases home if the items are difficult to carry.

Airmail services to Europe, Africa and Australia takes at least a week and a little longer for the Americas. **Speed Post** (which takes about four days to the UK) is available at major towns. Specialist shippers deal with larger items, charging about US$150 per cubic metre.

At some main post offices you can send small packages under 2 kg as Letter Post which is much cheaper at Rs 220 than Parcel Post. Book Post (for printed papers) is cheaper still, about Rs 170 for 5 kg. Book parcels must be sewn in cloth (best over see-through plastic) with a small open 'window' slit for contents to be seen. The parcel process can take up to two hours. Check that the post office holds necessary customs declaration forms (two/three copies needed). 'Packers' outside post offices will do all necessary cloth covering and wax sealing for Rs 20-50. Write 'No commercial value' if returning used clothes, books etc. Address the parcel, stick stamps (after weighing at a separate counter) and one customs form to the parcel with the available glue (the other form/s must be partially sewn on). Post at the parcels counter and get your registration slip (receipt). Maximum dimensions: height 1 m, width 0.8 m, circumference 1.8 m. Airmail is expensive (Rs 775 for the first kilogramme and Rs 200 for each subsequent kilogramme); sea mail is slow but reasonable (Rs 775 for the first kilogramme and Rs 70 for each extra kilogramme).

Poste restante facilities are available in even quite small towns at the GPO, (General Post Office), where mail is held for one month. Ask for mail to be addressed to you with your surname in capitals and underlined. When asking for mail at 'Poste Restante' check under your first name as well as your surname. NB Any special-issue foreign stamps are likely to be stolen from envelopes in the Indian postal service and the letters may be thrown away. Advise people who are sending mail to you in India to use only definitive stamps (not commemorative).

Well-known **courier** companies (eg DHL) operate from the larger towns. Documents take a minimum of four days to the UK and cost Rs 1500 approximately up to 500 g, Rs 300 for each additional 500 g. Other parcels take an extra day; Rs 1700 up to 500 g.

International direct dialling is widely available in privately run call 'booths', usually labelled on yellow boards with the letters 'PCO-STD-ISD'. You dial the call yourself, and the time and cost are displayed on a computer screen. They are by far the best places from which to telephone abroad. Varying cheaper rates operate from 2100-0600, which means long queues may form outside booths in the evening.

> ‡ *The international phone code is +91 for India and +91 832 for Goa. The whole state now has 0832 as its code.*

Telephone calls from hotels are usually more expensive. Ringing tone: double ring, repeated regularly; engaged: equal length, on and off. Both are similar to UK ringing and engaged tones.

Mobile phones Major global mobile phone companies have partner servers in India, but coverage remains uneven. You can buy a local pay as you go card from Rs 500 if you are going to make heavy local use of the mobile. NB One disadvantage of the tremendous pace of the telecommunications revolution is the fact that millions of telephone numbers go out of date every year. Current telephone directories are often out of date and some of the numbers given in this guide will have been changed even as we go to press. **Directory enquiries**, 197, can be helpful but works only for the local area code. Fax services are available from many PCOs, (public call offices), and larger hotels, who charge either by the minute or per page.

Media

Newspapers and magazines

India has a large English-language press. In Goa, there are three local English-language newspapers, *The Herald* (probably the best written and the most popular), the *Gomantak Times* and the *Navhind Times*. Goa news can be accessed at www.goanews.com which has useful links and a search facility by keywords.

The major Indian papers now have websites: *The Hindu*, www.thehindu.com; *The Hindustan Times*, www.hindustantimes.com, *The Times of India*, www.indiatimes.com. *The Economic Times* is possibly the best for independent reporting and world coverage, etc. *The Asian Age* gives good coverage of Indian and international affairs. Most of these are difficult to get hold of, even in Margao or Panjim. The weekly/fortnightly magazines, *The Week, India Today* and *Frontline* are widely read current affairs journals; *Outlook* is excellent for both current affairs and general interest stories. There are newsagents and bookshops in Margao, Panjim, Mapusa and Colva.

Radio and TV

India's national radio and television network, **Doordarshan**, broadcasts in national and regional languages. Many Indians have now switched off 'DD', as it is known, to watch satellite TV, including the **BBC World**, **CNN** and others. Some international channels are currently relayed through the Star Network. **BBC World Service** radio has a large Indian audience in both English and regional languages.

● *Telephone codes: Goa 0832; Mumbai 022; Gokarna 08386; Hampi 08394;*
● *Hospet 08394; India (from abroad) +91.*

Panjim & Old Goa

Mormugao (Marmagao)	**56**
Vasco da Gama and Dabolim airport	56
Listings	57
Panjim (Panaji)	**58**
The Waterfront	60
West Panjim and the Campal	63
City centre	64
Sao Thome and Fontainhas	64
Around Panjim	66
Goa Velha	68
Listings	70
Old Goa and around	**77**
Ribandar, Divar and excursions from Old Goa	82
Listings	85

⁑ Footprint features

Don't miss...	55
24 hours in Panjim and Old Goa	67
Braganza Cunha	63
The scattering of St Francis' remains	79
Sun salutations and downward dog	83

Introduction

The Portuguese moved their capital during their 450-year rule in Goa, but they didn't go far. Old Goa was their first base and it flourished when the Lisbon Empire was at its zenith and its missionaries at the height of their zeal. Its huge churches and giddyingly ornate baroque basilicas bear testament to the church's grand ambitions – this was an affluent city every bit as serious about converting souls as selling spices and trading Arabian horses. Today it is a city ravaged by time, empty but for those glorious giant, desolate, relics to a proselytizing past.

Panjim, just 10 km away to the west, was adopted as the colony's capital when Old Goa became a breeding ground for disease. It remained very much a pragmatic capital: the religious side of the Portuguese colonial project diminished as their empire's power waned. Consequently there are no great feats of architectural ambition but it's in that same very human scale that the city's charm lies today.

The pace of life in Panjim is at odds with what you would expect from any Indian capital city. You'll find streets of wide tree-lined boulevards, or winding residential alleys; the waterways are pretty clean, and the people warm, friendly and with time to gossip. The whole place behaves like a village and people still slope off for a siesta at lunchtimes.

The city's 19th century residential quarters in Fontainhas and San Thome speak of the past, filled with green, yellow, ochre or indigo-washed houses. Even the city's commercial hub is gentle, with colonial bungalows sitting beside taller structures of the 60s. Next door Vasco is a little different, as the state's fastest urbanizing town. One of the busiest ports on the Indian west coast, it ships iron ore these days in place of spices.

★ Don't miss...

1 **San Thome and Fontainhas** Spend an afternoon zig-zagging your way through the charming streets of these districts, page 64.

2 **Altinho** Watch the sun set from the top of the Altinho for a panorama over Panjim and the Arabian sea, page 64.

3 **Socializing** Shoot the breeze, Panjim-style, in one of the city's many shoebox-size bars, page 73.

4 **The MV Caravela floating casino** India's gamblers favourite, this very plush casino is docked at Panjim, page 73.

5 **A songboat cruise** Take a crash course in the Indian holiday-maker's entertainment of choice: a rowdy sunset cruise along the Mandovi, page 75.

6 **Old Goa** A city of sprawling convents, churches and chapels. November 2004 marks the exposition of St Francis Xavier's remains, page 77.

7 **Chorao Island** Embrace nature with a tour of one of India's most important mangrove complexes, page 82.

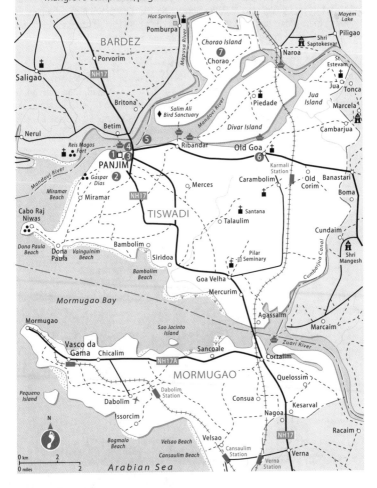

Mormugao (Marmagao) → *Colour map 1, grid C2.*

Mormugao taluka, a barren-looking laterite projection into the Arabian Sea, is the industrial heart of modern Goa. After independence the harbour's rocky headland became an important port for the Indian Navy who then developed Dabolim airport on the upland immediately behind. It's now the main direct entry point into the state for charter and internal flights. Today, Vasco da Gama has become Goa's largest town with a population growth of up to 10% a year. The once barren peninsula is rapidly being converted into the commercial core of a state where over half of the population is urban-based rather than depending on agriculture. ➤➤ *For Sleeping, Eating and other listings, see pages 57-58.*

Background

Mormugao was the location for the passenger terminus of Goa's oldest railway line, the metre-gauge of 1888 that connected the state with the interior and the south. Although the agricultural potential of the district has always been limited, its coastal position and good natural harbour periodically tempted the Portuguese to move their capital there. In the 17th century repeated Maratha attacks on Old Goa prompted authorities in Lisbon to issue orders for the destruction of that city's buildings so the stone could be used to build anew in Mormugao – more remote and more readily defensible.

Vasco da Gama and Dabolim Airport

Ins and outs   Vasco is 30 km from Panjim. There are taxis or an airport coach direct to Dabolim. Alternatively, cheap local buses pass along the main road. Trains via Londa can now bring visitors from the north (Delhi, Agra) or the south (Hospet, Bangalore). **Information   Tourist office** ① *at Tourist Hotel, T0832-2512673*, with a touchscreen help point on Goa (zoom in maps, hotel telephone numbers etc).

Vasco da Gama (Vasco for short) is the passenger railway terminus of the Central Goa branch line, and is the capital of the industrial heart of modern Goa. Its only pull for a

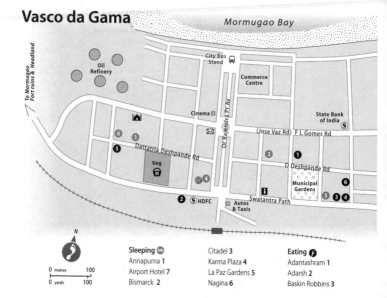

Vasco da Gama

Mormugao Bay

Sleeping 😴		Eating 🍴
Annapurna **1**	Citadel **3**	Adantashram **1**
Airport Hotel **7**	Karma Plaza **4**	Adarsh **2**
Bismarck **2**	La Paz Gardens **5**	Baskin Robbins **3**
	Nagina **6**	

0 metres 100
0 yards 100

visitor is in its proximity to Dabolim airport, 3 km away, which was developed by the Navy, and is now uncomfortably shared between the military's needs and the escalating demands of tourism. The squeeze has upped calls for a standalone civil aviation strip in the northeastern district of Pernem, but the issue is still being debated at government level. In the meantime, there are counters at the airport for car hire, foreign exchange (check rate and money carefully) and tourist information, all of which are normally open to meet flights.

⬤ Sleeping

Vasco de Gama *p56*
B La Paz Gardens, Swatantra Path, T0832-2512121, www.hotellapazgardens. com. 67 rooms, restaurants, bar, health club.
C-D Citadel, near Tourist Hotel, Jose Vaz Rd, T0832-2512222, epson@bom2.vsnl.net.in. 42 rooms, half a/c, restaurant, bar, friendly.
C-D Maharaja, FL Gomes Rd, T0832-2514075, mahahotl@goa1.dot.net.in. 40 smallish rooms, 18 a/c, Gujarati *thalis*, bar.
E Annapurna, D Deshpande Rd, T0832-2513735. 33 rooms with bath, cool Udipi dining hall.
E Gladstone, FL Gomes Rd, near railway station, T0832-2510005. 18 clean functional rooms, some a/c, restaurant, bar.
E Nagina, D Deshpande Rd, T0832-2511670. 21 rooms, some a/c, Goan restaurant.

Dabolim airport
A-B Majestic, just across the Mandovi bridge, Alto Betim, Porvorim, T0832-

2410378, themajestic@vsnl.net. Rooms with bath, safes, pool, excellent gym, sauna, restaurant and coffee shop. Panjim's top business hotel.
B Hotel Airport, aimed at business travellers, 28 small but functional a/c rooms, pool.

⬤ Eating

Vasco de Gama *p56*
$$ Goodyland, La Paz. Western fast food joint, pizza, cakes and sweets.
$$ Ginza, Karma Plaza, Rajendra Prasad Av. Japanese, Chinese and continental, pleasant split level a/c dining area. Good service.
$ Adarsh, Swatantra Path, 100 m south of railway station. Excellent *masala dosa*.

⬤ Transport

Vasco de Gama *p56*
Air
Air India, T0832-2224081, **Mumbai**, **Thiruvananthapuram**.
Indian Airlines, T0832-2223826, Reservations 1000-1300, 1400-1600, Airport T0832-513863. Flights to **Bangalore**, **Delhi** (some via **Agra**) and **Mumbai** daily; also **Chennai**; and from **Tiruchirapalli** and to **Pune**.
Jet Airways, T0832-2431472, Airport T0832-2510354, to **Mumbai** and **Bangalore**. Sahara, to **Mumbai** daily, and **Delhi**.
    Package tour companies and luxury hotels usually arrange courtesy buses for hotel transfer. The pre-paid **taxi** counter immediately outside the arrivals hall has rates clearly displayed (eg Panjim Rs 340, 40 mins; north Goa beaches from Rs 450; Tiracol Rs 750; south Goa beaches from Rs 240; Palolem Rs 700). State your destination at the counter, pay and get a receipt which will give the registration number of your

Goodyland **4**
La Goesta **5**
Nanking **6**

Panjim & Old Goa Mormugao Listings

taxi. Keep hold of this receipt until you reach your destination. There is theoretically no need to tip the driver. The taxi driver may insist that the hotel you have asked for has closed down or is full and will suggest another in order to get a commission from the hotel. Say that you have a reservation at the hotel of your choice (even if you don't!). The public **bus** stop on the far side of the roundabout outside the airport gates has buses to Vasco da Gama, from where there are connections to all major places in Goa. If you want to go straight to the nearest beach, go to the right of the round- about, cross the road for buses to Bogmalo.

Bus

From City bus stand near market. Frequent, non-stop service to **Panjim**, and **Margao**, Rs 15, via Airport.

Kadamba Bus Stand, northeast of town, with a very helpful information booth, has services to major towns in Goa (not non-stop), and to **Bangalore** via **Hubli**: 1500, 1645 (15 hrs), Rs 240; **Belgaum**, many, Rs 57; **Hospet**: 1130 (10 hrs) Rs 100; **Hubli** many (6 hrs) Rs 65; **Mangalore**: 1700 (10 hrs) Rs 156; **Mumbai**: 1330 (16 hrs) Rs 325. Check timetable in advance.

Taxi to and from Londa, about Rs 1,500.

Train

3 daily stops at: **Dabolim** for the airport and Bogmalo; **Cansaulim** for Velsao beach, Seraulim; **Majorda** for Utorda, Majorda, Betalbatim beaches; **Madgaon (Margao)** for Colva, Benaulim and the southern beaches; **Chandorgoa, Sanvordem, Calem, Kulem (Colem), Dudhsagar** for the waterfalls.

Long distance Reservations, T0832-512833. Services via Londa to **Belgaum, Bangalore, Delhi via Agra**, and with **Hospet** (for **Hampi**) among others. To **Londa Junction**: by Goa Exp 2779, depart 1400, arrive 1745; by Vasco Bangalore Exp 7310, depart 2030, arrive 2353; both 4¼ hrs. To **Delhi (Nizamuddin)** via Agra Cantt: Goa Exp 2779, depart 1400, arrive 0635 (after 2 nights), 41¾ hrs. To **Hospet** (for **Hampi**): Vasco-da-Gama Vijayawada Express 7228, Wed, Sat, 0640, arrive Hospet 1600. To **Pune** Goa Exp, 2779, depart 1400, 14 hrs.

⊙ Directory

Vasco de Gama *p56*
Ambulance T0832-2512768. **Fire** T0832-2513840. **Internet** Cyberdome, Karma Plaza, T0832-2518687, Mon-Sat 0930-2200, Sun 0930-1200, Rs 35 per hr, 8 terminals. **Medical services** Salgaocar Medical Research Centre, T0832-2512524. **Police** T0832-2512304.

Panjim (Panaji) → *Colour map 1, grid C2. Airport: 29 km.*

This small city tucked into the narrow strip of land between the Altinho (meaning 'hill') and the coastal banks of Goa's most important river, the Mandovi, has to be a contender for most laid-back state capital in India. It's all the more surprising considering the fact that, on paper, Goa is the subcontinent's wealthiest state per capita, but the population has stayed small and there's been no rush of urban migration. Goans complain bitterly about increasing urban sprawl and about the influx of out-of-state entrepreneurs who come to trade, but on the surface the city's feathers seem pretty unruffled. In Panjim's relaxed commercial hub, the biggest business seems to be in the sale of kaju (cashews), gentlemen-shaves in the barbieris and feni-quaffing in the booths of pokey bars. It's a tiny, clean city that's great to walk around. Gloriously uncommercial, only one gleaming block has showrooms selling Nike, Adidas, Lacoste and Benetton, while the rest of the 'complexes' and 'malls' are reassuringly ramshackle affairs.

There's something rather splendidly old world and genteel about the city today, but its fallen grandeur is on the cusp of getting a lift: if all goes to plan, from November 2004 it will host an international film festival which will make it India's answer to Cannes. Panjim already has a leafy waterside promenade to mould into its version of Cannes' Croisette, so now the government is busying itself in refurbishing the dilapidated, waterfront remains of what was Asia's first medical college into a movie multiplex. The event is bound to prompt the cranking open of many pots of much-needed paint for Panjim's peeling buildings and hotels, but there's already plenty of small scale, accessible, old world culture here, particularly focused around the Kala Academy. A riverside pink and orange candy confection of a building, like a downsized version of London's South Bank, it has an arts café and excellent musical and dance performances most evenings.

> **‡** Panaji is the official spelling of the capital city, replacing the older Portuguese spelling Panjim. It is still most commonly referred to as Panjim, so we have followed usage.

When you couple Panjim's position, so enticingly close to Goa's beguiling beaches, with the fact that it's the arrival point for neither planes nor trains to the state, it's easy to see why Goa's capital gets by and large bypassed by travellers. It's actually well worth giving yourself the breathing space to soak in the character of the city by staying overnight and Panjim makes the perfect base for a dawn raid on the remains at Old Goa: after all, the earlier you get there, the less likely it is that your every step will be dogged by chattering tour groups and hawkers. ►► *For Sleeping, Eating and other listings, see pages 70-75.*

Ins and outs

Getting there Prepaid taxis or buses run the short distance from Dabolim airport across the Mormugao Bay. The Konkan Railway's main terminus is at the headquarters of South Goa district, Margao, for trains from Mumbai and the north or from coastal Karnataka and Kerala to the south. Taxis and buses run to Panjim, but more often take tourists to the resorts or choice of beach. Karmali station (see Old Goa) is the closest to Panjim, where taxis wait to transfer you. The state Kadamba buses and private coach terminals are in Patto to the east of town. From there it is a 10-minute walk across the footbridge over the Ourem Creek to reach the city's guesthouses.

Getting around Panjim is very easy to negotiate on foot, but auto-rickshaws are handy and readily available. Motorcycle rickshaws are cheaper and more risky. Local buses run along the waterfront from the city bus stand past the market to Miramar.

Orientation and Information Panjim holds the archbishop's palace, a modern port, and government buildings and shops set around a number of plazas. It is laid out on a grid and the main roads run parallel with the seafront. The riverside boulevard (Devanand Bandodkar Marg) runs from the 'new' Patto bridge, past the jetties, to the formerly open fields of the **Campal**. Along it are some of the town's main administrative buildings. **Department of Tourism Office of the Government of Goa** ① *North bank of the Ourem Creek, opposite Fontainhas and beside the bus stand at Patto, Panjim, T0832-2438750, Mon-Sat 0900-1130, 1330-1700; Sun 0930-1400.* **Goa Tourism Development Corporation** (GTDC) ① *Trionora Apartments, Dr Alvares Costa Rd, T0832-2226515, gtdc@goacom.com,* for GTDC accommodation.

History

The Portuguese first settled Panjim as a suburb of Old Goa, the original Indian capital of the sea-faring conquistadores, but its position on the left bank of the Mandovi river had already attracted Bijapur's Muslim king Yusuf Adil Shah in 1500, shortly before the Europeans arrived. He built and fortified what the Portuguese later renamed the Idalcao Palace, now the oldest and most impressive of downtown Panjim's official buildings.

The palace's service to the Sultan was short-lived: Alfonso de Albuquerque seized it, and Old Goa upstream – which the Islamic rulers had been using as both a trading port and their main starting point for pilgrimages to Mecca – in March 1510. Albuquerque, like his Muslim predecessors, built his headquarters in Old Goa, stationed a garrison at Panjim and made it the customs clearing point for all traffic entering the Mandovi.

The town remained little more than a military outpost and a staging post for incoming and outgoing viceroys on their way to Old Goa. The first Portuguese buildings, after the construction of a church on the site of the present Church of Our Lady of Immaculate Conception in 1541, were noblemen's houses built on the flat land bordering the sea. Panjim had to wait over two centuries – when the Portuguese Viceroy decided to move from Old Goa in 1759 – for settlement to begin in earnest. It then took the best part of a century for enough numbers to relocate from Old Goa to make Panjim the biggest settlement in the colony and to warrant its status as official capital in 1833.

The Waterfront

Devanand Bandodkar (DB) Marg runs along the Mandovi from near the New Patto Bridge on the east of town to the once open fields of the Campal to the southwest.

Panjim (Panaji)

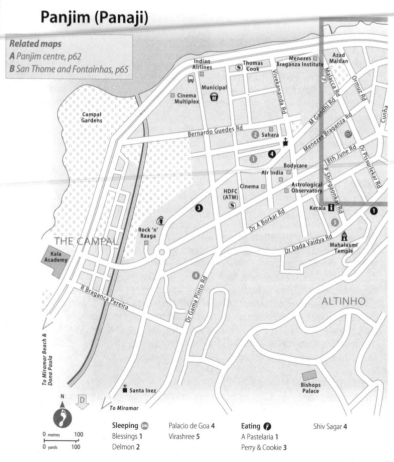

Related maps
A Panjim centre, p62
B San Thome and Fontainhas, p65

Sleeping	Palacio de Goa 4	Eating	Shiv Sagar 4
Blessings 1	Virashree 5	A Pastelaria 1	
Delmon 2		Perry & Cookie 3	

When Panjim's transport and communication system depend- ed on boats this was the town's busiest high- way and it still holds the city's main administrative buildings.

Walking from the east, you first hit **Idalcao Palace** ① *behind the main boat terminal, DB Marg*. Once the castle of the Adil Shahs, the palace was seized by the Portuguese when they first toppled the Muslim kings in 1510 and was rebuilt in 1615 to serve as the Europeans' Vice- regal Palace. It was the official residence to Viceroys from 1759 right up until 1918 when the Governor-General (the viceroy's 20th century title) decided to move to the Cabo headland to the southwest – today's Cabo Raj Niwas – leaving the old palace to become government offices. After independence it became Goa's secretariat building (the seat of the then Union Territory's parliament) until that in turn shifted across the river to Porvorim. It now houses the bureaucracy of the state passport office, but their days too could be numbered if the heritage campaigners have their way. The main entrance gate is a pilastered Romanesque arch in the south wall facing away from the river. The crest of the Viceroys that once adorned it has been replaced by the Ashokan 'Wheel of Law', the official symbol of India.

Next to it is a striking dark statue of the **Abbé Faria** (1756-1819) looming over the prone figure of a woman. José Custodio de Faria, who went on to become a celebrated worldwide authority on hypnotism, was born into a Colvale Brahmin family in Candolim. On separating shortly after their son's birth, his parents' gaze turned firmly towards heaven: his father became a priest, his mother a nun. The former took the

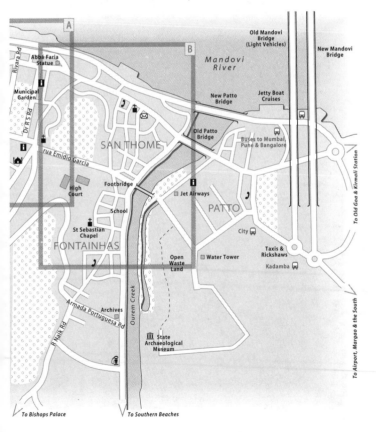

15-year-old José to Lisbon – a journey that then took over nine months and from which the adolescent boy was never to return. His father found patronage in the Portuguese court, and José was given a scholarship to study in Rome where he completed a doctoral thesis and was ordained a priest. So it was as Abbé Faria that José went on to Paris to wade into the French Revolution. His fame for hypnotism, or 'magnetizing power', came after he wrote *On The Causing Of Lucid Sleep*. Very little is known of his later career, apart from that he gave public lectures and demonstrations in Paris in the first two decades of the 19th century on curing little-understood conditions like hysteria. He died in 1819 in the French city at the age of 64.

> ‼ The character in Dumas' *Count of Monte Cristo* may have been based on Faria.

Further west, on Malacca Road, almost opposite the wharf are the **central library** and public rooms of the **Braganza Institute** ① *Mon-Fri 0930-1300, 1400- 1745*. It was established as the **Instituto Vasco da Gama** in 1871, on the anniversary of the date that the Portuguese explorer da Gama sailed round the Cape of Good Hope, to stimulate an interest in culture, science and the arts. It was renamed for Luis Menezes de Braganza

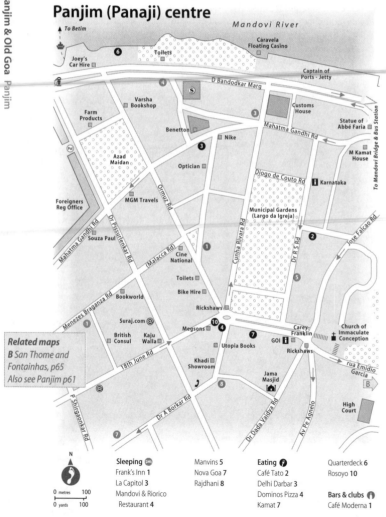

Panjim (Panaji) centre

Mandovi River

To Betim

Caravela Floating Casino

Joey's Car Hire

Toilets

Captain of Ports - Jetty

D Bandodkar Marg

Varsha Bookshop

Farm Products

Customs House

Statue of Abbé Faria

Benetton

Mahatma Gandhi Rd

M Kamat House

Nike

Azad Maidan

Optician

Diogo de Couto Rd

Karnataka

Foreigners Reg Office

MGM Travels

Mahatma Gandhi Rd

Municipal Gardens (Largo da Igreja)

Souza Paul

Cunha Rivara Rd

José Falcão Rd

Cine National

Toilets

Bike Hire

Bookworld

Rickshaws

Suraj.com @

Megsons

Carey-Franklin

Church of Immaculate Conception

British Consul

Kaju Walla

Utopia Books

GOI

Rickshaws

Related maps
B *San Thome and Fontainhas, p65*
Also see Panjim p61

18th June Rd

Khadi Showroom

Jama Masjid

rua Emidio Garcia

@

Dr A Borkar Rd

High Court

Dr Dada Vaidya Rd

Av Pe Agnelo

N

0 metres 100
0 yards 100

Sleeping 🛏
Frank's Inn **1**
La Capitol **3**
Mandovi & Riorico Restaurant **4**

Manvins **5**
Nova Goa **7**
Rajdhani **8**

Eating 🍴
Café Tato **2**
Delhi Darbar **3**
Dominos Pizza **4**
Kamat **7**

Quarterdeck **6**
Rosoyo **10**

Bars & clubs 🍸
Café Moderna **1**

⦂ Braganza Cunha

Braganza Cunha was born on 2 April 1891 in Chandor village. He returned to Goa in 1926 after an education in Pondicherry and then an electrical engineering degree in Paris. From that point until his death in 1958 he was a fierce opponent of colonialism and an advocate of full independence within India, becoming a radical rationalist despite the deep roots of conservative Catholicism in his landed-gentry background. The Portuguese arrested him as a leading subversive in 1946: he was jailed first at Fort Aguada then Vasco da Gama before being shipped to prison in Portugal. He broke the terms of his release in 1950 by escaping Lisbon for Paris, only finally making it back to India in September 1953. The post-Independence political climate he found was much changed: the success of freedom fighters against the British Empire in greater India had left the pockets of resistance against Portuguese rule in Goa isolated and its people largely apathetic. From then until his death five years later, Braganza Cunha fervently pressed the case for Goan independence through newspaper articles. Disowned by the Catholic Church, he was buried in a Church of Scotland cemetery in Mumbai, just short of glimpsing the free Goa he fought so ardently for.

(1878-1938), an outstanding figure of social and political reform in early 20th century Goa, whose palace of an ancestral home in Chandor, South Goa, is stuffed with furniture that wouldn't look out of place in Buckingham Palace. Here, though, the blue tile frieze in the entrance, hand-painted by Jorge Colaco in 1935, is a mythical representation of the Portuguese colonization of Goa. Read the three-metre-high *azulejos* (tiled) panels clockwise from the entrance on the left wall to follow the narrative sequence. Each picture is set over a verse from an epic poem by the great Portuguese poet Luis Vaz de Camões, whose statue stood in front of the Sé Cathedral until the post-colonial Goan government packed it off to the Old Goa museum. Camões had served in North Africa before travelling to Goa in 1553, staying in India and the Far East for 17 years.

An art gallery upstairs (often closed) has paintings by European artists of the late 19th and early 20th centuries and Goan artists of the 20th century. The central **library** ① *downstairs, free, 0930-1300, 1200-1700*, dating from 1832, has a rare collection of religious and other texts.

The small patch of grassland outside the Braganza Institute is the rather pompously named **Azad Maidan**, 'Freedom Park'. The statue of Albuquerque which once stood here was moved to the Archaeological Museum in Old Goa to make way for a memorial to Dr Tristao de Braganza Cunha, one of Goa's most venerated freedom fighters and founder of the Goa Congress Committee, see box, page 63.

West Panjim and the Campal

Further west still, just past the bustling **municipal market** ① *visit early in the morning for its colourful fish and vegetables sections, Mon-Sat*, lies the grand façade of the **Goa Medical College**, currently being refurbished to house an international film festival. Carry on to reach the **Campal**. Old residences lie on the south side of the boulevard while on the riverside are the lovely Campal gardens with their grand views across to the Reis Magos fort and church. To the south of the gardens is the cultural institute the **Kala Academy**. The name is an abbreviation of Campo de Dom Manuel, the viceroy who was responsible for reclaiming this area from the sea in 1833. Here you'll find one of the first cannons to be made in Goa that guarded the crossing from Tiswadi to Ponda at Banastari. The avenue leads on to Miramar and Dona Paula.

City centre

The giant white-washed 16th century **Church of the Immaculate Conception (Panjim church)** ① *Church Sq, Emidio Gracia Rd, Mon-Sat 0900-1300, 1530-1800, Sun 1030-1300, 1915-1900, free*, looms pristine and large over the main square, Largo Da Igreja. Its dimensions were unwarranted for the population of what was then, in Panjim, little more than a marshy fishing village; its tall, Portuguese Baroque twin towers were instead built both to act as a landmark for and to tend to the spiritual needs of arriving Portuguese sailors, for whom the customs post just below the hill at Panjim marked their first step on Indian soil. The church was built in 1541 then enlarged in 1600 to reflect its standing as the parish church of the capital; in 1619 it was completely rebuilt to its present design.

Before the hill was cut and the imposing stairway built in the 1780s, access was by a narrow staircase to the west. In 1871 the central arch had to be modified and strengthened to support the great bell, Goa's second largest after that found in the Sé Cathedral. Originally from the tower of the Church of St Augustine in Old Goa, it hung above Fort Aguada in the mid-19th century until it crashed down to fatally wound a member of the congregation.

Inside the church the main altar *reredos* (screens) and the altars on either side to Jesus the Crucified and to Our Lady of the Rosary, are typically ornate gilded baroque, in turn flanked by marble statues of St Peter and St Paul. The panels in the Chapel of St Francis, in the south transept, came from the chapel in the Idalcao Palace in 1918. The Feast Day is on 8 December.

In 1945, the statue of Our Lady of Fatima was installed for whom parishioners gifted a crown of gold and diamonds five years later. This statue is carried in a candlelight procession each year on 13 October.

The Hindu **Mahalaxmi Temple** ① *Dr Dada Vaidya Rd, free*, (originally 1818, but rebuilt and enlarged in 1983) is now hidden behind a newer building. It was the first Hindu place of worship to be allowed in the Old Conquests after the close of the Inquisition. Even then permission was slow to be granted and the project faced vehement opposition from Archbishop Galdino. He swam against the liberalising tide of the time to remain steadfast in his opposition of Hindu temple-building, and in 1827 ordered his priests to announce it a "very grave sin of idolatry for anyone to engage himself in the works of Hindu temples even when ordered to do so by the Government". The deity, which had been smuggled to Bicholim in the 16th century, was restored only after a temporary home was found in the house of Mahamay Kamat, near the Secretariat. The **Boca de Vaca** ('Cow's Mouth') spring, is near by.

San Thome and Fontainhas

On Panjim's eastern promontory, at the foot of the Altinho and on the left bank of the Ourem Creek, sit first the San Thome and then, further south, Fontainhas districts filled with modest 18th and 19th century houses. The cumulative prettiness of the well-preserved buildings' colour-washed walls, trimmed with white borders, sloping tiled roofs and decorative wrought-iron balconies make it an ideal area to explore at

● *Portuguese law decreed that owners colour-wash the outsides of their homes after each*
● *year's monsoon: the only buildings painted all white were churches, while secular buildings came in ochre with windows and door frames picked out in other colours.*

walking pace. You can reach the area via any of the narrow lanes that riddle San Thome or take the footbridge across the Ourem Creek from the new bus stand and tourist office that feeds you straight into the heart of the district. A narrow road that runs east past the Church of the Immaculate Conception and main town square also ends up here. But probably the best way in is over the Altinho from the Mahalaxmi Temple: this route gives great views over the estuary from the steep eastern flank of the hill, a vantage point once used for defensive purposes. A footpath drops down between the Altinho's 19th and 20th century buildings just south of San Sebastian Chapel to leave you slap bang in middle of Fontainhas.

San Thome & Fontainhas

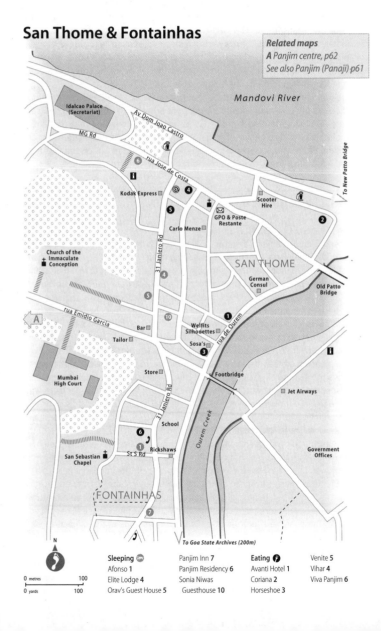

Related maps
A Panjim centre, p62
See also Panjim (Panaji) p61

Sleeping		Eating	
Afonso **1**	Panjim Inn **7**	Avanti Hotel **1**	Venite **5**
Elite Lodge **4**	Panjim Residency **6**	Coriana **2**	Vihar **4**
Orav's Guest House **5**	Sonia Niwas	Horseshoe **3**	Viva Panjim **6**
	Guesthouse **10**		

0 metres 100
0 yards 100

Fontainhas was first drained in the 18th century to yield rich alluvial soil for coconut cultivation and so came to be known as Palmar Ponte (bridge of palms). In the early 19th century, when the land belonged to the Catholic Carmelite community, the shift of capital from Old Goa (already in decline) put this part of Panjim under pressure to absorb a sudden influx of people. The place grew into a congested quarter sustained by the clear spring water of the Fonte Phoenix (beefed up by a basalt reservoir built by the then Governor); hence the change of name.

The chief landmark here is the small **San Sebastian Chapel** ① *St Sebastian Rd, open only during mass which is held in Konkani Mon and Tue, Thu-Sat 0715-0800, Wed 1800-1900, Sun 0645-0730, English mass Sun 0830-0930, free*, (built in 1818, rebuilt in 1888) which houses the large wooden crucifix that until 1812 stood in the Palace of the Inquisition in Old Goa where the eyes of Christ watched over the proceedings of the tribunal. For 100 years it rested in the chapel in the Idalcao Palace in Panjim before being moved on here. The church seems scarcely large enough to house the highly ornamented altars, themselves originally from the Church of Mother of God in Davim, together with the statue of Our Lady of Livramento.

The **Goa State Museum** ① *Patto, 0930-1730, free, head south of Kadamba Bus Stand, across the Ourem Creek footbridge, right across the waste ground and past the State Bank staff training building,* is an impressive building that contains a disappointingly small collection of religious art and antiquities. Most interesting are the original Provedoria lottery machines built in Lisbon that are on the first floor landing. A few old photos show how the machines were used.

Around Panjim

Miramar and Gaspar Dias

Further south along Panjim's seafront boulevard, DB Marg, from the Kala Academy, the site of the small fortress of **Gaspar Dias**, built to pair the fort at Reis Magos on the other side of the Mandovi estuary (see page 101), marks the start of Miramar beach. Jutting out west past here is the promontory of **Cabo Raj Niwas** – the State Governor's House and one-time fort of the Portuguese – with its excellent views, then the land swings back to meet the mouth of the Zuari river and **Dona Paula beach**.

Miramar is 3 km along the Mandovi from the centre of Panjim, not far enough to stop the place soaking in a great deal of the feeling of the city. The water is dirty and the beach holds little allure, so it's hardly the ideal spot for a beach holiday. Even so, it's a pleasant drive with good views over the sea and, if you've got a little time to kill, offers the best quick escape from the city, as used by many locals at sunset.

Gaspar Dias Fortress was finished around 1606. The Panjim-Ribandar causeway, built in 1634, gave it direct land access to the capital at Old Goa and its significance grew accordingly. The walls, likely laterite blocks 1½ m thick and 5 m high, made space for 16 cannons. These saw repeated action against the Dutch until the middle of the 17th century, but the fortress' importance waned after the Maratha onslaught and it fell into disrepair under 15 years of occupation by a British garrison in the early 19th century. It was made new but the Portuguese army finally abandoned it in 1870 as a result of further damage sustained during the mutiny against the Prefect of 1835. For a while the military still stationed soldiers here to convalesce but by the 20th century it had crumbled beyond recognition. All that is left is one cannon at the Miramar circle that marks the possible site of the fort. Four more cannons of the original 16 were excavated and are now at the Directorate of Archives and the Abbé Faria monument in Panjim, and at the Farmagudi roundabout near Ponda. Most of Miramar's hotels are on, or just off, the main DB Marg road to Dona Paula along the coast. Inland, the Taleigao Church inherited the image of Our Lady of Loreto from Vainguinim when the eviction of the Jesuits from Goa in 1759 left its original chapel to fall into disrepair.

24 hours in Panjim and Old Goa

Once you're set up in a guesthouse or hotel in Panjim – plump for somewhere in Sao Thome or Fontainhas – cross the Ourem Creek for the 15-minute bus or taxi drive to Old Goa along the causeway road.

Head furthest east first and climb up to the beautifully-restored **Chapel of Our Lady of the Mount,** best at first light, for its 360-degree views over the former capital of the Portuguese. Back down the hill is the main complex (turn right for the stunning **Convent of St Cajetan**).

From here it's a gentle stroll down towards the river to take in the **Viceroy's Arch** and **Gate of Adil Shahi Palace** then walk due south along the **Rua Direita ou dos Leiloes** for a cup of chai at the corner tea stall or a bottled mango juice at one of the many stalls. Double back, crossing Senate Square, to reach the **Sé Cathedral** and the **Convent of St Francis of Assisi**. Make time for the brilliant Viceroy portrait gallery upstairs at the **Archaeological Museum**.

Next you should head for the interior of the **Basilica of Bom Jesus** and the **Tomb of St Francis Xavier** – a government tour guide can bring the place alive for a fistful of rupees. As the central monuments start to fill up from 1100 you can take your pick of the churches on Holy Hill, to the west, or carry on down into **Ribandar** to wander round a 17th-century-style village.

If you've had your fill of architecture, get a food parcel from a local stall and take the ferry crossing here to see some wildlife on **Chorao Island** at the **Salim Ali Bird Sanctuary**. Otherwise head straight on for a slap up lunch back in Panjim: **Venite** for atmosphere, **the Horseshoe** for a tasty, upmarket introduction to Goan Portuguese flavours or go for a more down-at-heel option like **Café Tato** for authentic Goan.

Slip into the Panjim way of life by taking a siesta, then, as the heat subsides around 1600, take a turn about the Sao Thome and Fontainhas districts, including the **San Sebastian Chapel**, following 31 Janiero Road to reach the **Church of the Immaculate Conception**, the **Idalcao Palace** and the rest of Panjim's central sights.

Come dusk a handful of Panjim's population picks its way through the city's shady shoreside parkland in the **Campal Gardens** (opposite the market) to reach a small patch of sand and great views of the river water meeting the Arabian Sea.

Walk back along the riverfront to hop on board one of the brilliantly kitsch **evening cruise ships** or stay south for more highbrow culture at the **Kala Academy**.

Dinner can be a grand affair at North Indian **Delhi Durbar** or something snappy and fried before your eyes at any number of feni-stalls. Panjim does not keep especially late hours: if you want to keep drinking, as with many places in India, the drinks licenses are held by the five stars. Try the Marriott or nip across the Mandovi to the Taj's Fort Aguada nightclub.

Cabo Raj Niwas

From the roundabout by the **National Oceanography Institute** at the southern foot of Miramar beach, the road runs 600 m up to **Cabo Raj Niwas**, now Raj Bhavan, the **State Governor's House** ① *closed to visitors but passes are given at the gate for mass, Sun 0930*. Inside the private grounds, six cannons and some sections of wall are all that is left of the Portuguese Cabo fort which stood on top of the cliffs of this rocky promontory. The first small Our Lady of Cabo shrine was built in 1541 before the fort was built. It was a landmark for ships and gave Franciscan friars a toehold in the territory. A convent was built in 1594 then extended in the 17th century. The chapel has a simple white façade while the side altars inside have unusual eight-point stars (some say that the number eight signified regeneration and baptism); a memorial to Dona Paula de Menezes (see Dona Paula below) is in a niche. The door to the sacristy has carvings similar to Hindu temple art. The ancient, heavily carved door that leads to the back of the chapel might have come from a ruined convent in Old Goa. The Feast coincides with Independence Day, 15 August.

Documents of 1633 refer to both the chapel and various buildings of an incomplete fort with only four guns. During the Napoleonic Wars British troops garrisoned in the fort from 1799-1813 constructed more buildings for themselves (subsequently demolished by the Portuguese). A fair number of overgrown graves stand in the nearby **British Cemetery** ① *always open*, which still has a gate and four walls, to serve as a stark reminder. Around 1844, after the religious orders were abolished, the Archbishop of Goa was given the convent. He converted it into an impressive residence. Later, the Governor-General of Goa acquired the building and, after further upgrades, it became his official residence in 1918. Its grand interior was left intact after the Portuguese left in 1961. The splendid glassed-in veranda on the seaward side is a special feature.

If you don't make it inside the residence for mass, it's still worth a detour up here for the **viewing platform** near the entrance that gives superb views over the sweep of the coastline across the Mandovi estuary to Fort Aguada. This is where some local Goans come to canoodle at dusk.

Dona Paula

Dona Paula has a small palm-fringed beach with casuarina groves. The low laterite cliff forms a headland joined to the mainland by a short causeway. There's a platform that gives good views across the bay to Vasco da Gama and the busy shipping lanes that lead to the port of Mormugao. Fisherfolk turned local vendors sell cheap seaside knick-knacks and give speedy boat rides. It's a popular local picnic spot.

As is often the case in India, there is more than one story of who the Dona of the village's name could have been. Some say she was Paula de Menezes (the wife of a nobleman, Antonio de Souto Maior, and reputedly a mistress of the Viceroy), who died a young woman, in 1682: a black granite memorial stone is on a wall in the Chapel of Our Lady of Cabo and the family summerhouse still survives. Others link the village's name to a Paula who jumped from the cliffs when refused permission by her father to marry Gaspar Dias, a fisherman.

Vainguinim beach to the east of Dona Paula is backed by a part of Tiswadi district which the Jesuits enjoyed as highly productive agricultural land. There is a small beach but swimming is upset by the noise and exhaust fumes from motor boats.

Bambolim's dark-sand beach, south off the NH17 and 8 km from Panjim, is secluded, free of hawkers and shaded by palms. Goa University is nearby.

Porvorim

The **Houses of Goa Museum** ① *Tue-Sun 1000-1930, Rs 25, cross the Mandovi river from Panjim to Mapusa turning right at the Saligao junction at Alto Porvorim to travel 2 km on the road towards Torda; the museum is on your left*. This is the first public museum on Indo-Portuguese houses and was set up by a Goan publisher/architect.

Goa Velha

① *Twice hourly buses running along the NH17, the Panjim-Margao Rd, stop north of Agassaim near the site of Goa Velha and from here you can walk uphill to get to Pilar*

Goa Velha was the ancient port capital destroyed by the Bahmani Muslims in 1470. All you'll find now of this splendid city of fine houses, gardens, temples and its smart trade in spices, jewels, silks, muslins and Arab horses is a faded notice board standing on a pedestal near the main road north of Agassaim. It was the centre of international trade along the Zuari in the eighth century and grew to become capital of the Kadambas in 1052 but as Gopakapattana or Govapuri it had already suffered repeated attack – including a siege at the hands of the Delhi Sultans in 1312 – and long term decline due to heavy silting. There is little left of the place, and it is not to be confused with Old Goa (confusingly, also known as Velha Goa) whose inhabitants had christened this Goa *Velha* when their capital was young and flourishing. On Monday of Holy Week each year a colourful and unique **Procession of Saints** dating from the 17th century starts from the St Andrew's Church of the Franciscan third order, just north of the dispersed village. The only festival of its kind outside Rome, it has 26 lifesize, mostly 19th century statues of saints borne on floats and trailed by a motley collection of village elders, school children and members of the order. The procession winds down the main roads of Goa Velha village before returning to assemble in the dusty church square for a candlelit service. The statues remain in view in the church for two days to remind all of their good deeds. There is also a fair selling old-fashioned hand-held fans, a local handicraft, and actors and musicians perform in the villages.

Pilar

In **Agassaim**, not far from the Zuari Bridge, the simple façade of the 18th-century **Church of St Lawrence** hides a heavily gilded, rococo altar and reredos. Close by, the **Pilar Seminary**, which is still an active centre of religious instruction, stands on a commanding hilltop site once occupied by a Siva temple. It was founded in 1613 by Capuchin monks who remained here until their expulsion in 1835. The 17th-century church, dedicated to Our Lady of Pilar still shows faint remains of frescoes on the church walls, and also along the cloisters around the enclosed courtyard of the monastery.

The Carmelites took over and restored the monastery in 1858, but from 1890 it became the headquarters of the Missionary Society of St Francis Xavier. Father Agnelo de Souza (1869-1927) who spent 10 years in meditation here before dedicating his life to tireless service, awaits canonization. He is revered and remembered by worshippers at his tomb, especially at services on Thursdays throughout the year. The more recent extension, which houses the present seminary, has a small chapel with a fine marble altar and some German stained glass.

The **museum** ① *on the first floor of the seminary, 1000-1700*, displays finds from the Kadamba period and relics from the Siva temple including a headless Nandi (bull) and a rock carving of a Naga (serpent). From the rooftop you can get good views of Mormugao harbour and the Zuari.

Talaulim

Just north of the Pilar Seminary is the **Church of St Anna (Santana)** at Talaulim by the river Siridado, a tributary of the Zuari. Built around 1695, its elaborate baroque façade is similar in design (though smaller) to that of the great Church of St Augustine at Old Goa (of which only part of one tower remains). The parish church once had a large congregation but it fell into disrepair when nearby Old Goa declined, and had to be refurbished in 1907. It is described as a masterpiece of Indianized Portuguese baroque; a long overdue restoration will make it possible to appreciate its status more fully. If the door is locked, ask a villager to point you in the direction of the church member who holds the key.

The five storeys provide an interior with great space under a high barrel-vaulted ceiling lit by two upper rows of windows, which show off a profusion of stucco work. The shell-heads to the doors and niches on the lower floor attractively echo the design on the ornate façade. The church also has the unique feature of hollow side walls through which people secretly went to confession, which was heard in 'semicircular hollows'. The wooden image of St Anna above the chancel arch is particularly interesting. She appears as an elderly lady in a hat and carrying a stick, portrayed as she was reported to have appeared in separate visions to a Christian and a Hindu villager during the 17th century. The latter was also miraculously cured by her and both said that the lady had requested a home in the village. St Anna is similarly portrayed in the choir grill and the nave.

❦ This church is on the list of the 100 most endangered sites according to the world momuments fund.

St Anna's feast day (26 July) is celebrated by both Christian and Hindu communities who come to seek blessing from the mother of the Virgin Mary. Her intervention is traditionally sought by childless couples. It is known popularly as the Toucheam (Konkani for 'cucumber') Feast because those who come to pray for a baby boy (*menino*) bring with them a cucumber (*pepino*). Unmarried boys also come to pray for partners, bringing with them spoons (*colher*) to plead for wives (*mulher*); girls bring mung beans (*urid*) in exchange for husbands (*marido*)!

⬤ Sleeping

Panjim has a wide choice of accommodation and the director of tourism, T0832-2226515, has a list of families hosting paying guests. There are upmarket options south of town in Miramar and Dona Paula, but for most character it's best to book into one of the guesthouses in the atmospheric Fontainhas district. Old Goa, although it's on every tourist's itinerary, is very undeveloped in terms of places to stay and eat – places like Ribandar, Divar and Charao have even fewer tourist facilities. It's best to base yourself in Panjim. If towns really don't do it for you, you can still see everywhere listed above from places as far afield as Palolem and Arambol as (admittedly punishing) daytrips.

Guesthouses have 0800-0930 checkout to accommodate new arrivals on trains and buses. A 3rd person in a double room with or without mattress costs Rs 50-100.

Central Panjim *p58, maps p61 and p62*
A-B Mandovi, D Bandodkar Marg, T0832-2426270, www.hotelmandovigoa.com. Old building with hints of art deco, relaxing but lacks great character. 66 large a/c rooms (more expensive river-facing), rates include breakfast. 1st floor **Riorico** restaurant, popular pastry shop, terrace bar, exchange, good bookshop.
B Nova Goa, Dr Atmaram Borkar Rd, T0832-2226231, www.hotelnovagoa.com. 85

good a/c rooms with bath, some have fridge and bath tub, best with pool views, rooms and corridors dull and dirty.
B-C Delmon, C de Albuquerque Rd, T0832-2226846, www.alcongoa.com. 50 clean rooms with TV and desk, some a/c, breakfast included. Modern, comfortable hotel with popular restaurant.
C La Capitol, MG Rd, next to Custom House, T0832-2231050, lsons@goatelecom.com. 12 renovated rooms (some smallish), TV, neat, clean, restaurant, friendly and willing staff, but noisy during the day, check out 0900.
D Manvins, 4th floor, Souza Towers, T0832-2224412, www.goamanvins.com. 40 good-size, clean rooms, compact bathroom, TV, stunning views over Municipal Gardens and river Mandovi beyond. Terrace at the rear has a good view of Panjim Church and is a relatively private place to relax, good for city photos. Access via colourful passageway and lift to 4th flr. Recommended for the views alone.
D Palacio de Goa, Gama Pinto Rd, T0832-2221785. Modern 6-storey building, 55 decent rooms with phone, TV, (good value 4 or 5-bedded) a/c extra Rs 100, top floor best views, restaurant, check out 0800, far from bus stand.
D Rajdhani, Dr Atmaram Borkar Rd, T0832-2225362. 35 smallish clean rooms with bath, some a/c (Rs 100 extra), in

modern Indian business-style hotel, good a/c, pure vegetarian restaurant (closed afternoons).

D-E Blessings, MG Rd, behind Bhatkar House, T0832-2224770, hotelblessings@ yahoo.com. 18 ordinary rooms, TV (extra Rs 50), 2 have huge terraces instead of balconies, restaurant, quiet back yard full of trees.

D-E Panjim Residency (GTDC), near Secretariat, overlooking the river, T0832-2227103. 40 good-size rooms with balcony, some a/c (overpriced at Rs 950), best views from top floor, good open-air restaurant, often full.

D-E Virashree, opposite Mahalaxmi Temple, Dr Dada Vaidya Rd, T0832-2226656, virashree@hotmail.com. 12 large, comfortable rooms with TV but lacking quality finish.

E Orav's Guest House, 31 Janeiro Rd, T0832-2426128. 16 good rooms with shower, some with pleasant balcony, clean modern block in old part of town.

F Frank's Inn, 83 Menezes Braganza Rd, T0832-2226716. 10 rooms, shared baths, clean.

San Thome and Fontainhas *p64, map p65*
A The Panjim Peoples, opposite the Panjim Inn, www.panjiminn.com. The 3rd heritage project from the Sukhija family behind the Panjim Inn, this one is properly top end with just 4 rooms, antique 4-poster beds and bathtubs, plus internet access. There are plans for an upmarket restaurant.

C Panjim Inn, E212, 31 January Rd, Fontainhas, T0832-2226523, www.panjiminn.com. Goa's first heritage hotel is idiosyncratic, even in the context of the historic Fontainhas district. 14 rooms of varying size all fitted with 4-poster beds, a/c comes for an extra Rs 250.

C Panjim Pousada, just up the road from Panjim Inn. Slightly cheaper sister hotel to the Panjim Inn with double rooms set around a permanent art gallery in a courtyard. It is an evocative, attractive renovation. Best rooms at the back overlook another courtyard. Recommended.

E Afonso, near San Sebastian Chapel, Fontainhas, T0832-2222359. 8 clean rooms with bath, shaded roof terrace for breakfast, a family-run guesthouse, obliging and friendly, reserve ahead. Recommended. Others in Fontainhas (usually rooms

belonging to local families), include **Elite Lodge**, T0832-2422093 and **Sonia Niwas Guest House**, with 7 rooms with bath.

Miramar *p66*
AL-A Goa Marriott Resort, Mandovi River, T0832-2463333, reservation@goamarriottresort.com. 153 large rooms, good facilities, Barracuda Diving centre, pool (close to public beach), best hotel in Panjim area. Weekend buffet lunches popular with Panjim residents.

B Swimsea Beach Resort, T0832-2464481, swimsea@satyam.net.in. 28 a/c rooms with small balconies (in need of a makeover), sea facing best, pool, close to black sandy beach.

C Blue Bay, Caranzalem beach, T0832-2464881 bluebay@sancharnet.in. 12 simple modern rooms, some a/c, well kept grounds, friendly owner, quiet and isolated.

C-E Bela Goa, T0832-2462275. 11 simple rooms in an uninspiring building, surprisingly light and airy though no balcony, 2 a/c rooms (more expensive), restaurant, bar, enthusiastic staff.

D Miramar Beach Resort, close to the beach, T0832-2227754. 60 clean rooms, some a/c, there are better (and cheaper) rooms in newer wing by shaded groves, good restaurant.

F Youth Hostel, at the far end of Caranzalem beach, away from the beach, T0832-2225433. 3 rooms (Rs 60 per person), 5 dorms, max 3 nights, YHA members Rs 20, also non-members (except in Dec and Jan) Rs 40, canteen.

Dona Paula *p68*
B Prainha Cottages, T0832-2453881, www.prainha.com. 42 rooms, 'Madeira cottages' best (a/c, nearer beach and with sea view), spacious, simple but comfortable and quiet (reports of poor sound insulation on upper floor), good views, palm-shaded garden, good restaurant, small pool, beautiful secluded beach, helpful staff. Highly recommended.

B-C O Pescador, Dona Paula Beach, T0832-2453863, www.opescador.com. 25 large pleasant rooms in small buildings around a garden (need repainting), rate doubles for a/c and sea-facing balcony, restaurant, good pool, on the beach, quiet, young friendly management.

⊙ Eating

Panjim *p58, maps p61 and p62*

$$$ **Rioricoi** at the *Mandovi*, D Bandodkar Marg. Good seafood (tiger prawns Rs 600), Portuguese and Goan dishes, great buffet breakfast Rs 150.

$$ **Avanti Hotel**, Rua de Ourem, T0832-2427179, near Old Patto Bridge, Mon-Sat. Popular local Goan food and chilled beers, a/c, outdoor balcony. Recommended.

$$ **Delhi Durbar Restaurant and Bar**, MG Rd, T0832-2222544. Mughlai delicacies in plush environment. Kebabs, mutton rogan gosh, paneer shashlik etc. Panjim's finest North Indian food.

$$ **Goenchin**, off Dr Dada Vaidya Rd. Tasty Chinese with spicy seafood (Rs 80-140).

$$ **Horseshoe**, Rua de Ourem, T0832-2431788, Mon-Sat 1200-1430, 1900-1030. Low key Portuguese/Goan restaurant set across 2 orange and white high-ceiling rooms with exceptionally good service. Most meals are excellent value (Rs 60-80) but daily fish specials like red snapper are far more costly (from Rs 300). The cashew cake, Bolo San Rival (Rs 50), trumps all the great main courses; unique to the Horseshoe, it is worth a pilgrimage in itself. Highly recommended.

$$ **Quarterdeck**, next to Betim ferry jetty, T0832-2432905. Goan, Indian, Chinese. Riverside location is the best in Panjim, very pleasant in the evening when brightly lit cruise boats glide gaudily by. Occasional live music.

$$ **Venite**, 31 Janeiro Rd, T0832-2225537, Mon-Sat 0800-2200, closes in the afternoon. The most charming of Panjim's eateries has 1st floor balconies overlooking the Sao Thome streetlife and good music. Simple breakfasts and good Goan food, Rs 80+ for main dishes, pricier lobsters. Beer.

$$ **Viva Panjim**, house no 178, signposted from 31 Janeiro Rd, T0832-2422405. This family-run place dishes up specials of Goan food along with seafood plus take-away parcels of Indian, Chinese and continental.

$ **Annapurna**, Ormuz Rd. South Indian. Good *thalis* and *dosa* in large, clean eatery upstairs with families relaxing over *chai*.

$ **Café Tato**, off east side of Church Sq, closed evenings. Something of a local institution, Tato is always busy at lunchtime when office workers descend for favourite genuine Goan grub. Upstairs is a/c.

$ **Coriana**, in the lea of New Patto bridge, Mon-Sat, Goan. Dark purple decor and high backed booths give a slightly seedy feel, but the food is genuine, pleasant owner, excellent fresh fish, chilli fry, *sorpotel*, roast tongue.

$ **Kamat**, south end of Municipal Gardens. Very popular dining hall (quiet a/c upstairs), excellent *masala dosa* (Rs 18) and *thalis* (Rs 28), no alcohol.

$ **Rosoyo**, 18th June Rd. Serves a choice of excellent Gujarati *thalis*, Rs 40-50, generous refills (1130-1530), plus evening special, Rs 80. Recommended.

$ **Shiv Sagar**, MG Rd. South Indian vegetarian. No *thalis*, tasty Mysore *masala dosa* (Rs 20), clean, popular, a/c upstairs.

$ **Vihar**, R José de Costa. South Indian vegetarian. Well-prepared tasty *thalis* (Rs 50) and good choice of snacks, clean smart a/c upstairs.

Bakeries, cafes and fast food

If you fancy an alternative to endless *thalis* and Goan seafood these joints are popular in the evenings when the young go out on the town.

$ **A Pastelaria**, Dr Dada Vaidya Rd. Good variety of cakes, pastries and breads behind clean glass cases. **Mandovi Hotel** has a branch too (side entrance).

$ **Chicky Chocky** near Church of the Immaculate Conception. Good fast foods. '*Sizzle Point*' for speciality sizzlers.

$ **Dominos Pizza**, T0832-2231166, Church Sq corner. Bright plastic environment, good choice of pizzas (Rs 100-200), delivery service.

$ **Perry & Cookie**, MG Rd, west end of town. Take-away kebab house and roast chicken.

Miramar *p66*

$$ **Beach Boogie**, Caranzalem beach, towards Miramar bus stand. Garden restaurant, varied menu, live music.

$ **Foodland**, Miramar Beach Resort. Fast food.

$ **Goa Marriott's pastry shop,** Mandovi River, T0832-2463333. Has real continental delights (truffle torte, tiramisu).

Dona Paula *p68*

$ **Goan Delicacy**, Hawaii Beach, T0832-2224356. Look for the sign by the rickshaw stand on NIO Circle, follow track to left of Dona Paula road, turn left at the bottom and follow sandy path. Seafood, good local dishes, Tandoori oven, bar, family-run, very friendly. Relaxing atmosphere.

$ **White House**, near NIO Post Office T0832-2221239. Goan and seafood with great views over the Dona Paula shoreline.

♠ Pubs, bars and clubs

Panjim *p58, maps p61 and p62*
There's certainly no prohibition in Goa: you can't go 20 paces in Panjim without finding a bar: brilliantly pokey little rooms with tacky tables and chairs and some snacks being fried up in the corner. Many are clustered around Fontainhas. The *feni* (Goa's cashew- or coconut-extracted moonshine) comes delivered in jerry cans, making it cheaper than restaurants. Solitary women are rare.
Café Moderna near Cine National, food none too good, claustrophobic upstairs dining area, quality atmosphere.

☺ Entertainment

Panjim *p58, maps p61 and p62*
Read the today's events columns in the local papers: it often happens that some great concerts and performances are underpromoted.
Astronomical Observatory, 7th floor, Junta House, 18th June Rd (entrance in Vivekananda Rd), open 14 Nov-31 May, 1900-2100, in clear weather. Rooftop 6 inch Newtonian reflector telescope and binoculars, plus enthusiastic volunteers. Worth a visit on a moonless night, and for views over Panjim at sunset.
Kala Academy, D Bandodkar Marg, Campal, T0832-2223288. This modern and architecturally impressive centre designed by Charles Correa was set up to preserve and promote the cultural heritage of Goa. There are exhibition galleries, a library and comfortable indoor and outdoor auditoria. Art exhibitions, theatre, and music programmes (from contemporary pop and jazz to Indian classical) are held, mostly during the winter months. There are also courses on music and dance.

MV Caravela, Fisheries dept. building, D Bandodkar Marg, Panjim www.casinocity.com/in/panjim/caravela. India's first floating casino is docked on the Mandovi, 215 ft of high-rupee-rolling catamaran casino, all plush wall-to-wall carpets, chandeliers and saree-wearing croupiers. The boat accommodates 300 people, has a sun deck, swimming pool and restaurant and the Rs 1,200 entrance includes short eats and dinner and booze from 1730 till the morning.

☸ Festivals

Panjim *p58, maps p61 and p62*
Jan Fontainhas Festival of Arts. 30 old homes around Panjim are converted into galleries.
Feb/Mar In addition to the major festivals in Feb, the **Mardi Gras Carnival** (3 days preceding Lent in Feb/Mar) is a Mediterranean-style riot of merrymaking, marked by feasting, colourful processions and floats down streets: it kicks off near the Secretariat at midday. One of the best bits is the red-and-black dance held in the cordoned off square outside the old world Clube Nacional on the evening of the last day: everyone dresses up (some cross-dressing), almost everyone knows each other, and there's lots of old-fashioned slow-dancing to curiously country and western infused live music. The red and black theme is strictly enforced.
Mar-Apr Shigmotsav is a spring festival held at full moon (celebrated as Holi elsewhere in India); colourful float processions through the streets often display mythological scenes.
First Sun after Easter Feast of Jesus of Nazareth.
Nov/Dec Food and Culture Festival at Miramar beach.
Dec 8 Feast of Our Lady of the Immaculate Conception. A big fair is held in the streets around Church Sq and a firework display is put on in front of the church each night of the week before the feast (at 1930). After morning Mass on the Sun, the Virgin is carried in a procession through the town centre.

○ Shopping

Panjim *p58, maps p61 and p62*
Mapusa and Margao's **municipal markets** may have the edge in terms of local colour, but there's an incredibly clean new municipal market that's just been put up in Panjim that has piles and piles of lentils and veg and fruit spotlessly signposted, next to the old market which still stinks of fish and meat and draws clouds of flies. The first is great for practical food buying, the second for character. Western labels like Levi's, Pepe, Lee and Nike can make good investments.

Books
Mandovi Hotel bookshop has a good range including American news magazines.
Utopia, Dr A Borkar Rd, near Dominos Pizza, 1000-2000. Goa tourism booklets and maps, and books on Goan and Indian cuisine, helpful staff.
Varsha, near Azad Maidan, carries a wide stock in tiny premises, and is especially good for books on Goa. Obscure titles are not displayed but ask knowledgeable staff.

Clothes and textiles
Madame Butterfly, opposite Azad Maidan. For carefully-crafted designer wear for women plus accessories.
Sosa's, E 245 Rue De Ourem Panjim, T0832-2228063. Clothes as well as jewellery in papier mâché and silver.
Velha Goa Galeria, 4/191 Rua De Ourem, Fountainhas, T0832-2426628. Hand-painted ceramics, tiles used as wall hangings to tabletops.
Wendell Rodricks Design Space, B5 Suryadarshan Colony, T0832-2238177. Rodricks is probably Goa's most famous fashion designer who built his name making minimalist clothing. Here you'll find his luxury clothes and footwear.
Carey Franklin, Church Sq, next to GOI Tourist Office. Smart a/c shops near Delhi Durbar restaurant have genuine stock of international brands Adidas, Benetton, Jordache, Lacoste, Lee, Levi's (jeans Rs 1200-1600), Nike, Wrangler.
Government Emporia on RS Rd. Good value for fixed-rate clothes, fabric and handicrafts.

Khadi Showroom, Municipal (Communidade) Building, Church Sq, good value for fixed-rate clothes, fabric and handicrafts. Nehru jackets, Rs 250, plus perishable items such as honey and pickles.

Food
Farm Products, north of Azad Maidan, cheese, cooked cold meats, Goan sausages and sweets.
Megsons, 18 June Rd, sell cheese, cooked cold meats, Goan sausages and sweets.
Kajuwalla chain has good cashews (around Rs 250 per kilo).

Handicrafts
Goa Government handicrafts shops are at the tourist hotels and the Interstate Terminus. There are other emporia on RS Rd.
Kohinoor, 14 Patto Plaza, Shiv Towers. For high class pieces, beautifully displayed.

Music
Music Sinari's, 18 June Rd. CDs.
Rock 'n' Raaga, Rizvi Towers, 18 June Rd, T0832-2422841. Good CDs (around Rs 575).

Photography
Film costs about Rs 100. Developing is fast and high quality (Rs 250 for 36 exp).
Kodak Express, MG Rd. Central Studio, Panjim Residency.
Lisbon Studio, Church Sq.

▲ Activities and tours

Panjim *p58, maps p61 and p62*
Diving
Barracuda Diving India, Dive Center, Hotel Marriott, Panjim, T0832-2463333 www.barracudadiving.com. Daily dive trips, wreck dives, PADI certificates, diving and snorkelling from Goan and British couple.

Football
Goans are fanatical about football: professional matches are played at the stadium; season Oct-Mar, check the listings pages in local papers.

River cruises
River cruises by launch are organized on the Mandovi river, sometimes with live bands

and sing-along entertainment. Evening cruises are brilliantly corny but recommended. A bar also operates.
Santa Monica (GTDC), Santa Monica Jetty (east of New Patto Bridge): 1 hr cruise 1800-1900, 1915-2015, Rs 100, to Miramar and back.

Tour operators
Alcon International, D Bandodkar Marg, T/F0832-2232267. Quick, efficient and friendly flight bookings.
MGM Travels, MG Rd, T0832-2421865, opposite Azad Maidan, reliable and professional, Rs 100 for all rail bookings.
Sita, 101 Rizvi Chambers, 1st flr, C Albuquerque Rd, T0832-2220476, www.sitagoa .com, Mon-Fri 0900-1800, Sat 0930-1330.
Thomas Cook, 8 Alcon Chambers, D Bandodkar Marg, 'ferociously efficient' if slightly expensive.
TCI, 'Citicentre', 1st flr, 19 Patto Plaza, T0832-2237117, TCI.goa@gnpun. Travel agents charge Rs 100-150 to reconfirm international flights. Easy to call the airlines yourself.

Walking
There are some beautiful walks through the forested areas of Goa. Contact the **Hiking Association of Goa**, 6 Anand Niwas, Swami Vivekenanda Rd.

Watersports
Some large beach resorts such as Cidade de Goa, Vainguinim Beach and Fort Aguada Beach Resort have sailing, water-skiing, windsurfing etc.

Yoga
Brahma Kumari, E98 Mala, T0832-2226044, 0600-1100, 1600-2000.
Sri Aurobindo Society, Institute Menezes Braganza Building.
Vivekananda Society, 6th floor, Junta House, T0832-2224098, 1000-1300, 1500-1800.

⊙ Transport

Panjim *p58, maps p61 and p62*
Air
The airport is at Dabolim, see page 56. From Dabolim airport, 29 km via the Zuari Bridge from Panjim, internal flights can be taken

through **Air India** to **Mumbai** and Thiruvananthapuram.
    For pre-paid taxis, see under 'Touching down' (page 24).

Airline offices
Air India, 18th June Rd, T0832-2431101.
Indian Airlines and Alliance Air, Dempo House, D Bandodkar Marg, T0832-2237821, reservations 1000-1300, 1400-1600, airport T0832-2540788, flights to **Bangalore**, **Delhi** and **Mumbai** daily (US$ 95), and **Chennai**.
British Airways, 2 Excelsior Chambers, opposite Mangaldeep, MG Rd, T0832-2224573.
Jet Airways, Sesa Ghor, 7-9 Patto Plaza, T0832-2431472, airport T0832-2510354. Flights to **Mumbai** (US$ 103), and **Bangalore**.
Kuwait Airways, 2 Jesuit House, Dr DR de Souza Rd, Municipal Garden Sq, T0832-2224612.
Sahara, Live-In Appt, Gen Bernard Guedes Rd, airport office, T0832-2540043. To **Mumbai**, US$ 95, daily, and **Delhi**.

Auto-rickshaw
Easily available but agree a price beforehand (Rs 20-35), more after dark. Motorcycle taxis and private taxis are a little cheaper.

Bus
Local Crowded **Kadamba (KTC)** buses and private buses operate from the bus stand in Patto to the east of town, across the Ourem Creek, T0832-2222634. Booking 0800- 1100, 1400-1630. The timetable is not strictly observed: buses leave when full.
Frequent service to **Calangute** 35 mins, Rs 7; **Mapusa** 25 mins, Rs 5. Via Cortalim (Zuari bridge) to **Margao** 1 hr, Rs 8; **Vasco** 1 hr, Rs 8. To **Old Goa** (every 10 mins) 20 mins, Rs 5, continues to **Ponda** 1 hr, Rs 8.
    Long distance 'Luxury' buses and 'Sleepers' (bunks are shared). **Private operators**: Laxmi Motors, near Customs House, T0832-2225745; company at Cardozo Building near KTC bus stand; **Paulo Tours**, Hotel Fidalgo, T0832-2226291.
State buses are run by Kadamba TC, Karnataka RTC, Maharashtra RTC. Check times and book in advance at Kadamba Bus Stand. Unlicensed operators use poorly maintained, overcrowded buses; check out beforehand.

Panjim & Old Goa Panjim Listings

Buses to **Bangalore**: 1530-1800 (13 hrs), Rs 300; **Belgaum**: 0630-1300 (5 hrs); **Gokarna** and **Hospet (Hampi)**: 0915-1030 (10 hrs), Rs 150 (Rs 350 sleeper); **Hubli**: many; **Londa**: 4 hrs, Rs 60; **Mangalore**: 0615-2030 (10 hrs), Rs 180; **Miraj**: 1030 (10 hrs); **Mumbai**: 1530-1700 (15 hrs+), Rs 550 (sleeper), others (some a/c) Rs 300-450; **Pune**: 0615-1900 (12 hrs), Rs 200, sleeper Rs 400.

Car hire

Sai Service, 36/1 Alto Porvorim, north of the Mandovi Bridge, T0832-2417063, or at airport. **Hertz**, T0832-2223998; **Joey's**, town centre opposite the Mandovi Hotel, T0832- 2422050, Rs 700 per day (80 km) with driver. **Wheels**, T0832-2224304, airport, T0832-2512138.

Ferries

Flat-bottomed ferries charge a nominal fee to take passengers (and usually vehicles) when rivers are not bridged. Panjim-Betim (the Nehru bridge over the Mandovi supplements the ferry); Old Goa-Diwar Island; Ribandar-Chorao for Salim Ali Bird Sanctuary.

Tourist taxi

White vehicles. Can be hired from Goa Tourism, Trionora Apts, T0832-2223396, about Rs 700 per day (80 km). **Share-taxis** run on certain routes; available near the the ferry wharves, main hotels and market places (max 5). **Mapusa** from Panjim, around Rs 10 each. **Airport** about 40 mins; Rs 380.

Train

Some Konkan Railway trains stop at **Karmali**, T0832-2286398, near Old Goa (20 mins taxi). **Rail Bookings**, Kadamba Bus Station, 1st flr, T0832-2435054, 0930-1300; 1430-1700. The South Central Railway serves the Vasco-Londa/Belgaum line; for details see Transport under Vasco on page 57, and under Margao (Madgaon), page 149.

Miramar p66

Bus Buses from Panjim to Miramar continue to **Dona Paula**, Rs 8. Note: in Miramar they turn inland and follow the old road, rejoining the new road just before climbing the hill to Dona Paula.

ⓘ Directory

Panjim *p58, maps p61 and p62*
Ambulance T0832-2223026, T0832-2224601. **Banks** Many private agencies change TCs and cash. **Sita** transfers money worldwide (see activities and tours); **Thomas Cook**, 8 Alcon Chambers, D Bandodkar Marg, T0832-2431732, Mon-Sat. Also for Thomas Cook drafts, money transfers; **Wall Street Finance**, MG Rd, opposite Azad Maidan; **Amex**, at Menezes Air Travel, Rua de Ourem, but does not cash TCs. Cash against certain credit cards from **Central Bank**, Nizari Bhavan; **Andhra Bank**, Dr Atmaram Borkar Rd, opposite EDC House, T0832-2223513; **Bank of Baroda**, Azad Maidan; **HDFC**, 18 June Rd, T0832-2421922, 24 hr ATM, most convienient way to obtain cash in Panjim. **Fire** T101, T0832-2225500. **High commissions and consulates** Germany, Hon Consul, c/o Cosme Matias Menezes Group, Rua de Ourem, T0832-2223261; Portugal, LIC Bldg, Patto, T0832-2224233; UK, room 302, 3rd flr, Manguirish Bldg, 18th June Rd, T0832-2228571, bcagoa@goa1.dot.net.
Internet Among many charging Rs 35-40 per hr: **little.dot.com cyber cafe**, 1st floor, Padmavati Towers, 18th June Rd, T0832-2427811, 0930-2300. Best in town: **Suraj Business Centre**, T0832-2232510, 5 terminals upstairs, excellent fast connection (128 Kbps ISDN line), 0900-2300. **Medical services** Goa Medical College, Av PC Lopez, west end of town, T0832-2223026, is very busy; newer College at Bambolim; **CMM Poly Clinic**, Altinho, T0832-2225918. **Post office** Old Tobacco Exchange, St Thome, towards Old Patto Bridge, with Poste Restante on left as you enter, Mon-Sat 0930-1730, closed 1300-1400. **Telegraph office** Dr Atmaram Borkar Rd. **Tourist Police** T0832-2224757. **Police** T100. **Useful addresses** Foreigners' Regional Registration Office: Police Headquarters. **Wildlife** Chief Wildlife Warden, Conservator's Office, Junta House, 3rd flr, 18th June Rd, T0832-2224747, and Deputy Conservator of Forests (Wildlife), 4th flr, T0832-2229701, for permits and accommodation in the sanctuaries. **World Wildlife Fund**, B-2, Hillside Apartments, Fontainhas (off 31 January St), T0832-2226020, advises on trekking with a guide.

Old Goa and around → *Colour map 1, grid C3.*

When the British explorer Richard Burton arrived in Goa on sick leave from his Indian army unit in 1850, he described Old Goa, once the oriental capital of Portuguese empire-building ambition and rival to Lisbon in grandeur, as a place of 'utter desolation'; its people 'as sepulchral-looking as the spectacle around them'. Today, Old Goa has a flagging melancholy beauty, revived by a steady flow of tourists and pilgrims to the remains of St Francis Xavier housed in the giddying baroque of Basilica of Bom Jesus, the only church you'll find in Goa to have escaped bright whitewashing.
▶▶ *For Eating and other listings, see page 85.*

Ins and outs

Getting there Old Goa lies on the south bank of the Mandovi on the crest of a low hill 8 km from Panjim. The frequent bus service takes 15-20 minutes. Buses drop you off opposite the Basilica of Bom Jesus (Rs 5); pick up the return bus near the police station. Auto-rickshaws charge Rs 25, taxis, Rs 150 return. Karmali station on the Konkan Railway, just east of the centre, has taxis for transfer.

Getting around The major monuments are within easy walking distance of the bus stop. All the monuments are open daily, throughout the year, from 0830-1730.

History

Old Goa is to Christians the spiritual heart of the territory. It owes its origin as a Portuguese capital to Afonso de Albuquerque and some of its early ecclesiastical development to St Francis Xavier who was here, albeit for only five months, in the mid-16th century. Before the Portuguese arrived though it was the second capital of the Muslim Bijapur Kingdom. Today, all the mosques and fortifications of that period have disappeared and only a fragment of the Sultan's palace walls remain (see also Goa Velha, page 68).

Old, or 'Velha', Goa – one time 'Rome of the East' – was a flourishing port with an enviable trade even before the Portuguese arrived. The bustling walled city was peopled by merchants of many nationalities who came to buy and sell horses from Arabia and Hormuz, to trade silk, muslin, calico, rice, spices and areca nuts from the interior and other ports along the west coast. It was a centre of ship-building and boasted fine residences and public buildings.

After the arrival of the Portuguese Old Goa swelled still further in size and significance. In the west lay barracks, mint, foundry and arsenal, hospital and prison. The banks of the Mandovi held the shipyards of Ribeira des Gales and next door lay the administrative and commercial centre. Streets and areas of the city were set aside for different activities and merchandise, each with its own character. The most important, Rua Direita ou dos Leiloes ('Straight Street') was lined with jewellers, bankers and artisans. It was also the venue for auctions of all manner of precious goods, held each morning except on Sundays. To the east was the market and the old fortress of Adil Shah, while the true centre of the town was filled with magnificent churches built by the Franciscans, themselves joined by waves of successive religious orders: first the Dominicans in 1548, the Augustinians from 1572, the Carmelites from 1612 and finally the Theatines from 1655. By the middle of the 17th century the city, plagued by cholera and malaria and crippled economically, its was abandoned for Panjim.

Sights

The Basilica of Bom Jesus

The renaissance façade of Goa's most famous church, the **Basilica of Bom (the Good) Jesus**, a World Heritage Site, reflects the architectural transition to baroque taking place in Europe. Apart from the elaborate gilded altars, wooden pulpit and the candy-twist Bernini columns the interior is very simple.

Originally lime-plastered like the others, this was removed in 1956 to reveal the laterite base. The granite decorative elements have always been unadorned. The façade is the richest in Goa and also the least Goan in character. There are no flanking towers. It appears that the church was modelled on the earlier church of St Paul (now destroyed) which was in turn based on the Gesu, the mother church in Rome. There is only one tower in the building and that is placed at the east end, giving it a more Italian look. On the pediment of the façade is a tablet with IHS ('Jesus' in Greek, or Iaeus Hominum Salvator – 'Jesus, Man's Saviour' – in Latin).

The church contains the treasured remains of **St Francis Xavier**, a former pupil of soldier-turned-saint Ignatius Loyola, the founder of the Order of Jesuits. In 1613 St Francis' body was brought to the adjoining Professed House (see below) from the College of St Paul. It was moved into the church in 1624, and its present chapel in 1655 where it has remained ever since. St Francis was canonized in 1622.

The tomb, which lies to the right of the main chancel, (1698) was the gift of one of the last of the Medicis, Cosimo III, Grand Duke of Tuscany, and was carved by the Florentine sculptor Giovanni Batista Foggini. It took 10 years to complete. It consists of three tiers of marble and jasper: the upper tier has panels depicting scenes from the saint's life. The casket is silver and has three locks, the keys held by the Governor, the Archbishop and the Convent Administrator. You can look down on to the tomb from a small window in the art gallery next to the church.

After his canonization, St Francis' body was exposed for viewing on each anniversary of his death, but this ceased in 1707. Thereafter a few special private expositions were held until 1752, when the body was again put on public view, to quash rumours that the Jesuits had removed it. Since 1859, the exposition has taken place on the saint's death anniversary every 10 to 12 years: the next is scheduled for November 2004-January 2005. The relics are taken to the Sé Cathedral during this period to allow easier viewing for the vast numbers who attend. Feast Day is 3 December.

There is a **modern art gallery** ① *only sporadically open*, next to the church with rather amazing surrealistic paintings by Goan painter Dom Martin alongside wooden statues of Christian saints. Next to the church, and connected with it, is the **Professed House for Jesuit fathers**, a handsome two-storey building with a typically Mediterranean open courtyard garden.

Sé Cathedral

Across the square sits the **Sé Cathedral**, dedicated to St Catherine on whose day (25 November) Goa was recaptured by Afonso de Albuquerque. Certainly the

Basilica of Bom Jesus

N

0 metres 20
0 yards 20

1 Chapel of the Blessed Sacrament
2 Our Lady of Hope
3 Main Altar
4 St Michael
5 Sacristy
6 Chapel of St Francis Xavier
7 St Anthony
8 Pulpit

The scattering of St Francis' remains

St Francis has suffered many degradations over the years, and his body has been gradually reduced by the removal of various parts.

Soon after his death a 'small portion of the knee had been removed to show the captain of the ship on which his body was being carried its unusually fresh condition.

The neck was broken in Malacca by placing the body in a grave that was too short. In 1554 one devotee, a Portuguese lady, Dona Isabel de Carom, is supposed to have bitten off the right leg's little toe – carrying it in her mouth all the way to Lisbon where it is still supposed to be kept by her descendants.

Part of the arm was sent to Rome in 1615 where it is idolized in the Gesu church; the shoulder blade was divided between the three colleges of Cochin, Malacca and Macau, and part of the right hand was sent to the Jesuits in Japan in 1619.

In 1890 Xavier lost a second toe when it fell off (it is now displayed in an urn in the sacristy of the Basilica); a third fell off in 1910.

largest church in Old Goa, it could even be the biggest in Asia and was built on the ruins of a mosque by the Dominicans between 1562 and 1623. It is Tuscan on the exterior and Corinthian inside, with a barrel-vaulted ceiling and east-facing main façade. One of the characteristic twin towers collapsed in 1776 when it was struck by lightning. The remaining tower holds five bells including the Golden Bell (cast in Cuncolim in 1652). The vast interior, divided into the barrel-vaulted nave with clerestory and two side aisles, has a granite baptismal font. On each side of the church are four chapels along the aisles: on the right these are dedicated to St Anthony, St Bernard, The Cross of Miracles and the Holy Spirit, and on the left, starting at the entrance, to Our Lady of Virtues, St Sebastian, The Blessed Sacrament and Our Lady of Life. The clerestory windows are protected by a shield crowned by a balustrade to keep out the sun. The main altar is superbly gilded and painted, with six further altars in the transept. The marble-top table in front of the main altar is where, since 1955, St Francis Xavier's remains have been held during the exposition of the saint's relics. The main reredos has four panels illustrating the life of St Catherine. There is also an **art gallery** ① *Mon-Thu, Sat 0900-1230, Sun 0900-1030, closed during services, Rs 5.*

Around the cathedral

Southwest of the cathedral's front door are the ruins of the **Palace of the Inquisition**, where over 16,000 cases were heard between 1561 and 1774. The Inquisition was finally suppressed in 1814. Beneath the hall were dungeons. In Old Goa's heyday this was the town centre. f

There are two churches and a museum in the same complex as the Cathedral. The **Church (and Convent) of St Francis of Assisi** is a broad vault of a church with two octagonal towers. The floor is paved with tombstones and on either side of the baroque high altar are paintings on wood depicting scenes from St Francis' life while the walls above have frescoes with floral designs. The original **Holy Spirit Church** in the Portuguese gothic (manueline) style was begun by Franciscan friars in 1517: everything except the old doorway was replaced by the larger present

The ASI booklet on the monuments, Old Goa, by S Rajagopalan, is available from the Archaeological Museum here, Rs 10. See also Further Reading, page 256.

structure in the 1660s (itself restored in 1762-65). The convent now houses the **Archaeological Museum and Portrait Gallery** ⓘ *To832-2286133, 1000-1230, 1500-1830, Rs 5*, whose collection of sculptures covers the period from before the arrival of the Portuguese. Many date from the 12th-13th centuries when Goa came under the rule of the Kadamba Dynasty. There are 'hero stones', commemorating naval battles, and 'sati stones' marking the practice of widow burning. There is also a rather fine collection of portraits of Portuguese Governors upstairs that is particularly revealing both for its charting of the evolution of court dress as well as the physical robustness of the governors inside that dress. Some governors were remarkable for their sickly pallor, others for the sheer brevity of their tenure of office, which must have set the portrait painters something of a challenge.

‼ *No photography, although this appears to be totally ignored by all.*

To the west is **St Catherine's Chapel.** It was built at the gate of the old city on the orders of Albuquerque as an act of gratitude after the Portuguese defeat of the forces of Bijapur in 1510. The original mud and thatch church was soon replaced by a stone chapel which in 1534 became the cathedral (considerably renovated in 1952), remaining so until Sé Cathedral was built.

On the road towards the Mandovi, northeast from the cathedral compound, lies the **Arch of the Viceroys (Ribeira dos Viceroys)**, commemorating the centenary of Vasco da Gama's discovery of the sea route to India. It was built at the end of the 16th century by his great-grandson, Francisco da Gama, Goa's Viceroy from 1597 to 1600. Its laterite block structure is faced with green granite on the side approached from the river. This was the main gateway to the seat of power: on arrival by ship each new Viceroy would be handed the keys and enter through this ceremonial archway before taking office. The statue of Vasco da Gama above the arch was originally surmounted by a gilded statue of St Catherine, the patron saint of the city.

Walking east towards the convent from the arch you pass **the Gate of the Fortress of the Adil Shahs**, probably built by Sabaji, the Maratha ruler of Goa before the Muslim conquest of 1471. The now-ruined palace was home to the Adil Shahi sultans of Bijapur who occupied Goa before the arrival of the Portuguese. It was the Palace of the Viceroys until 1554 after which it served as both the hall of trials for the Inquisition and to house prisoners.

Convent and Church of St Cajetan (Caetano)

A little further still stands the splendid, domed baroque **Convent and Church of St Cajetan (Caetano).** Pope Urban III dispatched a band of Italian friars of the Theatine order to spread the Gospel to the Deccani Muslim city of Golconda near Hyderabad but got a frosty reception so headed back west to settle in Goa. They acquired land around 1661 to build this church, which is shaped like a Greek cross and is partly modelled on St Peter's in Rome. It is the last remaining domed church in Goa.

The main altar, dedicated to Our Lady of Divine Providence, has a free-standing reredos, which is elaborately decorated with gilded angels, cherubs, pilasters and scrolls while this rises to shafts of light beneath a golden crown. The oil paintings illustrate the life of St Cajetan whose altar is the larger one on the right. The small niches above have an attractive shell motif and along the walls there are carved wooden statues of saints. In the centre, under the dome, a curious platform covers a 'well' that may have belonged to a Hindu temple on this site: ask the guardian to show you. Some think the device was incorporated into the building to give the massive structure greater stability in difficult soil conditions.

The crypt below the main altar, where the Italian friars were buried, has some sealed lead caskets that are supposed to contain the embalmed bodies of senior Portuguese officials who never returned home. Next door is the beautiful former convent building which is now a pastoral foundation (closed to the public).

Chapel of Our Lady of the Mount

On a hill a good way further east is this chapel (1510), restored in April 2001 with help from the **Fundação Oriente,** and floodlit at night. It can be reached from the east or south of the hill. At the top, an impressive broad flight of steps leads up to the simple chapel which has a red tiled roof and porch across its façade. It gives you a good idea of how the other churches here must originally have looked. It is a peaceful spot with excellent panoramic views across Old Goa, recalling a more turbulent past when Albuquerque and Adil Shah vied for control of the surrounding area; early morning is best for a visit. The altar gilding inside has been beautifully restored. In front of the principal altar lies the body of architect Antonio Pereira whose burial slab requests the visitor to say an Ave Maria for his soul.

Holy Hill

Between the domineering central monuments of Old Goa's broad tree-lined centre and Panjim stands Holy Hill with its cluster of churches. The first building you reach (on your left) as you leave the central plaza is the **Church and Convent of St John of God,** built in 1685 and abandoned in 1835. To the right is the **Museum of Christian Art** ⓘ *Sun-Thu 1000-1700, Rs 5,* with 150 items gathered from Goa's churches, convents and Christian homes to show a rich cross-section of Indo-Portuguese sacred art workmanship in wood, ivory, silver and gold.

Next door sits **The Convent of St Monica** (1607-27), the first nunnery in India and the largest in Asia. A huge three-storey square building, with the church in the southern part, it was built around a sunken central courtyard containing a formal garden. At one time it was a Royal Monastery, but in 1964 became a theological institute, the Mater Dei Institute for Nuns. It was here in 1936 that Bishop Dom Frei Miguel Rangel is believed to have had a vision of the Christ figure on the Miraculous Cross opening his eyes, his stigmata bleeding and his lips quivering as if to speak. The vision was repeated later that year in the presence of the Bishop, the Viceroy Dom Pedro de Silva and a large congregation.

Take the left fork of the road to reach **The Royal Chapel of St Anthony** (1543) – dedicated to Portugal's national saint and restored by its government in 1961 – and, opposite, **the tower of St Augustine**. Although it is an uphill hike, it is very atmospheric and well worth the effort. The Augustinians came to Goa in 1572; the

Old Goa (Velha Goa)

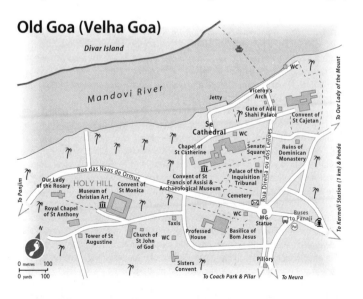

church they immediately began, bar the belfry, lies now in ruins. It once boasted eight chapels, a convent and an excellent library and was enlarged to become one of the finest in the kingdom. It was finally abandoned in 1835 because of religious persecution. The vault collapsed in 1842 burying the image; the façade and main tower followed in 1931 and 1938. Only one of the original four towers survives. The large bell now hangs in Panjim's Church of the Immaculate Conception. The Archaeological Survey of India is spearheading extensive repairs.

Behind is the **Chapel of Our Lady of the Rosary** (1526). Belonging to the earliest period of church building, it is called Manueline after Manuel I, the Portuguese king who oversaw a period of great prosperity that coincided with the country's conquest of Goa. The use of Hindu and Muslim craftsmen in building the chapel led to an architectural style that borrowed from Iberian decoration but also absorbed both local naturalistic motifs and Islamic elements (seen on the marble cenotaph). The church here has a two-storey entrance, a single tower and low flanking turrets. It was from here that Albuquerque directed the battle against the Adil Shahi forces in 1510.

Ribandar, Divar and excursions from Old Goa

Ins and outs At the start of the causeway back to Panjim is the attractive preserved village of Ribandar. Buses between Panjim and Ponda on the NH4A stop at the village's ferry wharf. One of the jetties takes you to Chorao Island's bird sanctuary, while the other takes you to Divar Island (ferries also go direct to Divar from Old Goa and Narao).

Ribandar

Ribandar (pronounced 'Re-bunder') or 'Royal Harbour' is possibly named after the arrival of the Vijayanagar King in the 14th century. The old houses along the road, some substantial, some modest and painted in evocative colours, still conjure up an image of 17th-century Portuguese Goa. The **Church of Our Lady of Help**, constructed in 1565, was built to give thanks for the safe arrival of a Portuguese vessel after a fierce storm at sea. The town provides the shortest route across to Mayem and Bicholim.

Chorao Island and Dr Salim Ali Bird Sanctuary

ⓘ *1000-1700, Rs 1, best Nov-Feb, ferry from Ribandar to Chorao. The ferry from Ribandar runs every 15 mins from 0600-2400, taking about 10 mins, fare Rs 2 (higher at other times). The bird sanctuary is a short walk from the ferry ramp but is not signposted. The best way to look around is to get local fishermen to row you quietly along the river – pay no more than Rs 100. Forest Department motor boats are supposed to operate but are rarely seen.*

This is still one of the most important mangrove complexes in India even though today it covers less than 20 ha. Sea water penetrates a long way inland, especially in the dry season and there are many species of mangroves here, including some rare ones.

The 2 sq km bird sanctuary on the west tip of **Chorao island** sits opposite Panjim at the confluence of the Mandovi and Mapusa rivers and is the focus of a range of conservation measures after it was snatched from the jaws of sure ecological disaster when the Konkan Railway route was proposed to run straight through it. The 14 species making up the mangrove forests here form a protective habitat for coastal fauna and they are home to a large colony of flying foxes, crocodiles, turtles and jackals as well as a rich birdlife: winter visitors include pintails, shovelers, snipes and terns. You can also see blue-winged teals, maddar ducks, grey and purple herons and adjutant storks from a viewing watchtower. You are likely to see a variety of birds according to the time of day and the season, as well as freshwater crabs and mudskippers.

Sun salutations and downward dog

Yoga, once seen as a politicized act of rebellion against British imperial rule, is not particularly popular among contemporary Indians, and they look with not a little curiosity on the lithe foreign yogis yearning to pick up extreme postures from the various 'gurujis' scattered about their country. "For them, it's the equivalent of having hoards of middle class Indians rocking up in Yorkshire to study something we consider as outmoded as morris dancing," admits Phil Dane, who runs a yoga-centric hotel near to Goa's foremost western-style yoga school, Purple Valley.

While some Indians look askance at the vast numbers of firangi yogis, others are making good coin from the trade. Devotees of Sri Pattabhi Jois, the venerated octogenarian who developed the 'ashtanga vinyasa' (dynamic) practice, joke that he has a new-found fondness for Louis Vuitton luggage sets. His disciples have been quick to cash in too and everywhere yoga, once the physical strand in the eight paths towards a Hindu spirituality, is fast becoming commercial. Danny Paradise, one of the first generation of western yoga teachers, today includes Goa on a year-round, global, and no doubt lucrative, yoga-teaching tour and has his own merchandising range that includes an 'asana CD' featuring cameos from students like Sting.

India remains, nevertheless, one of the best places to study the ancient art. If you want to include some informal, and inexpensive, practice in Goa, you'll find that teachers are as ubiquitous as fish curry. Like Goa's staple dish though, quality is far from assured. Look for posters and you might strike gold: Arambol in Goa is a good starting point. If you are travelling to India specifically to practice it's worth doing your homework first. The state's most high profile centre is Purple Valley, whose email newsletter (sign up at www.yogagoa. com) will also keep you up to date of the movements of the latest celebrity yoga teachers. You need to book far in advance, both for courses and flights. See under Activities and tours in the listings sections of each individual towns for further information.

Carambolim Lake (Karmali)

Carambolim Lake ① *12 km east of Panjim, near the NH4A*, is a wide and shallow lake (less than 3 m deep) that lies between the estuaries of the Mandovi and Zuari. It has a wide range of fauna, including 120 species of migratory and local birds similar to those found on Chorao. Siberian pintail ducks, barbets, herons, woodpeckers, swallows, orioles, drongos and marsh harriers can be seen most of the year.

Home to a wide range of varieties of wild **rice**, the lake has remarkably rich concentrations of detoxifying algae, some of which are believed to be responsible for the complete absence of mosquitoes in the surrounding area. In winter it plays host to the Coccilellid predator, which feeds on rice pests.

Heavily silted up, the lake has been managed for many years, being emptied just before the rains for fishing and later re-filled through channels. The lake water is auctioned every April for its fish, although numbers have deteriorated in recent years. Environmental groups suggest that a large section (nearly 20%) of the wetland may have been reclaimed by the Konkan Railway.

Getting there and around   The island, just 9 km long by 4 km wide, is approached by ferry from the Old Goa jetty (below the Arch of the Viceroys) to the south; the Naroa ferry to the northeast; and from Ribander to the southwest (the second ferry ramp when driving out of Panjim). Ferries are free for foot passengers and operate every 15-30 mins (Rs 7 cars).

A couple of local buses run between the three ferry points, but the best way to explore the island is with a scooter. A bus runs from Piedade up to Naroa village, turn round just by the church a short walk from the ferry. (The village on the other side of the river is also known as Naroa.) There is a ferry every hour. From the ferry it is just a 10-minute drive to the Shri Saptakotesvar Temple (see page 84). At Naroa the first ferry from Divar is at 0600, the last back to Divar 2130. As you drive up to the Naroa ferry and cross the river you get a good view of the scar on the landscape made by the Konkan Railway as it cuts across the northeastern corner of the island.

Divar Island is a deceptively quiet backwater: fertile paddy fields ring the steep wooded hill at the centre of the island to create a feeling of rural calm. It is in fact a site of great cultural significance to Hindus and was subject to both Muslim and Christian invasion.

Divar has several small peaceful villages (Navelim, Goltim, Malar and Naroa). At the centre of the island is **Piedade** on the slopes of an isolated hill. A Ganesh temple, an important Hindu pilgrimage place, once stood on here. **Nossa Senhora de Piedade** (Our Lady of Piety), which replaced the second church to Our Lady of Divar, now stands here. There are wonderful panoramic views from this hilltop site; the park is sadly over grown.

The insignificant looking cemetery chapel to the south has an interesting heavily carved stone ceiling and two perforated windows in stone which almost certainly belonged to the Ganesh temple; if locked ask the resident priest to open it for you. The Ganesh image was initially taken to Khandepar (Ponda taluka), then to Naroa (Bicholim taluka) and finally to its present location in Candola in Ponda (see page 172). The lettering above the arched gateway reads 'Tuji Vatt Pollet Assam', which is Konkani for 'Waiting for you'.

The other place of pilgrimage was the 12th-century **Saptakotesvar temple** to Siva built by the Kadambas, which stood in the northeastern corner of the island at Old Naroa but was ransacked by Muslim invaders in the mid-14th century. However, like the Ganesh image and many other Hindu deities within Goa, the faceted *dharalinga* made out of five metals (*pancha dhatu*) – gold, silver, bronze, copper and iron – was hidden in a field and reinstalled nearby by a Vijayanagar king in 1391. Again, a wave of Portuguese temple destruction around 1540 saw the end of the new temple. The remains of the temple tank can be seen near the small Portuguese **Chapel of Our Lady of Candelaria** (1563), which originally incorporated the ruins of the Siva temple in its unusual circular structure, and was later extended on either side. The Siva linga was subsequently smuggled across the river to Bicholim taluka to be placed in a rock-cut sanctuary in a village which adopted the old name Naroa (Narve). The popular pilgrimage was at the same time transferred to the deity's new location. The Shri Saptakotesvar temple in Bicholim taluka, which still attracts a large crowd of worshippers, was renovated in 1668 under instruction from the Maratha leader Sivaji after his visit.

In 1560 Divar was the scene of 'forced' mass baptisms of Hindu islanders converted to Christianity by the Portuguese. Many of the 1,510 new converts continued to make the pilgrimage to the rehoused deity in Naroa in spite of strong attempts by the Portuguese to stop the practice. The **Archaeological Museum** in Old Goa (see page 80) has some sections from the two Divar temples in its collection. Some temple parts found their way into Old Goa including the New Pillory, which was put up at the end of the 17th century at the foot of the hill of the Cross of Miracles on the Neura road.

Jua Island

Jua is immediately east of Divar and is approached by road from Banastari to the south. The rococo-style Santo Estevam (St Steven's Church) was built in 1759. With a false dome and lantern central to its plain façade, it is flanked by two smaller domes on the towers. On top of the hill immediately above the village, in the fort, there are excellent views from the modern shrine to Christ the King.

🍴 Eating

Old Goa and around *p77*
$$ Solar de Souto Maior, Sao Pedro (just short of Old Goa), www.siolimhouse.com. India's oldest existing colonial house (dating from 1585) is being renovated into an all-day restaurant (lunches from around Rs 200) serving veggie nosh inside and in the garden. There will also be a bookstore, lounge, tea room and bar, plus some boutiques on the ground floor. Opening Nov 2004.

Ribandar, Divar and excursions from Old Goa *p85*
Divar island
The **Gulf** supermarket sells cool drinks and snacks.

🔺 Activities and tours

Old Goa and around *p77*
Ketak Nachinolkar, conservation architect, leads walking tours around Old Goa and Panjim, Rs 250 per person, T0832-2125652, www.goaheritage.org.
Goa Tourism visit to Old Goa (included in the *South Goa* and *Pilgrim Tours*, see page 74), spends a short time visiting the sights. It is better to go by bus or share a taxi to give you time to see Old Goa at leisure.

❀ Festivals

Ribandar, Divar and excursions from Old Goa *p85*
Divar island
Aug Bonderam Feast is held to mark the harvest on the island at Goltim on the last Sat. Before the feast, the villagers process with colourful flags and then hold a mock battle with *fatass* (imitation guns made out of bamboo sticks).

🛍 Shopping

Ribandar, Divar and excursions from Old Goa *p85*
Ribandar
Camelot, H No 139, Fondvem, T0832-2234255, 0930-1830. A lovely shop selling good crafts, clothing, linen and textiles in contemporary designs – 'stylish and charming'. Shipping arranged.

🚌 Transport

Old Goa and around *p77*
Auto-rickshaws charge Rs 25.
Bus From Panjim, frequent buses take 15-20 mins (Rs 5). Buses drop you off opposite the Basilica of Bom Jesus; pick up the return bus near the police station.
Taxis Rs 150 return. Karmali station on the Konkan railway, just east of the centre, has taxis for transfer.

Panjim & Old Goa Old Goa & around Listings

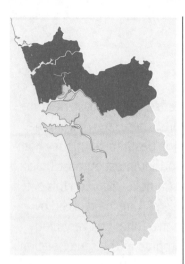

Mapusa and the Bardez beaches   **90**
  Mapusa   90
  Listings   92
Calangute and the beaches   **94**
  Calangute   95
  Baga   97
  Arpora   99
  Candolim and Sinquerim   99
  Saligao   99
  Reis Magos and around   101
  Listings   102
The party beaches   **112**
  Anjuna   114
  Vagator   116
  Chapora   117
  Listings   119
Coastal Pernem   **122**
  Arambol   123
  Morjim to Asvem   124
  Mandrem   125
  The Chapora river   125
  Keri (Querim) and Tiracol fort   126
  Pernem and the Tiracol river   128
  Listings   129

⁑ Footprint features

Don't miss...   89
Parties   113
Five minutes' peace   115
The trance dance experience   118
Tito's: from hippy hangout
   to hippodrome   127
Ready for take-off?   128

Introduction

North Goa packs a mean punch where it comes to diversity of scenery, landscapes and social scenes, and its coastline come littered with watchful war-torn forts. These stretch from the royal fort Reis Magos right up to the beautiful boutiquey hotel built into the ramparts of Goa's northernmost outpost Tiracol, whose church still serves the 350 Catholics living on this patch of Goa over the Maharashtra border. All are interspliced by some of Goa's most beautiful beaches, offering everything from outright yours-the-only-footprints-in-the-sand isolation to full-on blow-your-whistle hedonism, all within easy reach of the state's key cultural sites.

Bypass North Goa's developed beach resorts, Calangute et al, and head instead towards the North's busiest town of Mapusa for the slightly desolate, still-hippy strongholds of Anjuna and Vagator, or keep going north to Pernem district for the less built-up beaches in Morjim, Mandrem and Ashvem. There are still a few 'freaks' in Anjuna, although they are now far outnumbered by Israelis fresh out of military service and whose natural habitat is astride throbbing Enfield motorbikes largely en route to or from trance parties.

Feral hippies make their altogether quieter homes in the jungle above Arambol, and Morjim is home to both turtles and the most recent in the long line of successive colonizers of Goa, the Russians. Inland, the road east to the Western Ghats runs through a region of busy mineral development and industrialization, sat cheek by jowl with Bicholim's ancient Buddhist caves and Hindu temples tucked deep in densely forested slopes.

★ Don't miss...

❶ Shopping Have a flit through some of the fancy furnishings and lifestyle shops housed in Portugese colonial houses like Casa Goa and Sasigao, page 109.

❷ Amrita ayurveda centre, Candolim Enjoy a sesame oil rub-down under a technicolour dreamcoat canopy of saris, page 110.

❸ The party The unmissable beach party scene started in Anjuna and spread, page 114.

❹ Anjuna flea market Shelter from the madding crowds of the Wednesday flea market at the mellow section run by Tibetans, page 114.

❺ Purple Valley One of the most respected yoga schools in India, page 119.

❻ Getting out of Baga and Calangute Beaches to the north and south are far prettier and less congested, page 122.

❼ Tiracol Fort, Pernem Take mass here, a beautiful, compact church stowed away inside this military outpost, page 126.

❽ Tito's Have a night out to remember at this nightclub, page 127.

❾ The state's culture Explore inland by bicycle or motorbike and experience the heartbeat of the unmanufactured life of the state, page 128.

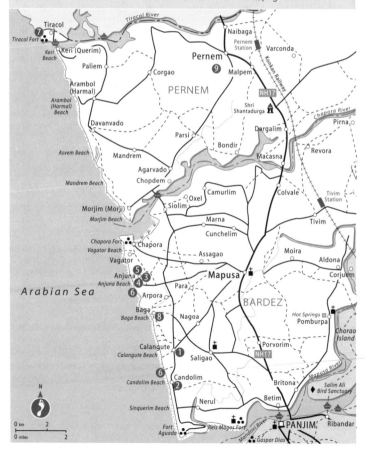

North Goa

Mapusa and the Bardez beaches

The faultless fawn sands of coastal Bardez – particularly Calangute – that until 40 years ago lay at the feet of a string of fishing villages now act as sandpit to the headquarters of Goa's booming travel trade. It follows that the place is chock full of accommodation, eateries, travel agents, money changers, beggars and charter tourists. The roads quickly become snarled up with tourist minivans, and unchecked development has made for a largely concrete conurbation that is home to the majority of Goa's 20,081 charter tourists come peak season in December/January. For all that, if you squint hard, or come in monsoon, you can see what once attracted the freaks: wonderful coconut-fringed sandy beaches backed by dunes that are only occasionally punctuated by rocky headlands and coves; you can walk ankle-deep in the Arabian sea almost uninterrupted all the way from fort to fort between Aguada and Vagator. Don't expect unbroken horizons though: huge rusty haulage freighters tread water off this coastline waiting to whisk cargoes of iron ore from Goa's interior and neighbouring mining states off to construction crazed China – after tourism, this is Goa's most profitable industry.

▸▸ *For Sleeping, Eating and other listings, see pages 92-94.*

Background

The name Bardez may have come from the term *bara desh* (12 'divisions of land') – a reference to the 12 Brahmin villages that once dominated the region. Another explanation is that it refers to 12 *zagors*, celebrated to ward off evil. Or it could be *Bahir des*, meaning 'outside land' – ie, the land beyond the Mandovi river. It was occupied by the Portuguese as part of their original conquest, and so bears the greatest direct imprint of their Christianizing influence.

The beach between Candolim and Baga is backed by a series of sand dunes, stabilized by grasses and casuarinas, which form a shelter belt for the flat river plains inland. The road and settlements all lie to the landward side of this strip. Inland the short rivers meander across the flood plain between Mapusa and the sea. The Mapusa river itself was once an important transport artery, its banks offering rich and fertile soils for the production of vegetables that were then moved to market in Mapusa or down to the Mandovi.

Mapusa → *Colour map 1, grid B2.*

There's no beauty in Bardez's administrative headquarters: a buzzy, unruly market town filled with 60s low-rise buildings. The banks of the Mapusa river, once a transport artery, have been reclaimed for building and its waters now come sadly clogged by urban waste. It's a friendly town though and, however small and messy, manages to also stock pretty much everything under the sun in its shops. It stands in the nape of one of Goa's many long east-west ridges: every inch of the flat valley's fertile agricultural land cultivated right up to the very edge of the town, interrupted only by the odd screaming billboard and furniture shack. This was once all seeping marshland: *maha apsa* means 'great swamps'. While the daily municipal market (particularly packed on Fridays, but more laid-back the rest of the week) is a treat to wander round, there's no real reason to stay here overnight, particularly with the north's stunning beaches so close.

Getting there The town is an important junction both for interstate buses and local bus routes including those to the northern beaches. **Buses** pull in at the market square opposite the taxi stand, while the local State Kadamba Bus Stand is a bit further south. The nearest **train** station, Tivim, is on the Konkan railroad just a couple of kilometres inland.

Getting around You can walk around the small town; Rs 10 should be ample for short hops on an auto.

Information and orientation However little town planning seems to have gone into Mapusa, it's difficult to get lost. Tourist information is available from the **Tourist Shopping Complex** ⓘ *T0832-2262390*.

Sights

The **municipal market** ⓘ *Mon-Sat, opens from early morning; peters out between noon and three, then gathers steam again till night*, has giant rings of chourica sausage, tumbles of spices and rows of squatting fruit and veg hawkers.

Walk east for the small 16th century **St Jerome's Church**, or 'Milagres', Our Lady of Miracles (1594), rebuilt first in 1674 then again in 1839 after a candle sparked a devastating fire. In 1961 the roof was badly damaged when the Portuguese blew up a nearby bridge in their struggle with the liberating Indian army. The church has a scrolled gable, balconied windows in the façade, a belfry at the rear and an interesting slatted wood ceiling. The main altar is to Our Lady, and on either side are St John and St Jerome: the *retables* (shelves behind the altar) were brought from Daugim. The church is sacred to Hindus as well as Catholics: not only because it stands near the site of the Shanteri Temple but also because 'Our Lady of Miracles' was one of seven Hindu sisters converted to Christianity. Her lotus pattern gold necklace (now kept under lock and key) may also have been taken from a Hindu deity who preceded her.

North Goa Mapusa & the Bardez beaches

Mapusa

0 metres 100
0 yards 100

Sleeping ●
Satyaheera 2
Vilena 4

Eating ●
Ashok 1
Casa Bela 2

▸ North Goa's best restaurants

→ **Delhi Durbar Restaurant and Bar**, Panjim. For North Indian delicacies in the capital, Durbar is unrivalled. See page 72.

→ **Casa Portuguesa**, Baga. The lush leaf-heavy garden location would be enough to recommend it, but the fusion food's top notch too. See page 106.

→ **J&A's Ristorante Italiano House**, Baga river. The best place to sate any pasta cravings. See page 106.

→ **Le Restaurant Français**, Calangute. Some say the best French nosh money can buy in Goa. See page 106.

→ **Plantain Leaf**, Calangute. Jumbo thalis that won't break the bank. See page 106.

→ **Sublime Bistro Bar Panchayat**, Calangute. Has an outright evangelical following. See page 106.

→ **Xavier**, Anjuna.One of the first restaurants founded for the freak business, go for the history and for the fish. See page 107.

→ **Lila's Café**, Baga river. If only for the deep European bread alone. See page 107.

→ **Bean Me Up**, Anjuna. Yummy fast-food vegan where you'll have to queue for a table. Grows addictive. See page 120.

→ **Olive Ridley**, Morjim.A laid-back sandy lounge on the seashore. See page 131.

The **Maruti temple** ① *west of the market opposite the taxi stand*, was built on the site of a firecracker shop where Rama followers in the 1840s would gather in clandestine worship of first a picture, then a silver image, of monkey god Hanuman after the Portuguese destroyed their Hindu temples.

Barely 5 km east of Mapusa finds you in **Moira**, deep in the belly of a rich agricultural district that was once the scene of Portuguese mass baptisms. The town is ancient – some say it was the site of a sixth or seventh century AD Mauryan settlement – and until the arrival of the Portuguese it must have been a Brahmin village. There were once seven important temples, but all were destroyed during the Inquisition and six idols moved to Mulgaon in Bicholim district (immediately east). Today the village is dominated by the unusual **Church of Our Lady of the Immaculate Conception**. Originally built of mud and thatch in 1619, it was rebuilt during the 19th century with square towers close to the false dome. The balustrades at the top of the first and second floors run the length of the building and the central doorways of the ground and first floors have Islamic-looking trefoil arches that contrast with the romanesque flanking arches. There is an interesting outside pulpit. Inside, the image of the crucifixion is unusual in having its feet nailed separately instead of together. A Siva linga recycled here as the base of the font after its temple was razed is now in the Archaeological Museum at Old Goa. Moira's famous long red bananas (grown nearby) are not eaten raw but come cooked with sugar and coconuts as the cavity-speeding sweet *figada*.

● Sleeping

Mapusa *p90, map p91*
None of the hotels here hold any special charm for the tourist: they are firmly geared towards the domestic business traveller. Try to avoid spending the night – nice hotels on the beach are near enough to get yourself to or from even to meet the most antisocial bus or train departures or arrivals – but should you get stuck, the following list may help.
C-E Satyaheera, near Maruti Temple, T0832-2262849, satya_goa@sancharnet.in.com. 33 reasonable rooms, some a/c, enclosed rooftop restaurant (shared with mosquitoes and the odd mouse!), bar.

D-E **Mandarin**, near Alankar Cinema, T0832-2262579. 21 basic rooms with bath (few a/c), clean rooftop restaurant.
E **Vilena**, opposite the Municipality, T0832-2263115, ticlotel@satyam.net.in. 16 neat, clean rooms, some a/c, good restaurants, bar, very friendly.

🍴 Eating

Mapusa *p90, map p91*
Food is also unlikely to be the highlight of a trip to Mapusa.
$$ **Ashok**, opposite the market's entrance. Serves genuine South Indian breakfasts like *uttapam* and *dosa*.
$$ **Casa Bela**, near Coscar Corner, specializes in Goan food.
$$ **Hotel Vilena** has 2 restaurants, 1 on the rooftop and 1 a/c indoors. They serve some of the best food in town.
$$ **Mahalaxmi**, Anjuna Rd. A/c, South Indian vegetarian.

Cafés
From 1630 until late, carts and stalls near the Alankar Cinema sell meat and seafood dishes.
Royal-T, Shop 96, near the Shakuntala Fountain, municipal market, Goan snacks etc.

✹ Festivals

Mapusa *p90, map p91*
Mon of the 3rd week after Easter Feast of Our Lady of Miracles The *Nossa Senhora de Milagres* image is venerated by Christians as well as Hindus who join together to celebrate the feast day of the Saibin. Holy oil is carried from the church to Shanteri temple and a huge fair and a market is held.

🛍 Shopping

Mapusa *p90, map p91*
Books
Other India Bookstore, 1st floor, St Britto's Apartment, above Mapusa clinic, T0832-2263306, is unconventional and excellent. It is heavily eco-conscious, has a large catalogue and will post worldwide.

Food
The **municipal Mapusa Bazaar**, on the south edge of the fruit and vegetable

market, has fixed-price basic food supplies like rice, spice, lentils and cereals: useful if you're here for the long term.

Photography
Remy Studios, Coscar Corner and Shop 8, KTC bus stand.

⊖ Transport

Mapusa *p90, map p91*
Bus
To **Calangute** (every 20-30 mins), some continue on to **Aguada** and **Baga**, some go towards **Candolim**; check before boarding or change at Calangute. Non-stop mini- buses to **Panjim**; buy tickets from booth at market entrance. Buses also go to **Vagator** and **Chapora** via **Anjuna** and towns near by. Buses to **Tivim** for Konkan Railway and trains to Mumbai, Rs 8 (allow 25 mins).
   Long-distance buses Private operators, lined up opposite the taxi stand, offer near-identical routes and rates. To **Bangalore**: 1830, 12 hrs, Rs 250 (Luxury), Rs 450 (Sleeper). **Hospet** (for Hampi): 1800, 10 hrs, Rs 350 (Sleeper). **Mumbai** 1600, 14 hrs, Rs 300 (Luxury), Rs 500 (Sleeper).
   Tivim train station on the Konkan railway is convenient if you want to head straight to the northern beaches (Calangute, Baga, Anjuna and Vagator), avoiding Panjim and Margao. A local bus meets each train and usually runs as far as the Kadamba bus stand in Mapusa. From here you either continue on a local bus to the beach or share a tourist taxi (rates above). Enquiries and computerized tickets: T0832-2298682.
   To **Ernakulam** (for junction): Mangalore Exp 2618, 1952 (arr 1345), 18 hrs. To **Jaipur** (from Ernakulam): Exp 2977, 1138, Mon. To **Margao**: Mandovi Exp 0103, 1650, 90 mins; Konkan Kanya Exp 0111, 0924, 90 mins. To **Mumbai (CST)**: Mandovi Exp 0104, 1113, 10 hrs; Konkan Kanya Exp 0112, 1846, 11 hrs (via Pernem). To **Mumbai Kurla (Tilak)** (from Trivandrum): Netravati Exp 6346, 0747, 11 hrs. To **Thiruvananthapuram (Trivandrum)**: Netravati Exp 6345, 2152, 19 hrs (via Margao and Canacona for Palolem beach).

Car hire
Pink Panther, T0832-2263180.

Motorcycle hire

Peter & Friends Classic Adventures, Casa Tres Amigos, Socol Vado 425, Parra, Assagao, 5 km east (off the Anjuna Rd), T0832-2254467, www.classic-bike-india.de, recommended for reliable bikes and tours of Southern India, Himachal and Nepal. Also has some quality rooms.

Taxis

(often shared by up to 5); to **Panjim** Rs 70; **Calangute/Baga**, Rs 100; **Chapora/Siolim**, Rs 80. Auto to **Calangute**, Rs 50. Motorcycle taxi to **Anjuna** or **Calangute**, about Rs 40, but open to bargaining.

❶ Directory

Mapusa *p90, map p91*

Ambulance T0832-2262372. **Banks** Bank of India, opposite Municipal Gardens, changes TCs, cash against Visa and Mastercard. Mon-Fri 1000-1400, Sat 1000-1200. **State Bank of India** exchanges cash and TCs, 15-20 mins. Foreign exchange on 1st floor, Mon-Fri 1000-1600, Sat 1000-1200. **Pink Panther Agency** changes Visa and Mastercard, Mon-Fri 0900-1700, Sat 0900-1300. **Couriers** Blue Dart, T0832-2263208. **Fire** T0832-2262900. **Hospitals and medical services** Asilo Hospital, T0832-2262211. Pharmacies: including Drogaria, near the Swiss Chapel, open 24 hrs; Mapusa Clinic, T0832-2262350; Bardez Bazar. **Internet** several across town, well signed. Most charge Rs 90 per hr. Best at LCC 3rd Flr, Bhavani Apartments, Rs 15 per 15 mins; 6 terminals, 0700-2130, 7 days a week. **Police** T0832-2262231. **Post office** The sub-post office is opposite the police station.

Calangute and the beaches

Baga beach bleeds all the way down to Fort Aguada in one fairly relentless seam of sun-loungers, beach shacks and fast-sizzling flesh. Independent-minded travellers are wont to compare the strip to Blackpool, Costa Del Sol or Tenerife, and it's true that it's unlikely you'll find much that's culturally challenging in Bagadorm: what passes for the norm in this area, like hitting the high-street in bikinis, say, would be frowned on elsewhere in Goa and utter anathema in broader India. Similarly, the Goans who live here have more western attitudes and mindsets to those you'll meet in the rest of the state. Love or hate it, it is likely you'll wash up here at some stage on your trip. On the positive side, as the most developed stretch of the state it offers a huge array of possibilities when it comes to dining, partying, shopping, sleeping and arranging onward travel. Plus, if you have the craving, many years of British charter flights mean fish, chips and mushy peas are easy to find on roads like the imaginatively named Holiday Street. Amazingly, if you delve into the dust tracks that criss-cross behind the main tourist-trodden arteries, among the chicken and pigs and waste and elegantly crumbling Portuguese houses, there's still the ghost of the area's village past. ▸▸ *For Sleeping, Eating and other listings, see pages 102-111.*

Ins and outs

Getting there The NH17 acts as the main arterial road between all of Goa's coastal belt. From Panjim, the highway crosses the Mandovi Bridge, taking you, via the ugly and wealthy suburb Alto Porvorim, to the area's main hub, Calangute (16 km from Panjim, 10 km from Mapusa). Buses run frequently to all points along the highway and they are a thrifty, if sometimes paint-dryingly slow, way to travel. Those from Mapusa (20 mins) and Panjim (35 mins), arrive at Calangute bus stand near the market towards the beach steps; a few continue to Baga to the north, from the crossroads. You can charter tourist minivans from Panjim, Dabolim, etc. If you have your own transport, turn left at the north end of the Mandovi Bridge and hug the coast through Reis Magos, then cross over to Aguada and travel up the coast road.

Train The closest stop on the Konkan railway route between Mumbai and Mangalore is Tivim near Mapusa. From Tivim hop in a rickshaw or minivan. On market days there are boats from Baga to Anjuna. There are buses from Mapusa and Panjim to Calangute, Anjuna, Chopora and Arambol but many prefer to hire a motorbike or bike to find their stretch of sand.

Ferry Goa is criss-crossed with rivers and estuaries, and plenty still rely on ferry crossings. The bridge at Panjim means it's not strictly necessary to take the ferry to the northern region (landing at the fishing village of Betim) but it does give you a neat introduction to how transport once was, and remains, in much of the state.

Northern beaches

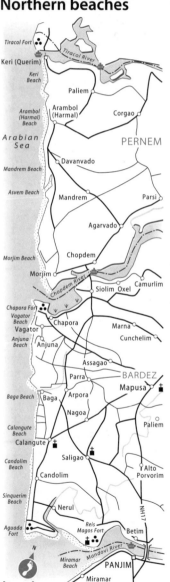

Getting around The roads in this area are pretty free from potholes so night riding on **bicycles, scooters and motorcycles** is okay – but beware the sudden unflagged speed-breaker. Despite the hazards, two-wheelers offer unparalleled independence in zipping spontaneously from one pocket of sand to the next, and packing a daysack and leaving the rest of your luggage in a cheap hotel here can be a fun way to explore the north's bays. It is still surprisingly hard to find push-bikes to hire in this area.

Bus Public buses run up and down the coast road, but for short distances it is often easier to charter motorcycle taxis or head for the sand and walk. **Taxis** and **motorcycle taxis** are ubiquitous, chiefly near the bus stand. Tourist vans and old ambassador cabs are also available; both cost Rs 8 per kilometre.

Orientation and information There are 9 km of uninterrupted starched sand between Fort Aguada and the tunnel-bridge over Baga river in the north. These are split into four beaches: Sinquerim, Candolim, Calangute and Baga, all of their sands doused with the Arabian Sea. Running parallel to the water on dry land there is one main thoroughfare that acts as an unofficial high street: of these, Calangute's is by far the most built up.

Calangute → *Colour map 1, grid B1.*

Bar the brilliantly quirky hexagonal *barbeiria* (barber's shop) at the northern roundabout, there is little to attract the aesthete's eye in Calangute. The main distinguishing feature of the streets is their commercialism: shops peddle

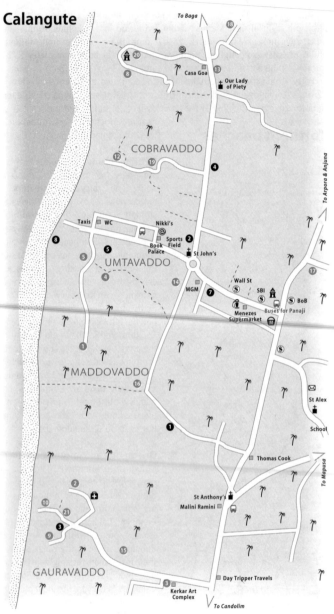

To Baga

To Arpora & Anjuna

Casa Goa

Our Lady of Piety

COBRAVADDO

Taxis WC

Nikki's

Sports Field

Book Palace

St John's

UMTAVADDO

Wall St

MGM

SBI

BoB

Menezes Supermarket

Buses for Panaji

MADDOVADDO

St Alex

School

Thomas Cook

To Mapusa

St Anthony's

Malini Ramini

GAURAVADDO

Day Tripper Travels

Kerkar Art Complex

To Candolim

N

| 0 metres | 100 |
| 0 yards | 100 |

Sleeping
Arabian Retreat 2
Ale-Pas 1
Coco Banana 4
Concha Beach Resort 5
Estrela do Mar 8
Goan Heritage 9
Golden Eye 10
Johnny's 12
Kerkar Retreat & Waves 3

Martin's Guest
  Rooms 13
Mira 14
Ondas do Mar 15
Paradise Village 16
Pousada Tauma 17
Santiago Resorts 18
Victorian Heritage 19
Villa Goesa 20
White House 21

Eating
A Reverie 3
Infanteria 2
Le Restaurant
  Français 4
Plantain Leaf 7
Souza Lobo 8
Sublime Bistro
  Bar Panchayat 1
Tibetan Kitchen 5

everything from cheap ethnic tat to extravagant precious gemstones with varying degrees of aggression. Most streets off the road to Baga empty onto the sea. The beach, to some, is perfect: rock-free, good for swimming (although beware the current) and littered with fishing boats, tackle and fishermen's huts. More frequent than these, though, are hawkers selling sarongs, offering massages, horoscopes or ear-cleaning and the predominantly British tourists, some of whom show no sign of interest in anything beyond where to watch tonight's game and how little cash they can spend while getting tanked up and tanned. All of this can be fun but if you're spending a while in Goa it's probably the type of place you'd prefer to dip in and out of rather than base yourself full-time. Licensed shacks line the beach, some of which have great nosh and make cool places to hang out in the evening: if you're travelling in a group, it's probably an idea to make an unofficial base in your own bar. Behind the busy beach front coconut trees still give shade to village houses; some offer private rooms to let. Any open space left over is being smeared with the concrete and steel to make new hotels, restaurants, money changers and shops. As well as attracting out-of-state beggars, the beach near the tourist resorts gets overrun on weekends with domestic day-trippers. Scantily-clad western women are the inevitable lure, after all most Indians cannot swim and tend instead to bob about in the shallows (signs put up in 2004 warned that 'To Swim Is To Commit Suicide', and drownings of domestic tourists are sadly routine). Just because you are in 'permissive' Goa it doesn't mean everyone overlooks what is tantamount to nudity: Indian women will all be wading into the water wearing full saris.

> ● *For casual yoga classes look for posters: you can find some very good teachers advertising themselves on tree trunks.*

Away from the town centre, the striking gold and white **Church of St Alex** (rebuilt in 1741) gives a great taste of rococo decoration in Goa, while the false dome of the central façade is an excellent example of 18th-century architectural development. The delicate decoration of the pulpit and the fine reredos are particularly fine. The **Kerkar Art Complex** ⓘ *Gaurawaddo, Calangute, T0832-2276017, www.subodhkerkar.com*, is also worth visiting. Medic-turned-contemporary artist Subodh Kerkar is on a one-man crusade to reverse Calangute's full-tilt slide into cultural vacuum. His relaxed complex is an exhibition space for the work of many artists passing through Goa, while next door sits a gallery reserved for his own paintings and installation work, some of which are like lovely Indian interpretations of nature artist Andy Goldsworthy.

Baga → *Colour map 1, grid B1.*

The very distinct identity for which Baga was once a byword has been almost wholly engulfed to make it little more than Calangute north. Here too, away from the paddy marshes, water tanks and salt pans, it's very much the same story of congestion, shacks, fishing boats and sun loungers (prices doubling to Rs 100 a day during high season). However, the beach is still clean, there's good live music and the river that divides this commercial strip of sand from Anjuna in the north also brings fishermen pulling in their catch at dawn, and casting their nets at dusk. The north bank, or **Baga river**, is all thick woods, mangroves and birdlife: it has quite a different, more village feel, with a few classy European restaurants looking out across the river. You can take an hour to wade across the river at low tide, then walk over the crest of the hill and down into Anjuna South (there's no access for motorbikes). The uncommonly ugly box suspension bridge (its nickname: 'the nuclear bunker') across the river adds about 1 km to this walk. Take care when using the bridge at night as there are no lights and not even the full moon can penetrate this architectural breeze-block.

North Goa Calangute & the beaches

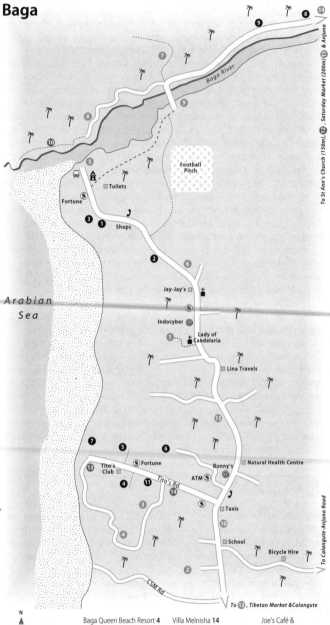

Arabian Sea

Baga River

To St Ann's Church (150m), 12, Saturday Market (200m) 11 & Anjuna

Football Pitch

Toilets

Fortune

Shops

Jay-Jay's

Indocyber

Lady of Candelaria

Lina Travels

Tito's Club

Fortune

Tito's Rd

Bunny's

Natural Health Centre

ATM

Taxis

School

Bicycle Hire

CSM Rd

To Calangute-Anjuna Road

To 12, Tibetan Market & Calangute

0 metres 100
0 yards 100

N

Sleeping 🛏
Alidia Beach Cottages **1**
Andrade Guest House **2**
Angelina **3**

Baga Queen Beach Resort **4**
Baia do Sol **5**
Cavala **6**
Lina's **7**
Nani's & Rani's **8**
Riverside **9**
Ronil Beach Resort **10**
Sun Village **11**
Venar **12**
Villa Fatima Beach Resort **13**

Villa Melnisha **14**

Eating 🍴
Apple Pie **6**
Britto's **3**
Casa Portuguesa **2**
Citrus **11**
Domingo's **4**
Fiesta **5**
J&A's Italiano House **8**

Joe's Café &
  Health Food Shop **1**
Lila Café **9**
Zanzibar Beach Shack **7**

Bars & clubs 🍸
Club Cubana **12**
Kamaki **14**
Mambo's **13**
Sunset **10**

Arpora → *Colour map 1, grid B1.*

The chief reason the small village of Arpora is on the map, apart from some lovely luxury hotels, is for its sanitized version of its coastal neighbour Anjuna's flea market. The Saturday night experience, **Ingo's**, is made much more pleasant (or anodyne) with urchins and beggars barred and bands and food stalls shipped in in their stead. The whole thing has the feeling of a mini festival and it's the social event of the week for long-staying foreigners and locals alike who either come to work or just to hang out. There's a brilliant, eclectic range of stuff for sale: along with the usual Rajasthani blankets, embroidered saris and Mahabalipuram stone carvings are Californian rave wear, home-made neon booties, or 'cotton shoes of Ninja' we should say, and Che Guevaras printed – who knows why? – onto tie-dye t-shirts. Food stalls include the punning '*Il fungo magico*' Italian, baked tatties and **Bean Me Up**'s legendary veggie fodder. Outside though, the scrum is the same, as 4wds, jeeps, minivans, Honda Kinetics and Enfields all fight for road and parking space. There is a second Saturday market, **Mackie**'s, that has more standard fair from identikit Karnatakan gypsy shacks.

Saligao → *Colour map 1, grid B2.*

Coconut palm-heavy Saligao, just east of Calangute, becomes a familiar crossroads for anyone spending time on one of the nearby beaches. As the home to Saraswat Brahmins many centuries before the arrival of the Portuguese it has several beautiful Goan houses standing in shady gardens. Saligao either takes its name from the *sal* trees that once grew thick here or from the *sall* rice cultivated in this rich agricultural belt.

The imposing **Our Lady Mother of God** (Mae de Deus) church was built in 1873, replacing five earlier chapels. It is an unusual neo-gothic structure but painted white like the traditional baroque churches in Goa. The prominent horizontal ribbed surface, all crenallated parapets and stylized flying buttresses, makes it quite unique. Inside is the unusual but attractive wooden ceiling with its pierced star design. The miraculous statue of the Virgin, originally found in a ruined convent in Dauji Village, Old Goa, was enshrined here when the plague forced the population of Dauji to move out.

Candolim and Sinquerim beaches → *Colour map 1, grid C1.*

The wide unsheltered stretch of beach here, backed by scrub-covered dunes, is marginally more staid and classy than Baga and Calangute to the north, chiefly because of the relatively expensive price of its restaurants and hotels. The ratio of burnt flesh per square inch is certainly a little lower. This is probably the best place to get togged up for your quality watersports: jetskis, windsurfers, catamaran and dinghy hire shops are clustered around here.

Fort Aguada
ⓘ *To reach the jail's gate take the road away from the beaches towards Reis Magos then turn hard right back towards the headland.* In 1612 the Portuguese built what was to be the strongest of their coastal forts to keep the Dutch navy at bay on the northern tip of the Mandovi estuary with the Nerul river. Two hundred guns were stationed here along with two magazines, four barracks, several residential buildings for the officers and two prisons. It saw repeated action against the

Marathas - Goans fleeing the onslaught at Bardez took refuge here, but its ramparts proved time and again impregnable. The main fortifications (laterite walls nearly 5 m high and 1.3 m thick) are still intact: the buildings lower down where the waves crash formed what must be a contender for most beautifully positioned jail in the world, still in use and which you can visit with the – admittedly rarely-granted – permission of the superintendent A large well and number of springs provided the fort and ships at harbour with drinking water and gave it its name 'aguada', meaning watering place.

> ‡ To see an example of Portuguese mansions (if you can't get to Chandor or Loutolim) take a walk down Monteiro Road to admire the 17th-century Monteiro family home.

The road to the fort passes the small **Church of St Lawrence** (or Linhares Church, 1630-43), which has an unusual porch with a terrace and balustrades on the towers and parapets. A 13-m high **oil lamp lighthouse** ⓘ *1030-1730, Rs 3*, was added at the top of the fort (84 m above sea level) sometime in the 18th century. There are good views from the top. Next to the fort, there is the 'new' 21-m high **concrete lighthouse** (1975) ⓘ *1600-1730, Rs 1, no photography*. Another unavoidable landmark that the travel agents have been keener to airbrush from their catalogues over the past five years is the huge oil tanker lying woefully grounded like a lumbering iron beached whale at the junction of Candolim and Sinquerim beaches. The Taj must be most sore: the ship's full hull dominates the views everywhere from their reception through to each sea-bent room and every

Candolim & Sinquerim

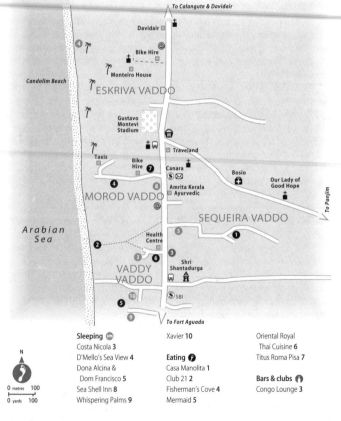

N

0 metres 100
0 yards 100

Sleeping 💤
Costa Nicola **3**
D'Mello's Sea View **4**
Dona Alcina &
 Dom Francisco **5**
Sea Shell Inn **8**
Whispering Palms **9**

Xavier **10**

Eating 🍴
Casa Manolita **1**
Club 21 **2**
Fisherman's Cove **4**
Mermaid **5**

Oriental Royal
 Thai Cuisine **6**
Titus Roma Pisa **7**

Bars & clubs 🍸
Congo Lounge **3**

restaurant (there's even a conspiracy theory among staff that the ship is owned by a rival upmarket hotel consortium). **'The River Princess'** washed up during a monsoon storm when its skeleton crew was unable to start its giant engines fast enough as the ship groaned towards the coast. It has been an equally large political hot potato as it is an eyesore ever since, and although parts worth several *crores* of rupees from inside have been stripped from the vessel, the shell remains a looming environmental threat. The dolphins don't seem too perturbed, though, and continue to fin along at the mouth of the Mandovi.

Reis Magos and around → *Colour map 1, grid C2.*

Reis Magos stands over the Mandovi river from Panjim like a sentry and gives matchless views over Goa's diminutive capital city. This charming little town was so strategically vital that Albuquerque stationed troops on this shoulder of headland from day one of Portuguese rule. It is interesting today for the angular and crumbling **Royal Fort** built by the viceroy Don Alfonso de Noronha between 1551 and 1554, overrun with jungle but with its canons still pointing pluckily out to sea. It remained as second line of defense after Panjim in case any enemy, notably the Dutch, managed to sail past the forts at Aguada round the corner to the north and the Cabo in the south. In 1703, it was rebuilt; 35 years later it had to face the Maratha attack on Bardez and alone with Fort Aguada stayed in Portuguese hands. The spring below the fort, like that at Aguada, was a valuable year round watering hole for ships. You can delve into the fort's bowels, revealed through archaeological digs, by climbing down a long stretch of steps.

The **Reis Magos Church** ⓘ *Mon-Sat 0900-1200, 1630-1730,* (1555), named after the 'Magi Kings', next door is one of the earliest of Goa's churches and was, some believe, built on the site of a Hindu temple (the old water tank and a granite tiger remain). A Franciscan friar, Joao Noé, is supposed to have crossed the Mandovi in 1550, put up a temporary altar in what was then the village of Verem and there celebrated the first ever Mass on Goan soil: Noronha had handed Bardez to the Franciscans and the church was a launching pad for the conversion of the district. Dedicated to the three Magi, Gaspar, Melchior and Balthazar, the reredos tell the kings' chapter in the nativity story on wooden panels painted with vignettes of them offering frankincense, myrrh and gold to the baby Jesus. From 1597 to 1793 the prestigious **St Jerome Seminary** took in Portuguese viceroys and governors on their way to or from Old Goa as guests. **The Festival of Three Kings** accompanied by a big fair is celebrated here as at Chandor on January 6 each year, see page 180. It is a pretty, though dead-end, drive to the end of the peninsula beyond Reis Magos, past muddy sands, rocks and shellfish pickers to Campal Beach.

Nerul and Coco beach → *Colour map 1, grid C2.*

The temple in Nerul dates from 1910 when special permission was given to return the deity of Shri Shantadurga, which had been removed to Mandrem in Pernem (see page 125). The present village **Church of Our Lady of Remedies** was built in 1569 on the site of the Shantadurga Temple: workers restoring the parish house in 1893 found a 1 m statue of the Hindu deity Betall in the holy well. An underground passage in the church was probably part of the former temple, as were the stone tigers that adorn its entrance. The big tank that now stands in ruins in its orchard likely once belonged to the temple too. The nearby estuary beach, which today can be slightly scuzzy with the swilling foam of landing fishing boats, draws holidaymakers from Calangute and beyond for more secluded sunbathing and sometimes Sunday night partying.

● Sleeping

You can hardly move in this stretch for accommodation options and the choice can be a little bewildering. As a general rule of thumb, prices fall the further north you move, so Sinquerim and Candolim have the snazziest hotels and the steepest tariffs; while when you travel to the south, prices fall to suit slimmer wallets in Baga and charter-central Calangute. North and inland, Arpora, with its special hilltop panoramas across the ocean, is home to a second clump of exclusive resorts.

Calangute p95, map p96

LL Pousada Tauma, Porbavaddo, T0832-2279061, www.pousada-tauma.com. 12 unique rooms set in a lush garden around a pool, a luxurious setting where the management and staff are used to dealing with people who value their privacy. Easily the best accommodation in Calangute; some would argue, in the whole of Goa.

A-B Ondas Do Mar, Gauravaddo, T/F0832-2277526, www.alfrangoa.com. Beachfront location, rooms set around pool, some a/c, most with balconies, restaurant.
B Goan Heritage, Gauravaddo, towards Candolim, T0832-2276253, www.goanheritage.com. 70 large, pleasant rooms but can get stiflingly hot, a/c and fridge (Rs 400 extra when used), some have sea view, expensive restaurant (more nearby), good pool, beautiful garden, close to beach.
B Kerkar Retreat, Gauravaddo, T0832-2276017, www.subodhkerkar.com. 5 double bedrooms with an overspilling library set above local artist Subodh Kerkar's art gallery. Sedate for Calangute but creative with it.
B Villa Goesa, Cobravaddo, off Baga Rd, T0832-2277535, alobo@sancharnet.in. 57 clean rooms, some a/c, some very shaded, excellent restaurant,

Sinquerim Beach & Fort Aguada

To Candolim Beach

Sinquerim Beach

Dando Chapel

Kashmir Fair

Rock Your Blues

Nerul River

Cannon Emplacement

Taj Sports

Bike Hire

Fishing Boats

Helipad

Arabian Sea

New Lighthouse

Fort Aguada

Jail

St Lawrence

Mandovi River

N

0 metres 200
0 yards 200

Sleeping ●
Aldeia Santa Rita **3**
Fort Aguada Beach Resort & Hermitage **1**
Kamal Retreat **4**
Marbella Guesthouse **5**

Marfran **6**
Palm Shade & Restaurant **7**
Par Avel **8**
Summerville **9**
Taj Holiday Village **10**
Village Belle **11**

Eating ●
Banyan Tree **1**
Palms 'n Sand **5**

lovely gardens, pool, quiet, relaxing, very friendly owners, 300 m walk from beach. Recommended.

B-C **Paradise Village**, Tivai Vaddo, South Calangute, near the beach, T0832-2276351, www.paradisevillage.org. 64 comfortable rooms in 2-storey chalets, pleasant restaurant, large pool, excellent service and management.

C **Concha Beach Resort**, Umtavaddo, T/F0832-2276056. 8 good-sized, clean, comfortable rooms, nets, best at front with large verandas, close to beach.

C **Estrela do Mar**, Calangute-Baga Rd, T0832-2276014. 10 clean, well-kept rooms with nets (rare in these parts), size varies, restaurant, pool, pleasant garden, peaceful location with no buildings near by, close to beach. Good value, highly recommended.

D **Ale-Pas**, Maddovaddo, T0832-2277479, len_dagama@rediff.com. 10 rooms with bath, fan, small balcony, spartan but clean, pleasant breakfast terrace. Peacefully set among tall palms a short walk from beach.

D **Arabian Retreat**, Gauravaddo (near Goan Heritage), T0832-2279053, www.arabianretreat.com. 10 rooms, some a/c, 1st floor better, includes breakfast served in a cramped yard, often full with Danish groups in peak season, set back from the beach. The manager can organize simple en-suite cheaper room, with balcony in a modern bungalow next door owned by an old Goan lady. Recommended.

D **Coco Banana**, 5/139A Umtavaddo, back from Calangute beach, T/F0832-2276478, cocobanana@ rediffmail.com. 6 spotless en-suite bungalows with nets, airy, light and comfortable, the Goan/Swiss owners have lived through all the changes in Goa and are caring and helpful. One of the best local guest houses. Highly recommended.

D **Golden Eye**, Philip's Cottages, Gauravaddo, T0832-2277308, www.hotelgoldeneye.com. 10 clean, comfortable rooms, half price singles, right on the beach (built before restrictions) with genuine sea views.

D **Martin's Guest Rooms**, Baga Rd, T0832-2277306, martins@goatelecom.com. 5 rooms in family house, clean, attractive verandas, use of kitchen but on the busy main road.

D **Mira**, Umtavaddo, near the chapel, 10 mins' walk from beach, T0832-2277342, mira1@satyam.net.in. 17 rooms, restaurant, 24-hr coffee shop, pool, email facilities.

D **Souza Lobo**, on the beach, T0832-2276463, www.souzalobo.com. 8 rooms in well-known restaurant that has managed to retain a good reputation for years.

D **Victorian Heritage**, Cobravaddo, T0832-2276216. 21 compact a/c rooms, TV, small balcony, very clean, pleasant shaded central dining area but stark pool surrounds. Rates include continental breakfast and mineral water. Quiet area, but a few mins' walk from beach.

D **White House**, Gauravaddo (near Goan Heritage), T0832-2277938. 8 rooms with seaview, very pleasant.

E **Johnny's**, Cobravaddo, T0832-2277458, johnnys_hotel@rediffmail.com. 12 rooms (1 a/c) with bath, rooftop terrace, good restaurant, interesting garden (fruit and spices), yoga, peaceful location, short walk to beach, call for collection from bus stand. Recommended. Also, 2-bed furnished apartments, Rs 8,000-10,000 per month.

Baga *p97, map p98*
Of the family guest houses on the northern side of Baga river, up towards Arpora, those to the left of the bridge (west or seaward) are quieter. Rooms in houses/cottages are available for about Rs 300 but good discounts are possible for weekly or monthly rental. Standards vary so check room and security first. Try Wilson Fernandes at **Nani's & Rani's** or ask at **Four Seasons Restaurant** at Jack's Corner.

B **Ronil Beach Resort**, T0832-2276099, ronil@sancharnet.in. 58 a/c rooms, pool, well run with a good local reputation, ideal for all Baga and Calangute nightlife, small grounds. Recommended.

B-C Santiago Resorts, close to Le Restaurant, T0832-2276491, desouza@ goatelecom.com. Spacious rooms with TV, bar, fridge, balcony. Continental restaurant and bar by the pool, Chinese restaurant. Convenient for beach. Excellent attentive service, good-value resort hotel.

C Baia Do Sol, by bus stand, top end of Baga, T0832-2276084, www.ndnaik.com. 23 very clean rooms, a/c cottages, good restaurant with views (excellent seafood), riverside location.

C-D Cavala, Sauntavaddo, top end of Baga village, T0832-2276090, www.cavala.com. 30 clean rooms with bath (some a/c), best at rear, overlooking fields, pool across road. Banana Republic restaurant, relaxed bar, popular live music evenings, friendly and attentive management, short walk to beach, good all-round value. Recommended.

D Alidia Beach Cottages, behind the church, Sauntavaddo, T0832-2276835, alidia@goaworld.com. 16 good clean rooms with attached bath, restaurant, secure, friendly owners, beach 2-min walk, excellent value off-season. One of the best of its kind, book ahead for Christmas, highly recommended.

D Riverside, next to the bridge, 5-min walk from beach, T0832-2277337, riverside@salyara.net. 8 rooms with river view, restaurant, garden setting, pool, peaceful location.

D Villa Fatima Beach Resort, Main Rd, Baga-Calangute, Sauntavaddo, Calangute, T0832-2277418, villa.fatima@sympatico.ca. A pretty ramshackle three storey affair plonked at the bottom of Antonio Mascarenhas' elegant old house with a nice atmosphere, national flags fluttering and books piled high from former guests. 25 clean, attached bathrooms, separate balconies, deals for long-stayers.

D-E Angelina, Sauntavaddo, T0832-2279145, angelinabeachresort@ rediffmail.com. 12 clean and secure rooms in family-run guest house.

E Baga Queen Beach Resort, T0832-2276880. 15 good-sized, clean rooms with bath, close to beach, better value than others near by.

E Lina's, north of Baga River, T0832-2281142. 4 good-value rooms in a secluded guest house. Recommended.

E Villa Melnisha, T0832-2277805. 4 simple, clean rooms with bath, kitchenette, good cheap *thalis*, owners live upstairs.

E-F Nani's & Rani's, T0832-2277014. 8 spartan rooms (shared or own bath), budget meals served in pleasant garden, bar, email, STD/ISD. One of the few local budget options with a sea view and a relaxing quiet location. Short walk across Baga Bridge for nightlife.

F Andrade Guest House, Cobravaddo, behind Linda Goa, rooms are really basic but have mosquito nets, Mrs Andrade is very friendly and amusing, cheap option near the beach.

F Venar, Cobravaddo, T0832-2276867. 4 basic but clean rooms with shared bath in an old house.

Arpora *p99*

L Nilaya Hermitage, Bhati, T0832-2276793, www.nilayahermitage.com. An eccentric, bright-blue luxury resort tucked 5 mins' drive up a scorched dirt track from the town: bungalows squat among trees and shrubs. The retreat's main resources, including a beautiful high-ceilinged music lounge, are built about a big pool that has unmatched views across the *taluka*'s floor onto the sea. Swirling cracked mosaic bathrooms wouldn't look out of place in Gaudi's Barcelona.

B Sun Village, T0832-2279409, www.desouzahotels.com. 135 spacious suites in well-thought out and maintained but very resorty resort, with TV, bar, fridge, good-size balcony, 2 restaurants plus a BBQ area, 2 pools with children's area, pub, health club, beauty parlour, good selection of shops. Minimum 3 nights stay, good value if you like all-you-can-drink booze.

Candolim and Sinquerim beaches *p99, map p100*

Sinquerim

L Fort Aguada Beach Resort, T0832-2479123-36, www.tajhotels.com. The self-confessed sprawling Taj complex, divided into 3, spills across 88 acres of Sinquerim. In descending order of cost these consist of the 17 hilltop family villas that make up the Aguada Hermitage, the 130 rooms with sea views at the Fort Aguada Beach Resort, actually built in the fort's ruins, and the scores of cottages for up to 8 people on the beach in the Taj Holiday Village. The complex has all sorts of 5-star facilities including 2 freshwater pools, 9 restaurants, ayurvedic and other spa treatments, plus golf, tennis and a crèche.

B-C Marbella Guesthouse, left off the road to the Aguada Beach Resort, T0832-22479551, shrisai@goatelecom.com. Mock-Portuguese period mansion with 6 lovingly-decorated rooms. Its owners have scavenged bona fide antiques and furnishings like mosaic tiles from old villas to create this elegant and unpretentious homestay. The penthouse has 3 large rooms.

D Ludovici Tourist Home, Dando, T0832-2379684. Just inland of the road leading to the fort sits this family home with 4 double rooms, all with fan and en suite and including breakfast. There's also a bar and restaurant and a lovely porch scattered with chairs that gives onto a spacious garden.

D Marfran, T0832-2279274, private house with a few simple rooms. Good peaceful budget option.

D Palm Shade, T0832-2277429. 5 rooms arranged around a small garden at the back of a popular beach restaurant. Quiet location, direct access to beach.

D Village Belle, near the main road by Taj Holiday Village, T0832-2276151, vbelle@vsnl.com, 8 rooms (some a/c), good, cheap restaurant, among palms, 500 m from the beach, friendly owners, good value for the area. Recommended.

Candolim

A Whispering Palms, 300 m from beach (looks a bit like a fortress), T0832-2479140, www.whisperingpalms.com. 66 well-equipped rooms, best in 2-storey villas, good restaurant overlooking excellent pool (non-residents Rs 150), pleasant garden, mainly packages, good but pricey.

A-B Dona Alcina/Dom Francisco, opposite Health Centre, T0832-2476936, alfran@goa telecom.com. Neighbouring package-orientated hotels, most rooms with balcony

overlooking pool, more privacy on upper floors, choice of restaurants, cyber café, ayurvedic massages. Indian dance performance on Sat at Dom Francisco, T0832-2479034.

B-C Kamal Retreat, Dando, towards Aguada, T0832-2476320, kmehra@ goatelecom.com. 23 large, quality rooms (half a/c) on a spacious site with immaculate grounds, large pool, direct beach access, one of the few hotels in Candolim not to be hemmed in, nor will it be, charming owner ensures high standards. Recommended.

C Aldeia Santa Rita, towards Aguada, T0832-2479356, www.desouzahotels.com, 32 rooms with balcony (better upstairs) in colourful 'street' of villas in attractive setting, some a/c, good restaurant, bar, small pool, well-maintained grounds, good value. Recommended.

C-D Costa Nicola, near the health centre (500 m from beach), T0832-2276343, costanicola@ yahoo.com. 7 rooms of varying size in old Goan house, full of character, 13 rooms in a functional new block, some with kitchenette, plus 9 rooms in Sandy Villa next door. Well kept-grounds, pool, friendly owners. Old house rooms excellent value in off season.

D Par Avel, 100 m from beach towards Aguada, T0832-2479074, www.paravel/ hotel/goacom.com. 6 simple rooms (Rs 650, a/c Rs 200 extra), courtyard garden for breakfast, friendly.

D Sea Shell Inn, opposite Canara Bank, Candolim-Aguada Rd, T0832-2281555, seashellgoa@ hotmail.com. 8 spotless, comfortable rooms with fan, in a new block behind the house, popular restaurant serves excellent sizzlers and seafood, residents may use pool at Casa Sea Shell.

D Summerville, towards Aguada, T0832-2479075, www.summerville beachresort.com. 15 well-kept rooms in a compact triangular block, breakfast on rooftop, sunbathing terrace, swimming pool at back in simple gardens.

D Xavier, down a lane and round the corner from the State Bank of India, T/F0832-2479911, www.goacom.com/ hotels/xavier. 10 spacious, well-furnished rooms, fan, balcony, sensible peak rates, excellent restaurant, close to beach, friendly, call in advance during monsoon season. Recommended.

E D'Mello's Sea View, Escrivaovaddo, turn at Monteiro Rd, T0832-2275050. 15 rooms, good food (tandoori specials), pleasant area. Recommended.

⊘ Eating

Calangute p95, map p96
$$$ A Reverie, next to Hotel Goan Heritage, Holiday St, T0832-3174927, areverie@ rediffmail.com. All white tableclothes and quiet garden, this is a splash-out venue. Pricey and out of the way, it is popular with the ex-pat crowd. Great chocolate mousse.

$$$ Le Restaurant Français, Baga Rd, T0832- 2121712. Extremely pragmatically, the daytime dairy curd café the Milky Way gets a wave of a magic wand to become Le Restaurant by night. Sofas are wheeled in, huge paintings of French street scenes are erected to serve as backdrop to the Gallic menu: all winning a thumbs up from the French community themselves.

$$$ Oceanic, Gauravaddo. Well planned setting in neat gardens, varied seafood, pasta, good fun when busy.

$$$ Souza Lobo, on the beach, excellent fresh seafood, lobster (Rs 550) and sizzlers served on a shaded terrace, well-known restaurant that has managed to retain a good reputation for years. Recommended.

$$$ Sublime Bistro Bar Panchayat, 3/22 Tivaivaddo, behind the Falcon Beach Resort, T0832-2484051. This hidden gem is designed very Zen and has a dogged following.

$$$ Waves, Kerkar Art Complex, Gaurawaddo, T0832-2276 017. One of the few places to showcase Hindu Goan cuisine, Waves serves some homely dishes including mackerel *Uddmethi* (infused with fenugreek) and *khathatem* (root veg stew steeped in a local berry).

$ Infanteria, 'the breakfast place' to locals, has Rs 125 set breakfast, eggs, coffee, juice, toast. Bakery and confectionery includes butterscotch swiss rolls.

$ Plantain Leaf, near petrol pump, Almita III. T0832-2276861. Mean *dosas*, jumbo *thalis*, sizzlers and a full range of curries: near unbeatable for your pukka pure veg Indian.

$ The Tibetan Kitchen, 0900–1500, 1800-22.30. This airy garden restaurant at the bottom of a track leading off Calangute Beach Rd is part tent, part wicker awning, part open to the skies. Tibet's answer to the ravioli – *momos* – are good here, but more adventurous starters like prawns, mushrooms and tomatoes seeping onto wilting lettuce leaves are exceptional.

Baga p97, map p98
$$$ Fiesta, Tito's Lane, T0832-2279894. Only open for dinner, closed Tue. One of Baga's destination eateries serving mediterranean nosh in stylish surroundings, unusual Portuguese and Italian dishes (Rs 200), and great desserts. Tends to attract the wealthy crowd before they move on to Tito's.

$$$ J&A's Ristorante Italiano House, 560 Baga river, T0832-2282364, www.littleitalygoa.com. Jamshed and Ayesha Madon's operation – along with their pizzas and pastas – has earned them an evangelical following in Goa. Next door is Bisque, their new foray into Spanish tapas. Both are open only for dinner between Oct-Apr.

$$ Apple Pie, opposite Tito's, Tito's Lane, Sauntavaddo, T0832-2638898, 1200-2400. French-managed Apple Pie isn't short of repeat customers prepared to pick their way across the sandy wasteland running to it from Tito's Lane. Chicken dijonnaise and lemon cheesecake are first rate.

$$ Britto's Bar and Restaurant, Baga beach, T0832-2277331. Cajie Britto's puddings are an institution and his staff (of 50) boast that in high season you'll be pushed to find an inch of table space from the restaurant's inside right out to the seashore. Seafood platters come for Rs 170, or plump for a breakfast of Heinz beans on toast for Rs 60. Good fish curry and rice too.

$$ Casa Portuguesa, Baga Rd, a real institution of a restaurant run by German/

Goan couple with live music in the gloriously overgrown jungle of a garden. Strongly recommended.

$$ Citrus, Tito's Rd, www.citrusvegetarian .com. Impeccable vegetarian med-style food in simple surround: prides itself on hygiene, European-run.

$$ Domingo's, Tito's Rd, just off the road next to Zinho's Guesthouse. International. Well cooked and tasty food, safe, one of few not to play background music of any kind. A friendly, family-run concern. Strongly recommended.

$ Joe's Café and Health Food Shop, Baga beach, T0832-2276838. Joe has been here on the road to Baga for 10 years and has come over all new age and started to focus solely on health food. 72-year old Yoga Baba, who hangs here during the season before going back to Rishikesh for monsoon, promises to teach *asanas* and the other 7 limbs of the life science of yoga on the upstairs veranda if he's still alive.

$ Lila's Café, north bank of Baga River T0832-2279843, lilacafe@sify.com. Slick German-run restaurant, good selection of European dishes, check blackboard for specials, smoked kingfish Rs 110. Homemade cheeses and jams, muesli and orange juice Rs 60, fresh bread, good coffee. Also serves beers. Shaded terrace overlooking the river. Closed evenings. Recommended.

Beach shacks

Zanzibar Beach Shack, 3rd shack on the right down Tito's Lane (park outside Mambo's), Baga, T98323274707. There's been an unusual amount of orange-and -black design consideration thrown at this shack: furniture, for a start, is cane not plastic. Zanzibar has great grub on its menu (fish and Indian food are strengths) and loads of music, particularly lounge. Open from 0900 for breakfast till the last person drops.

Candolim and Sinquerim beaches *p99, map p100*

$$ Casa Manolita, behind Dona Alcina resort. European bistro run by Anglo-Indian couple, meals served on balustraded veranda of

restored 19th-century Portuguese villa. Recommended.

$$ Fisherman's Cove, opposite Alexandra Tourist Centre, excellent tandooris cooked to order.

$$ Mermaid, opposite Whispering Palms Hotel, run by a Swedish-Goan couple, superb international and Goan cuisine at reasonable prices. Highly recommended.

$$ Oriental Royal Thai Cuisine, Candolim Holiday Beach Rd, next to Holiday Beach Resort. T0832-2121549. Although they play live music this is a relatively sedate restaurant for the neighbourhood, but has impeccable service and authentic Thai, buffet every Sun from 1900. Cooking classes held 1400-1700 on Mon (Rs 1,100 including a 5-course dinner).

$$ Palms 'n Sand, near the beach. Has to merit a mention on the basis of its signature dish alone - roast piglet – which you need to order the day before.

$$ Titus Roma Pisa, Candolim Beach Rd. More than just pizzas. Well-prepared food, very friendly staff (good place to ask about fishing trips, flea market etc), soccer bar for live football, but not rowdy at all, so not just for the younger crowd. Also has internet access. Highly recommended.

$$ Xavier. Western. Excellent meals (owner/chef spent 30 years in England), very attentive service, roast dinner on Sun. Cocktail bar with a happy hour, 1800-1900. Recommended.

$ Club 21, on the beach, now crowded in with other shacks, does good breakfasts for about Rs 75, snacks (seafood, pancakes) and drinks.

Fort Aguada

$$$ Banyan Tree, Taj Holiday Village. Exotic backdrop to delicious Thai food: a wide veranda, water garden and a great banyan tree; expensive though almost reasonable if you think in foreign tender.

Saligao *p99*

$$ Florentine's, Chogm Rd, Saligao T0832-2278122. A Goan café that Goans recommend: scores particularly high for its *cafreal*, chicken in spicy marinades, and caramel custard dessert.

🍸 Pubs, bars and clubs

Locals know which way their bread is buttered, and in this neighbourhood, it's beer up. Many bars here have a happy hour from 1700-1930 and show live Premier League football, in a bit of a home-from-home for many visitors. Along the beach, shacks also serve a wide range of drinks and cocktails to sip while watching the sunset.

Baga *p97, map p98*
Cavala, Sauntavaddo, top end of Baga village. One of the few genuine bars, with friendly atmosphere, attentive staff, great cocktails, and occasional live music evenings.
Kamaki, Tito's Lane. 'You've survived Kamaki's', reads the sign on this bar. Most do, but it's at your liver's peril that you enter here. Gets busy from 3am when the bigger venues down Tito's Lane start chucking out.
Mambo's, Tito's Lane. The slow crawl of the Tito's empire towards the beach continues with Mambo's, a touch more laid back than the original, no entrance fee.
Sunset, north of Baga river, a great place to watch the goings-on of Baga beach as dusk falls. Prime location but less hectic as it's north of the river bridge.
Tito's, Tito's Lane, www.titosgoa.com. So good, it got its own lane. From 2005, Tito's, one of Goa's first nightspots, will become the first venue to build itself a proper, international standard club. After a legal hiccup in 2004, it means that the club, famous among hip young things the length of India, should be back to full house music strength – the venue also serves excellent food through the night including reasonaby priced wood-fired pizzas.

Arpora *p99*
Club Cubana, Arpora Hill, T0832-2279799, www.clubcubana.net. Technically Cubana is a private residence, albeit with a built-in bar, so it's only open a handful of days a week and is sometimes prone to police raids. In club incarnation it is a big, brash, commercial party venue that mops up the charter holidaymakers. Ladies nights on Wed, after the flea market, are popular, then it's hip hop on Fri, club music on Sat, and funk, house and hip hop on Sun.
Nilaya. Has awesome panoramic views that make it a contender for best sundowner. There's also a fancy restaurant that carries a steep price tag.

Candolim and Sinquerim beaches *p99, map p100*
Congo Lounge, 242 Souzavaddo (Fort Aguada Rd), T0832-5644226. Snazzy super-modern venue serving breakfast, lunch and dinner. It's popular with the Mumbai/MTV crowd.
Rock Your Blues, south end of Candolim near Taj complex, open 2030. Playing retro music and selling sensibly priced drinks, this new venture is aimed not just at the Taj clientele.

🎭 Entertainment

Calangute *p95, map p96*
Heritage Kathakali Theatre, at the Hotel Sunflower, opposite the football ground, Calangute Beach Rd T0832-2588059, daily in season, 1800-2000. The breathtakingly elaborate mimes of 17th century Keralan mime dance drama take over 12 hours to perform in the southern state. Here, however, it comes abbreviated for tourist attention spans: you watch the players apply their make-up, are spoon-fed a brief background of the dance, then performed a snatch of a classic dance-drama.

Candolim and Sinquerim beaches *p99, map p100*
Satya's Garden, behind Oceanic Shack. An intimate living room screening room with Hollywood or Indian (mostly arthouse) films starting at 2130.

✿ Festivals

March Carnival is best celebrated in villages or in the main district towns but Calangute has brought the party to the tourists.

May (2nd week). The Youth Fête attracts Goa's leading musicians and dancers.

○ Shopping

Do your homework before you buy: prices in tourist shops are massively inflated, and goods are often worth less than a third of the asking. 92.5 silver should be sold by weight: prices are quoted on the international market and in 2004 a biscuit would go for Rs 11 per g; pay a little more for elaborate workmanship. The bigger Kashmiri shops, particularly, are notorious both for refusing to sell by weight, instead quoting by the 'piece'; taxi and rickshaw drivers routinely get Rs 100 per tourist delivered to shops plus 10% commission on anything sold.

Calangute *p95, map p96*
Book Palace, Beach Rd, near the bus stand, is a relic from the old days when long-term residents spent their weeks reading.
Casa Goa, Cobravado, Baga Rd, T0832-2281048, cezarpinto@hotmail.com. Cezar Pinto's shop is quite a razzy lifestyle store: beautifully restored reclining plantation chairs next to plates brought over by the Portuguese from Macau plus modern-day dress from local fashion designer Wendell Rodricks. Cool modern twists on old Goan shoes by local Edwin Pinto too.
Malini Ramini, 156, opposite St Anthony's Chapel, T0832-2275305, www.malini ramini.com. Threads for the eccentrically ethnic – much here is for the hip Mumbai crowd but there's good bikinis, bags and beaded dresses. International price tags.
Menezes supermarket, near petrol pump, T0832-2279993. A real treasure trove of a supermarket: all the usual plus adaptor plugs, water heating filaments, quince jam, wine, cashew feni in plastic bottles to take home, full range of sun lotion factors and brands, tampons etc and money change.

Association. During the season the Tibetan community in exile gently sell silver from 2 markets in Calangute.

Baga *p97, map p98*
Jay-Jays. Mostly secondhand novels; 50% back if you return the book.

Arpora *p99*
Tabra Arts Pvt Colonial Photo, Viegas Vado 32, T0832-2277699, silviogoa@ yahoo.com. Bollywood posters from the 40s and 50s, old sepia family line-ups and aquatints of maharajas reprinted and then laminated (prices from Rs 200) or buy an original for a far higher price tag.
Ingo's Saturday Night Bazaar, bagaingo@yahoo.com, 1630 till midnight. Snappily dubbed the 'artisan and hippie market-cum-beer garden and international food stalls'. Ingo, one of the founding freaks of the 80s Goan scene, has made a tidied up and much edited version of Anjuna's Wednesday flea market. Stalls are leased out at 4 times the price of stalls at Anjuna's market and fees for goods soar accordingly. The beggars and aggressive hawkers are kept out, most of the area's good restaurants pitch up, bands play live and there's nowhere better to find neon cotton booties next to stone chillums.

Candolim and Sinquerim beaches *p99, map p100*
Camelot, 139 Fondvem, Ribandar, T0832-2234255. Classic countryside furniture.
Rust, 409A Fort, Aguada Rd, Candolim, T0832-2479340. Everything from wrought-iron furniture to clothes.
Sangolda, Chogm Rd, opposite Mac de Deus Chapel, Sangolda T0832-2409309, sangolda@sancharnet.in, Mon-Sat 1000-1930. Lifestyle gallery and café run by the owners of Nilaya Hermitage selling handcrafted metalware, glass, ethnic wooden furniture, bed and table linen, lacquerware and wooden objects.
Sankar's, Acron Arcade, Fort Aguada Rd, Candolim, T0832-5643674, www.sankars books.com. Probably North Goa's best bookshop: Indian fiction and history, spirituality and yoga, management and

general fiction, both highbrow and pulp.
Yamini, Acron Arcade, Fort Aguada Rd,
Candolim. Next door to Sankar's, selling
some great, reasonably priced silk cushions,
throws and beach mats.

▲ Activities and tours

Calangute *p95, map p96*
River cruises
Floating Palace. If your trip begins and
ends in Goa then try a backwater cruise,
Keralan-style, by staying overnight in
this 4 cabin wooden houseboat. The
bamboo, straw and coir structure was
laboriously built in Kerala then shipped
up the coast. You depart from Mandovi in
the late afternoon, are fed a high tea
then a feast of a continental dinner
passing the Chorao Island bird sanctuary.
International standards of safety.
Bookings can be arranged through
Amazing Images Tour Operators,
opposite Milky Way, Khobravaddo.

Yoga
Holystamina Yoga Ashram, Naikavaddo,
T0832-2497400, www.cyril yoga.com. 3
classes held each day, first
class costs Rs 150, then price rises to
Rs 300 per class thereafter. Various
courses for all abilities, beginners
to advanced. Inner healing yoga
meditation, juice bar, yoga camps and
good karma-promoting volunteer
activities also on offer.

Tour operators
Many double as money changers.
Day Tripper, Gauravaddo, T0832-2276726,
daytrip@ goatelecom.com. Offers tours all
over Goa, best deals in the region, Palolem
beach Rs 350; spice plantations Rs 700;
backwaters Rs 1010, with pick-ups from
your hotel. Recommended.

Baga *p97, map p98*
Boat trips and wildlife cruises
Fiesta Yacht, Fiesta Restaurant opposite
Tito's, Tito's Lane. 36 ft, morning and sunset
cruises for dolphin watching, Rs 400-800.
Contact Maneck Contractor.
Mikes Marine, Fortune Travels, Sauntavaddo
by the bus stand at the top end of Baga,

T0832-2279782. Covered boat, dolphin trips,
river cruises and bird watching.

Diving and snorkelling
Goa Dive Center, Tito's Rd, T0832-2157094.
Goa isn't really on the diving map, chiefly
because it has only 2 dive sites, both of
which have what's known as 'variable', ie less
than great, visibility. However, the Dive
Center offers inexpensive PADI courses.
Options range from half day Discover Scuba
programme (from 10 years and up) for Rs
2,700 to the 4-day Open Water Diver
programme, Rs 14,500. The centre also runs
snorkelling tours.

Yoga
Natural Health Centre, opposite Tito's Rd,
offers alternative therapies including
ayurvedic massage and yoga lessons.

Candolim and Sinquerim beaches *p99, map p100*
Candolim
Ayurveda and massage
Amrita Kerala Ayurvedic, next to Lawande
supermarket, Annavaddo, T0832-3125668/9,
www.vedamassage.com, 0730-2000. This
massage centre, set inside an old Goan villa,
is neatly geared towards the foreign tourist.
Westerners are on hand to explain the
philosophy behind the Indian life science.
As well as treatments the centre teaches
massage. A basic course, scheduled for the
morning to give you more time on the
sand, takes 7 days. Panchakarma courses
last 6 months (Rs 7,500). Rs 750 for 75
min massage.

Dolphin watching
John's Boats, T0832-2277780, promises
'guaranteed' dolphin watching, morning
trips start around 0900, Rs 550 (includes
meal and hotel pick-up). Also
crocodile-spotting river trips with lunch.

Parasailing
Occasionally offered independently on
Candolim beach, costing around Rs 600-850
for a 5-min flight.

Fort Aguada
Taj Sports Complex, Fort Aguada Beach
Resort. Has excellent facilities that are open

to non-residents at the Taj Holiday Village, and a separate access between Aguada Beach Resort and the Holiday Village. Rs 450 per day for the complex, Rs 350 for the pool. Tennis (Rs 450 per hr); squash and badminton (Rs 150 for 30 mins); mini golf (Rs 200). Yoga classes. Scuba diving, sailing/ water skiing/windsurfing/rod fishing Rs 450-500 per hr; parasailing/jet ski Rs 900-950 per hr.

Arpora *p99*
Ayurveda and massage
Most top-end hotels offer spas both to residents and day treatments including: **Spa Aguada** at Taj Holiday Village, Fort Aguada for full body massage, facials, heat wraps and scrubs and **Nilaya Hermitage Wellness Spa**, Arpora: 60 min oil massage from Rs 950, 3 day *dhara* course from Rs 5,000.

Yoga
Rashnu Yoga, Viegavaddo, T0832-2276691, maggiehughesyoga@hotmail.com. Equipped to Iyengar specifications, 30-day courses (US$200-250). Rooms (**D**) for students only, simple, fan cooled, mosquito net, relaxing garden. Recommended.

Saligao *p99*
Ayurveda and yoga
The Ayurvedic Natural Health Centre, Chogm Rd, T0832-2409036, www.healthand ayurveda.com. Also in Baga, Baga-Calangute Rd, Villa 2, Beira Mar Complex. The ANHC is not for the faint-hearted: the centre was originally built for the local community that it continues to serve and hasn't made many concessions to western sensibilities. Those checking into the 2 week *panchakarma* can expect almost every cavity to be flushed. They do offer smaller, less daunting packages, like 2½ hr rejuvenations (Rs 300), and have a herb garden where you can taste first-hand leaves that tingle your tongue (used to stop stuttering) or others that eliminate your sense of sweet taste. Yoga is taught on the rooftop, some basic

accommodation is on site (11 rooms) or pick-up provided from most of Goa's northern beaches.

⊖ Transport

Baga *p97, map p98*
Cycle hire
The only place in Baga is 200 m down a small lane past the Hacienda, on the left. Rs 40 per day, a little extra to keep it overnight.

Motorbike hire
Almost every guesthouse owner or hotelier can rustle up a scooter at short notice – expect to pay Rs150 for one day or Rs100 per day for longer periods. Recycled water bottles of lurid orange liquid balanced in glass display boxes at roadsides denote your local gas station. Petrol is Rs 40 per litre.

❶ Directory

Calangute *p95, map p96*
Banks State Bank of India, Baga; Bank of Baroda, Baga. **Internet** I way, NetXcess Cyber Café, Shop No 1, Sunshine Complex, Baga Rd, T0832-2281516, netxcess@ mail.com. Broadband internet chain I way's branch is faster than most. **Nikki's Internet Café**, Calangute Tourist Resort Annexe, T0832-2281950, 8 terminals, forex, pool table, café, 0900 to midnight, Rs 40 per hr. Useful during periods of frequent power cuts. **Police** T0832-2278284. **Telephone** Look for the yellow STD ISD signs.

Candolim and Sinquerim beaches *p99, map p100*
Candolim
Medical services Health Centre, Main Rd; Bosto Hospital, Panjim Rd.
Photography Many outlets do quick processing of holiday snaps; fairly good quality, usually same day (processed at Calangute). Foto Finish, next to Stone House, stocks slides, black/white films and camera accessories.

The party beaches → *Colour map 1, grid B1.*

Anjuna was where the freaks headed when the squares got hip to Baga; it in turn has now spawned hedonistic ghettos in Vagator and Chapora, their labyrinthine layout making them still more difficult for a shuttle bus of tourists from Baga to daytrip. This neck of the coast is hilly and bursts with lush greenery during monsoon, but the same hills act as huge sound boards when the parties pounding through the area pick up once or twice a week. If total tranquility is paramount think twice or pack earplugs. If you've come to party, you're in good company. Where the strip south of Baga is more about the bottle, Anjuna and up is inevitably fuelled on drugs, both in terms of entertainment and economics.

Although parties still happen a few times a month, Anjuna, with the Wednesday flea market firmly etched in every holiday itinerary, has gone way too mainstream for most of its erstwhile exponents. The Anjuna exodus has slowly scattered old freaks, junkies and hippies up and down Goa's coast from Patnem in the south to Arambol in the north. But those still plugged into the party scene, and ergo, drugs, are mostly hidden in the hills of Chapora and Vagator or tucked away in inaccessible South Anjuna. Chapora particularly is now where westerners pitch up to stay for the long-term. The whole village has a bit of an edge: if you have neither dreadlocks nor an introduction you can expect a sharp swig of hostility.

Inland, the wealthy Brahmin convert village of Assagao has beautiful houses belonging to the more traditional Goa – illustrious landowners and the intelligentsia – and is the site of Goa's best established yoga centre, Purple Valley: health and spiritual tourists are spreading out their towels in increasing numbers alongside those chasing stoned sunsets. ▶▶ *For Sleeping, Eating and other listings, see pages 119-122.*

Ins and outs

Getting there There are frequent buses from Mapusa and a daily bus from Panjim which stop along the main Mapusa road. Get down at Starco's crossroads for Anjuna's hotels and guesthouses, for Chapora and Vagator you can walk or wait for a connecting bus. After climbing the Chapora hill, the three roads to the left (west) lead to the beaches. Local boats ferry passengers from Baga and Arambol for the Wednesday market.

Getting around Motorcycles are the most popular mode of transport and are available for hire everywhere, but the surrounding land is reasonably flat, making bikes a good option.

Background

Few of Anjuna's visitors know anything of its pre-hippy past, yet it has a history of which the local population is very proud. Anjuna was an important Arab trading post in the 10th and 12th centuries. As was common with many such ports on the west coast of India, Arab Muslim traders represented only a small minority of the population, and Hindu influences were also important, as both the lineage of some of the important Hindu castes and the existence of ancient temples illustrates.

Most traces of such temples have now been obliterated by years of Christianization, for Anjuna, along with the rest of Bardez, was deeply affected by Portuguese determination to convert everyone who lived in its Old Conquest territories. Ceded to the Portuguese by the Bijapur Sultans in 1543, it was allocated to the Franciscans as their sphere of missionary activity. Five years after the Franciscans began working in Bardez they established the parish of Nagoa, which

Parties

The availability of drugs inevitably attracts local police during the high season who carry out raids on travellers' houses and harass partygoers, often demanding large bribes. Not all international peddlers get away and some foreigners are serving long sentences.

The party scene is very much harnessed to local politics. Before each local election there is a general ban or a curb on loud music after 2200, as politicians seek to shore up the support of the local community. Once the elections are over, it's party time again. Goa's stop-start party cycle means that most of those that play music here live local. This makes for a rather insular musical orbit. Even so, Wednesday and Friday nights are most reliably rocking: sound systems are set up around a floor marked with neon-daubed coconut trees. For great stretches around the al fresco dancefloor, women wrapped in rugs sit at gas stoves surrounded by coir mats where overheated, overbreakbeated dancers can flake, drool into *masala chai* and pack their *chillums*. Inside the throng, where feet pummel into the sand, one-legged beggars hang at sleeves and pre-teen pick pockets zag between bodies. Daybreak brings renewed vigour to dancing, when parties often shift venue down to one of the Anjuna beach shacks till sunset.

There has been a surge in the reports of rapes and/or harassment around parties: stay in a group and if not driving yourself certainly make an arrangement to meet a reliable taxi driver whose registration plates you've written down. It may not sound overly like spontaneous holiday fun, but it's infinitely better than the worst case alternative.

included modern Anjuna. Local people still talk of the ghosts of this era inhabiting particular groves. Between 1546 and 1567, 300 temples were destroyed in Bardez and the income that had previously gone from temple lands to the temples was transferred to Christian education. The Anjuna shrine of Bhumika Devi was moved across into Pernem. The rectorate of Anjuna was established in 1603 when the Church of St Michael was dedicated. It was subsequently rebuilt on a much grander scale, in 1613.

A well-attested story tells how in 1628 a Portuguese vicar who had told a Hindu woman to have her child baptised was severely attacked by furious villagers. They were found guity of assault and executed. Their houses were confiscated, salt was mixed with the soil on their lands, and a warning account was carved in stone on a *padrao* (monument), and set up in the village. Gomes Pereira recounts that many years later the stone fell and broke in two, and that Hindu villagers would often light candles on the stone in memory of the victims.

Over the next three centuries Anjuna produced a series of notable figures in Goa's history, both in church and in secular life. The best-known cleric was Fr Agnelo Gustav de Souza (1869-1927). Born and brought up in the village, Fr de Souza trained for the priesthood in Mapusa and Rachol before joining the Missionary Society of Pilar. He developed an extraordinary reputation both for his preaching and for his pastoral work. Twelve years after his death his body was moved to Pilar, which became a place of pilgrimage. In 1986 he was raised by the Pope to the rank of Venerable, the final stage towards canonization.

Anjuna → *Colour map 1, grid B1.*

Against all the odds, and in spite of the thousands who descend here every Wednesday in season for its flea market, many corners of Anjuna still cling to something of the alternative life. People, mostly European, often English, who've had it with home for any number of reasons continue to come here, rent a house, buy a bike, meet a girl, start some small scale business to keep them in spliffs and booze or just plain food, water, flipflops and motorbike fuel and proceed to pay less attention to hours and days than to seasons and sunsets. Decide for yourself whether it's idyllic or deluded, but it's likely you'll find it outright insular: don't expect casual tourists to be necessarily greeted with open arms - every backpacker passing through wants an eyewitness account of the freak scene and the probing has made some just jaded, others plain hostile. It is a strong community, no doubt, but a judgmental one. What they have in common is a love for the beautiful lifestyle lived cheap here and Anjuna still has plenty to offer in that regard, and that counts for the passer-by as much as for the adopted resident.

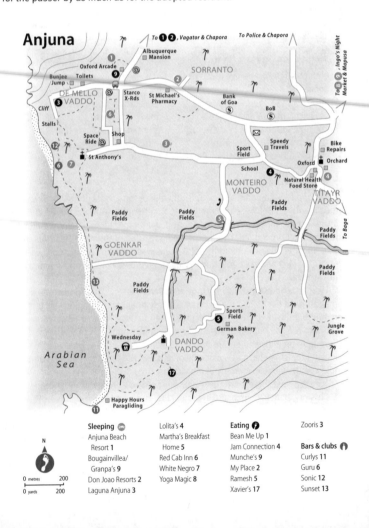

Sleeping 🛏
Anjuna Beach
  Resort **1**
Bougainvillea/
  Granpa's **9**
Don Joao Resorts **2**
Laguna Anjuna **3**

Lolita's **4**
Martha's Breakfast
  Home **5**
Red Cab Inn **6**
White Negro **7**
Yoga Magic **8**

Eating 🍴
Bean Me Up **1**
Jam Connection **4**
Munche's **9**
My Place **2**
Ramesh **5**
Xavier's **17**

Zooris **3**

Bars & clubs 🍸
Curlys **11**
Guru **6**
Sonic **12**
Sunset **13**

N

0 metres   200
0 yards   200

Five minutes' peace

If you are unlucky enough to look 'just landed' on the beach you are likely to be thronged and harrassed by hawkers there.

The Hindi word *chaio* means 'go away' or, if, that's too abrupt, try the Konkani phrase *mhaka naka tem* (or just *naka*) to say you don't want what it is they're selling.

If you're still feeling henpecked, there are two swimming pools nearby where you can pay to sunbathe in solitude: Hotel Bougainvillea and Lotus Inn both do daily rates.

The Flea Market ① *Dandovaddo, south Anjuna, Oct-Apr Wed 0800 till sunset, water taxis or shared taxis from anywhere in Goa*, is tourist India in overdrive: over 2,000 stalls descend on Anjuna every week during the season, coughing up Rs 200 rent apiece to hawk everything from Gujarati wooden printing blocks to Bhutanese silver and even Burberry-check pashminas. The trade is so lucrative that for six months several thousand Rajasthani, Gujaritas, Karnatakans and Tibetans, chiefly women, up sticks, leaving their families behind, to make their livings off the tourist dollar. The flea had very different origins, though, and was once an intra-community car boot-style bric-a-brac sale for the sixties freaks.

The rest of the week Anjuna remains a busy beach with laterite rocks in the sea swell and lots of bat and ball in g-strings on the sand. The approach roads to the different regions of Anjuna (the south being the most untouched by the vagaries of tourism whereas the north has a big club and a bungee jump) all end abruptly to give way to a series of tyre-wide sand paths that wind behind residential houses. It's amazing, considering the number of bikes that weave through here each year, that there's been no effort to pave or tarmac. Stalls along the beach front sell 'hyperethnicware', UV paintings glow lurid at the roadsides, and it's probably the best place in the world to pick up *poi* – the fire-twirling that lights up the free parties. You're never far from someone hissing you offers of hash. Indian tourists also get shipped in here by the busload and ask directions to the nearest freaks like western tourists might ask after the Taj Mahal.

South Anjuna to Chapora Fort

If this stretch of land were in the UK it's a safe bet that it would have picked up a stamped certificate of outstanding natural beauty by now. Once you've had enough of dunking yourself in the sea, pick your way along the coastal path for a sunset stroll from South Anjuna all the way to **Chapora Fort**, which has one of the grandest sunset vantages in Goa. There's a footpath just inland of the bungee jump in north Anjuna that takes you over the headland to Spaghetti Beach in Vagator where you'll have to thread your way down the gravelly terracing, climbing again to get onto the wide sands of Big Vagator beach: either stop here for an ear-rinsing sundowner at Nine Bar or keep on for the romantic desolation around the Fort.

The fort commands the hilltop at the north end of the bay, a short but steep walk immediately above the timeshare Sterling Resorts. Now in ruins, the fort stands on the south bank of the Chapora river and dominates the estuary. It was first built by Adil Shah, hence its original name *Shahpura*, or Chapora. Aurangzeb's son Akbar (not Akbar the Great) used it as his headquarters when plotting against his father in a pact with the Mughal's greatest enemies, the Marathas. The Portuguese built it in its present form in 1717 as a secure refuge for the people of Bardez in the face of Maratha attacks, as well as in defence of the river mouth. The fort, with its irregular walls, one major gateway on its eastern side and a series of octagonal battlements, was once served by a series of underground tunnels that were used to provide supplies to the besieged. You can still see old Muslim tombs, huge ramparts and two tunnel entrances. Don't miss the views from the sea-facing walls – they're spectacular.

The flat arc of the estuary inland from the fort is both a docking point for fishing boats and a boat building and repair workshop. It's ideal for exploring by bicycle: the rim-side road will take you all the way out to the bridge at Siolim where you can loop back to take a look at the **Church of St Anthony** that dominates Siolim Square close to the village market. Built in 1606, it replaced an earlier Franciscan church (1568). St Anthony, the patron saint of Portugal, is widely venerated throughout the villages of Goa (prayed to both by Hindus and Catholics in the hope of good fishing catches). The high, flat-ceilinged church has a narrow balustraded gallery and Belgian glass chandeliers. The attractive and typically gabled west end has statues of Jesus and St Anthony. Some extremely fine Portuguese houses are scattered about the village's shadows in varying degrees of disrepair: it's worth walking around to take in some of the facades (you can stay in peerless boutique luxury inside Siolim House, one which has been happily refurbished, see page 119).

Vagator → *Colour map 1, grid B1.*

The gravelly windswept red earth on the approach to Vagator makes the village feel somewhat apocalyptic. The black tarmac approach road snakes through a desolate rusty headland whose chief landmark is the up-juttings of a half-built hotel and the concrete shells of other developments abandoned midway. The beaches here, muddied sand bays upset by slabs of gray rock, quite different from the bubblings of porous laterite in Anjuna, fall at the bottom of terraced red cliffs planted with coconut trees that lean out towards the crashing waves, some of their bellies painted neon. The main access road ends at a car park. To your right in the foreground is the long sweep of **Big Vagator beach**, behind it the profile of the wide outer rim of the ruined **Chapora Fort** against a stunning backdrop of India's western coastline, running well past Goa's northern-most state line and up into Maharashtra. Look for the silhouette of the hilltop factory that lies parallel to Tiracol fort for a visual signpost of the Goan border.

To your left, running inland, is the sometime free party venue **'disco valley'**, threaded through with a creek that opens onto the central **Little Vagator beach**, its terracing lorded over by Nine Bar, a giant venue with an unswerving musical loyalty to trance. Just out of sight is **Ozran** or **'spaghetti beach'** a scrappy, atmospheric bay with great swimming that ends with rocks and jungle. Most people turn right to Big Vagator. Spaghetti, christened by Anjuna's British residents after all the Italians settled here, though dogged by very persistent sarong sellers, is both more sheltered, more scenic and more remote. One of the shacks here has rooms but otherwise it's strictly a daytime hang out.

Vagator to Mapusa

If it's classic Indo-Portuguese architecture you're after, on the way from Vagator to Mapusa sits the splendid yellow and white **Albuquerque Mansion**. The house, an exact replica of the Royal Palace of Zanzibar, was built in the 1920s by workers brought from the East African country specifically for the job. Manuel F Albuquerque had worked as a doctor in Zanzibar and was honoured by its sultan for his service. The home he built on his retirement and repatriation has been referred to as 'the pride of Anjuna'. Unfortunaley, it now houses a symptom of its neighbourhood's decline: a drug rehabilitation institute. If you keep on the Vagator-Mapusa road you'll reach the Catholic village of Assagao – dawn and dusk here are still marked by residents walking along the tropical roadside greeting neighbours taking the air from their traditional porches. The landowners here are unquestionably wealthy: their custom even prompted one of the traditional houses to become a particularly ramshackle branch of the State Bank of India.

Chapora → *Colour map 1, grid B1.*

The shady fishing village that swings along the crescent harbour under the fort's walls is a bit seedy for some to stay in – it's supposedly the centre of what locals, perhaps melodramatically, call the Israeli drugs 'cartel'. It is undeniably pretty though: the wide bowl of a bay has old wooden canoes bobbing about in the shallows, the picturesque fishing dock is full of stocky little ships and the village is full of kooky bars where travellers graze elbows with local fisherfolk.

Badem Church sits on the road between Chapora and Siolim, overlooking the estuary. It's great for views of sunsets.

Vagator & Chapora

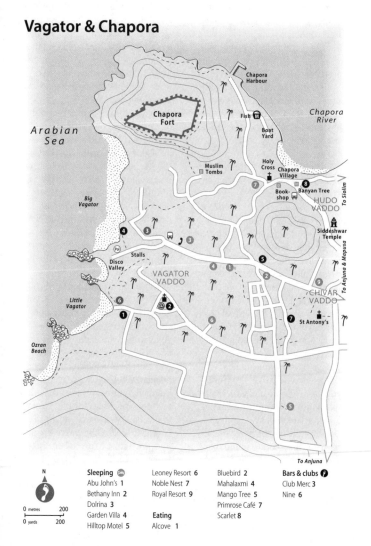

N

0 metres 200
0 yards 200

Sleeping
Abu John's 1
Bethany Inn 2
Dolrina 3
Garden Villa 4
Hilltop Motel 5

Leoney Resort 6
Noble Nest 7
Royal Resort 9

Eating
Alcove 1

Bluebird 2
Mahalaxmi 4
Mango Tree 5
Primrose Café 7
Scarlet 8

Bars & clubs
Club Merc 3
Nine 6

The trance dance experience

When the freaks – not hippies but beatniks with super nomadic genes, giant drug habits and names like Eight Finger Eddie – first kicked their scuffed shoes into Goan sand shortly after the departure of the Portuguese, some of them had guitars that they'd strummed across their overland pilgrimages through Asia slung over their shoulders. These, once they'd absorbed a bit of Hindu spirituality on the route down, were charged with picking out devotional songs by the beach campfire.

By the end of the 60s, thousands of freaks were swarming into Goa, often spilling down from Freak HQ in Kathmandu, and word had got back to proper paid-up acid rock musicians about the scene. Some more substantial entertainment was called for. People started playing records after the Flea Market.

The first music to run through the speakers was rock and reggae. Led Zeppelin, The Who and George Harrison rocked up and played live, but the freaks' entertainment was mostly recorded: Santana, Stones and Marley. Kraftwerk and synth had filtered in by the late 70s but the shift to electronica only really came in the early 80s when musicians got bored of the lyrics and blanked out all the words on albums of industrial noise, rock and disco, using the fully lo-fi production method of taping between two cassette decks. Depeche Mode and New Order albums were stripped down for their drum and synth layers. Some of the rock faithful were angry with the change in the soundtrack to their lives: at those early 80s parties, when the psychedelic-meets-machine- drum sound that still defines Goa trance was first being pumped out, legend has it that the decks had to be flanked by bouncers.

The music, developing in tandem to German nosebleed techno and UK acid house, locked into a worldwide tapestry of druggy drumscapes, but the Goan climate created its own sound. Because records would warp in India's high temperatures, music had to be put down on DATS rather than vinyl which in turn meant tracks were played out in full, ie unmixed. A track had to be interesting enough then, self-contained, so it could be played uninterrupted in full: producers had to pay more attention to intros, middles and outros – in short, the music had to have a story. It also meant there was less art to a Goan trance DJ's set than his opposite numbers in Manchester, Detroit and Paris, who could splice records together to make their own new hybrid sounds.

Many of the original makers of this music had absorbed a fair whack of psychedelia and had added the inevitable layer of sadhu thinking to this – superficially measured in incense, oms, dreads and the swirling dayglo mandalas that so unmistakeably mark out a Goa trance party. The music reflected this: sitars noodled alongside sequencer music to make the Goan signature sound.

By the 90s, though, ecstasy had arrived in Goa. The whole party scene opened right up, peopled by Spiral Tribe crusties as well as middle-class gap year lovelies and global party scenesters who came looking for an alternative to the more mainstream fare in Ibiza. Paul Oakenfold's Perfecto was a key label in fuelling the sound's popularity but there were more: Dragonfly, The Infinity Project, Return to the Source. Today the music comes from labels like Electrojump, Hux Flux, Errorhead, Color Drop, Wizzy Noise, Psycho+Trolls, Droidsect, Parasense, Peace Data, In-R-Voice. Although much of it hails from studios in Europe or Japan, there's the odd label that's more homegrown, like the resolutely Goan label 'Made In Chapora'.

At the budget end, the best options in Anjuna, Vagator and Chapora tend to be unofficial, privately owned residences leasing out rooms. Have a walk around looking for signs on trees or just ask people, but be careful about security because break-ins are common (padlocks are sold in a small shop next door to White Negro). Rs 2,000 per month is a reasonable monthly rent, but bear in mind that you run the risk of thumping techno beats at all hours.

Anjuna *p114, map p114*

AL-A Laguna Anjuna, Sorantovaddo, T0832-2274305, www.lagunaanjuna.com. Looking a little dog-eared, but still a mellow series of bungalows under 1 km from the hullabaloo of the beach. Not grandiose but happening: it has both a snooker table and a frangipani-fringed pool.

B Hotel Bougainvillea/Granpa's, Gaumwadi, T0832-2273270, www.goacom.com/hotels/granpas. Granpa Faria had a rather fine house for a postal worker. Lucindo and Betina no longer live on site, but the family portraits still stand proud on the wall of their 19th century manor. A billiard table stands off an airy reception hall and all rooms are set around a garden of some sort. TVs, fridges and phones are in most rooms. Stays open over monsoon. More likely to attract TV crews and yogis than the party crowd. Recommended.

C Yoga Magic, Chinvar, T0832-3565717, www.yogamagic.co.uk. A walk along from the Purple Valley drop-in centre at Hotel Bougainvillea gets you to just 7 tents under an awning of coconut trees. As well as providing every comfort imaginable and playing great music, its British owner has meticulously planned a system of solar lighting, heating and even composting to minimize environmental harm. A strong, but not evangelical, yogic philosophy prevails. Residents eat communally to create a beautifully calm, welcoming space. Special and highly recommended.

C The Tamarind, Kumar Vaddo, T0832-2274319 www.thetamarind.com. 22 rooms with flagstone floors and balconies in stone-built Portuguese-style house set in landscaped gardens with swimming pool 3 km inland from Anjuna. Courtesy bus service to beaches.

C-D Don Joao Resorts, Sorranto, T0832-2274325, luzco@sancharnet.in. 48 large rooms with balcony and fridge, some a/c, restaurant, exchange, small pool, friendly, away from beach.

D Anjuna Beach Resort, DeMello Vaddo, opposite Albuquerque Mansion, T0832-2274433. 14 rooms with bath, balcony, breakfast, snacks, bike hire, friendly, secure, quiet.

D Palacete Rodrigues, Mazal Vaddo, T0832-2273358, www.palacete rodrigues.com. Another chance to sleep in a little bit of history: the Palacete is a lovely living relic from the Portuguese era. Many rooms have wooden 4-poster beds inside and give onto verandas. A family house away from the beach.

D White Negro, near St Anthony's Church, T0832-2273326 mjanets@goatelecom.com. 14 rooms with nets, good restaurant and bar, very clean.

D-E Lolita's, by Oxford Stores, Monteiro Vaddo, T0832-2273289. 5 spacious, clean rooms with fridge and music system (own tapes), some with TV and a/c, friendly, secure.

D-E Martha's Breakfast Home, Monteiro Vaddo, T0832-2273365, mpd8650@hotmail.com. 8 clean, spacious rooms in separate block plus a couple of 2-bedroomed cottages, good brunch, waffles, crêpes. Small garden, quiet (except on Wed), friendly, well run.

D-E Red Cab Inn, De Mello Vaddo, T0832-2274427, redcabinn@rediffmail.com, 5-min walk from Starco crossroads. 4 newly-decorated rooms in old house, high ceilings, nice and cool, plus a room on the roof, good for long stay, plus a bright red cottage in the garden. Very clean and neat, own fresh water well, good evening restaurant. 15 mins walk from the beach.

Siolim

A Siolim House, Vaddy, opposite Vaddy Chapel, T0832-2272138, www.siolimhouse.com. This beautiful restoration of a 2-storey 300-year-old house once owned by the governor of Macau has 7 large, simply furnished suites. All walls are original, thus deciding the size of bedrooms and giving some giant bathrooms. Good Goan food, pool, gardens, video library: evocative of a past era. Strongly recommended.

Vagator *p116, map p117*

The village is quite spread out and most accommodation is hidden away down wooded lanes away from the beaches.

B Leoney Resort, T0832-2273634, www.leoneyresort.com. 13 rooms, 3 cottages, a/c extra Rs 400. Clean, modern, family run, low-key, quiet location, pool, 10 min walk from beach.

B-C Royal Resort, 500 m from beach, T0832-2274365. 28 rooms, 10 a/c (overpriced), new management, restaurant, jazz bar, pool.

D Bethany Inn, opposite Mango Tree, T0832-2273973, bethany@goatelecom.com. 7 clean, comfortable modern rooms with bath (some 4-bedded), central village location.

D-E Dolrina, T0832-2273382. 13 rooms, most baths shared between 2 rooms, newer rooms best, safe, secure, friendly.

E Abu John's, 6 small rooms with bath, good restaurant, garden, pleasant, quiet.

E Hilltop Motel, away from the beach, T0832-2273665. 14 small rooms, those with bath reasonable, popular late night venue.

E-F Garden Villa, T0832-2273571. 8 clean rooms, some with bath, restaurant with a decent choice.

Chapora *p117, map p117*

Caters mainly for long-term budget travellers.

F Noble Nest, opposite the Holy Cross Chapel, T0832-2274335. 21 rooms, 2 with bath but ample facilities for sharing, basic, but popular, exchange and internet.

⊘ Eating

Anjuna *p114, map p114*

$$$ Xavier's, Praias de San Miguel (follow signs from behind small chapel near flea market site; bring a torch at night), T0832-2273402. One of the veryfirst restaurants for foreigners has grown into a smart restaurant with 3 separate kitchens (Indian/Chinese/continental) excellent fresh seafood, tucked away under palm trees.

$$ Ramesh. Traditional family restaurant that's been running as long as Xavier's; particularly good for fish.

$ Bean Me Up, 875 2 Soranto, T0832-2273977, www.travelingoa.com/beanmeup. Open Sun-Fri 1200-1600, 1900-2300. Brilliant, world-standard soya station and salad bar with queues round the block as testimony to its tastiness. Vegetables come from its organic Osho Garden. Also does take away.

$ The Jam Connection, opposite Tin Tin in Tibet, nice garden for treats and cakes.

$ Munche's, De Mello Vaddo, 24-hr cafe next to Oxford Arcade on Vagator Rd. In peak season, an informal assembly point before heading off to parties, an 'in' place.

$ Yoga Magic Chinvar, T0832-3565717, www.yogamagic.net. Extraordinarily good home-cooked, health-conscious South Indian vegetarian supper served at this immaculately kept, eco-aware Rajasthani tent village. Meals are eaten communally in the middle of paddy fields and are prepared fresh chiefly for residents so visitors need to book before 1300 for the same evening.

$ Zooris, next to Paradiso, rather grand views of the sea and excellent Israeli eats. Owner has a sideline in making shoes.

Vagator *p116, map p117*

Several restaurants line the streets to the beach. Some serve good fresh fish including **Mahalaxmi**. **Primrose Café** serves tasty health foods and also hosts spontaneous parties.

$$ The Alcove on the cliff above Little Vagator. Smartish, ideal position, excellent food, pleasant ambience in the evening, sometimes live music.

$$ Bluebird, T0832-2273695, quietly placed, en route to Ozran, does real French food (inventive menu), to be washed down with pricey French wines; one of the best here.

$$ Mango Tree, in the village, offers a wide choice of continental favourites.

$$ My Place. Father-son act knocking out fresh gnocchi and ravioli. The kitchen is world class and it's unlikely its owners will baulk at any number of covers in the fairy-lit garden: they used to cook caterer style for the Osho camp in Pune.

Chapora *p117, map p117*

Scarlet, beside the Banyan in Chapora village, Huddovaddo. Good muesli, ice creams and chilled fruitshakes, the place for a morning 'pick-me-up' after a night on the dance floor.

🎧 Pubs, bars and clubs

Anjuna *p114, map p114*

Curlys at the very far south of Anjuna, a kind of unofficial headquarters of the scene, playing techno and ambient music.

Guru, along the beach, popular, mops up after the flea market.

Paradiso The biggest, looks like a wild Fred Flintstone flight of fancy. Although it advertises itself as a performance art space, it's dyed in the wool techno.

Sonic, by the beach, under the palms on a raised terrace.

Sunset, close to Shore Bar, good raised platform with comfortable sunbeds.

Beach parties

Wed and Fri nights tend to be the main evenings, but there is usually something going on each night during Christmas-New Year period – just ask around (taxi drivers invariably know where). Venues are often recognizable by illuminated trees and luminous wall hangings. It is best to walk there and back in a large group. Politicians have tried to impose a ban or a curb on loud music after 2200. A purpose-built set, 'Jungle Grove', has been created inland, south of Anjuna.

Vagator *p116, map p117*

Nine Bar, Ozran beach. A booming mud-packed bar with huge gargoyle adornments and a manic neon man carved out of the fountain. Great sound system and majestic sunset views.

Club Merc, close to Vagator beach, turns into a party venue.

🛍 Shopping

Anjuna *p114, map p114*

Flea Market, Wed, attracts hordes of tourists from all over Goa. By mid-morning all approach roads are blocked with taxis, so arrive early.

Natural Health Food Store, Monteirovaddo.
Orchard Stores, Monteirovaddo. Amazing selection catering for western cravings, at a price. Olive oil, pasta, fresh cheese, frozen meats etc.

Oxford Arcade, De Mellovaddo, next to Munche's. Good general store close to the beach.

Oxford Stores, for groceries, foreign exchange and photo processing.

Chapora *p117, map p117*

Narayan, bookstall, sells local newspapers.

⛰ Activities and tours

Anjuna *p114, map p114*
Ayurveda, massage and yoga

As in Calangute, there are a number of yoga teachers who flood in to teach in Goa during the season: look around for signs. You'll also stumble on practitioners of all sorts of alternative therapies: reiki healers, acupuncturists, chakra and even vortex cleansing can all be bought.

Healing Here And Now, The Health Center, St Michael's Vaddo, T0832-2273487, www.healinghereandnow.com. If you want an 'ultimate cleanse' sign up for a 5-day detox: fasting, detoxifying drinks and twice daily enemas. Also offers parasite cleansing, kidney cleanse and wheat grass therapy. Yikes.

Purple Valley, either drop-in at the Hotel Bougainvillea in Anjuna T0832-2981341 or book a residential at the Hillside Retreat Assagao, www.yogagoa.com. Purple Valley attracts the heavy-weight superstars of the ashtanga vinyasa yoga circuit such as the respected John Scott, Madonna's teacher Danny Paradise and there's even talk in hushed deferential tones of 'guruji', Sri Patabhi Jois, jetting in from his *shala* in Mysore. You need to book courses (which include accommodation) at the Hillside Retreat Center in Assagao well in advance but can drop in to the classes (ashtanga/ hatha and meditation/pranayama all offered) in Anjuna at the Hotel Bougainvillea on an ad hoc basis: single classes cost Rs 3,000 for 10, or Rs 400 per session.

Shri Dhanwantari's AyurSampada, church grounds, near Tamarind T0832-2268361, mayura_goa@sancharnet.in. Dr Laxmi Bharne has 4 years of experience in treating specific ailments, gives treatment only after check up, dietary advice, pure herbal treatments. Also offers full body massage, shirodhara, etc.

Bungee jumping
Offered by a Mumbai based firm with US trained staff, at Rs 500 per go. Safety is a priority with harnesses, carabinas and air bags employed. There are pool tables, a bar, an auditorium for slide/film shows and also beach volleyball. Open 1000-1230 and 1730 until late.

Paragliding
Happy Hours Café, south Anjuna beach, from 1230-1400; Rs 500 (children welcome), or at the hilltop between Anjuna and Baga, (and Arambol).

Windsurfing
Boards are sometimes available for hire at the south end of the beach for about Rs 100 per hr.

Tour operators
Speedy near post office Mazalvaddo, T0832-2273208, 0900-1830. Very helpful for all your onward travel arrangements, also a money changer. Very helpful, comprehensive service.

❶ Directory

Anjuna *p114, map p114*
Banks Bank of Baroda, Sorranto Vaddo, Mon-Wed, Fri 0930-1330, Sat 0930-1130, accepts most TCs, Visa/Mastercard, 1% commission (min Rs 50); also provide 'Safe Custody Packets'. There is no bank in Vagator or Chapora. Thomas Cook agent at Oxford Stores, central, quicker and more efficient. **Internet** Space Ride Internet, opposite St Anthony's Church, has high speed connections. In Chapora, **Sonya Travels** near Holy Cross, offers foreign exchange, money transfers, ticketing and internet. **Police** T0832-2273233. **Poste Restante** at post office, open 1000-1600, Mon-Sat; efficient, parcels are also accepted without a fuss. **Medical services** St Michael's Pharmacy, Main Rd, Sorranto, open 24 hrs.

Coastal Pernem → *Colour map 1, grid B1.*

The long bridge that spans the Chapora River and joins Bardez to the last, and so most heavily Hindu, of the new conquests, Pernem, also acts as the gateway to a series of serene, largely empty beaches that hug the coastal road in an almost unbroken strip right up to the border with Maharashtra. No sand in Goa is quite far enough to put it quite beyond the reach of busloads of daytrippers, and the impact the proposed airport in the northeast corner of Pernem would have on these gently uncommercialized beaches cannot be overstated, but so far, if you stay overnight up here, you're pretty sure of snaring yourself at the very least a secluded dawn. Arambol is the most developed of the district's five beaches but it has grown up in too much of a haphazard way for that development to have stopped it being resolutely mellow, meanwhile the overspill of more astute travellers is being gently soaked up by the pristine neighbouring sands of Mandrem and Asvem. ➔ *For Sleeping, Eating and other listings, see page 129-132.*

Ins and outs
Getting there The whole northern district of Pernem can easily be covered in one day's excursion from as far south as Panjim, but it's far better to give yourself a full day in each bay or plant yourself on one beach then go explore the rest. If you are crossing the bridge at Siolim on a motor- or push-bike turn left off the new main road immediately after the bridge to use the smaller, more scenic coastal roads. There are

also regular buses to the villages from Mapusa and from Chopdem. Travelling here, particularly if you are on a bike, is as much fun as arriving: there is truly stunning agricultural landscape, women leaning down to tend to their chilli crop, hoiking up water from wells, the amblings of rural village life, and each of the beaches is within a 20 minute hop of the next. One of the most beautiful stretches of scenery is where the road dips down from a lengthy plateau into the tiny hamlet of Paliem, down dense wooded slopes that turn along the sand-farming banks of the Tiracol to arrive at the ferry to the Fort and Keri beach.

Background
Sandwiched between the Tiracol and Chapora rivers and their estuaries, Pernem was incorporated into Goa in 1788 as the final part of the New Conquests. Before this it was alternately under Hindu and Muslim rule. The Bhonsles of Sawantwadi in modern Maharashtra were the last rulers of this hilly district on the north fringes of Goa before being ousted by the Portuguese, and Maratha influences remain strong here.

Arambol (Harmal) → *Colour map 1, grid A1.*

Arambol, which you reach when the plateau road noses down through paddy fields and cashew trees, is one of the beaches people used to whisper of in hushed tones when damning the deterioration of Anjuna. It's a beautiful long stretch of sand at the bottom of a bumpy dirt track (signposted from the village crossroads beside the bus stop) now fringed with stalls selling brightly coloured, heavily embroidered clothes – halternecks and pretty *lungis* flutter in the breeze – and has attracted longstayers wanting somewhere more *shanti* than Goa's central beaches. Because people have put down roots here, the village is abuzz with industriousness. Bits of A4 paper advertise *satsang* with smiling western gurus: there's also *tabla* teaching, yoga teacher training, reiki, belly-dancing even.

Arambol Beach

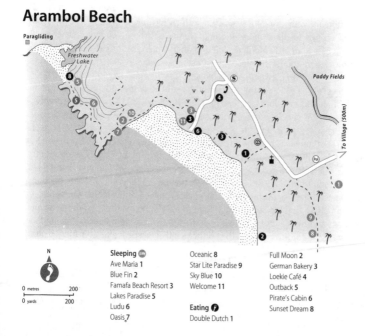

N

0 metres 200
0 yards 200

Sleeping
Ave Maria 1
Blue Fin 2
Famafa Beach Resort 3
Lakes Paradise 5
Ludu 6
Oasis 7

Oceanic 8
Star Lite Paradise 9
Sky Blue 10
Welcome 11

Eating
Double Dutch 1

Full Moon 2
German Bakery 3
Loekie Café 4
Outback 5
Pirate's Cabin 6
Sunset Dream 8

Skirt the beach's northern cliff and tiny basalt rocky bays by foot to reach the real lure: a second bay cut off from the roads and **a natural 'sweet water' lake** that collects at the base of a jungle spring. The lagoon collects just metres from the high tide line where the lush forest crawls down to the water's edge. You can walk up the spring's path to reach a belt of natural mineral clay: an idyllic spot for self-service **mud baths**. Further into the jungle is the famous **banyan tree**, its branches straddling 50 m, which has long been a point of Hindu and hippy pilgrimage. Black-faced monkeys swoop through the upper branches, keeping company with a few feral westerners who live here, occasionally clothed, for months at a time, keeping the cow-dung shrine at the banyan's base immaculate and doing *pooja*. If you are going to make the climb remember it's a temple and so it's right to take off your shoes. The shrine feels a world away from civilization, and it actually is physically far from shops: you might want to take some tea leaves, fruit or rice to leave with those living there.

If you spend some time in the village you may discover the main **village temple**, dedicated to the deity Shri Ravalnath, which also has eight affiliated deities. Arambol is a bit of an anomaly in the New Conquests in having a Christian community and a church.

Morjim (Morji) to Asvem → *Colour map 1, grid B1.*

The most southern of Pernem's beaches, Morjim has two wide sweeping beaches that both sit at the bottom of separate dead end streets. This inaccessibility means that, development-wise, they've got away relatively unscathed. The southern, protected, turtle beach appears at the end of the narrow track that winds along the north bank of the Chapora river mouth. Here grounded fishermen's boats and their heaped nets give way to broad swathes of sand stretching about 5 km north to a natural barrier of rocks. Birds spill over from the upstream sanctuary to dart over the clean, idyllic and still largely undeveloped beach, locals lie in the shade of shacks called names as incongruous as Harry Ramsden's. Loungers, mostly empty, are strewn haphazardly north of the official-looking **Turtle Nesting Control Room**. The wide shoreline with its gentle incline (the water is hip height for about 100 m) washed by easy rolling breakers makes it one of North Goa's best swimming beaches. The northern beach, or **little Morjim**, a left turn off the main coast road, is by comparison an established tourist hamlet with guesthouses and beach huts. Plans for an upmarket hotel complex here with a 'private' beach, which would deny local people free access to a section of the waterfront, have been dropped so this fine stretch of beach should be safe for some time to come. The **Shri Morja Devi Temple complex** in the village is of special interest because one affiliated shrine is dedicated to a Jain guru. This suggests an ancient heritage to the temple, since Jainism was sponsored by both the Chalukyas and the Rashtrakuta dynasties who ruled over the region from the sixth to 10th century AD. The principal festival, the month-long Kalas Utsav, takes place at intervals of three, five and seven years and closes with a large cultural fair.

The road from Morjim cuts inland over the low wooded hills running parallel to the coast through open farmland full of rice, chillies and onions whose harvest supports a few isolated settlements. After a few kilometres the road drops down to the coast and runs along the edge of northeast tilting **Asvem beach**. (Morjim faces Chapora to the south and west). The northern end of this peaceful palm fringed beach is divided by a small river.

● *Unlike the headlands around Anjuna, the rocks that run into the sea here are basalt, the*
● *hexagonal columns tilted almost horizontal but eroded into jagged shapes that are clearly*
visible for miles along the coast.

Mandrem → *Colour map 1, grid B1.*

Mandrem creek forces the road to feed inland where it passes through a small commercial centre with a few shops and a bank. Mandrem village has the **Shri Bhumika Temple** housing an ancient image. In the **Shri Purchevo Ravalnatha Temple** there is a particularly striking medieval image of the half-eagle, half-human Garuda, who acts as the *vahana* (carrier) of Vishnu. It is unusual in that the crouching Garuda is dressed as a soldier with wings protruding from his back.

A little further on, a lane off to the left leads down towards the main beach and a secluded hamlet in a beautifully shaded setting. The **beach** is one of the least developed along this stretch of coast: for the moment it is managing to tread that fine line between having enough facilities for comfort and enough isolation to guarantee idyllic peace. The southern end has the added boon of a river that yields a refreshing lush environment. Further north there is a lagoon fringed by palm trees and some simple rooms, virtually all with sea view. The beach has mercifully yet to draw hawkers, trinket sellers and tourist operators.

The Chapora river → *Colour map 1, grid B1-3.*

The bridge at **Colvale** (Kolvale) remains the lowest crossing point of the Chapora river. The first written record of the village goes back to an inscription dated AD 1011, and the name itself (*Kol*, from Koli, the Konkani name of the local fishing community, and *vale*, meaning 'creek') still describes one of the village's main activities. The area is believed to have come under the influence of Buddhism since a second-century (*Gautama*) Buddha image was found at Mushir near here in the 19th century by a historian, Fr Heras and one of the ancient deities of the village is 'Gauthama'.

Colvale's attractive **Church of St Francis of Assisi**, or Sacred Heart of Jesus Church, was originally built in 1591, and partly destroyed by the Marathas in 1683; the present building dates from 1713. The façade has a rather splendid plaster image of St Francis between two angels, looking down from above, his hands raised in the gesture of blessing. The principal altar inside is dedicated to the Wounds of St Francis. There's a fair on the feast day, September 17.

Dargalim (Dhargal) is 2 km north of Colvale, along the NH17. The **Shri Shantadurga Temple** is invisible from the national highway itself but the road leading 500 m to it is marked by a large yellow and white gateway and is just 200 m from the Konkan Railway line. The temple's main entrance at the east end leads through a romanesque arch into a large rectangular, walled and cloistered enclosure. A typical hexagonal lamp tower, *deepstambha*, stands near the entrance. The *mandapa* (central hall) has a red-tiled floor, pink-painted pillars and a tiled roof interior.

As you approach the shrine you see two small tomb-like enclosures housing two *linga*, opening towards the main shrine. The inner sanctum, which is open to all, has pale wooden doors, and a ceramic wall tiled in white interspersed with blue. The entrance steps are black marble, leading into the immaculate white marble flooring of the shrine room. The image is almost invisible in its ornately worked silver-fronted *garbagriha*. As with the typical inner shrines of Hindu temples, it is cool, pleasant and airy. Worshippers ring one of the bells hanging at the entrance to the shrine to announce their presence to the deity. The annual festival is in December.

The small hamlet of **Parsi** (Parchem, Parshem), 4 km from Chopdem, lies on the road between Agarvaddo and Pernem (6 km away), an attractive route that climbs steadily up on to the barren laterite plateau. The remarkable **Shri Bhagvati Senayan Temple** (rebuilt in the 19th century) has twin *deepstambhas* (lamp towers) in front and five romanesque arches. In addition to the shrine to Bhagvati, Siva's wife, also known as Parvati, there is a rare minor shrine to Brahma. The very elongated head dresses and the impassively smiling faces carved in black stone are a remarkable testament to the art of the seventh century. This image, discovered in the undergrowth near the temple, is worshipped today in one of the subsidiary shrines.

The Portuguese captured the important fort in the northeast corner of the state at **Alorna** from the Bhonsla in 1746. Located on the north bank of the Chapora river, it is now in ruins.

Keri (Querim) and Tiracol Fort → *Colour map 1, grid A1.*

Goa's northernmost beach is uniquely untouched. The drive towards Keri (Querim) along the banks of the Tiracol river from Pernem passes through some stunning rural areas that have been untouched by any tourist developments. One moment the road is lined with tall areca palm and banana plantations, the next, open flood plains are covered with verdant paddy fields. The road then turns inland and climbs up on to a dry plateau before dropping back to sea level by the river mouth and Tiracol Fort (see page 126). Look out for the small barges in the middle of the river collecting sand for all the building work in the *taluka*. Local villagers have exclusive rights to collect the sand and the barges are filled until they are only a few centimetres above the water level.

❖ At the top end of the beach there are strong currents near the estuary mouth so avoid swimming there; a 5-min walk south along the beach will get you to safe waters.

Walk across deep dunes to a casuarina thicket and out onto empty sand that stretches all the way from the mouth of the Tiracol river to the highland that splits it from Arambol. There's just one solitary shack at either end of the beach, both of which can arrange rooms with villagers from Rs 100. Querim is a popular weekend destination for bus-loads of domestic tourists but is not yet riddled with plastic bags and discarded water bottles. You can reach the beach from the north on foot from the Tiracol ferry terminal, or from the south by walking round the headland from Arambol. The Tiracol ferry runs half hourly from 0600 to 2130 taking 15 minutes. If you arrive outside these times you can charter a fishing boat for Rs 55.

Tiracol (Terekhol), at the northernmost tip of Goa, is an enclave of 350 Catholics on the Maharashtra border just 3½ km across where feni production is the biggest business. Its name probably comes from *tir-khol* (meaning steep river bank) and it's a jungly little patch of land full of cashew trees, banyans, orange blossoms, black-faced monkeys and squirrels.

The small but strategic **fort** ① *0900-1800, cross Tiracol river by ferry (half-hourly, 0600-2130) and walk the remaining 2 km. Ferries take cars and motorbikes*, stands above the village on the north side of the Tiracol river estuary on a rugged promontory with amazing views across the water. Its high battlemented walls are clearly visible from the Arambol headland. Built by the Maharaja Khem Sawant Bhonsle in the 17th century, it is protected from attacks from the sea, while the walls on the land side rise from a dry moat. It was captured by the Portuguese Viceroy Dom Pedro Miguel de Almeida (Marques de Alorna) in 1746, who renamed it Holy Trinity and had a chapel built inside (now St Anthony's). Tiracol was only fully and legally incorporated into Goa in 1788. The fort was armed with 22 cannons but saw a bloody massacre in 1835. During a military revolt, a ruthless Commandant, 'Tiger Killer' de Cunha, entered the fort and ordered the beheading of the garrison and civilians who were sheltering there, and went on to exhibit the heads on stakes. Far removed from the centre of administration in Panjim, Tiracol gained a reputation as a spot chosen by Goan freedom fighters to demonstrate their demands from time to time. A group entered the fort on 15 August (Independence Day) 1954 and succeeded in flying the Indian flag there for a day, before being captured and jailed.

Tito's: from hippies hang out to hippodrome

If you head to the built up areas of Calangute or Baga, it'll prove hard to escape the lure of Tito's, a multi-level restaurant/bar/nightclub complex that serves French haute cuisine, Goan curry, house music and cocktails. It's filled with rich and lecherous Bombay filmstars and social climbers who rub shoulders with Goa's new breed of charter tourists in their skimpy skirts and knee-high boots.

The Titos complex started life as a shack on the beach. Tito de Souza came home to Goa in the early seventies to find a growing hippie population hungry for western food. He rented a small house, turned the back room into a kitchen, put some rickety tables and chairs in the front and that was that: Tito's was open for business. The customers, mainly broke American hippies and the occasional British freak, would come to eat, drink, smoke chillums and watch the sun set over Baga Bay.

Tito died in 1985, the same year that the first British charter flight took to the skies introducing a new breed of visitor to Goa: people with more money than the freaks and different taste in drugs. Ecstasy had arrived, Goa trance was born and by the early 90s, Western travellers at Tito's – now run by his sons – were dancing on top of cake cabinets and beer coolers and cartwheeling outside in the sand.

As Tito's, and Goa's, reputation has grown, commercialism has crept in. *Midday*, Bombay's equivalent of the *London Evening Standard*, was the first to hold its launch in the club in 1995. Wealthy Goan socialites who'd shunned the place before because of its grungy reputation as a hippie hang-out stepped out to dance onto the flush new dance floor, the Baga sand buried under tiles. The millennium saw Tito's at the peak of its sassy popularity. Crowds of westerners and Indians churned to international djs, flirted with fire-eaters and knocked back cocktails at a cover charge of Rs 2,000 a head.

Tito's business ambitions have always run neck and neck with Goa's tourism development project and so it's little surprise that the club's original selling point – an unbroken view down to the sea – is today blocked out by its own new constructions. A state-wide ban on amplified music at night has driven those once uninhibited dancers inside into an air-conditioned underground disco and they are more likely to be rich Indian socialites and Bombay types lured to Goa by the promise of bare western midriff than hippies or fortnight charter tourists. Even so David, Tito's youngest son, still gives the odd free meal to a passing hippie. "Goa has had its heyday for Westerners," he says, "but Tito's spirit hasn't gone. There's still sand under these tiles."

St Anthony's Church ① *open on Wed and Sun for Mass at 1730*, inside the tiny fort, was built in the early 1750s soon after the Portuguese takeover. It has a classic Goan façade and is just large enough to cater for the small village. In the small courtyard, paved with laterite blocks, stands a modern statue of Christ. Inside, the church has several charming features. The Festival of St Anthony is held here at the beginning of May (usually on the second Tuesday) instead of on the conventional festival day of 13 June.

You can explore the fort's battlements and tiny circular turrets which scarcely seem to have been intended for the real business of shooting the enemy. The views from the fort looking south to Arambol, Chapora and Fort Aguada are magnificently

Ready for take-off?

Monohar Parrikar, Goa's chief minister, has publicly stated that the airport at Mopa in Pernem would be ready between 2007 and 2009. The state, he said, needed to handle more than the 14 flights accommodated daily at Dabolim. The plans could still be derailed though and have been a source of hot debate in the state. While the airport at Dabolim is "illegally occupied by the Navy", as commentators argue, precious bauxite deposits at Mopa will be lost if the airport deal goes ahead – at a potential loss of thousands of *crores* worth of revenue. Understandably, there are also fears in the southern districts of Goa that Mopa's development would be at their expense: Dabolim is far more central, and there are theories that Maharashtra has lobbied hard for the northern airport to get the green light so that their beaches could benefit from the overspill. All the while, Dabolim looks set to get its own facelift: the Civil Aviation Ministry has lined up an ambitious Rs 150 *crore* project for the airport's expansion.

atmospheric. Steps lead down to a terrace on the south side while the north has an open plateau. From here there is an enjoyable walk down the cliff to some caves; ask in the fort for directions. The fort hires out boats you can charter to Maharashtra's nearby ruined fort at Redi, which has a nice beach, or will ferry you up river to watch birds.

The short drive from Tiracol to the Maharashtrian town of **Shiroda** reveals a wholly different face of India, with a landscape bearing the marks of industrialization, and heavy lorries filling the roads. Yet the industrial plant has done little to spoil the rural peace of the fort itself.

Pernem and the Tiracol river → *Colour map 1, grid A2.*

Ins and outs The bus stand is just below the temple; private buses run to Keri.

Pernem (pronounced *Pedne*), ceded to the Portuguese in 1788, was among the last territories brought under Portuguese control. Today it is a small market town, just south of the Maharashtra border, with three major points of interest. This could all change if the controversial international airport goes ahead as planned.

St Joseph's Church in the heart of the town is a brightly painted white building on a hill with a statue of Christ in its forecourt and a Latin inscription that reads 'Christ reigns over all'. The date, 1864, is written on the central gable and there are two towers, one serving as the belfry. The interior is plain and largely undecorated.

Shri Bhagvati Temple ① *below the church, immediately to its north*, is entered through an ornamental gateway flanked by large dark-stone statues of trumpeting elephants. This temple is 500 years old and has a dark *ashtabhuja* (eight-armed) image of Bhagvati, a terrifying aspect of Siva's consort. Dasara celebrations here attract around 25,000 devotees.

Deshprabhu House ① *about 1 km from the bazaar, on the road that runs north from Pernem to join the NH17*. An arched gateway to a long drive marks the entrance. The great rambling 19th-century mansion belonging to the Deshprabhu family (whose descendants still reside here) has 16 courtyards enclosed by several buildings, which reputedly housed thousands of soldiers when required. Despite remaining Hindu, the influential family, whose members were the local rulers (nicknamed 'Viceroy of no longer open to the public, even by prior arrangement.

Just south of Pernem in Malpem is the small Hindu temple of **Mulvir**. Set in a heavily shaded compound, the low, tile-roofed temple is protected by a large banyan tree at its entrance. The chief feature is the wall paintings illustrating scenes from the Mahabharata. The main story panel, in rather faded, but still clear, colours shows the churning of the ocean of milk and the simple figures of people, animals and gods are charmingly represented. Sadly, the pictures have suffered extensive weathering damage.

⊜ Sleeping

Arambol p123, map p123

Touts meet newcomers at the bus stand, offering rooms close to the main beach for Rs 80-150 (bargain); other places to stay are clustered on a parallel road among trees (so more mosquitoes). Arambol is a budget place: you'll likely need your own sleepsheet, rooms are exposed and lack the security of a hotel compound but often have small metal lockers for valuables. Guest houses higher up on the rocky hills charge more but are poorly maintained and, what's more, there's a whiff of sewage.

D Famafa Beach Resort, Beach Rd, Khalchawada, T0832-2292516, famafa_in@hotmail.com. You don't head for Arambol for its swanky accommodation: Famafa, 25 rooms in an unimaginative development on the right of the stall-studded track down to the beach, is top of the range here. No a/c, but as pukka a hotel as it gets, just Rs 500 in high season.

E Ave Maria, inland, down track opposite police post, Modhlowado, T0832-2297674 One of the originals, offering some of the best accommodation. Simple but nevertheless recommended.

E Luciano Guest Rooms, Cliffside. Family house with toilet and shower: rooms on the cliffside get heavily booked up.

E Ludu, on the cliff path leading to northern beach. Modern block with basic rooms, little peace during the day.

E Oasis, far end of beach. 4 rooms, popular restaurant, bar on the cliff face. Impressive evening views. Look out for the hammock shop up the path at the back.

E Oceanic, inland at south end, T0832-2292296. Secluded guest house with simple rooms, all hidden behind wall in mature gardens, no drugs, popular. Recommended.

E Residensea Beach Huts, Arambol Beach, T0832-2292413, pkresidensea_37@hotmail.com. Basic bamboo shacks set around restaurant all have fans and secure locker facilities (outside toilets). German shepherd keeps watch.

E Star Lite Paradise has a simple compound overlooking a coconut plantation and the beach.

E Welcome, at end of road on seafront, T0832-2297733. Clean rooms, bath with hot water, serves the best muesli, taxi hire.

F Blue Fin, north end of beach. 3 rooms (Rs 150), tucked behind a shop, small courtyard, limited views but more privacy than others nearby.

F Lakes Paradise. Tiny place that also serves Goan curry and rice.

F Sky Blue. 4 small rooms in a cottage, shared veranda, great beach view, usually taken by long-term visitors.

Morjim to Asvem p124

You really need your own motorbike to make the most of staying here.

B The Olive Ridley, Morjim, has a rather lovely two-bedroom house just over the coast road from their restaurant which you can rent out for a pretty hefty Rs 4,000 per night: double beds are set on concrete bases.

C-D Montego Bay Beach Village, Vithaldas Wado, Morjim, T0832-2982753. Rajasthani-style tents pitched in the shade past beach shrubs at the southern end of the beach.

D Palm Grove, Asvem towards Morjim. 6 cottages, fan, in a discreet low-lying stone building with communal veranda (Rs 250), 5 well-built tree houses (Rs 450) close to the beach among casuarinas, plus 2 very basic huts. Communal wash facilities. Recommended for long stays.

North Goa Coastal Pernem Listings

E **Arabian Sea**, Marddivaddo, T0832-2297432. 2 brick cottages and 3 rickety bamboo huts on stilts (overpriced at Rs 300), all set back from the beach, limited sea views, communal wash block, beach restaurant.

E **Silent Cottages**, Marddivaddo. Huts on stilts with much better views.

F **Paradise Cottages**, closer to the main beach, Asvem. Basic rooms with cold showers.

F **Sawne**, Asvem. Tree houses and restaurant, little character.

Mandrem p125

B **Elsewhere Beach House**, T0832-3738757, www.aseascape.com. 3 lovely-looking bedrooms in the understated luxury of a redecorated 19th century house on a sandy spit with the sea on one side and a salt water creek the other. Living, dining room and kitchen are sea-facing, facilities include maid service, day and nightwatchman, stereo: extra for cook. Minimum rent period 1 week at £670. Another of the family's ancestral homes is currently under conversion.

B **Elsewhere Otter Creek Tents**. Under same ownership, 3 luxury Rajasthani tents each with 4-poster beds, hot showers en suite and private jetties and sit outs.

B-C **Villa River Cat**, Junasvaddo, T0832-2247928, www.villarivercat.com. 13 rooms in a 3-tiered round-house overlooking the river and a wade over deep sand dunes from the beach. The whole place is ringed with a belt of shared balconies and comes with big central courtyards that are stuffed with swings, sofas, plantation chairs and daybeds. There's a mosaic spiral staircase and a cavalier approach to colour: it's downbeat creative and popular with musicians and actors – in the best possible way, the poor man's Nilaya. Strongly recommended: booking essential.

C **Mandrem Beach Resort**, Junasvaddo, far end of village from junction with main road, T0832-2297115, http://ashextourism.com/ hotelsresorts/ Goa/MandremBeachResort.htm. 24

rooms in cottages (fan, lockers), river or sea view, good off-season discounts, al fresco restaurant, tranquil setting, friendly team, many repeat guests. Beach to yourself beyond the dunes. Recommended.

E **Dunes Holiday Village**, T0832-2247219, www.travelingoa.com/dunesholidayvillage. Calling itself a Holiday Village may be a bit jumped-up: Dunes has a few simple, although admittedly tiled-roof, shacks across Mandrem's river overlooking the beach, but you'd better like your neighbours because they're built so tight together. Well-kept communal wash facilities and yoga space under coconut palms. Money exchange.

E **Fantasy Guest House**, T0832-2297280. Modern block on the main road (not busy!), but away from the beach.

E **Merrylands Paradise**, T0832-2297446, merrylandsparadise@hotmail.com. Cottages and fragile-looking bamboo tree houses. Right on the lagoon behind the beach.

F **Sea Paradise**, simple bamboo huts on stilts, great location by the lagoon. Along the quiet lane leading off the main road.

F **Village rooms**, usually indicated by signs, rented out to foreigners for up to 6 months through the winter. Ask at one of the stores or the De Souza Pub.

Keri (Querim) and Tiracol fort p126

Around the Christmas, New Year period 3-4 shacks appear at the south end of the beach. Simple snacks are available from kiosks by the ferry at the north end of the beach, or buy mineral water and provisions back in the village.

L **Fort Tiracol Heritage Hotel**, Tiracol, T0832-66227631, nilaya@sancharnet.in. In 2003 the owners of Nilaya took over Fort Tiracol to create isolated, personalised luxury with unbroken views of the Arabian sea. Just 7 exquisite rooms, all with giant en suite, set in the fort walls that surround the Catholic Church which is still used by the 350 villagers of wholly Christian Tiracol for their mass. Goa's most romantic hotel.

E **Hill Rock**, 1 km from the ferry, T0832-2268264. Modern, 7 rooms in a family hotel, restaurant, good location overlooking fort and Keri beach but neglected.

F **Keri Forest Rest House**. The Forest Department's simple resthouse can be booked through the DCF, North Ponda, T0832-2312095.

F **Morning Star**, 4 very basic rooms with common bath (Rs 80).

● Eating

Arambol *p123, map p123*
There are beach cafés all along the main beach and around the headland to the north. A basic eatery in the village serves delicious authentic Goan fish curry and rice for Rs 20. Also doubles up as the village bar.

$ **Double Dutch**, from the beach turn left off the main beach road before Ganesh Stores. Arambol's best coffee shop – its cakes get distributed throughout the village – and is home to the 'bullshit info message board' where you can find information on the *bhajan* and *mantra* singing session group you'd always dreamed of. Excellent tea, coffee, good snacks through the day, imported journals.

$ **Eyes Of Buddha**, Cliffside, Arambol Beach. Long on Arambol's catering scene, Eyes Of Buddha has you well looked after with scrupulously clean avocado salads and an enviable cliffside position looking onto the Arabian sea.

$ **Full Moon**, secluded beach shack at south end. Seafood, drinks throughout the day. Recommended.

$ **German Bakery**, Beach Rd and beachfront, T0832-2292510. Nothing very obviously Teutonic in the management of either of these so-called German bakeries, but they do offer the sweet cakes the German Bakery pseudo-franchise is famous for among travellers the length of India. The beachfront shack is maybe more 'scene', but both are good places to take the pulse of the beach.

$ **Loekie Café** on the main beach approach road. Good varied menu and music in the evening.

$ **Outback**, on the path to second beach. Popular bar on spacious terrace perched above the rocks.

$ **Pirates Cabin**, Indian. Succulent tandoori grills, popular daytime hang-out.

$ **Sunset Dream**, around headland on 2nd beach. Great setting above the beach and rocks. Fruit juices, seafood. NB All 'fresh'

ingredients have to be carried by hand along the path but there's no sign of cool boxes.

Morjim to Asvem *p124*
You're not spoiled for gastronomic choice in Morjim yet: **Hard Rock, Planet Hollywood** and, hilariously enough, **Harry Ramsden's,** are popular shacks on turtle beach and do decent, although average, fresh fish dishes.

$$ **Le Plage**, Asvem T0832-2121712. Gives the impression of being rather a fancy French restaurant what with its Tibetan waiters in their natty black uniforms, plus Le Plage serves lovely things like brochetta. Recommended: also has a range of beautifully designed clothes on sale.

$$ **Olive Ridley**, Vithaldas Vaddo, Morjim, oliveturtle@rediffmail.com. Catch of the day is one of the specials in this leafy restaurant: a seafood platter including chips and salad will set you back Rs 250. Organic salads too. The best on this beach.

$$ **The Other Side**, Morjim. Oddly enough, the Other Side is probably Goa's coolest bar, set in a neat pill box of a house surrounded by banana trees. It wouldn't look out of place in Ibiza but apparently has been slow to get a following here: the bar's well-stocked but it's a case of BYO when it comes to the crowd.

$ **Café Asvem**, at the southern end, perched slightly above the beach.

$ **Rock Bite** close to Café Asvem, is a good place for lunch.

$ **Silent Cottages** will dish up lovely grub laid out on the balconies of their private beach huts.

● Pubs, bars and clubs

Arambol *p123, map p123*
The southern end of Arambol's main beach is the only place to offer any real night life. **Butterfly**, plays house and techno and charges an entrance fee (itself something of a shock here).
Surfclub, T0832-2292484, which is run by an English guy and has rock and live jamming sessions. Both wind down by 2300 to meet Goan laws curbing music played outdoors.

▲ Activities and tours

Arambol *p123, map p123*

21 Coconuts Inn, 2nd restaurant on the left after stepping on to the beach. For dolphin watching trips or boats to Anjuna, Rs 150 for each.

Himalaya Iyengar Yoga Centre
T01892-21312, www.hiyogacentre.com.
Classes conducted on a hard floor shaded by a parachute with breezes from the sea. Tipis are provided for long-term students.
Paragliding can also be arranged from beach shacks.

⊖ Transport

Arambol *p123, map p123p*
Bike and taxi hire from **Welcome Restaurant**.

Bus

There are regular buses from **Mapusa** and a frequent service from **Chopdem**, 12 km along the main road (about 40 mins); the attractive coastal detour via Morjim being slightly longer. It's a 2-hr-walk north through Morjim and Mandrem by the coast. **Delight** and **Tara**, in the village, exchange cash and TCs, good for train tickets (Rs 100 service charge); also sells bus tickets.

Mandrem *p125*
Buses towards **Siolem** pass along the main road at about 0930 and 1345. Direct services also to **Mapusa** and **Panjim**.

Keri (Querim) and Tiracol fort *p126*
From **Panjim** direct bus at 1700, arrives 1930, returns to Panjim 0700 next morning.

● Directory

Arambol *p123, map p123*
Police T0832-2297614. **Post office** The small village post office is at the T junction, 1,500 m from the beach. **Medical services** **Chemists**, on the main road; **Health centre** T0832-2291249.

Mandrem *p125*
Banks Canara Bank, on the main road accepts TCs. **Hospital** T0832-2230081.

Margao and coastal Salcete 136
  Margao (Madgaon) 137
  Colva (Colwa) and around 139
  South of Colva 142
  Listings 144
Cabo de Rama and further south 153
  Cabo de Rama (Cape Rama) 153
  Agonda 154
  Palolem and around 155
  Partagali and around 158
  Listings 159

⚇ Footprint features

Don't miss... 135
Arresting development,
  Canacona style 157
Hot property 138

Introduction

The Southern districts have a wholly different character to those of the north, both in culture and in sand. The Zuari river has long acted not only as a great political and cultural divide between Christian Salcete and Hindu Ponda but also as a much wider economic and cultural marker. Here the landscape is doubly green: the coconut thickets that stretch along the coast are topped up with broad swathes of iridescent paddy, broken only by the whitewash towers of some of Goa's finest churches. Beneath the coconut fronds sit the wealthy villages of fishermen and agriculturalists. Some of the deepest imprints of Portuguese culture were embedded in the landscape and minds of Salcete and in the district's interior are the centuries-old mansion estates of some of those that prospered most under European colonial rule.

Today the region's rising affluence, harnessed much more to mining and agriculture than it is to tourism, has avoided the packaged pop culture of the northern coast. The pace, even of the beach-life, is gentler. While Colva acts as the beach magnet for the people of nearby district capital Margao, elsewhere long stretches of sand lie completely deserted but for fishermen sat crouched over their broken nets with needle and thread. The romantic ruins of the Cabo De Rama fort divide these long beaches from those in the deep south of Canacona taluka – and the unspeakably beautiful beaches at Agonda and Palolem.

★ Don't miss...

1. **Velsao and Betalbatim** The narrow rural lanes are some of the best places to pedal about on a bicycle, page 140.

2. **Cabo De Rama** One of Goa's most dilapidated and atmospheric forts, page 153.

3. **Chartering a fishing boat from Palolem** Escape the mainland and sleep under the stars in sandy solitude on Honeymoon beach, page 155.

4. **Home, Patnem** Candidates for nicest café on the west coast of India, page 155.

5. **Jungle fever** Be swallowed up by the steamy forests in the Cotigao Wildlife Sanctuary, page 158.

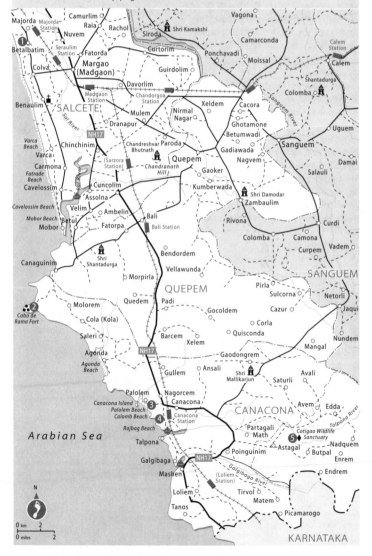

South Goa

Margao and coastal Salcete

→ *Colour map 3, grid A2.*

The lazy sweep of Salcete's tremendously long, wide belt of sand is less distinctive than the north's pockets of coves, embayments, and red cliff-backed beaches. But government regulations have kept almost all the rather snazzy hotels here at arm's length from the sea, and the character of the unbroken wide sand nonetheless varies. The road runs slightly inland for miles along the coast with the occasional spur leading down to the different sections of beach. Some, like Varca and Cavelossim, are little more than an empty stretch of dune-edged sand and an isolated fishing hamlet. In contrast, Colva's tall coconut palms spill over the beach, shading restaurants and a cluster of hotels and shops. Goa's most luxurious beach resorts are spread along this coastal zone.

The southern capital of Margao has falling-down dust-covered colonial houses being used as godowns and ugly concrete flyovers to measure against their misused elegance. It's richer, more haughty and both more brahminical and more austerely Catholic than the north. The elite landowners from the villages of south Goa are known for their high culture, the grace of their lifestyles and their Europeanization: if you can tear yourself from the beaches for long enough you can visit some of their quite literally palatial ancestral homes in the interior. ➤➤ *For Sleeping, Eating and other listings, see pages 144-152.*

Southern beaches

Ins and outs

Getting there The Konkan Railway connects Margao directly with Mumbai, Mangalore and Kerala. Madgaon/Margao station is 1.5 km southeast of the bus stands, municipal gardens and market area (where you'll find most of the hotels and restaurants). Rickshaws charge Rs 15 to transfer while locals walk the 800 m along the railway line. Interstate buses and those running between here and North Goa use the New Kadamba (State) bus stand 2 km north of town. City buses take you to the town bus stands for destinations south of Margao. Colva and Benaulim buses leave from the local stand east of the gardens. There are plenty of auto-rickshaws and eight-seater van taxis for hire in addition to city buses.

Margao (Madgaon) → *Colour map 3, grid A2.*

If you're travelling to Goa on the Konkan Railway, Margao may well be your first taste of Goa, but most people hotfoot it for the beaches, using Margao for an overnight stop only if they have to. This means that tourism has had little impact on what is Goa's largest commercial centre after Panjim and the capital of the state's richest and most fertile *taluka*, Salcete. You can still see examples of old Portuguese domestic architecture and fine churches against the backdrop of a fetching, bustling market town going about its everyday business. Pleasantly provincial, it was given the status of a *vila* (town) by royal decree in 1778. ⤷ *For Sleeping, Eating and other listings, see pages 144-152.*

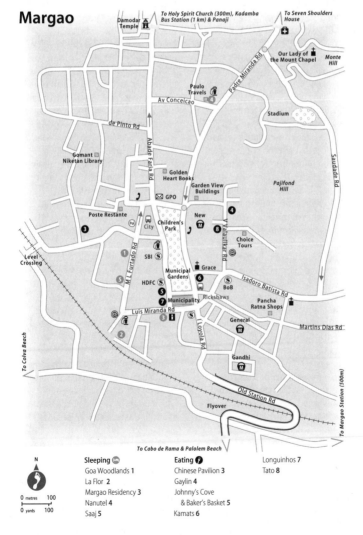

Margao

South Goa Margao & coastal Salcete

Sleeping 🛏
Goa Woodlands **1**
La Flor **2**
Margao Residency **3**
Nanutel **4**
Saaj **5**

Eating 🍴
Chinese Pavilion **3**
Gaylin **4**
Johnny's Cove
 & Baker's Basket **5**
Kamats **6**

Longuinhos **7**
Tato **8**

N

0 metres   100
0 yards   100

Hot property

There are a huge number of beautiful sweeping Portuguese-style houses – big porches, bright white lime shell walls, window-panes of oyster shell and red tile roofs – crumbling into disrepair all across Goa. They have fuelled many a fantasy of renting, or even buying, in the state, particularly when they carry a price tag of as little as £150 per month for a six bedroom place. This is easier in Goa than elsewhere in India after years of hippy and freak 'long-stayers' blazing the legal trail.

But while there are modern condos ranged round swimming pools where this whole process has been simplified, bear in mind that the more romantic dream of having your own 100 year old house carries a far higher investment in terms of both time and money.

If you plan on staying for a short spell (rather than an entire season) house-hunting is probably daft, unless you're lucky. The Goan property market is developing fast, but it's still a long way off the professionalism of the gite system in France or self-catering set-ups in the Med.

What's more, it's seldom that you'll find Goans actively hoping for their homes to fall into foreign hands. So, any house on the market will likely be vacant because children, emigrant or living elsewhere in the state, are squabbling about how best to divest themselves of the brick and mortar inheritance of their parents' ancestral homes.

There are other problems. One missing roof tile opens these old houses to a violent monsoon beating. Mud and lime walls dissolve quickly, wood rots and takes in termites, and shortly the wildlife (animal and vegetable) starts moving in. Firangi (foreigners) are convenient human agents to stem the tide of decay while the owner's family wrangles its way through lengthy court cases.

This means that, unless you're happy living in a scuzzy student-style atmosphere, on your shopping list on day one will probably be a fridge, gas stove, pots and pans, beds, mattresses, sofas, water filter system and, importantly if you have possessions you'd worry about losing, some form of security. Landlords, fingers often burned, will ask for a steep deposit for things like telephones (up to Rs 5,000), and you'll have to sign a short-term lease agreement. All of the above of course comes far cheaper than in England, Australia or America, but you could easily cough up £1,000 initially.

There are agents that are springing up to act as intermediaries in what is still a largely amateurish and deregulated industry, but you will pay pretty high charges to avoid the headache of having to handle all of this yourself. The best of these is probably the slick Homes & Estates, which also publishes a quarterly magazine, head office in Parra-Tinto, Bardez, T0832 2472338, www.homesgoa.com. They charge Rs 300 per house viewing. In 2004 they had four bedroom houses in Calangute with beach views for a monthly rent of Rs 20,000 with 3 to 6 month deposit. Also on their books was a two-bed house in Vagator, with garden, for a song at £64,000. Inland, in Assagao, this price falls to as little as £37,000.

The impressive Baroque **Church of the Holy Spirit** with its classic Goan façade dominates the Old Market square, the Largo de Igreja. Originally built in 1564, it was sacked by Muslims in 1589 and rebuilt in 1675. A remarkable pulpit on the north wall has carvings of the Apostles. There are also some glass cabinets in the north aisle

containing statues of St Anthony and of the Blessed Joseph Vaz. Vaz was Goa's
homegrown Catholic missionary who smuggled himself to Sri Lanka dressed as a
coolie when the Dutch occupation threatened the faith of the
Ceylonese. In the square there is a monumental cross with a
mango tree beside it. The church's feast day is in June.

> **❖** *Guesthouse owners with vacancies (rather than touts) meet new arrivals at the bus stand.*

The real gem of Margao is the glut of run-down
18th-century houses particularly in and around Abade Faria
Road. The **da Silva House** ⓘ *Da Silva's descendants continue to live in a small wing of the house and rarely give permission to enter: requests are fielded by the local tourist office at the GTDC Residency*, is a fine example of this regal type of town house. It was built around 1790, when Inacio da Silva stepped up to become Secretary to the Viceroy, and has a long façade whose roof was once divided into seven separate cropped 'towers' – hence its other name, **Seven Shoulders** - only three of these have survived. The house's grandeur is borne through in its interiors too: lavishly carved dark rosewood furniture, gilded mirrors and fine chandeliers. The first floor reception rooms that face the street are lit by large windows made of wood and oystershell that are themselves protected by wrought iron balconies.

Colva (Colwa) and around

Ins and outs From the airport, taxis charge about Rs 280. Those arriving by train at Margao, 6 km away, can choose between buses, auto-rickshaws and taxis for transfer. Buses pull in at the main crossroads and then proceed down to the beach about a kilometre away before turning around. Auto-rickshaws claim to have a Rs 30 "minimum charge" around Colva itself.

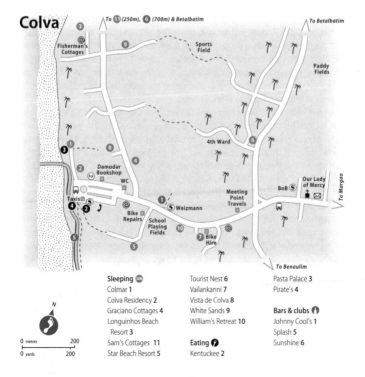

Colva

Sleeping 🛏
Colmar 1
Colva Residency 2
Graciano Cottages 4
Longuinhos Beach
  Resort 3
Sam's Cottages 11
Star Beach Resort 5

Tourist Nest 6
Vailankanni 7
Vista de Colva 8
White Sands 9
William's Retreat 10

Eating 🍴
Kentuckee 2

Pasta Palace 3
Pirate's 4

Bars & clubs 🍸
Johnny Cool's 1
Splash 5
Sunshine 6

0 metres 200
0 yards 200

Colva, the tourist hub of the southern beaches just 6 km from the city, has nothing on the development of its overgrown opposite number in the north, Calangute, which makes it pretty pleasant. The beach was once used as a summer retreat before the monsoon by Margao's elite, who rented the houses of local fishermen, as they moved out to live in their shacks.

The village itself is a bit scruffy, but the beach ticks all the right boxes: the requisite beautiful sands, gentle-swaying palms and blue waters which whip themselves into a broody grey-green when it's rough. There are three rather ugly little concrete crossings over a muddy stream to the beach, where the original dunes have all been removed to give direct access to the sea. During the season the area is lined with trinket stalls and a constant succession of beach vendors. It's popular with domestic tourists and day-trippers who are fond of parachute rides off the back of boats and leave lots of litter in their wake. Entertainment-wise, everything in Colva winds down by 2300 and it's hard to get a cab past midnight so it attracts a more mellow, and maybe a touch more mellowing, type of tourist. You're more likely to get middle-aged holiday-makers here, and live music is more frequent: a saxophonist from UB40 often pops up for an impromptu jam. A new night market (with music) is planned for every Monday and should do something to jazz things up a bit.

> ❖ *The hamlets between Colva and Benaulim retain their rural charm and many families run cheap guesthouses, often much better value than in the northern resorts.*

Refreshingly, this stretch is almost totally devoid of the sunloungers that so clog the Calangute-Candolim swathe of beach. Similarly though you can walk, or bicycle – the south's answer to the Enfield – north or south across miles of uninterrupted, beautiful, pale stiff sand. Teams of fishermen operate all along the coast, from here down to Benaulim further south. They draw their pitch-boarded boats – good for mackerel, squids and sardines – up on the beach and leave trawlers for kingfish, tiger prawns and pomfret anchored offshore. It is worth waking early to watch them haul in their nets. If you are very early you may even be invited out on a boat.

On the road into Colva from Margao you pass the large **Church of Our Lady of Mercy** (Nossa Senhora das Merces, 1630, re-built in the 18th century). The church has a relatively simple façade and a single tower on the south side that it is so short as to be scarcely noticeable, and the strong horizontal lines normally given to Goan churches by three of four full storeys is broken by a narrow band of shallow semi-circular arches above the second floor. However, the church is much less famous for its architecture than for its association with the miraculous **Menino Jesus**. Jesuit Father Bento Ferreira found the original image in the river Sena, Mozambique, en route to Goa, and brought it to Colva where he took up his position as rector in 1648. The image was found to have miraculous healing powers and became an object of special veneration. However, when religious orders were banned in 1834 it was removed to the Rachol Seminary for safekeeping although a diamond ring given as an offering to it was left behind. The church in Colva failed in its attempts to have the statue returned and so installed another figure in 1836 (which is still here today) and put the special ring on it. It was soon found to work miracles, whereas the original statue taken to Rachol ceased to have special powers. The story is celebrated today in the special annual festival, the *Fama of Menino Jesus* (Monday of 12-18 October), when thousands of pilgrims flock to see the statue in the hope of witnessing a miracle. Near the church, specially blessed lengths of string are sold, as well as replicas of limbs, offered to the image in thanks for cures.

Betalbatim to Velsao
Ins and outs The Margao-Vasco bus service also passes through the centre of Cansaulim. From Dabolim airport narrow village roads lead to all of the main resorts in Salcete. For the southern Mormugao beaches of Velsao and Cansaulim, which are no more than 20-30 minutes' drive from the airport, it is quickest to take the shorter route down off the plateau. Taxis take 20 minutes from the airport and under 15 minutes

from Margao. Cansaulim train station on the Vasco-Margao line is convenient for Velsao and Arossim beaches. Majorda station on the same line is convenient for Utorda and Majorda beaches. Auto-rickshaws meet all trains.

Betalbatim, named after the main temple to Betall which stood here before the deity was moved to Queula in Ponda for safety, is a pleasant stretch with a mix of coconut palms and casuarinas on the low dunes that separate the seaside from the resort development. It still retains a rural feel: trinket sellers and taxi ranks do not yet loiter outside every hotel. Colva, and a more upbeat pace of life, is only a short walk to the south along the beach. At low tide, when the firm sand is exposed, it is possible to cycle for miles along the beach in either direction.

The four beaches north, **Velsao**, **Arossim**, **Utorda** and **Majorda** – broad, flat and open – are among the least heavily used of these beaches. Around the resort hotels there are small clusters of beach shack restaurants, and occasional fishing villages scattered under the coconut palms. Northwards up the beach you can see the Mormugao headland when it is not concealed by haze. The only blot on the landscape is the large industrial complex.

Bogmalo, the nearest beach to the airport (4 km, and a 10 minute drive away) is small, palm fringed and attractive, yet seldom visited. The road from the airport forks about 2½ km before reaching Bogmalo. The right fork leads to Bogmalo while the left goes to **Hollant Beach**, 2 km away, a small rocky cove that is fringed with coconut palms. **Santra Beach**, further south, can be reached by going through the village

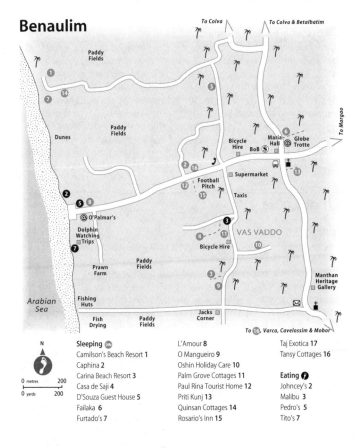

Benaulim

Sleeping
Camilson's Beach Resort 1
Caphina 2
Carina Beach Resort 3
Casa de Saji 4
D'Souza Guest House 5
Failaka 6
Furtado's 7
L'Amour 8
O Mangueiro 9
Oshin Holiday Care 10
Palm Grove Cottages 11
Paul Rina Tourist Home 12
Priti Kunj 13
Quinsan Cottages 14
Rosario's Inn 15
Taj Exotica 17
Tansy Cottages 16

Eating
Johncey's 2
Malibu 3
Pedro's 5
Tito's 7

behind the **Bogmalo Beach Resort**. Local fishermen can ferry passengers to two small islands for about Rs 350 per boat.

One of the distinctive features of this section of coast is the strip of land that lies between the main series of villages and the dunes which actually front the sea, used for intensive rice cultivation. The road runs through these villages, set back 1-2 km from the sea. Old mansions of wealthy families still standing in the villages include **Utorda House**. There are also some fine examples dotted about Velsao, in various states of repair. An afternoon exploring these quiet back lanes by bicycle gives a good window on village life. The villages from here southwards are noted for their high levels of emigration to the Gulf. Some have returned and invested money in the many new hotels.

Cansaulim village centre, just beside Utorda beach has a small selection of shops for basic provisions, cheap restaurants and email facilities.

Verna

Verna (the 'place of fresh air') is inland from the northern Salcete beaches on the NH17. The **church** here was initially built on the site of the Mahalsa Temple before being transferred. According to old Portuguese records the original Mahalsa Temple which housed the deity now in Mardol (see page 168) had some exquisite carvings. It was destroyed and marked by the cross to prevent it being re-used for Hindu worship. Serving as a sanctuary for widows who did not commit *sati* (see page 239), it became known as the 'Temple of Nuns'. Verna is also the place chosen in 1988 for re-siting the ancient 2.5 m **Mother Goddess figure** (fifth century BC) from Curdi (Kurdi) in Sanguem, which was under threat of being submerged by the Selaulim Dam project. Two megalithic sites were found in the area. It is surrounded by seven springs with special healing properties.

Immediately north towards Cortalim are the **Kersarval springs**, which have medicinal properties but are no longer a 'natural' remote watering place. They are very popular with Goans as a picnic spot. From the large car park, paths lead past several enclosures through the gently sloping wooded hillside. The covered resting areas for picnics are near the entrance. The path to the springs leads down a short but steep slope into a vertical walled grotto where bathers can stand under the trickling spring water. There is an extraordinary change in the atmosphere from the hot open plateau to the moist, cooler but lush semi-enclosed area surrounding the springs themselves. There is a small hotel and restaurant at the place where you turn off the NH17.

South of Colva → *Colour map 3, grid A2.*

Benaulim

Benaulim, according to the myth of Parasurama on the creation of Goa, is 'where the arrow fell'. Today it is the more tranquil and pleasant southern end of Colva beach, but during the season its approach road gets very busy and some complain of plagues of fruit and jewellery hawkers. It's easy to escape their advances by hiring a bike and peddling a little way south along the beach. Take the inland route for a walk or bike ride through the 4 km of idyllic countryside to Colva. Buses from all directions arrive at the hub of all the village activity at Maria Hall crossing, just over a kilometre from the beach. Autos and taxis wait at the crossing and at the end of the beach road.

The small **Church of St John the Baptist**, on a hill beyond the village, rebuilt 1596, is a superb example of Goan Christian architecture. The twin towers are surmounted by shallow domes while the typical scrolls are flanked by crosses. Although the gable façade is striking, the chief beauties of the church are inside. The magnificent altar reredos is uniquely decorated, and there is a wonderful rococo pulpit surmounted by a representation of the Lamb of the Apocalypse from across a river, painted in the nave opposite the baptistry. Fr Joseph Vaz, a mystic evangelist born in Benaulim, was baptised in the font here in 1651. After dedicating his life to the poor and downtrodden, Vaz died a missionary to Ceylon (Sri Lanka) where he preached for 24 years. See also Festivals and events, page 150. The village was noted for producing carved wooden furniture.

Varca to Mobor

The narrow and attractive road south from Benaulim runs about 1 km inland from the sea through small villages, some with superb white-painted churches. Paddy fields and palm groves alternate, and periodically roads run down to the sea, sometimes to small settlements, sometimes to deserted beaches. Benaulim beach runs into Varca, and then Fatrade. To reach **Cavelossim beach** involves a short walk through scrub vegetation and dunes.

Farthest south, **Mobor**, about 8 km from Varca, lies on the narrow peninsula where the river Sal joins the sea. Access to the beach near the river is somewhat restricted by the sprawling **Leela Palace** hotel complex. The Sal is a busy river and harbour for fishing boats, but it is also very pleasant place for boat rides. Over the last couple of years there seems to have been a non-stop building campaign in Cavelossim and this relatively quiet backwater has lost some of its charm to the boom. However, the development is still nothing like what has occurred on the north coast. It is well worth walking to the

Varca to Betul

To Benaulim · *To Margao* · Varca · Varca Beach · Orlim · *To Palolem* · Chinchinim · Fatrade Beach · Carmona · Cavelossim · Assolna · *River Sal* · *To NH17* · Betty's Place · *Fish Port* · Velim · Mobor Beach · *Arabian Sea* · Betul · Tarrie · *To Cabo de Rama*

N

0 km 1
0 miles 1

Sleeping
Club Mahindra **1**
Dona Sa Maria **2**
Dona Sylvia Resort **3**
Gaffino's & Hippo
   Cool **4**
Goa Renaissance
   Resort **5**
José Holiday Home **6**
Leela Palace **7**
Mobor Beach Resort **8**
Octima **9**
Resorte de Goa **10**
River Sal **11**
Sao Domingos **12**
Taj Exotica **13**

Eating
Grill Room **1**
Jazz Inn **2**
Mike's Place **3**
River View **4**

The large shopping mall opposite the Dona Sylvia houses a mix of shops, restaurants and travel agents. At present the only buses roaring past the resorts are public services from Margao.

Sal river estuary where a clean spur of sand dividing the river from the sea allows you to enjoy peaceful sunbathing. Be wary of the variable currents close to the river mouth though as the tide turns. The beaches here are quieter and cleaner than Colva: no rocks, mosquitoes or flies, little rubbish and occasional local day trippers. A bit exposed on windy days and with limited shade they are still good spots with good swimming.h

The **Nossa Senhora da Gloria Church** at Varca (1700), a short way north of the village, has a particularly striking façade, making use of a fan-like central feature based on the conch shell to give an effect of radiating light. Its twin towers are topped by semi-domes, but doors on the ground floor and the windows on its two upper storeys are romanesque. Cavelossim's small and relatively simple **Santa Cruz Church** (1763) has a highly decorated altarpiece, the gold leaf being set against a turquoise painted romanesque arch.

Ins and outs From Cavelossim the shortest route to Betul is by taking the ferry across the Sal (signposted, just southeast) to Assolna; turn left off the ferry, then turn right in the village to join the main road towards Betul. From Margao, the NH17 forks right (6 km) towards Assolna at Chinchinim. A further 6 km on, there is a second turning in Cuncolim for Assolna. Buses from Margao to Betul can be very slow, but there is a fairly regular service stopping in all the settlements along the way (a couple of them continue as far as Cabo de Rama). Confirm the route when boarding the bus in Margao.

Betul, which overlooks Mobor from the opposite bank of the Sal in Quepem taluka, is an important fishing village in an idyllic setting, delightfully shaded by coconut palms, jackfruit, papaya and banana. Just after the bridge, which crosses the mouth of a small river, a narrow road off to the right by the shops (some buses turn around here), zigzags through the village along the south side of the Sal. The village is dependent on fishing and coir production. A sand bar traps the estuary into a wide and protected lagoon. Cool breezes from the sea moderate the temperatures of the plateau above so that even in the hottest season it is perfectly bearable. A walk along the 'jetty' past dozens of many-coloured fishing boats will reveal busy fisherfolk loading fish into baskets and catches of tiny silvery fish glistening in the sun trapped under nets spread out on the bank. Walk on past the rusty iron ore conveyor belt and around the headland and you will find an isolated spot to pass an afternoon on the beach.

Cuncolim

Cuncolim saw the destruction of its three principal Hindu temples (including the Shantadurga), when the Jesuits were christianizing the area and later building churches and chapels on the sites.

Cuncolim is one of the few places in the area to have a petrol station.

Cuncolim was also the scene of the massacre of five Jesuits and several converts by local Hindu 'rebels' who had been incensed by the repeated destruction of temples and defilement of temple tanks. Most of them were subsequently captured by the captain of Rachol fort and 15 were killed by his soldiers. The Christian 'martyrs of Cuncolim' were initially buried in Rachol but were transferred to Old Goa where their relics are lodged in the Sé Cathedral. The golden bell, which is the largest in Goa, and which hangs in the remaining single tower of the Sé Cathedral, was cast here in 1652. ▶▶ *See also Festivals and events, page 150.*

Fatorpa

Fatorpa is no more than a tiny hamlet on the road from Bali to Cabo de Rama. Leaving the NH17 in Bali the road runs to a junction at Fatorpa, dropping down to the **Shri Shantadurga Temple**, partially concealed in its shallow valley. There are 14 affiliated deities. The image of Shantadurga, originally from Cuncolim in Salcete, was brought to Fatorpa (with several others) in 1583. The modern concrete temple has no trace of the original structure, although the deity is still lodged in her sanctuary behind a silver screen. ▶▶ *See also Festivals and events, page 150.*

🛏 Sleeping

Margao *p137 and map p137*
C **Nanutel**, Padre Miranda Rd, T0832-2733176, www.nanuindia.com. 55 smart rooms, comfortable business hotel, good food, nice pool but unattractive poolside area, bookshop.

D **Margao Residency** (GTDC), Luis Miranda Rd, T0832-2715528. 67 acceptable rooms in 6-storey building so some have good view over the city, a/c better, others are cramped, simple restaurant (good vegetable vindaloo), tourist information, travel desk.
D-E **Goa Woodlands**, ML Furtado Rd, opposite City Bus Stand, T0832-2715521,

woodland_goa@sancharnet.in. 35 rooms, 18 a/c, clean and spacious with bath, restaurant, bar, good value.

D-E Saaj, ML Furtado Rd (near the telephone exchange), T0832-2711757. 29 rooms, TV, basic singles, good options for 4-person rooms, restaurant, bar, near City bus stand, 24 hr check-out.

E La Flor, E Carvalho St, T0832-2731402, laflor@sancharnet.in. 35 rooms with bath, half a/c, restaurant, clean, on a side street away from the bustle of town.

E-F Railway Retiring Rooms, Margao Junction, 1st flr. 7 rooms (4 a/c), dorm beds.

Colva and around *p139*
Colva

Most hotels are 6-8 km from Margao railway station. Prices rise on 1 Dec. Discounts are possible for stays of a week or more.

B Vista de Colva, 4th Ward, T0832-2788144, colmar@satyam.net.in. 25 large a/c studio rooms, restaurant/bar with Goan specialities, small fish-shaped pool in an exposed paved area (non-residents pay Rs 50), live entertainment, very comfortable.

B-C Longuinhos Beach Resort, 1 km from 'Colva circle', T0832-2788068, lbresort@goatelecom.com. 52 clean rooms with balcony (nice views of local fishing fleet), 6 a/c (no TV) in an uninspiring modern block, but good location right on the beach, restaurant, pool, well-kept garden with hammocks, boutique.

B-C William's Retreat, 500 m from beach, T0832-2788153, www.goagetaway.com. 36 clean rooms, some a/c, restaurant, large pool (non-residents Rs 50), tennis, friendly, good value but tired.

C-D Star Beach Resort, just off Colva Beach Rd, T0832-2734921, www.starbeachresort goa.com. 41 large rooms, TV, some a/c, good value from mid-Jan (Rs 600), clean pool, children's pool, best rooms 1st floor poolside currently have uninterrupted views across paddy fields, restaurant.

D Colmar, on the beach (just beyond Colva Residency), T0832-2788043, atsfernandes@ colmarbeachresort.com. 127 rooms, dearer than similar in area but popular, restaurant (see below), travel desk, motorbike hire, bus to Anjuna flea market (Rs 95), exchange. Long-term fixture in Colva.

D Colva Residency (GTDC), by the beach, T0832-2788047. 47 pleasant, clean rooms (14 a/c), in 2-storey building or cottages, ugly complex but looks better after recent refurbishment, good restaurant, bar, garden, secure, popular with domestic tourists.

D Graciano Cottages, 4th Ward, within walking distance of bars and restaurants, T0832-2788787, gracianogoa@ rediffmail. com. 20 rooms (no cottages), upstairs with bath (a/c Rs 100 extra), seating areas a little exposed to passing traffic, pool planned, recent makeover and upgrade of facilities.

E Tourist Nest, 2 km from the sea, T0832-2788624, touristnest@indiatimes.com. Old Portuguese house, 12 rooms in secure new block, fan, Rs 200 with bathroom, 2 small self-contained cottages, good restaurant. Old part of house recommended for atmospheric long stay (Rs 8,000 per month for 2 bedrooms), spacious dining area, large lounge with antique furniture, private balcony, bathroom and cooking facilities.

E Vailankanni, H No 414/2, 4th Ward, near the crossroads, 500 m from beach, T0832-2788584, valiancottages@ rediffmail.com. 10 basic, clean rooms, 5 a/c flats, bath, TV, friendly, family-run, good-value restaurant.

F Maria Guest House, 4th Ward, near beach cafés. 7 rooms, some with bath, very friendly, helpful, car hire, popular with backpackers, good value. Recommended.

F Sam's Cottages, 3rd Ward, T0832-2788753. 16 good-sized clean rooms set around quiet garden courtyard, good value, restaurant, set back from beach.

F White Sands, H No 470, 4th Ward, T0832-2788080, set back from road. 8 clean comfortable rooms with mosquito nets (Rs 300 with fridge), friendly family-run guest house. Short walk to beach across the dunes.

Betalbatim

B Coconut Grove, Ranwaddo, T0832-2880123 www.goacom.com/ hotels/coconutgrove. New development beyond Alagoa Guest House. 36 clean a/c rooms with tasteful colour schemes and original pictures, all with small bath, TV, mini bar, 2 cottages, small gardens lead down to a pool area and 1st flr restaurant (see Eating). Short walk to the beach, peaceful setting.

B Nanu Resort, near the beach and paddy fields, T0832-2880111, www.nanuindia.com. 72 comfortable and spacious a/c rooms in 3-star, 2-storey 'chalet' complex, refurbished restaurant arranged in a neat terrace with sea views. Imaginatively planned, good pool with great beach views, garden, beach beyond a narrow stream, tennis, badminton, secluded and peaceful. Very good value from 1 May-30 Sep. Recommended.

D Alagoa Guest House, Ranvaddo, T0832-2880211. 12 very basic scruffy rooms, pleasant location surrounded by paddy fields, quiet.

D-E Manuelina Tourist House, behind Ray's. 5 spacious, clean rooms with bath, TV lounge, some food available, pleasant, secure, quiet. Recommended.

E Baptista, Beach Rd. 2 simple rooms with fan, 2 self catering flats with gas stove, use of fridge and utensils (Rs 350), good for long stays, short walk from beach.

E Ray's, Beach Rd, T0832-2880140. 3 clean upstairs rooms in family home, some a/c, use of kitchen, scooter hire.

Velsao

C Horizon Beach Resort, Aldeia Dona Lira, T0832-2754923, www.horizonbeach resort.com. 20 clean rooms in 2-storey blocks (most a/c), all with lounge area, pantry, mini bar, TV, balcony. Lots of character. Pool, restaurant, gardens. 5 mins' walk to an empty beach without having to brave taxi drivers and hawkers. Recommended if you want a quiet self-contained holiday.

Bogmalo

AL-A Bogmalo Beach Resort, T0832-2556222, www.bogmalo.com. 121 compact rooms with sea view (4th and 5th floors refurbished), restaurants, casino, pool, ayurvedic centre, no beach access, cycle hire.

A-B Coconut Creek, T0832-2538100 joets@sancharnet.in. 20 rooms (10 a/c) in 2-storey cottages, light and airy, pool, full of character, exemplary hotel with rotating theme nights, best in the area.

C-D Saritas, T0832-2555965, saritasguesthouse@rediffmail.com, near bus stand and beach. 13 rooms with bath, some a/c, restaurant.

D Joet's Guest House, right on the beach, T0832-2538036, joets@goatelecom.com. 12 small airy rooms with shower, excellent restaurant. Bar loans out huge stock of well-thumbed bestsellers to guests.

Arossim

LL Hyatt Regency Goa Resort and Spa, T0832-2721234, www.parkhyatt.com. 251 rooms, beachfront gardens, Sereno ayurvedic spa, restaurants, premium hotel.

A Heritage Village Club, at the northern end of the beach, T0832-2754311, www.select hotels.co.in. 3 star hotel with 2-storey blocks, 100 rooms. Good-size pool, health club, tennis, bullock cart rides, friendly and helpful staff, short walk to a deserted beach.

Utorda

AL Kenilworth Beach Resort, on a quiet stretch of white-sand beach 10 mins' walk north of Majorda, T0832-2754180, www.kenilworthhotels.com. 91 a/c rooms, 3 suites, dull design, rooms feel slightly on top of each other, health club, mini golf, tennis, library. The pool (the hotel's best feature) is reputed to be the largest in Goa, with plenty of quiet corners around the imaginative design. Slightly shabby feel.

Majorda

AL Majorda Beach Resort, 2 mins' walk from the beach, T0832-2881111, www.majordabeachresort.com. 120 rooms, 10 village suites, 10 cottages, 3 restaurants, pools, tennis, designed on a grand scale but with a barn-like public area, lush gardens. Quoted rates rather over-priced.

D Shalom Guest House, modern building on the corner of the road leading to the beach, T0832-2881016 (after 1800), shalome81 @satyam.net.in. 1 large family flat for 4 people, with cooking facilities, excellent value.

D Shangrila, Beach St, T0832-2881135, www.shangrilagoa.com. 12 reasonable rooms, some a/c, very dull, but fine for a budget option.

South of Colva *p142*
Benaulim

Budget hotels can be found along Benaulim Beach Rd, and in the coconut groves on either side. Rooms in private houses and 'garden cottages' go for Rs 80-150; south along the beach from **Johncy's**, rooms just off the beach with bath, are Rs 80-100.

LL Taj Exotica, Calvaddo, towards Varca, T0832-2771234, exoticabc.goa@ tajhotels.com. 56 acres of greenery and views of virgin beaches from each of its 138 luxurious rooms. Good choice of restaurants, including Mediterranean, plus coffee shop, nightclub, excellent pool, golf course, floodlit tennis, kids' activities, jacuzzi, watersports, gym and jogging track, library and bike hire. The Taamra Spa offers treatments like acupuncture, aromatherapy and Balinese massage.

C-D Carina Beach Resort, Tambdi-Mati, T0832-2770413, carinabeachresort @yahoo.com. 34 rooms, newer wing better with solar powered showers, some a/c (extra Rs 150), light and airy with balcony, restaurant, pool, quiet.

C-D L'Amour, end of Beach Rd, T0832-2770404. 20 rooms in a 2-storey block close to the sea, good terrace restaurant, handy for exchange and booking rail and bus tickets. Well-established hotel run by same team as Johncy's beach shack.

C-E Camilson's Beach Resort, Sernabatim, T0832-2771696. 20 simple rooms with bath, comfortable 2-storey villa (Rs 1500), shaded restaurant at the fringe of the beach, email access, away from most of the action.

D Failaka, Adsulim Nagar, near Maria Hall crossing, T0832-2771270, hotelfailaka @hotmail.com. 16 spotless, comfortable rooms (Rs 400), 4 with TV, quieter at rear, excellent restaurant, friendly family set up. Recommended.

D-E Palm Grove Cottages, Vas Vaddo, T0832-2770059, palmgrovecottages @yahoo.com. 14 clean spacious rooms. The newer block at rear with showers and balconies is better. Pleasant palm-shaded garden, good food, not on the beach but plenty of places to hire a bicycle just outside. Recommended.

E Caphina, T0832-2770573, slightly set back midway along Beach Rd. 8 spotless rooms on 2 flrs, no grounds to relax in, friendly and helpful owners (if not in, ask at **Tansy**), good value. Recommended.

E D'Souza Guest House, north of Beach Rd in the village, T0832-2770583. 5 very clean rooms, good food (see below), garden, friendly family. Recommended.

E Oshin Holiday Care, House no. 126, Vas Vaddo, T0832-2770069. 14 good large rooms with bath on 3 floors (room 11 best, Rs 400), breakfast, evening meals on request, friendly manager, excellent well kept grounds, you will need a bicycle to get to the beach but the peaceful location overlooking ponds is well worth it. Highly recommended.

E Paul Rina Tourist Home, in the middle of the activities along Beach Rd, T0832-2770591. 6 large, airy rooms with balcony, beauty parlour, good value.

E Quinsan Cottages, T0832-2771490, quinsancottages@yahoo.com. 7 rooms with cold shower, rooms at rear have views across countryside, no restaurant. Simple 1-storey cottage with a garden. Recommended. Call to see if open during monsoon.

E Rosario's Inn, just off Beach Rd by football pitch, T0832-2770636. 28 rooms, some with bath in a peaceful setting with plenty of mature trees, popular, simple restaurant, cycle/motorbike hire, camping possible.

E Tansy Cottages, Beach Rd, T0832- 2770574. 7 very clean, large rooms with bath, 2 cottages, good restaurant (super breakfast), friendly, good value. Recommended.

E-F O Mangueiro, next to **Carina**, Vas Vaddo, along a quiet lane, 10 mins' walk to beach, T0832-2770408. 5 spartan rooms, 10 newer with bath (Rs 400) next to the family house are much better, very clean, peaceful, safe and friendly. Very conscientious owners.

F Casa de Saji, 5 mins' walk from beach, T0832-2770228. 5 clean rooms, shared bath, those with balcony overlooking fields are better, very quiet.

F Furtado's, T0832-2745474. 6 basic rooms arranged around small garden with palms, in the dunes just above the beach. Popular budget option. Shacks for meals nearby.

F Priti Kunj, south of Maria Hall crossing, T0832-2732431, 15 m off the main road, behind **Caravan GH**. 4 clean, pleasant rooms, 3 with bath, also large 6-bed room in family house, meals to order, helpful owners, no sign in season as usually full with regulars.

Varca

L Club Mahindra, Varca Village, T0832-2744555, www.clubmahindra.com. 51 spotless rooms with tubs, 5 suites, spacious

public areas, excellent pool, gym etc, direct access to quiet beach, bit isolated. Top class.
B Resorte de Goa, T0832-2745066, resorte degoa@yahoo.com. 56 rooms and suites in main building and smaller rooms in colourful cottages, tennis, clean deserted beach with some shade, peaceful but a bit shabby.

Fatrade

AL Goa Renaissance Resort, Fatrade Beach, T0832-2745200, itstimefor@renaissance goa.com. 202 rooms, interesting design, watersports and 9-hole golf, high standards but expensive bland meals and drinks.

Tamborim

D Dona Sa Maria, T0832-2745290, www.donasamaria.com. 16 good-sized, clean rooms in modern colonial style villa with private balcony, 1 km from deserted beach, good food, pool, bike hire, internet, friendly family run, quiet. Recommended.

Cavelossim and Mobor

A-B Dona Sylvia Resort, T0832-2871321, info@donasylvia.com. 176 comfortable spacious cottages ('B' cluster closest to beach and most peaceful), some a/c, set in lush immaculate grounds with a 'village' feel, mainly packages and buffet meals, tennis. Direct path to the beach, 200 m.
C Mobor Beach Resort, T0832-2871167, moborbeachresort@rediffmail.com. 20 well-appointed rooms, fan, balcony, some with view of hills and the sea, restaurant, pool, spacious feel, new, well built, package oriented, aiming for high standards. Also the permanent base for **Cycle Goa**, the bicycle touring company.
C Sao Domingos, quiet lane opposite Dona Sylvia but built-up surrounds, T0832-2871461, www.saodomingosgoa.com. 15 comfortable rooms with fans or a/c and bath, balcony, rooftop breakfast area. Not close to beach.
D Gaffino's, opposite Dona Sylvia, Mobor, 5 mins' walk from beach, T0832-2871441, briangaffino@yahoo.com. 16 clean, simple rooms with bath on 4 flrs, 2 a/c, balconies overlook river or sea (far away), b&b, personal service, package oriented, in the centre of all the action.
D Hippo Cool, next to Gaffino's, T0832-2871201. 6 clean, very comfortable

rooms with fan (a/c on request) and shower, restaurant, 5-min walk from the beach. Recommended.
D Octima, next to Goan Village restaurant, T0832-2871462. 3 simple clean rooms, pleasant 1st floor breakfast balcony, down a quiet lane only a short walk from nightlife but not convenient for beach.
E José Holiday Home, T0832-2871127, fiell@goatelecom.com. 10 good clean rooms with attached bath, some a/c, friendly.

Mobor Beach

LL-AL Leela Palace, Mobor, opposite Betul village, T0832-2871234, www.ghmhotels. com. 137 rooms, luxury villas and pavilions blending eastern and western architecture, golf buggies for transport, top facilities, nightclub, casino, watersports, 9-hole golf, spacious lush grounds, very plush.

Betul

There is no accommodation in the village itself.
D River Sal, Kutbona, Zuem Velim, on the riverbank, T0832-2760276, 18 simple clean rooms (6 a/c), with perfect river views, bit isolated but very peaceful, offers excellent fresh river fish. Boatmen bring holidaymakers from Mobor to eat here in the evening.

🍴 Eating

Margao *p137 and map p137*
$$ **Chinese Pavilion**, M Menezes Rd (400m west of Municipal Gardens). Chinese. Smart, a/c, good choice.
$$ **Gaylin**, 1 V Valaulikar Rd. Chinese. Tasty hot Szechuan, comfortable a/c.
$$ **Longuinhos**, near the Municipality. Goan, North Indian. Open all day for meals and snacks, bar drinks and baked goodies.
$$ **Tato**, G-5 Apna Bazaar, Complex, V Valaulikar Rd. Excellent vegetarian, a/c upstairs.
$$ **Utsav**, Nanutel Hotel. Pleasant, serving a large range of Goan dishes.
$ **Café Margao**. Good South Indian snacks.

Bakery

Baker's Basket and **Johnny's Cove** at Rangavi Complex, west of Municipal Gardens, have Goan sweets including *bebincas*.

Colva

$ **Joe Con's**, 4th Ward. Excellent fresh fish and Goan dishes, good value.

$ **Kentuckee**, good seafood, select from fresh fish brought to table.

$ **Pasta Palace**, overlooking the beach at the Colmar. Good Italian with bar.

$ **Pirate's**, near the beach. Recommended for seafood.

Betalbatim

$$$ **Martin's Corner**, T0832-2131 676, www.martinscorner.com. Coming from the south, look for sign on left after village, 500 m down lane on right, opposite open ground. Accommodates over 200 under cover in front of an old house. Extensive menu, excellent lobster Rs 1500, tiger prawns Rs 500-700, crab Rs 300-500. Recommended.

$$ **Roytanzil Garden Pub**, set back from the beach at end of Majorda beach road past Martin's Corner (no sea views). Neat grounds, al fresco and small covered area. Seafood and Indian. Large set-up with seating for 200+ under cover in front of an old house. One of the best restaurants on the south coast.

$$ **Whining Riley's**, outside Nanu Resorts, with well-stocked bar, pool table, garden.

Bogmalo

$$ **Full Moon** and **Stiff Waves** near Bogmalo Beach Resort do excellent seafood.

$$ **Joet's**, great for seafood: tremendously popular with foreigners and Goans alike. It's a very friendly place; has sunbeds on the beach and hammocks among the palms.

South of Colva *p142*
Benaulim

Service can be tediously slow during the season. Most close in the monsoons.

$$$ **Taj Exotica's** speciality restaurants are faultless; spread of the Mediterranean, gourmet Goan or authentic Chinese.

$$ **Pedro's**, by the car park above the beach. Good seafood and tandoori. Imaginative menu, friendly.

$$ **Tito's**, the beach. English breakfasts, Rs 80.

$ **D'Souza's**, good juices, *lassis* and fast food.

$ **Johncy's**, varied menu, good seafood, big portions, tandoori recommended (after 1830) but service can be erratic, pleasant atmosphere though (backgammon, scrabble).

$ **Malibu**, nice lush garden setting for spicy fish/meat kebabs.

Varca to Mobor

Beach shacks offer Goan dishes and seafood at reasonable prices. Around **Dona Sylvia**, several come alive in the evening.

$$$ **Riverside**, Leela Palace. Serves Italian on an open deck overlooking the river Sal.

$$ **Grill Room**, Fatrade Beach Rd, open 1830-2230. Pleasant steak house with a simple menu. Tiger prawns Rs 400, steaks Rs 150.

$$ **La Afra**, Tamborin, Fatrade. Excellent steaks and fresh fish, sensibly priced. Boat-men ferry holidaymakers to **River Sal**, Betul.

$$ **River View**, Cavelossim. Tranquil, open air location, overlooking the river. Wide choice, international menu, good ambience despite being surrounded by ugly hotel developments. Cocktails Rs 100, sizzlers Rs 150-200, Tiger prawns Rs 500.

$ **Goan Village**, lane opposite Dona Sylvia, Tamborim, south of Cavelossim. The best here for all cuisines.

$ **Mike's Place**, Cavelossim. Recommended for good food, drink and service in a pleasant atmosphere.

For authentic Goan fish *thalis* (Rs 25), try the 1st house on the left past the church in Cavelossim if heading north.

☺ Pubs, bars and clubs

Colva

Johnny Cool's, half way up busy Beach Rd. Scruffy surroundings but popular for chilled beer and late night drinks.

Splash is 'the' place for music, dancing and late drinking, open all night, trendy, very busy on Sat (full after 2300 on weekdays in season), good cocktails, poor bar snacks – may not appeal to all especially unaccompanied girls.

Sunshine, bar and restaurant, north end of beach, popular evenings, hammocks over-looking beach, pool table, 60s music, small dance floor, gardens. Relaxed atmosphere.

South of Colva *p142*
Varca to Mobor

Aqua, Leela Palace, Mobor, is a gaming room and cigar lounge which turns into a late night disco after 2000.

▲ Activities and tours

Colva and around *p139*
Colva
Meeting Point, T0832-723338, for very efficient, reliable travel service, Mon-Sat, 0830-1900 (sometimes open even later, if busy).

Bogmalo
Bogmalo Beach Resort, T0832-2513291, and **Joet's**, T0832-2555036, offer watersports.
Goa Diving have a morning office at Joet's, and are based at Chapel Bhat, Chicalim, T0832-2555117, goadivin@goatelecom.com. PADI certification from Open Water to Assistant Instructor.
Splash Watersports, T0832-2409886. Run by Derek, a famous Indian champion windsurfer. Operate from a shack on the beach just below Joets, providing para-sailing, windsurfing, water skiing, trips to nearby islands; during the high season only.

South of Colva *p142*
Benaulim
Dolphin watching The trips are scenic and chances of seeing dolphin are high, but it gets very hot (take hat, water and something comfy to sit on). Groups of dolphins here are usually seen swimming near the surface. Boats from **Café Dominick** (signs on the beach) and several others charge about Rs 300.
Yoga At Taj Exotica indoors or on the lawn. Also aromatherapy and reflexology.

Varca to Mobor
Dolphin watching Most hotels arrange river trips and dolphin viewing, or call T0832-871455. River trips last from 1600-1730, dolphin trips 0800-1000 and sunset cruises depart at 1700. Expect to pay Rs 250.
Betty's Place, in a road opposite Holiday Inn, Mobor, arranges boat trips for fishing, dolphin viewing as well as trips up river Sal from 1030-1630 (food included), recommended.

✪ Festivals

Colva and around *p139*
Colva
Oct 12-18 (Mon that falls between these dates) **Fama of Menino Jesus** when thousands of pilgrims flock to see the statue in the **Church of our Lady of Mercy** in the hope of witnessing a miracle.

South of Colva *p142*
Benaulim
Jun 24 Feast of St John the Baptist (*Sao Joao*), gives thanks for the arrival of the monsoon. Young men wearing crowns of leaves and fruits tour the area singing for gifts. They jump into wells (which are usually full) to commemorate the movement of St John in his mother's womb when she was visited by Mary, the mother of Jesus!

Cuncolim
Dec-Jan Shantadurga jatra Annual event when thousands accompany the image in procession from Fatorpa to Cuncolim.

Fatorpa
Dec-Jan Annual jatra, once held on 20th day of Phalgun, when the deity is taken in procession by a large number of pilgrims. They travel from Fatorpa to the site of the original temple in Cuncolim, where the Chapel of the Sacred Heart stands.
Mar/Apr The Fatorpa Gulal is similar to *Holi*, when people throw coloured powder and water on each other.

✪ Shopping

Margao *p137 and map p137*
The Old Market was rehoused in the 'New' (Municipal) Market in town. The covered **market** (Mon-Sat, 0800-1300, 1600-2000) is fun to wander around. It is not at all touristy but holidaymakers come on their shopping trip to avoid paying inflated prices in the beach resorts. To catch a glimpse of the early morning arrivals at the **Fish Market** head south from the Municipal Building.

Books and CDs
Golden Heart, Confident Building, off Abbé Faria Rd, behind the GPO, (closed 1300-1500). Bookshop.
Nanutel Hotel. Small bookshop.
Trevor's, 5 Luis Miranda Rd. Sells CDs.

Clothes
MS Caro, Caro Corner, has an extensive range including 'suiting', and will advise on tailors.

J Vaz, Martires Dias Rd, near Hari Mandir, T0832-2720086. Good quality men's tailor.

Photography
Lorenz, opposite the Municipality.
Wonder Colour Lab, Garden View Building.

Colva and around p139
Bogmalo
Ritika Bookshop and Boutique, Bogmalo Beach Resort's veranda, a/c, good books and stationery, high quality gifts, good value.

South of Colva p142
Benaulim
Khazana at Taj Exotica, a veritable treasure chest (gifts, books, crafts, clothes) culled from across India. High class with prices to match.
Manthan Heritage Gallery, main road. Quality collection of art items.

⊖ Transport

Margao p137 and map p137
Auto-rickshaw
To Colva, Rs 30; beach, Rs 50.

Bus
The local bus stand is by the municipal gardens. You can usually board buses near the Kamat Hotel, southeast of the gardens.

The Kadamba (new) bus stand is 2 km north of town (city buses to the centre, or motorcycle taxi Rs 8); buses arriving before 1000 and after 1900, proceed to the centre. To Benaulim, Cabo da Rama 0730 (2 hrs); Canacona and Palolem, several; Colva: hourly; Gokarna, 1300 daily.

Non-stop KTC buses to Panjim: 1 hr. Buy tickets from booth at stand number 1.

Private buses (eg Paulo, Metropole Hotel, T0832-2721516), Padre Miranda Rd: to Bangalore (15 hrs); Mangalore 1800, 2130 (8-10 hrs), Rs 140; Mumbai (Dadar/CST) 1400, 1700 (16 hrs), Rs 600 (sleeper); Pune 1700 (13 hrs), Rs 450 (sleeper).

Car hire
Sai Service, T0832-2735772. Rs 700-900 per day with driver.

Train
Enquiries T0832-2732255. The new station on the broad gauge network is 500 m south of the old station. The reservation office on the 1st flr of the new station is usually quick and efficient, with short queues. Mon-Sat 0800-1400, 1415-2000, Sun 0800-1400. Tickets for Mumbai and Delhi should be booked well ahead. Confirm Indrail Pass reservations in Vasco, Mumbai or Mangalore.

Konkan Kanya Express (night train) and Mandovi Express (day train) from Mumbai also stop at Tivim (for northern beaches; take the local bus into Mapusa and from there catch another bus or take a taxi) and Karmali (for Panjim and Dabolim airport) before terminating at Margao. Both are very slow and take nearly 12 hrs. From Mumbai (CST): Mandovi Exp 0103, 0515 (arr 1815), (11 hrs, 2nd class 3-tier Rs 670), doesn't stop at Pernem; Konkan Kanya Exp 0111, 2250 (arr 1045). Delhi (Nizamuddin): Rajdhani Exp 2431, 1145, Wed, Fri; Goa Exp 2779, 1427, 35 hrs. Ernakulam (Jn): Mangalore Exp 2618, 2055, 17 hrs. Hospet (for Hampi): Vasco-da-Gama Vijayawada Exp 7228, 0720, Wed, Sat, 8½ hrs. Mumbai (CST): Mandovi Exp 0104, 1030, 11½ hrs (via Karmali, Tivim); Konkan Kanya Exp 0112, 1800, 12 hrs (via Karmali, Tivim, Pernem). Mumbai Kurla (Tilak): Netravati Exp 6346, 0640, 12 hrs (via Karmali, Tivim). Thiruvananthapuram (Trivandrum): Rajdhani Exp 2432, 1300, Mon, Wed, 18 hrs. Netravati Exp 6345, 2255, 18 hrs (via Canacona for Palolem beach).

The broad gauge line between Vasco and Londa in Karnataka runs through Margao and Dudhsagar Falls and connects stations on the line with Belgaum. There are services to Bangalore Vasco Bangalore Exp 7310, 2059, Mon, Thu.

The pre-paid taxi stand is to the right of the exit (charges are for 1 person with 1 piece of luggage); to Margao centre Rs 50, Panjim Rs 480 (45 mins), Anjuna Rs 670; Calangute Rs 600; Colva Rs 130, Palolem Rs 480; rates are clearly displayed outside the office. Autos to Colva Rs 100, to Panjim Rs 320. Avoid tourist taxis, they can be 5 times the price.

Colva and around p139
Colva
Bicycles mostly through hotels, Rs 20-25 per day (discounts for long term). Motorbikes for hire through most hotels (see also Panjim), Rs 200 per day (less for long term rental), more for Enfields, bargain hard.

Bus to **Anjuna** Wed for the Flea Market, tickets through travel agents, depart 0930, return 1730, Rs 90-100; to **Margao** half-hourly, take 30 mins, Rs 3 (last bus 1915, last return, 2000). Also to **Margao**, **motorcycle taxi**, Rs 20-25 (bargain hard); **auto-rickshaw**, Rs 30-40.

Betalbatim to Velsao
Bus

Buses from Margao (12 km), **motorcycle taxis** charge Rs 35. The **Margao-Vasco** bus service passes through the centre of Cansaulim.

Taxi

Taxis to/from **airport**, 20 mins (Rs 300); **Margao** 15 mins (Rs 200). From **Nanu Resort** Panjim Rs 500, Anjuna Rs 750, or Rs 700 for 8 hrs, 80 km.

Train

Cansaulim station on the Vasco-Margao line is handy for **Velsao** and **Arossim** beaches and **Majorda station** for **Utorda** and **Majorda** beaches. Auto-rickshaws meet trains.

From **Cansaulim** there are 3 trains a day to **Vasco** (Rs 6) via **Dabolim** for the airport; 0746, 1411, 1818. For **Kulem** (Dudhsagar Falls) (Rs 12) via Margao (Rs 6), 0730, 1330, 1750.

From **Majorda** there are 3 trains a day to **Vasco** (Rs 5) 0741, 1406, 1813. For **Kulem** (Dudhsagar Falls) (Rs 10) via Margao (Rs 5), 0737, 1337, 1757.

South of Colva *p142*
Benaulim

Buses from all directions arrive at Maria Hall crossing. **Bicycle** and **scooter** hire, Rs 35 and Rs 150 per day. **Taxis** and **autos** from the beach esplanade near Pedro's and at Maria Hall crossing. To/from **Margao**: taxis Rs 100; autos Rs 80; bus Rs 5. **Anjuna** Wed flea market: bus 0930, return 1530, about Rs 95, 2 hrs.

Varca to Mobor
Bike hire

Rocks outside Dona Sylvia, cycles Rs 10 per hr, Rs 150 a day; scooters Rs 300 a day without petrol, Rs 500 with 7 litres of fuel.

Bus

From Margao to **Cavelossim**, uncomfortably slow (18 km); autos transfer from bus stand to resorts.

Taxis

From Margao charge around Rs 200, from Dabolim airport to the resorts take under an hr.

Ferry

Crosses the river Sal, southeast of Cavelossim and **Assolna**, which sells petrol, and the lane from the river joins the main road, NH17.

⊕ Directory

Margao p137 and map p137
Banks Bank of Baroda, behind Grace Church; also in Market, Station Rd; **Bank of India**, exchanges cash, TCs, Visa and Mastercard; **State Bank of India**, west of the Municipal Gardens; **HDFC**, 24 hr ATM for MasterCard. Get exchange before visiting beaches to the south where it is more difficult. International money transfer is possible through **Weizmann**, 650 Costa Dias Building, NH 17 (Mon-Sat 1000-1800). There is also a branch in Colva. **Fire** T0832-2720168. **Internet** Cyber Link, Shop 9, Rangavi Complex; **Cyber Inn**, 105 Karnika Chambers, V Valauliker Rd, 0900-2000, Rs 30 per hr. **Medical services** Ambulance T0832-2722722; **JJ Costa Hospital**, Fatorda, T0832-2722586; **Hospicio**, T0832-2722164; Holy Spirit Pharmacy, 24 hrs. **Police** T0832-2722175. **Post office** north of children's park; **Poste Restante**, near the telegraph office, down lane west of park, 0830-1030 and 1500-1700 Mon-Sat.

Colva and around p139
Betalbatim

Monte Communications, next to Rays. Email and international phone calls.

South of Colva p142
Benaulim

Bank Bank of Baroda, near Maria Hall, best rates (better than at travel agents and STD booths). **Internet** GK Communications, Beach Rd. 24 hr phone, money exchange and internet with 4 terminals, book ahead when very busy, Rs 100 per hr. **Medical services** Late night **chemists** near the main crossroads.

Varca to Mobor

Banks Bank of Baroda, near the church in Cavelossim, accepts Visa, MasterCard, TCs; helpful staff, open Mon-Wed, Fri, Sat 0930-1330.

Cabo de Rama and further south

→ *Colour map 3, grid B2-3.*

Palolem is the closest you come to the picture postcard perfect beach ideal in Goa and naturally its beautiful curve of palm-fringed golden sand has not gone unnoticed. It's far from a deserted bay but remains lovely nonetheless: the narrow beach is top and tailed with rocky outcrops dubbed 'Pandava's drums' or 'footprints' by locals, there's a freshwater stream to the north and you can fetch up on the deserted jungle of the tiny Canacona Island with just a short swim or by wading across at low tide.

Palolem's popularity has led to tourism spilling out onto its neighbouring beaches. By and large there has been a southward drift to Colomb, Patnem and on to Galgibaga, skipping the beautiful Rajbag, whose charms are ringfenced by the new five-star development. Patnem, hemmed in by crags and river at either end, doesn't have the same rash of coconut trees that made Palolem so shadily alluring but the encroachment is already underway. Less visited, to the north, is the casuarina-backed bay of Agonda, a strung-out fishing village that pretty much ignores the few tourists lolling around in the sun. The sparsely visited but dramatic fort at Cabo de Rama lies midway between Agonda and Mobor to the north. ▸▸ *For Sleeping, Eating and other listings, see pages 159-162.*

Ins and outs

Getting there The nearest major transport junction for all these beaches is Canacona (pronounced Kannkonn, also known as Chaudi) on the NH17 between Panjim and Karwar in Karnataka with direct transport links, but there are also less frequent direct buses between the beaches and Margao (37 km north) that take roughly an hour. From here buses shuttle fairly continuously down to Palolem and less frequently to Agonda. Canacona Junction on the Konkan railroad between Mumbai and Trivandrum is only 2 km from Palolem. Canacona's main square has the bus and auto stands: rickshaws cost between Rs 50-150 to any of these bays.

Getting around

The area between the beaches is small and wandering between them becomes a leisure pursuit in itself. A motorbike is good for those with short beach attention spans. The drive to Cabo de Rama, although riddled with hair-pin bends, is particularly lovely and going under your own steam means you can look for the deserted beaches nearby and stop over at the fishing dock at the estuary north of Agonda. Buses run along this route between the bays on a roughly hourly basis.

Cabo de Rama (Cape Rama) → *Colour map 3, grid B2.*

Getting there From Salcete, the road that goes southwest from the crossroads at Bali towards Cabo de Rama first passes coconuts, breadfruit trees, then a really bleak landscape. After winding down into another valley for 1 km, a minor road forks off to the right to Cabo de Rama (the sign may be almost invisible). The fork left leads to and from Goa's southernmost beaches. After retracing your steps along the road from Cabo de Rama to the junction you can either return along the Betul/Bali road or go south to take the coast road to Agonda and Palolem (there are no signs to tell you this). It is an attractive alternative to the national highway.

On public transport, from Margao, buses leave at 0730 from the southeast corner of the Municipal Gardens (Rs 10, 2 hrs), return at 1200 or later. The bus runs to the small car park in front of the fort. Ask the driver for precise timings of the return service. From Palolem, you could hire a motorbike, but take care as there are a lot of blind corners.

❝❞ The sound here is the rattle of coconut fronds and bird song. Little puppies lie panting corpse-like in the bush. You can hear every voice and every flip-flop flap...

Capo de Rama is named after the hero of the Hindu epic Ramayana, who is said to have lived there with his wife Sita during their period of exile. It was obvious that the cape was the perfect site for a fort to any power whose interests might be threatened from the sea. Its origins pre-date the arrival of the Portuguese who captured it in 1763 and used it as a prison too.

The **gatehouse**, which was restored less than five years ago now looks more rundown than most of the original fortifications. Sadly, it is a grubby mess of broken timbers and walls covered with graffiti. The main entrance seems far from impregnable, but the outer ramparts are excellently preserved, with several cannons still scattered along their length. Despite the absence of buildings, other than the church, the magnificence of the site gives it an extraordinary atmosphere. There are stunning views from several of its major bastions, and you can walk virtually the entire outer length of the fort.

The beaches can be reached by taking any of the turnings off the fort approach road.

From the entrance follow the path to the right and climb the steps and ramp to a well-preserved bastion. From here there is a clear view of the rocky headland below and north along a totally unspoilt coastline. Just below this first bastion there are small gates within the wall and it is possible to scramble down to the sea – take great care on the crumbly laterite paths. Continuing anti-clockwise along the ramparts the path reaches a second bastion which has lost most of its protection; behind you is the freshwater tank standing in an atmospheric wooded dell. The path continues to follow the wall up to a derelict observation post. From here there is a 360° view which is particularly good to the south in the evening light, across bays stretching down past Palolem to Karnataka easily visible on a clear day. Retrace your steps keeping more to the right as you approach the thicker vegetation. A well-used path leads through the wood and comes out by the church and main entrance. The most dramatic of the walls is on the landward side, where it rises 10-15 m above the floor of the moat which was dug both to provide the laterite blocks from which the fort is constructed and to create the barrier around the fort.

The gatehouse is at the lowest point of the whole fort, the ground rising to its highest in the southwest and the wall then dropping down to the north. At its lowest it is only 20 m or so above the sea. At this point of the compound is the source of the fort's water supply. A huge tank was excavated to a depth of about 10 m, and even today it contains water right through the dry season. If the local herdsman is about, ask for directions to the two springs, one of which gives out water through two spouts at different temperatures. This tranquil place is well worth a visit.

Agonda → *Colour map 3, grid B2.*

Snake through forests and bright paddy south from Cabo De Rama towards Palolem to uncover artless Agonda, a windswept village backed by mountains of forestry full of acrobatic black-faced monkeys. Local political agitators thwarted plans for a five-star hotel and so have, temporarily at least, arrested the speed of their home's development as a tourist destination. Their success makes for a primitive holiday scene: a handful of internet points, less than a dozen restaurants and a small number of hotels and coco-huts are strewn out over the beach village's length. There's no house music, little throttling of Enfield engines and you need to be happy to make your own entertainment to stay here for any serious length of time. Less photogenic than Palolem, Agonda bay has pine-like casuarina trees lining the beach instead of coconuts and palms. The swimming is safe and the beach wonderfully calm. The northern end of the beach, close to the school and bus stop, has a small block of shops including the brilliantly chaotic original **Fatima stores & restaurant** (Fatima Rodrigues, not one to be a jack of all trades, has limited her menu to just spaghetti and *thali*) and **St Annes bookstore**, a video library.

Palolem and around → *Colour map 3, grid B3.*

For a short spell, when the police cracked down most severely on parties up north, Palolem looked like it might act as the Anjuna overflow. Today **Neptune's Point** has permission to hold parties once a fortnight, but so far, Palolem's villagers are resisting the move to make the beach a mini-party destination and authorities are even stumping up the cash to pay for litter-pickers. The demographic here is chiefly late-twenties and thirty-something couples, travellers and students: younger than Colva but less archly hip than Anjuna.

Canacona is the nearest settlement of any significant size to Palolem and has shops and direct transport links – it is the southernmost stop on the Konkan Railway in Goa and is the crossroads on the NH17 between Panjim and the Karnataka port city of Karwar. The large church and high school of **St Tereza of Jesus** (1962) are on the northern edge of town.

Shri Malikarjuna Temple, 6 km northeast of town, is believed to date from the mid-16th century and was renovated in the year 1778. The *mandapa* has carved wooden pillars. ▸▸ *See also Festivals and events, page 161.*

Beaches further south

Over the rocky outcrops to the south you come to the sandy cove of **Calomb**. Wholly uncommercial, its trees are pocked with longstayers' little picket fences and stabs at growing banana plants, their earthy homesteads cheek by jowl with fishermen's huts. The sound here is the rattle of coconut fronds and bird song. Little puppies lie panting corpse-like in the bush. You can hear every voice and every flip-flop flap. You could almost be on a different planet to Palolem.

At the end of the track through Calomb a collection of huts marks the start of the fine sweep of **Patnem beach**, which some

Agonda

Fatima Stores
St Anne's Bookstore
School
To Palolem
Arabian Sea
Dunhills Transport Store

N
0 metres 200
0 yards 200

Sleeping
Casa Maria **1**
Dersy Beach
Resort **2**
Eldfra **3**
Fatima Bar &
Restaurant Vall **5**
Sun Set Bar **4**

reckon to be the new Palolem. Here, the 500 villagers have both put a limit on the number of shacks and stopped outsiders from trading, and as a result the beach has conserved much of its unhurried charm. The deep banks of sand are whipped up by winds to catch kite-flyers' fancy and cushion the falls of volleyball-players: but fishing boats still far outnumber sun loungers. The place is something of a hit with old rockers, Israelis and long-stayers: so far there are no parties, no nightlife and, no coincidence, a healthy relationship between villagers and tourism.

⚏ Hindu temples in Patnem have music most Fri and Sat with tabla, symbols and harmonica.

Further south, wade across a stream (possible before the monsoon) to reach the dune and casuarina-fringed **Rajbag Beach**, its southern waters a-bob with fishing boats. Although it's virtually unvisited and has perfect swimming, the luxury five-star that opened here in 2004 has provoked a storm of protest and prevented anyone else from moving in. Local criticism of the development centres on

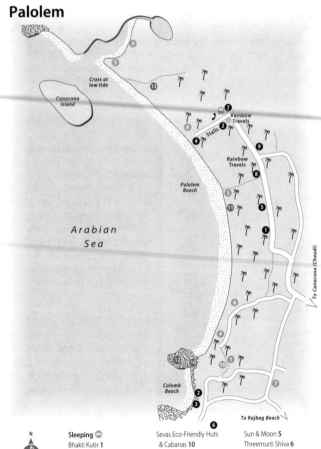

Palolem

Canacona Island

Cross at low tide

Rainbow Travels

Rainbow Travels

Palolem Beach

A r a b i a n S e a

To Canacona (Chaudi)

Colomb Beach

To Rajbag Beach

N

| 0 metres | 300 |
| 0 yards | 300 |

Sleeping
Bhakti Kutir **1**
Ciaran's Camp **3**
Cocohuts **4**
Cozy Nook **5**
Dream Catcher **9**
Hi-Tide Beach Huts **6**
Home Guesthouse **2**
Oceanic **7**
Palolem Beach Resort **8**

Sevas Eco-Friendly Huts & Cabanas **10**

Eating
Boom Shankar **3**
Brown Bread & Health Food **1**
Cool Breeze **2**
Dropadi **4**
Mamoo's **7**
Smuggler's **8**

Sun & Moon **5**
Threemurti Shiva **6**
Tibet **9**

Bars & clubs
Bridge & Tunnel
Living Huts **10**
Café del Mar **11**
Neptune's Point **12**
Rock It Café **13**

▮ Arresting development: Canacona Style

The only sign today of there ever having been a hard-fought war between the villagers of Agonda and outside developers is the shell of a huge five-star hotel complex that lies in the forest-clad hills to the south of the village: inside, instead of tourists, are snakes and monkeys and the roots and branches of trees bursting through walls. But fight there was.

In 1980 a Delhi-based hotel group, Seema, arrived among the small community of 60 families that live in Vall Agonda whose chief trade and industry is small farming, fishing from canoes and *toddy* tapping. The outsiders started to buy up land on the hillside: paying as little as four rupees per square metre. Villagers grew unhappy as the hotel group's plans seeped out: a five-star resort complete with golf course.

Dissent was whipped up by the Fernandez family, owners of a critical swathe of land from the road to the beach. It was the last piece in the developers' jigsaw and the Fernandez refused to sell up. Instead they mobilized enough resistance to ensure that the hotel's huts were torched and their electricity supply lines cut. In return the developers shipped in armed

goons from Maharashtra and Karnataka to police the property. Locals refused to vacate the plot.

Official arbitration in the dispute began. The Fernandez family demanded compensation for toddy tappers' loss of earnings (Rs 50,000 a pop) and that one member of each family be given a job in the hotel for a minimum of 20 years. The family, say that they, as the chief agitators, were approached with tempting offers to simmer down; they turned them all down.

"We made them go bankrupt," says John Fernandez. "For every 1 lakh they intended to spend on the hotel, we made them spend 100." All that's left of the hotel's ambitions is the concrete hulk and a few watchmen. A new resort is planned for the north of the village, but the villagers have been less quick to rally round to stop it. As Fernandez says: "People are greedy to do something here. At least on the site of the five star nobody can come and this corner is empty. It's all just forest and open palm trees and all. The other end of the beach it's a different story: north of the church every fisherman wants a bit...just now Agonda is very peaceful, but it's a fragile peace."

the whittling away of fisherfolk's access to the beach, the rebuilding of the ancient Shree Vita Rukmayee temple that villagers say is tantamount to the hotel 'swallowing our God' and the alleged flouting of the proviso that half the jobs created should go to local people. The isolated **Kindlebaga beach** is east of Rajbag, 2 km from Canacona.

Galgibaga

South of the Talpona river, which has a ferry crossing, a short strip of land juts out to sea. Galgibaga is a change from the fishing villages across the river as it has well-built houses among lucrative casuarina plantations belonging to the townspeople. Galgibaga beach, like Morjim in the north, is a favourite stop-over for Olive Ridley turtles which travel vast distances to lay their eggs here each November. Shacks are mushrooming here, much to environmentalists' concern.

● *Patnem is developing fast. In 1996 there were just two cafés. By 2001 there were 22. During Christmas 2003, demand for accommodation was so high that people were sleeping outdoors in hammocks, while huts were rented out at an amazing Rs 5,000 a day.*

Partagali and around → *Colour map 3, grid B4.*

Getting there 7 km south of Canacona (Chaudi) is a left (east) turn off the NH17. The massive concrete gateway here is to the Partagali temple, just further is a 2 km road that leads to the Cotigao wildlife sanctuary.

Partagali's **Shri Sausthan Gokarn Partagali Jeevotam Math** is on the banks of the river Kushavati. The *math* (religious establishment) was set up in AD 1475 at Margao when the followers, originally Saivites, were converted and became a Vaishnav sect. However, during the period of Portuguese Christianization (1560-68), the foundation was moved to Bhatkal (northern Karnataka). After a time, the sixth Swami (who was also responsible for the temple to Rama, Lakshman, Sita and Hanuman here), re-established the *math* at Partagali, where it has continued uninterrupted. The symbol representing the spiritual movement which is over 500 years old, is an ancient *Vatavriksha* (banyan tree) which spreads over an area of about 65 m x 70 m. Known as *Bramhasthan,* it has been a place for meditation, and the sacred tree with the *Ishwarlinga* (the *linga* of the Lord, ie Siva) in front of it is believed to have drawn worshippers from the surrounding area for over 1,000 years. Partagali has been developed into a centre of culture and learning, while continuing with its ancient traditions. The temple, which also has a typical tall Garuda pillar, celebrates its festival in March/April.

Cotigao wildlife sanctuary ⓘ *60 km south of Panjim, Rs 5, 2-wheelers Rs 10, cars Rs 50; still camera Rs 25; video Rs 100, 0730-1730 throughout the year (but may not be worthwhile during the monsoon),* is Goa's second largest and was established in 1969. In one of the most densely forested areas of the state, the 105 sq km sanctuary is hilly to the south and east and has the Talpona River flowing through it. There is a nature interpretation centre with a small reference library at the entrance. The vegetation is mostly moist deciduous with some semi-evergreen and evergreen forest cover. There are several small settlements of *Velip* and *Kunbis* forest-dwelling groups existing on subsistence farming, so it offers a good opportunity to observe traditional rural life. The villagers grow chillies and harvest cashew from the forest to take to the market in Cotigao. If you are a keen walker this is a great place to come and explore the forest and enjoy a small unspoilt corner of Goa. Make sure you wear sturdy shoes after the rains as there are many small streams.

The sanctuary claims to have a wide range of mammals including panther, sloth bear and hyena, and several reptiles, but you are only likely to see wild boar, the odd deer and gaur and many monkeys; birdspotting is more rewarding. Birds not easily seen elsewhere in Goa include rufous woodpecker, Malabar crested lark and white-eyed eagle.

You need your own vehicle to reach the treetop watch towers and water holes which are signposted, 3 km and 7 km off the main metalled road on a variable rough track. There are no guides but the forest office by the Interpretation Centre at the entrance has a map of the park roads on the wall. The forest paths are easy to follow but make sure you have drinking water and petrol. The chances of seeing much wildlife, apart from monkeys, however are slim, since by the opening time of 0730 it can be warm enough to reduce animal activity to a minimum. However, it can be rewarding to take a short walk through the forest and immerse yourself in the sounds of the jungle.

The first tower by a water hole is known as **Machan Vhutpal,** 400 m off the road. Unfortunately only if you are fit and have a good head for heights are you likely to venture up the steep wrought-iron ladder to the raised platform which offers a great view of the forest canopy. The second tower is far more substantial and the best place to spend a night if permission is granted (this should not be a problem).

Most visitors usually come for a day trip, but if you are keen on walking in the forest this a great place to spend a day or two. You can either stay near the sanctuary office or spend a night in a watch tower deep in the forest. A short way beyond the

kiosk for the villagers living within the reserve, which sells the usual array of basic
provisions. If you are planning to spend a few days in the park it is best to bring your
own fresh provisions and then let the staff prepare meals.

The cheapest way to visit the park is for a group to hire a taxi for a half-day in
Palolem. If you leave the beach just before 0700 you will be at the park gates when
they open. Motorbikes are also allowed in the sanctuary.

● Sleeping

Cabo de Rama p153
$ **Pinto's Bar**, near the fort entrance. Offers
meals and cool drinks on a sandy shaded
terrace, may also have rooms available. If
there are few visitors about (most likely) ask
here for a meal before exploring the fort to
save time waiting later.

Agonda p154, map p155
D-E Fatima Bar and Restaurant Vall
T0832-2647477. Attached/non attached
single and double rooms.
E Eldfra, T0832-2647378. 4 simple rooms
with fan, clean attached bathroom. Bar and
simple restaurant, basic roof terrace. A
purpose-built block but no direct seaview.
E Casa Maria, T0832-2647237. 4 rooms with
clean tiled bathroom, fan, veranda, sea views,
but overlooks the back of Eldfra.
E-F Dercy Beach Resort, T0832-2647503.
50-year-old family house developed to fit 12
clean rooms with bathrooms. Over the road
on the beach are 12 basic bamboo huts with
spotless shared wash block. Dynamic owner.
F Sun Set Bar, T0832-2647381. 7 simple
cottages (more planned) with great views,
shared facilities. The restaurant perched high
on the rocks has the prime location in
Agonda. Recommended.

Palolem and around p155, map p156
Palolem's popularity has soared inordinately.
Off-season, bargain hard and ask around for
rooms inside family houses. These can have
very basic facilities (eg 'pig' toilets, raised on a
platform where pigs do the necessary 'cleaning
out' below), some are lovely though and let
you use their kitchen and fridge, F price bracket.
B Ciaran's Camp, Palolem beach, T0832-2643
477, johnciaran@hotmail.com. Huts are spaced
wide apart in palm-covered landscaped
gardens. A library, lovely shop, ping-pong table
and great restaurant plus promises of live jazz
all make it the leader in Palolem cool.

B-C Bhakti Kutir, over the hill at the
southern end, T0832-2643472.
bhaktikutir@yahoo.com. A beautiful grove of
trees hanging over 22 huts with bucket
baths and compost toilets. Its German/Goan
owners are steeped in ecology and
spirituality. More than a place to stay, it's a
place to engage both brain and body. Away
from the beach and very quiet. Children
welcome. Highly recommended.
B-C Café Del Mar, Palolem Beach,
T0832-3276520. The only a/c bungalows on
the beach. Excellent restaurant and bar
makes this an uptempo place to stay.
C Oceanic Hotel, Palolem, T0832-2643059,
www.hotel-oceanic.com. 9 good rooms –
either large or small doubles (some with TV)
swimming pool and hot water. Massage
available, good cocktails and restaurant.
C Sevas Eco-Friendly Huts and Cabanas
opposite Bhaki Kutir, T0832-2311767,
sevasmicho@yahoo.com. Close to Bhakti
Kutir in distance as well as in spirit: but only
some of these huts have fan.
D Dream Catcher, riverbank, North Palolem,
T0832-2644873, lalalandjackie7@yahoo.com.
11 lovely huts all with fan. Dream Catcher is
the type of place that becomes addictive:
there's yoga, reiki courses, massage or just
big drawn-out afternoon talks. Jazz, funk,
soul, chill-out type music policy.
E Cocohuts, towards the southern end,
T0832-2643296. 15 breezy, shaded huts set
among palm trees on bamboo stilts, each
divided into 2 rooms by palm leaf partitions,
electricity and fan, separate shared toilets on
the ground; on the beach, restaurant.
E Cozy Nook, at northern end,
T0832-2643550. Plastered bamboo huts,
fans, nets, shared toilets, in a good location
between the sea and river, ayurvedic centre,
art and crafts, friendly. Recommended.
E Palolem Beach Resort, T/F0832-2643054.
9 rooms with bath, tents and basic cottages

with shared facilities, shower blocks, excellent seafood tandoori, ISD phones, reliable travel service and exchange. Clean, shaded site, book ahead.

E **Hi-Tide Beach Huts**, towards southern end, T0832-2643104. 18 huts, best on stilts at the beach front.

Camping

F **Palolem Beach Resort** and south of Cocohuts, camping and parking for campers and travellers (Rs 15-20 per day).

Calomb

C **Boom Shankar Restaurant**, T0832-2384634, www.boomshankar colomb.com. Rooms with showers attached to popular, beautifully placed restaurant.

Patnem

C–D **Home Guesthouse**, T0832-2643916, homeispatnem@yahoo.com. Just 8 rooms with fan and French linen close to the beach. Aims to become a forum for local artists and has occasional live music.

D **Hotel Sea View Bar Restaurant and Lodging**, T0832-2643110, seaview_1 @hotmail.com. Funnily enough doesn't have many sea views, as it's set back from beach on the road, but has rooms, internet and food.

D **Solitude Dream Woods**, T0832-2711186, ashper2002@yahoo.com. All-wood beach camp with pine and bamboo structures, one of the most advanced developments in Patnem.

Rajbaga

LL **InterContinental The Grand Resort Goa** Rajbaga, T0832-2644777, goa@ interconti.com. 85 acres of 5 star hotel between the Talpone river and the Sahaydri mountain range. 255 sea-facing rooms, 9 hole golf course, 5 restaurants, health spa, watersports, even a luxury yacht.

Kindlebaga

C **Molyma**, off NH17, west from the crossroads at Kindlebaga, T0832-2643028. 43 modern, large rooms, airy restaurant with limited menu, bar, friendly service, good value though rather deserted, 15 mins' walk to a good beach beyond dunes.

Partagali and around *p158*
Cotigao

E-F **Hatipaul Canacona** (eco-tourism complex), T0832-2644263, ask for the RFO Wildlife. A simple secure brick cottage with 2 beds, fan, clean (Rs 200). Separate wash block, no hot water, Indian-style toilet. There is also a 'tent' on a concrete platform, better to time your visit when the cottage is free (easily arranged). Canteen within the complex.

F **Forest Rest House**, Poinguinim, a short distance along the main road past the reserve entrance. Simple room. Contact the Conservator's Office, Margao, T0832-2735361, or enquire at the sanctuary interpretation centre.

🍴 Eating

Palolem and around *p155, map p156*

$$ **Bhakti Kutir.** Whole food restaurant that serves excellent fresh fish dishes, homegrown organic produce and fresh juices. Name any number of obscure nutritious grains and they're bound to have them. Recommended.

$$ **Dropadi Beach Restaurant and Bar.** Routinely packed out. Lobster and lasagne and North Indian food are the specials.

$$ **Cool Breeze**, Main Rd, T9422060 564, coolbreezegoa@hotmail.com. One of the perennial favourites like Dropadi that's probably got the best steaks in town.

$$ **Mamoo's**, on the corner where the road turns to meet the beach, T0832-2644261, mamoosplace@rediffmail.com. A 3rd long-standing favourite, famous for its grilled fish. Only comes alive in the evening.

$$ **Oceanic Hotel**, up on the hill north of the beach. Fresh soup on the menu every day and their chef spent last season moving through the Delia Smith recipe books. Excellent seafood and cocktails: popular in the evening.

$ **Brown Bread and Health Food**, near Syndicate Bank, T0832-2643604. Quite probably the best breakfast in Palolem.

$ **Smuggler's Inn**, Main Rd, T09822986 093. Traditional, home-cooked English fare with nice wines and lots of screens for football. Bangers and mash for Rs 90 and banoffie pie for afters.

$ **Tibet Bar and Restaurant**, Main Rd, T9822142775. Super fresh ingredients in these excellent Himalayan dishes. Small restaurant that's worth stepping back from the beach for.

Canacona

$ **Canacona Palace**, 50 m east of the cross-roads, serves good Udupi vegetarian food.

Beach shacks

$ **Silver Star**, with hammocks in the shade.
Sun & Moon, T0832-2643314, set back from the beach under palms, friendly, popular with great atmosphere and large helpings of well-cooked Goan food plus internet.

Calomb

$ **Boom Shankar** overlooks Calomb beach. Red snapper and tuna feature on the menu and the restaurant was built for sunsets.
$ **Threemurti Shiva**. Simple little restaurant serving tasty local meals.

Patnem

$$ **Home Beachfront Restaurant**, T0832-2643916, homeispatnem@ yahoo.com. Purified water-washed salad, blue cheese brought from Auroville, French cakes and Lavazza coffee. All under a wooden canopy with hammocks. Closed evenings and Wed.

🍷 Pubs, bars and clubs

Palolem and around *p155, map p156*
Bridge and Tunnel Pub Living Huts in the rocks towards Calomb, T0832-2633237, sera_goa@rediffmail.com. Pool for Rs 100/hr and a laid-back beach pub-lounge area filled with rugs and cushions.
Cuba Beach Cafe, behind Syndicate Bank, Palolem, T0832-2643449. Cool, upbeat bar for a sundowner, **Café Del Mar** next door does excellent fresh nosh too.
Neptune's Point Bar and Restaurant, T9822584968. Wide dance-floor for a mellow daily chill-out from 1700-2200 with a proper party on a weekly basis.
Rock It Café, north end of the beach, Palolem. Coffee from Bodum filters, backgammon, and Sade often on the playlist, it's a stoner's paradise shack.

🏃 Activities and tours

Palolem and around *p155, map p156*
Boat hire and trips
You can hire boats to spend a night under the stars on the secluded Butterfly or

Honeymoon beaches, and many offer dolphin watching and fishing trips. You can see the dolphins from dry land around Neptune's Point, or ask for rowboats instead of outboard motor boats if you want to reduce pollution. Mornings between 0830-1230 are best. Arrange through **Palolem Beach Resort**, travel agents or a fisherman. 4 people for about Rs 600 for 1-hr trip, Rs 1500 for 3 hrs (take sun-screen, shirt, hat and drinking water).
Ciaran's Camp, T0832-2643477, runs 2-hr mountain bike tours and you can charter a yacht overnight through Ciaran's bar for Rs 8,000.

Tour operators
Rainbow Travels, T0832-2643912. Efficient flight and train bookings, exchange, Western Union money transfer, safe deposit lockers (Rs 10 per day), good internet connection.
Bliss Travels 118/1 near main gate, Palolem beach, T0832-2643456, bliss_travels@ rediffmail.com. Air tickets (domestic and international), money change, bus services, speedy internet, ISD, plus package tours to nature reserves and retreat farm.

🛍 Shopping

Palolem and around *p155, map p156*
The approach roads are now hemmed in by the familiarly enticing flutterings of Kashmiri, Tibetan and Karnataka trinket shops selling clothes, *chillums*, music tapes and mineral water.
Chim at Ciaran's Camp, T982 9015263, mahaboy@hotmail.com. Classier stuff that Chim, herself a product designer, has painstakingly sourced from all over India.

⚜ Festivals and events

Palolem and around *p155, map p156*
Feb Rathasaptami The Shri Malikarjuna Temple 'car' festival attracts large crowds.
Apr Shigmo, also at the Shri Malikarjuna Temple, also very popular.

⊙ Transport

Agonda *p154, map p155*

From Palolem/Chaudi Junc, **auto-rickshaws** charge Rs 120-150; turn off the road by the Niki bar and restaurant. **Dunhills Hotel**, Agonda, hire out scooters, motorbikes and cars.

Bus

First direct bus for **Margao** leaves between 0600-0630, last at 1000, takes about 1 hr. Alternatively, arrange a lift to the main road and flag down the next bus (last bus for Margao passes by at around 2000, but it is advisable to complete your journey before dark). Hourly buses between **Betul** and **Palolem** call at Agonda (and Cabo de Rama). Easy to visit for the day by taxi, motorbike or bicycle from Palolem beach.

Palolem and around *p155, map p156*

Bus

6 daily direct buses run between Margao and **Canacona** (40 km via Cuncolim), Rs 9, on their way to **Karwar**. From Canacona, taxis and auto-rickshaws charge Rs 40-60 to **Palolem** beach only 2 km away. From Palolem, direct buses for **Margao** leave at around 0615, 0730, 0930, 1415, 1515, 1630 and take 1 hr. At other times of the day take a taxi or rickshaw to the main road, and flag down the next private bus. Frequent private services run to Palolem and Margao as well as south into Karnataka.

Train

From Canacona Junction station, 2 km away from Palolem beach. The booking office opens 1 hr before trains depart. Inside the station there is a phone booth and a small chai stall. A few auto-rickshaws and taxis meet all trains. If none is available walk down the approach road and turn left under the railway bridge. At the next corner, known locally as Chaurasta, you will find an auto-rickshaw to take you to **Palolem** beach (Rs 50) or **Agonda** beach; expect to pay double for a taxi.

To **Ernakulam Junction**, Netravati Exp 6345, 2325, 15 hrs, sleeper Rs 280, 3 tier a/c Rs 790, and on to **Thiruvananthapuram** (20 hrs); **Mangalore**, Matsyagandha Exp 2619, 0105, 6 hrs, Rs 49; **Margao**, 2 passenger trains a day, KAM 2up, 0630, KAR 2up, 1237, 45 mins, Rs 11; **Mumbai (Tilak)**, Netravati Exp 6346, 0548, 13 hrs, 2nd Cl sleeper Rs 300, 3 tier a/c Rs 800; via Margao 45 mins; **Mumbai (Thane)**, Matsyagandha Exp 2620, 1910, 12 hrs; via Margao 45 mins.

Canacona

Buses run to Palolem and Margao and also to Karnataka.

Calomb, Patnem and Rajbag

You can hire a **bicycle** from the village for Rs 4 per hr or Rs 35 per day. From Canacona (see below), **taxis** and **auto-rickshaws** charge Rs 40-60. Direct **buses** for Margao leave at around 0615, 0730, 0930, 1415, 1515, 1630 and take an hour. Alternatively, take a taxi or rickshaw to the main road and flag down the next private bus. Palolem is 3 km from Canacona Junction station, which is now on the Konkan line (Netravati Express).

⊙ Directory

Palolem and around *p155, map p156*

Banks Several exchanges along the beach approach road issue cash against credit cards, usual commission, 3-5%. **Internet** Widely available throughout the village, rates approximately Rs 60 per hr. **Medical facilities** T0832-2643339. Useful services **Police** T0832-2643357. **Post Office** Nearest is in Canacona.

Canacona

Banks State Bank of India, next to Canacona Palace, has no foreign exchange facility. **Internet** Baga cybercafé just beyond the bus station on the left and there are plenty of options in Palolem. **Medical services** Pai Chemists is 100 m east of the crossroads. **Post office** 200 m down the highway towards Karnataka. **Useful services** Petrol Aryadurga HP station 1 km north of the Palolem turning, towards Margao.

Calomb, Patnem and Rajbag

Banks No bank, but exchanges along the beach approach road give cash against credit cards, commission 3-5%. **Internet** widely available, Rs 60 per hr. **Medical facilities** T0832-2643339. **Police** T0832-2643357. **Post office** Nearest is at Canacona.

Ponda, interior Salcete & the eastern border

Ponda	**166**
Temples around Ponda	167
North of Ponda	171
Listings	175
West of the Zuari river	**175**
Chandor	175
Rachol	178
Loutolim (Lutolim)	179
Listings	179
To the Ghats	**180**
Bicholim and around	181
Sanquelim and around	182
Satari taluka	182
Listings	182
The central and southern interior	**184**
The Bhagwan Mahaveer Sanctuary	184
Southwest Sanguem	186
Listings	187

⚇ Footprint features

Don't miss...	165
Chartered Territory	169
The Braganza family	176

Introduction

There is enough spirituality and architecture in the neighbouring districts of Ponda and Salcete to reverse even the most cynical notions of Goa as a state rich in beach but weak on culture. Once you've had your fill of basking on the sand you'll find that delving into this geographically small area will open a window on a whole new, and richly rewarding, Goa.

The desecration of shrines that went with the 200 years of stop-start Inquisition led to the flight of many Hindu devotees from Portuguese missionary zeal and religion. They stole across the Zuari river on midnight rafts to Ponda. The building project that their relocation prompted sparked an entirely new blueprint for temple design and the hybrid forms you'll find here are totally idiosyncratic to the state: they bear Moghul-style domes and baroque balustrades. Here too there is the substantial pawprint of earlier conquering religions in the mosque of Ibrahim Adil Shah, whose dynasty's reign the Portuguese threw off to capture Old Goa at the opening of the 16th century.

Just over the water lies Salcete and the villages of Goa's most sophisticated and urbane elite, steeped in the very staunchest Catholicism. Here you can see the most eloquent symbols of the graceful living enjoyed by this aristocracy in the shape of palatial private homes, the fruits of their collusion with the colonizers in faith. Ironically, one of the finest – Braganza House in Chandor – is also the ancestral home of one of the state's most vaunted freedom fighters, Luis de Menezes-Braganza.

★ Don't miss...

① **Temples and shrines** Mug up on Goa's distinctive temple architecture style at the shrines of Mahalsa, Nagesh and Mangesh, pages 168 and 170.

② **Spice plantations** A day trip can offer a crash course in the medicinal values of plants, herbal Viagra, and a slap up Goan meal while you're at it, page 172.

③ **A tour of the Menezes-Braganza family home** Take Aida, herself the 87-year-old daughter-in-law of Luis, as your guide, page 175.

④ **Sunset** Best seen from Chandresvar Bhutnath temple hill, Paroda, page 177.

⑤ **The Alvares ancestral home in Loutolim** Much care went into the model village Big Foot next door but the real treat is this house, page 179.

⑥ **Mayem Lake** Charter a pedal boat to birdwatch on the lake, page 181.

⑦ **Tambdi Surla** The black basalt temple is the only major Hindu temple in Goa to predate the Portuguese, page 185.

⑧ **Dudhsagar Falls** Take a dunk and climb the river's mouth to bathe in the pools beneath the crashing falls, page 185.

Ponda → *Colour map 2, grid B3.*

Ponda, though Goa's smallest taluka, is also the richest in Goan Hindu religious architecture. A stone's throw from the Portuguese capital of Old Goa and within 5 km of the district's traffic-snarled and fume-filled town centre are some of Goa's most important temples including the Shri Shantadurga at Queula and the Nagesh Temple near Bandora. Ponda is also a pastoral haven full of spice gardens and wonderfully scenic views from low hills over sweeping rivers. The Bondla Sanctuary in the east of the taluka, though small and underwhelming in terms of wildlife, is a vestige of the forest-rich environment that once cloaked the entire foothills of the Western Ghats. ▶▶ *For Sleeping, Eating and other listings, see page 175.*

Ins and outs

Getting there Ponda town, once a centre of culture, music, drama and poetry, is now an important transport intersection where the main road from Margao via Borlim meets the east-west National Highway, NH4A. Buses to Panjim and Bondla via Tisk run along the NH4A, which passes through the centre of town: this is the main road you take through the Ghats to reach any of the rich ruins of Karnataka's Muslim and Hindu kingdoms at Bijapur, Hampi and Badami. The drive from Panjim via Old Goa to Ponda goes through a prosperous agricultural region with a mixture of beautiful rice paddies on the valley bottoms and a wide variety of tropical palms – the coconut and areca are particularly striking. The Zuari Bridge at Cortalim in Mormugao has been restricted to light vehicles (lorries are diverted through Ponda) and a ferry service has been reintroduced at that point. If the bridge closes for repairs, passing through Ponda will become a necessary part of the road journey for all routes between north and south Goa.

Getting around The temples are spread out so it's best to have your own transport: take a bike or charter an auto-rickshaw or taxi: you'll find these around the bus stand.

Background

The Zuari river, for most of its short course a broad, languid and becalmed river, represented the stormy boundary between the Christianized Old Conquests and the Hindu east for two centuries. St Francis Xavier found a dissolute band of European degenerates in the first settlers when he arrived in the headquarters of Luso-India and recommended the formation of an Inquisition. Although founded – in 1560 – to redress the failings within their own community, the Portuguese panel's remit quickly broadened as they found that their earliest Goan converts were also clinging clandestinely to their former faith. So the inquisitors set about weeding out these 'furtive Hindus', too, seeking to impose a Catholic orthodoxy and holding great show trials every few years with the public executions of infidels. Outside those dates set aside for putting people to death, intimidation was slightly more subtle: shrines were desecrated, temple tanks polluted and landowners threatened with confiscation of their holdings to encourage defection. Those unwilling to switch religion instead had to look for places to flee, carrying their idols in their hands.

Before the Europeans' arrival, the Goan Hindu population had dismissed Ponda, once ruled by the Muslim king of Bijapur – it had none of the resources of the wealthy, coastal district of Tiswadi. Their neglect had left it almost empty of stone-built temples. When the Conquistadores – or *descubridores* – took to sacking shrines and desecrating temple images, building churches in their place, the keepers of the Hindu faith fled for the broad river's banks and the Cumbarjua creek to its west, crossing it to build new homes for their gods. Almost every temple in Ponda tells the same story of

devastated religion, of gods snatched from the very jaws of Catholic looters and
marauders. Diogo Rodrigues, captain of Rachol Fort in 1567, was particularly zealous: he destroyed every temple in 58 villages and a mosque in Mormugao before moving on to torch the temple in Salcete from where the small half-man half-lion image in Velinga's Lakshmi Narasimha temple was carried.

Sights

Ponda wasn't always the poster-boy for Goa's Hindu identity that it is today. The **Safa Mosque** (Shahouri Masjid), the largest of 26 mosques in Goa, was built by Ibrahim 'Ali' Adil Shah in 1560. It has a simple rectangular chamber on a low plinth, with a pointed pitched roof, very much in the local architectural style, but the arches are distinctly Bijapuri. Because it was built of laterite the lower tier has been quite badly eroded. On the south side is a tank with *meherab* designs for ritual cleansing. Large gardens and fountains here were destroyed under the Portuguese, today the mosque's backdrop is all natural instead – it's set off by low rising forest-covered hills.

Meanwhile, for a picture of Goa's Buddhist history, travel 4 km east from Ponda on the NH4A to **Khandepar** to visit **Goa's best-preserved cave site** ① *the site is hidden on the edge of a wooded area near a tributary of the Mandovi: turn left off the main road from Ponda, look for green and red archaeological survey sign, just before the bridge over the river. Right after the football pitch then walk down the track off to the right by the electric substation*. Believed to be Buddhist, it dates from the 10th or 11th century. The first three of the four laterite caves have an outer and an inner cell, possibly used as monks' living quarters. Much more refined than others discovered in Goa, they show clear evidence of schist frames for doors to the inner cells, sockets on which wooden doors would have been hung, pegs carved out of the walls for hanging clothing, and niches for storage and for placing lamps. The first cave, probably intended for the senior monk, has deep (though rather crude) lotus carvings on the ceiling of the outer cell. There are further carvings on the ceiling in the rear cell. The much simpler fourth cave, which is a short distance away and faces the first cave, is only single-celled and was probably used as a prayer room. A Krishna image, a Nandi bull and a 15th-century Hanuman image found in Khandepar are now in the State Archaeological Museum in Panjim.

⁞ *The best time to visit Khandepar is in the morning when the sun partly shines into the 3 principal caves.*

Temples around Ponda → *Colour map 2, grid A/B3.*

Farmagudi
On the left as you approach Farmagudi from Ponda is a **Ganesh temple** built by Goa's first Chief Minister, Shri D Bandodkar, back in the 1960s. It is an amalgam of ancient and modern styles. Opposite is a statue of Sivaji commemorating the Maratha leader's association with **Ponda's fort** The fort was built by the Adil Shahis of Bijapur and destroyed by the Portuguese in 1549. It lay in ruins for over a century before Sivaji conquered the town in 1675 and rebuilt it. The Portuguese Viceroy attempted to re-take it in October 1683 but quickly withdrew, afraid to take on the Maratha King Sambhaji, who suddenly appeared with his vast army.

Velinga
Lakshmi-Narasimha Temple ① *from the north take a right immediately after crossing a small river bridge*, Goa's only temple to Vishnu's fourth avatar, the Lakshmi-Narasimha or Lakshmi-Narayana, is just north of Farmagudi at Velinga. The small half-man, half-lion image at this 18th century temple was whisked away from the torches of

Captain Diogo Rodrigues in 1567 Salcete. Its tower and dome over the sanctuary are markedly Islamic. Inside there are well-carved wooden pillars in the mandapa and elaborate silver work on the screen and shrine. The large spring-fed temple tank has steps down to the water on each side and is enclosed by a niched wall. A tall cosmic pillar with rings stands on the far side of the tank.

Priol

The Shri Mangesh Temple ① *to the northwest of Ponda set on a wooded hill at Priol on the NH4A leading to Old Goa* . This 18th-century temple to Siva's incarnation as the benevolent Mangesh is one of the most important Hindu temples in Goa. Its Mangesh linga originally belonged to an ancient temple in Kushatali (modern day Cortalim) across the river. After the opening of the Inquisition in 1561 the deity was spirited away across the water to save it from marauding soldiers intent on destroying Hindu temples throughout Salcete (Mukto, the man who saved it, got his own shrine inside the complex as a reward). It lay in a small shrine until the mid-18th century when an influential Hindu acquired the present estate.

The complex is typical of Goan Hindu temple architecture and the surrounding estate on which the temple depends provides a beautiful setting. Note the attractive tank on the left as you approach which is one of the oldest parts of the site. The bright white seven-storeyed octagonal *deepmal* in the courtyard is one of the most famous lamp towers in Goa. Around its base are colourful little red and yellow 'primitif' images painted on a blue background (lamps are placed in the niches at festivals). The sacred *tulsi vrindavan* (basil) plant stands nearby. The *mandapa* (assembly hall) has the typical red-tiled steeply-pitched roof. The highest tower with an octagonal drum topped by a dome is over the sanctum. At the entrance to the shrine itself is a beautifully carved wooden door. 19th-century Belgian glass chandeliers hang from the ceiling of the main hall, which is usually packed with pilgrims making offerings of flowers and coconuts. You'll find subsidiary shrines to the affiliated deities: the *nandi* (Siva's vehicle, the bull, particularly worshipped by the Gaud Saraswat Brahmins who are the temple mahajans or trustees), along with the silver *dwarpalas* (guardian deities) and shrines to Parvati and Ganesh: the deity itself is behind an elaborate silver screen. Cusped arches above the windows and moghul domes are the stamp of a strong Islamic architectural influence, while baroque balustrades and pilasters are more Catholic in design.

⚑ You can get a good view of the temple with its tank in the foreground by climbing the wall into the coconut grove.

The complex, with its *agrashalas* (pilgrims' hostel), administrative offices and other rooms set aside for religious ceremonies, is a good representative of Goan Hindu temple worship: the temple is supported by a large resident community who serve its various functions. February 25 is *Jatra*. During *Mangesh Jatra* the *rath* (temple car) with Shri Mangesh is pulled by crowds of attendants.

Mardol

Two kilometres on from Shri Mangesh, the early 16th century **Mahalsa Narayani Temple** is dedicated to Mahalsa, a Goan form of Vishnu's consort Lakshmi or, according to some, the god himself in female form *Mohini* (from the story of the battle between the *devas* and *asuras*). The deity was rescued from what was once a fabulous temple in Verna at around the same time as the Mangesh Sivalinga was brought to Priol. The entrance to the temple complex is through the arch under the *nagarkhana* (drum room). There is a seven-storeyed *deepstambha* and a tall brass Garuda pillar which rests on the back of a turtle, acting as an impressive second lamp tower. The half human-half eagle *Garuda*, Vishnu's vehicle, sits on top. A stone 'cosmic pillar' with rings, next to it, signifies the axis along which the temple is aligned. The new *mandapa* (columned assembly hall) is made of concrete, but is

Chartered territory

Over fifty thousand foreign tourists flood into Goa in December alone, and over a third of them are British.

Oddly, this doesn't mean that the state feels swamped. Even at peak season you can travel between plenty of inland *vaddos* without seeing another foreign face. This is because, according to (admittedly slightly questionable) government statistics, while over 100,000 foreign tourists holidayed in Bardez, much of the rest of the state – including Quepem and Sattari, Ponda and Canacona – saw barely a footprint.

Despite the fact that Britons outnumber the second most numerous visitors – Germans – by a factor of ten, they are hardly adored by their Goan hosts. In short, this is because the Brits have a reputation for tight-fistedness.

Christmas, New Year and Easter mean gold rush to the Goans who work in tourism. They work like dogs all hours of the day and night for days on end. Teachers and families that have to holiday at this time will have coughed up £1,000 for a ticket, and "when you've spent that much you're not going to be miserable about spending two quid on a meal", as a prominent Goan entrepreneur puts it. These Britons the Goans don't mind so much.

It's the others, the ones who get their flight and accommodation for two weeks for just £299 all in, who are significantly less popular. With these deals, the average holiday budget will be as little as possible, meaning the local economy hardly benefits from being the Brits' cheap lager, sun and fun playground. In Thomas Cook's tourism cost of living index for 2004 Goa ranked number one as the cheapest place for a slap up three-course meal, beating Tunisia and even Romania. Such publicity isn't helping the Goan tourist board make Goa an upmarket, and more income-generating travel destination.

Small wonder, then that the Russians are embraced with open arms. There, the demand for charter flights still far outstrips supply so it's the wealthy elite and the fast-emergent upper middle classes who can afford to jet in – the type who'll tip Rs 500 without blinking. There's also a great cultural sympathy – after India and the Gulf Russians are the largest consumers of Bollywood movies worldwide – and there's long been strong trade relations between the two countries. The Russian presence in Goa has been a late but fast developer. And unlike the British, the Russians "want to go everywhere, see everything, and have a live-fast-die-young approach to money so long as you can communicate with them". Small wonder, too, then, that many of the beach shack boys are learning Rusky.

More popular than both Brits and Russians, though, are Indians themselves. They are also more populous: one and a half million Indians holiday in Goa each year – more than the entire indigenous population of the state.

hidden somewhat under the red tiling, finely-carved columns and a series of brightly painted carvings of the 10 *avatars*, or incarnations, of Vishnu. The unusual dome above the sanctuary is particularly elegant. A decorative arched gate at the back leads to the peace and cool of the palm-fringed temple tank. A palanquin procession with the deity marks the February Mardol Jatra, Mahasivaratri is observed in February-March and Kojagiri Purnima celebrated at the August-September full moon.

A narrow winding lane dips down to this tiny hamlet and its **temple** ⓘ *head 4 km west from Ponda towards Farmagudi on the NH4A, looking for a fork signposted to Bandora*, to Siva as Nagesh (God of Serpents). The temple's origin is put at 1413 by an inscribed tablet here, though the temple was refurbished in the 18th century. The temple tank, which is well stocked with carp, is enclosed by a white-outlined laterite block wall and surrounded by shady palms. The five-storey lamp tower near the temple has brightly coloured deities painted in niches just above the base, the main *mandapa* (assembly hall) has interesting painted woodcarvings illustrating stories from the epics *Ramayana* and *Mahabharata* below the ceiling line, as well as the *Ashtadikpalas*, the eight Directional Guardians (Indra, Agni, Yama, Nirritti, Varuna, Vayu, Kubera and Ishana). The principal deity has the usual *Nandi* and in addition there are shrines to Ganesh and Laxmi-Narayan and subsidiary shrines with *lingas*, in the courtyard. The Nagesh Jatra, normally in November, is celebrated at full moon to commemorate Siva's victory.

In a valley south of the Nagesh Temple lies the **Mahalakshmi Temple**, thought to be the original form of the deity of the Shakti cult. Mahalakshmi was worshipped by the Silaharas (chieftains of the Rashtrakutas, AD 750-1030) and the early Kadamba kings. The sanctuary has an octagonal tower and dome, the side entrances have shallow domes. The stone slab with the Marathi inscription dating from 1413 on the front of the Nagesh Temple refers to a temple to Mahalakshmi at Bandora. The *sabhamandap* has an impressive gallery of 18 wooden images of Vishnu. Mahalakshmi is special in that she wears a linga in her head-dress and is considered a peaceful, 'Satvik', form of Devi: the first temple the Portuguese allowed at Panjim is also dedicated to her.

Around Ponda

Queula (Kavale)

Just 3 km southwest from Ponda's town centre bus stand is one of the largest and most famous of Goa's temples; dedicated to **Shantadurga** (1738), the wife of Siva as the Goddess of Peace. She earns the Shanti (Sanskrit for peace) prefix here because, at the request of Brahma, she mediated in a great quarrel between her husband and Vishnu, and restored peace in the universe. In the sanctuary here she stands symbolically between the two bickering gods. The temple, which stands in a forest clearing, was built by Shahu, the grandson of the mighty Maratha ruler Sivaji, but the deity was taken from Quelossim well before then, back in the 16th Century. It is neo-classical in design: its two-storey octagonal drum topped by a dome with a lantern, is a classic example of the strong impact church architecture made on Goan temple design. The interior of polished marble is lit by several chandeliers. Steps lead up to the temple complex which has a very large tank cut into the hillside and a spacious courtyard surrounded by the usual pilgrim hostels and administration offices. The temple has a six-storey *deepstambha* (lamp tower) and subsidiary shrines. The part-gilded *rath* (car) is housed in the compound. In December, there is a Sangeet Sanmelan (festival of classical singing) which honours the memory of Dinanath Mangeshkar, and in late January, a special ceremony is held to honour the Mhars or Harijans ('outcastes') who are not otherwise expected to enter temple precincts. The following day the temple goes through a 'purification ceremony'. Kavale Jatra (February) is marked by a procession of devotees accompanying the deity in a palanquin.

Shri Sausthan Goud Padacharya Kavale Math, named after the historic seer and exponent of the Advaita system of Vedanta was founded between Cortalim and Quelossim. This Hindu seminary was destroyed during the Inquisition in the 1560s and temporarily transferred to Golvan and Chinar outside Goa. After 77 years, in the early 17th century, the Math regrouped here in Queula, the village where the Shantadurga deity (which had also originated in Quelossim) had been reinstalled. There is a temple to Vittala at the Math. The foundation has another Math at Sanquelim.

Durbhat

The road southwest from Queula ends at Durbhat, once an important port on the Zuari. In nearby **Agapur** there's the – unusual for this area – pre-colonial, pre-Inquisition **Madhavdeo complex** of three small shrines on a low hill, built of laterite in the 11th century. This was the period when carpenters-turned-stonemasons were still imitating their work in wood on the new material: especially visible here where the mortar-less masonry has been spared later plasterwork. The stylized lotus-bud domes of the temples are well preserved and are unusual in being *sikhara*-style (as you find in the sanctuary towers of northern temples). Unlike later Goan temple domes, which were influenced by Islamic or Christian architecture, the corbelled dome here is thoroughbred Hindu. Their good condition suggests that the shrines were once protected from heavy rain by some kind of second roof, possibly supported originally on attractively carved wooden columns. The present tiled roof over the ancient structure is, of course, a more recent addition.

Siroda

The **Kamakshi Temple** ① *to the south of Ponda taluka*, is dedicated to a form of Shantadurga (see Queula above). The image, together with the affiliate deities Raieshwar Siva and Lakshmi Narayana, were once rescued from Raia across the Zuari around 1564, when the original temples were destroyed by the Portuguese. The temple has an unusual sanctuary tower with a tiled roof and four kneeling elephants at its base. The red pyramidal tiled roofs on the mandapas and atop the *nagarkhana* over the arched entrance gate are also attractive.

The 16th-century **Sivnatha Temple** was founded by a holy man named Sidha. The deity is taken out in a palanquin for Siroda Jatra.

North of Ponda → *Colour map 2, grid A3.*

Tucked right up close on the border with Tiswadi, just 5 km east of Old Goa on the national highway, is **Banastari**, the site of Albuquerque's hard fought battle against the Bijapuri Muslim Sultans in the 16th century. It is famous for its clandestine **night bazaar**, where trading in stolen Portuguese goods (along with the more mundane selling of fruit and vegetables) used to start at midnight on Fridays and continue until noon on Saturday. Banastari still holds a traditional local bazaar.

Marcela, north of Banastari, has a number of Hindu temples where most of the deities come from Ilhas (now Tiswadi) in the Old Conquest territory, in particular from Chorao Island. The village has several 'wedding halls' so is often busy, especially on auspicious dates of the Hindu calendar. Shri Ravalnatha-Devki Krishna has the most important deity in the village, which originally came from Chorao. The festival at full moon in January is celebrated with palanquin (covered litter) processions.

Candola has one of the two Ganesh temples in the state. The ancient Ganapati image in the **Ganesh Temple** was originally installed in the Kadamba Temple at Navelim (Divar Island) and was moved to a place of safety when Albuquerque ordered that a new church to Our Lady of Divar be built on the site of the Hindu temple. Sections of the ancient temple can still be seen in the centre of Divar Island, see page 84. Today the old Ganesh image has been replaced by a new one. The black Kalbhairav image of Siva here was found in a house in the village where it had been used as a weight for weighing rice on scales; since the block was a little too heavy a corner was knocked out to make it equal to a *maund*! Other temples in Candola also house deities with ancient origins, including Shri Bhagvati from Aldona (Bardez).

The Spice Hills

There are a number of spice plantations in the foothills around northeast Ponda that have thrown open their gates to offer in-depth tours that detail plants' medicinal and food uses during a walk through these cultivated forests. These are surprisingly informative and fun. Of these, Savoi Spice Plantation is probably the most popular (and the guide is excellent).

Taxis from the coastal resorts cost around Rs 700 return from Candolim, but it's better value to ask a travel agent as many offer competitive rates including entrance fees (eg **Day Tripper Tours**, T0832-2276726, near Kamat Complex, Calangute, Rs 700). Some also throw in a visit to a local cashew-nut processing plant nearby.

Savoi Spice Plantation ⓘ *6 km from Savoi, T0832-2340243, www.savoiplantation.com, 0800-1800, guided tour Rs 300, 1 hr, awkward to reach by public transport, ask buses from Ponda or Banastari heading for Volvoi for the plantation.* The plantation, now over 200 years old, covers 40 ha focused around a large irrigation tank. Half the area is wetland and the other half on a hillside, making it possible for a large variety of plants and trees to grow. The plantation was founded by Mr Shetye and is now in the hands of the fourth generation of his family, who regularly donate funds to local community projects such as the school and temple. All plants are grown according to traditional Goan methods of organic farming. The tour includes drinks and snacks on arrival, and concludes with the chance to buy packets of spices (good gifts to take home) and a tot of feni to 'give strength' for the return journey to your resort. You will even be offered several cheap, natural alternatives to Viagra, whether you need them or not!

♣ A large banyan tree stands here like a benevolent spirit; locals offer prayers along with feni, bread and bananas on Wed and Sun.

On your walk, you will pass grapefruit, areca palms (some over 150 years old), and coconuts with pepper vines growing up their trunks, bay, cloves, papaya, breadfruit and *cocum*. After the scarlet flesh of the *cocum* has been eaten the skin is cut into strips and sun-dried to turn into black *sola*, which is used for flavouring curries. *Bimla*, akin to starfruit, hang like bunches of large green grapes and are especially good for prawn curries and pickles. You will be shown soft and hard skin jackfruit, which can grow to giants weighing over 20 kg, and banana plants which can produce 250 bananas from a single flower; one flower is cut off each plant to be eaten as a vegetable delicacy. When used in curry, the unripe jackfruit has such a strong resemblance to meat that in some parts of the country it is called the 'tree goat'. As many as 200,000 pineapples are cut between June and September after maturing during the summer rains.

On the hillside grow pineapples, bamboo, basil, cardamom, cocoa, wood-apple, mangoes, and the surprising nutmeg (male and female), which are easily mistaken for lemons. No space is wasted on this densely cultivated plantation. Even the staple tuber (*suarn*) is grown under the surface, some weighing up to 2 kg. The ubiquitous coconut is not only prized for its fruit, which is cut off every three months, but also for its leaves which are used for thatching, and for its trunk which serves for building. Expert coconut pickers will climb up the straight trunk of a palm with a circle of rope around their ankles to cut fresh green coconuts, which provide a most welcome instant cool drink as well as a soft succulent kernel.

Outside Savoi village itself is the **Ananta temple** dedicated to Vishnu as Sheshashahi Ananta. The plain white exterior with pitched tiled roofs contrasts strikingly with the brightly coloured carvings on the wooden pillars and supporting beams of the mandapa. Visitors are allowed to view the principal deity, carved on a black stone. The reclining Vishnu, with a distinctive conical head-dress, rests on the coils of the serpent Ananta (or Shesha) protected by his hood. He is shown in the period between the creation of one world and the next, when a lotus emerges from his navel supporting Brahma the Creator. There is evidence of the village's ancient Hindu roots in the 10th-century medieval basalt image of Vishnu showing his 10 incarnations, which was found here and is now displayed in Old Goa's Archaeological Museum.

Pascoal Spice Plantation ① *near Khandepar between Ponda and Tisk, T0832-2344268, 0800-1800, tours Rs 300, signposted 1½km off the NH4A.* The plantation grows a wide variety of spices and exotic fruit and is pleasantly located by a river. A guided tour takes you through a beautiful and fascinating setting. Spices are available for sale.

⁝ *Try to visit a plantation at lunchtime.*

The **Sahakari Spice Farm** ① *Curti, on the Ponda-Khandepar road, T0832-2311394,* is also open to the public. The spice tour includes an authentic banana-leaf lunch.

Tropical Spice Plantation ① *Keri, T0832-2340329, tours Rs 300, boats for hire Rs 100, clearly signposted off the NH4A (just south of the Sri Mangesh temple).* This very pleasant plantation is situated in a picturesque valley in Keri. It has well-informed guides and friendly staff. It specialises in medicinal uses for the spices, the majority of which seem to be good for the skin. At the end of the tour an areca nut picker will demonstrate the art of harvesting by shinning up a tall palm with his feet tied together in a circle of rope. Having climbed up one palm, he will gracefully sway at the crown in order to transfer to the top of a neighbouring tree without having to waste any energy climbing down and up again! The demonstration ends with the equally impressive art of descent, a rapid slide down the trunk like a fireman. After the tour a delicious lunch is served in the shade overlooking a lake where there are a couple of boats for hire. Visitors arriving in the early morning will find the boats an excellent opportunity for viewing the varied birdlife around the lake.

Bondla Wildlife Sanctuary

① *20 km northeast of Ponda, mid-Sep to mid-Jun, Fri-Wed 0930-1730; Nature Education Centre 0930-1300, 1400-1730, Rs 5, camera Rs 25, video Rs 100, 2-wheelers Rs 10, cars Rs 50, buses from Ponda via Tisk and Usgaon stop near the sanctuary where you can get taxis and motorcycle taxis. KTC buses sometimes run at weekends from Panjim. During the season the Forest Department minibus is supposed to do 2 daily trips (except Thu) between Bondla and Tisk: from Bondla, 0815, 1745; from Tisk, 1100 (Sun 1030) and 1900. Check at the tourist office first. If you are on a motorbike make sure you fill up with petrol – the nearest pumps are at Ponda and Tisk. Bondla is well signposted from the NH4A east of Ponda (5 km beyond Usgaon, a fork to the right leads to the park up a winding steep road).*

Bondla is the most popular of Goa's three sanctuaries because it is relatively easily accessible. The small, 8-sq km sanctuary is situated in the foothills of the Western

Ghats; sambar, wild boar, gaur (Indian bison) and monkeys live alongside a few migratory elephants that wander in from Karnataka during the summer:

The mini-zoo here guarantees sightings of 'Goa's wildlife in natural surroundings', although whether the porcupine and African lion are examples of indigenous species is another matter. Thankfully, the number of animals in the zoo has decreased in recent years and those that remain seem to have adequate space compared to other zoos in India. The small and basic Nature Education Centre has the facility to show wildlife videos, but is rarely used. You can take five-minute **elephant rides** between 1100-1200 and between 1600-1700. A **deer safari** (minimum eight people), between 1600-1730 costs Rs 10. The park also has an attractive picnic area in a **botanical garden** setting and a 2.4 km **nature trail** with waterholes, a lake and a tree-top observation tower (about one hour on foot, so take plenty of water). A single metalled road goes some distance into the sanctuary but the chances of seeing many animals are slim. You are most likely to see monkeys and attractive birds, and deer and gaur if you are lucky.

☁ Sleeping

Ponda p166
Ponda is within easy reach of any of Goa's beach resorts and Panjim.
C-D **Menino**, 100 m east of Bus Stand junction, 1st flr, T0832-2313148. 20 rooms, some a/c, pleasant, comfortable, good restaurant serves generous main courses, impressive modern hotel, good value.
E **President**, 1 km east of bus stand, supermarket complex, T0832-2312287. 11 rooms, basic but clean and reasonable.
E **Padmavi**, Gaunekar House, 100 m north of bus stand on NH4A, T0832-2312144. 20 large clean rooms, some with bath with TV.

Temples around Ponda p167
Farmagudi
C-D **Atish**, just below Ganesh Temple on NH4A, T0832-2335124, www.hotelatish.com. 40 comfortable rooms, some a/c, restaurant, large pool in open surrounds, gym, modern hotel, many pilgrim groups, friendly staff.
E **Farmagudi Resort**, attractively located though too close to NH4A, T0832-2335122. 39 clean rooms, some a/c, dorm (Rs 80), adequate restaurant (eat at Atish).

North of Ponda p171
The Spice Hills
B **Savoi Farmhouse**, T0832-2340243, is an idyllic traditional Goan-style farmhouse built from mud with 2 adjoining en suite double rooms each with private veranda. There is electricity and hot water and rates are for full board and include the plantation tour. A night in the forest is memorable and highly recommended. Ideally, stay 2 nights around the full moon; spend a day exploring deep into the forested hills, good for bird watchers.

Bondla Wildlife Sanctuary
F **Eco-Cottages**. 8 basic rooms with attached bath, newer ones better. Also 1 km inside park entrance (which may be better for seeing wildlife at night) are 2 12-bed dorms (Rs 30). Reserve ahead at Deputy Conservator of Forests, Wildlife Division, 4th Flr, Junta House, 18th June Rd, Panjim, T0832-2229701, although a room or bed is often available to anyone turning up.

❼ Eating

Ponda p166
$ **Amigos**, 2 km east of centre on the Belgaum road.
$ **Spoon Age**, Upper Bazaar, T0832-2316191. Garden restaurant, serving Goan meals for local folk, friendly new set up. Occasional live music at weekend.

North of Ponda p171
The Spice Hills
$$ **Glade Bar and Restaurant**, Pascoal Spice Plantation, 1130-1800, is good but a bit pricey. Tropical Spice Plantation also serves delicious lunches.

Bondla Wildlife Sanctuary
$ **The Den Bar and Restaurant** near the entrance, serves chicken, vegetables or fish with rice. A small cafeteria, inside the park near the mini-zoo, sells snacks and cold drinks.

⊚ Transport

Ponda p166
Buses to **Panjim** and **Bondla** via Tisk, but it is best to have your own transport to see the places nearby.

ⓘ Directory

Ponda p166
Internet Fun World.Com, Viradh Building, T0832-2316717. **Deputy Conservator of Forests** (North) T0832-2312095. **Medical services** Community Health Centre, T0832-2312115.

West of the Zuari river → *Colour map 2, B2-3 & C3.*

Beautiful, white, wide-veranda houses are commonplace all over Goa, and there's much to keep any architectural enthusiast on the prowl in almost any village, but guided tours around the stately homes of this area of Goa gives unparalleled insights into just how well the state's aristocracy once lived. You wouldn't ordinarily get to glimpse these castles, but some of the landed gentries' difficulties in adapting to post-Independence Goa, and their much-reduced economic situations, have resulted in estates being opened up to visitors. Interior Salcete is a hotbed of these huge 18th century buildings, some of which rival the chateaux of France and the most illustrious estates of England, stuffed with chandeliers from Belgium, ceramics from China and Japan, and polished Italian marble floors.→ *For Sleeping, Eating and other listings, see pages 179-180.*

Ins and outs

Getting there and around These villages are closest to Margao but can also easily be visited from Panjim or the beaches in central Goa. It would be an arduous day trip from the northern beaches. Buses from Margao Kadamba bus stand (45 mins) take you within walking distance of the sights but it is worth considering a taxi. The Madgaon railway station with connections to Mumbai and the Konkan coastal route as well as direct trains to Hospet is close by.

Background

By the late 18th century, an educated middle class elite had emerged in the villages of the Old Conquests. With newly established rights to property, well-to-do Goans began to invest in large homes and very fine living. The villages of Lutolim and Chandor are two of a number that saw the distinct development of estates and houses built on this grand scale. Their houses were stuffed with tokens of their Europeanization and affluence, mixed with traditions appropriated from their native ancestry, installing personal chapels instead of *devachem kuds*, or Hindu prayer rooms.

Chandor → *Colour map 2, grid B3.*

Although something of a backwater today, the once-grand village of Chandor nonetheless boasts several fine Portuguese mansions. Foremost among them the enormous **Menezes Braganza family house** ⓘ *13 km east of Margao, both wings are usually open daily 1000-1730 but it is best to confirm by telephone. West Wing: T0832-2784201 between 1300-1400 or early evening after 1830. The front door is usually open; go up the stairs and ring the bell by the door on the left (you may have to wait a few minutes). A donation of Rs 100 (Rs 50 for students) at the end of the tour will be greatly appreciated. East Wing: T0832-2784227. The East Wing is keener on donations.* Luis de Menezes Braganza was an influential journalist and politician (1878-1938) who not only campaigned for freedom from colonial rule but also

Ponda, interior Salcete & the eastern border West of the Zuari river

The Braganza Family

Southern Goans imagine themselves as both more cultured and more moneyed than their opposite numbers in the north, and the snooty southern demeanour certainly became second nature to the family Braganza. Claudeo, of the family's current generation, remembers his father as a man whose shirts were all stitched in Bond Street, London. His great grandfather, meanwhile, would be borne aloft on a palanquin all the way to Panjim on the occasion of the feast day of St Xavier, where he would have booked out a whole hotel for a month just for himself. "They had the money and they lived with a lot of style. People today don't know how to live, don't know what comfort and culture is," Claudeo says now.

But fate dealt his family a double-blow. The freedom fighter Luis de Menezes-Braganza and his descendants were at the forefront of the movement to end the Portuguese colonial occupation of Goa. Claudeo's great uncle was taken prisoner and jailed in Portugal, charged with incitement against the colonial enterprise. Those members of the family left in Goa fled the state in fear of reprisals in 1946, exiles in broader India until the Portuguese finally handed back sovereignty in 1961. The family returned to find 20 years worth of coconut and paddy looted in their absence. Shortly after, the incoming government put in place land reforms favouring tenant farmers over landlords.

Not only was the everyday upkeep of the home too costly to bear without their once grand income, the home itself had suffered horrible neglect: chandeliers and huge bracelets of gold had been looted and, worst, the caretaker had taken to burning antique, carved rosewood beds, tables and chairs for fuel. Even today, the yard is full of the shards of their once fine crockery collection. Aida, who married into the family, refused to let her opulent house crumble, and humbly took to guiding tourists through the house herself, 25 years ago. Her decision was met with furious tongue-wagging from the local community who took a dim view of such a fine family taking in foreigners. "I'm not robbing or assaulting anyone," Aida told herself in the face of extreme criticism. As she says now: "If the queen can do it why can't I?" Now in her 80s, Aida is handing over the responsibility for the upkeep of the house to her son Claudeo. "We can't let this fall," he says taking in the grand house with a sweep of his hand, "Let me try to do just 10 % of what my mother did."

became a champion of the less privileged sections of Goan society. The late 16th-century two-storey mansion he inherited, (extended in the 18th and 19th centuries), still complete with much of the family furniture and effects, shows the sheer opulence of the life enjoyed by the old Goan families who established great plantation estates. The two wings are occupied separately by members of the Braganza family who have inherited the property. The central staircase, which divides the house into two halves, leads upstairs to the public reception rooms in the front, and the private rooms at the back. The kitchen and servants' quarters were downstairs at the back around the courtyard. Typically, the reception rooms at the front are lit by large glazed windows.

The **West Wing**, which is better maintained and has finer antiques, is owned by Aida de Menezes Braganza. The guided tour by this elderly member of the family – when she resides here – is fascinating. She has managed to restore the teak ceiling of floor survived better since this native Goan timber can withstand water. In the dining room, the original polished *argamassa* floor has been replaced by new mosaic though a small section of old tiles has been retained near a window, as an example. The original ceiling of the grand salon (ballroom) has been cleverly refurbished with patterned fibreglass to imitate the original American zinc panels (some original ceiling panels can still be viewed in the East Wing). There is much carved and inlaid antique furniture and very fine imported china and porcelain, some specially ordered, and bearing the family crest.

The faded **East Wing**, occupied by Sr Alvaro de Perreira-Braganza, partly mirrors the West Wing. It also has some excellent carved and inlaid furniture and a similar large salon with fine chandeliers, which once reflected on polished coloured marble floors. Today it requires some imagination to conjure up the grand occasions it must have witnessed in the past: there's lots of dust and odd family bric-a-brac. The baroque family chapel at the back now has a prized relic added to its collection, the bejewelled nail of St Francis Xavier, which had, until recently, been kept guarded away from public view.

The guide from the East Wing of the Braganza House can also show you the **Fernandes House** ① *daily, phone ahead To832-2784245, suggested donation Rs 100*, if he's not too busy. It's another example of a once-fine mansion just to the southeast of the village, on the Quepem road. This too has an impressive grand salon occupying the front of the house and a hidden inner courtyard. Recent excavations have unearthed an underground hiding place for occasions when Christian families were under attack from Hindu raiders.

Back in Chandor village itself, the **Church of Our Lady of Bethlehem**, built in 1645, replaced the principal *Sapta Matrika* (Seven Mothers) temple, which was demolished in the previous century.

South of Chandor

Paroda, 15 km southeast of Margao (and about 4 km northwest of Quepem), is the start of the climb up the 350 m-high **Chandranath Hill** (only signposted in Hindi), which has the **Chandresvar Bhutnath Temple** at its top. The temple was referred to in copperplate inscriptions as early as the fifth or sixth century AD. The final climb on foot up some rough steps brings you to a superb open site for the brilliant white temple dedicated to Siva, as the Lord of the Moon. Water is believed to ooze from the rock linga, which has a face carved on it, when it is touched by moonlight at each full moon; the temple was reputedly designed to make this possible. The moon was worshipped by Bhoja kings who ruled south Goa from the pre-Christian era up to the mid-eighth century. There is a separate shrine to Siva Bhutnath, an unadorned tall linga. An enclosure houses two wooden temple chariots; the older one has some good carvings. There are distant views from the hilltop, particularly at sunset, across to the sea. It is also believed that the hill is one of the 180 holy ancient pilgrimage centres for Hindus. A second temple in the village, dedicated to Raibondkaranchem Deul, which has ancient sculpted images, is visited regularly by pilgrims from Ribandar in Tiswadi.

The tiny hamlet of **Cacora** in north Quepem, on the road between Sanvordem and Chandor, is noted for its **Shri Mahadeva Temple**. Although the temple is unremarkable in appearance it has some very unusual features. One is a shrine in the precincts to a Muslim *Pir* (saint) which Gomes Pereira notes is served by a Muslim who is permanently employed by the temple. Even more remarkable is the annual ritual during which a buffalo is sacrificed. This ceremony, known as *Reddebhogvoll*, is not uncommon in Maratha and Sudra villages, and is probably a relic of pre-Hindu animal sacrifice rituals often preserved in the worship of Betall. You need your own transport to reach Cacora.

Curtorim (Kurhtori) is a straddling village on the left (south) bank of the Zuari, 9 km from Margao and southeast of Rachol. The **Church of St Alex** (1597), possibly on the site of a Hindu temple, was rebuilt 50 years later and further renovated 200 years ago. Its position away from the village centre is unusual. It stands in an attractive open setting, with its huge square facing a tranquil tank edged by shady palms. The large ornamental piazza cross resembles the monumental cross in front of Margao's Church of the Holy Spirit. The church towers illustrate the influence of Hindu design in 18th-century Goan churches. The octagonal drums topped by domes and lanterns recall the principal tower over the *garbagriha* of the Shri Mangesh Temple at Mardol. The interior with its five altars is profusely and elaborately decorated with some very fine detail.

Rachol → *Colour map 2, grid B3.*

Rachol (pronounced *Rashol*) is set in a fertile valley, vivid green during the wet season and into the New Year, but burnt brown in the summer heat. A stone archway crosses the road marking the entrance to the settlement, the road coming to an abrupt end in a hamlet by the river bank. Rachol is 12 km from Margao near the Zuari, hourly buses from Margao run along the road below the seminary.

Rachol Seminary The seminary was established here in 1580 since the site had the protection of the fort (the earlier one at Margao was destroyed by Muslims the previous year). Originally known as the College of All Saints, it was rededicated to Ignatius Loyola in 1622. The Rachol complex, principally an ecclesiastical college, also includes a hospital, a primary school, an early printing press which printed the Bible in Konkani and is nearly a self-sufficient community. For successive generations the seminary has been the most prestigious centre of education in Goa producing some of Goa's secular as well as religious leaders, and now is a forward-looking institution which trains clergy able to meet the challenges of society today. The seminary also contains large galleries and a famous library of rare books on the first floor. The vast stone structure of the seminary is built round a large courtyard. There is an underground cistern which some suggest belonged to an ancient Siva temple, now destroyed, while an underground passage from the courtyard conjures images of an escape route through the fort in the precarious years of the 17th and 18th centuries.

The church ⓘ *daily church service at 0700, at all other times visits only by advance notice, contact Father Ivo de Souza, T0832-2776621, icsouza@goatelecom.com,* dating from 1609, was rebuilt in 1622. The impressive interior, beautifully restored and rich with gilding, has nine altars including one to St Constantine containing his relics, and one with the celebrated Menino Jesus statue (which was considered miraculous when it had been installed in Colva, see page 140). There are many murals in the Seminary and Church. The **Church of Our Lady of the Snows** (Nossa Senhora das Neves), now the parish church, is a short distance away on the riverside.

Little evidence remains of one of Goa's important early **forts** save a gateway and parts of some walls. Originally Muslim, it was captured by the forces of the Hindu Vijayanagar King in 1520 who then handed it over to the Portuguese in the hope that they would keep the Muslims at bay. During the Maratha Wars of 1737-39, and the siege that followed, the fort was badly damaged. Having lost the northern provinces the Portuguese paid a huge indemnity to keep the southern forts. The one in Rachol was repaired by the Marquis of Alorna in 1745. With the threat of aggression removed, the 100 cannons here were dispersed and most of the buildings gradually disintegrated over the ensuing years.

Loutolim (Lutolim) → *Colour map 2, grid B2.*

The small village of Loutolim also has several interesting Goan country houses around it. Sadly, after some priceless items were stolen from the chapel of one of these houses, they are no longer open to the public. The owners, who are often elderly, do not welcome visitors and would be grateful if tourists did not disturb them but simply viewed the houses from the road. From Margao take a bus to Cortalim (via Fatorda and Racaim), stop at the church square and it's a few minutes walk from the complex, Rs 6. There is a regular bus to Loutolim from Margao, Rs 5.

The only old house open to the public in Loutolim is **Casa Araujo** Alvares ① *To832-2777034, 1000-1230 and 1500-1800, Rs 100*, the original family home of Maendra Alvares, the founder of next door **Ancestral Goa**. Ask there to take the tour of the not yet fully restored house with a brilliant guide whose stories bring the past vividly to life. The house has the feel of a museum with a collection of typical fixtures and furnishings assimilated from other fine houses, including Bohemian chandeliers, Chinese porcelain, gilded mirrors, carved wooden furniture, English prints and Portuguese books. The private chapel contained precious figures, ivory and plate, while the grand salons and reception rooms for entertaining had highly polished wooden floors and painted tiles. There is also a growing collection of interesting domestic and agricultural artefacts.

Maendra Alvares, an artist/sculptor, has devoted considerable time, energy and finance to build the model village, **Ancestral Goa** ① *daily 0830-1830, Rs 20*, that replicates old town and village houses and artisans' huts on a woody plot next door. Well-informed guides steer you around the dwarf hillside village while they talk you through Goa's socio-historical background: good for children. There's also a display of Goa's spices and fruit trees. At the top of the site is Maendra Alvares' single-handed achievement *Natural Harmony*, a sculpture of Sant Mirabai carved out of a horizontal block of laterite (15 m x 5 m).

Also in the village, is the fine country house, **Miranda House** ① *at the end of a rough track which starts near the church square*, dating from around 1700. The Mirandas became wealthy as owners of areca plantations and the garden here still has specimen palms as reminders. The house has a typical garden courtyard at the back around which run the family rooms and bedrooms protected by shady verandas. There is also a family chapel with the kitchen and servants' quarters at the far end.

● Sleeping

Chandor *p175*
There was no accommodation in the village itself in 2004, but John at Ciaran's Camp in Palolem and Claudeo Braganza at the West Wing of Menezes Braganza House are both planning to set some up.

Rachol *p178*
C **Naari**, nearby in Maina-Curtorim village, T0832-6138316, naari@ del3.vsnl.net.in. A guesthouse for women among cashew groves, not far from the river, bed and breakfast (US$160 pw double/US$85 single), spacious living space, rooms with bath (hot water), home cooking, garden/terrace. Guests need to book and pay at least a month ahead.

● Eating

Loutolim *p179*
A bakery in a private house about 500 m from **Ancestral Goa** sells mouth-watering *Melting Moments* – macaroons made with ground cashew nuts. Ask for directions.

There is also a chai stall selling crisps and samosas located at the entrance to the model village.

Ponda, interior Salcete & the eastern border West of the Zuari river Listings

⊛ Festivals and events

Chandor *p175*

Jan 6 Three Kings Festival Crowds gather on each year at Epiphany for the Three Kings Festival, which is similarly celebrated at Reis Magos, with a big fair, and at Cansaulim (Quelim) in southern Goa. The three villages of Chandor (Cavorim, Guirdolim and Chandor) come together to put on a grand show. Boys chosen from the villages dress up as the three kings and appear on horseback carrying gifts of gold, frankincense and myrrh. They process through the village before arriving at the church where a large congregation gathers.

To the Ghats

Wherever you are in Goa, you are never more than 55 km from state's eastern border, taking the form of the high walls of the Western Ghats. Whether you're north or south, packing an overnight bag and heading inland towards these mountain ranges will give you vistas of stunning scenery overflowing with bird and wildlife as well as a picture of Goa's mining heartland. These forested foothills of the mountains carry the state's rich reserves of iron ore, bauxite and manganese, and these mineral seams run all the way down the inland territories, from the northeasternmost corner of Pernem through Bicholim and west Sanguem into the southern tip of Canacona. Their busy industrialization sits cheek-by-jowl with ancient Buddhist caves and Hindu temples tucked deep into slopes packed thick with forest. In the northern interior you'll find the paint-peeling faded elegance of Mayem Lake. From here, keep your compass set southeast to visit Tambdi Surla, the only early Hindu-temple to survive the Portuguese. There's the natural beauty of the forests next door at Bhagwan Mahaveer sanctuary, within whose borders lie the awesome Dudhsagar falls – at 600 m tall, they are one of the highest in India. ▶▶ For Sleeping, Eating and other listings, see pages 182-183.

Ins and outs

Getting there Roads now connect Bicholim with the headquarters of the Satari taluka, Valpoi, and south through the dense forest reserves of the Bondla Sanctuary to Tisk; and southeast via Tambdi Surla to Molem in Sanguem taluka.

Background

Bicholim and Satari talukas are two of the three most marginal talukas in Goa. Located on the edge of the Western Ghats, they have always been on the fringe of political developments elsewhere. Only brought into Goa as part of the New Conquests, they were previously a battleground in the constantly shifting borders of Hindu and Muslim power for three centuries before. Difficult terrain, dense forest cover and the scarcity of agricultural land meant that the population was sparse and towns few and far between. It was to these talukas that Hindus from the Old Conquests often escaped, taking with them the most sacred images and artefacts from the temples of their old villages. The remoteness of the forested hills here was virtually absolute, protected not only by their own inhospitable character but by the Mandovi river to the south and the Mapusa river to the west. The balance of resources is now fundamentally altered by the discovery of massive iron ore deposits, which are being extensively worked in Bicholim. In these forested hills, Buddhist and Jain communities survived resurgent Hinduism and the invasions of Islam, and Buddhism remained in the hills for some time after its elimination from most other parts of India in the early centuries AD.

Bicholim and around → *Colour map 1, grid, B4.*

Headquarters of the taluka, Bicholim town has little of interest in itself but is the crossroads on the main route between Mapusa and Valpoi and for the road from the south via Divar Island.

Mayem Lake is like a lost Victorian playground, its promenades crying out for walkers carrying parasols, and is the last oasis before the heavy mining area around Sanquelim. It is a peaceful spot, rich in birdlife, especially at the quieter, southern end of the lake away from the road. If you look closely, you may be able to spot monkeys in the surrounding forest. It isn't heavily visited or commercialized, and just a few souvenir stalls and bar/restaurants line the short stretch of road along the north bank. Pedal boats are not everyone's idea of a good time, but they make bird-watching at close range easier – carry binoculars and bring some oil too to fix the irritating sqeaking to which many of the boats are prone.

Sri Saptakotesvar Temple ① *Naroa (Narve) approached from Divar Island by Naroa ferry, shortly after the road veers away from the Konkan Railway there is a lane on the right. Drive past the first temple and look out for the temple on the left,* is one of Bicholim's main attractions. The scenery around here is particularly beautiful. The temple sits in a forested depression just off the road. Here, again, like so many of Goa's temples and small settlements, the deity originated some distance away and was re-established as a result of an enforced move. The faceted *dharalinga,* which is the chief image, was moved when the original temple on Divar Island was destroyed in order to build a church. The original site on Divar Island is now occupied by the Church of Nossa Senhora de Piedade, see page 84. The marks on the stone suggest that at one stage it was used as a pulley, probably for drawing water, but it was rescued and placed in its present setting as a result of Sivaji's visit in 1668. There is nothing ornate about either the design or the decoration of the temple. The simple and typical red-tiled roof and pale blue and yellow painted exterior walls house a simple five-pillared *sabhamandapa,* with side aisles where a miniature black stone *nandi* faces the *linga* in the small square, wood-panelled, sanctuary (*garbagriha*) covered by a squat, Islamic dome on an octagonal drum. Today, the structure stands as an example of a typical Goan Hindu temple; it has been recently restored with funding from the Fundação Oriente. The *deepstambha* outside, with 10 rings, is typical of the area. Near it the shrine to Kalabhairav has two rock carvings of sandals.

The **Lairaya Temple,** northwest of Bicholim, is well known for the firewalking that accompanies the Padvo festivities. If a dhond is injured by the flames, he is considered impure – he had either not prepared himself properly for the ceremony or hides a guilty conscience! ▶ *See Festivals and events, page 183.*

At the northern end of the taluka in **Kansarpal,** the **Shri Kalikadevi Temple** is about 100 years old. An unusual feature of the structure is that it has two *sabhamandapas* preceding the sanctuary with seven rows of four pillars. One has a sunken section where dance and theatre performances are held during festivals; the *nagarkhana* to seat the musicians is above. The three silver-covered temple doors and the sanctuary door are ornately decorated. The inner sanctuary has an image of Devi, the fierce form of the goddess Kali. The goldsmiths, the temple trustees, traditionally set aside the gold dust collected when they make jewellery to act as the reserve fund.

Sanquelim and around → *Colour map 1, grid B4.*

Southeast of Bicholim, the town is the 'home' of the Rajput Ranes tribe, who migrated south from Rajasthan in the late 18th century and spent the next century fighting for the Portuguese as mercenaries – then against them for arrears of pay! In 1895 one of their revolts necessitated the despatch of troops from Portugal. The **Datta Mandir** (1882) north of the bazaar, backed by a hillock covered with dense groves of areca palms, has the *trimurthi* (three-headed) image of Dattaraia, which is believed to cure insanity. The temple, with an interior of white marble, celebrates *Datta Jayanti* in December. It is one of two temples in Goa where *Devadasis* plays no part and are not permitted to enter (the other is the Ananta Temple in Savoi Verem).

The 14th-century **Temple of Vitthala to Vishnu**, built in the north Indian style, has been renovated but still retains some of the original carved wooden columns. Shri Vitthala is the ancestral deity of the Ranes who still live in the old family house next to the temple.

Arvalem

Two kilometres east of Sanguelim a turn goes south to this small settlement noted now for its **waterfalls** and small **Buddhist cave temples**. The latter were subsequently converted for Siva worship. The altars, which probably originally supported Buddha images, now have Siva *lingas* set into them. The caves are believed to date from the third to sixth century AD, though a Brahmi inscription found was dated to the first century. The two groups of caves were cut out of laterite outcrops, with the cells opening out into two pillared porches. No architectural detail survives.

In a pleasant shaded site with a temple near their foot, the **waterfalls** are formed at the end of a small gorge and are impressive during the monsoon when the river is in spate. They are concealed from view until the last moment. Steps lead down from the parking place to the foot of the falls, then a track goes along the river and crosses it by a footbridge, leading a short distance to an open cast mine less than 1 km away.

Next to the falls is the **Shri Rudreshwar Temple** which is important for funeral rites. Although the present building is comparatively modern, the temple itself is ancient, although no one knows exactly when it was founded.

Satari taluka

The second-largest and the second least densely populated taluka in Goa has always been a largely forested district. The steep hills of the Western Ghats rise to the east and the forests of the Bhagwan Mahaveer Sanctuary are to the south. The administrative headquarters, **Valpoi**, with a population of 7,900 is only a small town, 9 km northeast lies Carambolim, also known as Brahma Carambolim or Karmali because of its unusual Brahma temple.

⬭ Sleeping

Bicholim and around *p181*
Mayem Lake
D-E **Mayem Lake Resort** (GTDC), on the west bank, T0832-2362144. 17 good-sized but shabby rooms (some a/c), wildlife includes frogs in the bathroom. Having

said that, given a lick of paint this would be one of the most beautiful spots in Goa. Good restaurant although lunchtime is often reminiscent of Hitchcock's *The Birds,* with crows lining up for scraps.

D-E **Prabhu Smaran**, 100 m north of lake, T0832-2361222. 6 rooms, some a/c in a friendly, family-run guest house, clean and comfortable, well kept. Recommended.

🍴 Eating

Bicholim and around *p181*
Mayem Lake
$ **Government Restaurant** on the south side of the lake serves good food, though the buildings are rather run down. There are clean *sulabh* toilets in the compound.

🔺 Activities and tours

Bicholim and around *p181*
Mayem Lake
Rowing/pedalo boats, Rs 80 per hour, Rs 60 for 30 mins. **Polycat** (a lightweight pedal catamaran) Rs 60 per hour, Rs 40 for 30 mins.

✹ Festivals and events

Bicholim and around *p181*
Naroa (Narve)
Feb/Mar Mahasivratri is the special festival at the Sri Saptakotesvar Temple.

Sirigao (Shirgao)
Apr/May The Hindu **Lairaya Jatra** coincides with 'New Year' celebrations in at the Lairaya Temple. Local villagers gather firewood to build a pyre, about 10 m square at the base, and 6 m high. Hundreds of *dhonds* (the name given to a special group of worshippers who participate in the ceremony) enter the village, recognizable by the piece of coloured cloth they carry on their back and the entwined cane in their hands. During the day, the goddess Lairaya gives *darshan* and is worshipped. Excitement mounts as midnight approaches and a noisy crowd of devotees, accompanied by loud musicians, join the temple priest and the *dhonds* in a procession towards the pyre. They call first at a mango tree, which

is believed to contain an evil spirit that has to be appeased by an offering of red flowers. The pyre is lit by the priest and the *dhonds* continue with their rituals and reach a state of frenzy before preparing to walk on the red hot ashes of the pyre. Then, at a specified moment, early in the morning, they all step on to the ashes while some also dare to run through the tongues of flame. Excitement reaches fever pitch until the last *dhond* completes the act.

Sanquelim and around *p182*
Apr The annual festival is held at the Temple of Vitthala to Vishnu when the temple 'car' is used to transport a Hanuman image.

Arvalem
Feb/Mar The Mahasivaratri festival, when devotees honour Siva through the night, is celebrated at the Shri Rudreshwar Temple with processions, singing and theatre performances.

⊖ Transport

Bicholim and around *p181*
Mayem Lake
From **Panjim** or **Ponda**, travel via **Banastari**, although the most direct route is via the Ribandar-Chorao ferry from Panaji. There are direct buses from **Chorao** to **Mayem Lake** but they are few and far between so you may be forced to choose between a 2-hr wait or taking a motorbike taxi (Rs 100). From **Mapusa** there is a regular bus service via Bicholim.

Sanquelim and around *p182*
One road goes south to **Tisk** (25 km) at the intersection with the NH4A near a spice plantation. A longer circuit takes in **Arvalem** and the Tambdi Surla Temple, joining the NH4A at **Molem** which gives access to the Bhagwan Mahaveer Sanctuary. Buses between **Mapusa** and **Valpoi** pass through Bicholim and Sanquelim.

The central and southern interior → *Colour map 2, grids B&C 4-6.*

Sanguem, Goa's largest taluka, covers the state's eastern hill borderland with the south Indian state of Karnataka. The still-forested hills, populated until recently by tribal peoples practising shifting cultivation, rise to Goa's highest points. Just on the Goan side of the border with Karnataka are the Dudhsagar falls, some of India's highest waterfalls, where the river, which ultimately flows into the Mandovi, cascades dramatically down the hillside. Both the Bhagwan Mahaveer Sanctuary and the beautiful, small Tambdi Surla Temple can be reached in a day from the coast (about two hours from Panaji). ›› For Sleeping, Eating and other listings, see pages 187-188.

Ins and outs

Getting there Buses running along the NH4A between Panjim, Ponda or Margao and Belgaum or Bangalore in Karnataka stop at Molem, in the north of the taluka. Much of the southeastern part of Sanguem remains inaccessible. Trains towards Karnataka stop at Kulem (Colem) and Dudhsagar stations. Jeeps wait at Kulem to transfer tourists to the waterfalls.

If you are traveling to Tambdi Surla or the falls from north or central Goa, then the best and most direct route is the NH4A via Ponda. However, by going to or from the southern beaches of Salcete or Canacona you can travel through an interesting cluster of villages, only really accessible if you have your own transport, to see the sites of rock-cut caves and prehistoric cave art.

Getting around There is no direct public transport between Molem and the sites, but the town is the start of hikes and treks in December and January (see Transport, page 188).

The Bhagwan Mahaveer Sanctuary → *Colour map 2, grid B6.*

ⓘ *T08324-2600231, 0830-1730 except public holidays, Rs 5, 2-wheelers Rs 10, cars Rs 500. Tickets are available at the Nature Interpretation Centre, 100 m from the police check post, Molem. Entrance to the Molem National Park, within the sanctuary, 100 m east of the Tourist Complex, is clearly signed but the 14 km of tracks within the park are not mapped.*

Goa's largest wildlife sanctuary holds 240 sq km of lush moist deciduous to evergreen forest types and a herd of gaur (*bos gaurus*, aka 'Indian bison'). The **Molem National Park** in the central section of the sanctuary occupies about half the area with the **Dudhsagar falls** located in its southeast corner; the remote **Tambdi Surla Temple** is hidden in the dense forest at the northern end of the sanctuary. Forest department jeeps are available for viewing within the sanctuary; contact the Range Forest Officer (Wildlife), Molem. Motorbikes can manage the rough track outside the monsoon period but not scooters. In theory it is possible to reach Devil's Canyon and Dudhsagar Falls via the road next to the Nature Interpretation Centre (from where entrance tickets are sold), although the road is very rough and it may require a guide. Make sure you have a full tank of petrol if attempting a long journey into the forest.

Sambar, barking deer, monkeys and rich birdlife are occasionally joined by elephants that wander in from neighbouring Karnataka during the summer months, but these are rarely spotted. Birds include the striking golden oriole, emerald dove, paradise flycatcher, malabar horbill and trogon and crested serpent eagle.

Devil's Canyon is an impressive gorge through which the Dudhsagar river flows and can be visited after getting permission from the Nature Interpretation Centre (see above). The centre will also give directions to it. The river is believed to hold crocodiles, but some visitors nonetheless choose to jump off the river's rocky outcrops into the water below.

Dudhsagar falls

The spectacular Dudhsagar falls on the border between Goa and Karnataka, are the highest in India and measure a total drop of about 600 m. The name meaning 'the sea of milk', is derived from the white foam that the force of the water creates as it drops in stages, forming pools along the way. They are best seen just after the monsoon, between October and December, but right up to April there is enough water to make a visit worthwhile.

Until quite recently it was possible to visit Dudhsagar by rail as the line runs across about the mid-point of the vertical drop of the cascades, and the small **Dudhsagar railway station** ⓘ *at present the trains run twice a week (Tue and Sat from Margao), but there are no return trains on these days*, allowed you to step down and then walk back to the opening between the two train tunnels, offering a route to the beautiful pools. As the road route described below is in some ways tougher and less attractive than visiting by train we have retained the following description in case the station re-opens in the near future. When arriving by train, a

‡ *Whether you visit the falls by train or road you need to be fit and athletic.*

rough, steep path takes you down to a viewing area which allows you a better appreciation of the falls' grandeur, and to a beautifully fresh pool which is lovely for a swim (take your costume and towel). There are further pools below but you need to be sure-footed. The final section of the journey is a scramble on foot across stream beds with boulders; it is a difficult task for anyone but the most athletic. For the really fit and adventurous the arduous climb up to the head of the falls with a guide, is well worth the effort. Allow three hours, plus some time to rest at the top.

By road, motorbikes, but not scooters, can get to the start of the trail to the falls from Molem crossroads by taking the road south towards Kulem. From there it is 17 km of rough track with at least two river crossings, so is not recommended after a long period of heavy rain. The ride through the forest is very attractive and the reward at the end spectacular, even in the dry season. A swim in the pool at the falls is particularly refreshing after a hot and dusty ride. Guides are available but the track is easy to follow even without one.

Tambdi Surla

ⓘ *A taxi from Panjim takes about 2½ hs for the 69 km. There is no public transport to Tambdi Surla but it is possible to hike from Molem. From the crossroads at Molem on the NH4A, the road north goes through dense forest to Tambdi Surla. 4 km from the crossroads you reach a fork. Take the right fork and after a further 3 km take a right turn at Barabhumi village (there is a sign). The temple is a further 8 km, just after Shanti Nature Resort. Make sure you have enough petrol before leaving Molem. It is also possible to reach the site along minor roads from Valpoi. The entrance to the temple is a short walk from the car park.*

This Mahadeva (Siva) Temple is a beautifully preserved miniature example of early Hindu temple architecture from the Kadamba-Yadava period. Tucked into the forested foothills, the place is often deserted, although the compound is well maintained by the Archaeology Department. The temple is the only major remaining example of pre-Portuguese Hindu architecture in Goa; it may well have been saved from destruction by its very remoteness.

The 12th to 13th-century black basalt temple stands on a platform with three plain mouldings. The stone used must have been transported some distance as basalt is not available locally. The exterior walls have little decoration save for the breaks provided by the vertical pilasters. However, there are some good miniature reliefs and sculptures on the *shikara* above the *garbagriha*, showing deities including Brahma with Swarasvati above, Siva with Uma-Mahesh above and Vishnu with Kumarashakti above. The low wall near the open-sided entrance has finely carved lozenge-with-rosette motifs which still appear crisp.

The entrance/main hall (*sabhmandapa*), vestibule or middle hall (*antaralaya*) and sanctuary (*garbagriha*) are aligned on the same east-west axis. The 10 pillars, all different, are relatively plain, but four monolithic pillars that support the stone ceiling with a very fine example of the conventional floral design, are deeply incised. The carving showing an elephant trampling a horse (on the lower section of the first pillar on the right) may have political significance, since horses were the favoured animals of war of the Muslim invaders, in contrast to the elephants used by Hindu kings.

The *shikharas* of the four niches in the *mandapa*, which contain images including *Nagas*, throw light on how the original temple must have looked with its tower over the *garbagriha* complete. A *Naga* with two hoods appears on a separate slab.

Southwest Sanguem → *Colour map 2, grid C4.*

Pandava caves ① *Rivona, ask for directions in the village and carry a torch – beware of snakes.* The rock-cut **cave sites**, where a statue of the Buddha was found, are referred to locally as the Pandava Caves. The headless stone statue, said to date to the seventh century and missing the left arm, was found seated on a throne with three lions in front; it is now in the Archaeological Museum, Panjim. The caves were later taken over by Hindus, who left carvings on stones, including a stylized long-tailed *Hanuman* holding a tree in one hand.

Just south of the bazaar along the main road through the village, a dirt path opposite the water pump leads to the first cave site after about 100 m. The small set of excavated cells, which may have been used as a monastery to accommodate 25 to 30 persons, is approached by steps that lead down to a vestibule, with a well that has a funnel-shaped hole channelled through to the surface to provide light and air. Another entrance porch, facing a pool, also gave access to the cells through the vestibule. Natural springs supplied water that was stored in tanks.

To find the second cave site, return to the main road and follow a path for about 400 m down to the river and along it. The cave shelter near the valley bottom, which is more open, has a platform at the back. Here too, there was no shortage of water. The hole to the right of the cave entrance is believed to have been the start of a tunnel to Curdi, some 8 km. It is best not to attempt to enter either cave. Carry a torch and keep a safe distance away as they are likely to harbour snakes.

The **Damodar Temple** ① *Zambaulim, north of Rivona, 22 km southeast of Margao*, is attractively set along the banks of the Kushavati (Panti) River. The deity – originally from Margao – was transferred here in 1567 but the temple structure is fairly modern, dating mainly from the 1950s to the 1970s. The water of the river here is believed to be especially blessed and to have medicinal properties, so attracts pilgrims from both the Hindu and Christian communities. The surrounding area around also came under the influence of Buddhism. A monk called Punna is believed to have lived in the village preaching the doctrine of Buddhism. A statue of the Buddha was found in Rivona.

● The name Pandava may be derived from Rishi-vana (forest of saints), recalling a period
● around the seventh century when groups of Buddhist monks are believed to have
   established cave retreats in this part of Goa.

The road inland from Rivona to the west, passes through **Colomba** where there's the **Shantadurga Temple**, one of the few places in India where Brahma is worshipped, here as an affiliate deity.

Head south for **Usgalimal** on the banks of the Kushavati River, where the latest discoveries of **prehistoric rock carvings** were made in the 1990s. Some of the finds are displayed in the Panjim Archaeological Museum. The Archaeological Survey of India sign – green with a red dash – directs visitors towards the site of the rock carvings down a rough path off the road. The prehistoric art depicts animal and human figures as well as intriguing concentric circles, which are not all easy to decipher (so may disappoint).

Follow the road east to reach **Curdi (Kurdi)**, known as a **megalithic site** where a 2-m laterite Mother Goddess statue (fifth century BC) was excavated. The statue was taken to Verna (also a megalithic site) by the Directorate of Archaeology and re-sited on the spot where an old Mahalsa temple stood until 1560. Also discovered were sections of a Kadamba Temple to Siva (11th century). The **Mahadeva Temple** was threatened by the Salauli Irrigation Project and was re-sited in the new settlement. A short distance away, rock-cut steps led down to a stream where a small rock shelter was found, with two statues of Siva. The shelter is now under water.

Eight kilometres north is **Sanguem**, the headquarters of Sanguem district which, although inland, has a 'backwaters' feel. The town's 19th century **Jama Masjid** was renovated in 1959.

⊜ Sleeping

Bhagwan Mahaveer Sanctuary *p184*
There is no accommodation inside the sanctuary; carry provisions. The nearest GTDC accommodation is the Tourist Complex in Molem, east along the NH4A from the Molem National Park entrance.

Tambdi Surla
C **Shanti Nature Resort**, 500 m from the temple. Contact ahead **Passive Active Tourism** (Freedom Holidays), Hotel Four Pillars, Panjim, T/F0832-2222986.. 9 large mud huts with palm-thatched roofs, electricity and running water in natural forest setting, emphasis on rest, ayurvedic treatment and meditation. Restaurant for all tastes, visits to spice gardens, bird-watching, hikes, trips to Dudhsagar, etc, arranged (2 nights, US$120). Highly recommended for location and eco-friendly approach.

Molem
E **Tourist Resort** (GTDC), 300 m east of police check post, about 500 m from the temple, T0832-2600238. 23 simple but well-maintained, clean rooms, some a/c, dorm, check-out 1200, giving time for a morning visit to Tambdi Surla, uninspired restaurant with limited menu serving north Indian food and beer.

F **Molem Forest Resthouse**, can be booked through the Conservator's Office, 3rd flr, Junta House, 18th June Rd, Panjim, T0832-2224747.

Southwest Sanguem *p186*
Sanguem
F **Sanguem Forest Rest House**. Can be booked through the Conservator's Office, 3rd flr, Junta House, 18th June Road, Panjim, T0832-2224747.

⊛ Festivals and events

Southwest Sanguem *p186*
Zambaulin
Mar/Apr Zambaulim Gulal is celebrated like Holi at Damodar temple. Festivities continue for a week with much feasting, cultural shows and a big fair.

▲ Activities and tours

Bhagwan Mahaveer Sanctuary *p184*
Molem
Popular hiking routes lead to **Dudhsagar** (17 km), the sanctuary and Atoll Gad (12 km), Matkonda Hill (10 km) and Tambdi Surla (12 km). Contact the **Hiking Association**, 6 Anand Niwas, Swami Vivekenanda Rd, Panjim.

⊖ Transport

Bhagwan Mahaveer Sanctuary *p184*
Train From the southern beaches, you can get the Vasco-Colem Passenger from Vasco at 0710, or more conveniently Margao (Madgaon) at 0800, arriving at **Kulem** (Colem) at 0930. Return trains at 1640, arriving **Margao** at 1810; leave plenty of time to enjoy the falls. Jeep hire is available from Kulem Station.
Road If coming from the south, travel via Sanguem. The road from Sanvordem to the NH17 passes through mining country and is therefore badly pot-holed and has heavy lorry traffic. From Kulem, **jeeps** do the rough trip to **Dudhsagar** (Rs 300 per head, Rs 1800 per jeep). This is a very tough and tiring journey at the best of times.

Molem
Buses between **Panjim**, **Ponda** or **Margao**, and **Belgaum/Bangalore**, stop at Molem for visiting the Bhagwan Mahaveer Sanctuary and Dudhsagar Falls.
From Molem, a road to the south off the NH4A leads through the forested hills of Sanguem taluka to **Kulem** and **Calem** railway stations and then south to **Sanguem**. From there, a minor road northwest goes to **Sanvordem** and then turns west to **Chandor**.

Beyond Goa

Mumbai (Bombay)	192
Gateway of India and Colaba	195
Central Mumbai	197
Around the CST or VT	199
Marine Drive, Malabar Hill and around	200
Listings	202
Coastal excursions	**215**
The Maharashtran border villages	215
Karnataka's coast	216
Gokarna	217
Listings	218
Interior Karnataka	**220**
Hospet	220
Hampi	221
Bijapur	224
Hindu temples around Bijapur	226
Hospet to Bidar	229
Listings	231

⦂ Footprint features

Don't miss...	191
24 hours in the city	193
Bright lights of Bollywood	199
Card sharps	216
Half day in Hampi	221

Introduction

Goa makes a brilliant stepping-stone from which to delve into the chaos and riches of all that lies just beyond its borders. Seeing life seethe in an Indian city is invariably eye opening. Mumbai has all the swagger and speed you'd expect of India's financial capital, and has both markets, and slums, that you wouldn't believe.

Smaller overnight forays can easily get you as far as the pristine beaches of Maharashtra in the north or Gokarna's Om beach in the south, the shoreline to one of the holiest patches of land on the west coast. Inland, Maharashtra also has jaw-dropping landscapes that look like the rockies or the grand canyon – all unjustly bypassed in the well-worn route between the gateway of Mumbai and the allure of Goa.

For ancient culture, though, push through Karnataka on Goa's eastern border and you'll meet with the sprawling ruins of long-vanquished empires: from the Hindu Vijayanagar kindgom at Hampi to the forts and tombs of the Islamic sultans at Bijapur and stonemasons' playgrounds at Badami, Aihole and Pattakanal.

★ **Don't miss...**

❶ Chor Bazaar, Mumbai Stock up on Bollywood trinkets here, page 200.

❷ Mumbai panoramas Great views from the top of two of the swankiest hotels, the Taj or the Oberoi, pages 202 and 203.

❸ Redi A near-empty Maharashtran bay, page 215.

❹ Gokarna Hindu pilgrims come for the temple, western ones for the hammocks along Om Beach, page 217.

❺ Echoes of Hampi Hear every sound for miles bouncing off giant boulders around Hampi's ruins, page 221.

❻ Hanuman's birthplace, Hampi Cross the river in a coracle, then cycle through paddy to climb the whitewashed steps to the temple, page 221.

❼ Sculptures Visit the dainty-as-doilies sculpture at Pattadakal and Aihole, pages 226 and 227.

❽ Badami temples Investigate cave temples wedged up the sandstone ravine of Badami, page 228.

❾ Thanksgiving Share a picnic at the tomb of the Sufi saint Khwaja Bande Nawaz at Gulbarga, page 229.

Beyond Goa

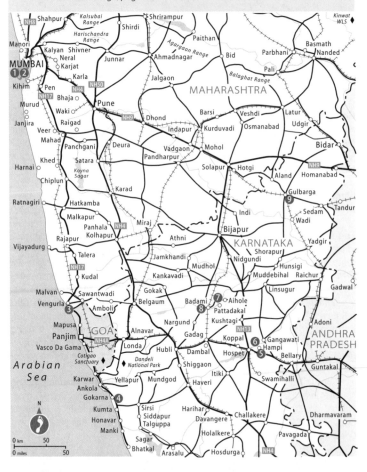

Mumbai (Bombay)

→ *Phone code: 022.*

You are always in a crowd in Mumbai. Stand at Churchgate station or VT terminus any time after 0600 on a weekday and be overwhelmed with the tidal waves of humanity washing out of the walls. The city, India's economic capital for over 150 years, is the subcontinent's outward-looking commercial face and its melting pot. From the cluster of fishing villages first linked by the British East India Company, it has swelled to sprawl across seven islands joined into an artificial isthmus. Its problems – a population of 20 million over two-thirds of whom live in slums – are only matched by the enormous drive which makes it the centre of business, fashion and film-making in modern India and the great repository for the country's hopes. Its skyline is a combination of gothic towers, skyscrapers, mill chimneys and shanties. The streets are giddying, aswarm with panel-beaten English double-deckers, waspish yellow and black taxis, long wooden carts stacked with hessian-stitched blocks of cargo and mangoes carried in reverential pyramids on plates. ▶▶ *For Sleeping, Eating and other listings, see page 202-215.*

Ins and outs

Getting there Chhatrapati Sivaji International air terminal is 30 km from Nariman Point, the business heart of the city. The domestic terminals at Santa Cruz are 5 km closer. Pre-paid taxis to the city centre are good value and take between 40 minutes and 1½ hours, depending on traffic but there are also cheaper but slower buses. If you arrive late at night without a hotel booking it is best to stay at one of the hotels near the domestic terminal before going into town early in the morning or making for Goa.

Getting around The sights are spread out and you need transport. Taxis (yellow top and blue, air-conditioned) are metered and generally good value. There are frequent buses on major routes, and the two suburban railway lines are useful out of peak hours on some routes, but get horrendously crowded. Auto-rickshaws are only allowed in the suburbs. ▶▶ *See Transport, page 211, for further details.*

Climate The hottest periods are March-May and October-December. Rainfall is very heavy June-August (June over 900 mm). Best time to visit is November-March.

Tourist information **Government of India** ⓘ *123 M Karve Rd, opposite Churchgate, T022-2093229, Mon-Sat 0830-1730 (closed 2nd Sat of month from 1230). Counters open 24 hrs at both airports, and at Taj Mahal Hotel, Mon-Sat 0830-1530 (closed 2nd Sat from 1230).* Helpful staff who can also issue liquor permits (essential for Gujarat); printouts given from computer database of many destinations.
　　Maharashtra Tourist Development Corporation ⓘ *www.mtdcindia.com, CDO Hutments, opposite LIC Building, Express Towers, 9th flr, Nariman Pt, T022-2024482; Madam Cama Rd, T022-2026713. Information and booking counters at international and domestic terminals. Also at Koh-i-Noor Rd, near Pritam Hotel, Dadar T022-4143200; CST Railway Station, T022-2622859 and Gateway of India, T022-2841877.*
　　Goa ⓘ *Mumbai Central Station, T022-3086288.* **Gujarat** ⓘ *Dhanraj Mahal, Apollo Bunder, T022-2024925.* **Madhya Pradesh** ⓘ *74 World Centre, Cuffe Parade, Colaba, T022-2187603, mptourism@b01.net.in.* **Himachal Pradesh** ⓘ *Himachal Emporium, 36 World Trade Centre, Cuffe Parade, T022-2181123.* **Rajasthan** ⓘ *230 Dr DN Rd, T022-2075603.*

⁞ 24 hours in the city

One of the world's great humbling experiences is watching India go to work. Rush-hours stretch between 0800 and 1100 (then again 1700 and 2000) so you can start your day like everyone else does in Mumbai: with the commute at **Victoria station**. Commuter trains pull in with people hanging out of every door, women at the front in the separate-sex compartments. Take a simple breakfast here, and kill two birds with one stone by investigating trains to Goa.

From Victoria station, walk down **Bazaar Gate Fort Road** where *bindi* stalls and *chai wallahs* rub shoulders with circus performers, and sugar cane carts jangle their bells to divert your attention to their lemon and ginger sharp juice. Carry on south – passing the Bombay Stock Exchange – to end up at **Horniman Circle**, a jungly disc presided over by the grand old Asiatic Society, and the **Fort area**. It's an interesting walk down to the **Gateway of India**, from where you can take a boat to the **Elephanta Caves**.

On your way back, pop in to the **Taj** for its excellent bookshop, then tear yourself away from air-conditioning again to browse everything from cheap junk to elaborate saris on **Colaba**

Causeway or head for the pricey but excellent antique shop **Phillips** opposite the Regal Cinema. Peckish again? For Indian food, eat at Shiv Sagars; for European, try Basilico.

Culture comes in the excellent **Chhatrapati Sivaji Museum** and the **Jehangir Art Gallery**, only a short walk away. To speed up, get a taxi to the **Gandhi Museum** at Mani Bhavan, the **Hanging Gardens** and **Jain Temple**, stopping on the Mahalaxmi Bridge to see the extraordinary activity at the **Dhobi Ghats**, then back south for kite-flying at Chowpatty and an evening stroll along **Marine Drive** where the sunset draws huge crowds.

Then dust yourself down (you'll be well overdue for a shower by now, by the standard of most Mumbai days) and take your pick of the best eateries. If having a window on the city isn't a big deal, go to **Trishna's** for garlic butter crab (the logical first step in a night that should end at **Red Light**), or stay on Marine Parade to eat at the **Pearl of the Orient** revolving restaurant (the Hotel Intercontinental's terrifyingly glamorous bar your next stop) or back to the amazing views from **Souk**, the top floor of the Taj, before rubbing shoulders with Bollywood royalty at **Athena**.

Beyond Goa Mumbai

Background

Hinduism made its mark on Mumbai long before the Portuguese and then the British transformed it into one of India's great cities. The caves on the island of Elephanta were excavated under the Kalachuris (AD 500-600). Yet, only 350 years ago, the area occupied by this great metropolis comprised seven islands inhabited by Koli fishermen. The British acquired these marshy and malarial islands as part of the marriage dowry paid by the Portuguese when Catherine of Braganza married Charles II in 1661. Four years later, the British took possession of the remaining islands and neighbouring mainland area and in 1668 the East India Company leased the whole area from the crown for £10 a year, which was paid for nearly 50 years. The East India Company shifted its headquarters to Mumbai in 1672. Until the early 19th century, Mumbai's fortunes rested on the shipbuilding yards established by progressive Parsis.

Mumbai remained isolated by the sharp face of the Western Ghats and the constantly hostile Marathas. However, it thrived on trade and, in the cosmopolitan

Mumbai

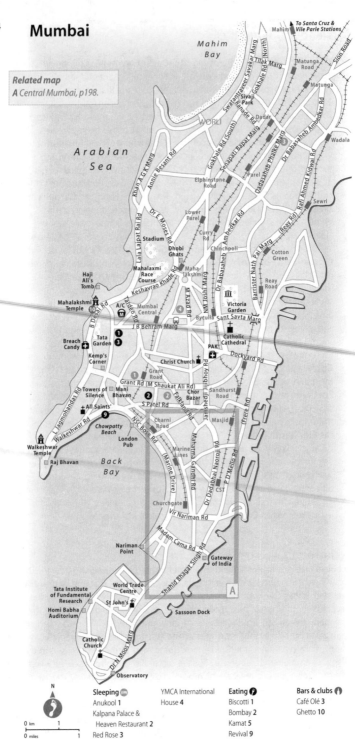

Related map
A Central Mumbai, p198.

Mahim Bay

Arabian Sea

To Santa Cruz &
Vile Parle Stations

WORLD

Matunga
Road

Matunga

Sivaji
Park

Dadar

Wadala

Sewri

Cotton
Green

Reay
Road

Dockyard Rd

Elphinstone
Road

Lower
Parel

Curry
Rd

Chinchpoli

Stadium

Dhobi
Ghats

Mahalaxmi
Race
Course

Maha-
Lakshmi

Mumbai
Central

Byculla

Victoria
Garden

Haji
Ali's
Tomb

Mahalakshmi
Temple

Breach
Candy

Tata
Garden

Kemp's
Corner

J B Behram Marg

Christ Church

Grant
Road

Catholic
Cathedral

PAK

Chor
Bazar

Sandhurst
Road

Grant Rd (M Shaukat Ali Rd)

S Patel Rd

Towers of
Silence

Mani
Bhavan

All Saints'

Chowpatty
Beach

London
Pub

Charni
Road

Masjid

Walkeshwar
Temple

Raj Bhavan

*Back
Bay*

Marine
Lines

CST

Churchgate

Vir Nariman Rd

Nariman
Point

Madam Cama Rd

Gateway
of India

Tata Institute
of Fundamental
Research

World Trade
Centre

St John's

Homi Babha
Auditorium

Sassoon Dock

Catholic
Church

Observatory

Beyond Goa Mumbai

N

0 km   1
0 miles   1

Sleeping 🛏
Anukool **1**
Kalpana Palace &
  Heaven Restaurant **2**
Red Rose **3**

YMCA International
House **4**

Eating 🍴
Biscotti **1**
Bombay **2**
Kamat **5**
Revival **9**

Bars & clubs 🍸
Café Olé **3**
Ghetto **10**

city this created, Parsis, Sephardic Jews and the British shared common interests and responded to the same incentives.

After a devastating fire on 17 February 1803, a new town with wider streets was built. Then, with the abolition of the Company's trade monopoly, the doors to rapid expansion were flung open and Mumbai flourished. Trade with England boomed. After the opening of the Suez Canal in 1870, Mumbai's greater proximity to European markets gave it an advantage over Kolkata. The port became the commercial centre of the Arabian Sea.

Mumbai rapidly became the centre of an entrepreneurial as well as a commercial class. Mumbai has become the home of India's stock exchange (BSE) and headquarters for many national and international companies and is also a major industrial centre. With the sponsorship of the Tata family, Mumbai has also become the primary home of India's nuclear research programme, with its first plutonium extraction plant at Trombay in 1961 and the establishment of the **Tata Institute for Fundamental Research**, the most prestigious science research institute in the country.

Mumbai is still growing fast. One third of the population live in the desperately squalid *chawls* of cramped, makeshift hovels. There are also many thousands of pavement dwellers. Due to heavy demand for building space, property values are exceedingly high. New Mumbai across the Thane Creek has been developed to ease the pressure on the isthmus, but Great Mumbai remains a magnet to people from across India.

Gateway of India and Colaba

The Indo-Saracenic-style Gateway of India (1927), designed by George Wittet to commemorate the visit of George V and Queen Mary in 1911, is modelled in honey-coloured basalt on 16th-century Gujarati work. The great gateway is an archway with halls on each side capable of seating 600 at important receptions. The arch was the point from which the last British regiment serving in India signalled the end of the empire when it left on 28 February 1948. The whole area has a huge buzz at weekends. Scores of boats depart from here for **Elephanta Island,** creating a sea-swell which young boys delight in diving into. Hawkers, beggars and the general throng of people all add to the atmosphere. A short distance behind the Gateway is an impressive statue of **Sivaji**. The original red-domed **Taj Mahal Hotel** has been adjoined by a modern skyscraper, the **Taj Mahal Inter-Continental**. It is worth

‼ *Sadly, increasing numbers of beggars target foreign visitors here.*

popping into the **Taj** for a bite to eat or a drink, or to go to the disco with its clientele of well-heeled young Indians. Unfortunately, drug addicts, drunks and prostitutes frequent the area behind the hotel.

South of the Gateway of India is the crowded southern section of Shahid (literally 'martyr') Bhagat Singh Marg, or Colaba Causeway. The Afghan Memorial **Church of St John the Baptist** (1847-1858) is at the northern edge of Colaba itself. Early English in style, with a 58-m spire, it was built to commemorate the soldiers who died in the First Afghan War. Fishermen still unload their catch early in the morning at **Sassoon Dock**, the first wet dock in India; photography prohibited. Beyond the church near the tip of the Colaba promontory lie the **Observatory** and **Old European cemetery** in the naval colony (permission needed to enter). Frequent buses ply this route.

● *860 Bollywood films are made each year, of which 854 fail.*

Gateway of India & Colaba

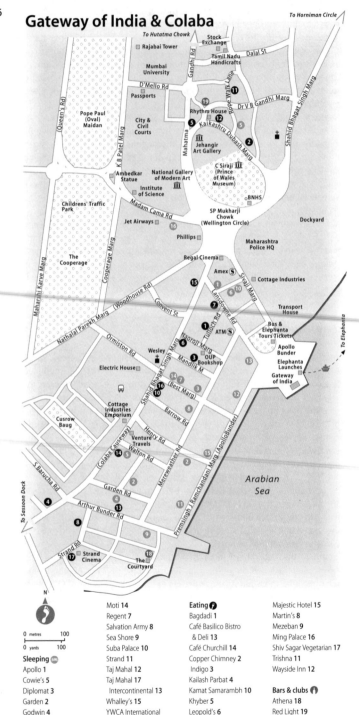

Sleeping

Apollo 1
Cowie's 5
Diplomat 3
Garden 2
Godwin 4
Gordon House 6
Moti 14
Regent 7
Salvation Army 8
Sea Shore 9
Suba Palace 10
Strand 11
Taj Mahal 12
Taj Mahal 17
Intercontinental 13
Whalley's 15
YWCA International
Centre 16

Eating

Bagdadi 1
Café Basilico Bistro
& Deli 13
Café Churchill 14
Copper Chimney 2
Indigo 3
Kailash Parbat 4
Kamat Samarambh 10
Khyber 5
Leopold's 6
Ling's Pavilion 7

Majestic Hotel 15
Martin's 8
Mezeban 9
Ming Palace 16
Shiv Sagar Vegetarian 17
Trishna 11
Wayside Inn 12

Bars & clubs

Athena 18
Red Light 19

Central Mumbai

The area stretching north from Colaba Causeway to CST (Victoria Terminus) dates from after 1862, when Sir Bartle Frere became Governor (1862-1867). Under his enthusiastic guidance Mumbai became a great civic centre and an extravaganza of Victorian Gothic architecture, modified by Indo-Saracenic influences.

Chhatrapati Sivaji (Prince of Wales) Museum ⓘ *Oct-Feb Tue-Sun 1015-1730, Jul-Sep Tue-Sun 1015-1800, Mar-Jun Tue-Sun 1015-1830. Foreigners Rs 350 (includes taped guide); Indians Rs 15. Camera fee Rs 15 (no flash or tripods).* This impressive building was designed by George Wittet to commemorate the visit of the Prince of Wales to India in 1905. The dome of glazed tiles has a very Persian and Central Asian flavour. The archaeological section has three main groups: Brahminical; Buddhist and Jain; Prehistoric and Foreign. The art section includes an excellent collection of Indian miniatures and well displayed *tankhas*. There are also works by Gainsborough, Poussin and Titian as well as Indian silver, jade and tapestries. The Natural History section is based on the collection of the **Bombay Natural History Society**, founded in 1833. Good guidebooks, cards and reproductions on sale. **Jehangir Art Gallery** ⓘ *in the Chhatrapati Sivaji Museum complex*, holds small short term exhibitions of contemporary art, available to buy. The **Samovar café** is good for a snack and a drink including chilled beer in a pleasant garden-side setting. There are phones and toilets. Temporary members may use the library and attend lectures.

National Gallery of Modern Art ⓘ *Sir Cowasji Jehangir Hall, opposite the Chhatrapati Sivaji Museum, T022-852457.* Three-tiered gallery converted from an old public hall which gives a good introduction to India's contemporary art scene.

St Andrew's Kirk, (1819), just behind the Chhatrapati Sivaji Museum, is a simple neo-classical church. At the south end of Mahatma Gandhi (MG) Road is the renaissance-style **Institute of Science** (1911) designed by George Wittet. The Institute, which includes a scientific library, a public hall and examination halls, was built with gifts from the Parsi and Jewish communities.

The **Oval garden** has been restored to a pleasant public garden and acts as the lungs of the southern business district. On the east side of the **Pope Paul (Oval) Maidan** is the Venetian Gothic-style **old Secretariat** (1874), with a façade of arcaded verandas and porticos faced in buff-coloured porbander stone from Gujarat. Decorated with red and blue basalt, the carvings are in white *hemnagar* stone. The **University Convocation Hall** (1874) to its north was designed by Sir George Gilbert Scott in a 15th-century French decorated style. Scott also designed the adjacent **University Library** and the **Rajabai Clocktower** (1870s) next door, based on Giotto's campanile in Florence. The sculpted figures in niches on the exterior walls of the tower were designed to represent the castes of India. Originally the clock could chime 12 tunes including *Rule Britannia*. The **High Court** (1871-1879), in early English gothic style, has a 57-m high central tower flanked by lower octagonal towers topped by the figures of Justice and Mercy. The **Venetian Gothic Public Works Office** (1869-1872) is to its north. Opposite, and with its main façade to Vir Nariman Road, is the former **General Post Office** (1869-1872). Now called the Telegraph Office, it stands next to the original Telegraph Office adding romanesque to the extraordinary mixture of European architectural styles.

The old buildings of the centre are floodlit after 1900.

Beyond Goa Mumbai

🟢 *Greed is nothing new to Mumbai, say its inhabitants. The city has always worshipped*
⚫ *money in the shape of Mahalaxmi, the temple to the goddess of wealth.*

Central Mumbai

Related map
B Gateway of India and
Colaba, p196.

Beyond Goa Mumbai

0 metres   300
0 yards   300

Sleeping
Ambassador **9** C1
City Palace **1** C3
Chateau Windsor
  Guest House **2** C2
Grand **8** C3

Manama **3** B3
Oberoi &
  Oberoi Towers **4** D1
Rupam **5** B3
Supreme **6** E1
West End **7** B2

Eating
Apoorva **15** C3
Balwas **1** C2
Berry's Chopsticks **2** C1

Croissants & British
  Airways **4** C2
Gaylord **5** C2
George **6** D3
Kamling & Flavors **7** C1
Mahesh Lunch
  Home **8** C3
May Rose **9** B2
Piccolo Café **11** D3
Santoor **13** E1
Sapna **14** C2

Satkar **18** C2
Sidewok **19** D1
Thacker's **16** C2
West Coast **12** C3
Woodlands **17** E1

Bars & clubs
Copa Cabana **3** A1
Intercontinental **20** C1
Not Just Jazz by
  the Bay **10** C1

⦂ Bright lights of Bollywood

Mumbai produces nearly 200 films a year, making Bollywood the world's second largest film-maker after Hong Kong. The stars live in sumptuous dwellings, many of which are on Malabar Hill, Mumbai's Beverley Hills, and despite the spread of foreign videos, their popularity seems to be undiminished.

It is difficult to get permission to visit a studio during filming but you might try **Film City**, Goregaon East, T022-8401533 or **Mehboob Studios**, Hill Road, Bandra West, T022-6428045. Alternatively, the staff at the **Salvation Army Hostel** (see Sleeping) may be able to help foreigners get on as 'extras' (blonde and tall preferred!); Rs 500 per day.

Fort area

Horniman Circle was laid out in 1860. On the west edge are the Venetian Gothic **Elphinstone Buildings** (1870) in brown sandstone. The **Cathedral Church of St Thomas** was begun in 1672, opened in 1718, and subject to a number of later additions. Inside are a number of monuments forming a heroic 'Who's Who of India'. The **Custom House** is believed to incorporate a Portuguese barrack block of 1665. Over the entrance is the crest of the East India Company. Parts of the old Portuguese fort's walls can be seen and many Malabar teak 'East Indiamen' ships were built here. **The Mint** (1824-1829), built on the Fort rubbish dump, has ionic columns and a water tank in front of it. The **Town Hall** (1820-1823) has been widely admired as one of the best neo-classical buildings in India. The original idea of paired columns was abandoned as being too monumental, and half the columns – imported from Britain – were used at Christ Church, Byculla. The Corinthian interior houses the **Assembly Rooms** and the **Bombay Asiatic Society**. From the imposing Horniman Circle, Vir Nariman Road leads to Flora (or Frere) Fountain (1869), now known as **Hutatma Chowk**.

Around the CST or VT

The **Chhatrapati Sivaji Terminus**, formerly Victoria Terminus or VT, (1878-87), the most remarkable example of Victorian Gothic architecture in India, was opened during Queen Victoria's Golden Jubilee year. The first train in India left from this terminus for Thane in April 1853. Known today as 'CST', over half a million commuters use the station every day.

The station was built at a time when fierce debate was taking place among British architects working in India as to the most appropriate style to develop to meet the demands of the late 19th-century boom. One view held that the British should restrict themselves to models derived from the best in western tradition. Others argued that architects should draw on Indian models, trying to bring out the best of Indian tradition and encourage its development. By and large, the former were dominant, but the introduction of gothic allowed a blending of western traditions with Indian (often Islamic Indian) motifs, which became known as the Indo-Saracenic style. The giant caterpillar-like walkway with perspex awnings looks incongruous against the gothic structure of 'VT'. The frontage is symmetrical with a large central dome flanked by two wings, capped by a 4-m high statue of Progress. The booking hall with its arcades, stained glass and glazed tiles was inspired by London's St Pancras station.

Opposite the CST station are the grand **Municipal Buildings** (1893), built by Stevens. In Mahapalika Marg (Cruickshank Road) are the **Police Courts** (1888), **Cama**

Albless Hospital, which has interesting gothic windows with conical iron hoods to provide shade, **St Xavier's College** founded in 1867, and **Elphinstone High School** (1872). On the opposite side of the road is the **Azad Maidan**.

St Xavier's School and **Gokuldas Tejpal Hospital** (1877), built by Parsi benefactors, are in Lokmanya Tilak Marg (Camac Road). On the southeast and southwest faces are medallions by Rudyard Kipling's father Lockwood Kipling.

Crawford Market, Mumbai (1865-1871), now **Jyotiba Phule Market**, was designed by Emerson in the 12th-century French gothic style. Over the entrance is more of Lockwood Kipling's work; the paving stones are from Caithness. The market is divided into sections for fruit, vegetables, fish, mutton and poultry.

Between Crawford Market and Mumbai Central Railway Station is **Falkland Road**, the centre of Mumbai's red-light district. Prostitutes stand behind barred windows, giving the area its other name 'The Cages' – many of the girls are sold or abducted from various parts of India and Nepal. Medical reports suggest that AIDS is very widespread.

Marine Drive, Malabar Hill and around

You can do an interesting half-day trip from Churchgate Station, along Marine Drive to the **Taraporewala Aquarium**, **Mani Bhavan** (Gandhi Museum), the **Babulnath Temple**, past the **Parsi Towers of Silence** to **Kamla Nehru Park**, the **Hanging Gardens** and the **Jain Temple**. If you wish, you can go further towards Malabar Point to get a glimpse of **Raj Bhavan** and the **Walkeshwar Temple**, before returning via the **Mahalaxmi Temple** and **Haji Ali's tomb**.

Churchgate Station (1894-1896) was designed by FW Stevens for the Mumbai, Baroda and Central India Railway. Stevens was a great protagonist of the indo-saracenic style. With its domes and façades, Churchgate Station is byzantine in flavour. The statue on the western gable shows a figure holding a locomotive and wheel, symbols of technological progress.

> Join the crowds at sunset for an entertaining walk: hawkers and sand sculptors mingle with joggers and Mumbai's high society walking their dogs.

Chowpatty Beach, a long stretch of white sand, looks attractive from a distance, but is polluted. Swimming here is not recommended but there is a lot of interesting beach activity in the evening. Chowpatty was the scene of a number of important 'Quit India' rallies during the Independence Movement. At important festivals like **Ganesh Chaturthi** and **Dasara** (see Festivals), it is thronged with jubilant Hindu devotees. Netaji Subhash Road, better known as Marine Drive, runs round Back Bay along Chowpatty from just below the Hanging Gardens on Malabar Hill to **Nariman Point.** At night, lined with lights, it is a very attractive sight from Malabar Hill.

Mahatma Gandhi Museum (Mani Bhavan) ⓘ *west of Grant Rd, 19 Laburnum Rd, 0930-1800, Rs 3, allow 1 hr*, is further north towards Nana Chowk, at Mani Bhavan. This private house, where Mahatma Gandhi used to stay on visits to Mumbai, is now a memorial museum and research library with 20,000 volumes. There is a diorama depicting important scenes from Gandhi's life; slides without a mount are available, Rs 100. The display of photos and letters on the first floor is more interesting, and includes letters Gandhi wrote to Hitler in 1939 asking him not to go to war, and those to Roosevelt and Tolstoy; there are also letters from Einstein and Tolstoy.

In the heart of the Muslim quarter where agate minarets mingle with the upper storeys of 1960s residential towers lies **Chor Bazaar**. The atmosphere here is totally different from the crumbling colonial architectural glory of the Colaba and Fort area, and at sunset the ramshackle roads hum with yellow and black taxis, adolescent boys

● *Bombay, named after the Portuguese for good harbour (bom bahia), was rechristened*
● *Mumbai after Mumba Devi, a Koli goddess, following fierce lobbying from Shiv Sena.*

wielding wooden carts through traffic at a run, and Muslim women at a stroll. The jumble of the bazaar is a brilliant place to poke around in, there are tonnes of dealers in old watches, film posters, Belgian- or Indian-made temple lamps, enamel tiles and door-knobs. The area around Mutton Street is popular with film prop-buyers and foreign and domestic bric-a-brac hunters. Further out the produce is more local: tarpaulins and tools, Mecca paintings, and burqas with gold geometric embroidery. Balconies come bedecked with fairy lights on faded apartment blocks and wooden shutters lie over grilling, pollution stains streaked over the pastel buildings.

The **Towers of Silence**, Mumbai (Parsi 'temple') are in secluded gardens 500 m west of Mani Bhavan. This very private place is not accessible to tourists but it can be glimpsed from the road. Sir Jamshetji Jeejeebhoy gave a large area of land around the towers, thus affording them privacy and allowing the creation of a tranquil garden. Parsis believe that the elements of water, fire and earth must not be polluted by the dead, so they lay their 'vestments of flesh and bone' out on the top of the towers to be picked clean by vultures. The apparent depletion in the number of vultures is a cause for concern.

The **Hanging Gardens (Pherozeshah Mehta Gardens)** immediately south of the Towers of Silence, on top of a low hill, are so named since they are located on top of a series of tanks that supply water to Mumbai. The gardens are well kept with lots of topiary animals and there are good views over the city from the children's park across the road. Snake charmers operate from the roadside. Worth a visit.

Nearby is the Church of North India **All Saints' Church** (1882). Across the road from the Hanging Gardens is the **Kamla Nehru Park**, laid out in 1952 and named after the wife of India's first Prime Minister. Very good views over Back Bay.

The **Jain Temple** (1904) was built of marble and dedicated to the first Jain Tirthankar. Much of the decoration depicts the lives of the Tirthankars. Visitors can watch various rituals being performed. Jains play a prominent part in Mumbai's banking and commerce and are one of the city's wealthiest communities.

One of the oldest buildings in Mumbai, the **Walkeshwar Temple** ('Lord of Sand') was built about AD 1000. In legend this was a resting point for Rama on his journey from Ayodhya to Lanka to free Sita from the demon king Ravana. One day Rama's brother Lakshman failed to return from Varanasi at the usual time with a *lingam* which he fetched daily for Rama's worship. Rama then made a *lingam* from the beach sand to worship Siva.

On Bhulabhai Desai Road, Cumballa Hill are the **Mahalakshmi temples**, the oldest in Mumbai and dedicated to three goddesses whose images were found in the sea.

Haji Ali's Tomb and the mosque here are devoted to a Muslim saint who drowned here. They are reached by a long causeway usable only at low tide. The moneychangers are willing to exchange 1 rupee coins into smaller coins, enabling pilgrims to make several individual gifts to beggars rather than one larger one, thereby reputedly increasing the merit of the gift.

From Haji Ali's Tomb go along Keshavrao Khade Road to **SG Maharaj Chowk (Jacob's Circle)**. From the Mahalakshmi Bridge there is a view of the astonishing Municipal dhobi ghats.

Go down Maulana Azad Road then turn left into Clare Road. On your right is **Christ Church**, Byculla (1835), which incorporated half the pillars originally intended for the Town Hall. Clare Road leads down the side of the **Victoria Gardens**. They are very attractive – marked as Jijamata Udyan on some maps and signs. A list at the entrance shows which trees are in bloom.

"The unregarded millions have multiplied and now, flooding into the cities, cannot be denied. The illegal hutments in which they live are knocked down; but they rise again, a daily tide wrack on the margin of cities and beside the railway lines and the industrial highways." VS Naipaul 'A Wounded Civilization'.

North of Byculla Station is the **Victoria and Albert Museum (Bhav Daji Laud Museum)** ① *Mon and Tue, Thu-Sat 1030-1700, Sun 0830-1645*. Inspired by the V&A in London and financed by public subscription, it was built in 1872 in a palladian style. The collection covers the history of Mumbai and contains prints, maps and models. In front of the museum is a clocktower (1865) with four faces (morning, noon, evening and night), and a stone statue of an elephant found by the Portuguese in the harbour. Elephanta Island was named after it.

◉ Sleeping

There's no low-season when it comes to accommodation in Mumbai: whenever possible make reservations in advance. If you have not, arrive as early in the day as possible. Most hotels are concentrated in the central area (Marine Drive, Nariman Point, Apollo Bunder and Colaba). See page 204 for convenient places to stay for the airport.

There are stacks of moderately priced hotels immediately behind the Taj Mahal Hotel. Backpackers usually head for the Colaba area to the south. The alternative is to look around CST and Dadar railway stations. There are several 5-star hotels on Juhu beach and close to the airports. For paying guest accommodation contact India Tourist Office, 123 M Karve Rd, T022-2032932. Some E-F category hotels are clustered around the Taj Mahal Hotel. On Arthur Bunder Rd, Colaba, there are several, often on upper floors, usually shared facilities, cold water only, some windowless rooms; arrive early and inspect room first.

Gateway of India and Colaba *p195, map p196*
Rooms with seaview are more expensive. There are few budget hotels left in the area charging under Rs 400 though you may get a dormitory bed for Rs 250.

LL Taj Mahal Apollo Bunder, T022-56653366, www.tajhotels.com. The grand-dame of Mumbai lodging, over a centuryold, with 294 rooms on the Gateway to India and 306 in the **Taj Mahal Intercontinental**, its newer wing. So good, even the corridors look like art galleries. 9 restaurants and bars, plus full fitness centre and there's even a yacht on call.
L-AL Fariyas, off Arthur Bunder Rd, Colaba, T022-2042911. 80 upgraded rooms, good restaurants, 'pub', roof garden, pool (open to non-residents), obliging service.

L-AL Gordon House Hotel, 5 Battery St, Apollo Bunder, Colaba, T022-2871122, www.ghhotel.com. Amazingly, a spiffingly spruce boutique hotel in the rundown Colaba district, 3 themed floors that really do leave India outside: yellow med-style walls in some, quilts in the country cottage rooms and all blonde wood in the Scandinavian floor.
A Strand, 25 PJ Ramchandani Marg, T022-2882222. Friendly, clean, decent rooms, some with bath and seaview.
A-B Garden Hotel, 42 Garden Rd, T022-2841476, gardenhotel@mail.com. Sister hotel to the Godwin next door, with similar facilities plus all rooms have bath tubs. Efficient.
A-C Godwin, 41 Garden Rd, T022-2872050. 48 large, clean, renovated, a/c rooms (upper floors have better views), good rooftop restaurant (full of wealthy Mumbaiites on Fri and Sat night), very helpful management. Recommended.
B Apollo, 22 Lansdowne Rd, Colaba, behind Taj, T022-2020223. 39 rooms, some a/c, some with amazing sea views. Tatty linen and walls, but helpful, friendly service.
B Diplomat, 24-26 BK Boman Behram Marg (behind Taj), T022-2021661, diplomat@vsnl.com, 52 a/c rooms, restaurant, quiet, friendly, relaxed atmosphere, good value. Very simple furnishings, small beds. Recommended.
B Gulf Flower, Kamal Mansions, Arthur Bunder Rd, T022-2833742. Off-putting exterior but modern and clean rooms inside.
B Regency Inn, 18 Lansdowne Rd behind Regal Cinema, Colaba, T022-2020292. Spacious a/c rooms, fridge, good value.
B Regent, 8 Ormiston Rd (Best Marg), T022-2871854. 50 rooms in modern hotel that's popular with sheiks, hence the camels and pastels theme. Well-furnished a/c rooms, no restaurant but good room service.

B **Suba Palace**, Apollo Bunder, T022-2020636, just behind Taj. Clean, modern, well run. Recommended.

B-C **Hotel Cowie's**, 15 Walton Rd, near Electric House, Colaba T022-2840232. 20 rooms, all with central a/c, en suite, television and phone, in old world hotel on one of the tree-lined residential streets off Colaba Causeway. Excellent value.

B-C **Shelley's**, 30 PJ Ramchandani Marg, Colaba, T022-2840229, shelleyhotel @vsnl.com. Large comfortable, bright airy a/c rooms, some sea-facing with TV and fridge (more expensive), a 'heritage' building with character, breakfasts only, helpful and friendly owners. Recommended.

C **Moti Hotel**, 10 Best Marg, opposite Electric House, Colaba, T022-025714. 8 a/c rooms with slatted wood doors in ground floor of a mansion block, yellow walls made of ply, original mosaic flooring. Extremely narrow bathrooms with plastic mirrors, 24-hr hot water, TV.

C-D **Sea Lord**, , 1/49 Kamal Mansion, Arthur Bunder Rd. 15 bright gloss-pink rooms and purple corridors, shower in room but no sink, 7 with window and TV and fan, 8 without. Sea view room has 4 beds. 2 rooms come with toilet, TV and hot water.

C-D **Whalley's**, 41 Mereweather Rd, T022-2834206. 25 rooms (inspect first), some good, a/c with balcony and bath, includes breakfast, accepts TCs, old-fashioned.

C-D **YWCA International Centre**, 2nd Flr, 18 Madam Cama Rd (entrance on side), Fort, T022-2020122. For both sexes, 34 clean, pleasant rooms with bath, breakfast and dinner included, essential to write in advance with Rs 1,300 deposit. Recommended.

C-F **The Salvation Army**, Red Shield House, 30 Mereweather Rd, T022-2841824, red-shield@vsnl.net. With A/c (more expensive), includes all meals. Dormitory F rate includes breakfast only. Mostly dorm about Rs 130 including breakfast, Rs 200 including meals), some double rooms (Rs 450, all meals), lockers Rs 30 per item 0800-2200, showers, check out 0900, book in advance or arrive early when others check out, bus ticketing (eg Goa) at reception. Recommended as convenient, friendly, best value but could be cleaner. See also box, page 199.

D **India Guest House**, 1/49 Kamal Mansion, Arthur Bunder Rd. 20 rooms along long corridor, white partitions that you could, at a push, jump over. Fan, no toilet or shower. The corner room has a neat panorama over the bay. Sound will travel.

D **Sea Shore**, top floor, 1/49 Kamal Mansion, Arthur Bunder Rd, Kitsch as you like, pink and white moulding clad ceiling, desks and mirrors, TV, plastic flowers down the corridor.

Around the CST or VT *p199, map p198*

B **Grand**, 17 Sprott Rd, Ballard Estate, T022-2618211. 73 a/c rooms, exchange, book counter, old-fashioned, built around a central courtyard, helpful service, very relaxing.

B-C **City Palace**, 121 City Terr (Nagar Chowk), opposite CST Main Gate, T022-2615515. Tiny though clean, functional rooms (some without windows), with bath (Indian WC), some a/c, helpful staff, convenient location. Recommended.

D **Popular Place**, 104-106 Mint Rd, near GPO, Fort Market, T022-2695506. Clean rooms with bath (hot water), some a/c, helpful staff good value.

D-E **Manama** , 221 P D'Mello Rd, T022-2613412. Reasonable rooms, few with bath and a/c, popular.

D-E **Rupam** , 239 P D'Mello Rd, T022-2618298. 37 rooms, some a/c with phone, clean, friendly, comfortable beds.

Marine Drive, Malabar Hill and around *p200, map p198*

LL **Intercontinental Marine Drive**, 135 Marine Dr, T022-56399999, www.intercontinental.com. 59 rooms in boutique hotel overlooking Marine Drive. Bose stereo, plasma TV screens, Bulgari toiletries, personal butler service and beautiful rooftop pool.

LL-AL **The Oberoi**, Nariman Pt, T022-2325757. 350 large rooms, the newer Oberoi combining modern technology with period furniture, excellent restaurants.

LL-AL **Oberoi Towers**, Nariman Pt, T022-2324343. 650 rooms, superb views from the higher floors, good buffets, garden and swimming pool, excellent shopping complex. Recommended.

LL-AL **President**, 90 Cuffe Pde, T022-2150808. 317 rooms, most business facilities, good service but poor value, informal but lacks character.

L-AL **Ambassador**, Churchgate Extn, Vir Nariman Rd, T022-2041131. 127 rooms, all facilities, revolving restaurant and pastry shop, slightly run-down feel.

AL **Nataraj**, 135 Marine Dr, T022-2044161. 83 rooms, some with views over bay, food and live music in restaurant, good but a bit noisy and overpriced.

A-B **West End**, 45 New Marine Lines, T022-2039121, westhotel@vsnl.com. 80 small, pleasant suites but need refurbishing, good restaurant, excellent service, very efficient front desk, well located, good value. Recommended.

B-C **Chateau Windsor Guest House**, 86 Vir Nariman Rd, T022-2043376, info@chateau windsor.com. 36 rooms (some a/c) vary, some very small and dark, room service for light snacks and drinks, friendly, clean, good value. Recommended. Cash only.

C **Sea Green**, 145 Marine Dr, T/F022-2822294. 34 rooms, 22 a/c, pleasant breezy informal sitting area.

C-D **Astoria**, 4 J Tata Rd, Churchgate, T022-2852626. 75 a/c rooms, restaurant, bar.

C-D **Supreme**, 4 Pandey Rd, near President, T022-2185623. Clean rooms with bath, good service but can be a little noisy.

Dadar, Mumbai Central Station & Grant Rd area

Dadar can be a good option to stay – plenty of restaurants and good trains to Churchgate and CST.

A-B **Midtown Pritam**, 20-B Pritam Estates, Senapati Bapat Marg, 2 mins from Dadar station, T022-4145555. 63 rooms, terrace garden.

C **Sagar**, Nagpada Junction (Bellasin Rd/JB Behram Marg corner), Byculla, T022-3092727. Very clean rooms, good restaurant, friendly. Recommended.

C-D **Red Rose**, Gokuldas Pasta Rd, (behind Chitra Cinema) Dadar East, T022-4137843. 31 rooms, some a/c, mostly shared but clean baths, flexible checkout, friendly – "welcoming at 0530 with no booking". Recommended.

D **Anukool**, 292-8 Maulana Saukat Ali Rd, T022-30814013, hotelanukool@hotmail.com. 23 rooms, some a/c, friendly, helpful, good value, but inspect room first.

D **Heritage**, Sant Savta Marg, Byculla, T022-3714891. 84 a/c rooms, restaurant (good Parsi), bar.

D **Kalpana Palace**, 181 P Bapurao Marg, opposite Daulat Cinema, Grant Rd, T022-3000846. 30 decent rooms, some a/c.

D **Railway Retiring Rooms**, Mumbai Central, T022-3077292. Some a/c with bath.

D-E **YMCA International House**, 18 YMCA Rd, near Mumbai Central, T022-3091191. Decent rooms, shared bath, meals included, temp membership Rs 60, deposit Rs 1,300, good value, book 3 months ahead.

Outskirts of Mumbai

Juhu Beach (20 km from the centre) used to be quite an attractive and relaxed seaside area but the sea is now polluted. On Sunday evenings the beach takes on a fairground atmosphere. Most airport hotels offer free transfer. Tourist information at the airport will help to book.

Airport

LL-L **Leela Palace**, near International Terminal, T022-56911234, www.theleela. com. 460 modern rooms, excellent restaurants, pricey but excellent, bar (closed to non-residents after 2300).

L **Renaissance**, near Chinmayanand Ashram, Powai, 9 km from international airport, T022-6928888, www.renaissance hotels.com. 286 stylish rooms, excellent restaurants, pleasant green surroundings, large pool, relaxing.

L-AL **Orchid**, 70C Nehru Rd, Vile Parle (east), T022-6100707, 5 mins' walk from domestic terminal. Totally refurbished, attractive rooms, eco-friendly. Boulevard restaurant boasts a '15 min lightening menu' and good midnight buffet. Recommended.

AL **Centaur Airport**, Santa Cruz, has had poor reports.

B **Metro Palace**, Hill Rd, near Bandra station (W), T022-6427311. Convenient, close to domestic airport and shops, good restaurant.

B **Pali Hills**, 14 Union Park, Pali Hill, Bandra, T022-6492995. Quiet location, near market, continental restaurant (see below).

B-C **Atithi**, 77A Nehru Rd, Vile Parle (east) 7 mins' walk from domestic terminal, T022-6116124. 47 rooms, functional, clean, set meals included, good value, efficient desk, popular.

B-C **Residency**, Suren Rd, Andheri (E), T022-6923000, residency@hotmail.com. New hotel 3 km from the airport (request free pickup). 72 smallish a/c rooms, good restaurant, on quiet back street, friendly staff. Recommended (often full).

B-C **Transit**, off Nehru Rd, Vile Parle (east), T022-6105812. 54 rooms, modern, reasonable overnight halt for airport, excellent restaurant (good food and service, draught beer), airport transfer.

D **Airport Rest Rooms**, old Domestic Terminal, Santa Cruz. For passengers with connecting flights within 24 hrs of arrival, comfortable, clean, but often full.

Juhu Beach

L-AL **Holiday Inn**, Balraj Sahani Marg, T022-6204444. 190 rooms, 2 pools, courtesy coach to town, reliable.

AL **Sun-n-Sand**, 39 Juhu Beach, T022-6201811. 118 rooms, best refurbished, comfortable, though cramped poolside, good restaurant.

A **Citizen**, 960 Juhu Tara Rd, T022-6117273, citizen@bom2.vsnl.net.in. Despite unexciting appearance, 45 smallish but very well appointed rooms, suites, efficient airport transfer. Recommended.

B **Juhu Hotel**, Juhu Tara Rd, T022-6184014. Spacious comfortable cottage-style rooms, sea-facing lawns, good restaurant (try seafood and *Mughlai*), soundproofed disco.

B **Sands**, 39/2 Juhu Beach, T022-6204511. 40 rooms, excellent restaurant. Recommended.

❶ Eating

Gateway of India and Colaba *p195, map p196*

$$$ **All Stir Fry**, Gordon House Hotel, oriental nosh served up in *Wagamama*-style at long shared benches. DIY food too.

$$$ **Copper Chimney**, 18 K Dubash Marg, T022-2041661. Indian. Subdued lighting and quietly tasteful, excellent North Indian dishes, must reserve.

$$$ **Indigo**, 4 Mandlik Rd, behind Taj Hotel, T022-2856316. Excellent Mediterranean in smart new restaurant, good atmosphere, additional seating on rooftop.

$$$ **Khyber**, 145 MG Rd, Kala Ghoda, Fort, T022-2632174. North Indian. For an enjoyable evening in beautiful surroundings, excellent food, especially lobster and *reshmi* chicken kebabs, try *paya* soup (goats' trotters!), outstanding restaurant, reserve.

$$$ **Ling's Pavilion**, 19/21 KC College Hostel Building, off Colaba Causeway (behind Taj and Regal Cinema), T022-2850023. Stylish decor, good atmosphere and delightful service, colourful menu, seafood specials, generous helpings. Recommended.

$$$ **Souk**, Taj Mahal Apollo Bunder, T022-56653366, www.tajhotels.com. Taj's top floor is now home to a North African themed restaurant. Open from 1900, great views. You can just have a drink but a glass of imported red wine, excellent though it may be, costs Rs 500 before tax.

$$$ **Tides**, Gordon House Hotel, seafood restaurant, bar, wines and coffee shop with submarine theme.

$$$ **Trishna**, Sai Baba Marg, next to Commerce House, Fort T022-22614991, behind Kala Ghoda, by Old Synagogue. Indian. Good coastline cuisine, seafood, excellent butter garlic crab. "Swinging, crowded and fun". Recommended.

$$ **Bagdadi**, Tullock Rd (behind Taj Hotel), T022-2028027. *Mughlai*. One of the cheapest, first class food, fragrant biryani, delicious chicken, crowded but clean. Recommended.

$$ **Café Basilico Bistro & Deli**, Sentinel House, Arthur Bunder Rd, T022-56345670, www.cafebasilico.com. Very *chi-chi*, European-style café with waffles from Rs 85, soups, salads, pastas and smoothies.

$$ **Ming Place**, Apsara Building, Colaba Causeway, T022-2872820. Chinese. Big a/c place with cosmic murals and heavy wooden chairs. Try 'Shanghai potatoes'.

$ **Bade Miyan**, behind Ling's Pavilion. Streetside Kebab corner but very clean. Try *baida roti*, *shammi* and *boti* kebabs

$ **Café Churchill**, T022-22844689, 1000-2400. A tiny little caff with 7 tables crammed with people basking in a/c, towered over by a cake counter and a Winston Churchill portrait. Great breakfasts, club sandwiches, whoppers, seafood, fish and chips, lasagne, irish stew and so on.

$ **Kamat Samarambh**, opposite Electric House, SB Singh Marg. Indian vegetarian. Very good *thalis* and snacks, try *chola battura* (*puri* topped with spiced chickpeas).

$ **Majestic Hotel.** Bustling, cheap columned and boothed canteen doing a fast business in *thalis* and the old South Indian favourites like *iddly/sambar*.

$ **Martin's**, near Strand Cinema. Goan. Simple, authentic Goan food, excellent seafood and pork *sorpotel*.

$ **Paradise**, Sindh Chambers, Colaba Causeway, Tue-Sun. Parsi and others. Spotless, excellent dhansak; try *sali boti* (mutton and 'chips'), not a/c.

$ **Shiv Sagar Vegetarian Restaurant**, mouth of Colaba Market, Mistry Chambers, Opp Telephone Bhawan, Near Strand Cinema, Colaba, T022-2811550. Excellent very simple veg restaurant, hygienic and clean that does South Indian snacks outside normal restaurant mealtimes.

Cafés and fast food

Many serve chilled beer; prices have gone up and waiters care too much for large tips from tourist groups:

Food-Inn, 50 m from Leopold's. Mainly Indian (some western) snacks. Pleasant (a/c upstairs), reasonably priced, friendly, recommended.

Kailash Parbat, 1st Pasta La, Colaba. Excellent snacks and chats. In an old-style eatery serving Punjabi *thalis*, tooth-rotting sweets from the counter.

Leopold's, Colaba, T022-2830585. An institution among Colaba backpackers and Mumbai shoppers, good western food and drink (limited Indian veg), but it's pricey too. Similar cafés nearby are far better value.

Mondegar, near Regal Cinema, T022-2812549. Similar, but a little cheaper and with a loud rock soundtrack.

Wayside Inn, 38 K Dubash Marg, T022-2844324. Quaint country inn-style place, good breakfast menu, average continental but perfect for an afternoon beer in heart of the city. Breezy, laid back and leisurely, moderately priced.

Around the CST or VT *p199, map p198*

$$ **Apoorva**, near Horniman Circle, Fort, T022-2881457. Very good seafood, especially crabs and prawns (menu is cheaper downstairs).

$$ **Bharat**, 317 SB Singh Marg, opposite Fort Market, T022-2618991. Excellent seafood and crab as well as naans and rotis: or try fried, stuffed Bombay Duck.

$$ **George**, 20 Apollo St (near Horniman Circle). Pleasant quiet atmosphere, colonial feel, good service, lunchtime biriyanis and *thalis*.

$$ **Sadanand**, opposite Crawford Market. Excellent *thalis* and veg food, popular with Indian families.

$$ **Wall Street**, 68 Hamam St, behind Stock Exchange. Coastal cuisine, excellent seafood, try spicy Malabari prawns, squid green garlic, fish *patta*.

$ **Icy Spicy**, off PM Rd, next to Fort Central Restaurant. Veg snack bar. Great light meals (from Rs 25).

$ **Ideal Corner**, Hornby View, Gunbow St, Fort, CST. Lunchtime Parsi food and snacks in clean café.

$ **Mahesh Lunch Home**, Sir PM Rd, Fort. Excellent for Mangalorean, Goan and tandoori seafood, a/c, bar, very popular.

$ **West Coast**, Rustom Sidhwa Rd, off Sir Perin Nariman Rd. Very good meals. On MG Rd (north end), you can have a traditional breakfast, often served as early as 0600.

Marine Drive, Malabar Hill and around *p200, map p198*

$$$ **Gaylord**, Vir Nariman Rd, T022-2821231. Indian. Good food (huge portions) and service, tables inside and out, barbecue, pleasant, good bar, tempting pastry counter.

$$$ **Indian Summer**, 80 Vir Nariman Rd, T022-2835445. Indian. Excellent food, tasty kebabs, interesting modern glass decor, smart dress, reserve.

$$$ **Pearl of the Orient**, Ambassador Hotel, T022-2041131. Excellent Chinese, Japanese and Thai. The revolving restaurant offers stunning views especially at night. For a less expensive stationary view try the bar on the floor above which does simple meals.

$$$ **RG's Kitchen**, Intercontinental, Marine Dr, T022-56399999. 3 open kitchens, one Indian, one Oriental and one Western. Where Mumbai's posh socialites eat.

$$$ **Santoor**, Maker Arcade, Cuffe Parade, near President Hotel, T022-2182262. North Indian. Small place, *Mughlai* and Kashmiri specialities: creamy chicken *malai* chop,

chana, Peshawari (*puri* with chickpeas),
Kashmiri soda made with salt and pepper.
$$$ Sidewok, next to NCPA theatre,
T022-2818132. Interesting south
east Asian/fusion cuisine. Innovative
menu, imaginative cocktails (try
non-alcoholic too), surprise
entertainment by staff, "longest mosaic
mural in Asia", a special, fun dining
experience. Reserve.
$$ Berry's, Vir Nariman Rd, near Churchgate
Station, T022-2875691. North Indian.
Tandoori specialities, good *kulfi*.
$$ Chopsticks, 90A Vir Nariman Rd,
Churchgate, T022-2832308. Chinese, good,
hot and spicy. Offering unusual dishes (*taro*
nest, date pancakes, toffee bananas).
$$ Kamling, 82 Vir Nariman Rd,
T022-2042618. Genuine Cantonese. Simple
surroundings, but excellent preparations, try
seafood, often busy.
$$ May Rose, Cinema Rd (next to
'Metro'), T022-2081104. Chinese. Clean a/c,
very good food.
$$ Sapna, Vir Nariman Rd. Indian,
very traditional Mughlai delicacies,
bar, some tables outside, attentive service,
good value.
$$ Satkar, Indian Express Building,
opposite Churchgate station, T022-
2043259. Indian. Delicious vegetarian,
fruit juices and shakes; a/c section
more expensive.
$ Balwas, Maker Bhavan, 3 Sir V
Thackersey Marg. Inexpensive, well-
prepared food.
$ Thacker's, corner Maharshi Karve Rd and
1st Marine St. Indian. Good *thalis*.
$ Piccolo Café, 11A Sir Homi Mody St.
Parsi. 0900-1800, closed Sat afternoon
and Sun, profits to charity, homely, clean,
good *dhansak*.
$ Purohit's, Vir Nariman Rd. Indian. Excellent
veg *thalis*, also Parsi.
$ Woodlands, Mittal Chambers,
Nariman Pt, Mon-Sat. South Indian.
Excellent *idli* and *dosai* and good *thalis*,
busy at lunchtime.

Cafés and fast food
Croissants, Vir Nariman Rd, opposite
Eros Cinema. Burgers, sandwiches,
hot croissants with fillings, ice cream,
lively atmosphere.

Fountain, MG Rd. For sizzlers and apple pie
in a café atmosphere.

Dadar, Mumbai Central Station and Grant Rd area
$$$ Biscotti, Crossroads, Haji Ali,
T022-4955055. Excellent Italian. Wholesome,
leisurely dining, try batter-fried calamari,
giant prawns in liqueur, flavoured sugar-
free soda, zabaglioni, bistro-style complete
with fiddler.
$$$ Goa Portuguesa, THK Rd, Mahim.
Goan. Authentic dishes, taverna-style
with guitarist, try *sungto* (prawn) served
between *papads*, *kalwa* (oyster), *teesryo*
(shell) and clams, lobsters cooked with
tomatoes, onions and spices and
bebinca to end the meal.
$$$ Revival, Chowpatty Sea Face (near
footbridge). Classy, good Indian/Continental
buffets and desserts.
$$ Bombay A1, 7 Vadilal A Patel Marg (Grant
Rd Junc). Parsi. Cheerful, varied menu, try
Patrani *machli*.
$$ Copper Chimney, Dr AB Rd, Worli,
T022-4924488. Indian. Window into kitchen,
excellent food from extensive menu,
reasonable prices, undiscovered by tourists.
$$ Under the Over, 36 Altamount Rd (by
flyover). Bistro-like, for Mexican, Creole
dishes, sizzlers and rich desserts, reasonably
priced, no alcohol.
$$ The Village, Poonam Intercontinental,
near Mahalaxmi racecourse. Gujarati. 'Village'
setting, sea views, good authentic food.
$$ Viva Paschim, City View, Dr AB Rd, Worli,
T022-4983636. Quality coastal
Maharashtrian. Sunday lunch buffet great
value (Rs 225), folk dances at dinner often.
$ Heaven, corner of Grant Rd/P
Bapurao Marg. Very cheap, friendly
(*egaloo matar* Rs 10).
$ Kamat, Navrose Mansion, Tardeo
Rd. Indian. Very inexpensive *thalis* and
veg snacks.

Outskirts of Mumbai
Airport, Juhu Beach and Bandra
Bandra, the upcoming area of the moment,
has some exciting options.
$$ Gazalee, Kadambari Complex,
Hanuman Rd, Vile Parle (E), T022-8388093.
Finest coastal cuisine, try stuffed Bombay
Duck and shellfish.

$$ **Just around the Corner**, 24th-30th road junction, TPS III, Bandra (W). Bright casual American-style diner. Extensive breakfast menu (0800-1100). Pay by the plateful, lots of combination options, excellent salads, low-calorie.

$$ **Olive Bar & Kitchen**, Pali Hill Tourist Hotel, 14 Union Park Khar (W), T022-26058228, www.olivebarandkitchen.com. Olive caters to a very chic Bollywood Bombay crowd. This also means that they do not encourage male gawpers, so men need to be escorted by women to get in.

$$ **Out of the Blue**, at Pali Hills. Steak and fondue, great sizzlers, unusual combinations, flavoured ice teas, flambéed desserts, UV lit inside or outside smoke-free.

$$ **Trim with Taste**, 500 Sant Kutir, Linking Rd, Bandra (lane behind KBN store). Small, spotless, serving unusual health food. Try stuffed idlis, peach and yoghurt smoothies.

$ **Crunchy Munchy**, Agarwal Market, next to Vile Parle (E) station. Open-air café serving veg Indian and Mexican mini-meals. Very clean, good service and portions.

$ **Kanchi**, Mittal Industrial Estate, Andheri-Kurla Rd, Marol, Andheri (E). Excellent South Indian vegetarian, unusual daily specials. Recommended.

$ **Lucky**, 9 SV Rd (Hill Rd junction), Bandra (W). Good *mughlai* especially chicken biriyani and tandooris.

⊙ Pubs, bars and clubs

All major hotels and restaurants have bars, others may only serve beer. Many pubs expect couples Fri-Sun. Most pubs charge Rs 175-250 for a 'pitcher' (bottle); cocktails Rs 75-150. Pick up *Mumbai This Fortnight*, an informative free booklet on everything that is hot in the city, free from larger bookshops and stores.

Gateway of India and Colaba p195, map p196
Clubs
Red Light, Khala Gowda, sleazy as they come, see behaviour from Mumbaikars that would shock the hell out of you if you saw it on your local high street disco, but brilliant all the same – proper *bhangra* and Hindi pop plus western dance music.
Insomnia, Taj. Snazzy.

Polly Esther, Gordon House Hotel. A reggae, pop, rock disco, retro-themed nightclub.
Provogue Lounge, Phoenix Mills, Lower Parel. By day a boutique for natty fashion brand, by night they clad the clothes rails with white wood and the sales tills turn to ringing out tequilas. Very in-crowd Mumbai.
Athena, 41/44 Minoo Desai Marg ,Colaba, T022-2028699, www.athenaontheweb.com, 1930-0130, food served till 2345. At Chateau Indage, champagne cigar lounge and restaurant. A slick celeb-festooned hangout, 300 capacity joint. Rs1,000 per couple, Rs 300 to get in then Rs 700 redeemed against drinks. Slick lounge with drapes and white leatherette and pearly pink lounge beds. Lounge music.

Marine Drive, Malabar Hill and around p200, map p198
Intercontinental, 135 Marine Drive, T022-56399999, www.intercontinental.com. Extremely expensive, and trendy, nightclub that comes alive with house music on Fri and Sat night. For beautiful people.
Not Just Jazz by the Bay, 143 Marine Dr, T022-2851876. Modern chrome and glass, live music (varied), karaoke, good food menu (great starters, desserts), generous portions, wide selection of drinks, very lively, a fun place.

Central Mumbai p197, map p198
Flavors. Bright 24-hr coffee shop-resto-bar. Chic, interesting cocktails and starters (PSP prawns, corn and spinach toast), barbecue buffet lunch (Rs 300-800), happy hour (1800-2000), try Graveyard (huge) or Flavothon (a shooter race), big screen, DJ (weekends). Fun at a price.
Café Olé, Ground flr, Cross Rds, Haji Ali, T022-4955123. Classic sports bar, chrome and glass, interesting menu (some Indianized), try Cactus Passion or Red Ginger (non-alcoholic), mini dance floor, DJ at weekends, fun place, affordable drinks.
Copa Cabana, Dariya Vihar, 39/D Girgaum, Chowpatty, T022-3680274. Small, playing 70s hits and Latino music, packed at weekends so little space for dancing.
Ghetto, B Desai Rd (100 m from Mahalakshmi Temple). Western pop from 60s, 70s, 80s, free entry (couples only), neon graffiti.

Geoffreys, Hotel Marine Plaza, Marine Dr,
T022-2851212. Soft music, relaxing for a
drink and a bite, no dancing.
Juhu Paparazzi, opposite Juhu Bus Depot,
Juhu Beach Rd, T022-6602199, Tue-Sun.
Small, cosy disco bar, packed after 2300,
drinks and snacks.
Razzberry Rhinoceros, Juhu Hotel, Juhu Tara
Rd, T022-6184012. Disco, nightclub. Lots of
space for dancing, pool tables, live acts.

Entertainment

Cinema
Bollywood films are screened in dozens of
cinemas: try **Eros** opposite Churchgate
station or **Metro**, on MG Rd, northwest
corner of Azad Maidan.
English language films are shown at many,
including **Regal**, Colaba Causeway, **New
Empire** and **Sterling**, Marzaban Rd, southwest
of CST station. It is best for women to get
seats in the circle.

Theatres
Plays are performed in English, Hindi,
Marathi and Gujarati, usually beginning at
1815-1900. Check *Mumbai This Fortnight* for
details. See a modern Hindi play at **Privthi
Theatre** to sample local culture; cool café for
drinks and snacks outside.

Activities and tours

Adventure tourism
Maharashtra Tourism has been active in
encouraging adventure tourism (including
jungle safaris and watersports) by introducing 'rent-a-tent' and hiring out trekking
gear. Prices range from US$35-150 per
day/weekend depending upon season and
activity. Some sites provide electricity, linen,
bathrooms and authentic cuisine in rustic
restaurants. It has also set up 27 'holiday
resorts' providing cheap accommodation at
hill stations, beaches, archaeological sites
and scenic spots. Details from tourist offices.

Horse racing
Mahalaxmi Race Course, opposite Haji Ali.
Season Nov-Mar, Sun and holidays,
1400-1700. Many of India's top races are held
at the delightful course (1878), including the
Derby in Feb/Mar.

Swimming
Breech Candy Club, B Desai Rd, T022-
3612543. For the select set, 2 clean pools
including a large one; non-members Rs 250.

Tennis
**Maharashtra State Lawn Tennis
Association**, Cooper, Colaba, T022-2848102.

Yoga
Iyengar Yogashraya Mumbai, Elmac
House, 126 Senapati Bapat Marg, Lower Parel
91, T022-24948416, info@bksiyengar.com.
Iyengar drop-in centre.
Kaivalyadhama, next to Taraporewala
Aquarium, Marine Dr.
The Yoga Institute, Praghat Colony,
Santa Cruz (E).
Yoga Training Centre, 51 Jai Hind Club,
Juhu Scheme.
Yoga Vidhya Niketan, Sane Guruji Marg,
Dadar, T022-4306258.

Tours
If you wish to sightsee independently with a
guide, ask at the tourist office. See page 192.
City sightseeing Approved guides from
the India tourist office, T022-2036854.
City tour usually includes visits to The
Gateway of India, the Chhatrapati Sivaji
(Prince of Wales) Museum, Jain temple,
Hanging Gardens, Kamla Nehru Park and
Mani Bhavan (Gandhi Museum). *Suburban
tour* includes Juhu Beach, Kanheri Caves
and Lion Safari Park.
MTDC, Madam Cama Rd, opposite
LIC Building, T022-2026713. *City tour*
daily except Mon, 0900-1300 and
1400-1800, Rs 100. *Suburban tour* 0915
(from Dadar 1015-1815. *Fort walk* A
heritage walk around CST and Fort area
with the Kala Ghoda Association,
Army & Navy Building, T022-2852520,
www.artindia.co.in. *Elephanta tours* From
Gateway of India. Boat, 0900-1415, Rs 70
return; reserve at Apollo Bunder,
T022-2026364.
Ajanta and Ellora MTDC 4-day tour to the
famous caves at Ajanta and Ellora.

Festivals and events

In addition to the national Hindu and
Muslim festivals there are the following:

Jan 1st weekend Banganga Classical Music Festival at Walkeshwar Temple. Magical atmosphere around temple tank with fine musicians taking part; tickets Rs 50-150 (much in demand).

Feb Elephanta Cultural Festival at the caves. Great ambience. Contact MTDC, T022-2026713, for tickets Rs 150-200 including launch at 1800. **Kala Ghoda Arts Festival.** New annual showcase of all forms of fine arts. T022-2842520; also weekend festival, mid-Dec to mid-Jan includes food and handicrafts at Rampart Row, Fort.

Mar Jamshed Navroz. This is New Year's Day for the Parsi followers of the Fasli calendar. The celebrations which include offering prayers at temples, exchanging greetings, alms-giving and feasting at home, date back to Jamshed, the legendary King of Persia.

Jul-Aug Janmashtami celebrates the birth of Lord Krishna. Boys and young men form human pyramids and break pots of curd hung up high between buildings

Aug Coconut Day. The angry monsoon seas are propitiated by devotees throwing coconuts into the ocean.

Aug-Sep Ganesh Chaturthi. Massive figures of Ganesh are worshipped and immersed in the sea on several days following the festival.

Sep Mount Mary's Feast, celebrated at St Mary's Church, Bandra. A fair is also held.

Sep-Oct Dasara. During this nationwide festival, in Mumbai there are group dances by Gujarati women in all the auditoria. There are also Ramlila celebrations at Chowpatty Beach. **Diwali** (The Festival of Lights) is particularly popular in mercantile Mumbai when the business community celebrate their New Year and open new account books.

25 Dec Christmas. Christians across Mumbai celebrate the birth of Christ. A pontifical High Mass is held at midnight in the open air at the Cooperage Grounds.

Ⓞ Shopping

Most shops are open 1000-1900 (closed Sun), the bazaars sometimes staying open as late as 2100. Mumbai prices are often higher than in other Indian cities, and hotel arcades tend to be very pricey but carry good quality select items. Best buys are textiles, particularly tie-and-dye from Gujarat, hand-block printed cottons, Aurangabad and 'Patola' silks, gold bordered saris from Surat and Khambat, handicrafts, jewellery and leather goods. **Crossroads** and **Pyramid**, Haji Ali, are modern shopping centres.

Bazaars
Crawford Market, Ambedkar Rd (fun for bargain hunting) and **Mangaldas Market**. Other shopping streets are South Bhagat Singh Marg, M Karve Rd and Linking Rd, Bandra. For a different experience try **Chor (Thieves') Bazaar**, on Maulana Shaukat Ali Rd in central Mumbai, full of finds from Raj left-overs to precious jewellery. Make time to stop at the **Mini Market**, 33-31 Mutton St, T022-34724257 (closed Fri), minimarket@rediffmail.com and nose through the Bollywood posters, lobby cards, and photo-stills. On Fri, 'junk' carts sell less expensive 'antiques' and fakes.

Antiques
It is illegal to take anything over 100 years old out of the country.
Natesan in Jehangir Gallery basement and in Taj Hotel. For fine antiques and copies.
Phillips, Madame Cama Rd opposite Regal Cinema. An Aladdin's cave of bric-a-brac and curios.

Books
There are lines of 2nd hand stalls along Churchgate St and near the University. An annual book fair takes place at the Cross Maidan near Churchgate each Dec.
Crossword, 22 B Desai Rd (near Mahalakshmi Temple), smart, spacious, good selection.
Danai, 14th Khar Danda Rd. Good for books and music.
Dial-a-book, T022-6495618, for quick delivery.
Nalanda, Taj Mahal Hotel, excellent art books, western newspapers/magazines.
Strand Books, off Sir PM Rd near HMV, T022-2061994. Excellent selection, best deals, shipping (reliable), 20% discount on air freight.

Clothes
Benzer, B Desai Rd, Breach Candy (open Sun), good saris and Indian garments.
The Courtyard, 41/44 Minoo Desai Marg, Colaba. Very new, very elite and fashionable

mini-mall includes boutiques full of stunning heavy deluxe designs (Swarovski crystal-studded saris, anyone?) by **Rohit Bal**, www.balance.ws. **Rabani & Rakha** (Rs 17,000 for a sari) but probably most suitable to western eye is textile designer Neeru Kumar's **Tulsi** label, a cotton textiles designer from Delhi. Beautiful linen/silk stoles and fine *kantha* thread work. There's also a store from Indian designer **Pratap**, spelt à la Prada.
Ensemble, Great Western Bldg, 130-132 South Bhagat Singh Marg, T022-2872882. Superb craftsmanship and service for women's clothes – Indian and 'east meets west'.
Fabindia, Navroze Bldg, 66 Pali Hill, nr HDFC Bank, Bandra (W), handloom *kurtas* etc, Bamboo earthenware and jute home furnishings, *khadi* and *mulmul* cloth.
Michele Boutique, shop no 21, Shah House, Mandlik Rd, T022-22885312. 25 tailors, 24-hr turnaround, fabric on site includes linen, raw silk and cashmere.
Melange, 33 Altamount Rd, T022-23854492. Western-tailored, Indian embroidery clothes. Stocks designs from irresistible labels like Horn OK Please.

Crafts and textiles

Government emporia from many states sell good handicrafts and textiles; several at **World Trade Centre**, Cuffe Parade. In Colaba, a street **Craft Market** is held on Sun (Nov-Jan) in K Dubash Marg.
Cottage Industries Emporium, Apollo Bunder. Represents a nationwide selection, especially Kashmiri embroidery, South Indian handicrafts and Rajasthani textiles. Shop at Colaba Causeway, next to BEST, with fabrics, ethnic ware, handicrafts.
Anokhi, 4B August Kranti Marg, opposite Kumbala Hill Hospital. Good gifts.
Bombay Store, Western India House, 1st flr, PM Rd, Fort. Spacious, ethnic lifestyle, gifts (open Sun), value for money.
Contemporary Arts and Crafts, 19 Napeansea Rd, T022-23631979. Handicrafts, weaves and crockery, ethnic, traditional or modern.
Curio Cottage, 19 Mahakavi Bhushan Rd, near the Regal Cinema, T022-22022607. Silver jewellery and antiques.
Good Earth, 104 Kemp's Corner. Smart, trendy, pottery, glass and handmade paper stationery.

Yamini, President House, Wodehouse Rd, Colaba, especially for vibrant textiles.
Sadak Ali, behind Taj Hotel. Good range of carpets, but bargain hard.

Jewellery

Popli Suleman Chambers, Battery St, Apollo Bunder, T022-2854757. Semi-precious stones, gems, garnets and pearls.
Le Bijou Mahavir Bhuvansh, 37 Hill Rd, Bandra, T022-26443473. Trinkets and junk jewels.

Music

Groove, West Wing, 1st flr, Eros Cinema, Churchgate. Has café.
Hiro, SP Mehta St. Good Indian classical CDs.
Planet M, opposite CST station. Also has book/poetry readings, gigs.
Rhythm House, north of Jehangir Gallery. Excellent selection of jazz and classical CDs.

Musical instruments

On VB Patel Rd, **RS Mayeka** at No 386, **Haribhai Vishwanath** at No 419 and **Ram Singh** at Bharati Sadan.

Photography

Kodak Express, 1B East and West Court, Colaba Causeway (near Churchill café).
Mazda at 231, T022-3004001. Hasselblad, Metz, Nikon, offers free pick up/delivery.
Remedios, opposite Khadi Bhandar, between CST and Flora Fountain, reliable repairs. Best buy cameras from DN Rd.
Heera Panna Shopping Arcade, Haji Ali, T022-24946318. All things electrical: minidisc gadgets, camera, phone accessories etc.

Silks and saris

Many including **Kala Niketan**, MG Rd and **Juhu Reclamation**.
Sheetal, Tirupati Apartments, B Desai Rd, saris from all over India; fair prices.
Vama, in Kanchenjunga (next to Kemp's Corner), tailoring possible.

⊖ Transport

Air

International Departure Tax, Rs 500 (Rs 250 within south Asia) is often included in the price of your ticket. Look for 'FT' in the tax column.

Beyond Goa Mumbai Listings

Chhatrapati Sivaji International airport
T022-6329090. Left luggage counter, across the drive from end of departure terminal, Rs 35-45 per item per day. The tourist office counter helps to book rooms in upmarket hotels. There is an Indian Railways reservations and car hire counters inside, and domestic airlines' counters just outside the exit. The new domestic terminal (1A), exclusively for Indian Airlines, is about 400 m from the old terminal (1B), used by others. Enquiries: T140, 143.

Touts are very pushy at both terminals but the hotels they recommend are often appalling. It is worth making your own telephone call to hotels of your choice from the airport. The rest rooms in the old domestic terminal are clean, comfortable (rooms Rs 500, dorm Rs 200); available for those flying within 24 hrs, but are often full; apply to the Airport Manager.

Transport to and from the airport Pre-paid taxis into town, from counter at the exit at the Chhatrapati Sivaji International terminal (ignore taxi touts near the baggage hall). Give the exact area or hotel, and the number of pieces of luggage. Hand the receipt to the driver at the end of the journey. There is no need to tip.

To **Nariman Point** or **Gateway of India**, about Rs 260, 1 hr. During 'rush hour' it can take 2 hrs. Late at night, taxis take about ½ hr – hair-raising! To **Juhu Beach** Rs 150. From Santa Cruz: metered taxis should charge around the same. Dispatchers at the airport claim that each taxi can take only 3 passengers. Stand firm as this law is totally disregarded elsewhere.

Buses The red BEST buses connect both terminals with the city. No buses at present to New Mumbai.

Airline offices
Domestic Air India Flies to **Chennai, Delhi, Hyderabad, Kolkata, Thiruvananthapuram.**
Indian Airlines Nariman Pt, T022-2023031, flies to all major cities.
Jet Airways B1 Amarchand Mansions, Madam Cama Rd, T022-2855788, airport, T022-6156666, www.jetairways.com. To 23 destinations.

Sahara, Tulsani Chambers, Nariman Pt, T022-2882718, airport T022-6134159. **Bangalore, Bhopal, Delhi, Goa, Indore, Jaipur, Kolkata, Lucknow, Patna, Varanasi.**
International Air India, 1st flr, Nariman Pt (Counters also at Taj Mahal Hotel, Centaur Hotel and Santa Cruz), T022-2024142, Airport T022-8366767.
Aeroflot, Tulsani Chambers, Nariman Pt, T022-2871942.
Alitalia, Industrial Assur Bldg, Vir Nariman Rd, Churchgate, T022-2045023, airport T022-8379657.
Air Canada, Amarchand Mansions, Madam Cama Rd, T022-2027632, Airport T022-6045653.
Air France, Maker Chamber VI, Nariman Pt, T022-2025021, Airport T022-8328070.
Biman, 199 J Tata Rd, Churchgate, T022-2824659.
British Airways, 202-B Vulcan Ins Bldg, Vir Nariman Rd, T022-2820888, weekdays, 0800-1300, 1345-1800. Sat, 0900-1300, airport T022-8329061.
Canadian, Taj Intercontinental, T022-2029112, Airport T022-8366205.
Japan, Raheja Centre, Nariman Pt, T022-2874940.
Delta, Taj Mahal Hotel, T022-2885660, Airport T022-8349890.
Emirates, Mittal Chamber, Nariman Pt, T022-2871649.
Gulf Air, Maker Chambers, 5 Nariman Pt, T022-2021626.
KLM, 198 J Tata Rd, T022-2886973.
Kuwait, 2A Stadium House, 86 Vir Nariman Rd, Churchgate, T022-2045351.
Lufthansa, Express Towers, Nariman Pt, T022-2023430.
PIA, Mittal Towers, Nariman Pt, T022-2021455.
Qantas, 42 Sakhar Bhavan, Nariman Pt, T022-2020343.
Royal Jordanian, 199 J Tata Rd, T022-2823065.
Saudia, Express Tower, Nariman Pt, T022-2020199.
Singapore Airlines, Taj Intercontinental, T022-2022747.
Sri Lanka, Raheja Centre, Nariman Pt, T022-2844148, Airport T022-8327050.
Thai Airways, 15 World Trade Centre, Cuffe Parade, T022-2186502.

Auto-rickshaw

Not available in central Mumbai (south of Mahim). Metered; about Rs 8 per km, revised tariff card held by the driver (x8, in suburbs) 25% extra at night (2400-0500). Some rickshaw drivers show the revised tariff card for taxis! It's worth buying a card for a couple of rupees from hawkers at traffic junctions.

Victorias (horse-drawn carriages), available at Mumbai Central, Chowpatty and Gateway of India. Rates negotiable.

Bus

Red **BEST** (Bombay Electrical Supply Co) buses are available in most parts of Greater Mumbai, T022-4128725. Within the Central Business District, buses are marked 'CBD'.

Maharashtra RTC operates bus services to all the major centres and District HQs in the state as well as to **Ahmadabad**, **Bangalore**, **Goa**, **Mangalore**, **Indore**, **Vadodara** and **Hyderabad** in other states. Information on services from **MSRTC**, central bus stand, Mumbai Central, T022-3076622.

Private buses also travel long distance routes. Some long distance buses also leave from Dadar where there are many travel agents. Information and tickets from **Dadar Tourist Centre**, just outside Dadar station, T022-4113398.

Car hire

For 8 hrs or 80 km: Luxury cars cost a/c Rs 1,500; Maruti/Ambassador, a/c Rs 1,000, non a/c Rs 800.
Auto Hirers, 7 Commerce Centre, Tardeo, T022-4942006.
Blaze, Colaba, T022-2020073.
Budget, T022-4942644, and **Sai**, Phoenix Mill Compound, Senapati Bapat Marg, Lower Parel, T022-4942644. Recommended.
Wheels, T022-2822874.
Holiday caravans with driver, T022-2024627.

Taxi

Metered yellow-top or blue a/c: easily available. Rs 12 for first km and Rs 12 for each Re 1 on metre. Revised tariff card held by drivers. Taxis called by hotel doormen often arrive with meter registering Rs 12. Always get a prepaid taxi at the airport.

Train

Suburban electric trains are economical. They start from Churchgate for the west suburbs and CST (VT) for the east suburbs but are often desperately crowded (stay near the door or you may miss your stop!); there are 'Ladies' cars. Trains leaving Mumbai Central often have seats at the terminus but soon fill up. Avoid peak hours (southbound 0700-1100, northbound 1700-2000), and keep a tight hold on valuables. The difference between 1st and 2nd class is not always obvious although 1st class is 10 times as expensive. Inspectors fine people for travelling in the wrong class or without a ticket.

Times for trains are published each Sat in the Indian Express newspaper. To book trains foreign tourists must have either foreign currency or an encashment certificate and passport.

Mumbai is the HQ of the **Central and Western Railways**, enquiries, T134/135; reservations, T022-2659512, 0800-1230, 1300-1630 (Foreigners' Counter opens 0900; best time to go). **Western Railway**, Churchgate, and Mumbai Central, 0800-1345, 1445-2000. All for 1st class bookings and Indrail Passes.

Foreign tourists: Tourist Quota counter on mezzanine floor above tourist office opposite Churchgate Station for Northern Railways. Otherwise, queue downstairs at reservations. For **Southern Railways**, at CST, the tourist counter is on the ground floor (towards the left), credit cards upstairs. **Railway Tourist Guides** at CST and Churchgate, bus 138 goes between them.

The following depart from CST unless specified by these abbreviations: Bandra (B), Central (C), Dadar (D), Lokmanya Tilak (LT): **Ahmadabad** (all from Mumbai Central): Shatabdi Exp 2009, 0625, except Fri, 7 hrs; Karnavati Exp 2933,1340, except Wed, 7¾ hrs; Saurashtra Mail 9005, 2025, 9 hrs; Gujarat Mail 2901, 2150, 9 hrs. **Allahabad** : Howrah Mail 3004, 2110, 23½ hrs; Mahanagari Exp 1093, 2355, 24¼ hrs. **Agra Cantonment**: Punjab Mail 2137, 1910, 21½ hrs. **Aurangabad** (for **Ajanta** and **Ellora**): Tapovan Exp 7617, 0610, 7½ hrs; Devgiri Exp, 1003, 2120, 7½ hrs. **Bangalore**: Udyan Exp 6529, 0755, 24¾ hrs; Coimbatore Exp 1013, 2220 (LT), 23¾ hrs.

Bhopal: Pushpak Exp 2133, 0810, 14 hrs; Punjab Mail, 2137, 1910, 14 hrs. **Chennai**: Dadar Chennai Exp 1063, 2020 (D), 23¾ hrs; Chennai Exp 6011, 1400, 26¾ hrs.

Ernakulam (for **Kochi**): Netravati Exp 6345, 2300 (LT), 29½ hrs. **Guntakal** (for **Hospet/Hampi**): Dadar Chennai Exp 1063, 2020 (D), 15 hrs; Udyan Exp 6529, 0755, 16¾ hrs; Coimbatore Exp 1013, 2220 (LT), 16¼ hrs; Kanniyakumari Exp 1081, 1535, 17¾ hrs. **Gwalior**: Punjab Mail 2137, 1910, 19¾ hrs. **Hyderabad**: Hussainsagar Exp 7001, 2155, 15¼ hrs; Hyderabad Exp 7031, 1235, 17½ hrs. **Kolkata** (**Howrah**): Gitanjali Exp 2859, 0600, 33 hrs; Howrah Mail 8001, 2015, 35½ hrs. **Lucknow**: Pushpak Exp 2133, 0810, 25½ hrs.

Madgaon (for **Goa**): The day train is a good option, the night service is heavily booked. Special trains during the winter. Mandavi Exp 0103, 0515, 11 hrs; Konkan Kanya Exp 0111, 2240, 12 hrs; Netravati Exp 6635, 1640, 13½ hrs (LT). **New Delhi**: Rajdhani Exp 2951, 1655 (C), 17 hrs; Golden Temple Mail 2903, 2130 (C), 21½ hrs; August Kranti Rajdhani Exp 2953, 1740 (C), 17¼ hrs (to Hazrat Nizamuddin). **Pune**: deluxe trains Shatabdi Exp 2027, 0640, 3½ hrs; Deccan Queen Exp 2123, 1710, 3½ hrs, among many. **Thiruvananthapuram**: Netravati Exp 6345, 2300 (LT), 35 hrs. **Ujjain**: Avantika Exp 2961,1925 (C), 12½ hrs. **Varanasi**: Lokmanya Tilak Varanasi Exp 2165, 0520 (LT), Mon, Thu, Sat, 26 hrs; Muzaffarpur/Darbanga Exp 5217/5219, 1125 (LT), 27¼ hrs.

❶ Directory

Ambulance T102. **Banks** Most are open 1000-1400, Mon-Fri, 1000-1200, Sat. Closed on Sun, holidays, 30 Jun, 31 Dec. Best to change money at the airport, or at Bureau de Change (upstairs) in Air India Building, Nariman Pt or at **Thomas Cook**, 324 Dr DN Rd, T022-2048556; also at 102B Maker Tower, 10th flr, F Block, Cuffe Pde;TCI, Chander Mukhi, Nariman Pt; A/2 Silver Arch, JB Nagar, Andheri; and at International Airport. **American Express**, Regal Cinema Building, Colaba. ATMs for Visa card holders using their usual PIN at **British Bank of the Middle East**, 16 Vir Nariman Rd; **Citibank**, Air India Building, Nariman Pt, 293 Dr DN Rd; **Hongkong Bank**,

52/60 MG Rd, Fort; Standard Chartered, 81 Ismaili Building, Dr DN Rd, 264 Annie Besant Rd and elsewhere. **Credit cards** **American Express**, Lawrence and Mayo Bldg, Dr DN Rd; **Diners Club**, Raheja Chambers, 213 Nariman Pt; **Mastercard**, C Wing, Mittal Tower, Nariman Pt; **Visa**, Standard Chartered Grindlays Bank, 90 MG Rd. Usually open 1000-1700. Sahar Airport 24 hrs. Post offices all over the city and most 5 star hotels. **Embassies and consulates** Australia, Maker Tower East, 16th flr, Cuffe Pde, T022-2181071. **Austria**, Maker Chambers VI, Nariman Pt, T022-2851066. **France**, Datta Prasad, NG Cross Rd, T022-4950918. **Germany**, 10th Flr, Hoechst House, Nariman Pt, T022-2832422. **Indonesia**, 19 Altamount Rd, T022-3868678. **Israel**, 50 Deshmukh Marg, Kailas, T022-3862794. **Italy**, Kanchenjunga, 72G Deshmukh Marg, T022-3804071. **Japan**, 1 ML Dahanukar Marg, T022-4934310. **Malaysia**, Rahimtoola House, Homji St, T022-2660056. **Netherlands**, 1 Marine Lines Cross Rd, Churchgate, T022-2016750. **Philippines** , Sekhar Bhavan, Nariman Pt, T022-2814103. **Spain**, 6 K Dubash Marg, T022-2874797. **Sri Lanka**, 34 Homi Modi St, T022-2045861. **Sweden**, 85 Sayani Rd, Prabhadevi, T022-4212681. **Thailand**, 43 B Desai Rd, T022-3631404. **UK**, Maker Chamber IV, Nariman Pt, T022-2830517. **USA**, Lincoln House, B Desai Rd, T022-3685483. **Fire** T101. **Internet** Among many: British Council, 'A Wing' 1st flr, Mittal Tower, Nariman Pt, T022-2823560, 1000-1745, Tue-Sat; **Cybercafé**, Waterfield, Bandra; **Infotek** , Express Towers, ground flr, Nariman Pt, I-way, Barrow Rd junction with Colaba Causeway and branches across Mumbai. Easily the fastest access, in this 2nd flr shop with heaps of terminals. You must first register as a member but it's well worth it. **Medical services** The larger hotels usually have a house doctor, the others invariably have a doctor on call. Ask hotel staff for prompt action. The telephone directory lists hospitals and GPs. Admission to private hospitals may not be allowed without a large cash advance (eg Rs 50,000). Guarantees from insurers may not be sufficient. **Prince Aly Khan Hospital**, Nesbit Rd near the harbour, T022-3754343, has been recommended. **Chemists** several open day/night especially opposite Bombay

Hospital. **Wordell**, Stadium House, Churchgate; **New Royal Chemist**, New Marine Lines. **Police** Emergency T100. **Post office** Nagar Chowk, Mon-Sat, 0900-2000 (**Poste Restante** facilities 0900-1800) and Sun 1000-1730; parcels from 1st flr, rear of building, 1000-1700 (Mon-Sat); cheap 'parcelling' service on pavement outside; **Central telegraph office** Hutatma Chowk, Churchgate PO, 'A' Rd, Colaba PO, Colaba Bus Station and also at Mandlik Rd, behind Taj Mahal Hotel. Foreign PO, Ballard Pier. Counter at Santa Cruz. **Travel agents** Cox and Kings, 270-271 Dr DN Rd, T022-2073066; **Everett**, 1 Regent Chambers, Nariman Pt, T022-2845339; **Mercury**, 70VB

Gandhi Rd, T022-2024785; **Sita**, 18 Atlanta, Nariman Pt, T022-2840666; **Space Travels**, 4th flr, Sir PM Rd, T022-2864773, for discounted flights and special student offers, Mon-Fri, 1000-1700, Sat 1030-1500; **TCI**, Chandermukhi, Nariman Pt, T022-2021881; **Thomas Cook**, Cooks Building, Dr DN Rd, T022-2813454; **Venture**, Ground flr, Abubakar Mansion, South Bhagat Singh Marg, T022-2021304, efficient, helpful and friendly. **Useful addresses Foreigners' Regional Registration Office** Annexe 2, Police Commissioner's Office, Dr DN Rd, near Phule Market. **Passport office** T022-4931731.

Coastal excursions

Crossing the borders of the old Portuguese enclave over the Tiracol river to the north takes you to deserted beaches and ruined Maratha forts along this little-visited but often beautiful coastline. After the Keri ferry, the road takes you into Maharashtra with its quite different atmosphere: the coastal belt here is full of salt pans rather than Keri's ubiquitous cashew trees and stench of their fruit being fermented to make feni. Meanwhile, in the opposite direction, a few hours travel from the south will bring you to Karnataka's jewel, Gokarna, an ancient pilgrimage site and alternative drop out hang out since Goa got pricey. Broad estuaries, bridged by both the National Highway and the Konkan Railway, and long stretches of golden sand mark the coastline. Inland, low-wooded hills rise rapidly into the Western Ghats. ▸▸ *For Sleeping, Eating and other listings, see pages 218-219.*

The Maharashtran border villages

The southernmost tip of Maharashtra, Sidhudurg district, is spearheading the state's tourist ambitions. The government *babus* know what they're on about too: not only is this region perfectly poised for expansion should the proposed airport at Mopa in Pernem go ahead, but it has natural bounty aplenty with serene and beautiful beaches, temples, forts and rich folk traditions.

Ins and outs So far, Dabolim remains the nearest **airport**. The region has four stops on the Konkan Railway: Kankavali, Sindhudurgnagri, Kudal, and Sawantwadi.

Redi and around
Just 3 km north of the Goa border and Tiracol, a turn off from the NH17, south of Shiroda, leads to **Redi Village and beach**. An old Maratha Fort, the ruins of which are being turned into a boutique hotel by the owners of Nilaya (also behind the transformation of Fort Tiracol), dominates the view over a stunning and almost unvisited bay. An idyllic picnic spot (and one-time trance party venue), and the perfect day trip from Tiracol, Redi has no facilities or shops so pick up water and food on the way.

There is a **Ganesh temple** at Redi that was found inside the village's mines. Legend has it that Ganesh appeared to a mineworker in a dream and asked him to

Card sharps

Sawantwadi was once noted for the production of hand-painted *gangifa* (playing cards) but this is a dying tradition. The Sawantwadi royal family is actively keeping this ancient art and other local crafts alive, allowing a few artists and craftsmen to work in the once- impressive palace durbar hall. They also produce painted lacquer furniture, chessmen, board games and candlesticks.

The brightly coloured *gangifa* were originally produced by pasting layers of cloth together, using tamarind seed gum then coating the 'card' with chalk before polishing it with a stone to provide a smooth white base for decorating the face with natural pigments, while the back was stiffened with lacquer. The packs of circular cards come in various sizes and suits. The ten suits of the *Dasavatara* (featuring Vishnu's 10 incarnations), for example, forms a pack of 120 cards while the *Navagraha* (nine planets) has nine suits. The miniature paintings with patterns drawn from mythology, history and nature, often reflect folk traditions. A few towns in Bengal and Orissa continue to produce *gangifa*. Prices range from Rs 800 to Rs 3,000.

search the ground. The huge idol (with only two hands) was indeed unearthed when the mines were dug. A giant mouse (Ganesh's vehicle) was found nearby. Port traffic at Redi would increase dramatically if a $493 million planned agricultural shipment facility gets the go-ahead.

Nearby is **Vengurla**, a former trading settlement on an island that is now joined to the land again just off the national highway. The coast here is lined with beautiful white sand beaches. Saltpans provide an important product for export from the region. The 10th-century deity within the **Shri Devi Navadurga temple** of Kayale-Redi was shifted here from the Tiswadi taluka of Goa over 450 years ago. Inland, **Sawantwadi** is a large market town, centred on the big tank and palace buildings. From Sawantwadi a state road goes up the ghats to the minor hill station of **Amboli** at an altitude of 690 m. Set on the flat, open-topped heights of the Western Ghats overlooking the coastal plain below, Amboli is a quiet and little-visited resort. There are attractive walks and several waterfalls. You can also take a look at bauxite mines, 10 km away. The road continues on to **Belgaum**.

Karnataka's coast

The coastal road to the hippy stronghold and mass pilgrimage site of **Gokarna** – literally 'cow's ear' – passes through **Karwar** and its **Project Seabird**, the hugely futuristic defence city being built across 8,000 acres of coastal land by the Indian Navy to secure their western fleet against Karachi's missiles. Further on you reach this tremendously sacred Hindu centre Gokarna, little more than one narrow street, lined with traditional wooden houses and temples, and packed with pilgrims. The whole place was adopted, along with Hampi, by the Goa freak overspill, lured by spirituality and the beautiful, auspiciously-shaped Om beach. Days, however, are very much numbered for those still drawn to no-frills beachfront huts and hammocks costing Rs 20 a night: the snazzy, eco-conscious Keralite hotel group **CGH Earth** have just bought up 50 acres of the beach to turn into a boutique yoga hotel. ➤➤ *For Sleeping, Eating and other listings, see page 219-219.*

and Karwar 23 km. Buses run from all of these railheads. It is 2 km to Gokarna from the NH17. KSRTC buses run between Gokarna and Canacona in Goa, Hospet for Hampi and other towns along the Kannada coast. Karwar is the nearest major transport intersection.

Gokarna → *Phone code: 08386.*

The narrow streets, traditional houses and temples together with its long wide expanse of beach, lure growing numbers of backpackers to this alternative hideaway on the five unspoilt beaches (Om, Gokarna, Kudle, Half Moon and Paradise) to the south. There is a somewhat curious mix of Hindu pilgrims and castaways from the hippy era here who are tolerated rather than welcomed. Visitors should respect local sensibilities and dress suitably in town. Ganesh is believed to have tricked Ravana into putting down the famous *Atmalinga* on this spot now sanctified in the Mahabalesvara temple. As Ravana was unable to lift the *linga* up again, it is called Mahabala (the strong one). Tambraparni Teertha stream is particularly sacred for casting the ashes of the dead. Today Gokarna is also a centre of Sanskrit learning.

Most travellers head for the beaches to the south. The path from town passing **Kudle** (pronounced *Koodlee*) **Beach** is well sign-posted but quite rugged, especially south of the Om Beach (about 3 km), and should not be attempted with a full backpack during the middle of the day. Also, though parts are lit at night, stretches are isolated; single women especially should take a companion. Boats from Gokarna to Om charge around Rs 200 one-way. **Om Beach** can now also be reached by a motorable track which can be accessed from near Mayura Samudra Hotel. It is no

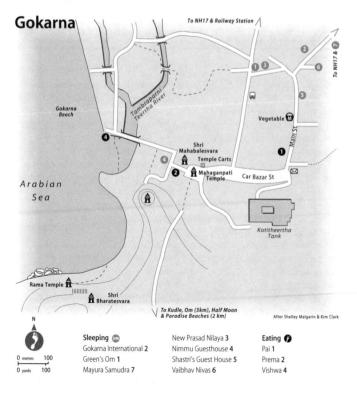

Gokarna

Arabian Sea

Gokarna Beach

Tambraparni Teertha River

To NH17 & Railway Station

Vegetable Ⓜ

Shri Mahabalesvara Temple Carts

Main St

Mahaganpati Temple

Car Bazar St

Kotitheertha Tank

Rama Temple

Shri Bharatesvara

To Kudle, Om (3km), Half Moon & Paradise Beaches (2 km)

After Shelley Malgarin & Kim Clark

N

0 metres 100
0 yards 100

Sleeping		Eating
Gokarna International 2	New Prasad Nilaya 3	Pai 1
Green's Om 1	Nimmu Guesthouse 4	Prema 2
Mayura Samudra 7	Shastri's Guest House 5	Vishwa 4
	Vaibhav Nivas 6	

Beyond Goa Coastal excursions

longer quite the secluded paradise. As with Kudle, in season it can get extremely busy and the combination of too many people, shortage of fresh water and poor hygiene, results in the beaches getting rather dirty. **Half Moon** and **Paradise Beaches**, popular with long-stayers, can be reached by continuing to walk over the headlands and are another 2 km or so apart.

Karwar

Karwar is the administrative headquarters of North Kanara District on the banks of the Kalinadi River. **Devbagh beach** ① *Devbagh beach resort, T0832-2226596,* off the coast, has a deep-water naval port protected by five islands. One of these was 'Anjedive' of old, known to seafarers centuries before Vasco da Gama called at the island in 1498, and the Portuguese built a fort there. It was later used as a Goan penal colony. Since it is now under the control of the navy it is off-limits to all foreigners. From 1638 to 1752 there was an English settlement here, surviving on the pepper trade. The Portuguese held it for the next 50 years until the old town was destroyed in 1801. Today Karwar, strung out between the port and the estuary, has an unpleasant beach. However, the beaches a little to the south rival those of Goa but are still deserted. Of interest is the hill fort, an octagonal church, and a 300-year old temple.

Project Seabird India's Western Naval Command, which controls the 'sword arm' of the subcontinents powerful western fleet, has been planning to move here from Mumbai since the 1960s, but work on the immense project only began in October 1999. When complete (which could be as early as 2005) it will become the largest naval base this side of the Suez Canal and will hold 140 plus warships, aircraft and repair dockyards, while the hillsides will be put to use concealing submarines. Karwar, crucially, is located 900 nautical miles from Karachi versus Mumbai's 580. Since the area is under the control of the navy it is off limits to foreigners but driving past it gives a striking portrait of the subcontinent's military might and ambition.

◉ Sleeping

Gokarna *p217*
Around the beaches, mud and palm leaf huts with shared facilities charge Rs 30-60 (extra for a mattress). The lack of security in beach huts has prompted the guesthouses in town to offer to store luggage for a small charge. The exceptions are at the southern end of Kudle.
D-E Gokarna International, Main Rd, Kumta Taluk, T08386-656848, www.geocities.com/ hotelgokarna. 43 modern rooms (3 a/c) with bath and tubs, back quieter and have balconies, restaurant, bar, friendly staff, and the first lift in Gokarna! Recommended.
E-F Green's 'Om', Ganjigadde, 2-min walk from bus stand, T08386-656445. 20 clean, airy, well maintained rooms with bath, 2 a/c, restaurant (Nepali, Indian, Western) and bar operates in peak season. Very good value.

E-F New Prasad Nilaya, near New Bus Stand, Ganjigadde, T08386-657135. Spacious but very run-down rooms with shower, some balconies, upstairs slightly better, friendly staff.
E-F Shri Laxmi, Bus Stand Rd, T08386-560365. Clean, spacious rooms in newly-converted family house. Small scale but friendly and good value.
F Mayura Samudra (KSTDC), 2 km north on hilltop facing the sea, T08386-56236. 3 rooms, dining room, garden, helpful staff but quite a trek.
F Namaste, Om beach. Acceptable rooms, though far from the best swimming areas.
F Nimmu Guest House, near Temple, Mani Bhadra Rd, T08386-656730. 15 clean rooms with shared Indian toilets, 5 newest are better value as they are big, bright and catch the breeze, limited roof space for overspill, garden, laid-back and friendly, safe luggage storage. Recommended.

F **Nirvana**, Om beach. "One of nicest and cheapest" (Rs 40) but no beds so a hammock or inflatable mattress is recommended. Also has shower and restaurant.

F **Shastri's Guest House**, Dasanamath, T08386-56220. 24 rooms with bath, some 3-4 bedded, set back from road, quiet.

F **Shiva Prasad**, Kudle beach. Decent brick-built rooms with fan.

F **Vaibhav Nivas**, Ganjigadde off Main St (5 min walk from bazaar), T08386-56714. Family guesthouse, small rooms, annexe with 10 rooms, some with bath (Indian and western WC), meals, luggage store.

Karwar *p218*
An upmarket hotel is expected to be built here.

D **Bhadra**, on NH17 (4 km north of Karwar), T08382-25212. 20 rooms, some a/c, lovely views over estuary, restaurant, a modern hotel. A roadside stall outside the hotel serves very good value vegetarian food.

F **Anand Lodge**, near bus stand, T08382-26156. Rooms with Indian WC, basic but OK.

❼ Eating

Gokarna *p217*
Soft drinks can be wildly over-priced; check before ordering.

Cheap vegetarian *thalis* are available near the bus stand and along Main St, while shacks at the entrance to the town beach serve up the usual disarray of travellers' favourites. Standards are improving on the southern beaches with food, drinks and internet access becoming available, though often only in the peak season. The **Spanish Chai shop**, Kudle, and **Hotel Look Sea** are popular.

$ **Kinara**, near Gokarna Beach. Ice creams, Indian and some western food. Basic but clean and well-run.

$ **Pai**, near vegetable market. Good *masala dosa*.

$ **Prema**, opposite Mahabalesvar temple. Large room upstairs, does great fruit salads, ices, *gudbad* and its own delicious soft garlic cheese. Popularity has resulted in slow and surly service.

$ **Vishwa**, on the beach. Nepali-run, varied menu including Tibetan, large helpings.

❺ Transport

Gokarna *p217*
KSRTC **buses** provide a good service: **Chaudi** (2 hrs); **Karwar** (via Ankola) frequent (1 hr); **Hospet** 0700, 1425 (10 hrs); **Jog Falls** 0700, 1130 (6 hrs); **Margao**, 0814 (4 hrs); **Mangalore** via Udipi, 0645 (7 hrs); **Panjim** 0800 (5 hrs).

Gokarna Road **train** station is 10 km from the town, 2 km from the NH17; most trains are met by auto-rickshaws and a private bus. Rs 10 to Gokarna bus stand. State buses can be flagged down on the NH17. **Margao** (Madgaon): Mangalore-Madgaon Pass KR2 (K), 1110, (2¼ hrs); **Mangalore**: Margao-Mangalore Pass KR1 (K), 1532, (5 hrs).

Karwar *p218*
Buses run to **Jog Falls**, 0730 and 1500 (6 hrs). Frequent buses also go to **Palolem**, **Margao** (Madgaon) and **Panjim**, and there are also direct buses to **Colva**. Buses are often full – you may have to fight to get on. The road crosses the Kali river (car toll, Rs 5) then reaches the Goa border and check post (8 km north).

❶ Directory

Gokarna *p217*
Bank Pai STD opposite Ramdev Lodge, and **Kiran's Internet** change money.
Internet There are several in town and on Kudle and Om beaches; **Sriram**, near the post office, is your best bet.

Karwar *p218*
Bank State Bank of India changes money.

Interior Karnataka

After Goa's Dudhsagar falls, the train between Margao and Hospet climbs over jungle-covered mountains before reaching Karnataka's endlessly flat arable land. The most life you'll see will be a dog standing under a sapling, two miles on a tiny girl striding towards her herd of goats. Storks stand snowy pinnacles on top of clumps of earth or wade to their knees in swampy marsh. As you near Hospet, children, a dozen at each station, team direct to the tourist car windows, getting bolder with each others' bravado. Today sugar cane production dominates the workaday lives of most northeastern Karnatakans: these arid pockets are among the state's most 'backward'. But the harvesting of the thick sweet stalks takes place in towns overshadowed by some of India's hugest historical figures: the rulers of the Deccan. All that remains of their awesome egos is soft crumbling laterite brick arches and sudden plots of scores of the calm domes of tombs, their Persian inscriptions ghosted into the lime. Some come to look at Hampi alone, but give yourself time to see Aihole, Badami and Pattadakal too. The Islamic relics at Bijapur and Bidar are all the more striking for being lesser visited. ▸▸ *For Sleeping, Eating and other listings, see pages 231-236.*

Hospet → *Phone code: 08394.*

Ins and outs The station, about 500 m north of the town centre, has connections with Hyderabad and Bangalore. The bus stand is right in the town centre and most hotels are within easy walking distance. There are buses and auto-rickshaws to Hampi. Hire a bicycle on arrival as the site is spread out. Some paths are too rough to ride on. ▸▸ *For Sleeping, Eating and other listings, see page 231.*

Information   **Department of Tourism** ① *Taluk Office Compound, Hospet T08394-28537.* **KSTDC** ① *Old Fire Station, Taluk Office Circle, near bus stand, T08394-28537.*

Hospet is famous for its sugar cane: the town exports sugar across India, villagers boil the milk to make *jaggery*, and a frothing fresh-wrung cup costs you just Rs 4. Other industries include iron ore, biscuit-making and the brewing of Royal Standard rum. The **main bazaar**, with its characterful old houses, is interesting to walk around. Muharram, the Muslim festival that marks the death of Mohammed's grandson Imam Hussein, is celebrated with a violent vigour both here and in the surrounding villages and with equal enthusiasm by both the area's significant Muslim population and Hindus. ▸▸ *See Festivals and events, page 236.*

The beginnings or ends of livestock migrations to seasonal feeding grounds are marked with huge bonfires. Cattle are driven through the fires to protect them from disease. Some archaeologists suggest that Neolithic ash mounds around Hospet were the results of similar celebrations over 5,000 years ago.

The 2-km **Tungabhadra Dam** ① *Rs 5, local bus takes 15 mins, 6 km away*, is 49 m high and offers panoramic views. One of the largest masonry dams in the country, it was completed in 1953 to provide electricity for irrigation in the surrounding districts.

● Today Hampi holds a population of 3,000 people across its 62 sq km. Once that figure was closer to one and a half million and the city would sell diamonds by the kilogramme.

Half day in Hampi

Climb the giant piano key steps leading up **Matanga Parvat**, over the road from Hemakuta Hill, at 0530 for a spectacular dawn (take a torch and, if alone, a guide: there have been muggings). Devotional songs blow across a land emptied of humans in the one time empire capital with a horizon of great cleft cliffs and boulder piles that make up the mountain ranges. In the rush hour, each car engine reverbs through the temple tops as the mists lift over earth and green pool rivers.

Walk down via the two **Ganesh temples** and through the bazaar, stopping for breakfast at one of the budget cafes that once peddled pearls not *dosas*.

Head into the living temple of **Virupaksha** where women do their washing and slap their wet saris on the granite ground to dry. Make sure you see the inverted *gopuram*, a 15th century pinhole camera.

By **coracle**, cross the river to hire bicycles for pedalling round paddy-filled **Anegundi**: to the east is the **Hanuman temple**, to the west a **swimming lake**.

Lunch can either be at Boulder Hotel or cross back to the Sacred Centre for a shady lunch at the Mango Tree.

Shade from the heat till evening, when goats are driven along the roads. Blazing amber fire slips into mauve, hazy dark blue dusk.

Hampi → *Phone code: 08394. Best season: Oct-Mar.*

Climb any boulder-toppled mountain around the ruins of the Vijayanagar Empire and you can see the dizzying scale of the Hindu conquerors' glory – Hampi was the capital of a kingdom that covered the whole of Southern India. Little of the kingdom's riches remains for future generations: gypsy mudhuts squat under the boulders where noblemen once stood, and the double-decker shopfronts of the bazaar where diamonds were traded by the kilo are now geared solely to profiting from incoming western tourists and domestic pilgrims. Small boys beseech the former to buy their guidebooks, while their mothers yell at the latter to buy their parcels of coconut and jasmine flowers as offerings. It's a romantic kind of desolation that you find in Hampi – the remains, heaped across a vast area and still being unearthed, demand at least a full day to do them justice. » *For Sleeping, Eating and other listings, see page 231.*

Ins and outs Some find Hospet a handy base for visiting Hampi: it holds relatively plush accommodation options as well as the nearest railway station. However, it is not a cosmetic choice: Hospet has an industriousness that some won't find charming and it means a half-hour, Rs 250 rickshaw commute to Hampi. Hampi is quieter, more atmospheric and convenient if you are going to spend any length of time at the remains. Across the river by coracle (Rs 15) you can also reach the hamlet of Anegundi, a beautiful paddy-planted village with plenty of budget guesthouses, coco-huts and cottages to stay in. Inland are two excellent high range options amd Anegundi is recommended for those at either the top or bottom extreme, budget wise. You can hire bicycles from the main bazaar for Rs 75, a good way to explore the heritage city independently.

Information Regional tourist office ① *Old Fire Force Building, Hospet, T08394-428537.*

Hampi was founded in 1336 on the banks of the Tungabhadra river by two brothers, Harihara and Bukka, and rose to become the seat of the mighty Vijayanagara Empire and a major centre of Hindu rule and civilization for two centuries. The city, which held a monopoly on the trade of spices and cotton, was enormously wealthy, some put it greater than Rome, and the now-sorry bazaar was packed with diamonds and pearls, while the crumbled palaces were plated with gold. Although it was well-fortified and defended by a large army, the city fell to a coalition of Northern Muslim rulers, the Deccan Sultans, at Talikota in 1565. The invading armies didn't crave the city for themselves, and instead sacked it, smiting symbolic blows to Hindu deities and taking huge chunks out of many of the remaining white granite carvings. Today, the craggy 26 sq km site holds the ghost of a capital with aquaducts, elephant stables and baths as big as palaces.

The site for the capital was chosen for strategic reasons but the craftsmen adopted an ingenious style to blend in their architectural masterpieces with the barren and rocky landscape. Most of the site is early 16th century, built during the

Hampi - Vijaynagara

Sleeping
Mayura Bhuvaneswari 1
Shanti Guest House & Raju 3
Vicky 4

Eating
Shambhu & Suresh 1

20-year reign of Krishna Deva Raya (1509-1529) with the citadel standing on the bank of the river. Excavations undertaken by the Archaeological Survey of India are still in progress.

Sights

The road from the west comes over Hemakuta Hill, overlooking the **Sacred Centre of Vijayanagara** (the 'Town of Victory', 13 km northeast of Hospet town), the Virupaksha Temple and the Tungabhadra River to its north. On the hill are two large monolithic Ganesh sculptures: and some small temples.

The road runs down to the village, the once world-famous market place. You can now only see the wide pathway running east from the towering **Virupaksha (Pampapati) Temple** with its nine-storey *gopuram*, to where the bazaar hummed with activity. The temple is still in use; note the interesting paintings on the *mandapam* ceiling. The monkeys here can be aggressive.

You can walk along the riverbank (1,500 m) to the famous **Vitthala Temple** ① *foreigners US$5 (allows entry to Lotus Mahal on the same day 0600-1600)*, a World Heritage Monument dedicated to Vishnu. The path is easy and passes several interesting ruins including small 'cave' temples – worthwhile with a guide. Alternatively, a motorable road skirts the Royal Enclosure to the south, and goes all the way to the Vitthala Temple. It stands in a rectangular courtyard, enclosed within high walls. Probably built in the mid-15th century, it is one of the oldest and most intricately carved, with its *gopurams* and *mandapas*. The Dolotsava *mandapa* has 56 superbly sculpted slender pillars which can be struck to produce different musical notes. It has elephants on the balustrades and horses at the entrance. The other two ceremonial *mandapas*, though less finely carved have some interesting carved pillars, eg Krishna hiding in a tree from the *gopis* and a woman using a serpent twisted around a stick to churn a pot of buttermilk. In the courtyard is a superb chariot carved out of granite, the wheels raised off the ground so that they could be revolved! On the way back along the riverside you can visit the **Raghunatha Temple**, on a hill top, for its Dravidian style, quiet atmosphere and excellent view of the countryside from the rocks above, especially at sunset.

> ❖ *The dry arable land is slowly being peeled back by the archaeologists to expose more and more of the kingdom's ruins – 80 have been found so far.*

After passing **Achyuta Bazaar**, which leads to the **Tiruvengalanatha Temple** 400 m to the south, the riverside path goes near **Sugriva's Cave**, where it is said that Sita's jewels, dropped as she was abducted by the demon Ravana, were hidden by Sugriva. There are good views of the ancient ruined bridge to the east, and nearby the path continues past the only early period Vaishnavite shrine, the 14th-century **Narasimha Temple**. The **King's Balance** is at the end of the path as it approaches the Vitthala Temple. It is said that the rulers were weighed against gold, jewels and food, which were then distributed to Brahmins.

On the road between the Virupaksha Bazaar and the Citadel, you pass **Krishnapura**, Hampi's earliest Vaishnava township with a Chariot Street 50 m wide and 600 m long, which is now a cultivated field. The **Krishna Temple** has a very impressive gateway to the east. Just southwest of the Krishna Temple is the colossal monolithic statue of Lakshmi Narasimha in the form of a four-armed man-lion with fearsome bulging eyes sheltered under a seven-headed serpent, Ananta. It is over 6 m high but sadly damaged. The road south, from the Sacred Centre towards the Royal Enclosure, passes the excavated **Prasanna Virupaksha Temple** (misleadingly named 'underground') and interesting watchtowers.

At the heart of the Metropolis is the small **Hazara Rama Temple**, the Vaishnava 'chapel royal'. The outer enclosure wall to the north has five rows of carved friezes while the outer walls of the *mandapa* has three. The episodes from the epic Ramayana are told in great detail, starting with the bottom row of the north end of

66 99 The dawn rush hour consists of bullock carts wheeling along with sugar cane loads, squirrels scampering about the rocks and crows beginning to caw...

the west *mandapa* wall. The two-storeyed **Lotus Mahal** ① *0600-1800, foreigners US$5 (allows entry to Vitthala Temple on the same day)*, is in the Zenana or ladies' quarter, screened off by its high walls. The watchtower is in ruins but you can see the domed stables for 10 elephants with a pavilion in the centre and the guardhouse. Each stable had a wooden beamed ceiling from which chains were attached to the elephants' backs and necks. In the Durbar Enclosure is the specially built decorated platform of the Mahanavami Dibba, from which the royal family watched the pageants and tournaments during the nine nights of *navaratri* festivities. The eight-m-high square platform originally had a covering of bricks, timber and metal but what remains still shows superb carvings of hunting and battle scenes, as well as dancers and musicians.

The exceptional skill of water engineering is displayed in the excavated system of aqueducts, tanks, sluices and canals, which could function today. The 22 m square Pushkarini is the attractive stepped tank at the centre of the enclosure. The road towards Kamalapuram passes the **Queen's Bath**, in the open air, surrounded by a narrow moat, which had scented water filling the bath from lotus-shaped fountains. It measures about 15 m x 2 m and has interesting stucco work around it.

The **Archaeological Museum** ① *Sat-Thu 1000-1700*, at Kamalapuram has a collection of sculpture, paintings, copper plates and coins. The ASI booklet is on sale. There is a scale model of Hampi in the courtyard.

Bijapur → *Phone code: 08352. Population: 245,900.*

Mohammed Adil Shah was not a man to be ignored: the tomb he built from the first day of his rule in anticipation of his own death hovers darkly magnificent over Bijapur, so large it can be seen from over 20 km away. Bijapur has the air of a northern Muslim city with its mausolea, mosques and palaces. It has some of the finest mosques in the Deccan and retains real character. The *chowk* between the bus station and MG Rd is quite atmospheric in the evening. Overall it is a provincial, grubby but unhurried town. ⊁ *For Sleeping, Eating and other listings, see page 231.*

Ins and outs

The railway station is just outside the east wall of the fort under 1 km from the Gol Gumbaz while long distance buses draw in just west of the citadel. Both arrival points are close enough to several hotels. It is easy to walk or cycle round the town. There are also autos and tongas; negotiate for an 'eight sight tour price'.

Information Tourist office ① *opposite stadium, To8352-503592, Mon-Sat 1030-1330, 1415-1730*, next to useless. Better information from the manager of **Mayura Adil Shahi** (see below).

History

The Chalukyas who ruled over Bijapur were overthrown at the end of the 12th century. In the early years of the 14th century the Delhi Sultans took it for a time until the Bahmanis, with their capital in Gulbarga, ruled through a governor in Bijapur who declared independence in 1489 and founded the Adil Shahi Dynasty. Of Turkish origin, they held power until 1686.

Sights

The **Jama Masjid** is one of the finest in the Deccan with a large shallow, onion-shaped dome and arcaded court. It was built by Ali Adil Shah I (ruled 1557-1579) during Bijapur's rise to power and displays a classic restraint. The Emperor Aurangzeb added a grand entrance to the Masjid and also had a square painted for each of the 2,250 worshippers that it can accommodate. The Citadel with its own wall has few of its grand buildings intact. One is the **Durbar Hall**, Gagan Mahal (Sky Palace), open to the north so that the citizens outside were not excluded. It had royal residential quarters on either side with screened balconies for the women to remain unseen while they watched the court below. Another worth visiting is the **Jal Manzil**, or the water pavilion, a cool sanctuary.

Ibrahim Rauza ① *0600-1800, foreigners $2, Indians Rs 5, video camera Rs 25, early morning best to avoid crowds*, the palatial 17th-century tomb west of the city wall, is beautifully proportioned. It has slender minarets and carved decorative panels with lotus, wheel and cross patterns as well as bold Arabic calligraphy, bearing witness to the tolerance of the Adil Shahi Dynasty towards other religions. Built during the dynasty's most prosperous period (after the sacking of Vijayanagara) when the arts and culture flourished, it also contains the tomb of Ibrahim Adil Shah II (ruled 1580-1626) who had it built for his wife but died first. Near the Rauza is a huge tank, the **Taj Bauri**, built by Ibrahim II in memory of his wife. The approach is through a giant gateway flanked by two octagonal towers.

Gol Gumbaz ① *0630-1730, foreigners US$2, Indians Rs 5, video camera Rs 25 (complaint book available!), some choose to just view it from the gate*, the vast whitewashed tomb of Mohammad Adil Shah buried here with his wife, daughter and favourite court dancer, has the world's second largest dome (unsupported by pillars), and one of its least attractive. Its extraordinary whispering gallery carries a message across 38 m which is repeated 11 times, but noisy crowds make hearing it near impossible (it is quietest in early morning). Numerous narrow steps in one of the corner towers, lead to the three-metre-wide gallery. The plaster here was made out of eggs, cow dung, grass and *jaggery*. There is an excellent view of the city walls from the base of the dome.

The **Nakkar Khana**, the gatehouse, now houses the **Archaeological Museum** ① *1000-1700, Rs 2*, and has an excellent collection of Chinese porcelain, parchments, paintings, armoury, miniatures, stone sculpture and old Bijapur carpets.

The **Asar Mahal** (c. 1646) was built with a tank watered by the old conduit system. It was used as a court house and has teak pillars and interesting frescoes in the upper floor. The **Mehtar Mahal** (1620), with its delicate minarets and carved stone trellises and brackets supporting the balconies to form a decorative gateway, was supposed to have been built for the palace sweepers.

To the west, **Sherza Burj** (Lion Gate) in the 10-km-long fort wall, has the enormous 55 tonne **Malik-i-Maidan** (Ruler of the Plains) cannon on the west. To avoid being deafened the gunner is believed to have dived into the tank off the platform! It was cast in the mid-16th century in Ahmadnagar, and was brought back as a prize of war pulled by "400 bullocks, 10 elephants and hundreds of soldiers". Note the muzzle – a lion's head with open jaws with an elephant being crushed to death inside. Inside the city wall, close by, is **Upli Burj** , the 24-m-high watch tower on high ground with its long guns and water tanks.

The **Bara Kaman** was possibly a 17th-century construction by Adil Shah III. Planned as a mammoth 12-storey building with the shadow of the uppermost storey designed to fall onto the tomb of the Gol Gumbaz, construction was ended after just two storeys with the death of the ruler. An impressive series of arches on a raised platform is all that remains.

Hindu temples around Bijapur

Although Bijapur became an important Muslim regional capital, its surrounding region has several villages which, nearly 1,500 years ago, were centres of Chalukyan power and the hearth of new traditions in Indian temple building. At a major Indian crossroads, the temples at Aihole represent the first finely worked experiments in what were to become distinct North and South Indian temple styles.

❧ Some prefer to wander around the many deserted (free) temples around town instead of joining the crowds in the park.

Ins and outs Since it takes a half day to see Badami, visiting the sites by bus doesn't allow time for Mahakuta. It is well worth hiring a car in Bijapur which allows you to see all the sites quite comfortably in a day. If travelling by bus it is best to visit Badami first, followed by Pattadakal and Aihole. By car it is best to start at Aihole and end at Badami.

Aihole → *Phone code 0831.*
Aihole was the first Chalukyan capital, but the site was developed over a period of more than 600 years from the sixth century AD and includes important Rashtrakuta and Late Chalukyan temples, some dedicated to Jain divinities. It is regarded as the birthplace of Indian temple architectural styles, and the site of the first built temples, as distinct from those carved out of solid rock. Most of the temples were dedicated to Vishnu, though a number were subsequently converted into Saivite shrines.

The **main temples** are now enclosed in a park ① *open sunrise to sunset, foreigners US$2, Indians Rs 5, flash photography prohibited.* There are about 140 temples – half within the fort walls – illustrating a range of developing styles from Hoysala, Dravida, Jain, Buddhist, Nagara and Rekhanagara. There is little else. All the roads entering Aihole pass numerous temple ruins, but the road into the village from Pattadakal and Bagalkot passes the most important group of temples which would be the normal starting point for a visit.

Durgigudi Temple is named not after the Goddess Durga but because it is close to the durga (fort). Dating from the late seventh century, it has numerous superb sculptures, a series contained in niches around the ambulatory: walking clockwise they represent Siva and Nandi, Narasimha, Vishnu with Garuda, Varaha, Durga and Harihara. **Lad Khan Temple** has been dated from approximately AD 700, not from AD 450 as previously suggested. Originally an assembly hall and *kalyana mandapa* (marriage hall), it bears a striking resemblance to the megalithic caves which were still being excavated in this part of the Deccan at the beginning of the period. The roof gives an excellent view of the village. **Gaudar Gudi Temple**, near the Lad Khan temple, is a small, rectangular Hindu temple, probably dating from the seventh century. Its roof of stone slabs is an excellent example of North Indian architecture. Beyond the Gaudar Gudi Temple is a small temple decorated with a frieze of pots, followed by a deep well. There are others in various states of repair.

To see the most important of the remaining temples you leave the main park. Turning right out of the main park, the Bagalkot road leads to the **Chikki Temple**. Similar in plan to the Gaudar Gudi, this temple has particularly fine carved pillars. The beams which support the platform are also well worth seeing.

Ravan Phadi Cave Temple is reached from the main park entrance on the left, about 300 m from the village. The cave (formerly known as the Brahman) itself is artificial, and the sixth century temple has a variety of carvings of Siva both outside and inside. There are two small eighth century temples at the entrance.

The **Buddhist Temple** is a plain two-storeyed Buddhist temple on a hill beyond the end of the village on the way to the Meguti Temple. It has a serene smiling Buddha with the Bodhi Tree emerging from his head, on the ceiling of the upper floor. Further uphill is the **Jain Temple**, a plain structure with a statue of Mahavira in the shrine within. Climb up through the roof for a good view of Aihole.

The **Meguti Temple** (AD 634) is reached from the Buddhist Temple down a path leading to a terrace. A left hand route takes you to the foot of some stairs leading to the top of a hill which overlooks the town. This is the site of what is almost certainly the oldest building in Aihole and one of the oldest dated temples in India. Its 634 date is indicated in an inscription by the court poet to the king Ravikirtti.

The **Kunti Group** is a group of four Hindu temples (seventh to ninth centuries). To find them you have to return down to the village. The oldest is in the southeast. The external columns of its *mandapa* are decorated with *mithuna*, or erotic couples. The other two date from the Rashtrakuta period. Beyond these temples is the **Hucchappayya Math**, dating from the seventh century. There is a Tourist Rest House close to the temples should you wish to stay.

Pattadakal

On the banks of the Malaprabha River, Pattadakal, a World Heritage Site, was the second capital of the Chalukyan kings between the seventh and eighth centuries and the city where the kings were crowned. There is no suitable accommodation here although a new restaurant is opening. Stay either in Badami, Aihole or at Bagalkot.

Most of the **temples** ① *open sunrise to sunset, foreigners US$2*, cluster at the foot of a hill, built out of the pink-tinged gold sandstone, and display a succession of styles of the southern Dravida temple architecture of the Pallavas as well as the North Indian Nagara style, vividly illustrating the region's position at the crossroads of north and south Indian traditions. With one exception the temples are dedicated to Siva. Most of the site is included in the archaeological park. Megalithic monuments dating from the third-fourth centuries BC have been found in the area.

Immediately inside the entrance are the very small **Jambulinga** and **Kadasiddheshvara Temples** (eighth century). Now partly ruined, the curved towers survive and the shrine of the Jambulinga Temple houses a figure of the dancing Siva next to Parvati. The gateways are guarded by *dvarapalas*. Just to the east is the eighth century **Galaganatha Temple**, again partly damaged, though its curved tower characteristic of North Indian temples is well preserved, including its *amalaka* on top. A relief of Siva killing the demon Andhaka is on the south wall in one of three original porches. The **Sangamesvara Temple** dating from the reign of Vijayaditya (696-733), is the earliest temple. Although it was never completed, it has all the hallmarks of a purely Dravidian style. Above the sanctuary is a superbly proportioned tower of several storeys. To the southwest is the late eighth-century North Indian style **Kashi Vishvveshvara Temple**, readily distinguishable by the Nandi in front of the porch.

The largest temples, the **Virupaksha** (740-744) with its three-storeyed *vimana* and the Mallikarjuna (745), typify the Dravida style, and were built in celebration of the victory of the Chalukyan king Vikramaditya II over the Pallavas at Kanchipuram by his wife, Queen Trailokyamahadevi. The king's death probably accounted for the fact that the Mallikarjuna temple was unfinished, attested by the failure to do more than mark out some of the sculptures.

❖ *Note the ingenuity of the sculptor in making an elephant appear as a buffalo when viewed from a different side.*

However, the king's victory over the Pallavas enabled him to express his admiration for Pallava architecture by bringing back to Pattadakal one of the chief Pallava architects. The Virupaksha, a Saivite temple, has a sanctuary surrounded by passageways and housing a black polished stone Siva *linga*. A further Saivite symbol is the huge 2.6-m high chlorite stone *nandi* at the entrance. The three-storeyed tower rises strikingly above the shrine, the outside walls of which, particularly those on the south side, are richly carved.

In the ninth century the Rashtrakutas arrived and built a **Jain Temple** with its two stone elephants a short distance from the centre. The carvings on the temples, particularly on the *papanatha* near the village which has interesting sculptures on the ceiling and pillars, synthesizes northern and southern architectural styles.

Mahakuta, which was reached by early pilgrims over rocky hills from Badami 5 km away, is a beautiful complex of Chalukyan temples dating from the late seventh century; worth a detour. The superstructures reflect both northern and southern influence and one has an *orissandeul*.

Badami → *Phone code 08357.*

Badami occupies a dramatic site squeezed in a gorge between two high red sandstone hills. Once called Vatapi after a demon, Badami was the Chalukyan capital from AD 543-757. The ancient city has several Hindu and Jain temples and a Buddhist cave and remains peaceful and charming. The transcendent beauty of the Hindu cave temples in their spectacular setting warrant a visit. The village with its busy bazaar and a large lake has white-washed houses clustered together along narrow winding lanes up the hillside. There are also scattered remains of 18 stone inscriptions (sixth-16th century).

> ❖ *The area is well worth exploring by bicycle.*

The **caves and temples** are best visited early in the morning. They are very popular with monkeys, which can be aggressive, especially if they see food. End the day by watching the sun set from the eastern end of the tank.

The **South Fort** ① *foreigners US$2*, is famous for its cave temples, four of which were cut out of the hillside in the second half of the sixth century. There are 40 steps to **Cave 1**, the oldest. There are several sculpted figures, including Harihara, Siva and Parvati, and Siva as Nataraja with 18 arms seen in 81 dancing poses. **Cave 2**, a little higher than Cave 1, is guarded by *dvarapalas* (door-keepers). Reliefs of Varaha and Vamana decorate the porch. **Cave 3**, higher still, is dedicated to Vishnu. According to a Kannada inscription (unique in Badami) it was excavated in AD 578. It has numerous sculptures including Narasimha (man-lion), Hari-Hara (Siva-Vishnu), a huge seated Vishnu and interesting friezes. **Cave 4**, probably about 100 years later than the three earlier caves, is the only Jain cave. It has a statue of the seated Parsvanatha with two *dvarapalas* at the entrance. The fort itself above the caves is closed to the public.

The **Buddhist Temple** is in the natural cave near the ancient artificial Bhutanatha Lake (Agasthya Lake), where the mossy green water is considered to cure illnesses. The **Yellamma Temple** has a female deity, while one of the two Saivite temples is to Bhutanatha (God of souls); in this form, Siva appears angry in the dark inner sanctuary. The seventh-century **Mallegitti Sivalaya Temple**, one of the finest examples of the early southern style, has a small porch, a *mandapa* (hall) and a narrower *vimana* (shrine). Statues of Vishnu and Siva decorate the outer walls, while animal friezes appear along the plinth and above the eaves. **Jambulinga Temple** is an early temple in the centre of the town near the rickshaw stand. Dating from 699, as attested by an inscription, and now almost hidden by houses, the visible brick tower is a late addition from the Vijayanagar period. Opposite is the 10th century **Virupaksha Temple**.

The **North Fort temples** ① *Rs 2, carry water*, mainly seventh century, give an insight into Badami's history. Steep steps, almost 1 m high, take you to 'gun point' at the top of the fort which has remains of large granaries, a treasury and a watchtower. The Upper Sivalaya Temple, though damaged, still has some friezes and sculptures depicting Krishna legends.

An ancient **dolmen site** ⓘ *a local English-speaking guide Dilawar Badesha at Tipu Nagar charges about Rs 200*, can be reached by an easy hike through interesting countryside; allow 3½ hours.

Archaeological Survey's **Medieval Sculpture Gallery** ⓘ *Mon-Thu, Sat and Sun, 1000-1700, free, north of the tank*, has fine specimens from Badami, Aihole and Pattadakal and a model of the natural bridge at Sidilinapadi, 5 km away.

Hospet to Bidar

The dry and undulating plains are broken by rocky outcrops giving superb sites for commanding fortresses such as Gulbarga and Bidar. ▸▸ *For Sleeping, Eating and other listings, see page 231.*

Gulbarga → *Phone code 08472.*

Gulbarga was the first capital of the Bahmanis (from 1347-1525). It is also widely known among South Indian Muslims as the home of Saiyid Muhammad Gesu Daraz Chisti (1320-1422) who was instrumental in spreading pious Islamic faith in the Deccan. The annual Urs festival in his memory attracts up to 100,000 people.

The town sites and hotels are quite spread out so it is worth hiring an auto for half a day. The most striking remains in the town are the fort, with its citadel and mosque, the Jami Masjid, and the great tombs in its eastern quarter – massive, fortress-like buildings with their distinctive domes over 30 m high.

The **fort** is just 1 km west of the centre of the present town. Originally built by Ala-ud-din Bahmani, in the 14th century, most of the outer structures and many of the buildings are in ruins although the outer door of the west gate and the Bala Hissar (citadel), a massive structure, remain almost intact though the whole is very overgrown. A flight of ruined steps leads up to the entrance in the north wall. Beware of dogs. The whole area of **Jami Masjid**, 3,500 sq m, is covered by a dome over the *mihrab*, four corner domes and 75 minor domes, making it unique among Indian mosques. It was built by Firoz Shah Bahmani (1397-1432). Similarities with the mosque at Cordoba have contributed to the legend that it was designed by a North African architect from the Moorish court. The **tombs** of the Bahmani sultans are in two groups. One lies 600 m to the west of the fort, the other on the east of the town. The latter have no remaining exterior decoration though the interiors show some evidence of ornamentation. Please note that women are not allowed to enter the tombs.

Bidar → *Phone code 08357.*

Bidar's impressive fort is still intact and the town sprawls within and outside its crumbling walls, in places retaining some of its old medieval charm. The palaces and tombs provide some of the finest examples of Muslim architecture in the Deccan. The town is pleasantly traffic free and well worth exploring on foot.

The walled fort town, on a red laterite plateau in North Karnataka, was once the capital of the Bahmanis and the Barid Shahis and remained an important centre until it fell to Aurangzeb in 1656. The Bahmani Empire fragmented into four kingdoms, and the ninth Bahmani ruler, Ahmad Shah I, shifted his capital from Gulbarga to Bidar in 1424, rebuilding the old Hindu fort to withstand cannon attacks, and enriching the town with beautiful palaces and gardens. With the decline of the Bahmanis, the Barid Shahi Dynasty founded here ruled from 1487 until Bidar was annexed to Bijapur in 1619.

Ins and outs The branch railway line is too slow to be of much use. Travel instead by bus from Hyderabad or Gulbarga, both under four hours away, or Bijapur, eight hours away. The bus stand is 1 km west of the centre. There are no exchange facilities.

The **Inner Fort** built by Muhammad Shah out of the red laterite and dark trapstone was later embellished by Ali Barid. The steep hill to the north and east provided natural defence. It was protected to the south and west by a triple moat (now filled). A series of gates and a drawbridge over the moat to the south formed the main entrance from the town. The second gate, the **Sharaza Darwaza** (1503) has tigers carved in bas relief on either side (Shia symbols of Ali as protector), tile decorations on the walls and the **Nakkar Khana** (Drum gallery) above. Beyond this is a large fortified area which brings you to the third gate, the huge **Gumbad Darwaza**, probably built by Ahmad Shah Wali in the 1420s, which shows Persian influence. Note the decorated *gumbad* (dome).

You will see the triple moat to the right and after passing through the gateway, to your left are steps leading to the **Rangin Mahal** (Coloured Palace) where Muhammad Shah moved to, after finding the nearby Shah Burj a safe refuge in 1487 when the Abyssinians attacked. This small palace (an indication of the Bahmanis' declining years) was built by him, elaborately decorated with coloured tiles, later enhanced by Ali Barid with mother-of-pearl inlay on polished black granite walls as well as intricate wood carvings. If locked, ask at the museum for a key. The old banyan tree and the Shahi Matbak (once a palace, but served as the Royal Kitchens) are to the west, with the Shahi Hammam (Royal Baths) next to it, which now houses a small **museum** ① *0800-1700*. The exhibits include Hindu religious sculptures, stone age implements, cannon balls filled with bits of iron.

The **Lal Bagh**, where remains of water channels and a fountain witness its former glory, and the *zenana*, are opposite the Hammam. The **Sola Khamba** (16 column) or **Zanani Mosque** is to the west (1423). The adjacent **Tarkash Mahal** (possibly refurbished by the Barid Shahis for the harem), to the south of Lal Bagh, is in ruins but still retains some tilework. From behind the mosque you can get to the **Gagan Mahal** (Heavenly Palace) which once carried fine decorations and is believed to have allowed the ladies to watch animal fights in the moat below from the back of the double hall. Good view from the roof. The **Diwan-i-Am** (Hall of Public Audience) is to the northwest of the *zenana* which once held the 'Takht-i-Firoza' (turquoise throne). To the north stands the **Takht Mahal** with royal apartments, audience hall and swimming bath. The steep staircase will take you down to underground chambers.

South of the royal apartments is the well which supplied water to the fort palaces through clay pipes. Of the so-called (thousand) *kothri*, you can only see a few underground rooms and passages which enabled a quick escape to the moat when necessary. Further south, the **Naubat Khana** probably housed the fort commander and the musicians. The road west from the Royal Apartments leads to the encircling **Fort Wall** (about 10 km) with bastions carrying vast canyons, the one to the northwest being the most impressive. You can see the ammunition magazine inside the Mandu Darwaza to the east before returning to the main fort entrance.

Bidar old town

As you walk south from the fort you can see the ruins of the **Madrassa of Mahmud Gawan** (1472). It is a fine example of his native Persian architecture and still bears signs of the once brilliant green, white and yellow tiles which covered the whole façade with swirls of floral patterns and bold calligraphy. The **Chaubara** is a 23-m circular watchtower at the crossroads, south of the town centre (good views from the top). South of this is the **Jami Masjid** (1430) which bears the Barid Shahis' typical chain and pendant motif. The **Kali Masjid** (1694), south of the Talghat Darwaza, is made of black trapstone. It has fine plaster decorations on the vaulted ceiling. There are also a number of *khanqahs* (monasteries).

The road east from the Dulhan Darwaza, opposite the General Hospital, leads to the eight **Bahmani tombs** ① *Ashtur, 0800-1700, free.* The attendant can use a mirror to reflect sunlight but it is best to carry your own flashlight. These are best seen in the morning when the light is better for viewing the interiors. The square tombs, with arched arcades all round have bulbous domes. The exteriors have stone carvings and superb coloured tile decoration showing strong Persian influence, while the interiors have coloured paintings with gilding. On the way back, the **Chaukhandi of Hazrat Khalil-Ullah** is approached by a flight of steps. Most of the tilework has disappeared but you can see the fine carvings at the entrance and on the granite pillars.

The **Barid Shahi tombs** each of which once stood in its garden, are on the Nanded Road to the west of the old town. That of Ali Barid is the most impressive. A prayer hall, music rooms, a combined tomb for his concubines and a pool fed by an aqueduct are nearby. The road north from Ali Barid's tomb descends to **Nanak Jhera**, where a *gurdwara* marks the holy place where Sikhs believe a miracle was performed by Guru Nanak and the jhera (spring) rose.

Raichur → *Phone code 08532.*

The main road from Hospet to Hyderabad passes through the important medieval centre of Raichur, once dominant in the Tungabhadra-Krishna *doab* but now a dusty peninsula town. An important market town, it is in the middle of a cotton growing area.

The site of the **fort**'s citadel at Raichur gives magnificent views over the vast open spaces of the Deccan plateau nearly 100 m below. Built in the mid-14th century, Raichur became the first capital of the Bijapur Kingdom when it broke away from the Bahmani Sultans in 1489. Much of the fort itself is now in ruins, but there are some interesting remains. The north gate is flanked by towers, a carved elephant standing about 40 m away. On the inner walls are some carvings, and a tunnel reputedly built to enable soldiers access to barricade the gate in emergency. Near the west gate is the old palace.

There are some other interesting buildings in the fort below the hill, including the **Daftar ki Masjid** (Office Mosque), built around 1510 out of masonry removed from Hindu temples. It is one of the earliest mosques in the Deccan to be built in this way, with the bizarre result of producing flat ceilings with pillars carved for Chalukyan temples. The **Ek Minar ki Masjid** ('one-minaret mosque') is in the southeast corner of the courtyard, with its distinctively Bahmani style dome.

● Sleeping

Hospet *p220*

NB Station Rd has been renamed Mahatma Gandhi Rd (MG Rd).

B-D Shanbhag Towers, College Rd, T08394-425910, shanbhagtowers@ yahoo.com. 64 spacious rooms, 32 a/c with tub, TV, fridge, in brand new hotel, breathtaking Hampi theme, restaurants (one rooftop with great views), bar.

B-F Malligi, 6/143 Jambunatha Rd, T08394-28101 malligihome@hotmail.com. 140 rooms, 65 a/c, newer (D) are large with bath (4 B suites), always inspect first as standard varies enormously, restaurant and bar by pool (economy guests and non-residents pay Rs 25 per hr for pool), health club, exchange, travel (good Hampi tour Rs 80), creakingly slow internet and overpriced STD/ISD service.

C-E Priyadarshini, V/45 Station Rd, T08394-28838, www.priyainnhampi.com. 82 fairly good rooms, 25 a/c, rather bare and bit over priced, though friendly service, good restaurants, internet, parking.

D-E Karthik, 252 Sardar Patel Rd, T08394-426643. 40 good-sized, clean rooms, 10 a/c in quiet, modern hotel, garden, dining, friendly and good value.

D-E Nagarjuna Residency, Sardar Patel Rd, opposite Karthik, T08394-429009. Spotless, modern, excellent value rooms, some a/c, extra bed Rs 30-50, very helpful. Recommended.

E Shivananda, next to bus stand, T08394-420700. 23 rooms, 4 a/c, simple but clean, astrologer!

E SLV Yatri Nivas, Station Rd, T08394-421525. 15 bright, airy rooms in clean, well-run hotel. Good vegetarian restaurant and bar. Recommended.

F Viswa , MG Rd, opposite bus station, away from the road, T08394-427171. 42 clean rooms (some 4-bed) with bath, adjacent Shanthi restaurant. No frills but good value.

Hampi *p221, map p222*

A small selection from scores of guest houses are listed here. All are fairly similar: converted family houses, usually with common bathroom/toilet, some with roof-top restaurant. Few are purpose-built. Most are in the block to the north and northeast of the Virupaksha Temple, and behind the shops on the main street; some are nearer the bazaar bus-stand. Prices rise 30% during the 'season'. Power cuts are common so a supply of candles and a torch are essential. Mosquitos can be a real problem, especially at dusk.

Hampi Bazaar

D Ranjana Guest House, behind Government School, T08394-441696. A friendly guest house with 5 rooms with hot water.

E Aum Guest House, T08394-441431. 4 rooms.

E Padma Guest House T08394-441331. Family guesthouse, 4 doubles. Foreign exchange.

E Shakti Guest House, T08394-441953. 1 room in quiet family house with double bed.

E-F Archana, T08394-441547. 8 rooms, very clean, quiet, with nets and roof area, attached shop.

E-F Gopi, T08394-41695. 10 rooms with bath, nets, board games.

E-F Rahul, south of the bus stand but reasonably quiet. Basic sleeping under nets, and washing, clean, good simple veg food, good views from rooftop.

E-F Raju, T08394-41349. Two buildings on either side of river, 2 and 14 rooms. Old with character, and clean, rooftop restaurant.

E-F Shambhu, T08394-41383. 5 rooms with bath and nets, plenty of plants, rooftop restaurants (egg dishes), friendly.

E-F Shanti Guest House, down path to the right of the temple (signed), T08394-41568. 23 rooms with fans around pleasant courtyard with plenty of plants, common shower, roof for overspill, very clean, well run and friendly, cycle hire, good cakes (see below).

E-F Vicky, 200 m north of main road (turn off at tourist office), T08394-41694. 7 rooms (4 with bath), bucket hot water, Indian toilet, good rooftop restaurant, internet Rs 60 per hr.

Kamalapuram

D-E Mayura Bhuvaneswari, 2 km from site, T08394-41574. 32 redecorated rooms (8 a/c, Rs 450), fairly clean, decent food, chilled beer, poor cycle hire.

D Kishkinda Heritage Resort, T08532-367734, www.kishkindaheritage.com. Huts with swimming pool and internet.

Bijapur *p224*

There has been a sudden spurt in decent hotels and restaurants.

B Madhuvan International, off Station Rd, T08352-55571. 35 rooms, 10 a/c, very pleasant, good veg garden restaurant and rooftop terrace, travel desk, but a bit overpriced.

B-D Hotel Kanishka International, Station Rd, T08352-223788 www.kanishkabijapur. com. 24 rooms (10 A/C) with decidedly garish decor – giant mirrors – also has cable TV, telephone, en suite, laundry, plus the excellent Kamat Restaurant downstairs.

C-D Hotel Pearl, Opposite Gol Gumbaz, Station Rd, T08352-256002. 32 rooms (17 a/c) in 3-storey modern, scrupulously clean, modest mint pastel-coloured hotel set round central courtyard with pure veg basement restaurant (booze and non-veg through room service). Telephones, cable TV in all rooms, laundry and parking.

D-E Hotel Navaratna International
Station Rd, T08352-222771. Grand
colonnaded drive belies modest price
tag of the 34 rooms here (of which 12 a/c).
Communal areas scream with huge
modernist paintings and rooms are
done up with colour-coded care (TV,
phone, etc and smaller have nice sit-outs).
Very popular non-veg courtyard, bar and
pure veg restaurant. Best of all is the fact
that they have rooms and bath for drivers
– a giant leap in the humane direction for
an Indian hotel.
D-F Godavari, Athni Rd, T08352-53105. 48
good rooms, friendly staff, good veg and
non-veg food.
D-F Samrat, Station Rd, T08352-51620. 30
basic rooms, 6 a/c passable, rest battered,
good vegetarian garden restaurant but
mosquito feast at dinner.
D-F Sanman, opposite Gol Gumbaz, Station
Rd, T08352-51866. 24 clean, pleasant rooms
with shower, nets, 6 a/c. Very good value.
Separate veg restaurant and non-veg with
bar. Recommended.
D-F Santosh, T08352-52179. 70 good, clean
rooms including some a/c, quieter at back,
convenient, good value.
F Railway Retiring Room and dorm
Exceptionally clean, contact Ticket Collector
on duty. Recommended.

Bagalkot
E Circuit House. A/c rooms, 5 km from
centre on Bijapur Rd.

Badami
There is no formal money exchange but the
hotel Mukambika may be persuaded to
change small value TCs.
B Badami Court, Station Rd, T08357-20230,
www.hotelbadamicourt.com. 2 km from
town (pleasant stroll or frequent buses). 26
clean, modern, though cramped rooms
(bath tub), some a/c, good restaurant,
pool (small only knee deep; non-residents
Rs 80 per hr) gym, garden to relax, friendly,
well-managed, rates sometimes
negotiable, only accepts Rupees, tour of
all nearby sites Rs 800.
F Shree Laxmi Villas. Simple rooms, 3
with balconies with great views back to
the temples. Right in the thick of it so
interesting if noisy.

Gulbarga
D Pariwar, Humnabad Rd, near station,
T08472-21522. Some a/c rooms (Rs 450),
some good value. Old but clean, tidy, friendly
staff, tasty vegetarian meals (no beer).
D Santosh, University Rd (east of town),
T08472-22661. Some a/c rooms, good non
veg restaurant (beer). Best in town.
D-E Aditya, Humnabad Rd, T08472-202040.
Reasonable rooms, some a/c with bath,
clean vegetarian restaurant, very good value.

Bidar
E Ashoka, off Udgir Rd, near Deepak Cinema,
T08357-26249. 21 clean, good-sized rooms,
hot water, some a/c, restaurant ("bit of a
drinking den but good tandoori"), friendly,
only decent hotel in town. Recommended.
F Airlines Lodge, T08357-26883. 18 rooms,
some with TV, hot water in morning, clean
linen, OK despite first appearances.

🍴 Eating

Hospet *p220*
The hotels serve chilled beer.
$$ Waves, Malligi's, by pool. Multicuisine.
Good food, bar.
$ Iceland, Station Rd, behind the bus station.
Good South Indian meals.
$ Shanbhag, near the bus station. Good
South Indian meals.

Hampi *p221, map p222*
All restaurants are vegetarian, though eggs
are sometimes available. The following are in
Hampi Bazaar:
$ Boomshankar, on path to Vittahla Temple.
Well prepared, fresh river fish.
$ Gopi, for good simple, cheap *thalis*.
$ Mango Tree, river bank, 500 m west of
temple. Relaxed and pleasant.
$ Manju. Family-run, simple but enticing
food (apple *parathas*), take-aways for tiffin
boxes (will even lend boxes).
$ New Shanti. Good carrot/apple/banana/
chocolate cakes to order.
$ Om Shiva. Excellent western and
Middle-Eastern dishes. Good hygiene.
$ Shambhu, opposite Shanti. Fresh
pasta/noodles and espresso plus all
the usual; also sells bus/train tickets for a
small commission.

$ **Suresh**, 30 m from Shanti, down a small
alley. Very friendly family, made to order so
takes a while, but worth the wait.

Kamalapuram
$ **Mayura Bhuvaneswari**, does cheap
adequate meals. Snacks available near the
bus stand.

Bijapur *p224*
Eateries include **Kapali**, opposite bus stand,
decent South Indian; **Priyadarshini**, for veg
snacks; **Shrinidhi**, for quality veg meals.

Hindu temples around Bijapur *p226*
Badami
Sanman, near Bus Stand, has
non-vegetarian; **Laxmi Vilas**, near taxi
stand, does vegetarian meals; **Parimala** and
Geeta Darshini both do South Indian
breakfasts.

⊛ Festivals and events

Hospet *p220*
Muharram. 10 days of fasting is
broken with fierce drum-pounding,
drink, and frequent arguments –
sometimes accompanied by physical
violence. Each village clusters around
icons of Hussein, whose decapitation
is represented by a golden crown on
top of a face full of long strings of
jasmine flowers held aloft on wooden
sticks. Come evening, fires are lit. When
the embers are dying villagers race
through the ashes, a custom which may
predate Islam's arrival.

Hampi *p221, map p222*
Jan-Feb Virupaksha Temple Car festival.
Nov 3-5 Hampi Music festival at Vitthala
Temple. Hotels are packed.

Bijapur *p224*
Jan Siddhesvara Temple festival. Music
festival accompanied by Craft Mela.

Hindu temples around Bijapur *p226*
Bagalkot
Jan Nrutytsava draws many famous
dancers and is accompanied by a Craft Mela.
Mar-Apr Temple car festivals at Virupaksha
and Mallikarjuna temples.

○ Shopping

Hospet to Bidar *p229*
Bidar
Excellent *bidriwork* here, where it is said to
have originated, particularly shops near the
Ta'lim of Siddiq Shah. You can see craftsmen
at work in the narrow lanes.

▲ Activities and tours

Hospet *p220*
Tours From KSTDC, T08394-21008, and
SRK Tours and Travels at Malligi Hotel to
Hampi, Rs 75 (lunch extra); 0930-1630.
English-speaking guide but rather rushed.

Hampi *p221, map p222*
Malligi, 6/143 Jambunatha Rd,
T08394-28101, malligihome@hotmail.com,
does daytrips to Aihole, Badami, Pattadakal
0830-1930, Rs 275 per person. Long drive.
Local sightseeing costs Rs 700 per day.

⊖ Transport

Hospet *p220*
From Hospet to/from **Hampi** , travel via
Kamalapuram, especially in the rainy season
when the slower road to Hampi Bazaar
which winds through villages, is barely
passable.

Auto-rickshaw
Local to **Hampi**, demand Rs 150. Long
distance to **Hampi**, Rs 50. Cycle-rickshaw
from train station to bus stand about Rs 10.

Bus
Frequent buses to **Hampi**'s 2 entry points
(via Kamalapuram and Museum, Rs 4 and via
Hampi Bazaar, 30 mins, Rs 3.50), from 0530;
last return around 2000.

Express bus to/from **Bangalore** (road now
upgraded), several from 0700, 10 hrs; **Mysore**,
1830, 10½ hrs (Express buses to Belur/Halebid
from both). Services to other sites, eg **Badami**
(6 hrs), **Bijapur** (6 hrs), **Chitradurga** 0530 (3
hrs). Overnight Karnataka Tourism luxury
coaches to various towns. Direct buses to
Panjim (Goa); the road is being improved –
Luxury, 0630 (10½ hrs), State bus, 0830
(reserve a seat in advance); others involve a

change in Hubli (4½ hrs). **Paulo Travels** Luxury Sleeper coach from Hotel Priyadarshini, at 1845, Rs 350, daily; **West Coast Sleeper**, from Hotel Shanbhag, 1830, Rs 350; daily (Oct-Mar only); strangers may be expected to share a bunk. It is better to take a train to Londa (under 5 hrs) and get a bus to Margao or Panjim (3 hrs).

Taxi
KSTDC, T08394-21008, or from Malligi Hotel; about Rs 700 per day (possible to share).

Train
Bangalore, Hampi Exp 6591, 2010 (via Guntakal, 2½ hrs) 10½ hrs. **Guntakal**, Amaravati Exp, 7226, 1610, 2½ hrs. For **Belur/ Halebid,** Amaravati Exp 7225, 1050 to Hubli; then Hubli-Arsikere Pass 884 (S), 1440, arrive 2120. To **Badami**, via Gadag, 4 hrs. **Hyderabad** (via Guntakal): Hampi/ Rayalaseema Exp 6591/7430, 2010, 14 hrs. **Margao**, 7227, Tue, Fri, depart Hospet 1050, 9 hrs.

Hampi *p221, map p222*
Bicycle hire from Hampi Bazaar (try stall behind the temple, Rs 30 per day), and Kamalapuram.
Coracles take passengers across the river from the jetty west of the Virupaksha Temple, Rs 5 (Rs 10 with luggage).

Bijapur *p224*
Bus
A service runs between the **station** (2 km east) to west end of town. Horse drawn carriages ply up and down MG Rd; a fine change from autos but bargain hard.

Buses are frequent between Bijapur and **Bidar, Hubli, Belgaum** and **Solapur** (2-2½ hrs). Buses to **Badami** (3½ hrs). For **Hospet**, travel via Gadag or Ikal. Reservations can be made on the following daily services to **Aurangabad** 0600, 1830 (Rs 180), **Hospet, Bangalore**, 1700, 1800, 1930, 2130 (Rs 193, 12 hrs); Ultra fast at 1900, 2000 (Rs 252), **Belgaum**, 0630 (Rs 71), **Hubli**, 0900, 1400, 1600 (Rs 84), **Hyderabad**, 0600, 1800 (Rs 141); Deluxe at 2130 (Rs 203), **Mumbai** (CT), 0800, 1600, 1700, 2030 (Rs 215), **Mumbai (Kurla)**, 1900, 2000, 2100 (Rs 210), **Mysore**: 1700 (Rs 230), **Panjim**, 1900 (Rs 126) and **Vasco de Gama**, 0715 (Rs 131).

Several private agents also run services to **Bangalore** (Rs 220, 12 hrs), **Mumbai** (Rs 250, 11 hrs) and **Pune** (Rs 200, 7 hrs).

Train
Computerised reservation office open 0800-2000, Sun 0800-1400. **Solapur**, 0945, 1635 (2½ hrs); **Gadag**, 5 trains daily for long distance connections. Otherwise, buses are more convenient.

Hindu temples around Bijapur *p226*
Badami
Bicycle
Bike hire: stalls along the main road, Rs 4 per hr; pleasant to visit Banashankari, Mahakuta and Pattadakal.

Bus
Few daily to **Hospet** (6 hrs), very slow and crowded but quite a pleasant journey with lots of stops; **Belgaum** via Bagalkot, 4 hrs; **Bijapur**, 0645-0930 (4 hrs). Several to **Pattadakal** and **Aihole** from 0730. **Aihole** (2 hrs), from there to Pattadakal (1600). Last return bus from Aihole 1715, via Pattadakal.

Car hire
From Badami with driver for Mahakuta, Aihole and Pattadakal, about Rs 650.

Train
The station is 5 km north on the Bijapur-Gadag line, with 6 trains daily in each direction (enquire about schedules); frequent buses to town.

Hospet to Bidar *p229*
Gulbarga
Bus
There are bus connections to **Hyderabad** (190 km) and **Solapur**.

Train
Mumbai (CST), 8 trains daily, 13 hrs; **Bangalore**, Udayan Exp 6529, 1900, 13½ hrs; **Lokmanya Tilak** 1013, 0905, 13 hrs; **Chennai (MC)**, Chennai Exp 6011 (AC/II), 0130, 15 hrs; Mumbai Chennai Mail 6009, 1140, 18 hrs; Dadar Chennai Exp 1063, 0605, 14 hrs. **Hyderabad**, Mumbai-Hyderabad Exp 7031 (AC/II), 0020, 5¾ hrs; Hussainsagar Exp 7001, 0740, 5 hrs.

Bidar
Auto-rickshaw
Easily available, Rs 15 is the going rate for most short hops across town.

Bicycle
Cycle is the best way to get around and see the sights. 'Cycle taxis' can be hired for around Rs 20 per day from several outlets all over town and near the New Bus Station. You may have to ask 2 or 3 before you find a shop that will rent to you, but persevere. Don't waste time with **Ganesh Cycle Taxi**, near New Bus Station.

Bus
Services from New Bus Station to most regional destinations, but check timings since the last bus is often quite early. Private buses to **Mumbai**, 1700, 5 hrs, Rs 260. **Pune**, 1530, 3½ hrs, Rs 220. Taxi to **Gulbarga** Rs 800.

Train
Bidar is on a branch line from Vikarabad to Parbhani Junction. **Aurangabad**, Kacheguda-Manmad Exp 7664, 2140, 8½ hrs; **Bangalore**, Hampi Link Exp 6593, 1237, 18 hrs; **Secunderabad**, Manmad-Kacheguda Exp 7663, 0352, 5 hrs.

● Directory

Hospet *p220*
Banks State Bank of India, next to Tourist Office, only changes cash (US $ and UK £). **Monica Travel**, near Bus Station, changes TCs (3% charge). **Internet** Cybernet, College Rd, next to Shivananda. **Post office** Opposite vegetable market.

Hampi *p221, map p222*
Banks Several agents on main street. **Modi Enterprises**, Main Rd, near Tourist Office, changes TCs and cash; **Neha Travels**, internet, money change and tour agent.

Bijapur *p224*
Banks State Bank of India in the citadel; Canara Bank, north of market, best for exchange. **Internet** Cyber Park, 1st flr, Royal Complex, opposite GPO, 0930-2300 fast connections.

History	**238**
Early Goa	238
Contact with the Muslim world	238
The Portuguese	239
Independence	240
Recent political history	240
Culture	**241**
People	241
Language	241
Music and dance	242
Cinema	243
Architecture	243
Religion	**245**
Hinduism	246
Hindu society	248
Christianity	250
Islam	251
Buddhism	252
Land and environment	**252**
Climate	253
Wildlife	253
Vegetation	256
Books	**256**

History

Early Goa

Through its early history Goa often found itself on the borders of developments taking place in both North and South India. When the Mauryan Emperor Asoka (272 BC) extended his administration from the banks of the Ganges at Patna southwards across the Deccan plateau, the west coast may have been incorporated into the great Maurya Empire. Further south, other great kingdoms – the Cholas, Keralaputras and Pandiyas – all contested for power.

The Bhojas followed the Mauryas and based their kingdom in Chandrapur (modern Chandor). From the third to the eighth centuries AD the Kadamba Dynasty established itself on the western borderlands. Until the arrival of the Muslims from the north in AD 1312, their power was reduced to a narrow coastal and hill belt, and they were almost entirely subservient to the Chalukyas who controlled most of central peninsular India. In 1052, the Kadambas established their capital in the port town on the north bank of the Zuari (near Goa Velha), which had been developed by the Chalukyas as the port of Gopakapattana or Govapuri (Gove as it came to be known by traders).

Contact with the Muslim world

Since before the birth of Christ, the Arabs traded along the west coast of India and Arab geographers knew Goa as Sindabur. As the Arab world converted to Islam, the traders spread their new religion and many settled in Goa. However, while the Muslim-based coastal trade was largely peaceful, the penetration of Islam into the Deccan was anything but. In 1312, Muslim invaders from the Delhi Sultanate took power, destroying much of Govapuri and forcing the Kadambas to return to Chandrapur. In 1327 the Muslims under Mohammad Tughluq carried out further incursions into the interior, going as far as Chandrapur. However, their power was challenged 20 years later by the Bahmanis.

In 1347 Muslims in the Deccan peninsula broke away from the Delhi Sultanate to the north and established the Bahmani Dynasty (1347-1527). While the Bahmanis were in control of Goa from approximately 1348-1369 (and again for 26 years from 1470) they entered a renewed period of temple destruction and of terrorizing the Hindu population. Goa's territory was the subject of repeated contests between the Hindu and Muslim powers of the interior and subsequently the maritime Portuguese.

The Bahmanis were defeated by the Hindu Vijayanagars in 1378 and there followed nearly a hundred years of relative peace and prosperity. It was control of the maritime trade that attracted the peninsular powers into repeated conflict rather than ideological or religious competition. However, brutal attacks on the Muslim population of Bhatkal to the south of Goa by the Vijayanagar king encouraged the Bahmanis to return with renewed force in 1470. They destroyed what was left of the old capital Govapuri (which became known as Goa Velha) and moved the administration to the port of Ela on the Mandovi, taking the name 'Govapuri' (later Velha Goa). The Bahmanis themselves split into five different states, the largest of which, Bijapur (1490-1686) played a key role in Goa's political fortunes. The Adil Shahis of Bijapur took control from 1498-1510, and Yusuf Adil Shah, the Muslim Sultan of Bijapur, was the ruler when the Portuguese arrived. Under the Muslim Bahmanis, the new Govapuri developed into a town of great geopolitical significance, prosperous as a result of trade in horses and spices.

The Portuguese

For the first Portuguese, their encounter with the Muslims on the coast of India was an extension of the contest for power between Catholicism and Islam in the Iberian Peninsula. They had come not only to rescue the early Syrian Christians from the threat of Muslim dominance, but also to bring them under the influence of Rome. They also wanted to establish coastal stations on the way to the Far East to control the lucrative spice trade.

Although Vasco da Gama landed in India in 1498, Goa was only taken by Afonso de Albuquerque in 1510. Originally intending to take his fleet up from Karwar, just south of Goa, to Egypt, Albuquerque changed his plans when he obtained vital information about Goa. He discovered that the Muslims were building their ships in Goa, that the administration was fairly weak and that Bijapuri taxes were becoming increasingly unpopular among the local subjects.

He successfully took Goa on 1 March 1510. Yusuf Adil Shah died almost immediately after the defeat, but two months later his 13-year-old son and successor, Ismail Adil Khan (known to the Portuguese as the 'Idalcan'), blockaded Goa with 60,000 men and recaptured it. However, Adil Khan's victory was short-lived. He was no match to defend the city against Albuquerque who returned after the monsoon with reinforcements and recaptured the city on 25 November (St Catherine's Day) 1510, after a bloody struggle.

The territory over which Albuquerque gained control was a roughly triangular-shaped island with a rocky headland and two harbours which was given the name Ilhas ('island' in Portuguese), together with the islands of Chudamani (Chorao), Dipavati (Divar), Vamsim (the tiny island between the two) and Jua. In 1534 the adjoining lands of Bardez and Salcete, dependencies of Govapuri, came under Portuguese control. The two territories were annexed by the Portuguese around 1543 to make up the territory known as the 'Old Conquests'.

Once Albuquerque established his own control, the Portuguese started to develop Goa as a major Christian centre. To avoid conflict between missionaries in the Old Conquest territories, Bardez was offered to the Franciscans, while Salcete was under the Jesuits and Ilhas was principally allotted to the Augustinians and Dominicans. Although some Hindu practices, such as *sati* (the burning of a widow on the funeral pyre of her husband), were stamped out by Albuquerque, in other respects he did little to interfere with local custom. By 1570 the colony had become so wealthy that it had acquired the sobriquet Golden Goa. Goa became the capital of the Portuguese Empire in the east and was granted the same civic privileges as Lisbon.

Throughout the 100 years after their arrival the Portuguese were intent on trying to build an empire in Asia. In that effort Goa played a pivotal role between Portugal and its territories to the east. It was their misfortune that in 1565 the Vijayanagar Empire was suddenly – and unexpectedly – routed. Five years earlier the Portuguese had embarked on the Inquisition, attacking Hindus and Muslims alike within the Old Conquest territories. In 1570 Muslim rulers from Bijapur to Sumatra attempted a concerted attack on Portuguese interests, and Goa was subjected to a 10-month siege. The harassment from the Bijapur Sultanate was only finally ended by the overpowering dominance of the much greater Muslim power of the Mughals.

When the Dutch began to control trade in the Indian Ocean, Portuguese dominance of the sea declined. The fall of the Vijayanagar Empire in 1565 caused the trade between Goa and the Hindu state to dry up. The Dutch blockaded Goa in 1603 and 1639, weakening it but failing to take it. It was ravaged by an epidemic in 1635, and manpower was so severely depleted that the Portuguese resorted to bringing criminals from Lisbon's prisons to maintain the numbers.

By the early part of the 18th century Portuguese fortunes had already experienced wide fluctuations and the territorial base was still restricted to the Ilhas, Salcete in the south and Bardez in the north. The greatest threat to security had come through the latter part of the 17th century from Sivaji (1627-1680) and his Maratha confederacy (1674-1818). Sivaji and his son took the whole of the northern territories, only to be forced to withdraw in 1683 by the threat they faced from the Mughals on their own northern flank. Goa remained safe in its isolation, though it was threatened again briefly in 1739.

The risk of attack from both land and sea encouraged the Portuguese to establish a series of forts inland as well as on the coast. The forts are small compared with even the modest Indian forts, due to the small number of expatriate Portuguese available to man them.

Despite extraordinary cultural achievements, notably in the church building of Old Goa, Portugal's political base in Goa remained weak. In the mid-18th century a series of reforms were introduced under pressure from the Portuguese Government in Lisbon. These included the ending of the Inquisition and the confiscation of Jesuit property.

In 1741 King Joao V of Portugal (ruled 1706-1750) decided to extend Portuguese control to the provinces that were to become the 'New Conquests'. The implementation of this plan had to wait four decades, when a succession of military victories led to the integration of the New Conquests into Portuguese territory. Bicholim and Satari were conquered in 1781 and 1782, and the victories were celebrated by the first public display of the body of St Francis Xavier in 1782. Pernem was ceded to Portugal in 1788, while Ponda, Sanguem, Quepem and Canacona followed three years later, along with official acceptance by the Raja of Sunda of the capture in 1763 of the headland of Cabo de Rama. Portugal's hold on its Goan territory was complete.

Struggles in continental Europe however, notably between Britain and Napoleonic France, had an impact on alliances in India, and Goa itself was occupied by the British between 1799 and 1813. It was during this period that Goa experienced its most important revolt against the Portuguese. In 1787 a group of priests met in the house of the Pinto family in Candolim and formed a plot to overthrow the government; the escapade became known as the Pinto Revolt. Fifteen of the 47 conspirators who were arrested and tortured were subsequently executed in Panjim.

Independence

By the end of the Second World War, when the rest of India was on the point of achieving independence, there were fewer than 30 Portuguese officials based in Goa. The Portuguese came under increasing pressure in 1948 and 1949 to cede Goa, Daman and Diu to India, and in response despatched over 4,000 troops to hold on to the territory. In 1955 *satyagrahis* (non-violent demonstrators) tried to enter Goa. They were deported but later, when their numbers had increased, the Portuguese used force to repel them and some were killed. At a demonstration in Margao, Portuguese police fired on the unarmed mob, killing 32 and injuring 225. The problem festered until 19 December 1961 when the Indian Army, supported by a naval blockade, marched in and brought to an end 450 years of Portuguese rule. Originally Goa became a Union Territory, but on 30 May 1987 it became a full state of the Indian Union.

Recent political history

Goan politics remains sharply distinct from that of its neighbours. The Goa Legislative Assembly has 40 elected members while the state elects three members to the Lok Sabha, the Central Government. Although the Congress Party has been the largest single party for most of the period since Goa became part of independent India, political life is strongly influenced by the regional issue of the relationship with neighbouring Maharashtra. The debate over the role of Marathi led to the creation of the Maharashtrawada Gomantak Party, which was in power in the Union Territory of Goa from 1963 until 1979. Regional issues remain important, but there is now also a strong environmental lobby, in which the Catholic church plays a prominent part.

Culture

People

The four major *varna* groups of Hindus – the **Brahmins** or priestly caste, **Kshatriyas** (warriors), **Vaishyas** (merchants) and **Sudras** (agriculturalists) – retained their designations in only slightly modified form despite four centuries of Portuguese dominance. According to the **India's Anthropological Survey**, the different sub-castes of the Brahmin community in Goa merged into the single Catholic Saraswat group, the Vaishya sub-castes merged into one becoming the Charddo Catholic community, and the remainder became Catholic Sudras. There was a small community of Catholic Mestiços, most having left Goa for Portugal after Liberation. Today the two highest Catholic castes, the Brahmin and Charddo Catholics, have become a single group, inter-marrying and generally occupying high positions in society. Catholic Sudras, who include the Christian fishing communities, remain separate.

The Catholics are sub-divided into a number of occupational groups. In Salcete, Ponda and Quepem, for example, the Carpenter group (*Thovoi*) is common, and many continue to depend on making small items of furniture or decorative images for church buildings. Along the coast the Catholic *Kharvi*, or fishermen, claim to be Goa's original inhabitants. While their surnames – Rodrigues, Costa, Souza, Dias, Pereira – have all been adopted from the Portuguese, they are direct descendants of the Hindu fishing communities of the coast.

Unlike the Christian communities, the Hindu castes are still sub-divided along their original occupational lines. One of the most remarkable communities among the Hindus is that known today as the **Gomantak Maratha Samaj**. The group belongs to the former *devdasis*, dancing women and prostitutes who had been dedicated to temples and the service of their deities. Ancient Hindu scriptures had suggested that the most beautiful girls should be dedicated to temple service, and that they should be considered of high social status. There are also the tribal groups such as the **Gavdes** and **Kunbis**. Gavdes were originally nomadic hunters and fishermen who worshipped natural elements, while the Kunbis usually worked on the land, herding animals on the hillsides, and lived in villages with mud and thatch huts. Some continue to wear traditional tribal dress.

Language

There is a seemingly baffling variety of Indian languages, many with their own scripts. Goa is located precisely on the dividing line separating the Indo-European languages of North India from the Dravidian languages of the south.

The roots of nearly all the North Indian languages can be traced back to **Sanskrit**. By the sixth century BC Sanskrit had become the dominant language of North India. **Hindustani** developed from the interaction between the Persian of the court and the native Sanskrit-based language, separately identified as Hindi and Urdu. The following centuries saw the development of the major regional languages of North India, including **Marathi**, the language of Maharashtra.

In sharp contrast, the dominant language of Karnataka, the state bordering Goa to the east and south, is **Kannada**, one of the four Dravidian languages. Each has its own script and was heavily influenced by Sanskrit.

Portuguese was widely spoken in Goa until 1961 and even today many of the older generation can speak it, but Marathi and Konkani remained important. In 1991, **Konkani** was introduced as the language of instruction in church primary schools and was added to the list of recognized languages in the Indian Constitution in August 1992. Hindi is increasingly spoken, with the influx of non-Goan employees in hotel resorts. English and Hindi are widely used on road signs, bus destinations and tourism-related notices. In rural areas, however, Konkani predominates.

It is impossible to spend even a short time in India without coming across several of the different scripts that are used. The earliest ancestor of scripts in use today was Brahmi. Written from left to right, a separate symbol represented each different sound. For about a thousand years the major script of northern India has been the Nagari or Devanagari, and Hindi and Marathi join Sanskrit in their use of it. In Goa, you are likely to come across widespread use of Hindi, and of the Roman script for English. Although Konkani is written both in Roman and Devanagari scripts, it is the latter that has now become the official script for the language.

Music and dance

Goans are noted at home and abroad for their love of music. Although Indian classical music is often performed and Goa has a rich heritage of folk music and dance, Goan popular music reflects modern western popular influences.

Indian music can trace its origins to the metrical hymns and chants of the *Vedas*. Over more than 3,000 years of development, through a range of regional schools, India's musical tradition has been handed on almost entirely by ear. At some point after the Muslim influence made itself felt in the north, North and South Indian styles diverged, to become Carnatic (Karnatak) music in the south and Hindustani music in the north. However, they still share important common features.

Hindustani music probably originated in the Delhi Sultanate during the 13th century, when the most widely known of North Indian musical instruments, the *sitar*, was believed to have been invented as well as the small drums, or *tabla*. The other important instrument of the north are the stringed *sarod*, the *shahnai* reed instrument and the wooden flute.

Contemporary South Indian music, **Carnatic (Karnatak)** music, is traced back to Tyagaraja, Svami Shastri and Dikshitar, three musicians who lived and worked in the 18th and 19th centuries. They placed more emphasis on extended compositions than Hindustani music. Perhaps the best-known South Indian instrument is the stringed *veena*. The flute is commonly used for accompaniment along with the violin (played rather differently to the European original), an oboe-like instrument called the *nagasvaram* and the drums, or *tavil*.

India is rich with folk dance traditions and Goa has its own heritage. The rules for classical dance were laid down in the *Natya shastra* in the second century BC, and they still form the basis for modern dance forms, although there are many regional variations. The most common sources for Indian dance are the epics, but there are three essential aspects of the dance itself: *Nritta* (pure dance), *Nrittya* (emotional expression) and *Natya* (drama). Like the music with which it is so closely intertwined, dance has expressed religious belief and deep emotion.

Cinema

The hugely popular Hindi film industry comes mainly out of a tradition of larger-than-life productions with familiar story lines performed as escapist entertainment for the community. The stars lead fantasy lives, enjoying cult status and a following of millions. Unsurprisingly, should they choose to turn their hand to politics, they find instant support in an unquestioning, adoring electorate. The experience of a Bollywood film is not to be missed. Television is popular but it's always easy to find a cinema in any sizeable town and gaudy posters dominate every street. Be prepared for a long sitting with a standard story line, set characters and lots of action – the typical multi-million Rupee blockbusters attempt to provide something to please everybody. Marathon melodramas consist of slapstick comedy contrasted with tear-jerking tragedy, a liberal sprinkling of moralizing with a tortuous disentangling of the knots tied by the heroes, heroines, villains and their extended families. There are many examples of truly brilliant works by world-class Indian film-makers (Satyajit Ray, Mira Nair, Rithwik Ghatak, Shyam Benegal, Aparna Sen, to name a few), but they are not usually box office successes or made for popular consumption, and have to be sought out.

Architecture

All Goan architecture is in some sense atypical. Even church architecture is not a simple transplant from Europe, although the influence of the baroque on many of Goa's most famous churches is obvious. In their turn, Hindu and Muslim architecture in Goa are strongly influenced by the mixture of cultural traditions from which they grew. Yet the distinctiveness of both Christian and Hindu traditions remains clear, and the fundamental features of their design can be traced back to their wholly different roots.

Goan Christian architecture

Almost nothing remains of the first great development of Portuguese church building during the reign of the Portuguese King Manuel I (ruled 1495-1521). The doorway to the church of St Francis of Assisi in Old Goa, and the Church of Our Lady of the Rosary, the oldest church standing in Goa (1543), illustrate the incorporation of Indian features in a predominantly European model. Influences of both the Italian late renaissance and the early baroque are also evident.

The ornately gilded *reredos*, though usually on a much reduced scale, is typical of many of the Goan churches. Roman influence is clearly visible in one of the other great churches of Old Goa, the 17th-century Convent Church of St Cajetan, which took St Peter's in Rome as its model. Both its Michaelangelo-inspired façade and its interior, based on the form of a Greek cross with a central cupola, are strikingly effective.

In the second half of the 18th century rococo features began to be expressed in a new bout of church building. Indian architects played a significant part in decoration, especially of the *reredos* and the pulpit. In *Golden Goa*, Dr José Pereira lists five Goan churches as masterpieces of the Indian Baroque: the **Holy Spirit** (Old Goa) being the most sublime; **Holy Spirit** (Margao) the most majestic; the **Santana** (Talaulim) the most perfect; **St Stephens** (Santo Estevam, Jua Island) the most ornate, and the **Piedade** (Divar) the most luminous.

Domestic architecture

In the early 18th century Goa benefited directly from the huge wealth that Portugal gained from Brazil. Landed Goan families began to build houses to express their status and wealth.

They borrowed some of the fundamental features from the coastal architecture of the Konkan with sloping roofs of red Mangalore tiles to keep off the rain. The biggest houses had a private chapel (or oratory) where Mass could be celebrated and curved windows, sometimes filled not with glass but with translucent oyster shell (*nacre*), gave a warm, filtered light while also ensuring privacy. Central courtyards, another feature of Indian domestic architectural design, also gave families private space, although some of the newer grand houses also had outward-looking windows, in contrast to the entirely inward-looking courtyard houses of traditional Goan society.

Despite the innovations, Goan domestic architecture never entirely severed its links with earlier Hindu forms. One example was the universal practice of building private chapels, which can be seen as an extension of the Hindu tradition of every house having a shrine dedicated to the domestic deity. Outside the Old Conquests, domestic architecture retained stronger links with traditional Hindu coastal architecture.

Hindu temple building

The principles of religious building were laid down in the *Silpa- sastras* sets of rules on mechanics and building compiled by priests. Every aspect of Hindu, Jain and Buddhist religious building is identified with conceptions of the structure of the universe. This applies as much to the process of building – the timing of which must be undertaken at astrologically propitious times – as to the formal layout of the buildings. The cardinal directions of north, south, east and west are the basic fix on which buildings are planned. The east-west axis is nearly always fundamental to the plan. Number is also critical to the design of the religious building, the key to the ultimate scale of the building derived from the measurements of the sanctuary at its heart. Indian temples were nearly always built to a clear and universal design, which had built into it philosophical understandings of the universe.

This cosmology, of an infinite number of universes, isolated from each other in space, proceeds by imagining various possibilities as to its nature. Its centre is seen as dominated by **Mount Meru**, which keeps earth and heaven apart. The concept of separation is crucial to Hindu thought and social practice. Continents, rivers and oceans occupy concentric rings around the mountain, while the stars encircle the mountain in another plane. Humans live on the continent of **Jambudvipa**, characterized by the rose apple tree (*jambu*). The *shastras* show plans of this continent, organized in concentric rings and entered at the cardinal points. This type of diagram was known as a *mandala*. Such a geometric scheme could be subdivided into almost limitless small compartments, each of which could be designated as having special properties or be devoted to a particular deity. The centre of the *mandala* would be the seat of the major god. *Mandalas* provided the ground rules for the building of sacred, and highly symbolic, Buddhist funerary shrines (*stupas),* and temples across India, and gave the key to the symbolic meaning attached to every aspect of religious buildings.

Temple design

Hindu temples developed characteristic plans and elevations. The focal point of the temple lay in its sanctuary, the home of the presiding deity, known as the womb-chamber (*garbagriha*). A series of doorways, in large temples leading through a succession of buildings, allowed the worshipper to move towards the final encounter with the deity itself and to obtain *darshan* – a sight of the god. Both Buddhist and Hindu worship encourage the worshipper to walk clockwise around the shrine, performing *pradakshina*, regarded as an act of reverence and respect. In contrast to the extraordinary profusion of colour and life on the outside, in most Hindu temples the interior is dark and cramped, but it is the place where, it is believed, the true centre of divine power resides.

While some of the key principles underlying Hindu temple architecture remain the same in Goan temples, the differences are striking, and the outward forms are wholly distinctive and unique. Both in design and in decoration many Goan temples, most of which are 18th century or later, have borrowed liberally from both Muslim and Christian architecture. The transformation was initiated by the Maratha leader Sivaji, who rebelled against the Muslim political dominance of Maharashtra and encouraged the development of a new temple style. It took advantage of some features of Muslim architecture with which Sivaji was familiar including minarets, cusped arches and domes, or the beautifully curved *bangla* roofs loved by the Mughals. The Marathas also introduced long open pavilions in front of the temple, supported by columns, and the tall and often octagonal lamp towers, or *deepmal* or *deepstambha*.

Goan architects also added a drum tower, a 'room' with a pyramidal tiled roof, or *nagarkhana* (or *naubatkhana*), where temple musicians would sit, above the entrance gateway. Another distinctive feature was the prominent *tulsi vrindavana* (basil enclosure), which was similar in principle to the humbler container that is an integral part of Goan Hindu domestic architecture. The *tulsi* is believed to have many mystical properties and there are many myths relating to the *tulsi* plants origin; one suggests that Tulsi was a beautiful woman, who, after practising austerities for many years, was granted a favour by the gods. Vishnu's wife Lakshmi was furious to hear that Tulsi's desire was to become Vishnu's wife, and in anger she turned her into a Tulsi plant. In compensation Vishnu promised to stay near her forever in the form of a *shalagrama*, a multi-coloured fossil widely believed by followers of Vishnu to enshrine the God. The 'enclosure' next to a temple would sometimes assume monumental proportions, and adopt features imitating the more commonly seen piazza crosses in front of churches.

In place of the pyramidal or curving towers that signal the *garbagriha* (main shrine) in most Hindu temples, Goan temples are uniquely surmounted by the kind of dome unknown in the pre-Muslim period. Classical styles influenced by Europe, taking as their models churches in Old Goa such as the Sé Cathedral and Our Lady of Divine Providence, gave both classical scales and the specific feature of the dome. The typical Goan temple comprised a regular series of features. The entrance porch would have an arch, sometimes surmounted by a dome. Inside, the pillared hall (*mandapa*), which could be regarded as similar to the nave of a church, was topped by a steep-pitched tiled roof, while the sanctuary itself was crowned by a dome that would sometimes sit over a European-style drum and be topped by a lantern.

The full distinctiveness of Goa's Hindu temples can only be appreciated in their context. Often set in the heart of lush valleys surrounded by dense greenery, instead of proclaiming themselves like the great hilltop temples of Peninsular India, Goa's temples are often completely hidden from view until the last moment. The temple tank provides not only the means of ritual cleansing but a beautifully cooling stretch of fresh water, usually close to the temple entrance. The pilgrim or worshipper is thus presented with an element of surprise up to the moment of entry. At festivals, welcoming lamps flicker in the lamp tower and across the compound.

Religion

The visitor's first impression of the religion of Goa's peoples is likely to be highly misleading. Most books about Goa give prominence to the Portuguese Christian legacy, and the drive from the airport to Panjim or south to any of the coastal resorts would appear to confirm that the state is predominantly Christian. In the area of the Old Conquests, tens of thousands of people were indeed converted to Christianity, but the Zuari river represents a great divide between Christian and predominantly Hindu Goa. Today about 70% of the state's population is Hindu, and there is also a small but significant Muslim minority. Other noteable minority groups include Sikhs and Jains, although they exist in far smaller numbers than elsewhere in India.

Only when you get to Ponda or into the rural areas of the interior do you find significant Hindu temples, and these are mainly the product of the 18th and 19th centuries. Indeed, their curious blend of Muslim, Christian and Hindu features testifies to the distinctive influences on Hinduism in Goa over the last four centuries. There is no place in India where it is possible to define a 'pure' Hinduism, either in terms of belief or practice, but in Goa the interaction between the communities has blended features of each of the major religions. It is no accident that the only Hindu temple with a design rooted in the traditions of the peninsula is that of Tambdi Surla, deep in the forest and close to the border of Karnataka. Almost as far as it is possible to be from the Christianizing influences of the west, or the Muslim routes into Goa of military and political control, it seems to have survived by default.

The daily life of many Goan communities reflects a strong mutual respect for each other's traditions. Village festivals are often shared, deities or saints are venerated by both communities, and mutual respect for each other's religious beliefs is shown at all levels of Goan society. This is not to say that there are no tensions between the communities, but many Goans will say that these have been created artificially by outsiders. Yet if the people of Goa seem to follow hybrid versions of each of the major religions, the roots of each are nonetheless clearly discernible, and it is necessary therefore to appreciate the fundamental characteristics of each in its Goan context.

Hinduism

While some aspects of modern Hinduism can be traced back more than 2,000 years before the birth of Christ, other features are more recent. As early as the sixth century BC the Buddhists and Jains had tried to reform the religion of Vedism (or Brahmanism), which had been dominant in some parts of South Asia for 500 years. Great philosophers such as Sankaracharya (seventh and early eighth centuries AD) and Ramanuja (12th century AD) transformed major aspects of previous Hindu thought.

A number of ideas run like a thread through intellectual and popular Hinduism. One recurring theme is **'vision', 'sight'** or **'view'**. *Darshan* is used to describe the sight of the deity that worshippers hope to gain when they visit a temple or shrine. Equally it may apply to the religious insight gained through meditation or prayer.

Many Hindus also accept that there are **four major human goals**: material prosperity (*artha*), the satisfaction of desires (*karma*), and performing the duties laid down according to your position in life (*dharma*). Beyond those is the goal of achieving liberation from the endless cycle of rebirths into which everyone is locked (*moksha*). It is this search for liberation to which major schools of Indian philosophy have devoted most attention. Together with *dharma*, it is basic to Hindu thought. *Dharma*, an essentially secular concept, represents the order inherent in human life. The *Mahabharata* lists 10 embodiments of *dharma*, including truth, self-control, endurance and continence. These are inseparable from five patterns of behaviour: non-violence, an attitude of equality, peace and tranquillity, lack of aggression and cruelty, and absence of envy.

The idea of *karma*, 'the effect of former actions', is central to achieving liberation. As C. Rajagopalachari put it: "Every act has its appointed effect, whether the act be thought, word or deed. The cause holds the effect, so to say, in its womb. If we reflect deeply and objectively, the entire world will be found to obey unalterable laws. That is the doctrine of karma".

The belief in the transmigration of souls (*samsara*) in a never-ending cycle of rebirth has been Hinduism's most distinctive and important contribution to Indian culture. The earliest reference to the belief is found in one of the *Upanishads*, around the seventh century BC, at about the time when the doctrine of *karma* made its first appearance. Belief in transmigration probably encouraged a further distinctive doctrine, that of non-violence or non-injury (*ahimsa*). The belief in rebirth meant that all living things and creatures of the spirit – people, devils, gods, animals, even worms – possessed the same essential soul.

The abstractions of philosophy do not mean much for the millions of Hindus living across South Asia today, nor have they in the past. The Hindu gods include many whose origins were associated with the forces of nature, and Hindus have revered many natural objects. Mountain tops, trees, rocks and particularly rivers, are all regarded as sites of special religious significance.

In Goa veneration of the *tulsi* (basil plant) is illustrated by the profusion of *tulsi* enclosures in front of houses and in temples. In addition to warding off mosquitoes and being an air purifier the *tulsi* is also effective in warding off death, as an antidote to snake venom. With all these desirable attributes it is not surprising that the herb should play such an important role in Hindu rituals from birth to death.

For most Hindus today, worship (often referred to as 'performing *puja*') is an integral part of their faith. The great majority of Hindu homes will have a shrine to one of the deities. Individuals and families will often visit shrines or temples, and on special occasions will travel long distances to particularly holy places such as Varanasi. Goa's temples similarly are centres of periodic pilgrimage and of special festivals. The popular devotion of simple pilgrims of all faiths in South Asia is remarkably similar when they visit shrines, whether Hindu, Buddhist or Jain temples, the tombs of Muslim saints or even churches. Perhaps Goa's most famous shrine at which both Christians and Hindus worship is at the Church of St Jerome in Mapusa, better known as the Milagres Church, or Our Lady of Miracles.

The Hindu Trinity

Popularly, *Brahma* is interpreted as the creator in a trinity alongside *Vishnu* as preserver and *Siva* as destroyer.

In the early *Vedas* **Brahman** represented the universal and impersonal principle that governed the universe. Gradually, as Vedic philosophy moved towards a monotheistic interpretation of the universe and its origins, this power was personalized. In the *Upanishads* Brahman was seen as a universal and elemental creative spirit. Brahma, described in early myths as having been born from a golden egg and then to have created the earth, assumed the identity of the earlier Vedic deity Prajapati and became identified as the creator. Characteristically he is shown with four faces (each facing a cardinal direction).

It is from Brahma that Hindu cosmology takes its structure. The basic cycle through which the whole cosmos passes is described as one day in the life of Brahma – the *kalpa*. It equals 4,320 million years, with an equally long night. One year of Brahma's life – a cosmic year – lasts 360 days and nights. The universe is expected to last for 100 years of Brahma's life, who is currently believed to be 51 years old.

By the sixth century AD – before the great period of temple building – Brahma worship had effectively ceased. This accounts for the fact that there are remarkably few temples dedicated to Brahma. Goa is thus highly unusual in also having a Brahma temple, at Carambolim. On the other hand, images of Brahma are found in most temples.

Vishnu is seen as the god with the human face, sometimes presented as the god of creation or preservation. From the second century AD a new and passionate devotional worship of Vishnu's incarnation as Krishna developed in South India. By AD 1000 Vaishnavism became closely associated with the devotional form of Hinduism preached by **Ramanuja**, whose followers spread the worship of Vishnu and his 10 successive incarnations (*avatars*) in animal and human form. For Vaishnavites, God took these different forms in order to save the world from impending disaster.

By far the most influential incarnations of Vishnu are those in which he was believed to take human form, especially as **Rama** (twice) and **Krishna**. In the earliest stories about Rama he was not regarded as divine. Although he is now seen as an earlier incarnation of Vishnu than Krishna, he was added to the pantheon very late, probably after the Muslim invasions of the 12th century AD. Rama (or Ram, to rhyme with *calm*) is a powerful figure in contemporary India, and for Goans Parasurama, Vishnu's sixth incarnation, is responsible for the creation of Goa. He freed the world by fighting the all-powerful king of the Kshatriyas. After his triumph he flung his axe from the top of the Sahyadri Range out to sea and commanded the sea to withdraw so that he could perform the most powerful of sacrifices, the Yajna. Goa was thus created as pure, virgin land.

Siva is interpreted as both creator and destroyer, the power through whom the universe evolves. He lives on Mount Kailasa with his wife **Parvati** and two sons, the elephant-headed **Ganesh** and the six-headed **Karttikeya**. Siva is also represented in Shaivite temples throughout India by the *linga*, literally meaning 'sign' or 'mark', but referring in this context to the phallus. The *linga* has become the most important symbol of the cult of Siva. Although Siva is not seen as having a series of rebirths, like Vishnu, he nonetheless appears in very many forms, representing different aspects of his varied powers. In Goa his most common names are Nagesh, Mangesh or Saptakoteshwara. As Betall, who is shown naked with human skulls round his neck and covered in serpents, he is widely feared in Goan villages as having power over evil spirits. Other common names for Siva include **Chandrasekhara**, **Mahadeva** and **Nataraja**, the Lord of the Cosmic Dance. Siva is normally accompanied by his 'vehicle', the bull (*nandi* or *nandin*). **Nandi** is one of the most widespread of sacred symbols of the ancient world and may represent a link with **Rudra**, who was sometimes represented as a bull in pre-Hindu India. Strength and virility are key attributes, and pilgrims to Siva temples often touch the Nandi's testicles on their way into the shrine.

Other Hindu deities

Of thousands of Hindu deities, **Ganesh** is one of Hinduism's most popular gods, seen as the great clearer of obstacles. Shown at gateways and on door lintels, with his elephant head and pot belly, his image is revered across India. Meetings, functions and special family gatherings will often start with prayers to Ganesh, and any new venture, from the opening of a building to the inauguration of a company will not be deemed complete without a Ganesh *puja*.

Sarasvati, Brahma's consort, has survived into the modern Hindu world as a far more important figure than Brahma himself. In popular worship Sarasvati represents the goddess of education and learning, worshipped in schools and colleges with gifts of fruit, flowers and incense. She represents 'the word' itself, which began to be edified as part of the process of the writing of the *Vedas*, which ascribed magical power to words. Normally coloured white, riding on a swan and carrying a book, Sarasvati is often shown playing a *vina*. She may have many arms and heads, representing her role as patron of all the sciences and arts.

Commonly represented as Vishnu's wife, **Lakshmi** is widely worshipped as the goddess of wealth. Earlier representations of Vishnu's consorts portrayed her as **Sridevi**, often shown in statues on Vishnu's right, while **Bhudevi**, also known as Prithvi, who represented the earth, was on his left. Eight forms of Lakshmi are recognized, but she is popularly shown in her own right standing on a lotus flower.

Hindu society

Dharma (see page 246) is seen as the most important aim of individual and social life.

Caste

Although the word caste was given by the Portuguese at the end of the 15th century AD, the main feature of the system emerged at the end of the Vedic period. Two terms – *varna* and *jati* – used in India have come to be used interchangeably and confusingly with the word caste.

Varna, which literally means 'colour', had a four-fold division. By 600 BC it had become a standard means of classifying the population, with the fair-skinned Aryans distinguishing themselves from the darker-skinned earlier inhabitants. The priestly *varna*, the Brahmins, were seen as coming from the mouth of Brahma; the Kshatriyas (or Rajputs as they are commonly called in northwest India) were warriors, coming from Brahma's arms; the Vaishyas, a trading community, came from Brahma's thighs, and the Sudras, classified as agriculturalists, came from his feet. Relegated beyond the pale of civilized Hindu society were the untouchables or outcastes, who were left with the jobs regarded as impure, usually associated with dealing with the dead (human or animal) or with excrement.

Jati is the group into which the great majority of Indians put themselves rather than one of the four *varna* categories. There are thousands of different *jatis* across the country. Many used to be identified with particular activities, and occupations used to be hereditary. Caste membership is now decided by birth. You can be evicted from your caste by your fellow members, usually for disobedience to caste rules such as marriage, but you cannot join another caste; technically, evictees become outcastes.

Gandhi spearheaded his campaign for independence from British colonial rule with a powerful campaign to abolish the restrictions imposed by the caste system. Coining the term *harijan* (meaning 'person of God'), which he gave to all former outcastes, Gandhi demanded that discrimination on the grounds of caste be outlawed. Lists – or 'schedules' – of backward castes were drawn up during the early part of the last century in order to provide positive help to such groups. The term *harijan* itself has now been widely rejected by many former outcastes as paternalistic and as implying an adherence to Hindu beliefs that some explicitly reject. Today, many have adopted the secular term *dalits* or the 'oppressed'.

Since 1947 the Indian government has extended its positive discrimination (a form of affirmative action) to scheduled castes and scheduled tribes, particularly through reserving up to 50% of jobs in government-run institutions and in further education leading to professional qualifications for these groups. Members of the scheduled castes are now found in important positions throughout the economy.

Hindu calendar
While for its secular life, in common with the rest of India, Goa follows the Gregorian calendar, for Hindus much of religious and personal life follows the Hindu calendar. This is based on the lunar cycle of 29 days, but the clever bit comes in the way it is synchronized with the Gregorian solar calendar of the west by the addition of an 'extra month' (*adhik maas*), every two and a half to three years.

Hindu literature
Sanskrit was the first all-India language, and its literature has had a fundamental influence on the religious, social and political life of the entire region. Its early literature was memorized and recited, and it is still impossible to date with any accuracy the earliest Sanskrit hymns. They are in the *Rig Veda*, which probably did not reach its final form until about the 6th century BC, although the earliest parts may go back as far as 1300 BC – approximately the period of the fall of Mycenean Greece in Europe.

The **Rig Veda** is a collection of 1,028 hymns, not all directly religious. Its main function was to provide orders of worship for priests responsible for the sacrifices that were central to the religion of the Indo-Aryans. Two further texts that began to be created towards the end of the period in which the *Rig Veda* was being written down, the *Yajurveda* and the *Samaveda*, served the same purpose. A fourth, the *Atharvaveda*, is largely a collection of magic spells. Central to the Vedic literature was a belief in the importance of sacrifice. At some time after 1000 BC a second category of Vedic literature, the **Brahmanas**, began to take shape. The most famous and important of these were the *Upanishads*, probably written at some time between the seventh and fifth centuries BC.

The Brahmanas gave their name to the religion that emerged between the eighth and sixth centuries BC, Brahmanism, the still-distant ancestor of Hinduism. Two texts from about this period remain the best known and most widely revered epic compositions in South Asia. The **Mahabharata** and the **Ramayana**, are known and loved by Hindus in every town and village in India. Dating the *Mahabharata* is problematic as the details of the great battle recounted within it are unclear. Tradition puts its date at precisely 3102 BC, the start of the present era, and also suggests that the author of the poem was a sage named Vyasa. Evidence suggests, however, that the battle was actually fought around 800 BC, at Kurukshetra. It was another 400 years before priests began to write the stories down, beginning a process that was not complete until AD 400. The *Mahabharata* was probably an attempt by the warrior class, the Kshatriyas, to merge their brand of popular religion with the ideas of Brahmanism. The original version of the *Mahabharata* was probably about 3,000 stanzas long, but it now contains over 100,000 – eight times as long as Homer's *Iliad* and *Odyssey* put together. The Ramayana Valmiki is thought of in India as the author of the second great Indian epic, the *Ramayana*, though no more is known of his identity than is known of Homer's. Like the *Mahabharata*, the text underwent several stages of development before it reached its final version of 48,000 lines.

Sanskrit literature

Sanskrit was always the language of the court and the elite. Other languages replaced it in common speech by the third century BC, but it remained in restricted use for over 1,000 years after that period, essentially as a medium for writing. Sanskrit literature continued to be written long after sanskrit had ceased to be a language of spoken communication. One of the 'nine gems' of Chandragupta II's court, and one of India's greatest poets, **Kalidasa**, contributed to the development of Sanskrit as the language of learning and the arts. Vatsyana's *Kamasutra* not only explores the diversity of physical love but also sheds light on social customs.

Literally 'stories of ancient times', the *Puranas* feature the three major deities, Brahma, Vishnu and Siva. Although some of the stories may relate back to real events that occurred as early as 1500 BC, they were not compiled until the Gupta period in the 5th century AD. The stories are often the only source of information about the period immediately following the early *Vedas*. Each *Purana* concerns the five themes of the creation of the world; its subsequent destruction and recreation; the geneology of the gods; the reigns of the Manus; and the history of the solar and lunar dynasties.

Christianity

Although the Portuguese brought Roman Catholicism to Goa in the 16th century, Christians had probably arrived in India during the first century after the birth of Christ. Until the arrival of the Portuguese most Goans were either Hindu or Muslim. However, within 50 years of the Portuguese arrival, Christian influence became a force to be reckoned with. The Jesuit, St Francis Xavier, landed in Goa in 1542, and in 1557 Goa was made an Archbishopric. Xavier left an indelible imprint on Goa's religious life.

Although Goa remained almost entirely within the Catholic realm the influence of Catholicism varied greatly through time and in different parts of the Portuguese-ruled territory. The Inquisition was directed against the "unholy tendency" of these early converts to retain clandestinely their links with the Hindu faith, but it was unable to change certain phenomena, like caste. The Goan church eventually came to crystallize that institution in the form of the *confrarias*.

The **Inquisition**, which lasted from 1560 to 1812, represented the most intensive, long-term attempt to impose Catholic orthodoxy on the large, newly converted Christian population. Because of the enormous lengths to which the courts of the

Inquisition went to establish any heresy, its effective writ was geographically restricted to the area of closest Portuguese control – the Old Conquests – 'Ilhas' (comprising Tiswadi), Bardez and Salcete (including present-day Mormugao). Every two or three years the Inquisition held great public trials, the *auto-da fé* tests of faith, with executions of those proven to be infidels. Here, not surprisingly, large-scale conversions took place, and this area today retains by far the largest proportion of the Christian population. Today, although Christian services may be held daily in some churches, most Christian congregations in Goa meet for worship on Sunday, and services are held in Konkani and in English. They are open to all.

Islam

Islam reached Goa both by land and sea. Since before the birth of Christ, Goa, along with other ports along the west coast of India, from Surat in the north to Cochin in the south, was on the Arab sea trading route to Southeast Asia and China. When the Arab world converted to Islam in the seventh century AD many of the traders based in these Indian settlements followed suit. However, Goa was never more than a relatively minor port on this route and the size of the Muslim community was much smaller than in Kerala to the south.

Subsequently Islam played a very different part in Goa's history. From the 13th century Turkish power brought Islam to India from the northwest. Mahmud of Ghazni stormed into Punjab, defeating the Rajput rulers in 1192. Within the next 30 years Turkish Muslim power stretched from Bengal in the east to Madurai, in modern Tamil Nadu, in the south. On their way south the Muslims followed the path taken by generations of their predecessors who had migrated into the Deccan (meaning simply 'south'). A chain of Muslim kingdoms was established on the landward side of the Ghats who contested for power with each other and with the Hindu state of Vijayanagar. Some of the Muslim kingdoms retained important links with Persia and with the Arab world, and sea ports on the west coast became an important avenue for military supplies, especially horses, both for the Hindu Vijayanagar Empire and the Muslim courts. Even in the 15th and 16th centuries business was business.

The early Muslim rulers looked to the Turkish ruling class and to the Arab caliphs for their legitimacy, and to the Turkish elite for their cultural authority. From the middle of the 13th century, when the Mongols crushed the Arab caliphate, the Delhi sultans were left on their own to exercise Islamic authority in India, a role which was taken over from the 16th to the 18th centuries by the Mughals who shaped the greatest of the Muslim-led empires.

Muslim beliefs

The beliefs of Islam (which means 'submission to God') could apparently scarcely be more different from those of Hinduism. Islam, often described as having 'five pillars of faith', has a fundamental creed: 'There is no God but God; and Mohammad is the Prophet of God' (*La Illaha illa 'llah Mohammad Rasulu 'llah*). One book, the *Qur'an*, is the supreme authority on Islamic teaching and faith.

Islam preaches the belief in bodily resurrection after death, and in the reality of heaven and hell. Islam has no priesthood. The authority of religious scholars, *Imams*, learned men, judges, and so on, collectively referred to as the *Ulema*, derives from social custom and from their authority to interpret the scriptures, rather than from a defined status within the Islamic community. Islam also prohibits any distinction on the basis of race or colour, and there is a strong antipathy to the representation of the human figure. It is often thought, inaccurately, that this ban stems from the *Qur'an* itself. In fact it probably has its origins in the belief of Mohammad that images were likely to be turned into idols.

Buddhism

Despite its inaccessible location, at least after 250 BC Goa was home to Buddhist communities in the foothills of the Western Ghats. Emperor Asoka is believed to have sent a missionary monk called Dharmarak to the area and another monk named Punna is thought to have preached Buddhism in Zambaulim in Sanguem. Today Buddhism is practised mainly on the margins of the sub-continent, from Ladakh, Nepal and Bhutan in the north to Sri Lanka in the south. Although there are approximately five million Buddhists in Maharashtra, most are very recent outcaste Hindu converts, the last adherents of the early schools of Buddhism having been killed or converted by the Muslim invaders of the 13th century.

Buddhists developed cave sites as monasteries or temples such as at Arvalem in Bicholim, Khandepar in Ponda and Rivona in Sanguem. However, they have none of the exceptional murals and rock carvings found at Ajanta and Ellora in Maharashtra, north of Goa, or in Sigirya in Sri Lanka, and are comparatively small and insignificant. Today there are fewer than 400 Buddhists in the whole of Goa.

Land and environment

By Indian standards Goa is a tiny state. The coastline on which much of its fame depends is only 97 km long. The north and south of the state are separated by the two broad estuaries of the Zuari and Mandovi rivers. Joined at high tide to create an island on which Panjim stands, these short rivers emerge from the high ranges of the Western Ghats less than 50 km from the coast and then glide almost imperceptibly to the sea. On either side of the rivers are extensive tidal marshes, and to north and south a series of minor streams run through flat-bottomed valleys into the sea. From Tiracol in the north to Betul in the south these estuaries provided an important though far from wholly effective defence against invaders. Often overlooked by steep-sided hillocks rising to the flat tops of the laterite plateaus that make up much of the area between the marshes, some of the estuaries contain the last remains of mangrove swamp and its associated ecosystem in western India.

The long sandy beaches, which run for much of the length of both the north and the south coasts, are backed by parallel sets of dunes. Apparently barren and economically useless, the dunes play an important role in the wider ecosystem, providing shelter for housing and transport just inland. The beaches themselves are interrupted at various points by seaward extensions of the laterite plateaus, which sometimes form impressive headlands.

Inland from the coast, Goa occupies a shallow indentation in the Sahyadri Ranges of the Western Ghats. Rising to around 1,000 m along this section of their crest line, the Ghats were developed on the old fault that marked the separation of the Indian Peninsula from the ancient land masses of Gondwanaland – which today have become South Africa, South America and Antarctica. Separated from that great continental land mass less than 100 million years ago, the Indian Peninsula has been pushing northwards ever since. At its northern margins as it thrust under the Tibetan Plateau it was responsible for the creation of the massive mountain wall of the Himalaya. The movement caused huge instability along the northern margins of the peninsula, and earthquakes are frequent in the foothills of the Himalaya themselves. In contrast, the land on which Goa stands is largely stable.

Climate

At a latitude of 15°, North Goa lies well within the tropics. Throughout the year it is warm, but its position on the coast means that it never suffers the unbearable heat of India's northern plains. However, from mid-April until the beginning of the monsoon in mid-June, both the temperature and the humidity rise sharply, making the middle of the day steamy hot and the sand of the beaches almost untouchable. It is the monsoon itself which defines Goa's climate and its seasons, standing like a dividing wall between the heat of early summer and the beautiful warm clear and dry weather of its tropical winter, stretching from October to March.

What makes the Indian **monsoon** exceptional is not its regularity but the depth of moist air that passes over the sub-continent. In an average year Panjim receives around 1,500 mm of precipitation in just six weeks. On the coast this rain often comes as torrential storms accompanied by lashing winds, while up in the cooler air of the Ghats if it is not raining you can usually rely on the hilltops being cloaked in swirling cloud and mist. It's a good time of year for the waterfalls though. While heavy showers persist into August and September, and the high humidity can continue to make life unpleasant, the rainfall drops away and in October most of the state receives less than 100 mm.

Wildlife

Goa has a fascinating range of birds and animals and there are around 48 genera of mammals, 275 genera of birds and 60 genera of reptiles, seven of which are endemic to the Western Ghats. The wildlife sanctuaries are worth visiting, but can be disappointing if you are expecting to see a wide variety of exotic animals.

Mammals

There are several species of **deer**, including the magnificent **sambar** (*Cervus unicolor*). Sambar live on wooded hillsides in groups of up to 10 or so, though solitary animals are also quite common. The much smaller **chital** or spotted deer (*Axis axis*), only about 90 cm tall, are seen in herds of 20 or so in grassy areas.

By far the most visible member of the **oxen** family is the domesticated **water buffalo** (*Bubalus bubalis*), widely seen in the coastal districts. The **Indian bison** or **gaur** (*Bos gaurus*) looks superficially like a large buffalo. The 'state animal' of Goa, this massive animal can be up to 200 cm tall at the shoulder, with a heavy muscular ridge across it. It usually lives in forested uplands. There are large herds in the Bhagwan Mahaveer Sanctuary and as far south as Canacona. Although declining in numbers, **wild boar** are found in the foothills of the Ghats, and have a reputation for causing immense damage to paddy, banana and sugar cane crops.

One of the most important scavengers of the open countryside, the **striped hyena** (*Hyena hyena*) usually comes out at night.

The **sloth bear** (*Melursus ursinus*), lives in broken forest and has been seen in the Cotigao Sanctuary and Surla Ghat. Unkempt and mangy-looking, it has a distinctively long and pendulous lower lip.

The Bhagwan Mahaveer Sanctuary, Goa's largest wildlife park, is reputed to have 18 **panthers** (*Panthera pardus*). A few **tigers** (*Panthera tigris*, or *Vag*) are known to stray in occasionally from neighbouring Karnataka in the summer but are rarely seen. Smaller species of cat include include the **jungle cat** (*Felis chaus*), **leopard cat** (*Felis bengaliensis*), and **small Indian civet** (*Vivirrecula indica*).

The **Indian elephant** (*Elephas maximus*) is not normally found in Goa, though a wild one may occasionally be seen in the Bhagwan Mahaveer Sanctuary or the Bondla National Park when they wander in from neighbouring Karnataka in the summer months.

The **common giant flying squirrel** (*Petaurista petaurista*), which inhabits the Western Ghats, is found around Valpoi and the Bhagwan Mahaveer and Cotigao Sanctuaries. **Palm squirrels** are very common. The five-striped palm squirrel (*Funambulus pennanti*) and the three-striped palm squirrel (*Funambulus palmarum*), both about the same size (30 cm in length, about half of which is tail), look very similar.

In addition to the animals that still live truly in the wild there are many species that have adapted to village and town life. India's various **monkeys** are rare on the coastal strip but inland they are far more common. The **common langur** (*Presbytis entellus*) is a long-tailed monkey with a black face, hands and feet, which lives largely in the forest. The **bonnet macaque** (*Macaca radiata*) is more solid-looking with shorter limbs and a shorter tail, and has the distinctive whorl of longer hairs on the head. All monkeys can be aggressively demanding and are carriers of rabies, so should be kept at a distance.

The two types of **bat** most commonly seen in towns differ enormously in size. The larger is the **flying fox** (*Pteropus giganteus*) with a wing span of 120 cm. They roost in large noisy colonies, often in the middle of towns or villages, where they look like folded umbrellas hanging from the trees. The much smaller **Indian pipistrelle** (*Pipistrellus coromandra*), with a wing span of about 15 cm, is an insect eater.

The **common mongoose** (*Herpestes edwardsi*) lives in scrub and open jungle as well as in gardens and fields. Tawny-coloured with a grey grizzled tinge, it is about 90 cm in length, of which half is pale-tipped tail.

Dolphin spotting is an increasingly popular activity from several points on the Goa coastline, and boat rides are increasingly popular. Both the **long-beaked dolphin** (*Steno spa*) and the **finless black porpoise** (*Neomeris phocaenoides*) are common right along the coast and the endangered **dugong** or sea cow (*Dygong dugon*), rather like a large seal, is also found.

Birds

Like other parts of the Western Ghats and the west coast, Goa has a very rich birdlife. In the towns and villages, one of the most widespread types is the **Pariah kite** (*Milvus migrans*, 65 cm), an all-brown bird with a longish tail. The much more handsome **brahminy kite** (*Haliastur indus*, 48 cm) is also a familiar scavenger, but is largely confined to the waterside. Its chestnut and white plumage is unmistakable. The common **white-backed vulture** (*Gyps bengalensis*, 90 cm) is a heavy-looking, ungainly brown bird with a bare and scrawny head and neck. The **feral pigeon**, or **blue rock dove** (*Columba livia*, 32 cm), is generally a slaty grey in colour and invariably has two dark bars on the wing and a white rump. The **little brown dove** (*Streptopelia senegalensis*, 25 cm) is quite tame and shows little fear of man. It is bluey grey and brown above, with a pink head and underparts, and a speckled pattern on the neck. The **collared dove** (*Streptopelia decaocto*, 30 cm) is common especially in the drier parts of Goa, in gardens and open spaces. It has a distinct half collar on the back of its neck. The **red-vented bulbul** (*Pycnonotus cafer*, 20 cm), a mainly brown bird, can be identified by the slight crest and a bright red patch under the tail. The **common myna** (*Acridotheres tristis*, 22 cm) feeds on lawns, especially after rain. Look for the white under the tail and the bare yellow skin around the eye, yellow bill and legs, and in flight the large white wing patch. A less common, but more striking bird also seen feeding on lawns and in open country is the **hoopoe** (*Upupa epops*, 30 cm), easily identified by its sandy plumage with black and white stripes, and long thin curved bill. The marvellous fan-shaped crest is sometimes raised. Finally there is a member of the cuckoo family which is heard more often than seen. The **koel** (*Eudynamys scolopacea*, 42 cm) is commonly heard in gardens and wooded areas, particularly during the hot weather. The call is a kuoo-kuoo-kuoo.

Goa's marshes form an enormously rich bird habitat. **Cormorants** abound; the most common, the **little cormorant** (*Phalacrocorax niger*, 50 cm), is an almost entirely black bird with just a little white on the throat. It has a long tail and hooked bill, and is seen both on the water and in colonies in waterside trees. The **coot** (*Fulica atra*,

40 cm), another black bird, which has a noticeable white shield on the forehead, is found on open water, especially in winter. The **openbill stork** (*Anastomus oscitans*, 80 cm) and the **painted stork** (*Ibis leucocephalus*, 100 cm) are two of the commonest storks of India. The openbill stork is a white bird with black wing feathers, and a curiously shaped bill. The painted stork is also mainly white, with a pinkish tinge on the back, greenish black marks on the wings and a broken black band on the lower chest. The bare yellow face and yellow down-curved bill are conspicuous. By almost every swamp, ditch or rice paddy up to about 1,200 m you will see the inconspicuous buff-coloured **paddy bird** (*Ardeola grayii*, 45 cm). It is easily overlooked as it stands hunched up by the waterside but as soon as it takes off, its white wings and rump make it very noticeable. Goa is also home to wonderful **kingfishers**. The most widespread of the Indian species is the jewel-like **common kingfisher** (*Alcedo atthis*, 18 cm). With its brilliant blue upperparts and orange breast it is usually seen perched on a twig or a reed beside the water, or as a flash of eye-catching blue in flight. The much larger black and white **pied kingfisher** (*Ceryle rudis*) is adept at fishing from the air and can sometimes be spotted hovering over water.

In the open grassland and cultivated land, the **cattle egret** (*Bubulcus ibis*, 50 cm), a small white heron, is usually seen in small flocks, frequently perched on the backs of cattle. The all-black **drongo** (*Dicrurus adsimilis*, 30 cm) is almost invariably seen perched on telegraph wires or bare branches. Its distinctively forked tail makes it easy to identify. Weaver birds are a family of mainly yellow birds, all remarkable for the intricate nests they build. The most widespread is the **baya weaver** (*Ploceus philippinus*, 15 cm). These birds nest in large colonies, often near villages.

Reptiles and amphibians

India is famous for its reptiles, especially its snakes, which feature in many stories and legends. Despite its small size Goa has its fair share. The dense flora and heavy rainfall of the interior provide a perfect environment for **snakes**. Although about 200 people a year report being bitten in Goa, snakes generally keep out of the way of people.

One of the most common in the well-watered areas of the hills is the **Indian rock python** (*Python molurus*), which is about 4 m in length (and sometimes longer). Pythons are 'constrictors', killing their prey by suffocation. The bright yellow *Dhaman* or *Sodne Nagin*, or **Indian rat snake** (*Pytas musosus*) is often seen in houses. It grows to nearly 3 m and has an unpleasant smell. A common harmless snake in the forests of the foothills is the *Kalinagan*, or **golden tree snake** (*Chrysopelea ornata*), which can be almost black with greenish cross bars. Living on small mammals, geckos, birds and insects, it can swing and 'jump' up to 6 m from tree to tree.

There are several species of the poisonous cobra all of which have a hood, which is spread when the snake draws itself up to strike. The best-known is probably the *Nag*, or **spectacled cobra** (*Naja naja*), which has a mark like a pair of spectacles on the back of its hood. The largest venomous snake in the world is the *Raj Nag*, **king cobra** (*Ophiophagus hannah*), which grows to 5 m in length. It is usually brown, but can vary from cream to black. In their natural state, cobras generally inhabit forests. Equally venomous, but much smaller in size, the *Kaner* or *Maniar*, or **common krait** (*Bungarus caeruleus*), grows to just over 1 m. This is a slender, shiny, nocturnal, blue-black snake with thin yellowish bands across the body. The bands vary from very conspicuous, to almost indiscernible. The smaller and harmless *Pasko*, **kukri snake** (*Oligodon taeniolatus*), common on farmland, is very similar as its markings resemble the krait's bands. Another common non-poisonous snake mistaken for a krait is the *Kaydya*, or **common wolf snake** (*Lycodon aulicus*), which can be found near houses and in gardens. The grey-brown body has 12-19 darker cowrie-shaped markings that resemble the krait's cross bars.

In houses everywhere you cannot fail to see the small harmless **gecko** (*Hemidactylus*) on the wall. At the other end of the scale is the **monitor** (*Varanus*), which can be up to 2 m in length.

The most widespread **crocodile** in India is the **freshwater mugger** or **marsh crocodile** (*Crocodylus palustris*), which grows to 3-4 m in length. The enormous **estuarine** or **saltwater crocodile** (*Crocodylus porosus*), as much as 7 m long, is a much sleeker-looking species than the mugger. It is found in brackish waters and, unlike the rather docile mugger, has an aggressive temperament. Both are found in the wild in Goa, notably in the Cambarjua Canal that separates the island of Tiswadi from Ponda.

Although turtles are commonly found in ponds, ditches and wells, the **sea turtles**, including the **Olive Ridley** (*Lepidochelys olivacea*) which visit certain Goan beaches (Morjim, Calangute and Cabo de Rama among them) between September and February to lay their eggs, are being severely affected. Few baby turtles return to the sea since the eggs are prized as a culinary delicacy. The Forest Department has taken measures to prevent the nests being plundered by villagers.

Vegetation

None of Goa's original vegetation remains untouched. The **mangrove** forests of the tidal marshes have been steadily eroded by the need to drain land for agriculture, while the estuarine waters have been increasingly polluted by mining activity.

Of all Indian trees the **banyan** (*Ficus benghalensis*) is probably the best known. Featured widely in Indian literature, it is planted by temples, in villages and along roads. In a wall, the growing roots will split the wall apart. If it grows in the bark of another tree, it sends down roots towards the ground. As it grows, more roots appear from the branches, until the original host tree is surrounded by a cage-like structure, which eventually strangles it. The largest banyan in Goa is in a *math* (seminary) near the Cotigao Sanctuary. The **pipal**, **casaurina** and **ashok** trees are also varieties seen in Goa.

Goa's economy depends heavily on cashew and coconut, though other trees are also significant. Despite its haphazard cultivation, it is Goa's most important economic crop and the nut is a good foreign exchange earner. The **coconut palm** (*Cocos nucifera*) grows best along the coast and river banks of Goa and is a familiar sight along the country roads of coastal districts. The **areca palm** (*Areca catechu*), also known as betel nut, grows abundantly in the Ponda taluka in particular. The economically valuable **tamarind** (*Tamarindus indica*), which may have originated in Africa, is another handsome roadside tree with a straight trunk and a spreading crown. **Bamboo** (*Bambusa*) – strictly speaking a grass – is also an export crop. Goa has a unique thornless type. The **silk cotton tree** (*Bombax ceiba*), also known as the kapok, can grow to 25 m in height and its fruit produces the fine silky cotton that gives it its name.

The **banana** plant (*Musa*) is actually a gigantic herb arising from an underground stem. The very large leaves grow directly off the trunk which is about 5 m in height. The fruit grows in bunches of up to 100. **Breadfruit** trees are common, as is the **jackfruit, kokum, mango** and **papaya** trees.

Books

The literature on Goa is significant and growing. Most of the material listed here is available in English, though original sources were in some cases in Portuguese. Panjim has a few good shops, including the one at the **Mandovi Hotel** and Varsha near Azad Maidan. In Margao, **Bookmark** opposite Nanutel Hotel, has a wide collection. Mapusa's **Other India Bookshop** prides itself on covering environmental issues. A few suggestions are listed here.

Art and architecture

Archaeological Survey of India, (New Delhi, 1994). A short history and guide to the monuments with a few plans and photos, usually available at the site (Rs 10).

Anand, M R *In praise of Christian Art in Goa*, (Marg, Vol XXXII No 4, Mumbai).

Pereira, J *Baroque Goa, The Architecture of Portuguese Goa*, (Books & Books, New Delhi, 1955). A very detailed and technical analysis.

Pereira, J *Goa Shrines and Mansions*. Knowledgeable account of interesting temples and buildings.

Current affairs and politics

Alvares, C (ed) *Fish, Curry and Rice*, a citizen's report on the Goan environment. (Ecoforum publication, Other India Press, 3rd revised ed, 1995, Mapusa). Full of current environmental information, written from a perspective of continuous moral outrage.

Granta 57 *India: The Golden Jubilee*. Superb edition of the literary magazine devoted to India's 50th anniversary of Independence, 22 international writers give brilliant snapshot accounts of India today.

Silver, R B and Epstein, B *India: a mosaic*, (NYRB, New York, 2000). Distinguished essays on history, politics and literature including Amartya Sen on Tagore, Pankaj Mishra on Nuclear India.

Environment

Alvares, C *Fish Curry & Rice*. A citizen's report on Goa's environment, ecosystems and likelihood for survival.

Hall, R *Empires of the Monsoon: A History of the Indian Ocean And Its Invaders* (Harper Collins, 1998). An all-too vivid record of life on the Indian Ocean rim as tussled over by waves of Portugese, Dutch, British and Arab traders (Hall's bias is for Africa finally, but there is good detail on India too).

Early and colonial history

Basham, A L *The Wonder that was India*, (Sidgwick & Jackson, London, 1985). One of the most comprehensive, readable accounts of the development of India's culture.

Cabral e Sa, M, *Legends of Goa*, (IBH, Mumbai, 1998). A well researched collection.

Keay, J *India: A History*, (Harper Collins, 2000). A major new popular history.

Penrose, B *Goa – Queen of the East*, (Lisbon 1960). The story of Old Goa with interesting illustrations.

Richards, J M *Goa*, (revised ed. Vikas, New Delhi, 1993). A visitor's record of the State's history and culture.

Spear, P and Thapar, R *A History of India*, (2 vols, Penguin, 1978). Compact and authoritative history.

Xavier, P D *Goa: A Social History (1510-1640)*, (Rajhans, Panjim, 1993). Detailed chapters on social structure and institutions with full bibliographies.

Modern history

Couto, M A *Goa: A Daughters Story* (Penguin, 2004). Vividly researched new history of Goa and personal history that will overturn outsiders' assumptions.

Saksena, R N *Goa: into the mainstream*, (Abhinav Publications, New Delhi, 1972). An account of Goa's political integration with India after its incorporation in 1961.

Literature

Jack, I (ed.) *India The Golden Jubilee* (Granta 57, 1997) Contributors to this Indian edition of the literary magazine include Arundhati Roy, RK Narayan, Mark Tully, Vikram Seth plus pages xeroxed from Naipaul's diary.

Mascerenhas, L *In the Womb of Saudade*, (Rupa, 1995). A collection of Goan short stories, illustrated by Mario Miranda.

Menezes, A *Chords and Dischords*. Poems by a Goan writing in English.

Narayan, R K has written many gentle and humourous novels and short stories of South India, including *The Man-eater of Malgudi*, *Under the Banyan Tree and other stories*, and *Grandmother's stories*, among many. Also a 're-telling' of the *Mahabharata*.

Naipaul, VS *India: A Million Mutinies Now*, (1989, rep. Minerva 1991) *A Wounded Civilization* (1975, rep. Picador 2002) and *An Area of Darkness* (1964, rep. Picador 2002). A probing, far-reaching and sometimes depressingly stark trilogy from masterly member of Indian diaspora.

Roy, A *The God of Small Things*, (Indian Ink/Harper Collins, 1997). Booker prize-winning novel about family turmoil in a Syrian-Christian household in Kerala.
Rushdie, S *Midnight's Children*, (Picador, London, 1981). A novel of India since Independence.
Seth, V *A Suitable Boy*, (Phoenix House, London, 1993). Prize-winning novel of modern Indian life.
Shetty, M *Ferry Crossings: Short Stories from Goa*, (Penguin, 1998). A collection of social and political tales.

Music

Cabral e Sa, M *Wind of Fire*, (Promilla, New Delhi, 1997). A full coverage of Goan music and dance.

People and places

Albuquerque, T *Anjuna: Profile of a village in Goa.* (Promilla, New Delhi, 1988). An attractive illustrated account of the history of one of Goa's most famous villages.
Angle, P S *Goa, Concepts and Misconcepts*, (Goa Hindu Association, Mumbai, 1994). An account of Goa's place in modern India emphasising the significance of its Hindu traditions.
Cabral e Sa, M and Da Costa Rodrigues, L B *Great Goans*, (NNAP, Piedade, Goa, 1985). Brief but interesting account of 4 of Goa's major figures: Abbé Faria, Jose Vaz, Lata Mangeshkar, TB Cunha.
Guest, T *My Life In Orange* (Granta, 2004). Interested in gurus and life in the saffron-robed ashrams of Osho? Guest grew up in them and details his unconventional upbringing, along with the unraveling of the cult, with both insight and restraint.
Odzer, C *Goa Freaks: My Hippie Years in India* (Blue Moon Books, 1995). Often frustratingly narcissistic but a good window on the shift in the freak scene of the 1970s and 1980s: Odzer charts its members' gradation from smack to coke and back.
Singh, K S (ed) *People of India Goa*, (Vol XXI, Bombay, Anthropological Survey of India. Popular Prakashan, Mumbai, 1993). A traditional anthropological description of some of the major groups in Goa.

Religion

Gomes Pereira, R *Goa, Volume 1, Hindu Temples and Deities*, translated from the original in Portuguese by Antonio Victor Couto, (Panjim, Printwell, 1978). Detailed listing with some interesting accounts.
Waterstone, R *India, The Cultural Companion*, (Duncan Baird, Winchester, 2002). India's spiritual traditions brought up-to-date; profusely illustrated.

Illustrated books

Cabral e Sa, M *Goa*, (Lustre Press, New Delhi, 1993). Informative; attractive souvenir with colour photos by Jean-Louis Nou.
Hall, M *Window on Goa*, (Quiller Press London, 2nd ed 1995). Probably the best, most comprehensively illustrated text on Goa's religious and secular sights.

Travelogues

Burton RF *Goa and the Blue Mountains* (The Narrative Press, 2001). A different era of travel writing: Burton was stationed in India in the 19th century.
Dalrymple, W *The Age of Kali* (Flamingo, 1999). Wide-ranging travelogue includes masterly reconjuring of Portugese Goa plus a profile of Bombay's first lady of porn and of Bangalore's anti-globalization movement.
Dalrymple, W *White Mughals* (Perennial, 2003). The Nizam of Hyderabad's kingdom lies due east of Goa in Andhra Pradesh. This doorstop of a book is an insightful and painstakingly researched history.

Wildlife and vegetation

Ali, S and Dillon, R S *Handbook of the Birds of India & Pakistan* compact edition, (BNHS, Mumbai).
Bole P V and Vaghini, Y *Field Guide to the Common Trees of India*, (OUP). Good for identifying species.
Nair S M *Endangered Animals of India*, (National Book Trust, New Delhi, 1992). Attractively illustrated slim volume on the species of India's wildlife most at risk and their conservation.
Prater, S H *The book of Indian Animals*, (3rd ed, OUP/BNHS, Mumbai).

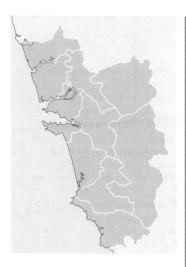

259

Footnotes

Glossary	**260**
Useful words and phrases	**266**
Konkani	266
Hindi	267
Eating out	**269**
Index	**272**
Map index	**276**
Advertisers' index	**276**
Map symbols	**277**
Credits	**278**
About the author	**279**
Acknowledgements	**279**
Complete title listing	**280**
Notes	**282**
Colour maps	**297**

Glossary

A

aarti (arati) Hindu worship with lamps

acharya religious teacher

Adinatha first of the 24 Tirthankaras, distinguished by his bull mount

agarbathi incense

Agni Vedic fire divinity, intermediary between gods and men; guardian of these

agrashala pilgrim resthouse

ahimsa non-harming, non-violence

ambulatory processional path

amrita ambrosia; drink of immortality

Ananta a huge snake on whose coils Vishnu rests

antaralaya vestibule between the temple hall and the sanctuary

apsara celestial nymph

apse semi-circular plan, in a church

architrave horizontal beam across posts or gateways

ardha mandapam chamber in front of main hall of temple

Ardhanarisvara Siva represented as half-male and half-female

Arjuna Hero of the Mahabharata, to whom Krishna delivered the Bhagavad Gita

arrack alcoholic spirit fermented from potatoes or grain

Aruna charioteer of Surya, the Sun God; Red

Aryans lit. 'noble' (Sanskrit); prehistoric peoples who settled in Persia and N India

asana a seat or throne

ashram hermitage or retreat

atman philosophical concept of universal soul or spirit

atrium court open to the sky in the centre in modern architecture, enclosed in glass

avatara incarnation of a divinity

ayah nursemaid, especially for children

B

bagh garden

baksheesh tip

balcao shaded wide veranda of a Goan house

bandh a strike

bandhani tie dyeing (W India, Rajasthan)

bania merchant caste

barrel-vault semi-cylindrical shaped roof or ceiling

Baroque (style) 17th century Italian, bold, exuberant, ornate decoration

bas-relief carving of low projection

basement lower part of walls, usually adorned with decorated mouldings

basti Jain temple

begum Muslim princess; Muslim woman's courtesy title

Bhagavad-Gita Song of the Lord; section of the Mahabharata

bhai brother

Bhairava Siva, the Fearful

bhakti adoration of a god or goddess

bhang Indian hemp

Bharata half-brother of Rama

bhavan building or house

bhumi 'earth'; refers to a horizontal moulding of a shikhara

bidi (beedi) tobacco leaf cigarette

Brahma Universal self-existing power; Creator in the Hindu Triad

Brahman (Brahmin) highest Hindu (and Jain) caste of priests

Brahmanism ancient Indian religion, precursor of modern Hinduism

Buddha The Enlightened One; founder of Buddhism

bund an embankment

burqa an over-dress worn by Muslim women observing purdah

C

cantonment planned military or civil area in town

capital upper part of a column

catamaran log raft, logs (*maram*) tied (*kattu*) together (Tamil)

chai tea

chakra sacred Buddhist wheel of the law; also Vishnu's discus

Chamunda terrifying form of the goddess Durga

Chandra Moon; a planetary deity

charka spinning wheel

charpai '4 legs' – wooden frame string bed

chattra ceremonial umbrella on stupa

chaudi town square

chaukidar night-watchman; guard
chauth 25% tax raised for revenue by Marathas
chhatri umbrella shaped dome or pavilion
choli blouse
chowk (chauk) a block; open place in a city where the market is held
circumambulation clockwise movement around a shrine
clerestory upper section of the walls of a building which allows light in
Communidade village assembly
corbel horizontal block supporting a vertical structure or covering an opening
cornice horizontal band at the top of a wall
crenellated having battlements
crore 10 million
cruzado Portuguese gold coin
cupola small dome

D

daal lentils, pulses
dado part of a pedestal between its base and cornice
dahi yoghurt
dais raised platform
dak post
dak bungalow rest house for officials
dargah a Muslim tomb complex
darshan (darshana) viewing of a deity
darwaza gateway, door
Dasara 10-day festival (Sep-Oct)
deepmal (deepstambha) temple lamp tower
Devi Goddess; later, the Supreme Goddess
dhansak Parsi dish made with lentils
dharamshala (dharamsala) pilgrims' rest-house
dharma moral and religious duty
dhobi washerman
dholi swinging chair on a pole
dhoti loose loincloth worn by Indian men
digambara lit. 'sky-clad'; Jain sect in which the monks go naked
dikpala guardian of one of the cardinal directions mostly appearing in a group of 8
Diwali festival of lights (Oct-Nov)
dosa thin pancake
dupatta long scarf worn by Punjabi women
Durga principal goddess of the Shakti cult
durwan watchman
dwarpala guardian deities at temple doorways (on silver doors of sanctuary)

E

ek the number 1, a symbol of unity

F

faience coloured tilework, earthenware or porcelain
festa Christian saint's day
feni spirit distilled from palm sap or juice of the cashew apple
fidalgo Upper class Portuguese noble
finial emblem at the summit of a stupa, tower, dome, or at the end of a parapet

G

gaddi throne
gadi/gari car, cart, train
Gandharva semi-divine flying figure; celestial musician
Ganesh (Ganapati) elephant-headed son of Siva and Parvati
Ganga goddess personifying Ganga river
garbagriha a temple sanctuary
garh fort
Garuda Mythical eagle, half-human, Vishnu's vehicle
Gaunkar settler in Goan village
ghat hill range, hill road; landing place; steps on the river bank
ghazal Urdu lyric poetry/love songs
ghee clarified butter for cooking
giri hill
godown warehouse
Gopala (Govinda) cowherd; a name of Krishna
Gopis cowherd girls; milk maids who played with Krishna
gopuram lit. 'cow gate'; gateway tower in Hindu temple
gram chick pea, pulse
gulal red colour (powder) thrown when celebrating Shigmo
gumbaz (gumbad) dome
gur palm sugar
guru teacher; spiritual leader, Sikh religious leader

H

Haj (Hajj) annual Muslim pilgrimage to Mecca
halwa a special sweet meat

Hanuman Monkey devotee of Rama; bringer of success to armies

harem women's quarters (Muslim), from 'haram', Arabic for 'forbidden by law'

Hari Vishnu Harihara, Vishnu- Siva as a single divinity

Hasan the murdered eldest son of Ali, commemorated at Muharram

hat (haat) market

hathi (hati) elephant

hidalgo Portuguese nobleman

Hiranyakashipu Demon king killed by Narasimha

Holi spring festival (Feb-Mar)

hookah 'hubble bubble' or smoking vase

hundi temple offering

Hussain the second murdered son of Ali, commemorated at Muharram

---

I

Id principal Muslim festivals

Idgah open space for the Id prayers

idli steamed rice cake (Tamil)

imam Muslim religious leader

imambara tomb of a Shiite Muslim holy man; focus of Muharram procession

Indra King of the gods; God of rain; guardian of the East

Ishana Guardian of the North East

Ishvara Lord; Siva

J

jaggery brown sugar, made from palm sap

jali any lattice or perforated pattern

jamb vertical side slab of doorway

Jami masjid (Jama, Jumma) Friday mosque, for congregational worship

jataka stories accounts of the previous lives of the Buddha

jaya stambha victory tower

-ji (jee) honorific suffix added to names out of reverence and/or politeness; also abbreviated 'yes' (Hindi/Urdu)

Jina lit. 'victor'; spiritual conqueror or Tirthankara, after whom Jainism is named

---

K

Kailasa mountain home of Siva

Kali lit. 'black'; terrifying form of the goddess Durga, wearing a necklace of skulls/heads

Kalki future incarnation of Vishnu on horseback

kalyanmandapa marriage hall

kameez women's shirt

kapok the silk cotton tree

karma impurity resulting from past misdeeds

Kartikkeya/Kartik Son of Siva, God of war

keystone central wedge-shaped block in a masonry arch

khadi woven cotton cloth made from home-spun cotton (or silk) yarn.

khana suffix for room/office/place; also food or meal

kharif monsoon season crop

Krishna 8th incarnation of Vishnu

kshatriya Hindu warrior caste, second after brahmins

Kubera Chief yaksha; keeper of the treasures of the earth, Guardian of the North

kumar a young man

Kumari Virgin; Durga

kumbha a vase-like motif, pot

kumhar (kumar) potter

kund lake, well or pool

kurta Punjabi shirt

kutcha (cutcha) raw; crude; unpaved; built with sun-dried bricks

---

L

lakh 100,000

Lakshmana younger brother of Rama

Lakshmi Goddess of wealth and good fortune, consort of Vishnu

lathi bamboo stick with metal bindings, used by police

lingam (linga) Siva as the phallic emblem

Lingaraja Siva worshipped at Bhubaneswar

lintel horizontal beam over doorway

lunette semicircular window opening

lungi loin cloth, normally checked

M

madrassa Islamic theological school

maha great

Mahabharata Sanskrit epic about the battle between the Pandavas and Kauravas

Mahadeva lit. 'Great Lord'; Siva

mahal palace, grand building

mahamandapam large enclosed hall in front of main shrine

maharaja great king

maharani   great queen

maharishi   (Maharshi) lit. 'great teacher'

Mahavira   lit. 'Great Hero'; last of the 24 Tirthankaras, founder of Jainism

Mahayana   form of Buddhism practised in East Asia, Tibet and Nepal

Mahisha   Buffalo demon killed by Durga

Maitreya   the future Buddha

makara   crocodile-shaped mythical creature symbolizing the river Ganga

makhan   butter

mandala   geometric diagram symbolizing the structure of the universe

mandapa   columned hall preceding the temple sanctuary

mandir   temple

mangesh   a form of Siva in Goa

Manueline   after King Manuel (1495-1521), ornate entrances and twisted piers often seen in Portuguese churches

Marathas   17th/18th century Maharash-trian power which challenged the Mughals and the British for supremacy in India

marg   wide roadway

masjid   lit. 'place of prostration'; mosque

mata   mother

math   Hindu religious seminary

maund   measure of weight, 40 seers

maya   illusion

memsahib   married European woman, term used mainly before Independence

Mestiços   of Portuguese-Indian parentage

mihrab   niche in the western wall of mosque

mitthai   Indian sweets

Mohammad   'the praised'; The Prophet; founder of Islam

moksha   salvation, enlightenment

mridangam   musical instrument, barrel-shaped drum

mudra   symbolic hand gesture

Muharram   period of mourning in remembrance of Hasan and Hussain, two murdered sons of Ali

Mulattos   of Portuguese-African parentage

mullah   religious teacher (Muslim)

N

Naga   (nagi/nagini) Snake deity; associated with fertility and protection

nagar khana   drum house; arched structure or gateway for musicians (also naubat khana)

nagara   city, sometimes capital

nallah   (nullah) ditch, channel

namaaz   Muslim prayers, worship

namaste   common Hindu greeting (with joined palms) translated as: 'I salute all divine qualities in you'

Nandi   a bull, Siva's vehicle and a symbol of fertility

Narayana   Vishnu as the creator of life

nata mandapa   (nat-mandir; nritya sala) dancing hall in a temple

Nataraja   Siva, Lord of the cosmic dance

natya   the art of dance

navagraha   9 planets, represented usually on the lintel or architrave of the front door of a temple

Navaratri   lit. '9 nights'; name of the Dasara festival

nawab   prince, wealthy Muslim, sometimes used as a title

nirvana   enlightenment; lit. 'extinguished'

niwas   small palace

P

padma   lotus flower, Padmasana, lotus seat; posture of meditating figures

paisa   (poisa) one hundredth of a rupee

palanquin   (palki) covered litter for one, carried on poles

pan   leaf of the betel vine; sliced areca nut, lime and other ingredients wrapped in leaf for chewing

panchayat   a 'council of 5; a government system of elected councils

pandal   marquee made of bamboo and cloth

pandit   teacher or wise man; Sanskrit scholar

pankah (punkha)   fan

parapet   wall extending above the roof

Parinirvana   the Buddha's state prior to nirvana, shown usually as a reclining figure

parishads   political division of group of villages

Parsi (Parsee)   Zoroastrians who fled Iran to W India in the 9th century to avoid persecution

parterre   level space in a garden occupied by flower-beds

Parvati   daughter of the Mountain; Siva's consort

Pashupati   lit. 'Lord of the Beasts'; Siva

pediment   mouldings, often in a triangular formation above an opening or niche

peon   servant, messenger (from Portuguese *peao*)

piazza cross cross in the church square

pice (old form) 1/100th of a rupee

pietra dura inlaid mosaic of hard, semi-precious stones

pilaster ornamental small column, with capital and bracket

pipal Ficus religiosa, the Bodhi tree

pir Muslim holy man

praça open square/area in a town

pradakshina patha processional passage

prasadam consecrated temple food

puja ritual offerings to the gods; worship (Hindu)

pujari worshipper; one who performs puja

pukka lit. 'ripe' or 'finished'; reliable

Puranas lit. 'the old'; Sanskrit sacred poems

purdah seclusion of Muslim women from public view (lit. 'curtains')

purnima full moon

Q

qibla direction for Muslim prayer

Quran holy Muslim scriptures

R

rabi winter/spring season crop

Radha Krishna's favourite consort

raj rule or government

raja king, ruler

Rajput dynasties of western and central India

Rama Seventh incarnation of Vishnu

Ramayana Sanskrit epic; the story of Rama

Ramazan (Ramadan) Muslim month of fasting

rani queen

rath chariot or temple car

Ravana Demon king of Lanka; kidnapper of Sita

reredos screen behind an altar

rickshaw 3-wheeled bicycle-powered (or 2-wheeled hand-powered) vehicle

rishi 'seer'; inspired poet, philosopher

rupee unit of currency in India

S

sabha columned hall (sabha mandapa, assembly hall)

sacristy place in church where vestments and vessels are kept

sadar (sadr/saddar) chief, main

sadhu ascetic; religious mendicant, holy man

sahib title of address, like 'sir'

Saiva (Shaiva) the cult of Siva

sal hardwood tree of the lower slopes of Himalayan foothills

salaam lit. 'peace'; greeting (Muslim)

salwar (shalwar) loose trousers (Punjab)

samadhi lit. 'concentrated thought', 'meditation'; a funerary memorial

sambar lentil and vegetable soup dish, accompanying main meal (Tamil)

samsara transmigration of the soul

sanyasi wandering ascetic; final stage in the ideal life of a man

saranghi small 4-stringed viola shaped from a single piece of wood

Saraswati wife of Brahma and goddess of knowledge

sarod Indian stringed musical instrument

sarvodaya uplift, improvement of all

sati (suttee) a virtuous woman; later applied to the act of self-immolation on a husband's funeral pyre

Sati wife of Siva who destroyed herself by fire

satyagraha 'truth force'; passive resistance

seer (ser) unit of weight equal to about 1 kg

sepoy (sepai) Indian soldier, private

seva voluntary service

Shakti Energy; female divinity often associated with Siva

shamiana cloth canopy

Shankara Siva

sharia corpus of Muslim theological law

shastras ancient texts setting norms of conduct for temple architecture

shastri religious title (Hindu)

shehnai (shahnai) Indian wind instrument similar to an oboe

Shesha (Sesha) serpent who supports Vishnu

shikhara (sikhara) curved temple tower or spire

shloka (sloka) Sanskrit sacred verse

shri (sri) honorific title, often used for 'Mr'; repeated as sign of great respect

sindur vermilion powder often used in temple ritual

singh (sinha) lion; also Rajput caste name adopted by Sikhs

Sita Rama's wife, heroine of the Ramayana

sitar classical Indian stringed musical instrument with a gourd for soundbox

Siva The Destroyer among Hindu gods

Sivaratri lit. 'Siva's night'; festival (Feb-Mar) dedicated to Siva

soma sacred drink mentioned in the Vedas

stambha free-standing column or pillar, often with lamps or banners

stucco plasterwork

sudra lowest of the Hindu castes

Sulabh washed clean (toilets with attendants)

sultan Muslim prince

Surya Sun; Sun God

svami (swami) holy man; also used as a suffix for temple deities

svastika (swastika) auspicious Hindu/Buddhist emblem

swadeshi homemade goods

swaraj home rule

swatantra freedom

syce groom, attendant who follows a horseman or carriage

T

tabla a pair of drums

tahsildar revenue collector

takht throne

Taluk (a) administrative subdivision

tamasha spectacle, festive celebration

tandava dance of Siva

tank lake created for irrigation; in temple architecture a masonry-lined body of water, often with stepped sides

tapas (tapasya) ascetic meditative self-denial

tempera distemper; method of mural painting by means of a 'body,' such as white pigment

tempo 3 wheeler vehicle

terracotta burnt clay used in building

thali South Indian vegetarian meal

tiffin snack, light meal

tika (tilak) vermilion powder applied by Hindus to the forehead as a symbol of the divine; auspicious mark on the forehead; now often simply decorative

tikka tender pieces of meat, marinated and barbecued

tirtha (teertha) sacred water

Tirthankara the title given to 24 religious teachers worshipped by Jains

topi (topee) pith helmet

torana gateway with two posts linked by architraves

Trimurti Triad of Hindu divinities, Brahma,

trisul the trident chief symbol of the god Siva

tulsi sacred basil plant

tulsi vrindavan basil enclosure

tympanum triangular space within the cornices of a pediment

U

Uma Siva's consort

untouchable 'outcastes', with whom contact of any kind was believed by high caste Hindus to be defiling

Upanishads ancient Sanskrit philosophical texts, part of the Vedas

ur village (Tamil)

ustad master

uttarayana northwards

V

vaddo (wado) ward, village 'area'

vaisya the 'middle-class' caste of merchants and farmers

Valmiki sage, author of the Ramayana epic

Vamana dwarf incarnation of Vishnu

Varaha boar incarnation of Vishnu

varna 'colour'; social division of Hindus into Brahmin, Kshatriya, Vaishya and Sudra

Varuna Guardian of the west, accompanied by Makara (see above)

vault arched roof (wood, stone or brick)

Vayu Guardian of the northwest; wind

Veda (Vedic) oldest known Hindu religious texts

Vedanta the final parts of the Vedic literature

veranda enlarged porch in front of a hall

vilas house or pleasure palace

vimana towered sanctuary containing the cell in which the deity is enshrined

vina (veena) plucked stringed instrument

Vishnu one of the principal Hindu deities; the creator and preserver of universal order

vyala leogryph, lion-like sculpture

W

-wallah suffix often used with a occupational name, eg rickshaw-wallah

Footnotes Glossary

Y

yagasala hall where sacred fire is maintained and worshipped; also place of sacrifice

yagya (yajna) major ceremonial sacrifice

Yaksha (Yakshi) a demi-god, associated with nature in folk religion

yali hippopotamus-like creature depicted in the ornamentation of Chalukyan temples

Yama God of death, judge of the living; guardian of the south

yantra magical diagram used in meditation; machine

yatra (jatra) pilgrimage

yoni a hole in a stone, symbolising the vagina or female sexuality

Z

zenana segregated women's apartments

Useful words and phrases

Konkani

Travellers in the 'tourist' areas of Goa can quite easily get by without any knowledge of Konkani or Hindi. Learning and using a few local words, as needed, when visiting a foreign country, is always received warmly.

Pronunciation

ā as in ah   ī as in bee
ō as in oh   u as oo in book
ū as in hub

t and d are usually soft (dental) eg dī as in thee
j is often pronounced like z
Nasalized vowels are shown as aṅ, iṅ, eṁ, etc. Place names often end with a nasal vowel eg Pernem.
NB these marks to help with pronunciation do not appear in the main text.

General

Hello	Hullo
How are you? (m)	Tuṅ kosso assa?
How are you? (f)	Tuṅ kosheaṁ (girl)/ koshi (woman) assi?
My name is...	Mhūjem nāoṅ...
Cheers!	Viva!
Goodbye	Bareṁ!/ Adeūs!
Pardon?	Kite-m mhalle-m?
Sorry	Tchūk zāli
Thankyou	Deo bareṁ korūn/obrigād
May I take a photo?	Photo kadum?
Yes/no	Hoi/Na
clean	līmp/sāf
closed	bandh

dirty	sooj
drink	pio-mche-m̄/pioṅk
food	khāneṁ
fruit	pholl
cashew	kazū
coconut	nāll
green coconut	ādsar
mango	ambō
orange	laranja
pineapple	ananas
good	bare-m
hot (temp)	hūṅ
hot (spicy)	tikh
shop	dūkāṅ
water	ūdak

Health

medicine	awkhad
Please get a doctor	Matso dotorac affoi
I have a fever	Mhaka zor āila
I feel unwell	Haoṅ baro nā
I have a stomach ache	Marjay pottan charpta
I have diarrhoea	Maka bhairī zalya

Hotel

I want a room please	Mhaka yek room zai mellat

...with a toilet	Rooman mhaka toilet zai
What is the room rate?	Roomachem̄ bhade-m kitte-m?
I'd like to see it	Mhaka room dekhūn zai
...larger room	...whodlō room
Please clean the room	Matso room sāf kor
There is no hot water/soap	Rooman gorom udak/sabu nā

Restaurant

Menu please	Matso menū dī
Bill please	Matshe-m bill dī
I'll have this	Haon̄ hem̄khatan̄
A bottle of water	Ūdkachi yek bātli
No chillies please	Mhaka tikh naka
No ice/sugar please	burf/sākhar naka
Sugar and milk please	Matsi sākhar āni dūdh dī
Spoon/fork/knife	tchomchō/kanttō/sourī

Shopping

How much is this?	Yay kitlay poishay?
I'll have this	Haon̄ hem̄ghetan̄
Too much	Ekdom mharaog
Make it cheaper	Matshemūnnay kor
I don't want it	Mhaka naka tem̄

Travel

I need a taxi	Mhaka taxi zāi
Can I share a taxi?	Taxi bhāgak korun̄ya?
How much to Colva?	Colwa kitlay podtollay?
Where is the bus station?	Bus station khain̄ assa?
Next bus?	Dusri bus kenna?

How far is Panjim?	Ponn̄ji kithli poiss assa?
How long will it take?	Kithlō wogauth?
I want to hire a cycle	Mhaka yek cycle bhadyak zai

Time and day

now	attan̄ts
morning	sakāl
afternoon	donpara
evening	sānz
night	rāt
at night	rātin̄
today	āz
tomorrow	fālya-m
yesterday	kāl
Sunday	Āi-tār
Monday	Somār
Tuesday	Mungllār
Wednesday	Būdhwār
Thursday	Birestār
Friday	Sūkrār
Saturday	Shenwār

Numbers

1	yek
2	dōn
3	tin
4	chār
5	pānts
6	so
7	sāt
8	ātth
9	nnov
10	dhā
20	wiss
100	shumber
1,000	hazār

Hindi (for use outside Goa)

Pronunciation

ā as in **ah**	ī as in **bee**
ō as in **oh**	u as oo in **book**

Nasalized vowels are shown as a**n**, i**n** etc
NB these marks to help with pronunciation do not appear in the main text.

Basic vocabulary

These are used locally but often pronounced differently (eg daktar, haspatāl): airport, bank, bathroom, bus, doctor, embassy, ferry, hotel, hospital, juice, police, restaurant, station, stamp, taxi, ticket, train.

General

Hello, goodbye	namaste
Thankyou	dhanyavād or shukriyā
No thankyou	nahīn'shukriyā
Excuse me, sorry	māf kījiye
Yes/no	jī hān/jī nahīn
That's all right	koī bāt nahīn
What is your name?	āpkā nām kyā hai?
My name is...	merā nām...hai
Do you speak English?	āp kō angrezī ātī hai?
a little	thorī-sī
Pardon?	phir batāiye
How are you?	kyā hāl hai?
I am well, thanks, and you?	main thīk hūn, aur āp?
Not very well	main thīk nahīn hūn
Where is the...	...kahān hai?
What is this?	yeh kyā hai?

Shopping

How much is this?	iskā kyā dām hai?
That is very expensive!	bahut mahangā hai!
Make it a bit cheaper	thorā kam kījiye!

Hotel

What is the room charge?	kirāyā kitnā hai?
Please show the room	kamrā dikhāiye
Is there an air-conditioned room?	kyā a/c kamrā hai?
Is there hot water?	kyā kamre men garam pānī hai?
...a bathroom/fan/mosquito net?	...bathroom/pankhā/machhar dānī?
Is there a larger room?	barā kamrā hai?
It's not clean	sāf nahīn hai
Please clean it	sāf karwā dījiye
Are there clean sheets/blankets?	sāf chādaren/ambal hain?
This is OK	yah thīk hai
Bill please	bill dījiye

Travel

Where's the railway station?	railway station kahān hai?
How much is a ticket to Agra?	Agra kā ticket kitne ka hai?
When does the Agra bus leave?	Agra bus kab jāegī?
How much?	kitnā?
Is it far?	bahut door hai?
left/right	bāien/dāhinā
go straight on	sīdhā chaliye
Is it near the station?	station ke pās hai?
Please come at 8	āth bajai ānā
stop	rukiye

Restaurants

Please show the menu	menu dikhāiye
No chillies please	mirch nahīn dālnā
...sugar/milk/ice	chīnī/doodh/baraf
A bottle of water please	ek botal pānī dījiye
sweet/savoury	mīthā/namkīn
spoon/fork/knife	chamach/kāntā/chhurī

Time

now	abhī
morning	suba
afternoon	dopahar
evening	shām
night	rāt
today	āj
tomorrow/yesterday	kal

Sunday	ravivār
Monday	somvār
Tuesday	mangalvār
Wednesday	budhvār
Thursday	vīrvār
Friday	shukravār
Saturday	shanivār

Numbers

1	ek
2	dō
3	tīn
4	chār
5	pānch
6	chhai
7	sāt
8	āth
9	nau
10	das
20	bīs
100	sau
1,000	hazār

Eating out

Eating out in India is normally cheap and safe, but menus can be dauntingly long and full of unfamiliar names. North Indian dishes are nearly universal. Outside their home states, regional dishes are normally only served in specialist restaurants.

Pronunciation
ā as in ah   ī as in bee
ō as in oh   u as oo in book
Nasalized vowels are shown as an, in etc
NB these marks to help with pronunciation do not appear in the main text.

Useful words in Konkani

Goan dishes
Ambok tik A hot, cour tamarind and chilli curry made with shark, squid or ray and eaten with rice.
Apa de camarão A spicy prawn pie with rice flour crust.
Balchão Prawn, king fish or meat in a red chilli and onion sauce served with bread.
Cafrial Meat marinated in pepper and garlic and braised over a slow fire.
Caldo/Caldinha Delicately spiced light fish and vegetable soup.
Chouriço Goan pork sausage boiled or fried with onions, chillis and feni, often eaten stuffed in bread.
Feijoada Haricot bean (feijão) stew; sometimes served with chouriço.
Guisado Tomato-based soup.
Kishmaur Ground, dried shrimp mixed with shredded coconut and chopped onion, served as an accompaniment.
Recheiado Whole fish stuffed with a hot masala sauce.
Seet corri Fish curry with coconut rice.
Sorpotel A highly spiced dish of pickled pig's liver and heart, seasoned with vinegar and tamarind. Perhaps the most famous of Goan meat dishes!
Soupa de carna Spicy soup made with meat and rice stock.
Vindaloo Spicy pork or beef, marinated in garlic, wine vinegar and chillis. Elsewhere in India, *vindaloo* often refers to a hot, spicy curry.
Xacutti 'Shakooti': Hot chicken or meat dish prepared with coconut, pepper and star anise (fr chacontine).

Goan bread
Goan bread is good and there are tasty European-style biscuits.
Kankonn Hard and crispy and shaped like a bangle; often dunked in tea.
Pāo Crusty bread rolls, soft inside.
Pollee Like a chapatti; often stuffed with vegetables.
Sannan Goan version of idli made with ground rice, coconut and fermented palm sap (toddy).
Undo A had crust round bread.

Goan sweets
Sweets are sometimes too sweet for the western palate.
Alebele A sweet pancake with a coconut filling.
Bebinca A layered coconut pancake and jaggery delicacy made with egg yolks, coconut milk, sugar, nutmeg and ghee.
Doce Fudge-like sweet made with nuts, chickpeas and milk.
Dodol A mix of jaggery and coconut with rice floud/semolina and cashew.
Neuro Semi-circular pastry.

Useful words in Hindi

Aloo Potato
Baingan Aubergine
Band gōbi Cabbage
Bhindi Okra, ladies' fingers
Dal Lentils, beans
Ghee Clarified butter
Gājar Carrots
Gosht, mas Meat, usually mutton
Jhinga Prawns
Khumbhi Mushroom
Lauki Green gourd
Macchli Fish
Mackkhan Butter
Matar Peas
Murgh Chicken
Panīr Drained curds
Piāz Onion

Phool gōbi Cauliflower
Sabzī Vegetables
Sāg Spinach
Saym Green beans

Methods of preparation

Many items on restaurant menus are named according to well-known methods of preparation, roughly equivalent to terms such as *Provençal* or *saute*.
Bhoona In a thick, fairly spicy sauce.
Dopiaza With onions (added twice during cooking).
Jhalfrazi Spicy, hot sauce with tomatoes and chillis.
Kebab Skewered (or minced and shaped) meat or fish; a dry, spicy dish cooked on a fire.
Kima Minced meat (usually mutton).
Kofta Minced meat or vegetable balls.
Korma In a fairly mild rich sauce using cream or yoghurt.
Madras Hot.
Makhani In butter-rich sauce.
Masala Marinated in spices (fairly hot).
Mughlai Rich north Indian style.
Nargisi Dish using boiled eggs.
Peshwari Rich with dried fruits and nuts (northwest Indian).
Tandoori Baked in a tandoor (special clay oven) or one imitating it.
Tikka Marinated meat pieces, baked quite dry.
Vindaloo Hot and sour Goan meat dish using vinegar.

Ordering a meal

A thali, for which you might pay Rs 20 (in small dhabas) to Rs 50, is usually the cheapest way of eating; the menu is usually fixed but refills are normally offered. You will be expected to eat with your fingers although a spoon is usually available. When ordering from the menu, you might like to try some bread and/or rice, a vegetable and/or meat curry, bhaji, dal, raita and papad. It is perfectly acceptable to order as little as some bread or rice and a vegetable dish or dal. Sweets are an extra. Gulab jamun, rashmalai and kulfi are popular.

Typical dishes
Aloo gobi Dry potato and cauliflower with cumin.
Aloo, matar, kumbhi Potatoes, peas, mushrooms in a dryish mildly spicy sauce.
Bhindi bhaji Lady's fingers fried with onions and mild spices.
Dal makhani Lentils cooked with butter.
Dum aloo Potato curry with a spicy yoghurt, tomato and onion sauce.
Kima mattar Mincemeat with peas.
Matar panir Curd cheese cubes with peas and spices (and often tomatoes).
Nargisi kofta Boiled eggs covered in minced lamb and cooked in a thick sauce.
Rogan josh Rich mutton/beef pieces in a creamy red sauce.
Sag panir (palak panir) Drained curd sautéd with chopped spinach in mild spices.

Rice
Biriyani Partially cooked rice layered over meat and baked with saffron.
Chawal Plain boiled rice.
Pulao/pilau Fried (and then boiled) rice cooked with spices (cloves, cardamom, cinnamon) and dried fruit, nuts or vegetables. Sometimes cooked with meat, like a biriyani.

Roti – bread
Chapati (phoolka, roti) Thin, plain whole-meal unleavened bread cooked on a *tawa* (griddle), usually made from *ata* (wheatflour).
Nan Oven-baked (traditionally in a tandoor) white flour leavened bread often large and triangular; sometimes stuffed with almonds and dried fruit.
Paratha Fried bread layered with ghee (sometimes cooked with egg or stuffed with potatoes).
Poori Thin deep-fried, puffed rounds of flour.

Accompaniments
Achar Pickles (usually spicy and preserved in oil).
Chutni Often fruit or tomato, freshly prepared, sweet and mildly spiced.
Dahi Plain yoghurt.
Papad, pappadom Deep-fried, pulse flour wafer rounds.
Raita Yoghurt with shredded cucumber, pineapple or other fruit, or *bundi* (tiny batter balls).

Sweets

These are often made with reduced/thickened milk, drained curd cheese or powdered lentils and nuts. They are sometimes covered with a flimsy sheet of decorative, edible silver leaf.

Barfi Fudge-like rectangles/diamonds.

Khir, payasam, paesh Thickened milk rice/vermicelli pudding.

Gubal jamun Dark fried spongy balls, soaked in syrup.

Halwa Rich sweet made from cereal, fruit, vegetable, nuts and sugar.

Kulfi Cone-shaped Indian ice-cream with pistachios/almonds, uneven in texture.

Jalebi Spirals of fried batter soaked in syrup.

Laddoo Lentil-based batter 'grains' shaped into orange rounds.

Rashgulla (roshgulla) Balls of curd in a clear syrup.

Rasmalai Spongy curd rounds, soaked in sweetened cream and garnished with pistachio nuts.

Snacks

Bhaji, pakora Vegetable fritters (onion, potatoes, cauliflower, aubergine etc) deep-fried in batter.

Chat Sweet and sour cubed fruit and vegetables flavoured with tamarind paste and chillies.

Chana choor, chioora ('Bombay mix') Lentil and flattened rice snacks mixed with nuts and dried fruit.

Dosai South Indian pancake with rice and lentil flour; served with a mild potato and onion filling (*masala dosai*) or without (*ravai* or plain *dosai*).

Idli Steamed south Indian ricecakes, a bland breakfast food given flavour by its spiced accompaniments.

Kachori Fried pastry rounds stuffed with spiced lentil/peas/potato filling.

Samosa (bengali shingara) Cooked vegetable or meat wrapped in pastry circles into triangles and deep fried.

Vadai Deep-fried, small savoury lentil doughnut rings. *Dahi vada* are similar rounds in yoghurt.

Drinks

Chai Tea boiled with milk and sugar.

Doodh Milk.

Kafi Ground fresh coffee boiled with milk and sugar.

Lassi North Indian cool drink made with yoghurt and water, salted or sweetened.

Nimboo pani Refreshing drink made with fresh lime and water, chilled bottled water, added salt and sugar syrup. Avoid ice! Also fresh lime soda.

Pani Water.

Index

A

Abbé Faria 62
accommodation 35
acknowledgements 280
activities 43
Adil Shah 115
Agapur 171
Agonda 154
  sleeping 159
  transport 162
Agonda 154
Aihole 226
air 22, 29
  internal flights 75
  airport 128
  airport information 24
  airport tax 25
Albuquerque
  Mansion 116
Albuquerque,
  Afonso de 239
ambulance 25
amphibians 255
animals 253
Anjuna 112, 114
  activities 121
  background 112
  directory 122
  eating 120
  nightlife 121
  shopping 121
  sleeping 119
Arambol 123
  activities 132
  directory 132
  eating 131
  nightlife 131
  sleeping 129
  transport 132
architecture 243
areca palm 256
Arossim 141
  Goa 141
  sleeping 146
Arpora 99
  activities 111
  nightlife 108
  shopping 109
  sleeping 104
Arvalem 182
  festivals 183
Assolna 152
Asvem 124
  eating 131
ATMs 21
author 280
auto-rickshaw 31
ayurveda 43
Azad Maidan 63

B

background 237
Badami 228
  eating 234
  sleeping 233
  transport 235
Baga 97
  activities and tours 110
  eating 106
  nightlife 108
  shopping 109
  sleeping 103
  transport 111
Bagalkot
  festivals 234
  sleeping 233
Bambolim beach 68
Bamboo 256
banana plant 256
Banastari 171
Bandora 170
banyan 256
Bardez beaches 90
bargaining 41
Basilica of Bom Jesus 78
baya weaver 255
beach parties 113
before you travel 17
begging 26
Belgaum 216
Benaulim 142
  activities 150
  eating 149
  festivals 150
  shopping 151
  sleeping 146
  transport 152
Betalbatim 140, 141
  directory 152
  eating 149
  sleeping 145
Betul 144
  sleeping 148
Beyond Goa 189
Bhagwan Mahaveer
  Sanctuary 184
  sleeping 187
  transport 188
Bicholim 181
  activities 183
  background 180
  eating 183
  festivals 183
  sleeping 182
  transport 183
Bidar 229, 230
  shopping 234
  sleeping 233
Bijapur 224

directory 236
eating 234
festivals 234
history 225
sights 225
sleeping 232
transport 235
birds 82, 83, 158, 254
birdwatching 43
Bogmalo 141
  activities 150
  eating 149
  shopping 151
  sleeping 146
Bollywood 199, 243
Bombay 192
  activities and tours 209
  background 193
  central Bombay 197
  CST or VT 199
  directory 214
  eating 205
  festivals and
    events 209
  Malabar Hill 200
  nightlife 208
  shopping 210
  sleeping 202
  transport 211
Bondla Wildlife
  Sanctuary 173
  eating 174
  sleeping 174
books 256
Braganza Cunha 63
Braganza family 176
Brahmanas 249
bread fruit 256
Buddhism 252
bus 24, 31
business hours 25

C

Cabo de Rama 153
  sleeping 159
Cabo Raj Niwas 67
Cacora 177
Calangute 95
  activities and tours 110
  directory 111
  eating 106
  entertainment 108
  shopping 109
  sleeping 102
Calangute and the
  beaches 94
Calem, San 188
Calomb 155
  directory 162

eating 161
sleeping 160
transport 162
Cambarjua Canal 256
Canacona
  directory 162
  transport 162
Candola 172
Candolim beach 99
  activities 110
  directory 111
  eating 107
  nightlife 108
  shopping 109
  sleeping 105
Cansaulim 152
Cape Rama 153
car hire 32
Carambolim Lake 83
caste 241, 248
Cavelossim
  sleeping 148
caves 182, 186
central and southern
  interior 184
Chandor 175
  festivals 180
  sleeping 179
Chandranath Hill 177
Chandresvar Bhutnath
  Temple 177
Chapora 117
  shopping 121
  sleeping 120, 121
Chapora Fort 115
Chapora river 125
charitable giving 26
charities 26
charter flights 169
children 16
chital 253
Chorao Island 82
Christianity 250
Church of Our Lady of
  Bethlehem 177
Church of Our Lady of
  Mercy 140
Church of Our Lady of
  Remedies 101
Church of Our Lady of
  the Immaculate
  Conception 92
Church of Our Lady of
  the Snows 178
Church of St Alex 178
Church of St Francis of
  Asissi 125
churches 243
cinema 243

climate 253
clothing 26
coastal Salcete 136
Coco beach 101
coconut palm 256
Colombo 53
Colva 139
  activities 150
  eating 149
  festivasls 150
  sleeping 145
  transport 151
Colvale 125
Colwa 139
communications 51
conduct 26
confidence tricksters 29
consulates 17
contents 9
Cortalim 142
Cost of living 21
Cotigao 158
  sleeping 160
credit cards 21
cricket 43
culture 241
Cuncolim 144
  festivals 150
Curdi 187
currency 20
Currency regulations 18
Curtorim 178
customs 18, 26
customs and
  traditions 26
cycling 32

D

Dabolim airport 24,
  56, 75
  sleeping 57
Damodar Temple 186
Dargalim 125
darshan 244
Datta Mandir 182
de Souza, Fr Agnelo
  Gustav 113
deities 247
Deshprabhu House 128
development issues 157
Devil's Canyon 185
Dhargal 125
disabled travellers 15
discount flight
  agents 23
Divar 82
Divar island 84
  eating 85
  festivals 85
diving 111
Dona Paula 68
  eating 72
  sleeping 71
drugs 27

Dudhsagar falls 185
dugong 254
Durbhat 171
duty free 18

E

early Goa 238
eating 27, 37
  glossary 269
embassies 17
emergency
  services 25
encashment
  certificates 21
entertainment 39
entry requirements 17
environment 252
essentials 11
etiquette 26
export restrictions 18

F

Fama of Menino Jesus
  140, 150
Faria, Abbé 61, 62
Farmagudi 167
  sleeping 174
Fatorpa 144
  festivals 150
Fatrade
  sleeping 148
fauna 83
Feast of St John, Goa 150
female travellers 16
fire 25
flights 22
food 37
football 43
footnotes 259
foreign currency 18
foreign exchange 20
Fort Aguada 99
  activities 110
  eating 107
Fort Tiracol 126

G

Galgibaga 157
Ganesh 248
gangifa 216
Gaspar Dias 66
Gateway of India and
  Colaba 195
Gavdes 241
gay and lesbian
  travellers 15
geography 252
getting around 29
getting there 22
glossary 260
Goa Velha 68
gods 247
Gokarna 216, 217

directory 219
eating 219
sleeping 218
transport 219
Goltim 85
greetings 26
Gulbarga 229
  sleeping 233
  transport 235

H

Hampi 221
  activities 234
  background 222
  directory 236
  eating 233
  festivals 234
  sights 223
  sleeping 232
  transport 235
Harmal 123
health 44
Hindi 15, 267
Hindu religion 241
  calendar 249
  deities 248
  literature 249
  society 248
  temples 226
  trinity 247
Hinduism 246
hindustani 241
history 238
holidays 39
Hollant Beach 141
Hospet 220
  activities 234
  directory 236
  eating 233
  festivals and
  events 234
  sleeping 231
hotels 35

I

Idalcao Palace 61
IDD code 25
immigration 17
independence 240
Indian tourist
  offices 25
Indrail Pass 31
innoculations 18
insurance 19
internal flights 75
internet 51
Islam 251

J

jackfruit 256
Jua Island 85

K

Kamalapuram
  eating 234
  sleeping 232
Kannada 242
Kansarpal 181
karma 246
Karmali Lake 83
Karnataka
  interior 220
  coast 216
Karwar 216, 218
  directory 219
  transport 219
Kavale 170
keeping in touch 51
Keri 126
  sleeping 130
  transport 132
kids 16
Kindlebaga 157
  sleeping 160
kokum 256
Kolvale 125
Konkani 15, 242, 266
Kunbis 241
Kurdi 187
Kurukshetra 250

L

Lairaya Temple 181
Lakshmi 248
land and
  environment 252
language 15, 25, 241
letters 51
Londa-Vasco train 58
Loutolim 179
  eating 179
Loyala, Ignatius, Rachol
  Seminary 178
Lutolim 179
  eating 179

M

Madgaon 137
  directory 152
  shopping 150
  sleeping 144
  transport 151
magazines 52
Mahabharata 250
Mahalaxmi Temple 64
Maharashtran border
  villages 215
mail 51
Majorda 141
  sleeping 146
Majorda, Bch, Goa 146
Majorda, Goa 141
Malabar Hill 200
Malpem 129
mammals 253

Mandrem 125
  directory 132
  sleeping 130
  transport 132
mango 256
mangrove 256
map symbols 276
maps 34
  colour maps 297
Mapusa 90, 116
  background 90
  directory 94
  eating 93
  festivals 93
  shopping 93
  sights 91
  sleeping 92
  transport 93
Mapusa and the Bardez
  beaches 90
marathi 241
Marcela 172
Mardol 168
Margao 136, 137
  directory 152
  eating 148
  shopping 150
  sleeping 144
  transport 151
Marine Drive 200
markets 42
Marmagao 56
  background 56
Mayem Lake 181
media 52
medicines 44
meditation 43
megaliths 187
Menino Jesus 140
Miramar 66
  eating 72
  sleeping 71
  transport 76
Miranda House 179
Mobor 143
  activities 150
  nightlife 149
  sleeping 148
Moira 92
Molem 184
  activities and tours 187
  sleeping 187
  transport 188
money 20
money transfer 21
mongoose 254
monsoon 13, 253
Mopa airport 128
Morjim 124
  eating 131
  sleeping 129
Mormugao 56
  background 56
motorbikes 33

Mulvir 129
Mumbai 192
  activities and tours 209
  background 193
  central Mumbai 197
  CST or VT 199
  directory 214
  eating 205
  festivals and
    events 209
  Malabar Hill 200
  nightlife 208
  shopping 210
  sleeping 202
  transport 211
Mumbai airport
  sleeping 204
Mushir, Bar 125
music 242
Muslim beliefs 251
Muslim world 238

N
Nandi 248
Naroa 84, 181
Narve 181
national holidays 39
Nerul 101
newspapers 52
north Goa 87
Nossa Senhora da Gloria
  Church 143
nudity 26

O
Old Goa and around 77
  activities and tours 85
  eating 85
  excursions 82
  history 77
  sights 78
  transport 85
Our Lady Mother of
  God (Mae de Deus)
  church 99

P
packing 18
Palolem 155
  activities 161
  eating 160
  festivals 161
  nightlife 161
  shopping 161
  sleeping 159
  transport 162
Panaji 58
  activities and tours 74
  city centre 64
  directory 76
  eating 72
  festivals 73
  history 59

nightlife 73
  San Thome and
    Fontainhas 64
  shopping 74
  sleeping 70
  the waterfront 60
  transport 75
  west Panjim and the
    Campal 63
Pandava 186
Panjim 58
  activities and tours 74
  around Panjim 66
  city centre 64
  directory 76
  eating 72
  festivals 73
  history 59
  nightlife 73
  San Thome and
    Fontainhas 64
  shopping 74
  sleeping 70
  the waterfront 60
  transport 75
  west Panjim and the
    Campal 63
Panjim and Old Goa 53
panthers 253
papaya 256
Parchem 125
Paroda 177
Parshem 125
Parsi 125
Partagali 158
party beaches 112
Patnem
  directory 162
  sleeping 160, 161
  transport 162
Patnem beach 155
Pattadakal 227
people 241
permits 17
Pernem 122, 128
  background 123
photography 27
Pilar 69
planning your trip 12
police 25
Ponda 163, 166
  background 166
  directory 175
  eating 174
  sights 167
  sleeping 174
  temples around
    Ponda 167
  transport 175
Portuguese 239
Porvorim 68
post offices 51
Priol 168
Project Seabird 218

property 138
public holidays 39
puja 247

Q
Querim 126
  sleeping 130
  transport 132
Queula 170

R
Rachol 178
  sleeping 179
Rachol Seminary, Goa
  178
radio 52
Raichur 231
rail 24, 30
Rajbag
  sleeping 160
  directory 162
  transport 162
Rajbag beach 156
Ramayana 250
Ranes tribe 182
Rathasaptami 161
reading 256
rebirth 246
Redi 215
Reis Magos 101
religion 27, 245
religious festivals 39
reptiles 255
responsible
  tourism 27, 28
restaurants 37
Ribandar 82
  shopping 85
rickshaws 31
Rig Veda 249
road 24, 31
rules 26
rupee 20

S
safety 28
Salcete 163
Saligao 99
  activities 111
  eating 107
Salim Ali Bird Sanctuary,
  Goa 82
sambar 253
San Thome and
  Fontainhas 64
  sleeping 71
Sanguem 187
  sleeping 187
Sanquelim 182
  festivals 183
  transport 183
sanskrit 241
Sanskrit literature 250

Santa Cruz Church 143
Santra Beach 141
Sanvordem 188
Sarasvati 248
Satari
  background 180
Satari taluka 182
Savoi 172, 173
  sleeping 174
Sawantwadi 216
scooters 33
scuba diving, see diving
  111
Sé Cathedral 78
sea 24
sea turtles 256
Shigmo 161
Shiroda 128
shopping 41
Shri Bhagvati Senayan
  Temple 125
Shri Bhagvati
  Temple 128
Shri Bhumika
  Temple 125
Shri Kalikadevi
  Temple 181
Shri Mahadeva
  Temple 177
Shri Malikarjuna
  Temple 155
Shri Morja Devi
  Temple 124
Shri Purchevo Ravalnatha
  Temple 125
Shri Ravalnath 124
Shri Rudreshwar
  Temple 182
Shri Sausthan Gokarn
  Partagali Jeevotam
  Math 158
Shri Shantadurga Temple
  125, 144

silk cotton tree 256
Sinquerim beach 99
  eating 107
  nightlife 108
  shopping 109
  sleeping 104
Siolim 116
  sleeping 119
Sirigao
  festivals 183
Siroda 171
sleeping 35
snakes 255
south Goa 133
Spice Hills 172
spice plantation
  Tropical 173
sports 43
St Anthony's church 127
St Francis Xavier 78, 79
St Joseph's Church 128
St Tereza of Jesus 155
student travellers 16

T
Talaulim 69
tamarind 256
Tambdi Surla 185
  sleeping 187
Tamborim
  sleeping 148
taxi 34
telephone 52
telephone directory 25
Temple of Vitthala 182
temples 244
the Ghats 180
theft 28
Three Kings Festival
  101, 180
tigers 253
time 25

tipping 27
Tiracol Fort 126
Tiracol river 128
Tito's 127
touching down 24
tour operators 13
tourist information 25
tours 13
train 24, 30
train travel 24, 30
trance music 118
transferring money 21
transport
  air 22, 29
  airport information 24
  rail 24, 30
  road 24, 31
  sea 24
travellers' cheque 20
travelling with
  children 16
tulsi 245
TV 52

U
Usgalimal 187
Utorda 141
  Goa 141
  sleeping 146

V
vaccinations 18
Vagator 116
  nightlife 121
  sleeping 120
Varca 143
  eating 149
  sleeping 147
Vasco da Gama 56, 239
  directory 58
  eating 57
  sleeping 57

transport 57
Vasco-Londa train,
  Panjim 76
vegetation 256
Velinga 167
Velsao 141
  sleeping 146
Vengurla 216
Verna 142
visa extensions 17
visas 17
voltage 25

W
water buffalo 253
watersports 44
websites 15
weights and
  measures 25
what to take 18
when to go 13
where to go 12
wildlife 83, 174, 253
women travellers 16, 29
words and phrases 266

Y
yoga 43, 83, 111, 150

Z
Zambaulim 186
  festivals 187
Zuari river 175
  background 17

Map index

A
Agonda   155
Anjuna   114
Arambol beach   123

B
Baga   98
Basilica of Bom Jesus   78
Benaulim   141

C
Calangute   96
Candolim and Sinquerim   100
Colva (Colwa)   139

G
Gateway of India and Colaba, Mumbai   196
Gokarna   217

H
Hampi-Vijaynagara   222

M
Mapusa   91
Margao   137
Mumbai   194
  Central Mumbai   198
  Gateway of India and Colaba   196

N
Northern beaches   95

O
Old Goa   81

P
Palolem   156
Panjim   60, 61
Panjim centre   62
Ponda, around   170

S
San Thome and Fontainhas   65
Sinquerim beach and Fort Aguada   102
Southern beaches   136

V
Vagator and Chapora   117
Varca to Betul   143
Vasco da Gama   56, 57

Advertisers' index

Direct Line Travel, UK   19
Indiatourism, London   Inside back cover

On the Go Tours, UK   14, 297
Travel Screening Services, UK   49

Map symbols

Administration

- ◻ Capital city
- ○ Other city/town
- International border
- Regional border
- Disputed border

Roads and travel

- — Motorway
- — Main road
- — Minor road
- - - - 4WD track
- ······ Footpath
- Railway with station
- ✈ Airport
- 🚌 Bus station
- Ⓜ Metro station
- - - - Cable car
- Funicular
- ⚓ Ferry

Water features

- River, canal
- Lake, ocean
- Seasonal marshland
- Beach, sand bank
- Waterfall

Topographical features

- Contours (approx)
- Mountain
- Volcano
- Mountain pass
- Escarpment
- Gorge
- Glacier
- Salt flat
- Rocks

Cities and towns

- Main through route
- Main street
- Minor street
- Pedestrianized street
- Ɔ Ͼ Tunnel
- → One way street

(Facilities)

- Steps
- Bridge
- Fortified wall
- Park, garden, stadium
- Sleeping
- Eating
- Bars & clubs
- Entertainment
- Building
- Sight
- Cathedral, church
- Chinese temple
- Hindu temple
- Meru
- Mosque
- Stupa
- Synagogue
- Tourist office
- Museum
- Post office
- Police
- Bank
- Internet
- Telephone
- Market
- Hospital
- Parking
- Petrol
- Golf
- A Detail map
- A Related map

Other symbols

- Archaeological site
- National park, wildlife reserve
- Viewing point
- Campsite
- Refuge, lodge
- Castle
- Diving
- Deciduous/coniferous/palm trees
- Hide
- Vineyard
- Distillery
- Shipwreck
- Historic battlefield

Credits

Footprint credits

Editor: Laura Dixon
Map editor: Sarah Sorensen
Picture editor: Claire Benison
Proofreader: Anita Sach

Publisher: Patrick Dawson
Editorial: Alan Murphy, Sophie Blacksell,
Sarah Thorowgood, Claire Boobbyer, Felicity
Laughton, Nicola Jones, Angus Dawson
Cartography: Robert Lunn, Claire Benison,
Kevin Feeney, Melissa Lin, Peter Cracknell
Series development Rachel Fielding
Design: Mytton Williams and Rosemary
Dawson (brand)
Advertising: Debbie Wylde
Finance and administration:
Sharon Hughes, Elizabeth Taylor,
Lindsay Dytham

Photography credits

Front cover: Salcete fishing baskets, Travel Ink
Inside: Travel Ink, Alamy, Powerstock.
Back cover: Anjuna flea market, Powerstock.

Print

Manufactured in Italy by LegoPrint
Pulp from sustainable forests

Footprint feedback

We try as hard as we can to make each
Footprint guide as up to date as possible
but, of course, things always change. If you
want to let us know about your experiences
– good, bad or ugly – then don't delay, go
to **www.footprintbooks.com** and send in
your comments.

Publishing information

Footprint Goa
4th edition
© Footprint Handbooks Ltd
October 2004
ISBN 1 904777 22 8

CIP DATA: A catalogue record for this book is
available from the British Library

® Footprint Handbooks and the Footprint
mark are a registered trademark of
Footprint Handbooks Ltd

Published by Footprint

6 Riverside Court
Lower Bristol Road
Bath BA2 3DZ, UK
T +44 (0)1225 469141
F +44 (0)1225 469461
discover@footprintbooks.com
www.footprintbooks.com

Distributed in the USA by

Publishers Group West

Neither the black and white nor colour
maps are intended to have any political
significance.

Every effort has been made to ensure that
the facts in this guidebook are accurate.
However, travellers should still obtain
advice from consulates, airlines etc about
travel and visa requirements before
travelling. The authors and publishers cannot
accept responsibility for any loss, injury or
inconvenience however caused.

About the author

Annie Dare is a freelance journalist and sub-editor based in London. She has travelled to India on assignment and independently since first spending four months in Jammu and Kashmir in 1995. She studied Indian literature, politics and British Imperialism on the sub-continent as part of her English Literature degree from the School of African and Asian Studies (AFRAS) at Sussex University, Brighton, then worked as a copywriter and on a number of British newspapers before writing for media magazines. When not researching Footprint guides to Goa and South India she writes about creative industries, specializing in the fields of photography, music video, advertising and film.

Acknowledgements

Thanks to everyone, and there are many, who supplied Footprint with hard fact, tall stories or just plain friendship in 2004. In Goa this goes double for the Tito's mafia – David and Mark of course – but chiefly Kennedy, for his outlandish generosity in giving both home and scooter, and for much fun besides.

Thanks also to Jack Ajit Sukhija at Panjim Inn and to the writer and conservationist Heta Pandit at Goa Heritage. To the writer and journalist Margaret Mascarenhas, for more leads than I could follow up. Thanks also to John Douglas Coutinho from Ciaran's Camp for a fine evening at his family house in Chandor. To Phil Danes at YogaMagic for being all-round unpaid editor and cartographer and particularly for letting me write from the house in Assagao.

In Mumbai, deep gratitude goes to Gopal, Geeta and Anu Gopalakrishnan for their warm hospitality. To MTV's Cyrus Oshidar, the master of the interesting aside, and also to Piyush Pandey and the Ogilvy gang for much insight washed down with much whisky-soda.

In England, thank you to Sarah Thorowgood and Laura Dixon at Footprint. More personally, thanks to my family – David, Jilly, Jenny, Lucy and Matt – and to Chris Lahr too.

The health section was written by Dr Charlie Easmon, MBBS, MRCP, Msc Public Health, DTM&H, DoccMed, Director of Travel Screening Services.

Complete title listing

Footprint publishes travel guides to over 150 destinations worldwide. Each guide is packed with practical, concise and colourful information for everybody from first-time travellers to travel aficionados. The list is growing fast and current titles are noted below.
Available from all good bookshops and online at www.footprintbooks.com

(P) denotes pocket guide

Latin America and Caribbean
Argentina
Barbados (P)
Bolivia
Brazil
Caribbean Islands
Central America & Mexico
Chile
Colombia
Costa Rica
Cuba
Cusco & the Inca Trail
Dominican Republic (P)
Ecuador & Galápagos
Guatemala
Havana (P)
Mexico
Nicaragua
Peru
Rio de Janeiro
South American Handbook
St Lucia (P)
Venezuela

North America
Vancouver (P)
New York (P)
Western Canada

Africa
Cape Town (P)
East Africa
Egypt
Libya
Marrakech (P)
Morocco
Namibia
South Africa
Tunisia
Uganda

Middle East
Dubai (P)
Israel
Jordan
Syria & Lebanon

Australasia
Australia
East Coast Australia
New Zealand
Sydney (P)
West Coast Australia

Asia
Bali
Bangkok & the Beaches
Bhutan
Cambodia
Goa
Hong Kong (P)
India
Indian Himalaya
Indonesia
Laos
Malaysia
Nepal
Northern Pakistan
Pakistan
Rajasthan & Gujarat
Singapore
South India
Sri Lanka
Sumatra
Thailand
Tibet
Vietnam

Europe
Andalucía
Barcelona (P)
Berlin (P)
Bilbao (P)
Bologna (P)
Britain

Cardiff (P)
Copenhagen (P)
Croatia
Dublin (P)
Edinburgh (P)
England
Glasgow (P)
Ireland
Lisbon (P)
London
London (P)
Madrid (P)
Naples (P)
Northern Spain
Paris (P)
Reykjavík (P)
Scotland
Scotland Highlands & Islands
Seville (P)
Spain
Tallinn (P)
Turin (P)
Turkey
Valencia (P)
Verona (P)

Lifestyle guides
Surfing Europe

Also available:
Traveller's Handbook (WEXAS)
Traveller's Healthbook (WEXAS)
Traveller's Internet Guide (WEXAS)

Footnotes Complete title listing

Notes

Footnotes Notes

Footnotes Notes

Goa

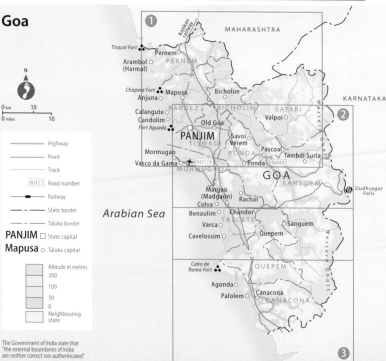

N

| 0 km | 10 |
| 0 miles | 10 |

MAHARASHTRA

Konkan railway

Tiracol Fort
Pernem
PERNEM
Arambol (Harmal)

Chapora Fort
Mapusa
Anjuna
BARDEZ
BICHOLIM
Bicholim
SATARI
Valpoi
KARNATAKA

Calangute
Candolim
Fort Aguada
Old Goa
PANJIM
TISWADI
Savoi
Verem
Pascoal
Western
Mormugao
PONDA
Tambdi Surla
Vasco da Gama
MORMUGAO
Ponda NH4A
GOA
SANGUEM

Arabian Sea

Margao (Madgaon)
Rachol
Colva
Benaulim
SALCETE
Chandor
Sanguem
Varca
Quepem
Cavelossim

Dudhsagar Falls

Western Ghats

Cabo de Rama Fort
QUEPEM
NH17
Agonda
Palolem
Canacona
CANACONA

Legend:

	Highway
	Road
	Track
NH17	Road number
	Railway
	State border
	Taluka border
PANJIM	State capital
Mapusa	Taluka capital

Altitude in metres
300
100
50
0
Neighbouring state

The Government of India state that "the external boundaries of India are neither correct nor authenticated"

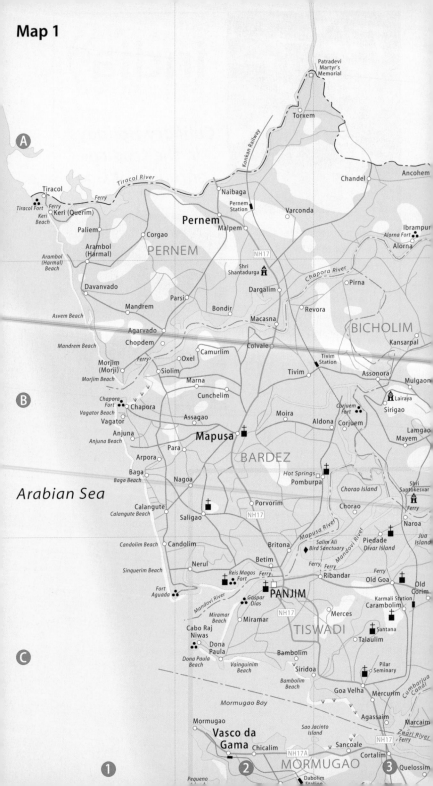

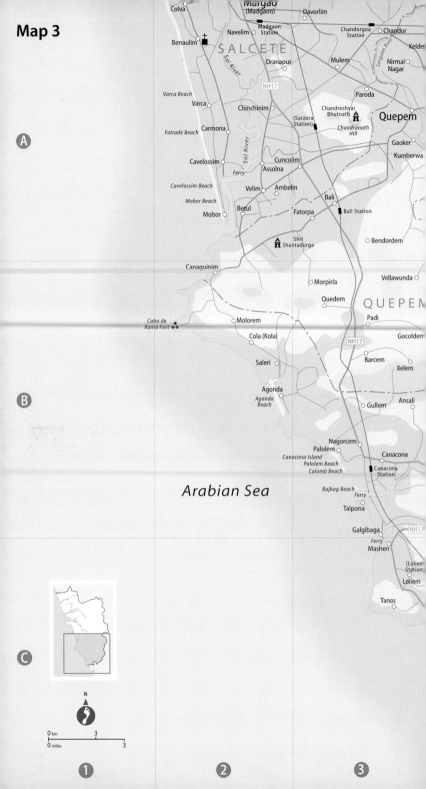

For a different view of Europe, take a Footprint

" " Superstylish travel guides – perfect for short break addicts.
Harvey Nichols magazine

Discover so much more...
Listings driven, forward looking and up to date. Focuses on what's going on right now.
Contemporary, stylish, and innovative approach, providing quality travel information.

THE BIOGF

OF

ALFRED DE MUSSET.

𝔗ranslated from the 𝔉rench of 𝔓aul de 𝔐usset

BY

HARRIET W. PRESTON,

AUTHOR OF "TROUBADOURS AND TROUVÈRES," ETC., AND TRANSLATOR
OF MISTRAL'S "MIRÈIO."

QUI LEGIT REGIT.

BOSTON:

ROBERTS BROTHERS.

1877.

Cambridge:
Press of John Wilson & Son.

PREFACE.

————•————

THE memoir of Alfred de Musset by his devoted brother Paul is, in many respects, a
model of what a biography ought not to be. It is
an ardent and tearful defence, a eulogy, a threnody,
a picturesque and highly idealized sketch: it is
any thing, in short, but a sober and truthful piece
of portraiture. But who would care to read a
brother's memorial of a life so brief and troubled.
a nature so richly endowed, and in many ways so
winning, if it were dispassionate? The whole of
the sad truth concerning the dissipations which
wrecked the poet's health, and the waywardness
and weakness which paralyzed his exquisite talent,
years even before he passed away, may be read
elsewhere. In particular, the study or series of
studies by Paul Lindau, published in Berlin almost
simultaneously with the present memoir, contains
a great deal of sound criticism, and is quite remarkable for its lack of reserve in details. But
the eager plea of M. Paul de Musset deceives as

little as eager pleas usually do.   We divine all that he avoids saying, at the same time that we like him the better for his chivalrous care of his brother's reputation.

The task of rendering into English his graphic and simple narrative has been a very pleasant one ; and, for an explanation of its few obscure allusions to matters connected with French literature and politics, I am indebted to my friend, Mme. George Harney, of Cambridge.

HARRIET W. PRESTON.

YORK, September 3, 1877.

THE BIOGRAPHY

OF

ALFRED DE MUSSET.

————•————

I HAVE long cherished the purpose of giving to
the admirers of Alfred de Musset the story of his
life. I have often felt moved to begin the task, but
have been withheld by the very vividness of my recollections. And yet it is no mere duty which I propose
to fulfil toward the man whom, of all men, I have best
loved, and whose most loyal friend and recipient of
confidence I have ever been. I regard it rather as a
complement needful to the perfect understanding of
his work. For his work is himself; and in it we perceive that daily transmutation of genius which belongs
only to those privileged poets in whom the imagination
is in constant communion with the heart. The creations
of these rare minds, their merest fancies, do not usually
wear the aspect of fiction for the reason that they reveal
the very workings of the poet's soul. Their history
becomes the history of the human heart, and nothing
can be uninteresting which makes them better known.
This it is which renders the curiosity of the public, about
the incidents of their lives, legitimate and intelligent.

Not only did Alfred de Musset receive the gift of keen feeling and forceful expression, but the sentiments and the thoughts to which he gave so fair a form were those of a whole generation. I know not if any other poet could be cited as being the poet of his era so thoroughly as was he. The first readers of "Rolla" and the "Nuit de Mai" may possibly have seen therein only a philosophic thesis, the doubts of an unquiet mind, the plaints of an unhappy lover; but ultimately men recognized, even there, the truthful expression of universal feelings. What the poet suffered, he suffered in common with all his contemporaries; and this is why his works were read in attics as well as in castles, and why his verses charmed the tedium of the bivouac on the remote frontiers of Kalybia.

It has often been said that the poetry of sentiment makes the envied possessor of this form of expression unhappy. Sensitive souls are sent into the world to be crowded and crushed. The loss of a mistress, the defection of a friend, a disappointed hope, an illusion dispelled, — all the ills, great and small, of which life is made up, — exasperate them, and would drive them to desire death if they could not find a solace for their woes in the poet's inspiration. So that those who afford us our highest intellectual pleasures and our sweetest consolations appear doomed to weariness and melancholy, even when they are not actually molested and tormented, as too often happens; and if their best friends sometimes irritate them unintentionally, how many others wound them on purpose, well knowing that a pin-prick will make them bleed. The biography which follows will not merely furnish an additional proof of these undeniable truths : it will help to establish another not quite so hackneyed ; namely, that sorrow makes great poets, as Alfred de Musset himself has said in the "Nuit de Mai."

Is it not plain that we owe the finest passages in the "Divine Comedy" to the bitterness of the exile, and to Dante's resentment against the injustice of his fellow-citizens? The "Misanthrope" of Molière might never have seen the light if Armande Béjart had been a virtuous and faithful wife. Happy is the poet who, like Petrarch, finds an inexhaustible source of sorrow and sensibility in the virtue of a gentle and compassionate woman!

Like his predecessors, Alfred de Musset drew from love and from grief his finest inspiration. A secret instinct forewarned him of those dangerous fellow-beings who were destined to put his affections to their hardest tests. But he had no need to go in search of suffering. Rather, it sought him out so often that his sensibilities were never allowed to sleep. Every one seemed to contribute something to the sum of his sorrows; and thus it is that the evil and invidious defeat their own end by rendering the poet's renown yet costlier, and more difficult for him to obtain.

If Alfred de Musset had been born in the age of Louis XIV., he would, of course, have belonged to the court, and shared the intimacy of the king. He would have enjoyed the privileges then reserved for nobility and genius; he would have held some important charge and been admitted everywhere, like Racine. Nor would

he have been indifferent to this kind of distinction.
Independent as his character was, he would have
yielded to the requirements of etiquette; he would
have taken an active part in the refined enjoyments
of the only sovereign who ever understood the great
art of grouping all manner of talents about himself,
and absorbing them for the augmentation of his own
glory.   He was essentially a man of the world, and
he might have been a genuine *grand seigneur.*   The
friendship of the Prince of Condé, the company of
Molière and Despreaux, would have charmed him more
than formal honors.   He would have had a far happier
life; but would he have been a greater man to day?
Would he have made, in an age when life would have
been so easy to him, the same deep impression which
he has left upon our own? I think not.   His weariness
and disgust in the midst of a society which is growing
every day more material have caused to vibrate in him
the more hidden strings.   For every wound which he
has received, he has mounted higher.   His renown has
been only the more solid and brilliant for being slowly
won, and an early death has but added to his fame.
That sad consecration was not needed.   He had had
time enough.

The De Musset family, which originated in the Duchy
of Bar, established itself at Blois and Vendôme, in the
fifteenth century, about the time of the siege of Orleans.
The first gentleman of that name mentioned in the
"Gallia Christiana" is a certain Rudolphe de Musset,
present as a witness at the ceremony of founding an
abbey in the diocese of Paris, in 1140. I have else-

where spoken of Colin de Musset, a celebrated poet and musician of the thirteenth century, the contemporary and friend of Thibaut, Count of Champagne.[1]

Other De Mussets are to be found in the council of Louis, Duke of Orleans, and brother of Charles VI.; in that of Dunois, bastard of Orleans; fighting in the army of Charles VII. at the battle of Pathay; and in the household of the Princess of Clèves, the mother of Louis XII. Several of them were lords-lieutenant of the province of Blois. Two of them commanded the companies of arquebusiers, and certain free companies of fifty men under Henry III. François de Musset was killed at Philipsbourg, in attempting to quell a revolt of the German troops in the garrison. The most celebrated soldier in the family was Alexander de Musset, a chevalier of Saint Louis, and lieutenant of the king at La Rochelle, who distinguished himself in all the battles of the war of the Succession, and became the comrade in arms of Maurice of Saxony. He received several wounds, and only retired after sixty years of active service.

Minister d'Argenson. and the Marshals of Saxony, Lowendal, Belle-Isle, and d'Estrées wrote him flattering letters, which his heirs have carefully preserved.

Certain interesting alliances of the De Musset family are also to be noted. An indirect one with Joan of Arc, through her niece, Catherine du Lys, whose marriage Charles VII. desired to arrange, and to whom he gave a dowry; others with the Bombelles, the Du Tillets, the

---

1 See a brief notice of the life of Alfred de Musset, in the large quarto edition of the poet's complete works published in 1866.

Du Bellays. The paternal grandmother of Alfred de Musset, Margaret Angélique du Bellay, the last female child of that name, belonged to a family which prized literary no less than military distinction. She married her second son. Joseph Alexander de Musset, to Jeanne Catherine d'Harville, an extremely clever woman. Victor de Musset, the father of Alfred, was the offspring of this marriage.

According to the peerage of France, the arms of this family are a golden hawk, hooded and jessed upon an azure field perched on a bar gules, with the device, "Courtoisie, Bonne-aventure aux preux." La Courtoisie and Bonne-aventure were two patrimonial estates : the first remained in the family until the middle of the last century ; the second, which formed a part of the patrimony of Alfred de Musset, was occupied by Antoine de Bourbon, the father of Henry IV., during the sojourn of the French court at the châteaux of Amboise and Blois. It lies two leagues from Vendôme, at the confluence of the Loir and a lesser river, at a place called Gué-du-Loir. It is well known that Antoine de Bourbon's was no edifying career. He frequently sought relief from the tedium of a life of show by retiring from the court to Bonne-aventure, where he gave shelter to certain damsels rather less virtuous than Queen Catherine's maids-of-honor. The secret of these pleasure parties was ill kept ; and the fame of them reached the ears of the poet Rousard, who chanced to be at Poissonière, not far from Vendôme. Rousard composed a song on the frolics of the king, the refrain of which was, "*La bonne aventure au gué, la bonne aventure !*" This satirical lyric went from one end of France to the other, and nurses sing the air of it to this day.[1]

The foregoing details are addressed to persons who are curious in matters of genealogy and heraldry. · Here are a few for those who interest themselves in the mysterious laws of hereditary transmission. It is only by an extraordinary concurrence of circumstances that Nature succeeds in producing a man of genius. *Savants* affirm that a single case of high intelligence will retard by three generations the progress of idiocy in a feeble-minded family. Apparently, the introduction of one inferior woman into an intellectual family is quite enough to debase the mental faculties of three generations: these facts are not sufficiently heeded in marriage. The maternal grandfather of Alfred de Musset used to relate that he said to himself, after his third interview with the lady whom he afterwards married, " There is the woman whom I *need*," and that a month before the marriage he knew nothing of the fortune of her parents, nor what dowry she would receive. But this same grandfather was an original character; a person of antique simplicity, a charming spirit, and a poet besides.

Claude Antoine Guyot-Desherbiers was of an old family in Champagne, and came to Paris to study law, under the reign of Louis XV. He was admitted to the

---

[1] In the collections of popular songs, this familiar refrain is variously given To insure correct spelling we must go back to Rousard, and remember that Bonne-aventure was situated on the Gué-du-Loir. The song quoted by Alceste in the first act of the " Misanthrope " is evidently derived from this of Rousard's; but the refrain, " *J'aime mieux ma mie augué*," is perfect nonsense.

bar, and afterwards made a magistrate. During the excitement which preceded the Revolution, he became the friend of the Abbé Morellet, of M. Suard, of the *savant* Cabanis, the astronomer Lalande, Merlin de Douai, De Barras, and others, into whose hands it was destined that power should presently fall. The tenth of August having abolished his seat on the bench, Guyot-Desherbiers lived in retirement till the end of the Revolution. After the 9th of Thermidor, he was appointed president of the committee on civil legislation. In this position he exerted his influence to save some heads from the scaffold ; among others, that of the Baron de Batz, who had tried to effect the escape of the queen and her children from their prison in the Temple. He even ran the risk of keeping M. de Batz hidden in his own house during the pursuit of the revolutionary tribunal.

M. Guyot-Desherbiers was endowed with a prodigious memory. At an advanced age, he amused himself by reciting whole comedies, playing all the parts with a degree of talent and spirit which delighted his audience, his grandchildren especially. I have heard that the excellent Carmontelle, several of whose proverbs he knew by heart, took especial pleasure in hearing him recite them ; and that this performance revealed to the author himself gleams of wit and shades of meaning of which he would not otherwise have dreamed.

Our grandfather's feeling for poetry was somewhat capriciously manifested; but that which especially distinguished M. Guyot-Desherbiers was a Gallic gayety, and a picturesque way of saying things, which imparted a peculiar charm to his conversation. This original turn of mind reappears in the comedies of his grandson, especially in the characters of Fantasio and Valentin and of Octave in the "Caprices de Marianne."

From the maternal side, also, Alfred de Musset derived qualities no less remarkable. M. Desherbiers had married Marie Anne Daret, a person of rare merit and excellent judgment, — a woman who gave good counsel, as her husband was fond of saying. Habitually grave and equable, our grandmother was at heart affectionate, tender, and impassioned; and, in moments of emotion, her eloquence carried one away. Her tall figure, the dignity of her countenance, the penetrating tones of her voice, and the unspeakable goodness of her heart have left a deep impression upon the minds of her grandchildren, — the memory of a kind of angelic creature. Her eldest daughter, who was very like her, transmitted to Alfred de Musset sensibility, eloquence, and pathos. It is through their union with distinguished faculties on the father's side, that these happy gifts have been enhanced to the utmost in the case of a single person.

Victor Donatien de Musset took a good rank in the military college at Vendôme, where he was a royal pupil. When he left school at eighteen, he had an elder brother already captain in a regiment at Bresse, and a sister who was queen's pensioner at Saint-Cyr with the promise of being made a canoness. On his return to his father's house, he found there a numerous and agreeable circle of relatives, friends, and neighbors. The eldest of the family was living at Cogners, near Saint-Calais. Other relatives and intimate friends dwelt at Tours, at Blois, and at Chartres. Vendôme was the centre where they often assembled. For the sake of spending a few days together, they would traverse abominable roads ; but the cheer was good, and the time passed gaily. The entire circle was occupied with plans for making life as pleasant as possible, without a suspicion that they were on the very verge of a political cataclysm. The father of Victor de Musset — called M. de Pathay in the province, to distinguish him from his two brothers — was so entirely preoccupied with the fortunes of the son who was a captain, that he made up his mind one day that his second son must not marry. Submissive to the fate of a cadet, Victor Donatien had resigned himself to the Church, when the Revolution arrived and snatched off those clerical bands of which he was so ready to be rid ; whence it is fair to conclude that the events of 1789 gave to France one great poet who else would never have seen the light.

About the same time that his future father-in-law saved the life of Baron de Batz, Victor de Musset met on the highway of Tours a condemned nobleman who was being escorted to Paris and the scaffold. The sight of this unfortunate man moved him to the deepest pity. He brought up a hay-cart under the windows of an inn where the *gendarmes* had stopped, deposited the prisoner in it, drove off with him by cross-roads with which he was familiar, and eluded pursuit. His prowess would have cost him dear, had not General Marescot taken a fancy to the youth, given him shelter under the folds of the flag, and received him into his own service. Em-

ployed at first in the inspection of fortified places,
Victor de Musset made the second Italian Campaign
with the general, and on his return from Marengo was
appointed chief inspector of engineers. His elder
brother, following a star very unlike his own, had emi-
grated and fallen by a republican bullet in the ranks
of Condé's army. During this interval, also, his parents
had both died, only a few months apart. To repair
these cruel bereavements he had recourse to marriage.
One of his friends introduced him at the house of M.
Desherbiers, whose eldest daughter he sought in marriage, and was readily accepted.

Victor de Musset remained in the War Department
until 1811, when he was made head of a division (*chef
de bureau*) in the Ministry of the Interior. Superseded
in 1818 by M. Lainé for the expression of liberal opinions, he took an active literary part in the Restoration
movement. In 1821, he published an excellent edition
of the works of J. J. Rousseau, and shortly afterwards a
careful and valuable work on the life and writings of the
Genevan philosopher, M. de Sémonville, who chanced to
meet and become attached to him, and caused him to be
appointed librarian of the Chamber of Peers. In 1828,
when General de Caux joined the political coalition which
goes by the name of M. de Martignac, Victor de Musset
was called to the War Department, in the capacity of
chief clerk (*chef du cabinet du ministre*), whence he
passed to the department of Military Justice, in which
he remained until his death.

During his long administrative career, Victor de
Musset was fortunate in being able constantly to exer-

cise the distinctive qualities of his disposition ; namely,
an inexhaustible kindness and serviceableness.   Never
did a man in power take so much trouble in the service
of others ; display such constant activity, energy, and
courage in assisting and protecting the unfortunate and
the persecuted.   It may well be supposed that occasions were not lacking.   I will cite but two.

Near the close of the Empire, an *émigré* named
D'Hotland returned to France, burdened with a numerous family, and stripped of all his resources.   He asked
employment and bread for his children of M. de Musset,
who appointed him inspector of the central police-station
at Melun.   Almost as soon as he was installed in office,
he was denounced to the Emperor as an old royalist,
and from the higher realms of government came the
order for his instant removal.   The minister summoned
the head of the bureau, who undertook an energetic
defence of his creature, in which he offered himself as
surety for the persons whom he employed, claiming that
he had the free choice of his subalterns, and was
responsible for them.   At the end of a month a new
complaint was lodged, and there was a fresh order for
immediate removal, this time in terms so peremptory
that the minister was terrified.   But M. de Musset refused to be intimidated.   At the risk of his own removal,
he addressed to the Emperor a second communication,
yet firmer than the first, in which he denounced with
indignation the scheme of the informers.   It was not
without hesitation that the minister M. de Montalivet
included this paper in his portfolio ; but it came back
the next day with this postscript in Napoleon's own

hand, — "The chief of the bureau is right," and the poor
official kept his place.

The other affair was more important than the preceding, and created some excitement. One Fabry — an
overseer or commissary of troops, I do not know which
— was accused of embezzlement, tried before a court-
martial, condemned to the galleys, and there died.
Fifteen years afterwards, the proofs of his innocence
were discovered. As the heirs of Lesurques, his wife
and children demanded his rehabilitation, which could
not however be effected without the passage of a law in
both Chambers. This was in 1831, and it was fortunate
for Mme. Fabry that she found M. de Musset in the
department of military justice. She made him enter
into her feelings and share them for a year. The minister of war positively shrieked when the chief of the bureau proposed to award her an indemnity of a hundred
thousand francs ; but, after repeated discussions, they
kept to that figure and proposed the law. The statement
of the case was a piece of genuine eloquence ; and the
day on which Mme. Fabry gained her cause before the
Chamber of Deputies was a holiday at home. This
obligingness, carried even to the point of self-sacrifice,
was once a peculiarly French quality, but is now no
longer in vogue. It has been replaced by the American
precept, " Time is money ;" and, ever since men began
to fancy that time can be estimated in cash, they have
ceased to spend it in the service of others.

To such qualities of heart Victor de Musset united
those graces of the mind which go to make up what we
call an amiable man,— a sparkling gayety, an astonishing

promptitude of repartee, and profound learning of which he made no parade. He would tell a story in a few words, and with a *bonhomie* which concealed great art. At table, among his intimate friends, when enlivened by wine and good cheer, his gayety would fly to his head, and a running fire of jests and droll sallies ensued ; but on these festive occasions, as on graver ones, the moment he perceived a trace of unfriendliness, his tongue became sharper, his eye flashed fire, his retort was biting, and he straightway became calm. And, as he never came out of such a skirmish otherwise than victorious, he became the terror of the snappish and surly.

On one of his visits to Vendôme, he took my brother and myself to see a country gentleman in the neighborhood when the mercury stood at twenty-five degrees.[1]

Our neighbor was penurious, and, in place of the refreshments which are invariably offered in the provinces to every visitor, he exhibited two ancient stone statues recently disinterred.

" You are one of the learned," said our host mockingly, " and will doubtless recognize at once the two saints whose images these are."

" Perfectly," replied M. de Musset. " One is evidently Saint Niggard and the other Saint Glutton ;" and, relieved by the delivery of this scratch, he smiled affably upon his neighbor. Victor de Musset wrote one comedy in verse, which was not found among his papers.

---

[1] Celsius ; that is, about 78° Fahrenheit.

PART FIRST.

FROM 1810 TO 1828.

I.

ALFRED DE MUSSET was born on the eleventh of December, 1810, in the heart of old Paris, near the Hôtel de Cluny, in a house which still bears the number, — 33 Rue des Noyers.[1] At thirty-seven in the same street lived our Grandfather Desherbiers, and a great-aunt, the proprietress of a garden which extended to the base of the ancient church of Saint Jean de Latran, now demolished. All the great-nephews of Mme. Denoux took their first steps in this garden. Alfred de Musset used to say, jestingly, that in his childhood he was just as stupid as another; but I do not hesitate to assert that he gave early evidence of a rarely precocious intelligence. After he had been to church for the first time, he asked his mother, as innocently as possible, whether she would take him again next Sunday to see the *comedy of the Mass;* nor had he any suspicion of the Voltairean character of his remark. If half the noteworthy things which children say are attributable to ignorance, there are others to which we give little heed, but which reveal, amid the simplicity of the child, the character of the future man. Here is one. When Alfred was three years old, some one gave him a pair of red shoes, which

---

[1] This street, partially destroyed by the recent embellishments of Paris, is no longer to be recognized. One may get an idea of what it was from other streets in the same quarter, as yet untouched by the hammer, — the Rue Galande, for example.

he admired exceedingly. He was being dressed, and was in a great hurry to go forth in the new foot-gear whose color took his eye. He quivered with impatience while his mother combed his long curls, and at last cried out in a tearful voice, "Oh, make haste, mamma, or my new shoes will be old!"

We can but laugh at this vivacity, but it was the first symptom of an impatience for pleasure, a disposition to devour the time, which was never calmed nor contradicted for a single day. Here is another in which the child plainly knows what he is talking about. He had committed some peccadillo or other; and his young Aunt Nanine, of whom he was especially fond, told him that, if he did so again, she should not love him any more.

"You think so," he replied; "but you can't help it!"

"Indeed I can, sir," was the aunt's reply; and, to give greater effect to her menace, she assumed as stern an air as possible. The child scanned her face carefully and a little uneasily, for a few minutes, until he detected an involuntary smile, when he cried out, "But I can *see* that you love me!"

Some other misdemeanor, graver apparently than the last, had led one day to his being shut up in the *dark closet*. When I was of his age, if a like misfortune overtook me, I never budged an inch, but endured my imprisonment in a transport of pride. He, however, the moment he was shut up, began to bemoan himself as if he had been *in carcere duro*.

"Oh, how miserable I am!" he cried. "How can I have deserved to be punished by so good and loving a mamma? I must be dreadfully naughty if she is angry

with me ! How can I make her forgive me ? What a
wicked child I am ! It is God who is punishing me."

He went on for a long while in the same pathetic
strain. Finally, his mother, touched by so deep a repentance, went and opened the door; whereupon the
prisoner, who had never dreamed of such success, cut
short his lamentations, and remarked in an indignant
and reproachful tone, "Pooh ! you are not very pitiful ! " (*attendrissante.*)

Among the recollections of childhood, this word remained as a memorable thing, and Alfred himself liked
often to quote it. He liked better still to recall another
remark, equally childish, but foretelling, to one disposed
to heed the indication, the man of imagination. In one
of the chambers of our old house there was an immense
beam in the ceiling, which the baby regarded with a sort
of terror. One day his Aunt Nanine wished to take
away from him a very young kitten which he was holding by the head, to the great displeasure of the animal.
After clinging long to the little beast, he saw that he
should be forcibly deprived of it, and gave it up ; exclaim-
ing furiously, however, in the style of Camille's male-
diction, "There ! Take your cat ! It will scratch you ;
it will tear your gown ; and the beam will fall on your
head ; and I shall go and dine at Bagneux."

At Bagneux, in the summer-time, the whole family
used to meet every Sunday at the house of our great-aunt
Denoux, — a beautiful country seat, where the children
enjoyed themselves exceedingly. Mme. Denoux was
greatly flattered when she learned that the utmost conceivable happiness to her small nephew was going to

dine with her.   Many and many a time since then, when
I have wanted to interfere and remonstrate with him,
Alfred has answered, "Yes, and the beam will fall on
my head, and you will go and dine at Bagneux!"

I am guilty of no wanton exaggeration, when I say
that his first love dates from the year 1814; and this
love was none the less intense for being juvenile,
although it had subsided into friendship before the days
of genuine amours.   Alfred was less than four years old
when he beheld enter his mother's house one day a young
lady, to him unknown.   She was from Liége, which had
then ceased to belong to France, and she rehearsed the
story of the invasion, the counter-strokes of which they
felt at Liége, where her father was an imperial magistrate.   The tale was a moving one, and the narrator
expressed herself with singular grace.   The baby was
smitten.   From the sofa where he sat surrounded by his
playthings, he heard her to the end without a word,
when he rose and requested to know the name of the
young lady.

"It is one of your cousins," they told him.   "Her
name is Clelia."

"Ah, she belongs to me!" he cried: "then I will
take her and keep her!"

He seized her in fact, and made her tell him, not only
the story of the invasion and the return to France, but a
hundred other tales which she invented to please him,
with the most captivating facility.   He could not exist
without his cousin Clelia.   The instant she arrived, he
drew her away to a corner, and began, "Now, then,
you see"— This was the signal for inexhaustible com-

munications, of which she never tired. Finally, he asked his cousin to marry him, in all seriousness ; and, not being refused, he exacted of her a promise that she would go with him to the Curé just as soon as he was old enough ; after which he considered himself to all intents her husband. Clelia was obliged to return with her parents to the province, and the separation cost floods of tears. The infant's fancy seemed to have all the characteristics of a violent passion. "Do not forget me !" he said, when his cousin was taking leave.

"Forget you," she cried : "why, you don't seem to understand that your name is engraved on my heart with a penknife !"

To qualify himself for correspondence with his lady, he flung himself into his reading and writing lessons with inconceivable enthusiasm. When the young maiden actually married a husband of less tender years, it became necessary to make a mystery of it, and to give the hint to some twenty persons. One day some one of them, forgetful of instructions, made some allusion to Mme. Moulin, — Clelia's new name ; when the child sprang impetuously into the midst of the circle.

"Whom are you talking about ?" he said. "Who is Mme. Moulin ?"

"This is she," was the answer, indicating a young lady whom he did not know, and whose presence was most opportune.

He looked attentively at the person designated, and then returned to his play. A few days later, our new cousin, M. Moulin, came to see us.

" I have seen your wife," said Alfred to him. " She isn't bad, but I like mine better."

The secret was kept in this way for a number of years. At last, when the serious business of education and the interests of school life had changed the current of his ideas, Alfred was informed that it had been impossible for his cousin to wait for marriage until he was old enough to take a wife. After the first shock occasioned by the revelation, he inquired, trembling, whether it were possible that Clelia had been mocking him. When they assured him that she still loved him as an elder sister, his anxiety was allayed. He reflected for a moment, and replied, " Well, I will be content ! " As if he could have understood the difference between a wife and a sister !

Mme. Moulin lived at Clermont, in Beauvoisis, with her husband and children. We were closely united by community of interests no less than ties of blood. But suddenly, in 1836, there arose a misunderstanding between us. We differed about a matter of business. Sharp letters were exchanged, and there was even talk of a lawsuit. Alfred set off by *diligence* for Clermont. He entered his cousin's house unannounced : they both burst into tears, and the lawsuit stopped there. From that time forward, our friendship was never interrupted. Alfred had great confidence in the taste and judgment of his Cousin Clelia. She came to Paris in 1852, to be present at his reception by the French Academy, and the very last time he saw her he said to her : " When they get up a gorgeous edition of my works on the thickest of paper, I shall have a copy bound for you in

white vellum with a gold band, as an appropriate memorial of our attachment."

I need but to recall my own first impressions, in order
to understand those of my brother, concerning the great
events of 1814 and 1815.   More than once we wept
together over the misfortunes of our country, without at
all comprehending their magnitude.   As the elder, I
undertook to have political opinions, which my brother
trustfully adopted, and I assisted his natural precocity.
We were brought up in the admiration of Napoleon, of
whom our mother spoke with an eloquence which filled
us with enthusiasm.   This great figure, which we appreciated after our own fashion, represented to us, first of
all, *the ideal soldier*, the warrior, always victorious. Before
we understood the quality of his genius, we regarded
him as infallible in every respect.

To us the Emperor was always right.   The snows of
Russia had conquered him to be sure, but the snows were
to blame ; and, sooner than acknowledge an imprudence
or mistake in the life of our hero, we would have
brought the charge against God himself.   Our idolatry
did not come quite to this pass, however, because we
found plenty of mortals to accuse.   One day a sack of
grain was brought to our house, and deposited in a
corner of the office.   The Emperor, they said, was coming to defend Paris ; and we must expect the miseries of
a besieged city.   These precautions amazed us.   If the
Emperor was coming to the aid of Paris, what was there
to fear ?   Was it not evident that the enemy could not
take it ?   But the Emperor did not come.   One day our
Uncle Desherbiers went off with his gun on his shoulder

to fight on the defences. That day, there was growling of cannon, and the servants were all in the street listening to the noise of the battle. The sound died away; and our uncle came back, black with powder, his clothes and hair in disarray. A few days later, the name of Marmont flew from mouth to mouth, coupled with a thousand curses. We learned with horror that men existed capable of betraying the Emperor and their country. What the charm of that could be, no one could make us understand. Good Sylvain Rondeau, a stalwart peasant whom our father had taken for a servant, tried vainly to explain it to us; but the results of treason appeared only too plainly, when we saw the Prussian soldiers setting up their cooking apparatus on the garden-beds of the Luxembourg, and defiling the lake water by washing their shirts in it. On the square of the Odéon, we found the first proclamation of Louis XVIII. The bill was slightly attached, and I sprang at it and tore it down. The prudent Sylvain was obliged to drag me away by force. Discord reigned in our mother's drawing-room: half of our friends had already declared for the new régime, and they quarrelled, tooth and nail. Happily the spring came, and we were taken to our great-aunt Denoux, at Bagneux.

There were some Hungarian hussars lodged among the servants in the house at Bagneux. One of them, an old subaltern officer, with a fine martial figure, took a fancy to me. The moment he caught sight of me, he would beckon me to approach. I used to put my foot upon the stone bench in the stable, and he would black my boots assiduously. During the process I would say, — well knowing that he understood no French, — " Black away, you old Cossack ! "

But the old soldier took us around the garden on horseback with such complaisance that by degrees he won our affection. The day the regiment left, we went to bid our old friend Martin good-by. Before mounting, he clasped us in his arms, and great tears rolled down upon his grizzled moustache. Perhaps the good man had left children in his own country, from whom he had parted more sorrowfully even than from us.

In the month of June of that year, 1814, I was separated from my brother for some days. Our father was looking for a wife for a cousin of his, and our mother had precisely what was required ; namely, a charming young unmarried cousin of her own. This cousin lived at Joinville. I was left with our great-aunt Denoux, while the rest went to Champagne, where the wedding was to take place. On the journey, my brother's blonde head, always at the opening of the post-chaise, attracted the attention of the peasants, who imagined him to be the King of Rome. There was a row in one village where they stopped to change horses, and they escaped with some difficulty from the hands of the Champagners, who were persuaded that they beheld the son of the great exile of Elba.

Our mother enjoyed, like the Emperor Napoleon, the privilege of infallibility. Our trust in the superiority of her knowledge, and the certainty of her conclusions, was boundless ; and in fact she was very seldom mistaken. One evening, in the winter of 1815, when she was putting me to bed, I heard her, through the open door

of the children's sleeping-room, pronounce these words,
— "This cannot last. The Bourbons do nothing but
blunder. We shall see the Emperor back again."

I sprang with one bound to my brother's bed, who was
already asleep. I woke him with the tidings that the
Emperor was immediately coming back. He asked me
how I knew, and when I told him that our mother had
just said so, he had no more doubt about it than I. We
awaited the advent of our hero with extreme impatience.
Finally, on the twentieth of March, he came ; and the
event which astonished the world appeared to us perfectly natural.

On the twenty-first of March, Sylvain took us into the
garden of the Tuileries. An innumerable multitude
blocked the approaches to the palace. The cheers, endlessly repeated by ten thousand voices, became one continuous sound, so that one could only hear the last syllable
eur in an immense murmur. We succeeded in slipping
into the crowd, just under the balcony of the pavilion
d'Horloge. There the Emperor presently made his
appearance, surrounded by his principal officers. He
wore the uniform of the dragoons, with white trimmings
and riding-boots. His head was bare, and he waddled
a little in walking, as though encumbered by his *embon-
point.* I can see, even now, the fat pale face, the
Olympian brow, the eyes set like those of a Greek
statue, the piercing look which he bent upon the
crowd. How unlike he was to the men around him !
What a contrast, in features and expression, to those
vulgar types ! It was verily Cæsar amid the blind instruments of his will. Alfred de Musset was then but

little more than four years old; but this poetic figure
struck him so vividly that he never forgot it. We
devoured it with our eyes for the fifteen minutes or
so that it posed before us, and then it vanished for
ever, leaving an indelible impress upon our childish
imaginations, and in our hearts a love that approached
fanaticism.

One day in the month of April we saw defile, under
the trees of a boulevard, a band of conscripts and en-
listed volunteers. No doubt they had come a long way,
and by forced marches. They were exhausted, gasping,
and all in tatters. The spectacle was heart-rending.
We had decided that Sylvain Rondeau ought to join the
army; but he was deaf to our appeals, and made great
sport of our reproaches. The six months which elapsed
after the passage of the troops appeared so long a time
to us, that we began, for very weariness, to interest ourselves in something beside the war. One morning our
mother came out of her chamber in a flood of tears, and
rent by agonizing sobs. We followed her to our father's
study, weeping and wailing too. It was thus that the
news of the Waterloo disaster spread through the house.
I can hear the clamor of the women now. A little
while after came two Prussian officers with their ticket
entitling them to quarters. Two rooms had been prepared for them on the second floor. They wanted to
see the drawing-room. Our mother came out upon the
staircase, closing the door behind her, and assured them
that they could not be admitted there. One of the
officers then attempted to snatch the key from her; but
she flung it out of the window into the court, and

declined to be intimidated by their threats and their
oaths. Our father entered in the midst of the alterca-
tion, took the Prussians back to their head-quarters,
and returned with two other officers of a more placable
temper.

Every evening the discussions between our parents
and our friends were renewed with more animation than
ever. My brother and I could not comprehend these
differences of opinion. All that was said about the
constitutional rights of the peers, and the claim of the
legitimate princes to the throne, was Hebrew to us.
It was unanimously decided in our own little councils
that we would remain true to our Emperor, that our
swords and our life-blood belonged to him alone, and
that he would certainly come back one day and require
them of us, and lead us to Vienna and Berlin as he
had done our fathers. Until a new miracle like the
return from Elba should come and restore to us the
object of our worship, we bade a temporary farewell
to politics.

Of the year 1816 we preserved only the memory of
an intolerable imprisonment, occasioned by the continuous rains. Our cook Eulalie laid the blame of the bad
weather and the destruction of the crops to the return
of the Bourbons, which seemed to us an incontrovertible
position, and strengthened us in our hopes of a better
future. However, in the next year, I was sent to a
boarding-school, where my brother came only in the
morning as a day pupil, and returned home at night.
Upon the narrow stage of that school, with its hundred
pupils, appeared all the political passions by which

France was then torn. There were royalists, liberals, hypocrites, and informers. The first held their heads high, and the local government, that is to say the head of the institution, showed them a marked partiality. They had all sorts of privileges, places of honor among the rest, awarded, not for good lessons or good conduct, but for the political and religious views which they paraded. The most exalted of these young extremists sat at a separate table in the recess of a walled-up door, where there was a gorgeous blue paper covered with gold *fleurs-de-lis*. We would not for the world have aspired to the privileges of this class, and our indifference in this matter caused us to be classed, by our orthodox comrades, among the lukewarm and *suspects*. This unpleasant position attracted to us affronts, injuries, and persecutions. Happily, the preceptor supposed us more devoted to the existing order of things than we really were, and his protection saved us some ill treatment. But, fifteen years later, Alfred found in the reminiscences of this period the germ of his " Confession d'un Enfant du Siècle." My sorrowful estate as a constant boarder rendered this life of constraint and suspicion a great deal more painful to me than it was to my brother. I could not understand how my mother could leave me so far away: I even doubted her tenderness, and became desperate. When it came time to resume the yoke, after vacation, I would gladly have died. Happily I came home one day with scarlet fever, and my brother took it. There was no more question of banishing us from the paternal roof, and we had a tutor.

It was during our convalescence that Alfred was informed of the marriage of his cousin Clelia. To console the young swain for the loss of his bride, and to supply the place of the charming stories which she used to improvise for his amusement, we had recourse to books. We devoured together all the Persian and Arabian tales on which we could lay our hands: the "Thousand and One Days," the "Thousand and One Nights," and the sequel by Calotte. Our appetite for the marvellous was not satisfied by reading these tales a thousand times: we wished to act them as comedies.

We therefore built, in the first place, an oriental edifice, approached by a spiral staircase of at least twenty steps, the lowest of which was a music-book, and the uppermost a writing-desk. The door was a folio volume which was made to turn on its hinges by means of a cord passed through the loose binding at the back. We descended into the interior of this labyrinth by means of a ladder of upholstery, disguised by fanciful architectural ornaments. The other outlet of this monument could be used for exits, but not for entrances. It was a long plank smeared with wax sloping steeply to a mattress, down upon which we slid, and whereby we executed precipitate flights, effective aerial voyages, and the sudden apparition of the genie with the wonderful lamp. This construction represented by turns the palace of the Calif Haroun, and that of the noble Aboul-Kasem, the cave with the bronze gate, the grotto of Ali-Baba, &c.

Our play-hours were presently insufficient for enjoyments so keen, and in vain did our tutor take us off to study. He could not withdraw us from the fantastic realms where we were living. The play went on all through our lessons, despite reprimands and punishments. We had talismans hidden in our pockets, and the red ring of Maugraby came out of our sleeves the minute our teacher's back was turned. In the evening, in our mother's drawing-room, we transformed into all sorts of animals the people who had not the good fortune to please us ; and, when we were sent to bed, we slept the sleep of Abou-Hassan, the better to play next morning the tale of the " Sleeper Awakened."

These amusements lasted throughout the year 1818. We were then living in the Rue Casette, in a house belonging to the Baroness Gobert, widow of a general who had died gloriously under the empire. Her son, the sole survivor of eight children, was of a silent and melancholy turn, and a request came that he might be allowed to join our fairy performances. Léon Gobert was a singular child, with a big head and a voice like a man's, and I did not then remember ever to have seen him laugh. He was just half way between Alfred and myself in age, being two years older than my brother. We considered him an excellent recruit for our company. He was carping and difficult at first ; but by and by he came to like it, and caught our oriental fever. The baroness, always absorbed in the health of her son, gave up to us her drawing-room, where a frightful disorder soon prevailed. At the end of a month, our new companion was no longer the same child. His bright face, his energy, his liveliness, confounded the physician who had thought him the victim of an incurable malady. It is certain that Léon Gobert passed without accident the age at which his brothers and sisters had been taken away. He survived his mother, and died in Egypt by his own imprudence, after having established a historical prize which furnished a life-annuity to Augustin Thierry.

II.

THE Baroness Gobert was so grateful for her son's restoration to life, that she was anxious to do us as great a favor as we had done her. She positively insisted on lending to our parents her estate of the Clignets, situated on the road to Viarmes, very near the forest of Carnelle. The house, which had been unoccupied and closed for many years, was queerly arranged and somewhat dilapidated. Outside, it looked like the fragment of some ruined convent, with its narrow and irregular windows. Buttresses sustained the walls, from which the stucco had fallen ; and in the evening we could see the rats and dormice scudding along by moonlight. Inside, there were some ten principal rooms, of which three or four were habitable, and in these were collected the best pieces of the worm-eaten furniture. In the garden, — which had been laid out in the English fashion, with winding walks, old trees, and dense thickets, — we were delighted to observe a rampart-like terrace, a long alley bordered by cherry-trees laden with fruit, and a mound of artificial rock-work, which might have been erected by the decorative artist of our oriental comedies. This hillock came near occasioning a serious accident. In climbing upon it, Alfred laid hold of a rock, which became loosened, and rolled with him to the bottom. I thought he was dead ; but he came off with a contusion of the leg, and a few bruises on his hands. The Duc

3

de Bourbon was not so fortunate. In one of our excursions in the great forest of Carnelle, we were follow-
ing·the chase at full speed. All at once, we heard a
strange noise in the copse, and what seemed a black
flying mass went by us, grazing the earth. It was the
boar. He flung himself upon a rearing horse, who fell
with his rider. The swooning prince was lifted up. He
had several dangerous wounds, and was long confined to
his bed ; but recovered at last, and was reserved for
a more terrible death behind closed doors.

Our residence at Clignets permitted us to display our
enterprising temper upon a broader stage. Dr. Espar-
ron had said to our mother, "What children need is
sun, air, and exercise." We were given loose rein, therefore, and made ample use of our liberty. Our greatest
delight was to propose some difficult expedition : like
making the circuit of the garden on the top of the wall ;
or climbing a tree as far as some branch particularly
designated ; or taking a bee-line from one point to
another, turning aside neither for hedges nor ditches.
Our tutor, who was twenty-five, sometimes accepted our
challenges. That was a happy day when he retreated
before a pool of water, which his pupils leaped by means
of poles. Our tutor was, however, an excellent man,
accomplished without pedantry, who found means to
teach us something even while he played with us. Our
history lesson was given during our walk. He understood Italian, and we learned it orally. In certain
hours, we were forbidden to speak French ; and, when
we did not know the Italian word, the master would
hand us his pocket-dictionary. As for geography, he

made that study most agreeable by introducing stories of celebrated travellers ; and Magellan, Vasco de Gama, and Captain Cook, took their turn in our fictions. The two years devoted to us by this excellent instructor were, to say the least, much pleasanter and more profitable than our school-years. His name was Bouvrain.

The farm of the Clignets lay alongside the mansion. The farmer, M. Piedéleu, was six feet high, with the shoulders of Atlas, although a little bent by age. His wife, who was but a few inches shorter than himself, looked like a giantess ; and, when they went to mass on Sunday with their sons around them, they looked like a family from Brobdignag. The first time that we penetrated the farm limits, — it was one evening after dinner, — one of the Piedéleu sons had by the horns a vicious young cow who wanted to get away, and was pushing her backwards into the stable. Two other boys were unbending after the labors of the day, by standing on its end a long stone of enormous weight, which served them for a bench. The father was contemplating with folded arms a new wheel which had just been put to his cart, and the mother and youngest girl were preparing supper. Nothing is so admirable to children as physical strength. The interior of the farm-yard and the assemblage of colossi impressed themselves so deeply upon the memory of the eight-year-old scholar, that they were afterwards faithfully reproduced in the little story of " Margot."

These Piedéleus, good folk as they were, did us an ill turn. They had built a huge hay-rick in the middle of the court-yard, and we discerned in the rick a small opening, a few feet above the ground, whence protruded the head of a cat. We started in pursuit of the animal, who came out on the other side of the rick by an interior passage. Enchanted by our discovery, we never went to the farm again without crossing the hay-rick by the cat's passage. One day two of the Piedéleu boys lay in wait for us, and seized the moment when we were in the centre of the gallery to stuff the two orifices with bundles of hay. To struggle with the colossi would have been useless. We thought of nothing but clearing a new passage at the side of the obstacle which opposed us. In a moment the air was exhausted, and I felt that we should be stifled. At last I succeeded by frantic efforts in clearing an opening, out of which I burst head-foremost upon the pavement of the court, crying to the peasants to save my brother. Most fortunately, he was directly behind, and came out by the same way as myself; for those good giants never budged, and only laughed at my fiery face and protruding eyes. When our tutor told them that if their fun had lasted five minutes longer we should have been suffocated, they asked what that was; nor could they ever be made to understand that there was any danger in being smothered with hay.

The Piedéleus also caused us another mischance. There was a great dove-cot at the farm, and the pigeons used to swoop down into the garden and upon the terrace of the mansion. One of these birds, less shy than the rest, honored us with his friendship. We used to give him grain, which he learned to take out of our very hands. One day a cook, from the village of Saint

Martin du Tertre, bought two pairs of pigeons, and besought the farmer's wife to kill him some more. When
the tidings reached us, the massacre had already begun.
We rushed to the farm, trembling lest we should recognize our friend among the victims. Unfortunately, our
mother also arrived during the execution ; and, when she
saw us eagerly watching the strangled birds and the
bloody hands of Mme. Piedéleu, she thought we were
enjoying the disgusting spectacle : her indignation was
equal to her grief, and she overwhelmed us with reproaches. I may as well confess here that my disposition was different from my brother's, and that his was
the better. He wanted to justify himself; but I held
back, and whispered to him to be silent. It was the
injustice that I resented. and I repelled the notion of
self-defence as a fresh outrage. My brother did not
share this feeling ; but he respected it, and we both kept
silence. Again and again, he asked me if it were not
time to explain that great affair of the pigeons, and my
answer was, "Not yet. We will see by and by." By
and by he forgot all about it, and left to me alone the
duty of arranging the vindication of our innocence.
But we were men before the misunderstanding was
removed.

The fogs and chill of November drove us from the
country. Once more in our apartment at the Rue
Casette, we were like wild plants in a hot-bed. Alfred
had attacks of frenzy from the want of fresh air and
space, very like those which are said to attend chlorosis
in young girls. In one day he broke one of the drawing-room mirrors with an ivory ball, cut the new curtains

with the scissors. and stuck an immense red wafer on the map of Europe, in the middle of the Mediterranean Sea. He got no reprimand for these disasters, because he appeared himself to regard them with consternation. It was I who undertook to keep them in his remembrance. When in our confabulations he asked my opinion about any thing which I did not approve, I used to say to him, "The glass is broken, but no matter; only try not to cut the curtains and stick wafers on the Mediterranean Sea." The reminder always made him laugh, and he heard me out with patience.

Among the books of our Grandfather Desherbiers, I found one day the "Legend of the Four Sons."

The perusal thereof plunged me into a deep reverie. A new world opened before me, — the world of chivalry. At the first word of it to my brother, he took fire. We cried aloud for romances. They gave us "Jerusalem Delivered," and we made but one mouthful of it. We must have "Orlando Furioso," and then "Amadis," "Pierre of Provence," and "Gérard of Nevers," &c. We were on the look-out for combats, deeds of prowess, and great feats with the lance and sword. Of the love-scenes we made little account, and when the Paladins began to bill and coo we were wont to turn the page. Our imaginations presently teemed with adventures. We rated far above the rest the heroes who owed their success to their own personal valor. For this reason, Renaud de Montauban bore off the palm from all his rivals, and became the type of an accomplished chevalier. All these fabulous people were weighed in our righteous balance, and received a rank in accordance with their merit, and each one was included in a category. Renaud alone could not be classified. From Charlemagne to Maugis, and Huon de Bordeaux, no one was forgotten. If the great Don Quixote himself could have been present at our deliberations, he would have approved our conscientious impartiality, and I do not hesitate to say that his Highness would have confirmed most of our judgments.

This labor of classification once completed, we felt our minds relieved, and resumed our dramatic representations. Léon Gobert played his parts admirably, and the character which he personated best was that of Roland. From the moment of entering the lists, he laid about him with positive fury. Alfred, as the weakest, was privileged to wield the enchanted lance, which unseated, by magic, the strongest and boldest knights. Whoever was touched by that was bound to fall, and thus an equality was maintained among the combatants. But our passion for chivalry put the patience of our tutor to a severe trial. Too often, instead of listening to him, we were prancing through the forest of Ardennes. He was quite right to be angry, but we were incorrigible. To avoid his penalties we invented a diabolical *ruse.* On each page of Noel's Latin Dictionary was inscribed the name of a cavalier. Whoever had a word to look out in the dictionary must assume the character whose name he found on the page containing the Latin word. The name of the braver of two knights caused the pupil who got it to score one, that of the inferior knight lost one to the other; and thus, under the pretext of Latin translation, our game went on under the master's very nose. One day our good M. Bouvrain was

himself looking in the dictionary, and chanced upon the
name of the traitor Ganelon ; whereupon, his two pupils
burst into a laugh as silly as that of Nicole in the
" Bourgeois Gentilhomme."

I should not dwell on these trifles, if I did not think
that they suggest subjects for reflection to those who
are devoted to the thankless calling of the teacher.
Instead of making war on our infatuation for the heroes
of chivalry, why might they not have turned our school-
boy passion to good account in our education?   All that
was needed was to offer to our starved imaginations a
better diet.   Would it not have been possible, by a little
tact and indulgence, to substitute the heroes of Plutarch
for those of the *Bibliothèque bleue?*   Our enthusiasm would
have fastened upon Themistocles or Paulus Emilius,
and we should have condemned the bad faith of Lysan-
der no less severely than the perfidy of Ganelon.   But
it costs a great effort to study the characters, tastes, and
instincts of children ; and I can well understand that it
is more convenient to treat them all alike.

The year 1819 was distinguished in our memories by
the important episode of a journey to Brittany.   After
staying a month in the little town of Fougères, where
Uncle Desherbiers was sub-prefect, we went to Rennes
to visit a friend of our father.   The artillery regiment
quartered in the town afforded the inhabitants the spectacle of a polygon by night.   On the day succeeding
the celebration, there was a party at the house of our
host, and several artillery officers were present.   The
colonel's son, who professed to know how to draw,
sketched upon a sheet of paper some mortars and can-

non ; and, to represent the curve described by a bomb-shell, he naïvely traced some regular semicircles.

"That is wrong," said Alfred. "The bomb is fired in a straight line, and then, as it loses its force, it changes its direction little by little, until the weight of it brings it down to the ground. And it doesn't go in a circle, but in a line that is curved in the middle and straight at both ends."

And he took the pen and drew some parabolas on the paper. The colonel's son, trained in the artillery, was vain and obstinate enough to defend his own work. But an officer to whom they appealed as umpire looked with amazement on the babe who had solved a problem in statics, and did not fail to assure our mother that her infant phenomenon would one day be a great mathematician. He was mistaken. Alfred had no taste for the exact sciences; but he had a correct eye, and could tell what he saw.

We had been promised a sight of the ocean ; and our host took us in a carriage to Dinan, where we embarked with other passengers upon a river which empties into the bay of Saint Servan. A violent storm broke upon us at nightfall, just as we were out on the open sea. A squall struck our bark and snapped the mast, and whirled away into the air the shako of a soldier. The passengers set up a doleful wail, and the captain lost his head. Fortunately, a large fishing-craft, just entering port, overhauled us off Cape Malo, where we arrived damp and chilled, but enchanted at having made the ocean's acquaintance through the medium of a slight shipwreck.

On our return to Paris, in the early days of October, our tutor expressed a wish to leave ; and the man who applied for the place was an ass who affected fashion, but whose ignorance soon became manifest. Our father thought a public education the only suitable one for boys, and he placed me in an institution. My brother remained at home and attended classes as a day-scholar in the college of Henry IV. He was but nine years old, but they thought him fit to enter the sixth form, which proves that good M. Bouvrain's lessons had not been so bad. On the day that he entered school, the spoiled child was greeted by the hootings of his companions. He had imprudently been allowed to retain his beautiful light curls, and a scalloped collar turned down upon his shoulders. He came home weeping, and insisted on having his hair cut at once. But, though he took this experience tragically, it was one of those mortifications which help to mould the character. It is altogether wholesome to come in contact with ridicule and ill-nature, when one is released from the maternal apron-string. We cannot learn too early to defend ourselves, and not to rely on the indulgence of others. This lesson, however, was followed by a far more cruel test, such as few have undergone at so tender an age.

Alfred early took a high rank in composition, and was noticed by the professor. The head of a large institution, where the course was very severe, wanted to take him gratuitously into his own house, declaring that he would be responsible for the boy's obtaining prizes at the general competition. Our mother rejected the offer decisively, fearing that her son's health would be sacri-

ficed to the reputation of the establishment. She never
repented her prudence. There was no need to stimulate
Alfred's ambition ; and, without working very hard, he
was sufficiently successful. Once, when he was not assigned a place on the *seat of honor*, he was so aggrieved
as to be almost inconsolable. He nearly cried his eyes
out, and was afraid to be seen ; but, when he found that
he was welcomed even more tenderly than usual, he realized, with a rapture which he never forgot, that he was
yet nearer to his mother's heart than he had supposed.
On the other hand, he was the smallest member of his
class ; and a ferocious hatred was excited among the baser
sort of his fellow-pupils against the little *blond* who was
always at the head, and whom the professor set above
the rest. The laziest formed among themselves an
offensive league against him ; and every day, when he
came out of the college-building, the model pupil was
saluted with a shower of blows. They chased him into
the very arms of the servant who waited for him at the
gate ; and the court-yard being a large one, he arrived
very ill-used, — his clothes in disorder, and sometimes
even with blood upon his face. The conspiracy lasted
for more than a month, and all that while the poor child
had to contend against the base passion of envy, under
its most brutal and cynical form ; so that he learned in
his very infancy that the vulgar do not bear themselves
toward superior men as they do toward the rest of the
world. It was Léon Gobert who brought this infamous
persecution to an end. He attended the school for
history lessons only. One day, seeing his friend fall
into one of these ambuscades, he flung himself into the

mêlée like a young lion, and dealt such terrific whacks on all sides that envy succumbed, and the league was dissolved for ever.

After my brother and I were separated, I saw him only on Sundays. On that day we returned to our chivalric romances ; but whether or no the cares of real life had shaken our faith and cooled our enthusiasm, it is certain that we did not bring to our make-believe the same ardor as heretofore. One day Alfred asked me seriously what I thought of magic, and particularly of the enchanter Merlin. I was obliged to allow that those stories were probably all made up by poets, and other ingenious writers ; that the wonderful adventures of Roland were fables, and that Merlin had never enchanted anybody.

"What a pity !" said Alfred, with a sigh. "But even if you can't make yourself invisible, or go in a flash from one place to another, or have a genie at your beck, there is nothing to hinder your making secret staircases in a thick wall, or having a hidden door in a wainscot panel, which will open by pushing a spring, if not by saying magic words."

I told him that I firmly believed in hidden staircases and secret doors.

"Well, then, what are we thinking about ?" he cried. "We have lived in this house several years, and how do we know that there isn't, even here, some mysterious passage or other, or some way of going from one story to another through the inside of the walls ?"

But a searching examination convinced us of the mournful truth that there was no mysterious outlet to our house. When I saw how disappointed my brother was, I wanted to afford him one moment of illusion. The dwelling of the Baroness Gobert had only a ground-floor and two stories.[1] We occupied the second; and we had, besides, a large kitchen under the roof, and two servants' rooms which looked into the gutter. At the risk of breaking my neck, I climbed by this gutter from one chamber to the other. The maid-servant had inserted in the wood-work a gilded copper hook with a screw, to hang her watch upon. I decided that this hook should be the key of a hinged panel; and I pompously informed my brother that there was a secret passage in the partition between the two attics. The news excited him so much that he turned pale with joy. Before unfolding to him the mystery, I required him to allow me to make the transit without seeing how I did it. We mounted to the attic. He shut his eyes and stopped his ears with all the simplicity and good faith of a true believer. I slid noiselessly along the gutter. When he heard me call him from the next room, his surprise was extreme. The idea did not occur to him to open his eyes and watch me, for he shrank from finding himself face to face with the flat reality. He wished, however, to traverse the wall for himself; and, under my directions, he turned the copper key eleven times one way, and thirteen the other; and I know not how many more times from right to left, and left to right. He stayed there half an hour, thinking that he had made some mistake. At last I revealed my stratagem,

---

[1] This house, No. 27 Rue Casette, has recently had another story added.

and the magic was dispelled. Alfred thanked me for
the deception as for a delicate attention ; but he felt the
illusion to have been too early lost. He promised
himself the pleasure of playing the same trick on our
neighbor Léon Gobert ; but that youth had no faith.
He made haste to open his eyes and dart at the gutter,
so that the trick was not even played out.

The adventure of the secret door was just before the
first of January. Whether by chance, or intentionally,
our parents gave us for our New Year's present the Don
Quixote of Cervantes, and that charming work dealt the
last blow to our demoralized taste for chivalry. We saw
more clearly than more rational readers that the work
of Cervantes is full of wisdom, moderation, and good
sense ; that it is calculated to clear the mind of extravagant and ridiculous rubbish ; and that it hits precisely,
without overpassing, the end at which the author aims, —
namely, as Cervantes himself says, to hold up to the
contempt of mankind a false and absurd school of literature. So ended, in Alfred de Musset's childhood, the
era of the marvellous and the *impossible ;* a sort of erup-
tion which his imagination had to undergo, — a malady
without danger for him, since he recovered from it at an
age at which others are barely attacked ; and all the
traces it left were a poetic and generous element, a certain inclination to look at life as a romance, a child-like
curiosity, and a sort of admiration for the unexpected, —
for concatenations of events and the caprices of chance.
This slightly fatalistic tendency may be recognized in
his novels and comedies, especially in the characters to
which he lends his own views and feelings.

III.

FOR those unfortunates who go to school, the year is reduced to the six weeks of vacation : the rest is but a series of insipid days during which one flounders in Latin, with one's elbows on a desk, and when it would not be worth while to live, were it not conceded that there is no other way of becoming a man. Alfred de Musset was too conscientious in his work, too desirous of success, and too much afraid of failure, not to be perpetually agitated and unhappy during the period of his classical studies. A low rank was his despair. If he had not been able to commit his lesson to the very last word, he set forth for the college trembling with apprehension. He was pursued by remorse for even the slightest failures, and always thought himself to blame. At the beginning of every school year, he was greatly exercised about the change of professors. We learn from one who was especially interested in him that he made one leap from the sixth to the fourth form, and even then bore off the first prize at the end of the year. He thoroughly corrected his timidity afterwards, but never overcame his tendency to nervous anxiety.

In the vacation of the year 1822, our father decided to take us to see his old friends in the vicinity of Vendôme, most of whom were unknown to us. At Chartres, a burlesque reception had been prepared for us. We descended from the diligence in the midst of a group

of peasants, who were apparently stupefied with amazement when they recognized *Monsieur de Pathay*. They
asked if the two striplings who accompanied him were
his sons, and addressed us with quirks and puns which
we did not at all know how to take. But M. de Pathay,
more acute than Pourceaugnac, recognized all the mum-
mers, one after another, except one wet-nurse, very loquacious and diabolically mischievous. It was a woman
who had been a young girl when he left, and whom he
found the mother of a family at the end of a dozen
years. We regarded this merry company with amazement; but they all played their parts wonderfully well,
and we retained a high opinion of the wit and liveliness
of the people of Chartres.

At Vendôme a less amusing reception awaited us.
Although the day and hour of our arrival had been announced to our old aunt the Canoness de Musset, she
professed not to have expected us. Her little house in
the faubourg Saint Bienheuré, with a tiny garden enclosed by a branch of the river, was very like those chill
and silent interiors which Balzac loved to describe.
There was an odor about it of penurious antiquity; and
the shutters, perpetually closed, defended the mould
and saltpetre on the walls from the sunlight. Three
dogs — one a hideous pug — replied to our pull at the
bell by inappeasable barkings. The mistress of the
house received us grimly. The breakfast, for which we
waited long, was so meagre that the good lady was
ashamed of it; and she condescended to add a cluster of
grapes, as sour as vinegar, which she plucked from the
trellis. During this light repast, she gave us clearly to

understand that she could have dispensed with our visit. At intervals the brother and sister became red with anger. They exchanged a few flings and parted coldly. In 1830, when the noise occasioned by the publication of the "Contes d'Espagne" had penetrated even that moist retreat, the canoness consoled herself by a reproachful letter. She had always blamed her brother for his excessive love of literature; but it was the extreme of humiliation to have a poet for a nephew. She disowned and disinherited the males of our family, on account of the disgrace.

A few days of freedom under the old trees of Bonneaventure effaced the painful impression made by our visit to the canoness. The remainder of the vacation was divided between the little Château de Musset —where was then living a cousin of ours, who was also a devoted friend — and the ancient manor-house of Cogners, the hereditary seat of the head of the family. Cogners, elevated to a marquisate, during the regency of Anne of Austria, was a feudal castle, which derived, from certain large additions made in the seventeenth century, a character at once picturesque and majestic. The great winding stone staircase is a blemish to both stories. The modern portion, where the state apartments are, contains immense rooms, with windows of an extravagant height. In the old part, the rooms are irregular in shape, the doors narrow, the windows have deep seats. Between the two layers of a double floor in one of the chambers a secret retreat had been contrived, approached by a trap-door, concealed under a huge, high-posted, canopied bed. Women and priests had sought refuge there during the storms of the Revolution. One of our fondest dreams was suddenly realized; but rather late, as often happens in this life. Great was Alfred's joy at being permitted to inhabit this chamber. Despite the fatigue of a day of travel, he could scarcely sleep for impatience to open the trap-door. He woke me at day-break, and we went down into the mysterious *entresol.* The room was low, but perfectly habitable. We came back covered with spiders'-webs, and when we discovered the subject of the fine tapestry which adorned our room to be Don Quixote taking the barber's tin dish for the helmet of Mambrino, we could not help laughing at our expedition.

Every thing, however, at the Château of Cogners, even the hospitable and patriarchal manners of the inhabitants, reminded us of by-gone times. We dined at two o'clock, and had supper at eight. The traveller, *curé,* physician, or military man who happened to be crossing the country, was sure of a plate at table, and room in the stables for his horse. In the evening, we gathered in a vast hall on the ground-floor, very dimly lighted in the far corners by a candelabrum with two arms, placed on a large stand in the centre. When one passed near the table, a gigantic shadow was projected upon the walls. While we waited for supper, the lord of the manor read aloud the lesson for the day. He declaimed certain passages with a solemnity truly comic, and never failed to take off his cap, when he came to the titles of Monseigneur the Dauphin, and her Royal Highness, Madame. It was no satire on the personages named, but merely his way of testifying his contempt for the new

power of the press, the importance of which he had not
learned to understand as an organ of public opinion.
The Marquis de Musset had been a member of the
Chamber of Deputies for 1814. His son served in the
king's body-guard, and his son-in-law in the guards of
Monsieur. He had himself served under the old régime.
At the age of eighteen, being then an officer in an
Auvergne regiment, his fine bearing attracted the attention of Louis XV., who made him step out of the
ranks that he might examine him more closely. His
grand-nephews could only admire in him the graces of
old age; but he was straight as a candle, and had a complexion of singular freshness, prominent eyes, an aquiline nose, and very handsome legs. He held his head
high when he walked, and flung his feet forward, as if
making his *entrée* into the royal drawing-room. His
grand air, his correct language, and the fund of old
stories which he told so well, inspired us with a mixture of curiosity and respect.

The marquis had had in his life one deep grief, aggravated by remorse, of which he never spoke, although
time and religion had consoled him. He had lost by
his own fault an eldest son of great promise. I remember that the subject was always avoided in the family
when the children were present; still we had heard
vague mention of our cousin Onésime, his fine parts
and pleasant disposition. Later, I learned the story of
his tragical death. His father had conceived the unfortunate idea of placing him, at fifteen, in the Institution
Liotard, where more attention was paid to the religious
sentiments of the pupils than to their intellectual de-

velopment. Onésime fancied that he was destined for
the clerical profession, toward which he felt an invincible repugnance. He imparted his fears to my father,
and besought him to intercede with the marquis and
induce him to explain his intentions. On his own part,
also, the youth wrote letter after letter ; but he received
only stern replies, and never the explanation which he
desired. The father, buried in his province, did not at
all comprehend the danger of these vague monitions.
He saw, in the prayers and entreaties of his son, only a
lack of submission. Onésime, never doubting that he
was to be made a priest, penned a last desperate letter.
The marquis was moved ; but he decided on principle
to make one more display, at least in words, of the rigor
of paternal authority. In a reply more severe than those
which had preceded it, he offered no explanation ; but
exacted a blind obedience. The fatal letter was hardly
in the post-office, before the father, as though he had
divined the consequences of his answer, set off in haste
from Cogners for Paris, determined to withdraw his boy
from the Institution Liotard. He arrived on the evening of the day when Onésime had committed suicide.

Our aged aunt, who was as devotedly pious as her
husband, had in the end consoled herself as well as him
for this terrible misfortune. She was an excellent lady,
a genuine figure of the past, with very slight knowledge
of the world, for she had never left her father's château
when she removed on her wedding-day to that of Cogners,
whence she never stirred. Her eldest daughter, who had
not married, devoted herself to charity on a great scale.
She had a kitchen and a dispensary for her paupers,

and read as many medical books as the parish doctor. She was often sent for in the middle of the night. At all hours and in all weathers, she would set forth, with her bundle under her arm, to carry aid to the sick. Neither fatigue nor failing health could stay her zeal for a single day. She led this devoted life in a lonesome region, with no reward save the blessings of the poor of the district, until the day when her strength sufficed only for praying to the God whom she had so nobly served.

Our good parents divided their caresses equally between my brother and me. Our uncle had an evident partiality for Alfred ; and so our aunt, actuated by a sense of justice, displayed the same for me. While the husband gave his favorite the finest fruit, the wife slipped tidbits into my plate. This milk-and-honey regimen was very satisfactory to hungry school-boys ; and, whenever we were asked where we wanted to spend our vacation, we clamored to go back to Uncle De Musset's. In 1824 we did so ; but this time an accident, of which any other child than my brother would not have made great account, mingled a fearful association with the delights of the castle of Cogners. Alfred was wild to go out hunting for the first time. A small single-barrelled shotgun was procured for him ; and, under the keeper's direction, he was permitted to kill rabbits in the warren. One morning he was walking behind me, carrying under his arm the gun which he had just loaded, and the muzzle of which was pointed at my heels. The gun was worthless, the trigger was worn out, and somehow it went off, the charge of lead making a hole in the ground close to my right foot. I turned at the noise ; and, across a puff of smoke, I saw my brother waver and fall. He had a nervous attack, followed by fever. The illness was short; but his passion for the chase was much diminished, his visit at Cogners was spoiled, and the number of the year, 1824, was always replaced by the periphrasis, — "the year when I almost killed my brother."

Alfred was then in his fourteenth year, and so far advanced in his studies that he might have graduated at fifteen, if he had not taken a double course in philosophy. The Duc de Chartres, who was his classmate, had received permission from his father, the Duc d'Orléans, to invite some of his school-fellows to the château of Neuilly on holidays. The best scholar in the class was, of course, among the invited guests. He found favor with all the Orléans family; especially with the mother of the young princes, who charged her son not to forget the little *blond*. It was a needless injunction. De Chartres, as he was called at school, had a marked partiality for Alfred, and during recitation used to write him heaps of billets upon bits of paper. They are mostly invitations to dine at Neuilly; but their tone is very free. I will quote the last only, which is in reply to a farewell note that the young prince thought too ceremonious.

"This is the last day that I shall come to school. As we shall not see one another for some time, I should be very much obliged if you would write to me. We are going on the 21st, and shall not come back before the 9th of August. We are going on a rambling tour to Auvergne, and Savoy, and the banks of the Lake of Geneva. Adieu, and ever yours.

"DE CHARTRES.

"P. S. I wanted something besides your respects."

During the trip here mentioned, the prince addressed to his old school-fellow two long letters. The first, dated at Clermont-Ferrand, contains a detailed description of the mountains of Auvergne. The other is the story of an excursion into Switzerland, told with all the artlessness of youth. But I find in the same bundle of papers still another letter, — much more original, and called forth by some ebullition of friendly and familiar mirth. I think that this last is worth publishing. It is dated Sept. 14, 1826.

"MY DEAR FRIEND, — It is only because I had nothing to say, that I have delayed writing to you so long. Nine study-hours — varied by horseback rides, and occasional stupid family parties at Montmorency, or the fair of Loges — do not offer much material for a letter. But to-day I have performed a splendid feat, and I must tell you about it.

"We went to the fair at Saint Cloud; and after we had been weighed, and had gone the round of the twenty-five-sou shops, and bought whatever we fancied, and eaten quantities of wafers, we went into the equestrian circus of M. le Chevalier Joanny. There were about a hundred persons present. M. le Chevalier Joanny, being five feet and eight inches high, came out in an old guardsman's uniform, made for a man of about five feet; so that the bottom of the waist was in the middle of his back. He had an embroidered waistcoat underneath, and his pantaloons were made to imitate Turkish trowsers. Then began a terrific noise, which was the overture. The inside orchestra — for, while the circus performance went on, they were all the time summoning spectators outside with trumpets — the inside orchestra consisted of six horns, all out of tune; and a trombone, played by a very young and very pretty woman. A Chinaman leaped into the ring. He had the top of a parasol for a hat, very dirty

drawers for breeches, and other things to correspond. As
for the other performers, *Ab uno disce omnes.*

"At last, after a great number of feats and gambols, they
all left the ring to make way for a monstrous elephant,
who was destined to be the *theatre* of my exploit. The
animal was very intelligent, and performed a number of
feats at the command of his driver. When he was ordered
to salute the company, M. le Chevalier Joanny explained
to us that in India, 'at sunrise, these creatures by a sort of
religious instinct salute the majestic orb of day.' What the
devil has religion to do with it?

"When the elephant took a broom to sweep the hall, M. le
Chevalier, who accompanied every act of the clumsy but
knowing animal by some judicious reflection, informed us
that, in India, little ladies of rank employ these creatures as
housemaids to clean their boudoirs. Finally, he invited all
who were so disposed to mount upon the elephant's back.
Nobody stirred. Seeing the general backwardness, I determined to set an example; so I climbed upon the creature's
back. along with the keeper and my brother Joinville. None
of the spectators cared to follow us. As we passed the
orchestra, I gravely removed my hat; and the musicians, not
to be outdone in politeness, struck up the air, — 'Où peut-
on être mieux.'

"Such, my dear friend, was the trait of heroism of which I
wished to inform you, confident that you would appreciate
it at its true worth.

"FERDINAND, P. D'ORLEANS."

IV.

THUS far we have seen in Alfred de Musset only a precocious child of vivid imagination, and an assiduous pupil, receiving with docility all that was taught him. But, in 1826, he began to give unusual signs of strength and independence of mind. He had been taught logic, analysis, and ratiocination ; and he began to reason. Often after the recitation in philosophy, when he had heard the lesson with attention, he would shake his head, and venture to say, " It does not satisfy me." He would then review in a hundred different ways the question under discussion, probe it to the bottom, and come to a fresh conclusion. His compositions were full of his aspirations after truth. The professor — an excellent man, · but extremely orthodox — was disturbed that his scholastic metaphysics were not received as Gospel-truth by his best scholar. He had, however, the good sense not to be angry. If only his fundamental principles were accepted, he would allow discussion of subordinate points. More than once, he gave a lesson to the whole class on the *duties* of the scholar. In the month of July, 1827, when Alfred had competed for the inter-collegiate prize, M. Cardaillac and another member of the university board came and told our father that his son would in all probability obtain the highest prize. The subject given out was a Latin dissertation on the Origin of Emotion. The essay of Alfred de Musset had at once been adjudged the best, both in thought and manner; but the religious side of the question had appeared to be insufficiently developed. Another pupil, whose work showed less talent, had dwelt more upon this important point; so that the opinions of the examiners were equally divided. The head-master of the university — who was also Bishop of Hermopolis — had caused the scale to incline toward the lad who seemed more devout. It could hardly have been otherwise under the reign of Charles X. Some years later, the first prize was given to Alfred; but now he only obtained the second. At the moment of distribution, Monseigneur d'Hermopolis smiled to see mount the platform a little *blond* of sixteen, with a head so small that the crown dropped about his neck.

A prize is of no great importance, save as a test of collegiate success. The works of Alfred de Musset show that he did not stop there in the study of philosophy, but pushed his metaphysical researches very far. The attentive reader knows that the thinker in him is always abreast of the poet.[1] It is important, however, to a clear understanding of the man, that we should examine his mode of procedure in the search for truth. When he came in contact with a great mind, he began by conscientiously taking the place of a learner, in order thoroughly to fathom the doctrine or the system. He

[1] M. Victor de Laprade, in the discourse on Alfred's reception by the French Academy, which he had the distinguished honor to pronounce, let fall in the course of his eulogium, whether in carelessness or levity, the strange remark, "Alfred de Musset obtained, if you can believe it, the philosophic prize!" It was astonishing to nobody but M. Victor de Laprade.

adopted it. He was ready to profess and even practise it. But presently his reason was outraged upon some point: doubts arose, and the disciple became first judge and then dissenter. It was thus that I saw him travel by successive stages from Descartes to Spinoza, then to the new philosophies of Cabanis and Maine de Biran, arriving finally at that haven where he found the "Espoir en Dieu." In his search for the beautiful he pursued the same method. He began by enjoying whatever pleased him, yielding himself with ardor to the delight of enthusiasm, and he ended by examination and exact appreciation. In this twofold exercise of seemingly incompatible faculties, — namely, enthusiasm and critical penetration, — he acquired, not in literature only, but in all the arts, a soundness of judgment which, if he had had nothing else to do, would have made him one of the foremost critics of his time.

In pursuance of the new plan of study which he had marked out for himself, Alfred began paying special attention to the reading of foreign authors, drawing, music, and law. Repelled by the dryness of the law, he had a passing fancy for medicine; but M. Bérard's lessons in descriptive anatomy, and the dissection of human bodies, inspired him with an insurmountable disgust. His father's one fear was that he would be an idler, and yet he did not press him to choose a profession. It was the student himself who was alarmed by the discovery that he had no taste for either of the two more distinguished of the learned professions. He shut himself up in his own room, and remained there several days, a prey to the most melancholy reflections; and,

when I inquired the cause of his sombre mood, his
answer was, "I shall never be good for any thing.
I shall never practise any profession.   Humanity in
general is only too insignificant on this grain of sand
where we live?   I shall certainly never consent to be
any particular kind of man."

He had no suspicion that he would, ere long, be
classed among men so rare that not more than three or
four of them appear in a century.   His mortification
was appeased when his drawing-master, amazed at his
progress, told him that he might be a painter if he chose.
At the notion that he might, after all, have a vocation,
his courage revived.   He spent his mornings in the
Louvre, and his portfolios filled with sketches.[1]   This
passion for painting was, however, only a digression
with which Nature amused herself, before revealing the
way by which she was to lead him.

In the spring of 1828, our mother rented a small suite
of rooms in a very large house at Auteuil.   Chance gave
us for a neighbor M. Mélesville, and charming relations
sprang up between his family and ours.   We acted
comedies and improvised charades.   We had sometimes
for spectators the elder Brazier and M. Scribe, and
Alfred enjoyed these reunions intensely.   He was off
to Paris early in the morning to pursue his studies, and

---

[1] Most of these sketches, among which were some original designs, were
destroyed by Alfred himself.   His friends often cut pages out of his album.
I have still two finished drawings.   One is a full-length portrait of Louise
Bouvier, — a celebrated thief, detained in custody at Clermont; the other a
head of Lord Byron.   Mme. Maxime Jaubert has about fifty of Alfred de
Musset's drawings.   An album full of caricatures was given me by a lady
cousin of mine, with whom he spent a month in 1842.

work in a studio ; but he returned to Auteuil for dinner, often on foot by the woodland alleys of the Bois de Boulogne, and with no companion save a book. The day when he had taken André de Chenier's little volume to read by the way, he arrived in the country later than usual. Under the spell of that elegiac poetry, he had chosen the longest way. From delighting to re-read and recite verses which one loves to aspiring to compose the like, there is but a step; and Alfred did not resist the temptation. He composed an elegy which he has not thought it worth while to preserve, but it began thus,—

> " Il vint sur les figuiers une vierge d'Athènes
> Douce et blanche, puiser l'eau pure des fontaines.
> De marbre pour les bras, d'ébène pour les yeux.
> Son père est Noémon de Crète, aimé des dieux ;
> Elle, faible et rêvant, mit l'amphore sculptée,
> Sous les lions d'airain, père de l'eau vantée,
> Et féconds en cristal sonore et turbulent," &c.

A youth came to the same fountain driving horses and mules, and while the animals crowded about the basin, the youth asked the maiden if she were the nymph of the spring. When he discovered that she was a mere mortal, he made love to her and invited her to share his home, of which he gave a poetic description. The maiden, whom her father had devoted to the worship of Diana, rejected the young man's proposals at first, but finally yielded. Then the jealous goddess pronounced a curse upon her, and the faithless priestess died just as the morning sun appeared above the horizon. This piece, which contained no less than a hundred stanzas, was finished in two days, or rather in two walks, and with the exception of a song composed at the age of fourteen for his mother's birthday, these are the first verses which Alfred ever wrote.

The history of his second attempt belongs to the age of romanticism, and the great civil war in French letters. The classics yet held possession of the stage, where they defended themselves as in a redoubt : but the " Henry III." of Alexander Dumas was already written, " Marion Delorme " was on the stocks, and " Cromwell " published ; and the famous preface to the latter work, in which the author had created a new school of poetry, had caused a fermentation in many a youthful brain.   Even before he had finished his studies, Alfred de Musset had been introduced, by his friend and school-fellow Paul Foucher, at the house of Victor Hugo.   There he had seen MM. Alfred de Vigny, Prosper Merimée, Sainte-Beuve, Émile, and Antony Deschamps, Louis Boulanger, &c.   All of these had already given proofs of genius, and won more or less reputation.   The time was spent in readings and literary conversations, in which everybody appeared to be of the same mind, although at heart they were often otherwise.   Alfred did not try to resist the contagious enthusiasm which one breathed in the very air of the Cénacle.   He soon became a neophyte in the new church, and was permitted to join the evening walks when they went to see the sunset, or to enjoy the view of old Paris from the towers of Notre Dame.   On the morning after a meeting, where a good many ballads had doubtless been recited, the young listener pacing along under the trees of the Bois de Boulogne, and haunted by the musical rhythm which still sounded in his ears, undertook to compose, first a ballad, and then a short romantic drama, both of which he afterward condemned to the flames. The scene was laid in Spain, in the castle of the old Sanchez de Guadarra. The daughter of this nobleman was singing one night at her window a plaintive song. Agnes had been twice affianced.

> " Une main dans sa main, deux fois s'était glacée,[1]
> Et, vierge, elle était veuve, en deuil de deux époux."

The two youths to whom she had been promised had died on the day after their betrothal. Her father had just proposed to her a third husband, Don Carlos, a brilliant cavalier, young and valiant. Old Don Sanchez had a high opinion of Don Carlos, and thus expressed his preference for the military profession : —

> " Homme portant un casque en vaut deux à chapeau,
> Quatre portant bonnet, douze portant perruque;
> Et vingt-quatre portant tonsure sur la nuque."[2]

The brilliant Don Carlos arrived with his long sword and his gold spurs. Agnes allowed herself to be betrothed for the third time. During the ceremony, a monk was saying his prayers in a corner. It was Don Juan, the brother of Carlos, a gloomy and mysterious person, who spoke seldom and always in vague prophetic terms, —

> " And ever gazed beyond the horizon's line. "

---

[1] She had twice held a hand which turned to ice in her grasp. She was a virgin and yet a widow, — in mourning for two husbands.

[2] A man in a helmet is worth two in a hat, four in a student's cap, twelve in a periwig, and twenty-four with the tonsure.

Don Juan was apparently indifferent to what went on around him. But, when the ceremony was over, he requested a moment's conversation with Don Carlos; and the two were left together. The monk then confessed his own love for Agnes, and that he had poisoned her two former lovers. Forbidden by his vows to aspire to her hand, he could not suffer her to belong to another man. He begged Don Carlos to give up the marriage; and, his prayer proving futile, the monk seized a sword suspended on the wall, turned back the sleeves of his frock, fought his rival and slew him briskly, after the manner of the romantic school, and subsequently killed himself, while Agnes went into a convent.

I need not say where the novice of seventeen found the subject, and whence he adopted the style of this performance. We detect the influence of the president of the Cénacle, and some of the verses need not have been disowned by the master himself. It should be observed that "Hernani" had not then seen the light, and that romantic Spain had but just been discovered by M. Merimée.

A tri-weekly journal of the narrowest dimensions was then appearing at Dijon, under the name of the "Provincial." Paul Foucher, who knew one of the editors, had published some of his own verses in this newspaper; and he proposed to submit to the same editor certain stanzas by another poet, as young and obscure as himself, who dared not as yet give his name. Sustained by Paul Foucher's recommendation, the youthful poet sent to the Dijon journal a ballad composed expressly for the "Provincial." This fragment, entitled "A Dream,"

appeared in the number for August 31, 1828, with no
signature but the initials A. D. M. It was in the woods
of Auteuil that the blond poet dreamed out this bit of
pleasantry. Paul Foucher's editorial friend, in an intro-
ductory note of twenty lines, asked pardon of the
readers of the "Provincial" for offering to them so
excessively romantic a composition ; but the editor-in-
chief, M. Charles Brugnot, declared in a foot-note that
this deprecatory preface was none of his, and that he
had no favors to ask for a piece of fanciful writing,
which he considered charming. The infant poet was
already the subject of a controversy between the two
editors, who quarrelled in the pages of their own journal.
Alfred, however, was overjoyed to receive the number of
the journal which contained his first printed verses.
Many a time since then his thoughts have awakened the
groanings of the press ; but the modest Dijon newspaper, preserved with religious care, has always held an
honorable place among his papers.

At the close of the year 1828, the literary war was
becoming livelier day by day. The louder the classical
camp cried "barbarism," the more audacious did the
romanticists become. Happy time, when men were
ready to fight for a sonnet, a fugitive verse, or a hemi-
stich ! Like a soldier who sees his friends rushing into
action, Alfred felt possessed by the longing to try his
strength. One morning he went and awoke M. Sainte-
Beuve with the laughing announcement, "I have been
making verses too!" M. Sainte-Beuve was not the
man to make a mistake about the worth of these
attempts, and the future reserved for their author. A

few days later, he wrote to one of his friends, "We have a child of genius among us." Alfred now determined to have his pieces read at the Cénacle. The elegy was a good deal applauded, but the poem of "Agnes" excited positive enthusiasm. The immense difference in style and movement between these two works could not fail to be remarked by so intelligent an audience. This versatility of talent gave the highest possible idea of the powers of the new recruit to the phalanx. It might have been foreseen that it would be impossible for him to serve long under any banner whatever, and that he would soon break ranks and follow his own fancy; but, as yet, nobody dreamed of that. Among other good traits, the members of the Cénacle had this admirable quality, that they knew not envy, and never stinted their praise of young aspirants. Alfred was welcomed on all sides.

But, despite these encouragements, the *débutant* would not yet allow that he was a poet. "If I were to mount the scaffold to-morrow," he said to his brother, "I might well strike my forehead, and repeat the words of André Chenier, 'I feel that I had something here'; but they are doing me poor service by assuring me that I am a great man. The public and posterity alone can confer that rank."

In order to have more verses to recite to his friends, he composed successively " Le Lever," "L'Andalouse," "Charles Quint à Saint Just," "Don Paëz," "Les Marrons du Feu," and " Portia." Then came the " Ballade à la Lune;" yet no symptom was observed of a revolution in his ideas, and great was the amusement excited by that carnival of wit. For even parodies were admitted by the Cénacle, and there was intolerance of nothing but classical works. No one dreamed that this lad had completely fathomed all the doctrines discussed in his hearing, and adopted an independent course ; and that he was neither to accept advice nor follow any model, from the day when, after deep reflection and long listening to the poetry of others, he uttered Correggio's cry, " I, too, am a poet ! "

While his muse yet lured him to the woods of Auteuil, the age of manhood arrived. On his first appearance in society the winter before, women had paid no attention whatever to the little fellow, who conscientiously executed the steps which his dancing-master had taught him ; but a few months later, his figure developed, and he lost his boyish air and his timid bearing. His countenance assumed a remarkable expression of pride and assurance, and his glance became steady, and, at the same time, so inquisitive and piercing that it was not easy to meet. The first woman who detected the change was a lady of much talent ; a fine musician, coquettish, and satirical, but attacked by an incurable affection of the chest. To visit her in the country, whither she continually invited him by notes of prudent brevity, Alfred missed his *rendezvous* with the Muses, and traversed the sterile plain of Saint Denis. When he saw that this lady did not regard him quite the same as formerly, while still she affected to treat him like a child, the manœuvre amazed him. It was some time before he learned that advantage had been taken of his innocence, and that he had been made to play the part

of Fortunio. The lady was provided with a Clavaroche;
but she had not the heart of Jacqueline. She remained
insensible to the tender reproaches of the youth whom
she cruelly mocked. He stopped his visits without betraying either anger or scorn. Another lady who had
a fancy for him tried to console him ; and when one
morning I observed him in spurs, and a tall hat inclin-
ing to the right side, while a long lock of hair waved on
the left, I perceived by these cavalier airs that his
vanity was safe.

Seven years later the memory of his first adventure
awoke, when Alfred de Musset thought himself taken in
a similar snare. He was mistaken this time ; but the
transient suspicion produced the " Chandelier,"—in my
opinion, his most perfect comedy, and one of the best productions of the French spirit since the days of Molière.

In the last days of 1828, as we were coming out of a
ball-room, where Alfred had displayed a keen ardor of
enjoyment, Prosper Chalas, editor of the "Temps" and
the "Pandora," a clever fellow with some knowledge of
mankind, seized my arm in the street, and whispered
in my ear,—

"You may be sure that your brother is destined to
become a great poet; but when I see his face, his delight in the pleasures of society, that air of his like that
of an escaped colt, the looks which he gives women
and the looks which they give him, I am afraid of the
Delilahs for him."

The presentiment was realized. The Delilahs came,
but they only made him the greater poet.

PART SECOND.

From 1829 to 1836..

V.

BESIDE the danger hinted at by Prosper Chalas, Alfred de Musset had freely run all sorts of other risks at the age of eighteen, and his position was defined. He had been intimate with young folk who were richer than he, and he had wished to adopt their ways of life. The first tailors in Paris had alone the privilege of approaching his person, and he gave them employment. Horseback exercise was in fashion among his friends, and he hired horses. They played high, and so did he. They turned night into day, and he kept vigil. But he had a constitution like steel, and incredible cerebral activity; and he often wrote fifty verses after his return from a supper-party. That which would have been excess for many people was really only exercise for him. When I spoke to him of the perils of *bouillote*,[1] and of the terrible day when the tailor would bring in the bill for his new clothes, he replied : —

" Just because I am young I want to know every thing. I want to learn by experience and not by hearsay. I feel as if there were two men in me, — one acting, and the other observing. If the first does a silly thing, the other will profit by it. Sooner or later, please God, I will pay the tailor. I play, but I am not a gambler; and when I lose money, the lesson is worth all the reproofs in the world."

[1] A game at cards.

Occasionally, to be sure, he had sombre mornings and evenings of vain regret. On these days of wretchedness, the poet liked to compose a costume corresponding with the situation. Out of the depths of a closet he would drag an old yellow coachman's coat with six capes, large enough to go round him three times. Thus muffled, he would lie down upon the floor of his room, and hum in a lamentable voice some ancient air, contemporary with the coat. Whenever I found him in this penitential garment, and in a melodramatic attitude, I knew that the cards had proved intractable. The moment I opened my lips to address him, "Let me alone," he would say, covering up his face. "Leave me to my rags and my despair."

But when evening arrived he would put off his rags and don his finest clothes. The mere change of raiment sufficed to turn the current of his thoughts; and he would set forth on a tour of Parisian drawing-rooms, where the pleasures of the world caused him to forget his reverses at play. Either because a ball-room made a singular impression upon him, or owing to some peculiarity connected with his taste for painting, he remembered with astonishing accuracy the order in which the ladies had been seated, the colors and fashion of their dress, the way their hair was arranged. Moreover, luxury gave him a kind of intoxication. He admired bright lights, laces, and jewels, as a child admires them. To dance with a real marquise, in real diamonds, in a vast saloon as light as day, seemed to him the summit of bliss. He had the same childish admiration for people who make a show of any kind. He could forgive Alexander for having burned Persepolis to amuse a courtesan. He liked Sylla because he was fortunate. Heliogabalus did not displease him at a distance in the robes of a priest of the Sun; and even Cæsar Borgia found some favor with him on the score of his mule shod with gold. I did not scruple to charge him with these weaknesses; and the best talks we ever had were when we quarrelled about such things, for he defended his bad cause admirably. I pause to note these details, because they belong to a period of three years only, in the career of one whose character was soon to change and become ennobled.

The winter of 1829 passed rapidly amid this complex life, in which, nevertheless, reading and study occupied a large place. The Muse now and then descended, taking him by surprise; but she was well received when she came. Among his pleasure-loving companions, Alfred was so fortunate as to find one true friend. Alfred Tattet, then making his first appearance in society, was exactly of the same age as himself. He was a lovable fellow and a very lively guest, regular in his devotions and extravagant in his language, finding every thing either entrancing or execrable; but yet keener after the pleasures of the mind than any others, and always ready to go into raptures over a fine verse. He easily obtained a sight of his friend's productions, and used to give little æsthetic evenings and *matinées* for the sake of hearing them read and re-read. There De Musset made the acquaintance of Olric Guttingeur, who one day took him to Havre and Honfleur. In consequence of a confidential conversation which they held

on this journey, Alfred wrote three stanzas which sufficed
to immortalize the friend to whom they were addressed.
The youngest disciple of the great Cénacle thus became
the god of a Cénacle not yet known.

In the drawing-room of Achille Devéria, where he
went a great deal, Alfred used to waltz alternately with
two young girls of the same age; both very pretty and
pleasing, equally ingenuous and great friends. He
talked delightfully about fashions and dress and trinkets,
and was as much a child as any of the three. He used
to dilate regularly to each on the beauty and the graces
of the other. On the morrow the maidens would exchange confidences, and they were somewhat scandalized
not to be able to discover which he preferred. These
drawing-room flirtations were renewed season after season, until they ended in an adventure which a few people must still remember. Gustave Planche, who was
very discriminating in his antipathies, detested Alfred
de Musset for no reason, but instinctively. Planche did
not dance; but, from the corner where he was seated,
he undertook one evening to depose that he had seen
the indefatigable waltzer furtively kiss the shoulder of
one of his partners. There was an immediate "Fie! fie!"
and the young lady received orders to refuse to dance
with her habitual partner. Alfred guessed, by the sorrowful looks of the victim, that she was acting under
authority, and having done nothing amiss, he demanded
an explanation so peremptorily that it was impossible to
refuse. The malicious speech was traced to its source,
and Planche attempted to deny it; but the matter was
pressed, and he was at last obliged to confess. The

father's wrath was turned against him, and when the
ball was over he waited for the calumniator and administered a sound caning. Planche learned the truth of the
proverb, "Ill luck follows an ill-wisher;" and it may
well be supposed that the adventure did not make him
love any better the poet to whom he owed the lesson.
The young girl's reputation was not to be affected by
any such flurry, and it was to her that Alfred de Musset
afterwards addressed the verses "To Pepa."

During this time, the collection of poems which was
to bear the title of "Contes d'Espagne et Italie," was
growing by degrees. That nothing may be omitted, we
will note, in passing, a first publication which is very
little known. At eighteen, Alfred was only too happy to
translate from the English a small romance for the publisher M. Mame. He had adopted the simple title of
"Le Mangeur d'Opium;" but the editor insisted on
"L'Anglais, Mangeur d'Opium."[1] This little volume, of
which it would probably be difficult to find a copy to-day,
was prepared in a month. The translator was not very
exact, and introduced into the reveries of the foreign
hero some of the impressions which he had himself received from M. Bérard's lessons in descriptive anatomy.
No notice was taken of this anonymous publication, and
it disappeared in the flood of literary novelties, like a
drop of water in the sea.

But now came a catastrophe of which the consequences
were serious, and which troubled the poet deeply. One
morning his father informed him that he had secured for
him a clerk's place in one of the offices of M. Febvrel,

---

[1] The title of the original was "Confessions of an English Opium-eater."

who had just obtained, through sealed proposals, the contract for supplying the military posts with fuel. The poor boy dared not wink. He suffered himself to be fettered by the bureaucratic ball and chain. No very great assiduity was required of him ; but he daily felt the weight of his fetters in every respect save that of salary. Impelled at length by a frantic desire to regain his liberty, he called on a devoted publisher of the romantic school. Urbain Canel examined the manuscript of the " Contes d'Espagne," and declared that it lacked five hundred verses of the length suitable for an octavo volume, which was the regulation form of the new literature.

" Five hundred verses ! " cried the poet. " I can soon give you those, if they will emancipate me ! "

It was the season of vacations, and Alfred obtained from his employers a leave of three weeks. On the 27th of August, 1829, he set out for Mans, where his Uncle Desherbiers was then residing. He returned on the 19th of September,[1] and that very evening repeated to me the entire poem of " Mardoche," which contained almost six hundred verses, some of the most audacious of which had, however, to be suppressed. Urbain Canel was particularly charmed by the length of the piece, and sent it at once to the printer. The compositors worked at these poems of an unknown author only in their leisure moments, and the last proof-sheets did not come till near the end of the year. On the 24th of December, Alfred besought his father to give a party, and invite MM. Merimée, De Vigny, Emile and Antony Deschamps,

[1] I find these exact dates in his note-books.

Louis Boulanger, Victor Pavie, De la Rosière and Guttingeur. To them he recited "Don Päez," "Portia," and "Mardoche." Most of the invited guests were already acquainted with the first two poems; but the last named, for all its freedom of language, carried off the honors of the night. There was but one opinion about the infallible success which awaited these poems.

A few days later, there appeared, under the title of "Contes d'Espagne et Italie," a volume of 232 pages, of which but five hundred copies were printed.[1] The effect which it produced is well known; but it is curious to-day to re-read the journals of that time. Some of them flew into a perfect rage against both the book and its author. One condemns the exaggeration both of characters and language; another, on the other hand, praises the young poet for not abusing his privilege of hyperbole. An opposition journal inquired with admirable gravity: "Whence comes this preference of the rising generation for Spain and Italy, countries where freedom does not exist, and where religion is degraded by superstitious observances." At the same time, a pious royalist critic votes an indulgence to the unbridled Muse on account of the second canto of "Portia," where he has discovered an edifying description of the awe inspired by the majestic aspect of a Gothic church.

[1] The smallness of the edition is not remarkable. In those days nobody bought new books. They only praised them in their neighbors' studies. Those five hundred books obtained, in a few days, ten thousand readers. Between 1828 and 1840 the fashion of publication changed. The 18mo displaced the 8vo, and people bought the books which they desired to read.

The celebrated " Ballade à la Lune " became at once the subject of clamorous discussion. Those who were sternly resolved to take it seriously, considered themselves absolved by this specimen from reading the rest of the book. Others saw in it much more than the poet had meant, and would have it that he was ridiculing both his friends and himself. It must be confessed that, on this occasion, professional connoisseurs and respectable middle-aged men were not exactly the most intelligent judges. But while they gravely discussed, with more or less of good faith, the exact meaning of the " Ballade à la Lune," the poet had conquered the public whom he desired to please, — the young of both sexes.

Alfred soon had numbers of adventures to confide to me. Some were " Boccaccian," and some romantic ; others had a spice of the dramatic. Several times, I was awakened in the middle of the night to give my serious opinion on some matter requiring the utmost prudence. All these anecdotes having been confided to me under the seal of secrecy, I forgot them as in duty bound ; but I am able to affirm that they would have stricken with envy Bassompierre or Lauzun. The women of those days were not absorbed in luxury and the toilette. Young people who desired to please did not need to be rich. To have at nineteen the prestige of genius and fame sufficed for some things. But for all his success, Alfred de Musset had the modesty and good sense to resist intoxication. He was always on his guard against foolish pride and infatuation about himself, — a vulgar shoal, on which nevertheless some of the greatest minds have grounded.

While the *servum pecus* of imitators flung itself upon
the " Contes d'Espagne," and made, as best they might,
a hundred different attempts to copy them, Alfred de
Musset himself was pondering a reform, and changed his
pace so completely that, in the "Vœux Stériles," "Octave,"
and the " Pensées de Rafäel," — the first pieces
which he published in the " Revue de Paris," after an
interval of serious reflection, — we find no more irregular
verses, no trace of carelessness in style. We know that
the poet asked forgiveness of his mother-tongue for
having sometimes offended her. He said that Racine
and Shakspeare met upon his table Boileau, who had
forgiven them ; and though he boasted of making
his Muse walk bare-foot, like truth, the classicists
might have supposed her shod with the golden buskin.
They might well have congratulated themselves on an
apology, so gracefully uttered ; but they pretended not
to have heard it, and came back to the " dot of the
i," [1] like Molière's marquis- in his refrain of " cream
tarts." At this epoch, the romanticists, wounded by
Raphael's profession of faith, complained of desertion,
and did not fail to say that the poet of the " Contes
d'Espagne " had deteriorated, and was not fulfilling his
early promise. Alfred de Musset suddenly found himself alone, all parties having turned against him ; but
he was young, and proud as Œdipus, and literary differ-

---

[1] Musset, in his famous " Ballad to the Moon," fantastically compares the
planet, hanging above a pointed spire, to the dot over an i, —

> " C'était dans la nuit brune,
> Sur le clocher jaune ;
> La lune,
> Comme un point sur un i," &c. — TR.

ences did not prevent friendly intercourse. He did not go as often as formerly to the Cénacle; but he met his old friends at the receptions of Achille Devéria, and at the Arsenal with good Nodier, who loved him devotedly.

But Alfred had obtained leave to resign his place; and the day on which he did so had been one of the happiest of his life. That his father might have no anxiety about the consequences of this rash step, he undertook to produce something more lucrative than poetry; and with this intent he composed a little dramatic piece in three tableaux, entitled "La Quittance du Diable." Each tableau was accompanied by a recitation in verse. It was a mere scintillation of fancy, yet not without originality. With the assistance of a musician of talent, he might have made of it a comic opera, which would have been as taking as many others. The piece was offered to the theatre of the "Nouveautés," where all kinds of things were played, and it was accepted; and some steps must have been taken towards its representation, for the distribution of characters is written out on the cover of the manuscript, in the manager's hand. M. Bouffet and Mme. Albert were to take the two principal parts, and they were the best artists in the company. I do not know what prevented the representation; but probably it was the Revolution of July, which broke out while the leader of the orchestra was arranging the music for the scenes. However that may have been, the author withdrew the piece, and consigned it to the portfolio where it still remains.

After the crisis of the 7th of August, Alfred de

Musset, who feared nothing so much as a public office, remained a passive spectator of the rush for places. Selfish congratulations poured from all quarters into the palace ; but he allowed himself to forget his old school-fellow, now become Duc d'Orléans. The gravity of the political prospect, and the counter-strokes of revolution in the north and south of Europe, did not suffice to arrest the literary movement, begun under the fallen dynasty. The general intellectual fermentation seemed to have turned to the advantage of letters. During the four years of the new régime, a generation of writers arose who have not yet been superseded. In the autumn of 1830, the theatres, less restricted now than ever before, seized upon a subject which had been forbidden under the previous government ; namely, the epopee of the Empire. Napoleon appeared upon every stage, even the most obscure. Harel, the enterprising director of the Odéon, brought out in superb style a drama of this kind, the principal part in which was given to Frédéric Le Maître ; and, to fill a void in his repertory, the same manager requested the author of the " Contes d'Espagne et Italie" to furnish him a piece as novel and audacious as possible. The manuscript of the " Nuit Vénitienne " was the result, and M. Harel appeared enchanted with it. The piece was carefully mounted, committed to memory in a few days, and announced as a godsend. M. Lockroy took the part of the Prince ; Vizentini, a capital actor, played the comic character ; an actress of moderate gifts, but extremely pretty, played Laurette ; and M. Lafosse, Razetta.

The first performance took place on Wednesday, Dec.

1, 1830.   I do not know the character of the audience ;
but in the second scene, which is nevertheless extremely lively, Vizentini found himself interrupted by
hisses.   Furious cries drowned the voices of the actors,
and the pit had paroxysms at all the finest points in the
dialogue, as though it had gone with the full intention
of hearing nothing.   The author was confounded by the
uproar, and could not believe but that the piece would
recover itself during the great scene between the Prince
of Eisenach and Laurette.   Mlle. Béranger, beautifully
dressed in white satin, was resplendent in freshness and
beauty, and for a moment the gigglers were actually
silenced.   Unhappily, the actress, in looking from her
balcony to see if the jealous Razetta were still at his
post, had to lean against a green trellis, the paint of
which was not dry, and she· turned toward the public
with a robe all crossed with green squares, from the
girdle to the hem.   This time the disheartened author
succumbed to his ill-luck ; and the scene between the
Prince and Laurette was fairly smothered in the yells of
the audience.   All the charming wit by which the young
" Vénitienne " allows herself to be cajoled, passed un-
heeded.   In that scene, there is one remark quoted from
a letter of Lovelace to Belford.   I hoped that this passage would conciliate the malcontents ; but it did not.
Richardson was hooted like all the rest.   Harel, convinced that all this tumult was deliberately planned,
insisted upon a second trial.   The fatal trellis was removed, Mlle. Béranger wore a new gown, and the author
besought M. Lockroy to add these words, after the quotation from Richardson, " as Lovelace says."   But all

was vain. The piece had almost precisely the same reception as at first, and the name of Lovelace was greeted by an ignorant and senseless titter. When the storm was at its height, the author cried out, " I would never have believed that there was material in Paris for so stupid an audience." Prosper Chalas wrote him the next day, and asked whether he proposed to throw himself to the beasts that evening, and he replied, "No, I have said farewell to the menagerie for one while."

The consequences of this sad mishap were incalculable. Disgusted by a rebuff of which he keenly felt the cruelty and injustice, Alfred de Musset wrote no more with a view to stage representation. If the public had awarded to the young author of twenty the consideration which was his due, how many more dramatic pieces might have followed this first attempt! His glorious revenge of the "Caprice" was not taken until seventeen years after this mortifying evening. Who can say how the theatre would have stood to-day if a handful of Bœotians had not alienated from it, for so many years, the only writer capable of arresting the decline of the dramatic art. Possibly that class of literature which, since the reign of Louis XIV., has always held the foremost rank in France, might have escaped the reproach of declining to a manufacture. The public has only itself to thank for the pleasure which it has lost.

Loève-Veimars, in the "Temps," had the courage to chide the Odéon pit for the brutality of its behavior. The young author was grateful, and paid a visit to Loève-Veimars, during which he was presented to

Jacques Coste, chief editor of the "Temps." The latter, by way of experiment, requested the author of the "Contes d'Espagne" to furnish him a few fanciful articles, and allowed him *carte blanche.* From Jan. 10, to the close of May, 1831, there appeared quite regularly every Monday a series of anonymous articles under the head of "Revue Fantastique," where Alfred treated such subjects as occurred to him. That of "Pantagruel, the Constitutional King," was remarkably opportune, and had a great success. But, though truly modest, the poet had too much independence long to submit to any species of slavery. He wearied of journalism, and his reviews soon ceased to appear.

Under the pretext of acquiring experience, he was leading a somewhat dissipated life. Young people of fashion used then to spend their evenings at the Café de Paris, and parties of pleasure were organized there on an extensive scale. They would set off at midnight in post-chaises for Enghien or Morfontaine. They laid extravagant bets, which created public excitement, and Alfred de Musset bore his part in all this nonsense. Occasions for more moderate pleasure also came to him. The *unforeseen,* for which he had a somewhat pagan veneration, reserved for him sundry special favors. Often bewildered by the choice offered him, he neglected a more obvious for a more doubtful pleasure, — for a simple card-party at his neighbor's the Marquis of Belmont, an informal visit, a cigar, a chat with a friend, or for nothing whatever. He found it extremely pleasant to stay at home and reflect that he might be enjoying himself abroad if he liked. His study was to him a haunt of delight, and there we often talked till three o'clock in the morning. Or sometimes the framing of an engraving purchased on the quays demanded our serious consideration; and, on such days, ours was an animated interior, and our family meals were as gay as possible.

Among those freaks of chance which the poet loved to regard with a whimsical reverence, there was one which deserves to be reported. Mme. La Duchesse de Castries wanted to read the "Contes d'Espagne," and ordered her companion, who was an Englishwoman, to buy a copy. Miss —— was not very well acquainted with the ways of the world, and knew no better than to write to the author the following note:—

"MONSIEUR,— A young English lady, wishing to read your poems, addresses herself immediately to you to obtain them. If you will send them to her, she will be deeply obliged."

This note, legibly signed and bearing the young lady's address, remained for a long time open upon a table, in company with others equally impertinent. One morning, however, Alfred read it over, and wrote the following reply:—

"MADEMOISELLE,— All young English ladies are pretty, and I shall not wrong you by fancying you an exception to the general rule. Since, therefore, you have freely confided to me your name and address, do not be surprised if I claim the privilege of offering to you in person the poems which you desire to read."

Poor Miss —— was terribly embarrassed. She ran to the duchess and confessed her blunder, and showed her

the cavalier reply which her imprudence had drawn
forth. Mme. de Castries comforted her, and told her
to await with composure the proposed call. Alfred de
Mussel soon came with his book under his arm. The
valet de chambre had had his orders, and conducted
him to the drawing-room, where the duchess received
him most graciously and invited him to sit down. She
then explained smilingly the mistake of her companion.
"There is no reason," she said, "why you should be
deprived of the pleasure of seeing this young English
girl, and I will presently introduce you ; but you must
begin by making my own acquaintance."

Thereupon, they began to talk. Alfred knew perfectly well that the Duchesse de Castries was one of
the most agreeable women in Paris. He, therefore,
put a good face on the matter, accepted the situation
merrily, and determined to shine ; and the result was
that the acquaintance, thus begun, ended in a life-long
friendship.

VI.

IT has been said of the author of the "Contes d'Espagne" that all he lacked in his various enterprises was good advice. I would have liked to see the honorable counsellors bringing their budget of maxims to that eager spirit, who knew much more about them than the old masters themselves, and who never treated a literary question, either in conversation or in writing, without improvising a whole art of poetry, full of genuine novelties. Nothing certainly would have been easier than to convince him that his verses were bad; but he would have flung them into the fire, and there would have been no gain. Advice about his way of life he never lacked. But it would have been a fine thing to hear reasonable people lecture this Fantasio, who even while he gave loose rein to his passions, yet scrutinized and studied himself so carefully that his fancy far outran all representations which could be made to him. Nothing but time, experience, and reflection can change the character of a poet's genius; and, if reflection can abridge time, never did poet advance faster than he of whom we speak.

His experience with the public had been enough to make Alfred de Musset resolve to reform his *manner*. Nor was this merely an affair of prosody and versification. A revolution far more important was in progress in his ideas and the character of his mind. He produced very little in the years 1830 and 1831; but he read and reflected much, and he lived more perhaps than is needful for a poet. One evening, in the month of October, I found him sitting moodily with his head in his hands, and I asked him what he was thinking of.

"I am thinking," he replied, "that I am approaching my majority. Two months from to-day, I shall be twenty-one; and that is a great age. Do I need to visit so many men, and chatter with so many women, in order to know mankind? Have I not already seen enough to have much to say, supposing that I am capable of saying any thing? Either we have nothing in us, and our sensations have no effect upon our minds; or we have the elements of all things in us, and then we only need see a little in order to divine the whole. And still I feel that I lack something, I don't know what. Is it a great love? Is it a great sorrow? Both perhaps. But I dare not crave that sort of enlightenment. Experience is a good thing, provided it does not kill you."

As if he scented in the air something which he dreaded, he formed schemes for retirement and hard work. He tried regularly to apportion his day. That he might be sure of quiet recreation, he took a season-ticket to the opera for six months. Sometimes he passed the time of the performance in a stage-box, where he met friends. Sometimes he retired alone to a remote corner, and gladly allowed the music to excite his imagination. Under this sort of stimulus, he composed the "Saule," the longest and most serious poem which he had yet written, and which represents what we call,

in the work of a painter, a period of transition. I
have elsewhere described the grotesque destiny of this
poem.[1]

The winter opened with gloomy auspices. The cholera,
which had been stayed for a short time in Poland, had
just appeared in the north of Germany. One morning we
learned that it had leaped with a single bound to London, and presently the tidings spread that it had broken
out in Paris. The whole aspect of the city was changed.
One could not stir abroad without meeting hundreds of
hearses. In the evening, the deserted streets, lighted
at long intervals by the red lanterns of the ambulances,
the closed shops, the silence, the few panic-stricken
passers-by who were hurrying for help, all revealed the
presence of the scourge ; and every morning the number
of the dead increased. Immense removal-carts encountered at every door one or more biers, sometimes
but half constructed. If the corpse was not ready, the
overworked agents complained of being made to wait,
and quarrelled with relatives and servants. Since the
days of the plague in the reign of Charles V., nothing
like it had been known in Paris.

Our father was then suffering from an attack of the
gout. On the 7th of April, when the physician questioned him, we observed his countenance change. He
did not mention the pestilence, but the prescriptions
which he ordered were enough. At nine o'clock in the
evening, cholera declared itself with frightful violence,
and at six in the morning all was over. Our consterna-

---

[1] See a brief notice of the life of Alfred de Musset, in the quarto edition
of his works, published by subscription in 1866. Paris: M. Charpentier.

tion was so great that we did not at first measure the
consequences of this great misfortune. I had seen my
brother shed tears over disappointments in love ; but now
his grief was quieter because deeper, and he was mute.
"This," said he, "is one of those tearless troubles which
are never assuaged, the memory of which will always
keep its first horror and bitterness. Death strikes us
otherwise than love."

Before examining the state of our father's affairs, it
seemed evident to us that, if the emoluments of a fine
office were subtracted from the family income, our position must necessarily be changed. It did not prove so.
Unexpected resources appeared ; but their extent was
yet uncertain, when my brother confided to me a resolution which will perhaps appear incredible to-day.

"Without comfort," said he to me one evening, "there
can be no leisure, and without leisure no poetry. I must
stop playing the spoiled child, and toying with a vocation
which is not a career. It is time for me to think and act
like a man. The notion of being a burden on the best of
mothers, or of prejudicing the future of a sister whom we
adore, and who will need a dowry in ten years, is revolt-
ing to me. I shall put the affection of those whom I love
best to no such test ; and this is what I have determined
to do. I shall make a last literary experiment with a volume of verses which will be better than the first. If the
publication of this work does not bring me in as much as
I expect, I shall enlist in Chartres' hussars, or in a regiment of lancers along with my old comrade the Prince of
Echmühl. The uniform will be very becoming. I am
young and in good health. I like horseback riding ; and,

with the influence which I can bring to bear, the devil is in it if I do not become an officer."

Considering the necessary delay, I was not overpowered by terror at this resolution. There was no prospect of immediate want at home. Alfred began his work, and it was not from work that I desired to dissuade him. The plan of the poem was suggested by that Oriental proverb of whose truth he was destined to have sorrowful experience, " Between the cup and the lip, there is room for a misfortune." He supposed himself obliged to work, and delighted to repeat that necessity is a muse whom courage can idealize. Sustained by the idea that this attempt would be his last, he felt perfectly free in his mind ; and, when he was satisfied with his day's work, he used to rub his hands and say : " I am not a soldier yet."

With no more information about the Tyrol than could be derived from the old geographical dictionary of La Martinière, he did not hesitate to lay the scene of " La Coupe et les Lèvres " in that unknown country, and he proved thereby that " the poet has within himself the elements of all things." This dramatic poem, which contains more than sixteen hundred verses, was finished in the course of the summer; and the author then read it aloud to his friend Alfred Tattet. During the autumn, he also wrote the comedy, " À quoi rêvent les jeunes Filles." Two sisters full of wit and grace whom he had known at Mans, and whom he called his first partners, served him as the models of those two charming figures, Ninette and Ninon.

It was I who undertook to offer to the publisher Renduel this volume, whose title, "Un Spectacle dans un Fauteuil," was suggested by the remembrance of that tumultuous night at the Odéon. Renduel seemed in no haste to conclude the bargain. Poetry, he said, was not a salable commodity, while prose sold like bread. Fortunately I myself had just engaged in bread-making; and, out of regard to me, Renduel consented to trade in the less popular form of food. The MS. was in the hands of the compositors, and the proofs were coming, when there was added at the foot of the page an exclamation of alarm, "More copy! more copy!" The publisher added, "There are but 203 pages, and we must have 300, or the volume will not be presentable."

The author set to work again. He wrote "Namouna" yet more expeditiously than he had written "Mardoche." Even then there were but 288 pages; but the article being rhymed, and consequently of the second class, the publisher was content with the smaller quantity. Alfred then assembled his friends, and made them listen to "La Coupe et les Lèvres," and the comedy "À quoi rêvent les jeunes Filles." The audience consisted of the very persons who had applauded the "Contes d'Espagne" three years before; but what a difference! He was heard in sombre silence. Was it admiration, shock, surprise, or dissatisfaction? I do not know. I only know that the *séance* was perfectly glacial, and that the publisher was in despair. M. Merimée alone drew near the author and said in a subdued tone: "You have made an enormous advance. The little comedy, especially, pleases me very much." The book appeared before the end of the year, but with the date 1833. It did not create nearly as great a sensation as the "Contes d'Espagne ; " but most fortunately the author had heard, the very day after it was offered for sale, two young men who were walking before him on the Boulevard de Gand laughingly repeat this verse from the part of Irus, —

"Spadille a l'air de oie, et Quinola d'un cuistre." [1]

And this trivial circumstance, made him feel entirely satisfied. The journals were apparently somewhat afraid to reverse their previous judgments ; but at length M. Sainte-Beuve, who himself owed no apology to the author of the "Contes d'Espagne," succeeded in attaching the bell. In the "Revue des Deux Mondes," for Jan. 15, 1833, he published an article in which the new volume of poems was compared with the first, progress noted, and the beauties of the two works illustrated, with that absolute correctness of eye, that skill in thoroughly searching and fathoming a subject and throwing its most delicate shades into relief, which make criticism, when sustained by disinterestedness and good faith, a truly fine and useful art. M. Sainte-Beuve quoted from both volumes passages with which he was peculiarly struck, and then added : "To my mind these verses have a poetical quality, the equal of which in its own way is not to be found in all the works of any one of a large number of estimable people whose verses have brought them to the Academy, — M. Casimir Delavigne himself, if you will. Images like these are found, not elaborated. I could cite at least a hundred as good, of which all plagiarists, manufacturers, verbal critics, and people of taste, are invited to partake."

[1] "Spadille looks like a goose, and Quinola like a fag."

One likes to see criticism turn animated and forget itself, cast aside its judge's cap in a moment of enthusiasm, and push to the verge of imprudence its disregard of consequences. At the close of his article, M. Sainte-Beuve delicately reminded his readers that he was a poet himself, by remarking that Marlowe and Rotrou, on the appearance of Shakspeare and Corneille, were saved from sorrow by admiration.

The example thus deliberately set by M. Sainte-Beuve found but few imitators. Articles appeared at long intervals. People were pretty generally agreed about the merit of the portrait of Don Juan in "Namouna." There was no longer any thought of denying talent ; but it was still possible to dispute originality. Every thing is like something else. Criticism fell back on the accusation, so often repeated since and with so little discernment, of having imitated Lord Byron and other poets whom my brother resembled but slightly. On this point, the author had well defended himself in the very dedication of the book thus criticised. This dedication contained a passage in which the doctrines of the romanticists, and the mania for curious rhymes, were sharply attacked. But it made no difference ; and the poet had flung at his head the names of Byron, Victor Hugo, La Fontaine, and Mathurin Regnier. In point of fact, a man who could have imitated successfully so many poets, differing so widely among themselves, must have come near originality. It would seem as if three years of intimate association with a mind as firmly tempered as that of M. Victor Hugo ought to have exercised some influence over a young *débutant ;*

but there was no trace of any such influence in the volume then in the hands of the critics.

As for Lord Byron, everybody imitated him in the sense that all contemporary poets heard his strains with emotion, and found echoes of the same awakened in their own souls. If Alfred de Musset responded to him better than the rest, it was because of a greater similarity of sentiment and life-experience between him and the English poet. On certain sides, in fact, these two fine organizations strongly resemble one another. They sacrifice to the same gods, and offer, "for incense, love and grief and melody; for a victim, the poet's heart." Both liked to represent themselves in their fictitious creations, because this was the only method which made it possible for the poet's heart to beat under the drapery of the character. In this respect, neither imitated the other; but they met upon ground which Dante, Shakspeare, Molière, La Fontaine, and many others, had traversed before them.

Can it be necessary now to say that, if Alfred de Musset studied Mathurin Regnier as well as Fontaine, it was for the purpose of fathoming the true genius of our language, and defending himself against that influx of English and Germanic elements which was inundating the new literature? Seriously, to imitate Regnier would have been to do him too much honor. What he liked in the old satiric poet, was his frankness; and he had the best of reasons for setting a high value on that Gallic quality, for he possessed it himself, and owed to it a large part of his power and influence.

Another reproach in which several of his critics

united, and which it is now curious to recall, was this:
"The poet of 'Namouna,'" said one, "has no convic-
tions about any thing. What sort of a man is he? What
are the objects of his worship? Whence does he come,
and whither is he tending? In times as serious as the
present, how can he practise art merely for his own
amusement? The moment is ill chosen for these free-
and-easy airs about all which troubles and disquiets
humanity. If he believes in any thing, let him say so;
otherwise, he is of no account in our generation. He
is but a poetical amateur." This reproof becomes positively comical when we reflect that the author of
"Namouna" is precisely the only poet whose doubts
and anguish, and yearnings toward the infinite and the
divine, fairly represent the most secret history of the
human heart in this age of scepticism. M. Sainte-
Beuve, more sagacious than the rest, began by expressing his own bewilderment about the meaning of a work
which appeared full of inconsistencies; but, when he
had succeeded in analyzing the great figure of Don
Juan, he exclaimed: "If I have said that this work
lacks unity, I retract the saying. Unity — the difficult
and impalpable — is here collected like a beam of light,
and falls full and with magic effect upon the countenance in question. This is the object of idolatry."

And yet it was a unity whereof only glimpses were
obtained by clairvoyant spirits. It is not discernible in
any isolated poem, nor even in any one volume; but it is
to be found to-day in the complete works of the poet.
For the fifteen years between 1830 and 1845, — that is to
say, from the "Contes d'Espagne" to "Il faut qu'une Porte

soit Ouverte ou Fermée,"—his last contribution to the portraiture of our society, short-sighted people never ceased
to reiterate on the occasion of every new book by Alfred
de Musset: "Who is this man, and whither is he tending?" To which he might have replied: "I am going
where my age is going, where we are all going, where
you are going yourselves, although you may not know
it." But he said nothing, and that was better still.

It may readily be supposed that Alfred abandoned
the idea of enlisting in De Chartres' hussars, notwithstanding the handsome uniform of that distinguished
corps. That public composed of the young of both
sexes which he had desired to please, had responded to
his appeal. It was not precisely for that public that he
deliberately undertook the immensely difficult task of
composing a poem in stanzas of six consecutive rhymes.
But his more serious object was attained. Shortly after
the publication of M. Sainte-Beuve's article, the chief
editor of the "Revue des Deux Mondes" engaged the
assistance of Alfred de Musset. This publication,
founded subsequently to the "Revue de Paris," had
just begun, in 1831, to appear twice a month. It had a
formidable opposition to encounter, and its fortune to
make. The young poet promised to contribute as much
as he could; and the reader will allow that the review
suffered nothing at his hands, for all that he wrote
appeared there.

On the 1st of April, 1833, Alfred de Musset made
his first appearance in the "Revue des Deux Mondes,"
by the publication of "André del Sarto." The
subject of this drama had been suggested to him by

7

the brief notices which accompany the engravings in
the "Musée Filhol," a favorite book of his, which he
was perpetually conning.   When he came to throw himself into the characters of the Florentine artists of the
Renascence, he conceived a strong desire to visit Italy.
He wanted, he said, to imitate the author of the " Histoire
des Croisades " who, after his work was complete, went
to the Holy Land to see what sort of places they really
were which he had described.

After an interval of six weeks, " André del Sarto "
was followed by the "Caprices de Marianne," the two
acts of which were thrown off in a kind of juvenile
transport, the logic of emotion supplying the place of a
formal plan.   When he came to the famous bottle
scene, and had put into Marianne's mouth the tirade in
which she taunts the young libertine with having lips
more dainty than his heart, and with knowing more of
beverages than of women, the author stopped short for
a while as though stupefied by the force of his own
reasoning.   " It isn't to be supposed," said he, " that I
am to be beaten myself by that little prude ; " and, after
a few moments of reflection, he conceived the triumph-
ant reply of Octave.   Now that this comedy is fully
accredited, both as a reading and acting piece, it is
played, but no longer judged.   The first person who
saw the printed proofs was a little startled by it ; nor
is this very wonderful.   It was like nothing else whatsoever, — an impassioned subject impregnated with the
very quintessence of wit and fancy.   The fragment was
inserted in the " Revue" without alteration, but not without apprehension.   It was, however, the last instance of

any thing like hesitation ; and every thing else which the
new poet offered to the " Revue des Deux Mondes " was
accepted forthwith.   I ought also to add that, when his
admission to the editorial staff of the magazine awakened jealousy, and was made the occasion of recrimi-
nation, the editor-in-chief undertook his defence, and
insisted upon retaining him, with a firmness which he
was obliged to push to the verge of obstinacy.   All who
ever knew Alfred de Musset realize how like he was
both to Octave and Cœlio, although these two characters
appear the very antipodes of one another.   Nowhere
but in himself did he find that humor, that inexhaustible
merriment, that careless raillery, which vivify the scenes
between Octave and Marianne.   That the author had
such a side may readily be conceived ; but to understand that the same man reappears in Cœlio, with all
his sustained passion, and the sad and sweet exaltation
of mind characteristic of the timid lover, one must
remember that love has a transforming power.   Once in
love, Alfred passed directly from the former to the latter
character.   Nor is it by any means incredible.   For the
pangs which our friends endure when in love, we are
readily consoled: we bear them like philosophers ; but
our own are no laughing matter, and our sufferings
from them are very real.   Once we were Octave, but
now we are Cœlio.   For the noble and tender figure
of Hermia, the author had not far to seek.   He had
his model before his very eyes in the person of our
mother, always intent on sparing him trouble, or adding something to his comfort.   As for Marianne,
when I asked him where he found her, he answered:

"Nowhere and everywhere. She is woman, not *a* woman."

One morning after the publication of the "Caprices de Marianne," Alfred was at a breakfast at the house of Mme. Tattet, the mother of his friend. MM. Sainte-Beuve, Antony Deschamps, Ulric Guttinguer, and several other distinguished literary men were present. The mistress of the house was asking Alfred about the health of his mother and sister, and he replied : "I suppose that they are well, but I must confess that I have not seen them for twenty-four hours." He was rallied on this answer, and submitted to the reproaches of his friends about his way of life ; but insisted, in self-defence, that he had some very serious ideas in his head. At dessert he was asked for some verses, and recited the first part of an unpublished poem. It was "Rolla," about which he had as yet said nothing to any one but his brother. The company welcomed the poem with transports of delight, and the author had the good taste not to revert to their late friendly remonstrances. He knew that he was justified.

"Rolla" appeared in the "Revue des Deux Mondes," Aug. 16, 1833. The next day, as Alfred de Musset was going in to the opera, he flung away a cigar on the steps of the theatre, and then saw a young man who was following him stoop instantly, pick up the fragment, and carefully wrap it in paper. He has told me a great many times that no compliment, or badge of reward, or distinction, ever touched his heart like that simple testimonial of sympathy and admiration.

At this period, Alfred met for the first time a person

who was destined to exercise a considerable influence over his life, and leave a deep impression on his works. It was at a great dinner given to the editors of the "Revue" at the Frères Provençaux. The guests were many, and among them there was one woman, next whom Alfred sat at table. She simply and pleasantly invited him to call on her; and, after going two or three times at intervals of a week, he became a constant guest. Some of his intimate friends were also on familiar terms there, and among them Gustave Planche. This cynical individual, who had neither tact nor good sense, had usurped a position which rendered him very annoying. He assumed airs of familiarity to which he had no sort of right, took the tone of a master, and affected an ease which the mistress of the house endured, out of weakness and good-nature, but with concealed impatience, as Mme. D'Epinay endured Duclos. Alfred, who knew Planche thoroughly, advised him to alter his manner. Planche pretended not to understand the hint, and it became necessary to be more explicit about the estimation in which he was held. Instead of changing his tone, he retired furious, and bore my brother an inextinguishable grudge ever after.

The *salon* from which Gustave Planche withdrew into exile lost nothing by his departure. Conversation never languished there, and it was a scene of reckless gayety. I have never seen so lively a circle, or one which cared so little for the rest of the world. There were chat, and sketching, and music. On certain days, the company disguised themselves and played different parts. They met in little committees and invented all manner of entertainments, less through dread of *ennui* than overflow of animal spirits. One day they took it into their heads to give an æsthetic dinner, with a tinge of politics and philosophy. The invited guests were certain editors of the " Revue," and, among others, Lerminier the professor of philosophy. In order to provide him with a suitable companion, they invited Debureau, the incomparable Pierrot of the " Funambules." Debureau, who was usually seen clothed in white and powdered with flour, put on for the occasion a black coat, a shirt with a very full ruffle, a stiff starched cravat, pumps, and tight gloves. He was ordered to personate a distinguished member of the English House of Commons, passing through France on his way to Austria, with extremely secret instructions from Lord Grey. When they were in full swing, Alfred wanted a part assigned him, and adopted that of a young supplementary servant-girl, freshly arrived from Normandy. He donned the peasant woman's short petticoat, ribbed stockings, short sleeves, and cross suspended from the neck. His rosy cheeks and blonde hair corresponded with this picturesque costume ; and when he had shaved off his moustache he looked like a fine slip of a girl, not too clever.

On the day appointed the guests arrived, to the number, if I remember rightly, of seven or eight. Debureau, as became so considerable a personage, arrived fifteen minutes later than the hour named. The guests were presented to him, and he responded to their salutations by slight bows, after which he planted himself before the fireplace, where he stood, stiff as a statue, with his hands behind his back, in glum silence. There was great curiosity to see the author of " Rolla ;" but at half-past six, Alfred de Musset had not arrived, and they sat down at table, leaving his place vacant. The place of honor was assigned to the Englishman, who opened his mouth only to eat and drink, but that largely. Nobody recognized Pierrot. In order to give him free play, and Lerminier a chance to display his knowledge, they turned the conversation upon politics. But vain were all allusions to Robert Peel, Lord Stanley, and the other renowned statesmen of Great Britain. The foreign diplomat replied only in monosyllables. At last, however, somebody used the phrase, "the equilibrium of Europe;" whereupon the Englishman waved his hand as if about to speak.

"Would you like to know," said he, "what I understand by 'the equilibrium of Europe,' in the present portentous state of English and continental politics? Observe me. I will illustrate."

The diplomat took a plate, flung it into the air with a rotary motion, and then caught it adroitly on the point of his knife, where it continued to spin, but kept its balance to the great admiration of the spectators. "There," said Debureau, "is an emblem of European equilibrium. There is no security elsewhere."

A universal peal of laughter succeeded, and it was redoubled when the hostess had named Debureau. But the young girl from Caux, whose taking ways had been remarked by some of the guests, did nothing but blunder from the commencement of the dinner. She dropped whatever she touched, put the plates upon the table wrong side up ; brought a knife when a fork was re-

quested, and *vice versâ*. The reproofs of her mistress
appeared to embarrass her, and increase her awkward-
ness.   At the moment, however, when the Englishman gave such energetic expression to his views on
the balance of power, the young waitress, the better
to testify her participation in the general hilarity,
seized a carafe as though she would drain it, and then
poured the water upon the head of Lerminier, who
began to swear at the pestiferous *Normande*. Alfred
then took his place at table, still in his peasant costume, and partook of his share of the dinner which he
had served so ill. The reader can guess whether the
remainder of the evening was lively. The story made
so much noise at the time that a good many Parisians
still remember it.

The same individuals will perhaps recall an almost
forgotten writer by the name of Chaudesaigues who was
then attempting literary criticism in the "Revue de
Paris," and some other journals. Having neither much
talent nor much influence, he was a little envious and
too simple to conceal the fact. He was a tall, pale
youth, with a face like the pictures of Christ, and he
stammered in talking. One day he came to make a
call in the drawing-room where Debureau had figured as
a diplomat. Near him in an arm-chair Chaudesaigues
saw a fair-complexioned young man, who spoke never a
word, but left the talk to him. He began an exceedingly
knowing criticism of "Rolla," "Namouna," and the rest,
without a suspicion of the general enthusiasm about
verses which he himself could barely tolerate. The
blonde youth smiled encouragement, seconded all his

remarks, and accompanied with nods of approbation the discourse of the iconoclast. Thus supported, Chaudesaigues was proceeding to personal criticism, when the mistress of the house abruptly interrupted him with, "I have the honor of presenting to you M. Alfred de Musset, whose acquaintance I have long wished you to make."

Chaudesaigues stammered, seized his hat, and rushed for the door, amid irrepressible laughter. But he was a better fellow than Gustave Planche. He returned and begged pardon for his offence, when he might justly have complained that a malicious trick had been played upon himself. They gave him the right hand of fellowship and he was admitted to a *coterie* where he continued to afford amusement by further blunders.

It would seem as if a relation which insured so merry a life, where talent, wit, grace, youth, and good-humor were thrown into a common stock, ought never to have been dissolved. Especially would it seem as if people who were so happy could not have done better than remain in an establishment which they had succeeded in rendering so attractive to themselves and others. But no: unrest, the foe of all well-being, and an incomprehensible turbulence of spirit seized upon them, and they began to pine for a wider sphere than a small *salon* in the first city of the world. That city became in their eyes no better than a heap of crumbling, smoking ruins, from which they must needs escape. They essayed at first an excursion to Fontainebleau ; but it did not suffice, and as winter approached they talked of Italy. Their talk soon resolved itself into a scheme of travel, and the project became a fixed idea.[1]

---

[1] It can hardly be necessary to say that M. Paul de Musset here describes, with a somewhat superfluous air of mystery, the beginning of the too famous relation between Alfred de Musset and George Sand. — TR.

VII.

ALFRED DE MUSSET felt that his Italian journey must remain but a half-formed purpose until he had obtained his mother's consent. One morning, at the family breakfast he appeared preoccupied. I knew what was on his mind, and was hardly less agitated than he. On rising from the table, he sauntered about with an air of hesitation. At last he plucked up courage, and made a cautious official announcement of his intentions, adding that his plans were subject to his mother's approbation. His request was received like a piece of undeniably bad news. " Never," said our mother, " will I give my consent to a journey which I regard as a dangerous and fatal thing. I know that my opposition will be overruled, and that you will go ; but it will be against my wishes and without my sanction."

For a short time, he hoped to overcome this resistance by explaining on what conditions the trip was to be made ; but, when he saw that his pertinacity served but to excite a flood of tears, he immediately altered his determination and sacrificed his project. " Reassure yourself," he said to his mother, " I will not go. If it is absolutely necessary that somebody should weep, it shall not be you."

And he actually went out to countermand the preparatory orders which he had given. The same evening, at about nine o'clock, our mother was sitting with her daughter by the fire, when word was brought her that a lady was waiting outside in a hackney-coach and very anxious to speak with her. Our mother went down accompanied by a servant, and the unknown lady gave her name. She then entreated the anxious mother to entrust her son to her, promising that she would herself show him a mother's care and tenderness. Promises not proving sufficient, she proceeded to vows. She employed all her eloquence, and it must have been great to have secured her success in such an enterprise. In a moment of emotion, consent was extorted ; and for all Alfred had said, our mother was the one to weep.

On a foggy, melancholy evening, I accompanied the travellers to the mail coach, where they took their places amid all sorts of evil omens. When people whom everybody knows undertake to travel together in this way, they may be sure that their reputation has everywhere preceded them, and that mystery is out of the question. Any one must have been mad to suppose that such an expedition could remain a secret. Their purpose was neither to avoid the judgment of the public nor to defy it, but simply to submit to it ; or rather they did not think about it at all. It can be no more of a secret to-day than the plot of a comedy ; and, as all the world knows, *that* comedy was a drama. I am not going to rehearse it. I shall only relate such circumstances as I learned at a distance of three hundred leagues, and which I should have known in any case, even if I had received no confidences.

Alfred's first letter to his family was dated at Marseilles. He was rejoiced to have fallen in with Stendhal (Henri Beyle), who was leaving for his consulate at Civita Vecchia, and whose caustic wit had enlivened the journey. The second letter, dated at Genoa, contained some details about manners, costumes, the women, and the famous picture galleries of that city, and also an account of a walk in the gardens of the Villa Palavicini, where Alfred had sat down to rest in a delicious spot beside a fountain, which was a great favorite with tourists. Other letters from Florence informed us that he had found in the Florentine "Chronicles" the subject for a drama in five acts, and was enjoying visiting the public squares and palaces which he meant to make the scenes of his characters' action. This was the drama of "Lorenzaccio."

From Bologna and Ferrara, which he merely passed through on his way to Venice, he did not write at all ; but on his arrival at the death-struck city of the doges, he fell into transports of childlike delight. The room which he occupied in the Danieli palace, on the Molo degli Schiavoni, seemed to him to merit a full description. He never wearied, he said, of gazing on those ceilings under which the head of some great Venetian family must have walked long ago, or of contemplating, through the window, the entrance to the grand canal and the dome of La Salute. He knew that he should not be able to resist the temptation of laying amid these surroundings the scene of a romance or comedy ; and he therefore took notes on Venetian customs and peculiarities of dialect, and made his gondolier chatter incessantly.

Near the middle of February, the letters which had

arrived regularly up to that time suddenly ceased.
After a silence of six mortal weeks, our mother and I
had determined to set out for Italy ourselves, when a
letter was forwarded to us, which only added to our
anxiety by its altered handwriting, its tone of profound
sadness, and the deplorable news which it contained.
The poor boy, hardly recovered from an attack of brain
fever, spoke of dragging himself home as best he might.
He wished, he said, to leave Venice as soon as he was
strong enough to get into a carriage. "I shall bring
you a sick body, a depressed mind, and a bleeding
heart, but one which loves you still." He owed his
life to the devoted care of two people who never left
his pillow until youth and nature had fairly vanquished his malady. For hours he had lain in the
very grasp of death, and had been conscious of it
himself, in the midst of his strange and utter prostration. He attributed his cure, in part, to a soothing
potion, opportunely administered by a young physician
of Venice; and he wanted to keep the prescription for the
draught. "It is a powerful narcotic," he added, "bitter
like every thing which that man gave me, — even the life
which I owe to him." The prescription was actually
found among Alfred's papers, with the signature of
Pagello.[1]

The sick man's return was heralded by a letter
which plainly revealed his nervous irritability. "For
pity's sake," he said, "put me in some other room than
my own. At the bare idea of awaking to the sight of

---

[1] During a trip which I made to Venice in 1863, I ascertained that M.
Pagello was still living and practising medicine at Bellune. — P. M.

that hideous, crude, green paper. I shrink as if the four walls were hung with *ennui* and disappointment."

To humor his invalid fancy, I determined to give him my room, which had two windows looking into the garden, and a paper of a peculiarly subdued tone. On the 10th of April the poor prodigal arrived, very much changed and emaciated; but, once under his mother's wing, recovery was only a matter of time. The severity of his attack may, however, be inferred from the slowness of his recovery, and the psychological phenomena by which it was accompanied.

The first time that my brother tried to tell us the true story of his illness, and his return to Paris, I perceived his face change suddenly, and he fainted away. He had an alarming nervous attack, and a month elapsed before he was able to recur to the subject and finish his recital.

Alfred kept his room for a long time, leaving it only in the evening to play chess with our mother. He had brought from Italy a sort of servant, a hair-dresser by trade, who had taken tolerably good care of him on the journey, without knowing a word of French. The lad was a poor enough valet; but his services were agreeable to Alfred, who often summoned Antonio and made him talk the dialect of his country. Antonio, however, contracted in these interviews a home-sickness so intense that it became necessary to send him back to Venice; and one morning he accordingly departed with a load of empty phials and old pommade-pots, which he proposed to fill with lard and spirits of wine, and sell to the inhabitants of the lagoons as specimens of Paris perfumery.

Our little sister, child as she was, already played the piano very well.   We observed that Hummel's fine *concerto* in B minor had the power of luring the sick man from his retreat.   When he had been shut up a good while, I used to ask for the Hummel *concerto*, and after a few minutes we would hear him open his door. Then he would come and sit down in a corner of the drawing-room, and when the piece was finished we often succeeded in detaining him by talking of music ; but if a word recalled his trouble he would return to his chamber for the rest of the day.

When his craving for solitude was partially appeased, he opened his doors to his friend Tattet and myself, from whom he had nothing to conceal.   We sometimes passed whole days in the invalid's chamber, and evenings which might as well be called nights.   At first, Alfred was determined to be brave.   He thought that pride would serve his turn, and plainly counted on that for subduing his grief and his regrets.   But he was not long in recognizing the impotence of this auxiliary, and then he thrust it away as a futile point of honor.   After a while he allowed us to see the depth of the wound which he had received.   Despite the fearful memories which oppressed him, he hugged his grief, and sometimes he was angry with us for venturing to chide him on this head.   At times he was morose, as though his very nature were changed.   He suspected us of I know not what treachery, or accused us of utter indifference ; and then, all in a moment, he would take shame for his suspicions, and revile himself for ingratitude with such exaggerated vehemence, that we could hardly soothe him. As for those who had destroyed his peace, it was not enough for him to forgive them. He tried to find excuses or at least extenuating circumstances, for them : so sick was he at heart, so fearful that the courier from Venice would bring him no more letters. He wrote several, in which he did not hesitate to take all the blame to himself ; some of them contained verses.[1]

When it became known in Paris that Alfred de Musset had returned without the companion with whom he had set out on his travels, the matter gave rise to much conjecture, and fables were invented which bore no resemblance to the truth. Alfred got wind of the gossip, and spared no pains to deny whatever might prove injurious to the lady whom he had left at Venice. In this respect, he merely did his duty as a chivalrous man : but he could not conceal his depression, nor the alteration in his looks ; and malicious conjectures continued to be raised in spite of him.

If we would know his real state of mind during this time of trial, it is to himself that we must apply for a faithful picture of it : we must give place to the patient, and hear him in his own words. This is what he wrote on the subject in 1839, — after a lapse of five years :

"I thought at first that I felt neither mortification nor regret at being deserted. I took my leave proudly ; but, when I came to look about me, I beheld a desert. An unexpected

1 In 1859, I requested the person with whom these letters were deposited to return them to the family of the deceased poet. He calmly replied that the sacred trust had been violated, and the letters restored to the hands of one who should never have seen them again. I inquired what had become of them, and learned that they had been burned. I have in reserve a package of autograph letters on this subject. — P. M.

8

anguish seized me. My thoughts seemed all to be falling around me like dead leaves ; and a feeling, hitherto unknown, awoke in my heart, — a feeling excruciatingly tender and strange and sad. I saw that I was powerless to struggle, and I gave myself up to despairing sorrow. I broke off all my customary occupations, and shut myself up in my chamber. There I stayed and wept for four months, seeing no one. and having no diversion save a mechanical game of chess in the evening.

"Little by little, however, my sorrow was assuaged, my tears were dried, my nights were no longer sleepless. I fell in love with melancholy. In this quieter mood I looked back at what I had left. No remnant of the past remained, — nothing at least which could be recognized. An old picture, a tragedy which I knew by heart, an utterly hackneyed romance, a talk with a friend, afforded me surprise. Such things had a new meaning : I knew then what experience is, and I saw that sorrow teaches us truth.

"That was a noble moment in my life. I love to pause at it ; a hard but noble moment. I have not told you the particulars of my passion. The story, if I were to tell it you. would prove very like another ; and what would be the use? My mistress was dark : she had large eyes. I loved her and she deserted me, and I suffered and wept for four months. Will not that suffice ?

"I presently perceived the change which was being wrought in me : but it was as yet far from complete. One does not become a man in a day. I began by indulging a ridiculous exaltation : I wrote letters after the manner of Rousseau, — no matter about all that analysis ! My sensitive and inquisitive spirit trembled incessantly like the magnetic needle : but what matter, if the pole is found? I had long been dreaming : now I began to think. I tried to say as little as possible, but I went back to the world. I wanted to see and learn things anew.

"One is captious when one is suffering. Sorrow is not easy to suit. I began like Cervantes' *curé,* by purging my

library and consigning my idols to the garret. I had in my
room a good many lithographs and engravings, the best of
which now seemed to me hideous. I did not care to climb a
staircase to rid myself of these. I was content to put them
in the fire. When my sacrifices were achieved, I counted up
what remained. It was not much, but that little inspired me
with a certain respect. My empty bookcase annoyed me ;
and I replaced it by one three feet broad, and containing three
shelves, where slowly and reflectively I arranged a small number of volumes. My frames, on the contrary, remained empty
a good while. Six months elapsed before I could fill them
to my taste. and then I put in them old engravings from
Raphael and Michael Angelo." [1]

All these details are precisely true. I was present at
the *auto-da-fé* of the engravings, and the dismantling of
the library. The books which he kept, and which he
called his old friends. were the French classics of the
seventeenth century, Sophocles, Aristophanes, Horace,
Shakspeare, Byron, Goethe, the four great poets of
Italy in one volume, Boccaccio, Rabelais, Mathurin
Regnier, Montaigne, Amyot's Plutarch, and André
Chenier. Leopardi's little volume was afterwards added
to this choice collection. The frames had been vacant
a good while when Tattet brought him, one day, a very
fine engraving of Raphael's Saint Cecilia.

" I hope," said he, "that this master will find favor
with your severity."

Alfred admired the engraving, and wished himself to
frame it ; and before long there grouped themselves
around the Cecilia, the Virgins of the Chair and the
Candles, the Poetry of the Vatican, Saint Catherine of

[1] From an unpublished work of Alfred de Musset's, entitled " Le Poëte
Déchu."

Alexandria, Michael Angelo's Surprise,[1] and the Goliath of Giulio Romano. Titian and Rubens were not admitted until long after.

When first our invalid had consented to seek for some amusement away from home, he said, as he was dressing : " Now that I am going to plunge again into the stream of life, I feel a mixture of joy and dread, for it seems as though the unknown were before me. I am like a goldsmith, who cautiously rubs a gold ring on his touch-stone. I am going to test every thing by my own half-closed wound."

And the first time that he returned from a visit where the conversation had been such as to make him forget his troubles, he experienced a sort of shame. " Such is human misery," said he. " A grief which has become torpid is as like enjoyment as a new pleasure."

When we asked him whether the desire to produce something would not soon revive, his answer was : " The *desire?* you mean the *faculty* of production. I know nothing at all about it. I am just as incomprehensible to myself as to others. I tremble already when I think how bad the first verse which occurs to me will look the next day when I come to examine it coolly."

We urged him as a mere pastime and proof of his mental recovery to write a prose proverb ; and the leading editor of the " Revue des Deux Mondes " showed him many marks of friendship. Naturally obliging, he

---

[1] Apparently the engraving by Marc Antonio of certain figures, from the cartoon of the Battle of Pisa, of soldiers surprised while bathing in the Arno. — TR.

did not like to refuse ; and, the editor needing something of an imaginative character for the magazine, Alfred made an effort to resume work. Some time before, he had sketched in a few lines the plan of a comedy, to which he had given the provisional title of "Camille et Perdican." He had even written an introduction to it in verse ; but nothing would have induced him to compel his Muse to descend by means of exorcisms, and he therefore translated his verses into prose.[1]

The piece which was entitled, "On ne badine pas avec l'Amour," bears marks, in some places, of the moral condition of the author. The singular character of Camille, certain speeches of Perdican's which are marked by a melancholy tenderness, and the conflict of pride between the two, suggest the influence of the sad recollections to which the poet had succumbed ; but the whole piece, from beginning to end, is imbued with a passion and fervor of feeling, before which the "Dépit Amoureux" of Molière — the subject of which bears some resemblance to the loving strife of Camille and Perdican — turns positively pale.

Before he went to Italy, Alfred de Musset had sent to M. Buloz the MS. of "Fantasio," and this comedy had been published in his absence. Those who had the good fortune to know the author in the flower of his youth, and his youthful follies, know how faithfully he has depicted himself in the original character of "Fantasio." But that which, in the comedy, suffices for a whole character, a perfect type, and the subject of a piece,

---

[1] The poetical form of the introduction to this comedy was published in the large quarto edition of 1866.

is found, when we examine the original closely, to constitute but a single facet of a brilliant mind, and one out of a thousand of the deep recesses of his heart. The Emperor Napoleon was right when, in a conversation on literary matters with the renowned Goethe, he said that there is not time in an acting play to develop a complex character, with all its apparent contradictions, its delicate shades, and infinitely multiplied incongruities; and that, if we would not confuse the spectator, we must represent only simple and legible characters, the clew to which is given in the first word they speak. Only in a biography and after the lapse of twenty years, can it be fully and convincingly shown that the tender Cœlio, the epicurean Octave, the frivolous Valentin, the light-hearted Fantasio, the impassioned Fortunio, and the philosopher in the " Confession d'un Enfant du Siècle," were one and the same man.

A more sustained work than the story of the loves of Camille and Perdican had been offered to the " Revue des Deux Mondes," but not inserted ; namely, the drama of " Lorenzaccio." Probably it was thought too long; or it may be that the editor preferred to reserve it unpublished for the collected dramatic works brought out in book form by the house which issued the " Revue."[1]

In order to surmount the melancholy which, under the guise of constancy in love, still weighed his spirits down, Alfred undertook, in the month of September, a journey to Baden. The trip proved most beneficial ; and he returned perfectly restored, both in mind

[1] "Un Spectacle dans un Fauteuil." Prose, 2 vols. 8vo. Paris and London : 1834.

and body. He was engaged in writing out that graceful episode of his "Sentimental Journey," which he entitled "Une bonne Fortune," when an unlucky accident destroyed the favorable effect of the journey, and the fruits of six months of struggle and reflection. The return of a person whom he had wished never to see again, but of whom he was forced to see much, plunged him anew into a life so full of exciting scenes and painful discussions that the poor boy had a relapse, from which it seemed as if he could not recover. Nevertheless, he drew from his very malady the means of cure. Where reason did not avail, suspicion and incredulity saved him. He wearied of emphatic recriminations, and resolved to shake off that unwholesome régime. A final rupture took place in 1835, as the result of some trifling disagreement; and this time, instead of abandoning himself to the voice of his grief, the patient consented to seek distraction. The world did not wish to lose him, his friends entreated him to take part in their amusements, and he yielded.

There is a vast difference between a party of pleasure where the wine, by rendering fools more loquacious, is productive only of noise and coarseness in speech, and a supper among choice spirits animated by good cheer, who recite verses, give excellent music, improvise songs, and exchange the gayest of sallies. A great deal has been said about the reunions of which Prince Belgiojoso was the soul; and some people have been pleased to remark that Alfred de Musset there plunged into excesses extremely dangerous for a poet. It is a most absurd exaggeration. The greater part of these "excesses,"

reduce themselves to entirely simple dinners after swimming parties ; and even in carnival times, when custom
sanctions noisier amusements, Alfred very rarely took
part in such.   He refused ten invitations where he accepted one, and often quitted a circle and went home
when the evening's mirth was at its height.

A new man, very unlike the old, had in fact replaced
the Octave and Fantasio in him.   The malice and stu-
pidity of the insinuations against his mode of life at
this period will be sufficiently evident from a list of
the works composed during the year 1835.   They were
" Lucie," the " Nuit de Mai," the " Quenouille de Barbarine," the " Chandelier," the " Loi sur la Presse," the
" Nuit de Décembre," and the " Confession d'un Enfant
du Siècle."   Where would he have found time for all
this writing, if he had passed his nights in convivial
entertainments, and his days in recruiting from the
fatigue of the night ?   I say nothing of his reading, which
nevertheless was not discontinued.   Strictly speaking,
however, he composed nothing during the first four
months of that prolific year.   One day in May, his
friend, Alfred Tattet, asked him in my presence, what
the fruits of his silence were to be, and this was the
answer he made : —

" For the last year I have been reading over again
what I had read before, and learning over what I
thought I knew.   Now I have gone back to the world and
plunged into some of your pleasures, for the sake of seeing again what I had seen before.   I have made the
most sincere and heroic efforts to drive away the memory
which obscured my vision, and to break up the per-

petually recurring habits of the old time. After having interrogated grief till it had nothing more to tell me, and quaffed my own tears, sometimes in solitude, sometimes before you, my friends who believe in me, I feel at last that I have surmounted misfortune, and wholly disengaged myself from my past. To-day, I have myself laid upon their bier my youth, my idleness, and my vanity. My thought seems to me like a plant which it has long been necessary to water, but which can now draw nourishment from the earth and grow in the sunshine. It seems to me now that I shall speak soon, and that I have something in my soul which must come out." [1]

It was the "Nuit de Mai" which was crying to come out. One spring evening, as we were returning from a walk, Alfred repeated to me the first two couplets of the dialogue between the Muse and the Poet, which he had just composed under the chestnuts of the Tuileries. He worked without interruption until morning, yet when he appeared at breakfast I detected no sign of fatigue upon his face. Like Fantasio, he had the color of the May in his cheeks. The Muse possessed him. All day long, he carried on simultaneously his work and his social intercourse, as one plays two games of chess at the same time. Now and then he quitted us and wrote a dozen verses or so, and then came back and resumed conversation. But, when night came, he returned to his work as to a lover's rendezvous. He had a little supper served in his own room, and he ought really to have ordered two covers, — one for his attendant Muse. He made a requisition of all the candlesticks in the

---

[1] These lines occur again, almost word for word in the "Poëte Déchu."

house, and lighted twelve candles. It must have seemed to the other inmates as if he were giving a ball. On the morning of the second day the piece was completed, and the Muse took wing ; but she had been so well received that she promised to return. The poet blew out his lights, went to bed, and slept until nightfall. When he awoke, he read over what he had written, but found nothing to retouch. Then out of the ideal world where he had lived for two days, the poet dropped abruptly down to earth, sighing as though he had been rudely awakened from some delectable fairy dream. His enthusiasm was succeeded by a sudden lassitude, a disgust with life and its petty troubles, and a profound depression. It seemed as if all the luxury of Sardanapalus, and all the refined amusements which Paris had to offer, would hardly be enough to rouse him from his dejection. But the sight of a pretty face, a strain of music, a graceful note opportunely received, dispelled the shadows, and he was obliged to own that he was resigned to living a little longer.

In the eyes of some, these alternations of high excitement and utter prostration are only a proof of weakness ; but they are mistaken. Insensibility is not strength. It better deserves the name of impotence. "The man who takes the strongest dose of life," said the philosopher Flourens, "is the man who feels most keenly." In more than one passage of his works, Alfred de Musset, who knew himself thoroughly, has described the exceptional organization which makes what we call a poet ; but among his papers I have discovered yet another definition, which may, I think, be appropriately inserted here.

" Be sure that the restless spark imprisoned in this paltry skull is a divine thing. You admire a fine instrument — a piano of Erard, a violin of Stradivarius ; but, great God ! what are they compared to a human soul ? In all the thirty years which I have lived, I have never used my faculties as freely as I desired. I have never been quite myself except when I have been silent. I have as yet only heard the opening bars of the melody which perhaps is in me. The instrument will soon crumble into dust, and I have but tuned it ; yet that has been a delight.

"Whoever you are, you can understand me if you have loved any thing whatsoever, — your country, a woman, a friend : nay, even your own welfare, a house, a room, a bed. Suppose that you are returning from a journey : you are coming back to Paris. You are at the frontier, — stopped only by the custom-house. If you are capable of emotion, do you not feel a certain pleasurable impatience at the thought that you are returning to *that* house, *that* room ? Does not your heart beat quickly when you turn the corner, when you approach, when at last you arrive ? Ah well ! it is but a natural pleasure and a vulgar impatience which you feel for the bed and table which you know so well. But suppose that you felt the like for all that lives, — noble and common, known and unknown alike. Suppose your life a continuous journey, every boundary your frontier, every inn your home, your children awaiting you on every threshold, your wife on every couch : you think that I am exaggerating ; but, no ! It is thus with the poet ! It was so with me when I was twenty ! " [1]

He might have added : " So I am still, and so I shall always be." As M. Saint René Taillandier has said of Goethe, he planted flowers of poetry at every step. Every keen and sweet impression which he received in life produced some piece of verse. After he had written

[1] Quoted from the " Pöete Déchu." This page was written in 1839. — P. M.

the "Nuit de Mai," as though there had been healing in the first kiss of the Muse, he declared to me that his wound was perfectly cured.   I asked him if he were quite sound and sure that the wound would not open again.

"Possibly," he replied, "but if it does open it will only be poetically."

Twenty years later, in our mother's drawing-room, the conversation turned on divorce, and Alfred said in the hearing of several people who never forgot the remark: "Our marriage laws are not so bad after all.   There was a moment of my youth when I would gladly have given ten years of my life to legalize divorce, so that I might espouse a married woman.   But if my vows had been heard, I should have blown my brains out in six months."

VIII.

IN the month of August, 1835, the "Quenouille de Barbarine" appeared, and the author immediately set to work on the "Confession d'un Enfant du Siècle," of which, however, the title was not yet determined. He was laboring with zeal, when he read one morning in a newspaper the text of a proposed law which created a new misdemeanor in the case of printed matter; namely, that of objectionable *intent or tendency.* The penalty affixed struck him as enormous. The then minister, profiting by the alarm, occasioned by the attempt of Fieschi, was demanding of the legislators new weapons against free discussion. Alfred did not resist the temptation to write an occasional poem, which those would seem never to have read who reproach him with habitual indifference to the welfare of his country and the events of the day. In truth, he defined his position in these words : —

> "Pour être d'un parti j'aime trop la paresse,
> Et dans ancun haras je ne suis étalon.[1]"

But the boasted idleness of an exceedingly busy and industrious young man was only self-respect, and the firm resolution never to abandon poetry. This wise line of conduct, from which he never swerved, did not pre-

---

[1] "I love idleness too well to belong to any party, and I am not the stallion of any stud."

vent him from feeling most acutely all which concerned
the safety and honor of his country.   The verses on
the new law were addressed in the form of a letter to
the prime minister, who was wise enough to cherish no
grudge against their author.   Politicians are wont to
smile when poets mix themselves up with the affairs of
this world; but the men who at that time held the
destinies of France in their hands are now reduced to
asking, on their own behalf, a little of the freedom of
which they so rudely deprived others, and against which
they so loudly declaimed.[1]   Fieschi's case proved that
there was no correlation whatever between the newspapers, books, and theatrical performances of the year
1835, and an obscure conspiracy hatched by mercenary
subalterns in a grocer's shop; but we were enriched by
the crime of moral complicity and the penalty of trans-
portation.

All this while, Alfred was working at the "Confession
d'un Enfant du Siècle."   He went continually into
society, yet wrote every evening an appalling number
of those pages, where we feel, as we read, the quivering
of his pen.   A novel incident interrupted him in the
midst of his work.   He came home one evening per-
plexed by some ambiguous words addressed to him by a
woman, and accompanied by looks more significant than
her speech.   Disgusted as he was with love, and barely
recovered from his previous attack, Alfred observed the
lady's associates with suspicion, and fancied he saw
traces of a conspiracy into which two people had entered
to destroy his peace.   He did not hesitate to bring the

[1] This was written under the reign of Napoleon III.

charge, and the younger lady exculpated herself completely: but, while she proved that she had had no wish to inspire affection, she proved equally that she did not feel it; and the accuser found his position, with reference to her, somewhat embarrassing.[1]

Obliged to retract his unjust suspicions, Alfred asked himself what would have happened if they had been well founded; and, in a flash, he imagined the whole comedy of the " Chandelier."

I was then a modest hack-writer, having but two hours in the day — the time from four to six — to give to my friends and social duties, while I worked all the evening in the hope of acquiring a little talent; that is to say, the independence for which I pined. One night I was at home scribbling on I know not what, while my more worldly brother was abroad. As usual, it was past midnight when he came home: but between two and three o'clock in the morning he came to my room with some loose leaves of paper in his hand; and, seating himself on the foot of my bed, he began to read that charming scene in which the rage of Master André is opposed by the *sangfroid* of the crafty Jacqueline. We both went into fits of laughter; and the second scene, the one in which Clavaroche devises his odious machination, was written before daybreak. I entreated my brother to think seriously about having this delicious comedy put on the stage; but he replied that its fate was fixed. " If any theatre wants to adopt it," said he, " they will

---

[1] I have already told this story briefly in the notice which accompanies the edition of 1866. There seems to be no reason now why I should not give it more in detail. — P. M.

find the 'Chandelier' in the pages of the 'Revue.'"
The piece actually appeared there Nov. 1, 1835; and
nobody ever suspected that it could be played until
thirteen years later.

This time the characters of the comedy were imaginary. There is no similarity whatever between Jacqueline and the lady who so innocently furnished the
theme of the piece. But the author continued to play
the part of "Fortunio" toward her, although he uttered
no reproaches. One morning as he was walking along
the Rue de Buci, with a thoughtful face and downcast
eyes, he began to dream of the hazard of making this
lady a declaration of love by letter. All at once, he
said aloud, "But what if I were to say that I love you?"
then lifting his head he met the eyes of a passer-by who
began to laugh at his outbreak. His doubts naturally
resolved themselves into a poem, and he composed the
stanzas to Ninon. That evening, in the lady's drawing-room, some ten persons being present, he took a
paper out of his pocket and handed it to the mistress
of the house, remarking, with an air of entire simplicity,
that he had been writing some verses, and wanted to
know what she thought of them. The lady read the
verses to herself with an indifferent air, and handed him
back the paper without a word. Afterwards she asked
him for it again, held it open in her hand for a while,
and then put it in her pocket, as if unconsciously.

On the morrow, at the usual calling hour, Alfred sal-
lied forth to receive the reprimand which he expected;
but he found nobody at home. He was avoided. When
at last he did obtain an interview, it was before witnesses;

and the lady apparently did not remember that any verses had been addressed to her. Alfred pretended to be equally oblivious, but his interest was only piqued. Their silence ended in an abrupt explanation, and a full and unreserved avowal of his sentiments. In this first episode, the lover's happiness lasted three weeks, at the end of which period Alfred was assailed by new suspicions. The taste of the poison which he had drunk at Venice the year before came back to him. If his friend had been gentle and patient, she might have cured him of his jealous distrust ; but unhappily she had a haughty spirit, susceptible and impulsive, which brooked neither precaution nor delay. After a stormy week, they resolved to part, and the resolution was formulated in terms of crushing force. Alfred wrote a desperate letter in which he acknowledged himself in the wrong, and received, in reply, a request for the return of the letters, ten or twelve at most, which she had written him. He wrapped them up in a piece of cloth along with a lock of hair, a few little things which had been meant for souvenirs, and a flower which had scarcely had time to fade. Only one hand might hold this "dear and fragile treasure." He sent it back with tears, and remained face to face with himself. It was verily an amputation. When he thought of the usual patience of women under such circumstances, of their weakness, and the manœuvres which they know so well how to try, he asked himself by what strange fatality he had encountered the only woman in the world capable of a course so hard and cruel.

But his Muse did not, as on the previous occasion,

9

wait six months before consoling him. Publication, moreover, was one way of calling the attention of his ungrateful mistress to the expression of his grief and regret. One fearfully stormy night I came in at about midnight, and saw so many lights in my brother's room that I thought he must have a large number of guests. He was, however, writing the " Nuit de Décembre." That poem, fraught with so deep a melancholy, belongs to the episode which I have just related, and the reader of it sees plainly that the poet has drunk of a new cup. That picture of solitude ; that conception of a pale, sable-clad figure, becoming visible only in moments of anguish and desolation, — could only have originated in a new situation and a recent sorrow. I am aware that many readers have seen, in the " Nuit de Décembre," only a reaction from the memories of Italy, and a sort of complement to the " Nuit de Mai ; " but this is an error which requires correction. No doubt should be suffered to linger about that passage of the poem in which the deserted lover reproaches the woman who " knows not how to forgive." I know the truth : and I will not permit the slightest confusion between two very different women ; one of whom had really something to forgive, and the right to refuse her pardon. This is why I have chosen to dwell on that new love affair ; the prologue to which gave rise to the " Nuit de Décembre."

We will now return to the " Confession d'un enfant du Siècle." The author had had a sorrowful fancy for ending the romance at the point where Brigitte confesses her love to Octave. " My hero," he said, " will be more fortunate than I have been, for I have myself brought him to the moment when he will receive consolation. Let us go no farther! To-morrow will be too painful." But it was urged upon him that a good ending would render the book insignificant; and, having consented to finish the second volume, he set to work assiduously.

In spite of its title, we must not expect to find in the "Confession," an autobiography. The sentiments expressed are indeed to some extent his own; but truth of incident is nowhere to be found, not even by disregarding chronological order. The author never meant to tell the story of his youth. He did not merely draw upon his own recollections; but he observed whatever of life and movement he saw around him, and collected whatsoever he thought might be presented as symptomatic of the moral malady which he was attempting to describe; whatsoever might strengthen that philosophic thesis which gives his work a higher range than properly belongs to any mere society romance. Many of the real incidents have been developed or modified, that they might serve as illustrations of character. The attempt to separate what is real from that which appertains merely to art and the necessities of the case would prove utterly futile, and even if successful would shed no light on the life of the author.

As regards "Desgenais," I need only remark that so strong a type could not have been a portrait. There is summed up in this character a whole class of young people with whom Alfred had been intimate, and whom he named "men of the flesh," to distinguish them from the men of sentiment typified by Octave. The "Confession," delayed by events of which the public knew nothing, was awaited with impatience. It finally appeared in the early days of 1836 ; but those who hoped for revelations were disappointed. It did not create the least scandal. And the best advice I can offer to those who read it now, is that they give up their conjectures, and endeavor to learn from it something about themselves and the times in which they live.

IX.

THE eleventh of December had been Alfred de Musset's twenty-fifth birthday. The new year upon which he was entering began as badly as the previous one had done. Precisely because no fearful memories, no painful associations, were mingled with his second disappointment in love, he felt less energy than on the former occasion for contending against *ennui* and dejection. A healthful heart can summon the strength needful to surmount a passion of which it is ashamed; but, when there is no help save in cold reason, the heart refuses to be healed. Alfred felt that he had made a vain boast when he said to his stern mistress in the "Nuit de Décembre," "He who loses you has not lost all." He fancied, on the contrary, that he had lost the happiness of his whole life; and he could not be resigned to so great a sacrifice, nor allow himself to be condemned without being heard. The first time he met the lady in question after the publication of the "Nuit de Décembre," she told him that she had been both amazed and affected by the reading of the poem; that she had not supposed him capable of suffering such distress; that when she saw him unhappy, she pitied him sincerely. Then, as though afraid of having said too much, she added that it could make no difference. Alfred profited by the occasion to let her know what he had suffered, and then asked to be allowed to resume his visits as a friend; adding that she might receive him without danger, since *it could make no difference.* She owned the justice of his reasoning, and gave the permission required; and that night the poor child came home as pleased as though he had won a great victory.

When I learned the nature of the success in which he was exulting, and which he immediately confided to me, I did not hesitate to declare it a bad piece of business. "You do not, either of you," I said jestingly, "know what you want. Your fair one is like a fish nibbling at the hook, and all the while saying to the fisherman, 'You need not expect to catch me.' And you are like a man sick with gastric fever who consents to be treated for inflammation of the lungs. It is easy to foresee the result. In obedience to your ungrateful lady, you will not whisper a word of love; but you will betray your feelings a dozen times in a day. She on her part will be moved by your constancy; and, in her gratitude to you for ceasing to love her, she will fall in love with you herself. And, after a fortnight of this sort of thing, your obedience and her determination will end like the reformation of that drunkard who went back to the inn to treat his resolution."

In the very height of his troubles, Alfred always enjoyed a laugh at his own expense. It was one of his consolations, and I knew it, and often availed myself of the fact; and in this case my brother, while he laughed at my grumbling, felt in his heart that it was just. In a few days my predictions were verified. Alfred saw his implacable mistress three or four times in a week, and scrupulously observed her orders. He said not a word of love, but inwardly he was in a rage. Then the temptation assailed him to break silence by another poem; and, this method having succeeded before, he composed some new stanzas for his own consolation, but resolved to wait a while before offering them to her. The following are the verses, which have never been published : —

TO NINON.

For all your wit, my lady cool and fair,
Your studied languors, and the lofty air
That suits you well, albeit it works us ill, —
'Tis certain that you cannot have your will.

Certain, though not a sign thereof be shown,
That in my heart's domain you rule alone ;
That love is not destroyed when love is hidden,
And that I love you, Ninon, though forbidden.

Certain it is that, in your own despite,
The love you would rebuke you still invite ;
That men elect to writhe beneath your scorn,
And pangs of loving you are lightly borne.

And when, O spirit, sensitive and shy,
Spurning our lightest touch, you start and fly,
The scattered radiance of your loveliness
Falls on us, and our torment turns to bliss.

Be what you will then! Shed your sweetest graces,
Scorn or allure us, or our woes deride ;
And like a diamond with a million faces,
Turn ever more a new and dazzling side,

One soul there is will yield you thanks unceasing,
And the glad remnant of its days unknown ;
For me, your blows are better than all blessing,
And yours I am, and never more mine own.

And one there is who knows my heart's whole story,
My Muse, Ninon! She knows, but never tells!
You are so like, I think when she's before me
I see yourself! I scarce could love her else!

And there are nights when on the dark arises
A sweet look, shifting like a meteor's ray.
A sweet dream comes and goes, returns, entices
(Poets and happy folk are mad, they say).

A visionary being I embrace,
A wordless music murmurs in my ear,
Dark, spirit eyes look soft on my disgrace :
I turn to heaven, Ninon, and see you there.

O my beloved, do not take away
My darling grief, my lone life's mortal charm!
Pity me not, but let me suffer, pray!
No plaint of mine shall work you any harm.

Once indited, these verses could not fail of ultimately
finding their way to the lady who had inspired them. If
the author had attempted to hand them to her himself,
as he had done with the first stanzas to Ninon, she
would perhaps have refused to take them ; but the post-
office was invented to surmount difficulties of this nature,
and, by way of the post, the second stanzas arrived at
their address.   Alfred awaited the result with some
anxiety, until through the same medium he received a
large envelope.   The lady was not much of an artist,
but the envelope contained a pen-and-ink drawing, representing a large drawing-room clock, which the lover
readily recognized, and the hands of which indicated
the hour of three.

That evening, in spite of all his efforts to appear sober and self-possessed, our poet was in a transport of delight. He was positively beside himself. The second verses to Ninon had been as successful as the first. The lady liked pretty poetry, and poetry had wrung from her the confession which love had failed to extort. She was an extremely clever person ; and, instead of absorbing all her friend's leisure she spurred him on to work, declaring that she should look upon his future performances as so many proofs of his affection. They were both confident of a long future ; and I augured well of these indications, so long as their good understanding should last.

It lasted a fortnight. Chance had already determined the issue of the affair. This time the rupture was no fault of the lover's, who had profited by his previous experience ; but, while he was on his guard against his own jealousy and unjust suspicions, some one else who was jealous had guessed the whole truth. The Ninon of the stanzas was destined to figure under another name in a prose narrative. The situation, as I have said elsewhere, was reproduced in " Emmeline."

The dangerous point in affairs of this nature is always that moment of internal conflict, when a virtuous and loyal woman fully believes that she is coming off victorious. Why should she dissimulate so long as her conscience does not reproach her ? To dissimulate her feelings would be to avow herself in the wrong. She does not wish to yield ; she is not going to yield : but the day comes when love is too strong for her, and prudence awakes too late. She catches a glimpse of the future, and a few hours suffice to break up and destroy happiness, purpose, every thing. Alfred might not perhaps have resigned himself to the second separation if he had had the jealous person only to deal with; but when he found that he must make a man wretched, and bring about an inevitable catastrophe, he insisted no longer, but yielded to the lady's entreaties, — respectfully and sadly.

So ended the love story of "Emmeline." Just as in the romance which bears that title, the affair was concluded sorrowfully, to the gay notes of a waltz, between two figures of a cotillon, by the intervention of a compassionate but inexorable friend. Alfred made the very promise which he put into the mouth of his fictitious Gilbert. "Any thing in the world, for your sake." The condition imposed was complete separation. Alfred intended to go away. He made his arrangements for so doing, and announced his purpose to his friends; but his courage failed him, and he asked for one day of grace, and then another. And then, suddenly, he was apprised that his departure would not be necessary.

Alfred was supported under the pain of this wrench by the very sacrifice which he was making. Ought he not to consider himself fortunate to be able to restore his friend's peace at the expense of his own? He wanted to give an example of a sorrow bravely borne. But when the negotiations were concluded, and his unhappiness was achieved, and he found himself left alone to struggle with his regrets, he began to ask himself why he should live any longer. I could see that he was dreaming of all that he had lost, and fairly luxuriating in his disappointment. He plunged into his sorrow as deeply as might be, preferring active pain to passive dejection. I told him that he was in a fair way to make his malady incurable, and he replied : " It is so."

Alfred de Musset used openly to profess for M. de Lamartine both sympathy and admiration. One day in the month of February, 1836, under the influence of a fresh attack of melancholy, I found him re-reading the " Meditations." This poem, whose tranquillizing power he had just experienced, inspired him with the desire to give poetical expression to his own gratitude to the author of the " Lac." He repeated to me the first part of the epistle to Lamartine, as far as the verse where he says that Lord Byron in his last days —

" Sur terre autour de lui, cherchait pour qui mourir." [1]

But he hesitated about going on with the poem, fearing that it would seem pretentious in him to assume that Lamartine would be interested in the story of his troubles. By way of disposing of his modest scruples, I undertook boldly to assure him that verses like these would reflect as much honor on Lamartine as on their author, and that all Europe would feel an interest in the sorrow out of which they had sprung. Accordingly we proceeded to the usual ceremonies which distinguished his days of inspiration, — the grand illumination and the supper. The Muse was only awaiting permission to descend. On the following day the epistle was far advanced ; and on the first of March, 1836, it appeared in the " Revue des Deux Mondes." Some time after-

---

[1] " Looked the world over, seeking some one for whom he might die."

wards Alfred received a note from M. de Lamartine, inviting him to call. He hastened to comply, and for three or four months there was constant intercourse between the two poets. Evenings after he returned from these visits, Alfred would rehearse in the family circle the talk of the morning. Among other things, I remember his saying the first time he came home that he had been promised a reply to his verses. M. de Lamartine had asked for time in which to express his gratitude, saying, with a charming good grace, that it would be no easy matter to devise a reply worthy of the letter.[1]

Until the day should arrive in which he was to be glorified by this reply, Alfred dwelt with pride and pleasure on the promise. We know how he loved to burrow in the picture and engraving shops. In one such he found a crayon copy of the " Poetry " of Carlo Dolci, the features of which were really very like those of the

---

[1] In the nineteenth instalment of M. de Lamartine's "Literary Conversations" we were told, in 1867, why this reply never appeared; but I must confess that I never perfectly understood the explanation. It was somewhat amazing to learn that M. de Lamartine totally forgot his interviews with Alfred, and that when he found him at the Institute in 1852, he supposed that he was addressing him for the first time. In the same nineteenth conversation we are told that M. de Lamartine had at first but a poor opinion of the lyrical ability of this young man, an opinion derived from reading the " Rhin Allemand;" but that some time later, *a shepherd* handed him in the park of Saint Point the number of the "Revue des Deux Mondes" which contained the verses addressed to himself, and that, when he read these, his prejudice vanished. Now the "Rhin Allemand" was not written until June, 1841, and the "Épître à M. de Lamartine" appeared March 1, 1836; consequently, it would seem as if M. de Lamartine's memory must have served him very ill when he attempted to account for his silence; or else that it took the shepherd who was charged with the delivery of his copy of the "Revue des Deux Mondes" five years to find him in the park of Saint Point. — P. M.

author of the "Meditations." He instantly bought the drawing, and gave it a place in one of the frames which adorned his study; and his friends remember to this day how highly he prized this ideal portrait, and the childlike pleasure which he took in the contemplation thereof. Afterwards, when all Paris was rushing to the performances of the "Caprice," Mme. Allan conceived a fancy for this crayon. Alfred dared not refuse it to the actress who had insured the success of the play; but he always regretted losing it, and in the very last months of his life he said repeatedly: "Why need Mme. Allan have taken away my Lamartine?"

The readers of the "Revue" remarked the peculiarly careful execution of the "Epistle." The author wanted it to be faultless. We know now the circumstances under which that flower of poesy was sown, and there need be no mistake about the feelings which caused it to blossom. How is it possible fully to comprehend the poet's yearning regret, without the knowledge that his love was one which a mere sense of personal dignity would not have compelled him to crush out? The story told in the letter to Lamartine is that of an evening of deep agitation, when Paris was resounding with the coarse uproar of the Carnival. Those who were mistaken about the subject of the "Nuit de Décembre" committed the same error with regard to the letter. Alfred smiled at their misconceptions; but, when asked by his friends to explain, his answer used to be: "You can think what you please."

His reserve was just and proper at the time, but now all is changed. A third of a century has elapsed, and

the letter to Lamartine has become something beside
the effort of a young poet of great promise serving
to embellish the last number of a review.   He who
uttered that cry of pain has been removed by an early
death; but the cry is echoing yet, and the heart of the
public is moved by it.   There is a peremptory demand
for an explanation, and it ought to be made.

There are subtle differences to be observed in the
reproaches addressed by lovers to their cruel mistresses.
Read, for example, the whole of the passage in the
"Lettre à Lamartine" which begins, —

> "O mon unique amour! Que vous avais-je fait?
> Vous m'aviez pu quitter, vous qui juriez la veille,
> Que vous étiez ma vie, et que Dieu le savait." [1]

Far otherwise did the poet talk in the "Nuit de Mai!"
These verses are the sequel to those of the "Nuit de
Décembre."   They are addressed to the same person, and
she has had no occasion to blush for them.   The time
for misapprehensions is past.   Let us render to every
one his due.   I would renounce the purpose of writing
my brother's life, were it not permitted me to shed a
little light on those finest passages in his poems, where I
can feel at every word the very throbbings of his heart.

She who inspired the letter to Lamartine needed no
assistance to recognize her own likeness in it.   Shortly
after it appeared, the author found in his room, one
night when he went home, two Sèvres vases accompanied by a note in which occurred the following
passage: —

"[1] My only love, what wrong had I done you that you cast me off, when
you had sworn, only the night before, that you were mine and God knew it?"

" If you knew the state into which I was thrown by reading your verses, you would be sorry for having said in them that your heart was caught by *a woman's caprice*. It was true love and no caprice from which we both suffered. Do not be so unjust to me as to doubt it. Even now, if I had only myself to think of, I would wipe away the tears which blind my eyes, and leave all and lose all for you. One word from you would be enough, and I have now no hesitation in saying so. But because you love me, you will let me weep."

These lines wrought a great change in the mind of the distressed lover. Under the seeming sternness of his treatment he recognized a sincere compassion. His grief was shared; and this thought comforted him. Twenty times he repeated: "She would have left all if I had said a word; but I never will say the word which might destroy her."

Destiny brought to Alfred de Musset a compensation for his sacrifices. If there is a being on earth to whom a woman's friendship may be useful, it is surely a poet or an unhappy lover. He fulfilled both conditions when he became the friend and *godson* of a highly gifted woman whom he had known for a long time. Hers was one of the most agreeable *salons* in Paris. Music was given there once a week, and on these days numbers of people came to hear Prince Belgiojoso, Géraldy, the Countess de Sparre, &c. On other days, there were fewer guests and conversation only.

One evening they were amusing themselves by bestowing on one another fanciful sobriquets. The mistress of the house had been appointed to find a name for Alfred de Musset, and she dubbed him " Prince Phosphor of the restless heart."

The lady who thus baptized him permitted him to call himself her godson, and her his godmamma.

From this graceful intimacy, and the influence which the godmother acquired over the mind of her boy, there resulted, on the one side, judicious advice and encouragement, consolation, and the stimulus to exertion ; on the other, a constant desire to deserve the approval of a reader who endeavored to be exacting, precisely because she was fond of him.

For years Alfred de Musset felt bound to keep his godmother fully informed of all the impressions which he received. Not an amusing idea entered his head, nor a fleeting sentiment his heart, but it was communicated to her. The introduction to " Silvia " shows that that story was written in answer to a letter in which the poet had been reproved for allowing his Muse too long a rest. I shall tell later how he replied to a more serious reproach, by a sonnet addressed to his godmother, which could not well have been made public while the author lived. " [1]

[1] The "godmother" was Mme. Maxime Jaubert, and the friendship between her and Alfred de Musset one of the sweetest, most healthful, and helpful influences of the poet's life. — TR.

X.

A BRIEF and unimportant episode in Alfred's career, took him for a time away from all literary labors and associations. When he first re-entered his study, he examined all the objects about him earnestly, as if they had been old friends. His natural vivacity made all contrasts pleasing to him. One day I found him there, promenading up and down, while he alternately hummed that *cavatina* of Pacini which Liszt's piano and the voice of Rubini had lately brought into fashion, and murmured under his breath lines which arranged themselves in hemistichs. Finally he paused before his writing-table, seized a large sheet of paper, and wrote as follows : —

LA NUIT DE JUIN.

(LE POËTE.)

Muse, quand le blé pousse il faut être joyeux,
Regarde ces coteaux et leur blonde parure ;
Quelle douce clarté dans l'immense nature,
Tout ce qui vit ce soir doit se sentir heureux.[1]

---

[1] Or thus : —

"O my Muse! the corn is up, 'tis the season of delight,
Look how the circling hills their snow-white mantle wear,
And a softened splendor throbs in all the infinite air :
All things that breathe rejoice on such a night."

10

"In fact," I said, as I perused these lines, "this is going to be one of those nights when there is no death in the soul."

He laughed, and promised that the "Nuit de Juin" should treat of love and pleasure only. Dinner-time was approaching, and knowing, as I did, that the Muse was fond of descending at the shepherd's hour,[1] I made no doubt that on the morrow the piece would be half done. Unluckily, Tattet came in, and wanted to take his friend off to dine at a restaurant. I besought him not to interrupt so important a work, representing the harm he might be doing to the poet, the public, and himself. Tattet allowed that I was right, but the dinner was ordered, and he had promised my brother to the other guests, among whom were MM. Alfred and Hippolyte Mosselman, De Jean, and Arvers.[2] Tattet assured me that they would break up early, and that poetry should not be the loser; and Alfred departed, to my great regret. He came home late, and his head was tired. The next day I made inquiries for the "Nuit de Juin," and his answer was that there were thirty days in the month. He knew, however, that the Muse was offended and would not return; so he took his hat and went off for a call. The occasion had passed, and the "Nuit de Juin" stopped there. To-day, as I look upon the broad blank sheet, discolored by time, which I found among the author's papers, and read again the

[1] L'heure du Berger is the hour when the gentle shepherd enjoys the company of his mistress. — TR.

[2] Felix Arvers, — a very clever original fellow of a melancholy temperament, who, nevertheless, wrote several very lively and successful *vaudevilles*. He died young. — P. M.

title and the four autograph lines, I can hardly be reconciled to the thought that the page will never be filled.

We have, however, a compensation for this loss.. Alfred, who had trained alternately in the two rollicking companies commanded severally by his friend Tattet and Prince Belgiojoso, stopped short one morning and announced that he had had dissipation enough. He compared himself to a shuttlecock, sent back and forth between two battledores, and was resolved to declare his independence by returning to his mother's lodgings. He brought back a quantity of new impressions, and, hence, of new ideas. He donned his dressing-gown, flung himself into his arm-chair, and proceeded to read himself a better lecture than his father or his uncle could have delivered. From this unspoken dialogue came the scene between Valentin and the excellent Van Buck, and afterwards a piece in three acts, entitled " Il ne Faut Jurer de Rien." So it is, that in the life of a true poet nothing is lost or useless. The characters in this little piece were so purely comic, and the dénouement so happily conceived, that when the author came to put it on the stage, there were very few alterations to be made.

This comedy appeared in the " Revue " of July 1, 1836, and immediately afterward the " elastic ball " resumed its flights. Then came another return to our home, the same pleasure at the sight of his study, the same desire to shut himself up there, the same allurements offered to a Muse who only feigned resentment; for our poet had now no serious offence with which to reproach him-

self. But something more important was now in question than the amusing conversation of Uncle Van Buck.

The "Nuit d'Août" was, for our poet, a night of
veritable rapture. He had decorated his room and
thrown open the windows. The light of the candles
played over the flowers that filled four huge vases symmetrically disposed. The Muse came in the guise of a
youthful bride. No festival or evening's entertainment
ever compared with these glorious hours of facile and
fascinating labor ; and since, on the present occasion,
the poet's thoughts were peaceful, his heart sound, his
mind vigorous, and his imagination full of sap, he enjoyed a pleasure inconceivable by the vulgar. To form
an idea of this poetic intoxication, we need neither recall
what has been told of the effect of opium, hashish, or
other inebriating poisons, nor that accumulation of the
more refined pleasures of sense which Oriental story-
tellers have lavished on the heroes of their fabulous
narratives. One must judge by the degree of enthusiasm and sensibility with which he is himself endowed,
by raising to the tenth power the pleasure which he
receives from reading this beautiful poem of the "Nuit
d'Août," what the author must have enjoyed in writing it.

No sorrowful or bitter leaven mingled with his poetic
intoxication this time, and his happy mood lasted for
several days. All through the composition of the
"Nuit d'Août," the poet felt himself in communion
with his unknown readers, and never more so than at
the close of the last stanza, —

"Aime et tu renaîtras; fais toi fleur pour éclore."

The spell remained unbroken until the publication of the piece ; but, on the morrow, I found him moody, trying in vain to read a chapter in some new novel or other. I asked what ailed him, and he replied: "By great good luck, the fish has passed some days in the water. At present he is sprawling in a corn-field."

I took him off to the swimming-school, where his body at least might be restored to its beloved watery medium.   There we met Prince Belgiojoso and his comrades, who invited us to go with them to Broggi's Italian restaurant.   After a dinner seasoned by exercise and keen appetites, we had some music, and the evening passed merrily.   We returned rather late ; but, before going to bed, Alfred attempted to finish the novel which he had laid aside in the morning.   He read aloud to me a sentence in which we counted an incredible number of adjectives.   Every substantive dragged two or three in its train, and the effect was most uncouth. The reader in high good-humor asked me what I thought of it all, and I replied in the words of Léandre: "It is very much the fashion."

"I wish I knew," rejoined Alfred, "what the good people of the Provinces think of such a style, and whether they suppose it a fair sample of Parisian literature."

After discussing this question until a very late hour of the night, Alfred conceived the notion of addressing a letter to the editor of the "Revue," in the character of a denizen of some small town.   We talked it over ; and he concluded that, instead of giving the views of one provincial, it would be better to compare the impres-

sions of two.   Stendhal, whom we numbered among our
friends, had published sundry articles, sometimes over
the signature of "Dupuis," and sometimes over that of
"Cotonet."   Alfred adopted these two names, enjoying
the idea of Stendhal's own mystification.   Soon after,
there appeared in the "Revue" the first letter of "Two
Inhabitants of Ferté-sous-Jouarre," on the abuse of
adjectives.[1]   Under a light and attractive form, this
letter treated with clearness and force a question of
literary taste, and it created a considerable sensation.
Stendhal was enchanted with the good sense of his
pseudonyms; but people persisted in attributing the
article to him, and he had great difficulty in convincing
them that he was not its author.   He even received
complimentary letters from a great distance.   But the
secret was soon divulged.   Franz Liszt learned it from
a lady to whom it was confided by the editor of the
"Revue," and Liszt took pleasure in imparting it to
his many friends.

A distressing piece of news reached Paris at about
this time.   The newspapers announced the death of
Mme. Malibran.   Alfred had been one of her passionate
admirers,[2] and her untimely death affected his poetic

[1] Alfred de Musset never saw "Ferte-sous-Jouarre," all statements to the
contrary notwithstanding of pretended biographers who deserve a different name.   He chose that town because the name struck his fancy.

[2] But only an admirer.   One day, in a railway-car, I heard some unknown persons conversing about my brother, and deploring the fact that
Mme. Malibran had never returned his affection for her; saying that, if
she had, it might have defended the charming young poet from another
and more perilous attachment.   The story was retailed freely as matter of
public notoriety; but the truth is that, except upon the stage, Alfred never
saw Mme. Malibran but once in his life, when she sang in a parlor, and that
he never spoke to her.

sensibilities keenly. On the fifteenth of October, he published the verses which one so often hears quoted, and which so many people know by heart. Perhaps the poet felt in himself the same fatal predilection for suffering with which he reproached the great singer when he wrote the famous verse, —

"Tu regardais aussi la Malibran mourir."

The same might have been said of him twenty years later.

The year 1836 closed amid the excitement caused by the attempt of Meunier. This was the fourth time that the king had narrowly escaped death. Alfred, who did not forget the hospitalities of Neuilly, shared the universal feeling. He wrote, merely for his own satisfaction, a sonnet, which he did not intend to publish, but of which his friend Tattet requested a copy. Tattet showed the copy to M. Édouard Bocher, who lent it to his brother Gabriel, the librarian of the Duc d'Orléans; and so it was that the verses on Meunier's attempt came to the notice of the Prince Royal. An express from the château soon brought their author the note which follows : —

"Our common friend M. Bocher has just shown me, my dear schoolfellow, a noble page extracted from your poetical portfolio. These truly fine verses, in which a dry and ungracious subject receives dignity from the elevation of the poet's thought and his noble simplicity of expression, would have touched me, even had their author been unknown. It is with real delight, however, that I recognize in them the sentiments of an old school-comrade ; and, as I read, I find myself carried back to younger and happier days.

"I wanted to thank you in person for this good gift, and I

seize the occasion offered by New Year's day to beg your acceptance of the token herewith offered by your old associate, and the sincere admirer of your beautiful gifts.

" FERDINAND PHILIPPE D'ORLÉANS.

" TUILERIES, Jan. 1, 1837."

When the exchange of official compliments was concluded, Alfred de Musset repaired to the palace. The prince received him with open arms and the sonnet in his pocket. He drew the author away into a bay window, that he might read it once more, and then, as if aglow at the perusal, he exclaimed : " I have not yet found an opportunity of showing your verses to the king ; but, if you will wait five minutes, I will take them to him now, and, if he likes them as well as I do, I shall tell him that you are here."

The prince went in search of the king. After a quarter of an hour or so, he came back with a disturbed countenance, looking both sorry and embarrassed, and said that the king was not visible just then, but would be so on some future day ; which, however, he did not fix. Alfred felt sure that the sonnet had been read, and that it had not given pleasure ; and he begged the prince to tell him what it was in his verses which had offended the royal ears. The Duke of Orleans acknowledged with a blush that it was the familiarity, — the *tutoiement.* " I should have guessed a thousand times before guessing that," replied the poet, blushing in his turn.

The school friends parted in equal consternation. When my brother had repeated to me this strange conversation, we proceeded to re-read the sonnet together ; and I asked myself if it were possible that the king —

a man of intellect and culture — had really been offended by language which Boileau might have addressed to Louis XIV. It did not seem so ; and the probability is that the prince, in his youthful impetuosity, had disturbed his father by appealing to him at an inconvenient time. The king heard with a divided attention, and sent his son off, on the first pretext which occurred to him. The prince bore himself gallantly in the matter towards his former comrade, and had him invited to the palace balls. A singular circumstance afterwards occurred, which proved that, when the sonnet had been shown to the king, the Duc d'Orléans, perceiving that it had not made a good impression, had the good taste not to mention the writer's name. On the day when he was actually presented, Alfred perceived that Louis Philippe looked pleased at the mention of his name. " Ah," said the king, coming forward as though agreeably surprised, " you are from Joinville. I am very glad to see you."

Alfred was far too well bred to betray the slightest astonishment. He made a reverential bow ; and, as the king passed on to address some one else, he cast about him to discover the meaning of the words which he had just heard, and the smile which accompanied them. It then occurred to him that we had at Joinville a cousin, a very accomplished and delightful man, inspector of forests on the private domain, and fully worthy of that genial welcome. The monarch had forgotten his son's school-days, and the names of the children who had visited him at Neuilly ; but he remembered perfectly the condition and aspect of his own estates. The name of De Musset represented to him an inspector, a trustworthy overseer of his own woods, by whom he set great store, and very properly. Throughout the last eleven years of his reign, he saw once or twice every winter the face of the supposed inspector of forests, and continued to bestow upon him smiles fit to arouse the envy of more than one courtier, and which passed, it may be, for compliments to poetry and belles-lettres. It is certain, however, that Louis Philippe never knew that there lived, during his reign, a great poet who bore the same name as the inspector of his woods.

PART THIRD.

FROM 1837 TO 1842.

XI.

THE contempt of literature which the sovereign unconsciously testified by his gracious words and smiles did not amuse Alfred de Musset as much as it might have done; for his thoughts would recur to the days of Louis XIV., and he felt with keen regret the difference between the two eras. In vain I reminded him that, in our time, the public is the true Mæcenas. The indifference of the chief of the nation weighed on his heart. He was ashamed of it, and unwilling to allude to it, save in the chimney-corner. Yet the kind attentions and affectionate expressions of the Prince Royal were some consolation. He observed one day that there was a prince who would bring to the throne other ideas than those of Louis Philippe. In fact, the Duc d'Orléans had a confidential conversation with his school friend, in which he expressed his views very freely about his father's politics, and the isolated position of France between the unfortunate nations whose cause she had abandoned, and those foreign governments which were ever hostile and suspicious. The prince did not hesitate to hint at war as a very probable event of the first year of his own reign. He even quoted, apropos of his remark, a speech of Fantasio's. "We will make a trip to Italy, and enter Mantua with no other torches than our swords. And when peace is concluded," added the prince, "we will proceed to amuse ourselves. We will give employment to the poets and artists, and you shall write verses and come and read them to us."

In the midst of these discussions, the Princess Hélène arrived from Germany. With what pomp the marriage was celebrated is well known. Amid the vast galleries of Versailles, Alfred dreamed of a future, fairer, and worthier of a great nation than the epoch of the golden mean, and peace at any price. His imagination, "sensitive as the magnetic needle," discerned afar a new Renaissance of arts and letters, a brilliant and chivalrous reign. At twenty-six, such dreams were in order, and their entertainment seemed justified by the purposes and opinions of the Prince Royal, the noble character of the Duchesse d'Orléans, and the remarkable talents of the Princess Marie. Side by side with the old court there was growing up, in the *salons* of the heir-apparent, another younger and more vivacious court, graced by the fair and fascinating figure of a new Margaret of Valois. Alfred wished to prepare himself for the advent, nearer or more remote of that splendid era, which would, he believed, give a name to the nineteenth century. He applied himself more zealously than ever before to the polishing and perfecting of his works, and the care of his reputation. During the years of 1837–38, he worked calmly, without any undue excitement; still under the inspiration of his heart, for he could not do otherwise, but of a freer, happier heart than his had formerly been. He bore the vexations of life more patiently; he preferred being shut up among his books. As he says himself in the "Nuit d'Octobre:" "Oh days of labor, sole days when I have lived! Oh! thrice blessed solitude!"

And, since this happy mood impelled him to works requiring patient application, he resolved to write a series of novels; no less for the public and his friends, than for the future court of Francis I. and the Queen of Navarre. Having stimulated his enthusiasm for the story-teller's art by reading once again the charming tales of Boccaccio, he desired himself to display that talent for narration with which he had not yet been credited. The "Confession d'un Enfant du Siècle," had been more of an impassioned appeal than a romance. In order to give variety to his works, he resolved to add another prose volume. Ever since the 18th of August, 1836, he had had an engagement in writing with the "Revue des Deux Mondes," to furnish that periodical a society novel. The subject which he intended to treat was that of "Emmeline;" but when time had removed that episode of his experience into the perspective of the past, he perceived that his own sorrow had magnified it. Now it resumed its true proportions, which were those of a novelette; and he promised to fill out the proposed volume with other tales of the same sort, if the first were well received.

Suddenly, a wholly different subject occurred to him. Among the little tokens which he was always receiving, there had been a net purse with no name attached, the giver of which he had never been able to divine. After having suspected all the ladies of his acquaintance, he drew from his conjectures the subject of a picture of Parisian life. This was the origin of the "Caprice."

Wishing to produce a fresh type of the perfect woman of the world, he took for a model his godmother, although she had nothing whatever to do with the adventure of the net purse. The conception of Mme. de Léry occurred to him, with her gayety, her malice, her picturesque language, her keen wit, her seemingly frivolous character. There are very few women in any land capable, like Mme. de Léry, of using in the interests of morality the whole arsenal of coquetry; of doing a good deed as one makes an April fool, and extricating herself completely from a dangerous situation, with as much cleverness as grace. If, however, the thing is possible anywhere, it is in Paris; and that clearly outlined figure has been accepted as the perfect picture of a Parisienne *par excellence.* Those who think the portrait flattered are free to consider that charming creation, Mme. de Léry, as the author's tribute of gratitude to those women of Paris whose suffrages he has always received.

When the "Revue" published the "Caprice" (June 16, 1837), it was talked about in the *salons;* but the literary world at large affected to disregard it, as though with a somewhat ill-natured sense that the appreciation of such a sketch did not come within its province. The author did not trouble himself about this silence, but proceeded to write "Emmeline," which was completed in a few days, and the MS. of which he delivered to the printer with some slight reluctance. This was, in fact, his first genuine romance. He had undertaken to arouse interest and move the hearts of his readers by the simple story of a disappointment in love and a sacrifice to reason and duty. Left to his own resources, the poet of youth found that in attempting merely to talk well without rhetoric he encountered an entirely new test. The moment his story was out, his family and friends reassured him completely about the result of the experiment, and the "Revue" called for more tales. He at once commenced the little story of the "Deux Maîtresses," which, in his modesty, he still regarded as an experiment. After having depicted himself in Valentin, he paused. The incidents which he proposed to recount had not happened to himself, although he had long before found himself in a situation very like that of the hero. How could he impart an air of truth to a tale the subject of which must seem paradoxical to so many people? That it is possible to love two women at one time could not, as his godmother remarked, be doubted by Prince Phosphor; but to prove it by an example was not so easy. The first six pages of the "Deux Maîtresses" were strewn about his writing-table. The wavering author had planted Valentin on that spot, and gone off with his friend Tattet. He chanced upon a *bouillote* party, lost his money, and came back and shut himself up in his chamber a sadder man. He was even sulky the next morning when his mother brought him a great bunch of roses in a glass of water, and set them down before him, saying, "All those for four sous!" His mother stole softly away, and Alfred felt the tears come into his eyes. "Ah," said he, "here at least, is something true! I can't go wrong if I write what I have really felt."

He wrote that page about the pleasures of the poor,

which finishes the first chapter of the novel. Once reconciled with his subject, he worked all day long, and boldly undertook to present, under the form of candid recital, the romantic scenes and events which had taken place in his own imagination only. He did not, however, quite finish his little romance, and the new detention occurred on this wise.

To conceive a novel, to imagine a fable, and arrange the plan of it, had been the affair of an hour of fireside chat; but Alfred realized with impatience how slowly the manual labor advanced. Often he would be dreaming of a poetical subject, even while he was writing prose. He even maintained that this twofold exercise of the faculties was rather profitable than injurious to both efforts. Knowing perfectly well beforehand what he wanted to say in prose, he economized the time required to put the words upon paper by turning over in his head a new idea. It was, he said, like turning your eyes to a more distant star, in order to see more clearly the sparkle of the nearer one. Moreover, a chance occurrence recalled him to poetry. One evening, after a long conversation with a lady who was really frankness and kindness personified, he began to suspect her — I do not know why — of deceit and hypocrisy. Convinced almost immediately of the injustice of his suspicions, he sought within himself for the origin of his odious distrust, and fancied he detected the cause of it in that first occasion of his life when he had come in contact with treachery and falsehood.

Even while he related the loves of Valentin and Mme. Delaunay, he was dreaming of early memories and sorrows now gone by. As his reminiscences became more poignant, he conceived the idea of a supplement and conclusion to the "Nuit de Mai." He felt in his soul something like a rising tide. His Muse smote him upon the shoulder, and refused to wait. He rose to receive her, and he did well; for she brought him the "Nuit d'Octobre," which is in fact the necessary sequel to the "Nuit de Mai," the last word of a great woe: a perfectly legitimate, as well as a most crushing, revenge; that is to say, — forgiveness. On the 15th of October, the "Revue" published the last of the "Nights;" and, on the 1st of December, the "Deux Maîtresses."

By way of profiting by a mood so favorable to work, Alfred searched among his memories for another romantic subject, and the gay figure of Bernerette, recurred to him. The veritable adventure was somewhat desultory in its action; yet he made of it one of his most attractive and popular stories. Feeling that death alone could expiate the faults of the wayward girl, and soften the reader's heart toward sins of youth for which so severe a penalty was paid, he condemned his heroine to a tragic end. While the true Bernerette was roaming the country, no one knew where, the ideal Bernerette died at twenty; and the amours, begun in laughter and nonsense, finished with despair and suicide.

Like the history of Valentin, that of Frédéric and Bernerette suffered an interruption. The author had long been tormented by the insoluble problem of the destiny of man, and the ultimate aim of life. I used often to find him with his head buried in his hands, determined by sheer force to pierce the impenetrable mystery, seeking some ray of light, either in the depths of space, or the spectacle of the external world or his own heart; calling on science, on philosophy, on all creation for proofs and way-marks, and finding only systems, reveries, negations, conjectures, and, at the end of all, — doubt.

The subject of his reflections became a fixed idea, he wanted me to discuss it with him, and we were frequently at it until three o'clock in the morning. He read with inconceivable eagerness, the ancients and the moderns, the English, the Germans, Plato, Epictetus, Spinoza, down to M. de Laromiguière himself; and, as may readily be supposed, he found himself none the better. Oftentimes, repelled by the overweening dogmatism of some, and the indecision and obscurity of others, he closed his books, and resumed where he had left it the story of his poor Bernerette. But, on the day when he laid his heroine in her grave, the tears came into his eyes; as he penned the last page his scepticism vanished, and he said a word to me which I shall never forget. " I have read enough," said he. " I have scanned and searched enough! Tears and prayer are essentially divine. It is God who gave us the faculty of weeping, and tears come from Him to us, and prayer returns from us to Him." On the succeeding night he began the " Espoir en Dieu."

The readers of the " Revue des Deux Mondes," when they read in that magazine, with only a month intervening between the dates of their appearance, the history of a grisette, and an invocation to the Creator, can hardly have suspected the correlation between these two so dissimilar efforts. [t is certain, however, that the death of Bernerette, by provoking in the heart of the author a fleeting compassion for an imaginary woe, drowned all the philosophies of the world in a single drop of water. The verses on the "Mi-Carême," which immediately followed the above-mentioned publications, furnish a yet more striking proof of the versatility of this young and impressionable mind. One evening, at some ball or other, the cotillon was very ill-managed, and Alfred seized the occasion to pronounce a eulogy on the waltz, which he had been meditating ever after reading in Lord Byron's poems a bitter criticism on the same dance. When he had avenged the "Belle Nymphe aux Brodequins dorés," he returned to his novels.

At the time when he discovered among the memorials of the Italian painters the story of "Andrea del Sarto," he had also been smitten by another subject, too metaphysical to be treated under the form of a drama or comedy, but which he kept in reserve. Encouraged by the manager of the "Revue" to continue his series of novelettes, he looked up among his notes the story of "Tizianello." After mastering an excellent style of painting in his father's studio, — says the history, whether true or false, — the son of the celebrated Titian produced only one work, the portrait of his mistress; but that work was a masterpiece.

In order to enter more completely into the views of his hero, the author adopted them, and maintained this theory, — that one masterpiece is enough for the glory of one man; and that when a genius has once proved

what he can do, he ought to stop there and not lay himself open to the charge of deterioration, like Corneille,
Guido, and Titian himself. In our discussions I took
the other side, and pleaded the cause of assiduity and
fecundity. The obscurity which shrouds the name of
Titian's son, and the immense reputation of his father,
were all in my favor ; but my brother undertook to convert me by the example of his hero, of whom nothing
is known except that he had a great deal of talent, and
only once condescended to prove it. Of all his brief
romances the " Fils du Titien " is undoubtedly the one
which was written with most enjoyment and enthusiasm.
He was determined to make it a gem, and he added the
ornament of two sonnets composed for the occasion,
which were supposed to furnish irrefragable proof of the
cleverness and poetic talent of the hero, who could be
proved a great painter only in writing. The whole
month of April was devoted to this effort ; and this time,
if I remember rightly, no interruptions occurred.

The " Fils du Titien " appeared in the " Revue " for
May 1, 1837. Some personal reminiscences may be
detected in the episode of the purse, and the behavior
of the hero's prodigal son. A good many readers will
doubtless be pleased to observe how skilfully some slight
reflection from the author's own experience is occasionally introduced in the midst of fictitious circumstances
belonging to a remote time. Alfred thought this romance one of his best productions, both by reason of the
sonnets which he considered faultless, and of the distinguished character of the subject. He had treated it
so conscientiously that he took a six months' rest after

its publication, somewhat after the manner of Tizianello. But the time had not yet arrived for him to take a vow of inaction, and offer reasons for his silence.

One evening his bile had been stirred by a discussion at the café, in the course of which, certain envious persons had more or less vilified every contemporary reputation; and the fancy occurred to him to translate into verse the doctrines which he had been opposing, and so carry war into the camp of his adversaries. The result of this satirical whim was the idyl of "Dupont and Durand."

At the house of the Duchesse de Castries, Alfred de Musset met an extremely beautiful woman who had just read the "Espoir en Dieu," and complimented him highly on the beauty of its versification. He replied lightly, but with the utmost respect, that he was sorry he could not wear so delightful a compliment, like a flower in his button-hole. The lady went into the country the next day; but, a few days later, Alfred received an envelope containing a little bouquet of white flowers, tied with a thread of silk. He was not the man to allow so graceful an attention to pass unnoticed, and he replied by the verses "To a Flower." Afterwards he saw the lady again at long intervals, and her beauty was always one of his great admirations. She died young, while still beautiful and very much the fashion; and her death was a sudden and terrible one.[1]

Pauline Garcia had recently arrived in France, a mere child, but already famous. She had been heard but once in Paris, at the Belgian minister's; the second time she

[1] She was accidentally burned. — P. M.

was to appear at a musical matinée at the house of Alfred's godmother, before an audience composed of genuine *dilettanti*.   Prince Belgiojoso was there, and so was Deasaüer, a composer of much talent, who died shortly afterwards in Germany.   Mlle. Garcia began by singing Deasaüer's lovely air, " Felice Donzella," in D minor.   The author accompanied her himself.   I fancy I can still feel the thrill of delight which ran through the audience at the opening measures.   We declared that it was the voice of Malibran herself, but with more freshness, more compass, a more velvet smoothness, and without that slight hoarseness which never quite wore off under a quarter of an hour.   Of course, our excitement reacted on the youthful singer, and the applause nerved her up to such a degree that she remained a long while at the piano, resisting her mother's attempts to draw her away.   After Deasaüer's piece, came an air of Bériot's and then one of Costa's, and finally the whole repertory of boleros and ariettas. The connoisseurs were simply ravished at the marvellous compass of that voice, the quality of tone, the excellence of her method.   Meanwhile, Alfred de Musset, presented by his godmother, undertook to converse with the young girl on the highest themes of art, and found her — so he liked to say — as deeply versed as any old professor.   He came home from that *séance* in the highest spirits, repeating over and over again, " Oh, what a glorious thing genius is! How fortunate we are to live in a time when it still exists, and we can observe it closely!"   Just as though he had not been full of it himself!

Subsequént talks with Pauline Garcia about music and the stage confirmed him in the conviction that, by care and prudence, she might become the worthy successor of Malibran. That year (1836) was a year of high hopes. Of course, there must be an idolized singer for the future court of France and that æsthetic revival to which we were all looking forward. Chance had ordained that she should be of the blood of the Garcias. It was a clear case of predestination. Two new events occurred which added lustre to the promises of the future, — the birth of the Comte de Paris, and the advent of Mlle. Rachel. In the early days of August, the booming of cannon informed the populace of the safe delivery of the Duchesse d'Orléans. There were already two generations of heirs to the crown of July. Alfred was moved to testify to the prince who had honored him with his friendship his own participation in the happiness of the royal family. He composed some verses on the subject that very day, and the tribute was finished before we learned from the "Moniteur" what were to be the names and titles of the newcomer. His father desired to place him under the special protection of the city of Paris.

Three days after the birth of the prince, on the first of September, 1838, the "Revue des Deux Mondes" published some stanzas, to which the friends of the author called the attention of the Duc d'Orléans; and a messenger from the palace brought to the poet a pencil-case ornamented with a diamond. It has been said, in several of the more or less trustworthy notices which have appeared since Alfred de Musset's death, that the place of Librarian of the Department of the Interior was given him in reward for his verses on the birth of the Comte de Paris. This is not exactly true. The place became vacant, and the minister offered it to M. Buloz. The manager of the "Revue des Deux Mondes" thought best to decline it, but suggested instead one of his associates. After assurances that the appointment would be a good one, he gave the name of his candidate.

It is hardly necessary to say that the minister had not read so much as a line by the writer recommended. He knew something by hearsay of the "Ballad to the Moon," and characteristically remarked to M. Buloz, "I have heard some talk about the *dot over an i*, and I thought it a rather hazardous expression. I should not wish to compromise myself."

When Alfred heard of the steps kindly taken by M. Buloz, he requested the support of the Duc d'Orléans. The prince promised to intercede with the minister, who had already another person in view. Then came six weeks of parleying. M. Edmond Blanc was somehow mixed up in it. Finally, on the 19th of October, the appointment was signed, and the author of the *dot over an i* became the Librarian of the Department of the Interior.

At that time there was living next us, in the same house, a certain physician, a very accomplished man, and professor of lithotrity, with whom Alfred liked to talk about physiology and medicine.[1]   One day our

---

[1] His name was Léon Labat, and his destiny a strange one. During a journey to the East, on which his wife had accompanied him, he cured the

neighbor brought in from the country an exceedingly pretty little serving-maid, about fourteen years of age, in the costume and head-dress of her native village. With the doctor's permission, Alfred questioned the child and made her tell him her story. She had not very much to say; but Alfred treasured in his memory a great store of conversations with children and young girls, having a positive adoration for innocence and ingenuousness. The image of the farm of Clignets, forgotten for almost twenty years, recurred to his mind. This furnished him with a landscape, and his poetic imagination supplied the rest. The fable was composed; and, on the first of October, the "Revue" published the story of "Margot."

Just at that moment, there dawned upon us one of those geniuses who sway the world. A child of seventeen had restored tragedy to life, — tragedy which had apparently been buried for ever in the tomb of Talma. It seemed as if this maiden had suddenly discovered the true meaning of verses which the whole world knew by heart. The attempt to rejuvenate, by a new interpretation, consecrated and even antiquated masterpieces, if

Shah of Persia of a chronic kidney complaint, which had been pronounced incurable. The Shah would not part with him; appointed him his own physician-in-chief, and loaded him with honors, decorations, and gifts. M. Labat consented to reside in Persia: but he did not forget his native land; and his ascendancy over the mind of the Shah became very serviceable to the Frenchmen resident in the domains of that prince. On a certain occasion, some French and English merchants were disputing about privileges, and M. Labat caused the balance to incline to the side of his compatriots. Shortly afterward he was poisoned by his servants. He treated his own case, and very skilfully, but his health was ruined. He returned to France, arranged his worldly affairs, and went calmly to Nice to die, persuaded that he was the victim of British vengeance. — P. M.

made by a great artist, always succeeds. The public
taste readily goes back a hundred and fifty years, although it is equally ready to resume upon the morrow
its onward motion.   Mlle. Rachel had but to open her
Corneille and Racine, and her fortune was at once
assured.   After she had twice or thrice lifted up her
voice in the desert where the faithful guardians of tradition preach, she found one night a few attentive listen-
ers.   The tidings were whispered from one to another.
The newspapers, unwilling to be behindhand, made
haste to announce the new planet.   All Paris flocked
in, with a curiosity which soon became enthusiasm , and
it was decided that tragedy must still exist, since we had
undoubtedly a great *tragédienne.*

Alfred de Musset was one of the first to recognize the
genius of Mlle. Rachel.   For two months he did not
miss a single one of her representations, and the very
first day I heard him joyously exclaim: "We have two
Malibrans instead of one !   Pauline Garcia has a sister !"
As might have been expected, the classicists raised
shouts of triumph.   They made haste to proclaim that
the resurrection of a class of works long since abandoned was the death-warrant of others which had
recently been introduced upon the stage.   The romanticists, on their part, dissembled their fears, insisted
that the public was beside itself, and that the phantom
of tragedy would speedily return to its grave.   Alfred
de Musset thought there was as much of injustice and
unreason on one side as on the other, and he undertook
to reconcile the contending parties.   He published a
dissertation in which he argued that tragedy and the

romantic drama could perfectly well exist side by side, and need ask nobody's leave to live. When he had defined the character of the young actress's genius, and demonstrated that *genius* was neither too ambitious nor too flattering a word to be applied to her, the author approached the literary question. He began by assuring the romanticists that they need not hope for the speedy disappearance of the new craze for tragedy; but neither did he allow the classicists to count upon the utter annihilation of the class which dispenses with the unities. He then took a rapid survey, both of antique tragedy and that of the seventeenth century, and showed how they were severally adapted to the tastes of Athens and Versailles. But now that all theatrical conditions were changed, the author expressed the hope that we might see a third variety of dramatic compositions, more in harmony with our own manners than either, and partaking of the qualities both of antique tragedy and the modern drama. He briefly sketched the plan of a new poetic school, and closed as follows: "These are the questions which I would like to propose to those writers who are justly in high favor among us, provided any of them are induced, as they probably will be, by the talent of the young artist who has restored the honors of the old repertory, to arrange a new part, specially for her." [1]

No one, however, profited by this poetical proclamation, which might have aroused the antique Muse without sacrificing to her the conquests of modern art. The

[1] "On Tragedy considered with reference to the *Début* of Mlle. Rachel," "Revue des Deux Mondes," Nov. 1, 1838.

author of the article himself was alone capable of putting its principles in practice. But it would be a mistake to suppose that he dreamed of saying to himself, "Do *you* write a tragedy for Mlle. Rachel." The pitiable insults of the Odéon pit had for ever banished the thought of the theatre from his head. Moreover, he was not one of those who, when they see an artist in high favor, have no scruple about thrusting forward their own talent, for the sake of attaching their fortunes to hers. He never would have thought of writing a part for Mlle. Rachel, unless she had begged him to do so. This did actually happen twice, as we shall see farther on, and it is exceedingly to be lamented that the project came to nought both times. Let this be added to the other signs of the times, — that any thing fine and good in the way of poetry or art will infallibly fail, provided its success require, I will not say the concurrence of several persons, but even the steadfast accord of two wills. So foreign to the modern imagination are all save monetary and material rewards! The great tragic actress herself did not escape the malady of her age, as the close of her career plainly shows. But nobody foresaw this at the point which we have now reached.[1]

When the article in the "Revue" appeared, Rachel had already restored to the stage five works out of the old repertory; namely, "Cinna," "Horace," "Andromaque," "Mithridate," and "Tancrède." During the last days of November, she added a sixth to this list, and appeared in the part of Roxanna. This time the journals all agreed in charging her with the grave blunder of having

---

[1] This page was written in 1862.

attempted a part which did not suit her. Her friends were more alarmed than she was herself, her only sentiment being one of anger. Precisely because he was not a professional critic, Alfred thought he ought to undertake her defence. He had no difficulty in showing that Rachel had displayed in Roxanna the same qualities and the same genius, as in her previous parts, and that here, as always, her peculiar conception of the character had brought out novel effects. He then asserted that, if she had made her first appearance in " Bajazet," the critics would have smothered her with praise, and poured out upon her devoted head all the riches of their complimentary vocabulary. But Roxanna was her sixth impersonation; and there was the difficulty, — epithets were exhausted. There were no more compliments in the bin; and, after we have admired, it always looks well to show ourselves doubtful and difficult to please. " And this," said the author, " is the way judgment is pronounced; at least, in the newspapers."

The ill-humor of the Monday papers was diverted from the actress to her champion; but Alfred was not disconcerted, for the public was of his mind.[1] The performances of " Bajazet" attracted the same crowds as the former tragedies had done, and the incensed Roxanna was avenged by their applause. Rachel continued as long as she lived to play that beautiful part, notwith-

---

[1] On the 6th of December, 1838, Jules Janin published in the " Journal des Débats," an attack on the defenders of Mlle. Rachel, in which he called Alfred de Musset a third-class poet. The same critic had the audacity to set up above Rachel a certain Mlle. Maxime, long since entirely forgotten. There is no excuse for enormities of this kind which are not committed in good faith. — P. M.

standing the charitable advice which she had received to abandon it; and those who persisted, whether for the sake of making themselves notorious or from whatever motive, in waging an impious and cruel war upon this highly gifted woman so long as she lived coined money afterwards over the body of the dead Rachel, strewed her grave with artificial flowers, and shed above it tears adulterated by speculation.

Amid this breaking of lances, by virtue of which Alfred lived absorbed in the happy life of art, he was informed that Mlle. Garcia was to sing in a concert at the Théâtre de Renaissance (at present the Italian theatre, Place Ventadour). Ever since the musical *matinée* to which the godmother had bidden us, some twelve or fifteen admirers of this precocious genius had formed among ourselves a defensive league to assist her first public appearance in Paris. Among the more ardent members of this band, were MM. Maxime Jaubert, counsellor in the Court of Appeals, Berryer, Auguste Barre, the sculptor, Prince Belgiojoso, Baron Denier, Alfred de Musset, and his brother, and a number of society men, who by their position, knowledge, and authority might exercise a considerable influence. We embraced every opportunity, not merely of hearing Pauline Garcia sing, but of conversing with her. We informed ourselves about the young girl's purposes; we were absorbed in her interests, which were to some slight extent our own, since we were determined to attract her to Paris and detain her there. In order to render her stay agreeable, we must secure her a success proportionate to her talent. When she deigned to consult us, we weighed the *pros* and *cons* of every question with extreme solicitude, and highly approved in these consultations the prudence, experience, and good sense of her mother, the widow of the great Garcia.

Summoned by circulars, we attended the concert in the Théâtre de Renaissance, some time in December, 1838. The sister of Malibran was disposed to be satisfied. She did not need the assistance of her friends. The public applauded her with a fervor which detracted nothing from the regrets bestowed on Malibran. Alfred de Musset was not able to be present at the concert, but he called on the young *cantatrice* at her lodging, and she sang him the whole programme. In an article in the " Revue," he said with his customary modesty that he was no musician, but gave proof of a profound feeling for the art of which he professed ignorance. I do not think that the talent of Pauline Garcia was ever more justly defined and appreciated than in those six pages of the "Revue des Deux Mondes." For the three months that he had been pleading the cause of the youthful Muses of tragedy and song, the sincere and impartial critic only had appeared. It was time for the poet to take his turn, and a very simple incident effected it.

Alfred has himself told the story in an article in the " Revue des Deux Mondes " for January 1, 1839, which closes with a well-known piece of verse addressed to Rachel and Pauline Garcia.

" Unhappily," said the too modest poet, " it is not for me to follow these gifted young creatures."

But who should follow them if not he? He might have said : " It is not for me to follow them, but to take them by the hand, and lead them into the right way of art and beauty and truth." But the sigh of regret which he heaved was perfectly sincere. The meaning of it was, "Ah, if I were only thought worthy, how gladly would I employ my talents in the service of such interpreters!"

So ended the year 1838, the most prolific and the happiest year of my brother's life, because it was the richest in illusions.

But there was something beside the poetic amours, the artistic pleasures, and the triumphs which I have detailed. His happiness could not have been complete, if the heart had not had its share therein. Ever since 1837, Alfred had met often in society a very young and very pretty woman of an enthusiastic and impassioned nature, and occupying an independent position, — one who actually bought the works of poets, although it was not then the fashion to do so. They talked together in Parisian drawing-rooms. They corresponded during a necessary absence of hers in the provinces.

The correspondence was literary when it began. Afterwards it became lover-like. I have seen fragments of it which might belong to the series of the Portuguese letters.

The frank and loyal spirit of the lady was something so new to Alfred that he was deeply enamored of it. The connection lasted two years, during which there was neither quarrel, nor storm, nor coolness of any kind, nor any occasion for jealousy or offence; and this is why there is no story to be told about it. Two years of unclouded love are not to be described. Real happiness has no history.

XII.

ONE evening in the month of January, 1839, after a good day's work, Alfred counted in my presence the pages of his novel of "Croisilles," which he had just completed. When he had estimated approximately the number of pages in the "Revue" which the MS. would fill, he exclaimed: "*Finis prosæ!*" I asked him what he meant.

"I mean," he said, "that anybody can tell a love story more or less charmingly, although there is a difference between Boccaccio and the light-literature column. But since I can express myself in a language not spoken by the first man you meet, I wish and intend to confine myself to that."

I respected his scruples, and the only argument in favor of prose-writing which I brought forward was the pecuniary one.

"Just look," he rejoined, "at those two inspired young girls, whose *débuts* we have just watched with so keen an interest. *They* would never disown their vocation. *They* could not be turned out of their course by any pecuniary offer whatever. Pauline Garcia would not take an engagement at the Opéra Comique. Rachel would not deign to recite a bit of melodrama. I propose to follow my own line as they do."

He proceeded to read me his novelette of "Croisilles," which I thought charming, although it evidently required

one more scene, which was so clearly foreshadowed that
it seemed impossible to relinquish the thought of it.
After taking the old aunt of Croisilles in a hired carriage to the financier's, to request the hand of his
daughter, he should not have stopped there. Why not
portray the old lady's grand airs, the father's excitement, then the cooling of the good man's wrath, the
change of his ideas from black to white, and finally
his granting through vanity what he had once refused
from pride. There was a comic situation all outlined,
which it would scarcely have taken him two hours to
fill out. But nothing would induce the naughty boy to
attempt it. " No," he persisted, " I have decided, and I
shall not go back." "Croisilles" came out on the
fifteenth of February, 1839, and when the author was
criticised for the abruptness of its termination, he only
rubbed his hands and repeated, " *Finis prosæ !* "

He was paying attention at that time to a female
artist of talent, who treated him with a hardness and
lack of confidence the more inexplicable because he
had done her genuine service. I did not understand,
until a long time afterward, why it was that this exceedingly clever woman should have allowed herself to entertain a prejudice against a man whose poetic gallantries
might have made her immortal. Her unjust and inexplicable sternness mortified Alfred de Musset, and in a
moment of spite he wrote the stanzas to Mademoiselle
———— which begin, " Oui, femme, quoi qu'on puisse
dire." But this terrific reproach was not his last word ;
for the ensuing year he addressed to the same person
the verses entitled " Adieu," in which his anger appears

greatly softened. At the actual moment of separation, the poet could feel nothing but regret. Moreover, neither of these poems was sent to its address, and the lady who inspired them may have read them ten years later without recognizing them. Alfred always communicated these personal poems to his godmother, who was the depositary of his inmost thoughts, and gave her copies of them. On the morrow, he was agitated about something else. Two other pieces of the same sort, which he composed in the spring of 1839, are probably still hidden away in ladies' drawers, and will come to light some day, if Heaven pleases.

Alfred continued anxiously to watch the progress of the two *noble children*, as he called Rachel and Pauline Garcia. On the twenty-sixth of March, the godmother issued a circular letter inviting all her friends to be present at the "Théâtre du Gymnase Dramatique," at a performance given for the benefit of Mme. Volnys, at which Mlle. Garcia was to sing with Mme. Damoreau. A few days later, Mlle. Garcia left for England; and the London papers soon apprised us that she had made her first appearance there in the part of Desdemona. A letter addressed to the godmother, and shown to us, contained the following passage : —

"The public wanted the air 'Che Smania,' in the second act, repeated. But I would not interrupt the dramatic action, and kept straight on. I contented myself with coming before the curtain. In the third act, they were determined to make me repeat the *romanza* of the 'Willow,' and the 'Prayer.' How could I ? I should have had to have a glazier come to Othello's house and mend the broken pane of glass, that he might break it anew ! So, in spite of the uproar of *encores*, I would not stop."

Alfred was never weary of lauding the courage and conscientiousness of this inexperienced young girl, more preoccupied with the right rendering of her piece than with her personal success, and coping thus with the London public on the very day of her *début.* He saw foreshadowed the future of another Malibran.

Rachel, all whose performances he attended, interested him no less.   One evening in May, he met her in the corridor of the Palais Royal, coming out of the Théâtre Français, and she bore him off to supper along with a band of artists and other friends.   In his posthumous works may be read a curious description of that supper. "It was," says the author, "a picture by Rembrandt, and a scene out of Wilhelm Meister in one."   Shortly afterward his table was heaped with the works of Sismondi and Augustin Thierry, and he was sketching the plan of the "Servante du Roi."   I have told elsewhere why this tragedy was never finished ; but when he was at work on the fourth act, — in July; 1839, — it would not have seemed possible that so fine a project should miscarry.   Rachel read the monologue of Frédégonde, and from this sample demanded the rest of the piece.   While the poet was dreaming over it, his friends, and particularly the manager of the "Revue" reproached him with his silence.   His idleness was not without a purpose ; nevertheless, it was injurious to his interests.

It is a notorious fact, that none but English editors pay largely for literary wares of a superior quality. With French publications, it is quite otherwise; and quantity is all in all.   Remuneration is very slight, unless one fills a great many pages. Alfred always managed his money matters badly. He knew as little about the balance between his receipts and his expenses, as about the modern science of numbers. The slightest incident, the most fleeting impression, was enough to make the Muse descend; but, if the result did not furnish much matter for the typographers, he got his credit extended, so that the fruits of his labor were often consumed in advance, and when the day of settlement came he experienced a sincere regret. Nevertheless, his novelettes, although they had not occupied much space in the " Revue," had produced sums round enough to be appreciable by the author, and a good many people in his case would have made this fact the basis of a speculation. In him, however, this work, which was better paid than his poetry, occasioned a kind of desperate vexation. It was a case of literary conscience such as no explanation could make quite clear to the men of the present generation.

One day I was trying to persuade my brother to return, at least for a time, to his prose novelettes. I represented to him that his affairs were in confusion, and that the misfortunes of Galsuinde and the ambition of Frédégonde could not set them straight. At first he repudiated the notion of interrupting his historical studies, and diverting the current of his ideas; but afterwards he became alarmed at the thought that his immense credits were about to be converted into pressing debts. Two or three tales might serve as a solution of all his difficulties. Alfred consented to look over his notes with me, and there he found the sketch, in six lines, of a brief romance, the hero of which was Christopher Allori, the Florentine painter. He instantly warmed to this subject, which was really very fine. We had been talking it over for an hour when M. Felix Bonnaire came in. He came, at a venture. to ask for something, either in prose or verse for the "Revue;" expecting only the habitual response, "I neither have hatched, nor will I hatch, any thing, O Bonnaire!" Hence he was agreeably surprised when he heard of the project which we had been discussing. Alfred felt that he was perfectly safe, when he promised in writing to furnish three novelettes in three months; and M. Bonnaire departed, pleased at having secured some pages of printed matter for the "Revue." Alfred congratulated himself on being free from two importunate creditors; and I was delighted to think that the "Fils du Titien" would soon have a worthy pendant.

But in the night the wind changed. When I went into his room next morning, my brother overwhelmed me with reproaches. "You have turned me," he said, "into a mere thinking machine, — a serf attached to the glebe, — a galley-slave condemned to penal labor!"

He proceeded, in his exaggerated style, to draw a terrible picture of the prose-writer, painfully bending over his table, with two hundred pages in his head, but barely able to produce a dozen in six hours: pausing, exhausted, with red eyes, and fingers stiff with fatigue, and dolorously regarding the scrawl before him, poor product of his day's labor; haunted by the rest he had to say, and appalled at having said so little, and falling from languor into complete disheartenment.

Like the wise father of La Fontaine's young widow, I suffered the torrent to flow on. I then attempted to make the infuriated poet understand that a novel was not to be summoned into existence by a drum-beat ; that the " Fils du Titien," " Emmeline," and " Croisilles " itself had been written with too much zest to betray the slightest effort ; that facility of execution enhanced the pleasure of the reader ; and, moreover, that I had never myself observed the author in that galley-slave condition of which he had drawn so formidable a picture.

" But I very soon should be in such a condition," he replied, " if I listened to you ! I need only fulfil the engagements which I have made ! Give me back my debts and my creditors ! I prefer to be in debt ! I will toil and moil when I see fit. Now I am going back to the race-course ! "

Convinced that this sublime despair would soon subside, I waited patiently for the return of his working mood. At the end of a fortnight, the poet was less excited, but more gloomy. When his money matters had been arranged in accordance with the aforesaid agreement, he owned that he felt relieved ; but did not immediately begin to work, and he would not so much as speak of the painter Allori. I felt positive remorse for having subjected him to the critical alternative of working against the grain, or failing to fulfil his engagement.

As ill luck would have it, Alfred lighted one morning upon a flat magazine-story, in which he detected several gross blunders. With an astuteness which amazes me even now, he divined, three years in advance, that this new style of literature would bring about a revolution, and seriously corrupt the public taste.

" Read that," he said, handing me the story, "and tell me how long the literature of the imagination is likely to survive, if it goes on stultifying itself and its readers at this rate."

I endeavored to show him that all writers were not jointly and severally responsible for the anachronisms contained in one tale; and that the author of " Emmeline " need not fear being confounded with the fashionable craftsmen.

" Don't you see," he said, "that this *portière* style of literature is evoking a whole new world of ignorant and semi-barbarous readers? I know very well that it will die of its own excesses; but it will first disgust all delicate minds with reading. Meantime, I renounce it. There shall be nothing in common between us, — not even the utensil. I wish I might never touch a pen again. Thank God, a bit of chalk or a burnt match will do to write a verse with ! "

The days and weeks slipped by. Felix Bonnaire called from time to time to inquire for the promised novelettes. One day, Alfred said to him : " Come again to-morrow. They will be all done."

Bonnaire gave me an inquiring look; and I signified that I knew nothing at all about it. After he was gone, my brother said : "When a man finds himself in a blind alley, and cannot turn back because he has a sword sticking in him, all he can do is to make a hole in the wall, and go through."

After dinner, during which he said little, Alfred shut

himself up in his room. In the middle of the night, I fancied I saw him come into my room on tiptoe, with a light in his hand; but he did not make noise enough fully to awake me. In the morning when I got up, I remembered the vision; and I glanced toward a certain shelf of my book-case, where I had deposited a pistol-case. The box was gone; but I had taken the precaution to put the caps and the powder away in a bureau drawer, where they still remained.

Alfred came down to breakfast, as usual. He appeared depressed, and made scarcely any reply to my inquiries about his nocturnal visit. A letter was brought him, which he read and re-read. It was from Mlle. Rachel, inviting him to spend some days with her at Montmorency, where she had rented a country-seat. He set forth in high spirits, forgetting to take the pistol-case, which I restored to its place. I do not know what there was in Rachel's note beside the invitation; but it is certain that, during his stay at Montmorency, the poet amused his hostess so well by his disquisitions on the arts, and by talk both grave and gay, that she was very unwilling to have him return to Paris. On his return, still in a happy frame of mind, he wrote a letter to his godmother, in which — contrary to his usual custom of giving a full account to that beloved lady of all the impressions which he received — he hardly alluded to the Montmorency visit, but described some more recent experiences, and wound up with this sentence: "How . captivating she was the other evening, running about her garden with her feet in *my* slippers!" I confine myself to quoting this passage, leaving the reader to

draw such deductions as he may choose.   He will at
least venture to conclude that this incident must have
made a pleasing variety in the life of an intellectual
galley-slave.   A gust of wind seemed to have dispersed
all his gloomy thoughts.   Nevertheless, the contract with
the "Revue" still existed; and, once at home again, the
slave felt the ball tugging at his foot.   The face of Felix Bonnaire soon reappeared; and, to avoid him, Alfred
ran away to the country with M. Berryer, where he met
his godmother, and forgot his cares in the society of a
large and delightful circle.   The manager of the "Revue" was too much his friend sternly to exact the fulfil-
ment of his engagement within the prescribed time; still,
it was necessary to give him some sort of satisfaction.

On his return from the Château d'Augerville, Alfred,
beset by the memory of his promise, yet unable to surmount his repugnance to keeping it, shut himself up in
his own room, and refused to see any one.   I saw him
only at meal-times, and did not dare ask what he was
doing.   One day, as he was leaving the table, he said to
me, with a strange expression of bitterness and vexation,
"You insist upon prose.   Well, I will give you some."
I besought him to tell me his plans.   His writing-table
was strewn with manuscript sheets; but there was no
title on the first page, and I asked him what his subject
was.   "You will know presently," he said, "what the
name of it is.   It is neither a reminiscence, for the
story is not precisely my own; nor a romance, for I
speak in the first person.   There is too much that is
imaginary for you to call it a confession, and too much
that is true for a mere made-up story.   It is a production

without a name. The genuine thing about it is, unhappily, the grief which dictated it, the tears which I have shed while putting it on paper." He then took up his MS., and read me his fantastic performance. The following is the introduction : —

"Although the motive which impels you is sufficiently contemptible (being only an idle curiosity), I will tell you all you wish to know. You are almost a stranger to me, and your sympathy or compassion would be of no use to me whatever. For what you may say I care still less, for I shall never know it. Yet I will show you the depths of my heart as frankly and fully as if you were one of my dearest friends. You need be neither surprised nor flattered by this. I carry a load which is crushing me ; and, when I talk to you, I give it a preliminary shake, before casting it off for ever.

"What a story I could tell you, if I were only a poet! Here, in the midst of this wilderness, in view of these mountains, what would not a man like Byron say, if he had my sufferings to describe ! What sobs you would hear ! And these ice-fields would hear them also. But Byron would talk to you in the open air, on the verge of some precipice. I, gentlemen, propose to close my window. It suits me to converse with you in the chamber of an inn ; and I make use, very properly, of a language which I despise, — a coarse instrument without strings, abused by every chance-comer. It is my business to talk prose, and to tell in the style of the newspapers, between a pallet and a handful of fagots, the tale of an ineffable, unfathomable grief. I like to have it so. It suits me to drape with rags the sad romance which was my story, and to fling into the corner of a hovel a fragment of the sword which was broken in my heart.

" Do not suppose that my woes have been of a very elevated kind. They are by no means those of a hero. They would merely furnish the subject of a novel or melodrama. Listen to me as you listen to the wind that whistles in the crack of the door, and the rain which beats against the windows, — not otherwise. I was a poet, a painter, a musician. My miseries have been those of an artist ; my misfortunes, those of a man. Read as if you were reading your own journal."

There followed the story of a young man of abundant gifts, the spoiled child of an affluent family, who made verses, composed music, and painted pictures for his own pleasure merely, but with success. This part of the narrative was made up out of the experiences of the author's own childhood and youth. By way of exhibiting in the strongest possible light the meanness and vulgarity of his present trouble, Alfred began with the story of his first grief, and the wound which he had received in Italy.[1] An unexpected reverse of fortune suddenly altered the hero's position. Obliged to support a grandmother and four young sisters, he turned his talents to practical account, and began to write novels. His first efforts were successful, and the publishers asked for more. He imposed upon himself a daily stint. His head soon became tired, and his invention was exhausted ; but his necessities were such that he could allow himself no relaxation. He must write, write incessantly. After a year of this torture, the young man lost heart, as will appear from the ensuing scene : —

" One night, — or rather one morning ; for I had written till day-break,— I was seated at my table, having just completed a volume. Not only must I deliver to the printer my pages barely dry, but I must re-read, with my weary eyes on that gray paper, the melancholy result of my vigils. My sisters

[1] Extracts from this portion of his MS. have been given in pages 128–136 of the second part.

were asleep in the next room; and, while I fought with drowsiness, I could hear their breathing through the partition. I was so weary that I felt completely disheartened. Still I finished my task, and, the moment it was done, I buried my head in my hands. I do not know why it was that every respiration of the children filled me with profound sadness. The last chapter of my book had described the death of two lovers. It was hurriedly and carelessly done, like all the rest ; and the chapter lay before me. Mechanically, I cast my eyes over it, and a strange association occurred to me. I got up half asleep, took down the poem of Dante from my library, and began to read over the story of 'Francesca da Rimini.' You know that the passage contains not more than twenty-five verses. I read it several times in succession, until the sentiment of it pervaded my entire being. Then, forgetful of my sleeping sisters, I repeated it aloud. When I came to the last verse, where the poet falls to the ground like one dead, I, too, sank weeping upon the floor.

"'Twenty-five verses,' I said to myself, 'may make a man immortal. How? Because he who reads these twenty-five verses, after a lapse of five centuries, if he have a heart, falls down himself and weeps, and a tear is the truest and least perishable thing in all the world. But where do we find these twenty-five verses? Drowned in three poems! They are not the only fine ones, it is true, and they may not be the finest ; but they would suffice, by themselves, to save the poet from annihilation. And who knows but their accompaniment, — the three long poems, — and all the thoughts, and all the journeys, and the expatriated Muse, and the ungrateful compatriots, were needful that these twenty-five verses might be found in a book which is not read from beginning to end by two hundred persons in a year? It is, then, the habit of sorrow and toil — it is misfortune, if not misery — which makes the fountain flow ; and it is enough (is it not?) if a drop be treasured up. But, if in lieu of this, grief and toil, poverty and custom, combine to dry up the living spring, to degrade and exhaust the man, what becomes of the drop which might have fallen,—the tear which might have been so fruitful? It will run out upon the pavement and be lost.' " [1]

At this point, the reader paused. His hearer was as much moved as himself, and felt a weight upon his heart. We both kept silence for a few minutes, and then I asked for the rest. After the picture of that night of anguish, came a dissertation on the poet and the prose-writer.[2] The rest was only projected; but this was what was to happen: The hero of the tale, disgusted with hack-writing, turned eagerly to painting, and soon became a tolerably skilful *genre* painter. But he presently found himself confronted by the old difficulties. Family expenses and every-day necessities obliged him often to lay aside his brush for the sake of giving lessons, or to wield the crayon of the lithographer. He went to the Louvre, and wept before the smiling face of the " Joconde," as he had wept before the shade of Francesca da Rimini. The next day, he abandoned painting, planted himself before the piano, and passed whole nights in the study of the great composers. But notwithstanding all his efforts, and two or three triumphal evenings, he could not surpass the common throng of concert musicians. He returned to Paris, and relapsed into obscurity. For the third time, he shed barren tears of despondency while performing on his piano the Requiem of Mozart.

It was during this third night of despair that the artist resolved to emancipate himself by suicide. But, before his death, he desired to prepare some memento

[1] From the " Poëte Déchu."
[2] It appeared in the posthumous volume.

of his passage through life. He wanted, just once, to yield to the impulse of his heart, and to make his last cry of anguish audible to those who had suffered like torments with himself.

With this purpose, he slipped away one morning on the imperial of a diligence, and made his way to Switzerland. There, in the chamber of an inn, he hurriedly wrote a fragment of his own Memoirs. To the tale of his sufferings, he added a few scraps of poetry, the last being a farewell to life. He composed music for these verses; and then opened his box of colors, and took his own portrait.

I demurred a little to the *dénoûment.* The author wanted to carry things to extremes; and either fling his hero over an Alpine precipice, arranging the circumstances so that his death might seem accidental, or simply light a chafing-dish. I objected to so gloomy an ending. It seemed to me an additional wrong to our poor century, already so loudly decried, to represent a young man of the finest gifts yielding to the pressure of undeserved misfortunes, while in the performance of honorable duties. I stated to the author the following dilemma: either the hero will not be thought to have had real talent, or he will be accused of lacking courage and perseverance. To which the poet replied: " It rests with me to prove that he had talent. If his verses are good, and his prose eloquent, that will be enough." We continued to discuss the question, and I expressed a wish that the last three works — the " Farewell to Life," the piece of music, and the portrait, all of them inspired by the same genuine sentiment — might come to the notice of some discerning person, and be recognized as masterpieces.

"But what will you do with the author's modesty?" interrupted my brother.

I replied that the author could very easily vindicate that, if he would only take the trouble.

"I see," he said, "only one way to content you. It would be to introduce upon the scene a young girl travelling in Switzerland with her father. She must have a fine ear, and must hear him singing the 'Adieu à la Vie.' The sentiment of the verses and the accents of the singer will show her that his music is no mere pastime. Poetry, music, and likeness will all appear admirable to her, and the young man himself yet more interesting. The hero will be rescued by love, and I shall escape the charge of fatuity; for the enthusiasm of a woman for her lover's lucubrations does not prove them to be masterpieces."

Without committing himself to this idea, Alfred promised to consider it. But when he said to me, one evening, speaking of Jacopo Ortis, "The world only pities the misfortunes of which one dies," I knew very well that he was reverting to his tragical termination. A few days later, he read me his "Idylle de Rodolphe et Albert;" and asked me whether that bit of verse, if it were slipped in among the papers of his hero, would not suffice to make the reader accept him for a poet. I told him the only trouble was that the "Idylle" was too beautiful, and that people would not readily believe but that such verses might have saved their author.

"And why should they not believe it?" he exclaimed.

"Either I deceive myself, or my creation is a genuine poet; that is to say, a child incapable of working out his own destiny. His pleasure or pain, his success or his wretchedness, depend upon circumstances, not upon his own will. He sings the air which Nature taught him, as the nightingale does; but, when you try to make him sing like a blackbird, he is silent, or he dies. Greater souls than Gilbert or Chatterton have never been appreciated until after their death. When poets are flung into the midst of a distraught or heedless world, they must either get out of it, or become clerks or soldiers, according as the time is one of peace or war. But their contemporaries must answer to posterity for their loss. There have been blunders enough made in that line to justify the addition to the list of one imaginary woe. Moreover, in this romance, I do not accuse society, as I might if I were treating of a historical character, and as Alfred de Vigny very properly did in 'Stello.' The very title must show that I do not intend to enter an action against any one; and this is why I am still deliberating whether I had better call the work the 'Stone of Sisyphus' or the 'Lost Poet.'"

I besought my brother to choose the first title; representing the delight the envious would take in saying that the work was a new "Confession of a Child of the Age." Alfred threw up his head haughtily, and replied, "They would not dare!" But the observation had struck him. He began to look up the numbers of the "Revue," to discover the date of his last contribution; and was frightened to perceive that, since the fifteenth of February, he had worked only for himself. Instead of reserving for his romance the fine verses which he had just written, he sent them to the manager of the "Revue." This took place in the last days of September. The "Idylle" appeared on the first of October, and that night the poet slept serenely.

⸱ We had just heard a piece of news highly important to the *dilettanti*, — the engagement of Pauline Garcia at the Théâtre Italien. The management of this theatre had been intrusted to M. Viardot ; and, in consequence of the burning of Favart's Hall, the first performance was to take place at the Odéon. Pauline Garcia made her *début* in "Othello," and her friends were all at their posts ; but, before the close of the second act, Malibran's younger sister might have counted on the entire audience as her friends. Alfred de Musset wanted to have his say about this performance ; and I would recommend to curious readers his analysis of the genius of Pauline Garcia, written in 1839. There are niceties of detail about it, which would apply perfectly to the interpretation of Glück's masterpieces in 1861.

The differences between Malibran's Desdemona and Pauline Garcia's were noted with rare acumen. It was not because custom prescribes a stint of praise in such cases, that the author allowed himself to offer the young *débutante* some advice ; but because the advice was good and needed.

"The moment," he said, "in which she falls on the floor, when repulsed by Othello, is a painful one to some persons. Why need she fall? There used to be an easy-chair at hand, and the *libretto* says merely that Desdemona faints. I do not lay any very great stress

on this point; but these striking effects, these sudden
sensational turns, are so much in fashion nowadays,
that I think we ought to be cautious about them.   Malibran made frequent use of them it is true.   She fell,
and always did it well ; but now the boulevard actresses
have also learned how to fall, and Mlle. Garcia appears
to me better fitted than any one else to demonstrate
that, if one can succeed without such means, one ought
to avoid them."

Where did Alfred de Musset learn that there "used to
be an easy-chair at hand"?   I do not know ; but he was
right, for I find among his papers a letter from Mme.
Garcia, dated Nov. 2 (his article came out on the first),
in which the widow of the great Garcia expresses herself thus : —

"The article is charming ; the criticism excellent. We
shall try to profit by its good suggestions ; and, first of all, we
will have the arm-chair at the next performance, although
Emilia says. 'Al suol giacente ; ' that is, lying on the ground
or the floor. But no matter. My poor husband used to enter,
absorbed in jealous and heart-rending reflections. He flung
himself into a chair of some sort — whatever they had in those
days — and when he rose, he turned it, without appearing to do
so, in such a manner, that Pasta might drop into it naturally.
But enough for the present."

Always afterwards, Mlle. Garcia fainted in the arm-
chair, and left to other Desdemonas, who felt much less
keenly than she, exaggerated movements and carefully
studied falls.   If the article in the "Revue" had done
no more than this, it would have been something : but in
the closing paragraph the author gave both the young
actress and the French public some advice which they

would have done well to heed ; and which, though originally put in the form of a wish, has since assumed the character of a prophecy :—

"And what is to become of Pauline Garcia? There is no more doubt about her future. Her success is established, proved. All she can do now is to mount higher. But what will she do? Shall we keep her with us, or will she, like her sister, appear in Germany, England, and Italy? Shall she roam the world for the sake of a few handfuls of louis, more or less? Shall we award her fame, or will she seek it elsewhere? What is a reputation, after all? Who makes it? What determines it? This is what I asked myself the other evening, as I left the Odéon after witnessing that triumph, after I had seen so many tearful eyes and agitated faces in the hall. I beg pardon of the pit which clapped so bravely. My question is not addressed to that. I ask your pardon, too, fair ladies in the proscenium, who dream so fondly of the airs you love, and tap your gloves sometimes ; and who, when your hearts thrill to the accents of genius fling lavishly your fragrant bouquets ! Nor was I thinking so much of you, O subtile connoisseurs, fine folk who know every thing, and are consequently amused by nothing ! I was thinking rather of the student and the artist, of the man who, as they say, has only a heart and but little ready money ; who comes here once of a Sunday, for an extraordinary treat ; the man for whom the mere exercise of his intellect is a stimulating and salutary pleasure ; the man who needs to see something noble and fine and to weep over it, that he may work gaily on the morrow, and have courage to come again ; the man in short who loved the elder sister, and knows the worth of truth." [1]

How much there is in these few words ! Was it the fault of the pit, or of the fair ladies, or of the languid connoisseurs ? Was it the fault of the young singer her-

[1] Débuts de Mademoiselle Pauline Garcia. Revue des Deux Mondes, Nov. 1, 1839.

self? Which one of all these failed to do his duty, or comprehend his true interests? However it came about, Pauline Garcia went to Russia, and was almost entirely forgotten ; and for the fifteen ensuing years we saw other Desdemonas correctly flinging themselves upon the floor, and the Théâtre Italien descending by degrees to what it is to-day. Not until twenty years had elapsed — twenty years of shrieks and simperings and bad taste, in short of radical and complete decadence — did pure art, and simple song, and dramatic music revive one fine evening, in a remote corner of Paris, at the Théâtre Lyrique. Malibran's sister had reappeared in the " Orpheus " of Glück.

While the admirers of Pauline Garcia were reading the article on her Othello, Alfred was writing, with all his wonted facility, the pretty rhymed tale of " Sylvia." When the "Idylle" appeared, the godmother made haste to tell her son what she thought of the piece. Her letter wound up with a friendly reproof, touching the long silence of his Muse. "Idleness," she said, "is lack of courage." Her godson responded gaily and triumphantly to her strictures, in verses which were also given to the public.

I knew nothing of all this when in the " Revue des Deux Mondes " for December 15, I read, on a detached leaf of blue paper, a list of forthcoming contributions, among which Alfred de Musset's prose work was announced, under the objectionable title of the " Poëte Déchu." I could not suppress a gesture of impatience, which my brother observed. He merely pointed with his finger toward the MS. of the tale imitated from

Boccaccio, more than two hundred verses of which were already written. " Look," said he, " that little poem is but half done yet : in three days I shall have finished it. What farther proof do you require of the vigor of my brain? One would never attempt any thing so bold if one thought about envious and ill-natured people."

I replied that I was perhaps too cautious, and that I would defer my opinion to that of Tattet, or the god-mother. Tattet came so often that I did not have long to wait for him. My brother read him the story of the lost poet, and he interrupted him again and again with admiring exclamations. I even saw tears in his eyes.

" Nothing more eloquent has been written," he said, " since the days of Jean-Jacques Rousseau."

When the reading was finished, I left him alone with his friend, and my brother informed him of my objections. Tattet did not think them well founded ; but the next day Alfred told me that he had burned several pages of the romance, which was not at all what I wanted. He put the rest away in a box, and said that the prose contained some ideas which would be good to put into verse. The poem of " Sylvia," which appeared on the first of January, 1840, caused the readers of the " Revue" to forget the promise of the previous number. A long while afterward other portions of the MS. were burned, and my brother charged me to destroy whatever remnants of the work he might leave behind him, with the exception of the passages quoted above, for which I earnestly interceded. Twenty odd pages of writing are all that remain of that precious document. They are admirable. I have read them with deep emotion ; and, if I might give them to the public, I would not hesitate ; convinced that they would reflect no less honor on the character of the man than on the gifts of the writer.   But, fine as they are, I have promised ; and they must be destroyed.

XIII.

WE must not smile at the sufferings of the poet. He alone can give his plaints audible expression ; but how many there are who suffer like him, yet cannot make it known ! How many young souls, forcibly turned aside from their true vocation, have shed by night just such bitter tears as the strains of "Dante" wrung from the author of the " Poëte Déchu ! " How many are made unhappy by the very fact that Nature has endowed them with more intellect than belongs to the vulgar ! The latter may envy the poet his pangs, his heart-sickness, and his fame ; but it is none the less certain that genius is a fatal gift, unless it have the safeguard of enormous vanity. Alfred de Musset had not received from Heaven that infallible defence against the sorrows of the heart and mind ; and the incidents related in the last chapter show how unhappy he was. His refusal to publish a work which had been announced by the "Revue" complicated the situation yet more ; nevertheless, neither the engagements which he had made, nor my own exhortations to diligence, availed to induce him to return to prose, for which the magazine story had given him an invincible repugnance. "In verse," he said, "a poet may permit himself to offer to the public the truthful expression of his feelings ; but, in the language employed by anybody and everybody, he may not ! "

The prose manuscript which contained this honest expression of his mind was thrown into a corner; but the author could not dispose of his anxieties after the same fashion. A review is a kind of Minotaur. Of the two hundred verses of "Sylvia," the number for January 1, 1840, made but one mouthful, and three times a week came M. Felix Bonnaire to chat at our fireside. These friendly visits were assuredly those of a most patient and inoffensive creditor; nevertheless, he was a creditor with a mortgage on one's thoughts and feelings and tears. It was in such terms that Alfred invariably described all contracts for future work. I must confess that I thought him extravagant and unreasonable. Like the manager of the "Revue," like Alfred Tattet and the godmamma, I occasionally stigmatized his disdainful silence as laziness or weakness. But we were all wrong. We had not the poet's second sight.

Alfred was always in love as a matter of necessity. When I omit to mention the fact, it may be understood. His twofold admiration for Pauline Garcia and Rachel passed from his intellect into his heart, every time he came out from hearing a performance by either one. This was the time when he should have written the story of Valentin's double passion for the Marquise and Mme. Delaunay. The narrative would then have contained much curious analysis of emotion; but, as it was, the novel was written three years too early. The ideal situation might have been made much finer, because the hero would have been only an *amoureux*, not an *amant*.

The agreeable period of this double attraction came

to an end in the winter of 1840. I perceived that the poet, preoccupied with his engagements, worn out with exhortations to industry, and a trifle disenchanted, no longer wanted to confide his griefs to anybody. At the gay parties to which his friends invited him, he still enjoyed the sprightliness of others, but the animation of Fantasio had deserted him. His depression betrayed itself in all he said, and made itself felt even at our family meals. One evening after we had messed at a restaurant with Tattet and several other friends, — we had had a good dinner and drunk more than was needful, — the feasters left the table, bent upon further amusement; but when they came to look for Alfred he was not to be found. He had escaped, and had been for some hours in my room. I asked him how he had employed his evening. "I have been doing my best," he replied, "to enjoy myself as other people do, and I have only succeeded in stultifying myself. The truth is I am no longer capable of enjoyment."

I asked him what he meant by that; and the reply which he gave struck me as so singular that I requested him to write down the substance of it. It was a piece of advice which I often gave him, and which, unhappily, he very seldom heeded : but this time he probably put his thoughts upon paper before going to bed ; for there is certainly a reminiscence of the conversation I have reported in the following lines, which I found among his papers : —

" Pleasure is the exercise of our faculties. Happiness is their exaltation. It is thus that, from the beast to the child of genius, the whole vast creation underneath the sun silently accomplishes its eternal task.   And thus, at the close of a feast, some, heated with wine, seize cards and fling themselves upon heaps of gold under the glare of lamps ; some call for horses and ride forth into the forest; the poet arises with eyes aglow, and draws his bolt behind him ; while one young man speeds noiselessly away to the home of his mistress.   Who shall say which of all these is the happiest? But he who stirs not from his place, and has no part in the whirl about him, he is the least of men, or else he is the most unhappy.

"So goes the world.   Among tavern-rovers, some are rosy and merry ; some pale and taciturn.   Can there be a more painful spectacle than that of an unhappy libertine ? I have seen some whose smile would make one shudder. He who would subjugate his soul with the weapons of sense may intoxicate himself indefinitely.   He may affect an impassive exterior ; he may repress his thoughts by the might of a steadfast will : those thoughts will roar incessantly inside the brazen bull."

The melancholy which inspired such reflections was not easily surmounted.   When one has lost the faculty of enjoyment, in the poet's sense of the term, dissipations are of no use.   During the carnival, Alfred conscientiously compelled himself once or twice to join the hilarious bands ; but he brought back from these excursions nothing but fatigue and a fresh access of despondency.

One day he resolved to begin again, although he felt no inclination to do so.   "I am going," he said, "to imitate the late Marshal Turenne.   My body refuses to go into battle ; but my will shall take it there in spite of itself."

This time Nature rebelled, and he came home with inflammation of the lungs.   M. Chomel, although one of the most skilful physicians in Paris, did not form a correct opinion of the disorder ; but took it, at first, for a brain fever. If we had followed his first prescriptions, the mistake might have cost us dear. Fortunately, a mother's instinct, clearer-sighted than science, divined the error and repaired it.

It required no less than three persons, assisted by a sister of charity, to nurse a patient so insubordinate and full of strength. Ten days of sleeplessness and excessive blood-letting seemed only to exasperate him. In one of his rebellious moments, when we were at our wits' end, the godmother arrived. She found her boy sitting up in bed in a transport of rage, and calling loudly for his clothes, that he might go to the baker's, he said, and get some bread, because they would not give him any at home. At first he would not listen ; but, by degrees, the persuasions of his godmother quieted him. At last she peremptorily ordered him to lie down, and he obeyed ; muttering still, but remaining motionless under the touch of her little hand which hardly covered half his forehead. Princess Belgiojoso, who never missed the opportunity to do a kindness, came also several times and sat by the sick man's pillow, and offered him drink which he dared not refuse from the hand of so great a lady. One day, when he was very sick indeed, the princess said to him with perfect composure : " Be calm. People never die in my presence." He pretended out of gratitude to believe her ; but, when she promised to come and see him again, he said quite seriously, " I shall not die on that day."

When his disease was abating, I observed a strange phenomenon. One morning, Sister Marcelline and I were sitting by my brother's bedside. He appeared calm and somewhat exhausted. Reason was still contending with the delirium occasioned by the loss of sleep and the remains of pulmonary congestion. Visions were flitting before his eyes ; but he took note of all his sensations, and questioned me to enable himself to distinguish real from imaginary objects. Guided by my replies, he analyzed his delirium, observed it curiously, amused himself with it as with a spectacle, and described to me the images which were generated in his brain. By and by, complete pictures were composed, and one of these dissolving views remained fixed in both our memories.

It was then March. The sunshine fell upon the writing-table in the centre of the room which, for the time being, was covered with phials. In spite of its being thus encumbered, the invalid seemed to see the table just as he had left it the day he took his bed, — that is to say, strewn with books and papers with a writing-desk upon it, and pens methodically arranged. Presently four little winged genii snatched up the books, the papers, and the desk ; and, when they had cleared the table, they brought on the phials and medicines in the same order in which they had come from the apothecary's. On the arrival of the famous Venetian potion, which M. Chomel had allowed to be tried, the patient saluted it with his hand in the Italian fashion, and murmured : "Pagello has saved me once more." The other medicines took their actual places ; and, for a brief moment, the dream and the reality were identical. Then, from among the army of phials, arose a champagne-bottle adorned with its metal stamp. It was borne pathetically upon a litter by two small genii, who assumed for the occasion a subdued and sorrowful attitude. The convoy moved off by an ascending path which wound away into the distance ; while by another path a decanter descended wreathed with roses, and surmounted by its crystal stopper. The decanter glided smoothly down the sloping pathway, while the genii scattered flowers before it, and the phials drew themselves up in a double line to receive it, and gave it the place of honor.

After this impressive entrance, the decanter laid aside its wreath, and installed itself modestly upon the mantel. The genii removed the traces of the ceremony, took away the now useless phials, and restored things to their pristine state ; so that the recovered poet might find his table in order for work. Each volume and every scrap of paper resumed the place which it had occupied the night before he was taken ill, and the pens arranged themselves symmetrically before the desk. Their duty discharged, the genii departed ; but the poet, after inspecting his table, exclaimed, "That is not quite right! There was a little dust in spots, particularly upon that lacquered writing-desk."

The instant that he made this reasonable complaint, he perceived a little man about three inches high with a perambulating *cocoa-seller's* urn upon his back. The Liliputian traversed the desk and books, turning the faucet of his urn, whence issued a fine dust, and in a few seconds the desired order reigned on the table. "That is perfect," said the master, drawing the coverlid over his eyes. "Now I can sleep, and I believe that I am cured."

And so he was; for, when next he woke, his brain had recovered the clearness and tranquillity of its normal condition. He told these particulars to the physician himself, and M. Chomel replied with a smile, " You have had a regular poetical pneumonia. I am convinced that you would never be like the rest of the world, whether sick or well. But try to profit by the advice which you have given yourself. The apotheosis of the decanter will not suffice. You must also remember that nature designed the day for waking, and the night for sleep."

"Your aphorism," Alfred replied, " is not so profound as that of Hippocrates; but I promise you that I will ponder it."

The word *convalescence* does not begin to express the curious state of beatitude in which the poet found himself during his recovery from this illness. It was a veritable new birth. He felt about seventeen, and enjoyed the " pleasures of childhood and the notions of a page," like the cherub in the " Marriage of Figaro." All the difficulties, all the causes of despondency, which had preceded his illness, had vanished, and his horizon was rose-color. In the evening, the family used to assemble around the famous writing-table, to chat or sketch, while Sister Marcelline knitted little jugs out of variegated wool. Auguste Barre, who lived near us, used to come to work upon an album of caricatures in the style of Toppfer's, representing the series of events and catastrophes attendant upon a marriage treaty repeatedly broken off and renewed. All Paris was laughing at it, and one did not need to be a convalescent to find amuse-

ment in these comical drawings.   Alfred and Barre
wielded the pencil, and the rest of us made up the ex-
planatory text, which was no less absurd than the drawings.   The album consisted of fifty-one sketches, more
than half of which were from Alfred's hand.   It was
not without a pang of jealous regret that I saw the prodigal godson bestow on his godmamma these nonsensical
productions, which, if I had them now, would recall one
of the sweetest periods of our home life.   Who shall
give us back those delightful evenings of laughter,
chatter, and jest; when, without stirring abroad and
with no help from outside, our household was so happy?

The convalescent's first sorrow came with the farewell
of Sister Marcelline.   Not only had the angelic sweetness and devoted care of that saintly girl attached us
all to her; but, quite unconsciously, she had acquired a
marked ascendancy over the mind of the invalid, by the
spectacle of the serenity of spirit which she brought to
the discharge of her duties, and by describing to him,
with affecting simplicity, some of the events of her life;
especially those which had induced her to take the veil.
In her eagerness to second the physician's efforts, she
advised the patient about the course he ought to pursue; first, for the health of his body, and then for that
of his mind.   How could he forbid one so pious and so
affectionate to interest herself in the religious experience of him whose life she had saved by her devotion?
Marcelline used her privilege discreetly, and her gentle
entreaties had more effect than those of a doctor of
divinity could have had.   He assured her that it was
so, and she left him well content, — with the promise

that she would pray for him. Always afterwards, when he wanted help, Alfred asked for Sister Marcelline; but, whether by accident or intentionally, she was never sent to him but once. Occasionally, at intervals of several years, she got leave to come out and ascertain the condition of her patient. She would talk with him for a quarter of an hour or so and then flit away. They were angel visits, — unhappily too rare ; but they always came so opportunely that Alfred regarded them as marks of the favor of some mysterious and consolatory power.

According to the customary working of his mind, the poet, when bereft of the sister whom he regretted, began to concentrate all his thoughts upon her, until his thoughts became words, and his words took the form of verse. One day he told me that he had composed some stanzas, "To Sister Marcelline," but he obstinately refused to write them out. "These verses," he said, "were made for myself alone. They concern only me, and no one else has a right to them. Why should I not compose a dozen stanzas for my private use, and recite them to myself if I choose. I will repeat them to you once, and you may remember them if you can."

Accordingly, he did so. Tattet heard them also, and besought his friend for a copy, but in vain. Afterwards, another lady, whose care had been no less assiduous than Sister Marcelline's own, repeated from memory a few of these verses. By comparing our recollections, we succeeded with great difficulty in reconstructing four stanzas ; but their order is by no means certain. When I owned this misdemeanor to my brother, he was not at all angry ; and, since he demanded no promise of secrecy, I

do not see why I should consign to eternal oblivion one
of the purest inspirations of his vanished Muse. Here
is all I have been able to recover of the stanzas to Sister
Marcelline : —

> " Poor child, thy beauty is all fled !
> Thy nightly vigils by the dead
>   Have left thee pale as they.
> As any delver's of the soil,
> Thy hand is hard with loving toil,
>   Men's anguish to allay.
>
> Yet brave amid its weariness
> Beside the pillow of distress,
>   Thy white brow shineth ; and
> Full well the wretch whose fevered grasp
> Enfolds it, knows how kind the clasp
>   Of that disfigured hand.
>
> .   .   .   .
>
> Pursue thy solitary way,
> And step by step, and day by day,
>   Draw nearer to thy God.
> While we bemoan life's cruel ill
> Who meanly use our coward skill
>   To fly the chastening rod.
>
> But naught of evil dost thou know,
> And nameless unto thee the foe
>   With whom thou strivest still.
> The strokes thereof cannot harm one
> Who hath forgotten how to moan,
>   Save for another's ill." [1]

[1] There is an allusion to the tender memory left by the care of Sister
Marcelline in a letter of Alfred de Musset's to his godmother, dated July
31, 1840. In reply to a previous letter in which the poet had alluded jok-
ingly to his flirtations with several young women, his godmother had asked

Apparently, Sister Marcelline must have obtained from the invalid a promise to engage in some religious exercise ; for, when she went away, she left him a pen on which she had embroidered, in parti-colored silk, the motto, "Think of your promise." Seventeen years later, this pen and one of the little knitted jugs were enclosed in the poet's coffin. It was one of his last requests.

After his recovery, Alfred conceived the desire of writing for Rachel a tragedy of Alcestis. He purchased the drama of Euripides, and applied himself to his Greek, so as to read it in the original. His friend Tattet ransacked the libraries, both public and private, in search of the sketch of a tragedy upon this theme, which some of the biographers of Racine had declared to exist among his papers. In his review of the " Alcestis " of Glück, J. J. Rousseau had made some very judicious criticism of the faults in the libretto of the Bailli du Rollet. These faults were a lack of variety in the situations, and a consequent monotony of language, so difficult to avoid that the Greek poet himself had fallen into it. Alfred was not discouraged, but accepted these

him what had become of his feeling for the sister in the midst of these love affairs. This is evidently her meaning in her remark about the "sacred story." We must not misinterpret the apparent levity with which the godson replies to this question. I think he was unwilling to have so serious a subject mixed up with the *badinage* by which he was trying to divert the mind of a lady whom he suspected of a slightly malicious feeling, not toward himself, but toward one whom he deeply reverenced. It was in a very different tone that he spoke of Sister Marcelline to the Duchesse de Castries, as may be seen by a letter to his brother, dated June, 1840. When he told the godmother that the "sacred story" was somewhat in the condition of the Old Testament, it was probably his way of refusing to answer her at all. — P. M.

criticisms as useful warnings. We shall see presently
why this project was abandoned.

Unwilling to recall his thoughts to painful themes, I
was careful, during his convalescence, not to allude to
the things which had disturbed him before he was ill.
M. Felix Bonnaire, in his morning calls, never breathed
a word about work or engagements. Whether it were
heedlessness or presentiment I cannot say; but Alfred
made the remark now and then, that every thing arranged
itself in this world, and that his affairs would do the
same. Sister Marcelline had predicted it, and so it
would be; and, in point of fact, the poet's embarrass-
ments were about to receive a most unlooked-for
solution. M. Charpentier had just effected a revolution in the book-trade. His 18mo editions brought
within the reach of people of moderate means books
which even the rich had previously found too dear. In the
two preceding years, M. Charpentier had brought out a
large number of books, and M. Buloz now suggested to
him the idea of publishing the works of Alfred de Musset
in the new form. To further the success of the scheme,
M. Buloz consented to sacrifice a certain number of
copies of his own 8vo edition of the " Spectacle dans un
Fauteuil," which still remained in the book-shop of the
"Revue." One morning, therefore, M. Charpentier came
and proposed to the author of the "Contes d'Espagne "
to collect all his poems in one volume of the new form.
This proposal quite altered the aspect of affairs. M.
Charpentier was not deceived in his expectations: a
large number of copies of the reprinted poems were sold,
and the other works by the same author came in their

turn to furnish occupation for the printers. It was a financial revolution for our poet, and he repeated many times, — "Sister Marcelline predicted this; and yet the poor girl hardly knows what a verse is."

For the complete enjoyment of his leisure and freedom of mind, our convalescent resolved to regale himself with some interminable reading. He read the whole of "Clarissa Harlowe" for the second time, and then he wanted the "Mémorial de Sainte Hélène," into which he plunged, and read and reread, until the pages were fairly disfigured. Afterwards he wished to make himself acquainted with all the memoirs which had been published concerning the empire; not forgetting the journal of Antomarchi. According to his wont, he exhausted the subject. When he was possessed by this sort of rage for a person, his reading, his thinking, and his conversation constituted a genuine monograph. I asked him what it was which had attracted him so powerfully toward the imperial epoch, and he replied, — "Its greatness. The pleasure of living in imagination in a heroic time, and the need of getting away from our own. I am tired of little things, and I turn toward the quarter where great ones are to be had. I care more to know how that man put on his boots, than for all the secrets of the present political situation in Europe. I know quite well that clever people nowadays dread nothing so much as being ridiculed for *chauvinisme*;[1] but, for my own part, I snap my fingers at that sort of ridicule."

[1] Military braggadocia, a loud and boastful type of patriotism. The name is derived from Chauvin, the veteran sergeant in Scribe's "Soldat Laboureur," and is especially applied to the worship of glory and the great emperor under the Napoleonic *régime*.

The month of June arrived, and the Parisians began to disperse. Tattet invited his friend to try the air of Bury. As in former years, they rode horseback night and day in the woods of Montmorency. On the spot where, in 1838, Alfred had composed the happy sonnet, beginning, "Quel plaisir d'être au monde," he realized the change which a short time had wrought in his opinions and tastes. The turbulent life which they led at Bury inspired him only with the desire to turn his horse into some solitary path. His friends have told me that one morning when he was late about rising, they went into his room, and found upon his table a sonnet to which, when he afterwards published it, he gave the name of "Tristesse." After having allowed the state of his mind to be suspected by the active companions whose zeal for pleasure he no longer shared, he was afraid of being a check upon them, and he came away.

At about this time there was a transient revival of interest in politics. War was thought to be imminent. France, finding herself once more alone and confronted by her old enemies, made as though she would resist a new coalition consolidated by England. So long as the government preserved its bellicose attitude, they continued to tack on the other side of the channel; but on the day when the king of France, who was considered able, made the blunder of announcing in his *ultimatum* that he would not go to the length of actual hostilities, his enemies, as might have been anticipated, redoubled their arrogance. There is no need to rehearse the pitiful part played by France in 1840. Her influence in the east was destroyed for a long time to come. Like all honorable men, Alfred de Musset grievously resented his country's humiliation ; and the day when the shameful conclusion was made known, he angrily exclaimed, " This reign has lasted too long."

When the policy of *peace at any price* had been fairly resumed, Alfred endeavored to forget it all.   He haunted the galleries of the Théâtre Français, whatever the play might be, and notwithstanding the heat of summer.   One evening when the audience was very small, — they were only playing Molière, — he came home and wrote that curious piece which he called " Une Soirée Perdue," and which is at once a satire and an elegy.   The " Revue des Deux Mondes " profited by this graceful flight of fancy.

Shortly after, Mme. Berryer invited my brother and me to come and meet the godmother and several other agreeable people whom she had collected at her house. Accordingly, we went to Augerville together about the middle of September.   The first part of our journey passed off gaily ; but while we were crossing from Fontainebleau to Malesherbes, my brother became dreamy, and his melancholy mood infected me.   Without confessing as much to one another, we both found ourselves carried back to the same time.   These mysterious shades, these lofty forests so like Gothic cathedrals, the dark walls outlined against a blazing sky, — all these things were unchanged in appearance since 1833.   What signified seven years more or less to trees three hundred years old ?   At every step Alfred felt the memories of his youth starting into more vivid life.   The few words which he said I found again five months later in the lines now so well known, —

" Que sont-ils devenus les chagrins de ma vie ?
   Tout ce qui m'a fait vieux est bien loin maintenant,
  Et rien qu'en regardant cette vallée amie
      Je redeviens enfant." [1]

While his thoughts lingered about the favorite ride
and all the charming spots, mine went farther, and I recalled the day of his departure for Italy, the horrible
winter of 1834, our desolated home, the six weeks of
suspense when we heard nothing from our absent one,
the return still sadder than the departure, — until the
beauty of the forest made me shiver.   Crushing the fine
sand and jolting over the pavements, our uncomfortable
vehicle brought us at last to the hospitable asylum
where a delightful circle was awaiting us ; and in the
evening, after dinner, we introduced into a charade the
frightful drama of " Pouch Lafarge," who was so ill fed
by his better half ; for the public was just then divided
into the accusers and the partisans of Marie Capelle.

Thanks to the pending lawsuit, there was a great deal
of discussion at Augerville about the art of poisoning
and the ways of proving death by poison ; out of which
arose the project of turning the story of Simone into
verse.   The last stanzas will be found to contain slight
allusions to the contest in the Court of Assizes ; while
the introduction betrays a good deal of anxiety about
the evil course that literature was taking.   Two months
later, the author had pointed out the deplorable vagaries
of the drama.   Recurring now to pages written so long

---

[1] Where are now the sorrows of my life?   That which has made me old
is now far away.   And the mere sight of this beloved valley makes me
a child once more.

ago, we are struck with the prophetic character of all that portion which consists of literary criticism and observations on mental condition. But alas! in vain have poets received the gift of second sight. The fate of their predictions is not precisely like that of Cassandra's. We listen and admire. We are amazed that they should be able to tell us so exactly what is thought by people of taste. And then the torrent rolls on.

At Augerville, Alfred was apparently as happy as a child in vacation; nevertheless, at the end of a fortnight, he brought forward a pretext of pressing business, and took his leave. Although Rachel needed no champion, I hoped that he was returning to Paris for her sake; but it was written that these two creatures whose perfect accord was so much to be desired should never remain good friends for more than two weeks at a time. Almost as soon as Alfred saw Rachel again, they fell out with one another.

These trifles derive serious importance from the fact that, in consequence of the quarrel, all thoughts were abandoned, both of the " Alcestis " and the " Servante du Roi," and the one completed act of the latter piece was thrust away in a box. Many people will think that the author did not very well understand his true interests; and probably there are those among living dramatic writers who would have prosecuted their task with entire indifference to the ungrateful comments of Rachel. " Let her say what she will of me," they would have said, " provided she accepts a part which I have arranged. If the piece brings a good sum of money, the rest matters little." But Alfred de Musset was not exactly like all the rest of the world ; and since the sensibility of poets, unreasonable as it seems, is the source of their genius, we must forgive them for it.

His method of banishing Rachel, Frédégonde, and the annoyances of the side-scenes, was to plunge into the ideal world, and work to please somebody else; in this instance his godmamma, who was greatly interested in the subject of " Simone." This little poem, which Alfred wrote with enjoyment and even enthusiasm, appeared in the " Revue " for Dec. 1, 1840.

On the eleventh of the same month, the author completed his thirtieth year. That morning his air and bearing struck me as graver than usual. He made inquiries about the precise hour of his birth. I knew how he was feeling, and we talked long together. " I have come," he said, " to one of my climacterics. It is ten years and something more since I said my first word to the public. You know what I have thought and suffered. You know what luggage I carry, and can estimate its value. You can appreciate better than I can myself the reputation which I have won. Now, answer me truly, — Do you think that justice has been done me ? "

Unhesitatingly, I replied " No."

" I have thought so myself," he replied, " but feared that I was mistaken. The public is behindhand with me. It is silent about the things I publish to a degree which amazes me. I have not the slightest wish to play the part of an unappreciated genius ; but after ten years of work I think that I have the right to withdraw inside my tent. I am quite willing to say to myself that I have been a child until now ; but I do not want others to say it of me. It is high time that I had my dues. If I do not get them, I will be silent."

Alfred sat up very late on the night of the 11th of December; which was not in itself remarkable, since he rarely went to bed before two in the morning. It was during that night apparently that he wrote out the following reflections, on a stray bit of paper which lay about his table for a long time afterwards : —

"Thirty years old!

"There is a mournful look to be turned upon the past, only to see there dead hopes and dead sorrows ; and a still more mournful one to be turned upon the future, there to see — the winter of life!

"There is a foolish thing to be attempted ; and that is to keep on being a child, and yet it was a fine thing with those who were beloved of the gods, with Mozart, Raphael, Byron, and Weber; who died at thirty-six!

"There is a chilling thing to be done, and that is to say to one's self, 'All is over ; ' yet, when Göthe said it, it was noble.

"There is a stupid thing to be done, — to fancy that one has risen superior to one's self ; to assume the style of an accomplished man ; to live like an experienced egotist.

"A languid, lazy thing to be done, — not to hear the clock when it strikes!

"A brave thing to be done, — to hear it, and yet to live on in spite of the gods. But in that case one could not believe in eternity!

"A sublime thing to be done ; and that is not even to know that the clock is striking. But in that case one would have to believe in every thing!

"However it be, it is certain that, at this age, the hearts of some crumble to dust, while those of others live on. Lay your hand upon your heart, for the moment is come. It falters. Has it ceased to beat? Become ambitious or avaricious, one or the other ; or else die at once ! Is it beating still ? Then let the gods do their worst ! Nothing is lost."

Thé poet had indeed laid his hand upon his heart, and listened attentively. But that heart was beating still, and nothing was lost.

XIV.

LORD BYRON said good-bye to youth at the age of thirty-six. Alfred de Musset, always eager to devour the time, had anticipated by a few years that crisis after which we see the future in a new light. Ever since the month of September, he had been dreaming over his excursion to the woods of Fontainebleau. The impressions which he received on that journey were both sweet and bitter ; but, by and by, the bitter element, which had never been powerful, disappeared altogether. His recollections would have faded away entirely but for an unforeseen circumstance, which emphasized them anew and turned them to the profit of poesy. In the corridors of the Théâtre Italien, Alfred met a lady whom he had wellnigh forgotten for many years ; but who had first crossed his path under the shades of that forest. He came home a good deal agitated. The Muse came with him, and invited him to labor. He resolved to entertain her as in happier days, by a grand illumination and a banquet. It was like the meeting of two reconciled friends ; and the Muse, touched by her welcome, gave herself up without reserve. Whole stanzas flowed out upon the paper at one pulse of the fountain. The poet did not lie down before daybreak, nor did his inspiration slacken even in sleep ; but the moment he awoke he seized the pen. The "Souvenir" appeared in the "Revue," Feb. 15, 1841.

When he had received the congratulations of his mother, those of his friend Tattet, and the letter from his godmamma, which never failed under such circumstances, Alfred said to me, "This is all I shall get by my sacrifice to the public. I have thrown to the beasts my bleeding heart. I have wrestled with my thought, to the end that a madman or a blockhead might hum these lines like any common song, —

> " ' Mes yeux ont contemplé des objets plus funèbres
> Que Juliette morte, au fond de son tombeau.' [1]

"I said these words aloud, alone in the silence of the night, and there they are flung away to be picked up by any idle passer-by. Why could they not have waited till I was dead? But you will see that nobody will say a word about them then."

In short, he was beginning to perceive that his most remarkable poems seemed, at the time of their appearance, to fall into a void. Ever since his genius had taken a bolder flight ; ever since his verses had acquired a world-wide range, so that any one with a heart might have felt their beauty, — the press had feigned unconsciousness of them : and, if haply the name of their author were mentioned, it was merely to quote, with disheartening levity, the poet of the Spanish tales, as though he had made no progress whatever since 1830.

For a long while, Alfred de Musset refused to believe in that conspiracy of silence, which every one else observed. He was too kindly readily to admit such a

---

[1] " My eyes have seen sights more funereal than that of Juliet dead in the tomb "

thought, too magnanimous to see meanness in others, too dignified to take a single one of those steps which are supposed to be indispensable to the success of any literary work. When, finally, the truth fairly stared him in the face, he failed to recognize it. Now and then, he felt the ill-will of those who award reputation. The injustice grieved him; but he was too proud to let his disappointment be known. His modesty always took the turn of self-disparagement. And, while he pronounced the funeral oration of poetry and the arts, he judged himself with incredible severity. In these moments of discouragement, he insisted that others should agree with him, and corroborate his own extreme views. After that, a word would suffice to produce a reaction in his mind; but, when you had restored him to a sense of his power, you had also restored his spirit of indifference. How many times when urged to work, his answer has been, "Why should I? Who cares? Who will thank me?"

We have seen that, in 1840, he had resolved for the future to write verse only. After the publication of the "Souvenir," he determined to write merely for his own pleasure. Thenceforward his table was strewn with sonnets, songs, and stanzas. He amused himself by writing in a hurry—sometimes in short-hand—on scraps of paper, the envelopes of letters, the margin of a lithograph, or the cover of a novel, as though to prove that what he wrote interested himself alone, and was never to see the light. I waited until some stimulant should rouse him; but, unfortunately, he received none but disagreeable impressions; for there are periods in life when one trouble invokes another as its complement, and our woes are mutually aggravated by a kind of logical connection.

I have told how the friendly relations between Rachel and her champion were interrupted. Just then, Pauline Garcia was absent. To the shame of the Parisians be it said, the mass of the public had not obeyed the impulse given by people of taste on the first appearance of the youthful singer. The sister of Malibran sang in her own style, and according to her own feelings. At that time, there were certain infallible methods of getting one's self applauded at the Théâtre Italien, certain noises, hiccoughs, and invariable pauses, which never failed of success. It was a routine equally convenient for the artists and the *habituées* of the theatre; since it rendered quite unnecessary any knowledge of music on the part of the audience. Pauline Garcia repudiated these vulgar recipes. She adopted a course just the reverse of the fashionable one, and disdained the old effects which were looked for at certain places in her parts. On the other hand, she had flashes of genius which passed quite unnoticed. In a word, she was original. She needed to be understood, and she was not understood. After having sung Desdemona, Rosina, Tancrède, and Cinderella, with decreasing success, she thought that she had tried long enough; and she departed to a foreign land, to the great regret of the poet, who had celebrated her *début*, and saluted that "new era" which two years had sufficed to extinguish.

A lady to whom Alfred de Musset had become much attached during his illness had also gone away for a long absence. The Princess Belgiojoso, whose *salon* was one of the pleasantest in Paris, was passing the winter in Italy. She was making a noble use of her large fortune, by founding an important charitable establishment some leagues from Milan. Like Sister Marcelline, she had talked very seriously with the poet. Alfred wrote to his fair monitress, and told her how keenly he regretted the affectionate sermons to which her voice had lent so much sweetness, adding that he would gladly have a slight illness for the sake of hearing more of the same. The princess replied by inviting him to come to Italy, where he would find a genial climate, a healthful regimen, and other sources of inspiration than were furnished by the Boulevard de Gand. She promised him entire freedom, a spacious lodging, a family library filled with rare books, and as many sermons as he might desire. This graceful invitation filled him with joy and gratitude. Again and again, during the winter of 1841, he repeated. — " I am not forgotten by everybody. When it becomes intolerably tedious here, I shall know where to look for hospitality."

But while he talked in Paris about going to Italy, he wrote to Milan that the project was a dream.

In the month of May, it was the godmother's turn. Usually her absences were brief ; but this year she went into the country, intending to remain nearly all summer. She took care not to confide her purpose to her godson ; but he, while expecting her return from day to day, went back to his sad refrain that his friends were falling off, and the desert widening around him.

He got up one morning, carrying in his looks that motto of Valentine of Milan which he was so fond of quoting.   It actually seemed as if nothing ever would rouse him out of his dejection, when his eye happened to light on the song of the poet Becker.   It proved the spur which woke him suddenly.   The Vicomte Delaunay, in one of his witty papers, has pleased himself by describing, in a very sprightly fashion, the origin of the "Rhin Allemand."   All this anecdote lacks is veracity. It is made up from beginning to end.   The truth is as follows : —

On the first of June, 1841, we were breakfasting at home, when a copy of the " Revue des Deux Mondes " was brought in, which contained both Becker's song and the "Marseillaise de la Paix."   Alfred, seeing some verses by Lamartine in the table of contents, turned at once to that page of the magazine.   When he read those six couplets of Becker's which contain in so few words so many insults to France, he knitted his brows ; but, when he had read the reply to them, he knitted them still more.   No doubt he would have approved the feeling which inspired the " Marseillaise de la Paix," if the piece had appeared by itself.   It is perfectly legitimate to invite all men to clasp hands without distinction of race, name, or geographical boundary.   As a philosophical proposition, it is as good as any other ; but to reply to an insolent challenge by opening one's arms to the challenger is to choose one's time ill.   This was the way Alfred de Musset looked at it ; and since, to his mind, the " Marseillaise de la Paix " was no answer to Becker's song, the desire seized him to answer it himself.   The more we discussed it at the breakfast-table, the more animated his face grew.   He flushed to his very ears.   Finally, he struck the table with his fist, retired into his own room and shut the door. At the end of two hours, he emerged and repeated to us the " Rhin Allemand." For all M. de Lamartine called it a "tavern-song," it made an immense stir. The Duc d'Orléans at once despatched his congratulations to the author; for, since the retrograde movement of the preceding year, the political situation had not been such as to allow the heir-apparent to express himself openly. It is no exaggeration to say that at least fifty composers wrote music for this song. One of these airs was adopted by the army, and sung in all the barracks. Prussian officers wrote the author taunting letters, some in German and others in French, making appointments at Baden, and inviting him to fight them there on such or such a day. As often as one of these letters arrived, he laid it carefully away in a drawer. "These are fine young men," he said: "I like their patriotism. It gratifies me to perceive that my verses have gone to the right spot. I have clinched Becker's nail. But why does he not write me himself? He is the man I would like to fight. As for my young Prussians, they may fight with the French officers who have challenged Becker, if there are any."

The "Rhin Allemand" was composed on the morning of the first of June. Out of respect for the author of the "Marseillaise de la Paix," Alfred refused to publish it in the "Revue." Moreover, the next number would not come for a fortnight. He therefore offered the piece to the "Revue de Paris," which was published weekly ; and there it appeared on Sunday, June 6th, while the Vicomte Delaunay's comments on it were printed in the "Presse."

From Tourraine, where she was spending the summer, came the godmother's congratulations to her child.
" The ' Rhin Allemand,' she wrote, " is better than the
best songs of Béranger. There is a breath of loftier
poetry in it." To compliments she added exhortations
to industry. The godson replied that his patriotic
fibres would not be stirred every morning, and that his
heart was fast asleep and would not wake easily. The
godmother again reproached him for his indolence, and
again he made a jesting defence. " It is all your fault,"
he answered, " if I am tired to death and don't know
what to do with my evenings. But *ennui* and indifference are the best possible remedies for the disease
called *poesy*. Consequently, I am very well ; and what
are you scolding about ? "

In fact, the summer of 1841 seemed to him interminable. The manager of the " Revue " had quite as good
a right as the godmother to exclaim against his indolence, and I emphasized all he said. Alfred was
sincerely fond of M. Buloz, and very sorry that he could
not satisfy him. Finally, after a silence of six months,
after being repeatedly and earnestly pressed to explain
his conduct, he wrote the verses, " Sur la Paresse,"
which he addressed in the form of a letter to the man
most interested in the question. Usually, a satire loses
its point in a little while : but these verses read as
if they had been written yesterday ; a fact which proves
that the author understood perfectly the eccentricities of
his age, and that the age has not yet overcome them.
Read over the passages about hypocrisy, the unbridled
love of money, pompous egotism, the importance of

bread and butter, and that mediocrity which understands nothing but itself. It is all seasonable at the end of thirty years. The epistle was published on the first of January, 1842. "There," said the author, "that is the cleverest thing I ever wrote."

I asked him where the cleverness lay. "Don't you see," he replied, "I·have given reasons for my silence; and these reasons, whether good or bad, imply a promise that that silence shall continue. Really, it remains to be seen whether I keep my word. But when the world perceives that my disdain is real and unaffected, as it certainly is, I shall no longer give umbrage to any one. Those who pretend to be unaware of my existence will consent to acknowledge it. Am I a clerk or a copyist, that people should pester me about the employment of my time? I have written a great deal. I have made as many verses as Dante or Tasso. Who the deuce ever presumed to call them lazy? If Göthe took it into his head to fold his hands, who ever reproved him for frittering away his time over science? I will follow Göthe's example to the day of my death, if it suits me! My Muse is my own; and I will show the public that she obeys me, and I am her master, and that, if it wants any thing of her, it must do as I like."

When Tattet, in his turn, requested his friend to explain the course he was taking, he received in reply the following verses, —

> " Le mal des gens d'esprit, c'est leur indifférence,
>   Celui des gens de cœur, leur inutilité." [1]

---

[1] " The trouble with people of mind is their indifference; with people of heart, their impracticability."

The next number of the " Revue des Deux Mondes," after that in which the letter on Indolence appeared, was to contain an article by M. Sainte Beuve.   In reading the proofs of this article, M. Buloz came upon a paragraph, the terms of which he thought calculated to put the modesty of Alfred de Musset to too severe a test.   On the eve of the publication of the number, he sent me a hasty note, begging me to come and see him. I complied, and he read me the paragraph.   It was a classification of living poets ; not in the order of their merit, but in what the critic conceived to be the order of their celebrity.   It was a perfectly useless thing, proving nothing whatever : and the least of the objections to it was the one that the author himself allowed ; namely, that it was sure to wound the persons mentioned, quite as much as those whose names were omitted.   In this classification, Alfred de Musset was assigned to the third rank, and to a class so numerous that there were even *ladies* in it.   The critic added, however, that if the young poet were often to write satires like the verses " Sur la Paresse," or meditations like the " Nuit de Mai," he would stand a good chance of promotion to another group.

M. Buloz asked me what I thought of this judgment : and I replied that, if the writer of it had stopped his readings at the " Nuit de Mai," it would be a good plan to send him the twenty copies of the "Revue " which contained the other Nights, and the various poems and " meditations " published during the last six years ; moreover, that I should hardly have expected to find the author of the letter on Indolence confounded with versifiers to whom the manager of the "Revue" had frequently returned their productions, with as little consideration for "ladies" as for gentlemen ; that I thought the judgment in question thoroughly unfair, even in respect of applying the word "meditations" to poems of unquestionable originality ; that it did not become the "Revue" to speak in such terms of one of its most popular editors ; but that, if they desired to transfix their readers by the insertion of a page which would give more pain to Alfred de Musset's admirers than even to himself, the article was perfectly adapted to its end, and ought not to be altered in the least. M. Buloz hastened to assure me that he had no such intention, and he promised that he would request M. Sainte Beuve either to modify or entirely suppress that passage in his article.

Nevertheless, I knew the irritable temper and impracticable vanity of M. Sainte Beuve so well, that, when the number came on the fifteenth of January, I had a presentiment that nothing would be changed. Alfred took the pamphlet, opened it at random, and lighted directly upon the page where his name occurred. After an instant, he laid the number on the mantel, saying, in a low tone, "Et tu, Sainte Beuve !"

He at once changed the subject, and refused to recur to it. As for me, I protested as I had a right to do, and took the consequences of my recriminations. 1 have been taking them ever since, for they have not yet come to an end. At present, a glance at the poems of Alfred de Musset will show that he has not added to his works, since 1842, many satires, or "meditations" either; yet

M. Sainte Beuve· has revoked his judgment.   He has
placed the author of the "Nuit de Mai" among the
gods, since his death be it understood, — which is
why I make this reparation to-day.   And if my apology
seem somewhat tardy, so was his.

Alfred did not go very much into society in 1842 ;
but he went back to two or three *salons* which were frequented by friends of his.   From these, he several times
returned with sonnets or *rondeaux* in his head, which he
addressed on the morrow to some lady or other ; but of
which, unfortunately, he did not always keep copies.   As
for the charming allegory of the " Merle Blanc," it was
composed for an illustrated publication, the author of
which had won his esteem, and he did not consider it
work at all.

The illness through which he had been so carefully
nursed by Sister Marcelline had left him with an unfortunate tendency toward diseases of the chest.   He
needed to take the utmost precaution ; and he would
take none.   To the numerous colds which he owed
to the organization of the national guard, were added
others caught through mere imprudence.   Often, to his
great annoyance, he was condemned to keep his room ;
but his constitution was so elastic that a few hours restored him.   I would leave him prostrate in bed, and,
coming back almost immediately to keep him company,
I would find him up, and pulling on his walking boots.
Twice during the winter we called in the physicians ;
but they bled him too profusely.

Whatever they may say to the contrary, I am
convinced that their lancets did him incurable harm.

One morning in March, when we were at breakfast, I perceived that my brother, at every pulse-beat, gave a slight involuntary toss of the head. He demanded to know why my mother and I looked at him curiously; and we told him what we had observed. "I did not know," he replied, "that that was visible; but I can set your minds at rest."

He pressed the nape of his neck in some way with his thumb and forefinger, and his head immediately ceased to mark the pulsations of his heart. "You perceive," he said, "that this terrible disorder can be cured by a very cheap and simple method."

In our ignorance, we were reassured; but in reality we had seen the first symptom of a most serious affection, to which, at the end of fifteen years, he was destined to succumb.

On the return of warm weather, Alfred expressed a wish to take a little rest in the country; and the doctors advised it. Our good friend and cousin, the inspector of forests, had quitted the woods of Joinville for those of Ivry; and, in the hope that this change of residence would be his last, he had purchased, near Pacy-sur-Eure, the little Château of Lorey, which had once belonged to the renowned Taglioni. Life was lively in the valley of the Eure. People danced and played comedies, not at Lorey alone, but also at Breuil-Pont, at Comte Louis Talleyrand's, and with the ladies Roederer at Mesnil; and Alfred repaired thither in response to our cousin's numerous invitations. On the 14th of July, at a large and gay party which he attended, he observed that the legitimists present were conversing in undertones.

Some startling piece of news had been received, which people did not venture to do more than whisper one to another. The master of the house changed countenance when he heard the tidings, and uttered an exclamation of grief and consternation: the Duc d'Orléans was dead. Alfred returned to Paris the same day; not to mingle the vain expression of his condolence with others more or less sincere, but to be present at the funeral ceremonies, and then to shut himself up and give way to his own personal sorrow and regret. The death of the prince who had honored him with the title of friend took away all his courage. A great many of his illusions had been dispelled within a brief period; but now his last hope deserted him. "Fate," he said, "has decreed that our poor France should have no future, — not a single day. As for mine, it is annihilated. I see nothing before me but weariness and disgust. I only want to go myself as soon as may be."

I reminded him of his passion for the unforeseen, and the interest which he often took in watching his own career. "Nobody ever knows," I said, "what destiny has in store for him. Nature and chance are inexhaustible." To which he replied, that it had been all very well to say so formerly; but that now the unknown had nothing to offer him,—not even in the way of new griefs and trials, which would be welcome if he could regard them as salutary "derivatives," alluding to the doctrine of Hippocrates that one inflammation destroys another.

When it was suggested to him that his attachment to the prince royal might seem to demand some public expression of his grief, he repudiated the idea of making verses on such a theme. M. Asseline, the secretary of the Duchesse d'Orléans, brought him the engraving of the prince after Ingres. Alfred begged him to express his gratitude; and added that, when the official mourners had dried their tears, he should have something to say.

It was at this time that Tattet formed the resolution of leaving Paris, and taking up his abode at Fontainebleau. The motives which impelled him thus to break with his past life were too serious to admit of discussion. Alfred found fresh matter of grief in this separation, and felt it more keenly than he had anticipated. It was no "derivative" (to use his own expression), but an aggravation. Tattet was not merely a charming companion and a faithful friend: he had also precious qualities as a confidant and a listener. His admiration for the character and genius of his favorite poet manifested themselves with a fervor of which every one who approached him felt the fascination; and how much more he who was the object of it! The pleasures, the pains, and the vexations of his friend, Tattet laid to heart as if they had been his own. At his house used to assemble a small circle of agreeable men, whom his departure scattered. There were promises of frequent meetings at Fontainebleau; but daily confidences, long talks, readings in common, and the perpetual interchange of ideas and impressions, were no longer to be expected. It was a real loss, added to the visionary one of so many illusions and hopes.

Strange as it may seem, this man, so depressed, so discouraged and disenchanted, — who reiterated with perfect sincerity, "Nothing remains for me;"

this drowsy heart " shut up," as he declared, " for ever," [1]
— was becoming daily more susceptible to the slightest
emotion, and consequently more poetic than before.
Misfortune, anguish, and regret seemed only to enhance
his susceptibility.   A word. a line of poetry, a strain of
melody, would bring the tears to his eyes.   At the very
moment when he was lamenting that he had not the
strength to live any longer, his impressions were becoming more vivid than ever, and external objects were
acting upon his organization with greater power.

One day, in his edition of the four great Italian poets,
he came upon some sonnets by Michael Angelo Buona-
rotti.   The depth of thought, the vigorous terseness of
their form, delighted him.   He amused himself by trying
to detect in the poet's manner the peculiar qualities of
the sculptor and the painter ; and, when he found a
verse in which the thought seemed to him to be com-
pressed into an unusually small number of words, he
would exclaim, " There's brevity ! "

He now conceived the desire of delineating, like
Michael Angelo, some grand statuesque figure.   He
was at that time on intimate terms with a beautiful and
very distinguished lady, for whom he had a strong friendship ; but who sometimes treated him with a curtness
and severity under which he was not always patient, so
that their relation was marred by clouds and misunder-
standings. [2]   I never knew what the last offence was ; but
I know he must have encountered some very harsh,
unjust, and injurious treatment on the day when he came

---

[1] See the sonnet to Alfred Tattet, on his departure trom Paris.
[2] See correspondence of Alfred de Musset for the year 1842.

home resolved to break with this lady for ever. In the mood of mind which I have described, he wrote the verses "Sur une Morte." The rupture was complete and irremediable. In order to judge whether the writer of those verses was to blame, one should understand the wound which he resented ; and no one knows how deep that was. No one ever blamed the great Corneille for yielding to an impulse of poetic wrath against a lady who was rash enough to ridicule him. The way not to feel the lion's claw is not to tease him.

Beside the sonnets of Michael Angelo, Alfred read and re-read, until he knew them by heart, the poems of Giacomo Leopardi, where the vibration between stern sorrow and tender melancholy corresponded with his present state of mind. When he struck the cover of the book, and said, "This little volume is worth a whole epic," he felt that Leopardi's soul was the sister of his own. The Italians have such keen intellects that they are not very fond of the poetry of the heart. They want long, high-sounding words. Less fortunate than Alfred de Musset, Leopardi did not receive justice from his countrymen even after his death. Alfred was outraged by the thought. He desired to write an article for the " Revue des Deux Mondes " on this man whom he regarded as the first of modern Italian poets ; and he even collected some biographical materials for this purpose. But, while he dreamed of this, he preferred to pay in verse his tribute of sympathy and admiration to the 'Sad friend of Death." Hence the piece entitled " Après une Lecture," which appeared on the fifteenth of November, 1842.

While allowing for his excessive sensibility and natural exaggeration, we must concede, that, during the fatal year of 1842, Alfred de Musset received terrible wounds. He complained that, from every quarter at once, came matter of sorrow, disenchantment, and disgust. "I can see nothing," he said, "but the reverse of every medal."

Every symptom of deterioration in letters, he sorrowfully resented. The magazine-story had just then touched its extreme of popularity, cynicism, and audacity; and every one who wielded a pen had a right to feel humiliated. Alfred blushed for the fact, as did all writers of refinement. On the one hand, he beheld the literature of the imagination soiled and polluted, and a general falling off in literary honesty, public taste, and an appreciation of what is really fine; on the other, men of genius losing courage. At thirty-two, he lamented that he had lived too long. Add, moreover, his broken idols, the image of Rachel defaced, Pauline Garcia far away and forgotten, Tattet's voluntary exile, Sainte Beuve relegating the author of the verses "Sur la Paresse" to the level of female versifiers, Lamartine making him wait six years for an answer, the Duc d'Orléans miserably slain by a vulgar carriage accident,— and it must be conceded that even a man of duller susceptibilities than Alfred might here have found cause of sadness and lament. It is certain that, at this epoch, all things seemed to combine to affect him, and every thing that in any way affected his mind or heart gave him occasion for distress. Finally, even I, who would gladly have consoled him by any means in my power,— even I contrib-

uted my pang, like all the rest. For some years I had
been dreaming of a trip to Italy, and just at the close
of this year, 1842, the journey so long desired became practicable, and I left home on the nineteenth of
November. Unwilling to mar my pleasure, Alfred said
not a word of the enormous void which my absence
would make in his life, at a time when he needed me so
much. He insisted on accompanying me to the coach-
office, although he was not well on that day, and he bade
me good-bye with a smile. A letter from the godmother
revealed what he had felt when he shook my hand at
the door of the vehicle. " I was still too happy," he said;
"for at any hour of the night or day I could tell my
troubles to a friend. Even this comfort had to be taken
away from me."

I had but come to the first halting-place on my route,
when I received this letter. I was stopping at Mirecourt, in the Vosges, where our good uncle Desherbiers
was sub-prefect. The godmother's information made me
very anxious. I wrote to my brother, and told him that,
if he really needed me, I would defer my Italian journey
to some other time, and go back and spend the winter
in Paris. Alfred replied by the letter which follows,
and which I copy in this place to give some idea of his
unselfishness and delicacy of feeling, and of the affection which united us : —

" Thank you from the bottom of my heart, my dear friend,
for your good letter. I will begin by answering your question, conscientiously, as you desire. Pray do not think of me
otherwise than as a brother and a friend, and forget entirely
my passing annoyances, which are of no account. I am very

16

well just now ; and having no cause of vexation, whether real or material, my melancholy is gone with my fever. Of course, our midnight talks were very precious, and you may be sure I shall never forget the friendship you showed me in that last time of trial. You have been both extremely kind and extremely helpful to me ; but I beseech you to set forth on your journey without a single regret, or any afterthought capable of troubling you for an instant.

"My mother is come back, and so is Mme. Jaubert. You see that I am not alone. Mme. de Lagrange has invited me again, in the sweetest possible manner.

"The good captain charged me to tell you that the matter of the correspondence was arranged. Letters for you will be forwarded hence to Mme. Aubernon, who will send them on to you. You will only need to give the address, or rather the addresses, of the places where you want them sent.

"I am not surprised that you are happy with our excellent uncle. Tell him that I love him, and should enjoy just as much with him as you do. Tell him that he remains in my memory as the man of all men for whom I have most sympathy and respect.

"Farewell. Do not fail to write. Your letters will do me a great deal of good. I embrace you,

"ALFRED.

"THURSDAY, Dec. 1, 1842."

PART FOURTH.

From 1843 to 1857.

XV.

ONE of our sister's earliest friends was a young girl
who had been obliged to return to her father's
house almost immediately after her marriage. All the
best society of Paris was interested in the misfortunes
of this truly amiable, discreet, and beautiful woman,
condemned at the age of twenty to perpetual widow-
hood. Her residence under her husband's roof had
been accompanied by circumstances so strange, that the
question was raised whether she ought not still to be
regarded as unmarried. Unable to regret a man who
had spared no pains to alienate her from him, she was
not long in drying her tears and resuming her wonted
grace and gayety. We were then living in her neighborhood.[1] She came frequently to see her former play-
mate, and to relate to our mother the lamentable causes
of her lawsuit. When she went home at nightfall, although she had not a hundred paces to go, a servant
came for her. Two or three times only did Alfred give
her his arm to escort her to her own door. But they
were observed, and it was enough to give occasion, not
for slander, but for significant smiles of envy and malice.
Alfred would not wait till the smiles had been translated
into speech. He wrote the sonnet, " Non, quand bien
même une amère Souffrance," to which I refer the

---

[1] Since the month of October, 1839, we had lived on the Quai Voltaire.

reader.   Reverence for innocence has never, I think, inspired purer or more perfect poetry.

At his godmother's, Alfred often met another young wife, who had been almost as unhappily married as the one I have just mentioned.   Her husband had just died most opportunely ; and death, in the words of Sganarelle, adjusts many things.   The year of mourning had passed. and the widow was taking off her weeds.   One evening when he was sitting by her, Alfred told her that she was too young and too beautiful not to marry again ; but apparently marriage had left such bitter memories that she cried out at the suggestion, " Never ! " speaking the word with an energy of horror which impressed the poet greatly.   This is the whole history of the sonnet which is entitled " Jamais ! "   The other incidents of the conversation will be found in the lines themselves.   The lady's reply was sincere, and her resolution perfectly well considered.   She kept her word.

Under the pseudonyme of P. J. Stahl, Jules Hetzel, editor and author, had recently composed a fanciful tale, illustrated by a large number of engravings by Tony Johannot.   To insure the success of this expensive work, Hetzel entreated my brother to contribute some verses, and allow his name to be associated with that of the prose author.   At first, Alfred obstinately refused ; but, among the sketches of Johannot which pleased him very much, there was a graceful figure of a young girl sitting at a piano and singing.   The piece of music which was to be interpolated in the text was a *lied* of Mozart's, not yet published in France, the refrain of which was " Vergiss mein nicht."   Alfred set it up on his sister's piano, and when she had sung it to him he liked it so well that he wanted to translate the words. Difficult as the attempt was to adapt words to music already written, he succeeded at one sitting. He felt as if he were bound to do so. Johannot's drawings also inspired him with a sonnet, and the editor asked no more. Marie, and the *lied* in three couplets, "Rapelle-toi," were inserted in the "Voyage où il vous plaira," and P. J. Stahl is responsible for the rest. What Alfred would not have done from interested motives, he furnished impulsively under the charm of Tony Johannot's talent, and especially of the genius of Mozart. He allowed his name to be inscribed on the frontispiece of the illustrated volume.

After spending the winter in Naples and the spring in Rome, I found myself in the month of July at Florence, and there one evening at Countess Orlow's. I heard them talking about some verses on the death of the Duc d'Orléans, which had appeared in the French papers. The daughter of Countess Orlow, Madame Orsini, quoted the two first verses of the tribute :—

"La joie est ici-bas toujours jeune et nouvelle,
    Mais le chagrin n'est vrai qu'autant qu'il a vieilli." [1]

I knew that my brother had meant to wait for the anniversary of the thirteenth of July, before paying his meed of regret to the prince whom he had loved, and to the Princess Marie, whose coffin was still at Pisa. I knew the mournful pleasure which he had promised himself in recurring to that almost forgotten misfortune, at

[1] "Joy is ever new and fresh in this world; but grief is genuine only in proportion to its age."

the risk of astonishing those who had wept so loudly at
the time, but who very probably might take no heed
of the first recurrence of the.fatal anniversary.   When I
saw the effect produced by this poem in a foreign land,
I never doubted that its author would receive some
token of remembrance and affection from the royal
family.   I was mistaken.   The king did not even read
the verses on the death of his son ; and it seems that the
Duchesse d'Orléans noticed only the word concerning
Laborderie, one of the school-mates of Alfred and the
prince at the college of Henry IV., whom the poet
speaks of as the *best of us three.*   A long while after the
publication of the stanzas on the anniversary of the
" Treize Juillet," when it was no longer possible to ignore such a tribute to the memory of the Duc d'Orléans,
a messenger from the palace brought the author a few
words of very frigid and ceremonious politeness.   From
the constrained manner of the messenger, and the tone
in which he inquired who Laborderie was, Alfred divined
that the princess had been offended by the too laudatory
mention of their old comrade.   On the other hand, he
received a letter in an unfamiliar hand, in which a lady
thanked him, in glowing and affecting terms, for having
made her brother's name immortal.   The letter announced the coming of a tea-service in Limoges porcelain, some pieces of which are still in existence.   As
long as the poet lived, the sister of Laborderie wrote
him once a year, and sent him a truffled fowl at carnival
time.

Before I went to Italy, I had made, in company with J.
Hetzel and M. Obeuf, the mayor of Bellevue, an excur-

sion to Pontchartrain, which abounded in comic incidents, and the story of which diverted my brother so much that he had amused himself by turning it into verse. Hetzel repeated some parts of it to Charles Nodier, who requested the whole, and we sent it to him. After the lapse of nearly a year, Nodier, in a fit of mirthfulness, addressed to the author of that burlesque Odyssey some verses in the same measure in which it was written. Alfred replied, also in the same metre. His mind was still full of this pleasantry when the board of discipline decided to punish with severity the neglect of national-guard duty, and sentenced him to several days' imprisonment. The culprit made interest, and obtained the room numbered either 11 or 14, whose walls the artists who had been as lawless as himself had covered with paintings and drawings. The prisoner enjoyed this dungeon immensely; and, by way of leaving there a *souvenir* of his own residence, he inscribed a few verses under a female figure which took his fancy; and, when he was released, still pursued by the rhythm of his rustic Odyssey, he composed the " Mie Prigioni," published by the " Revue," Oct. 1, 1843. The copy containing these lines fell into the hands of M. le Comte Molé, who, attracted no doubt by the originality of the title and the brevity of the piece, read it through, and was so much pleased with it that he charged a third person to be the bearer of his compliments to the author, and to tell him that if ever he, M. Molé, was in the ministry again, he would remember him. M. Molé was never minister again; but he did not forget " Mie Prigioni," when its author paid him a visit as candidate for the French Academy.

When I returned from Italy in November, 1843, Alfred wanted to celebrate the day, and he took me off to dine at the restaurant, although dinner was ready for us at home. We had to talk over that beloved Italy with which I was yet more in love than he. My fresh recollections awoke his own. We talked all dinner-time, and in the evening, over the fire, we talked on until two hours after midnight. The next day and for many days, we had to recur to the subject. Venice in particular was an inexhaustible theme. But when I spoke of Florence, and the Pitti museum, we always stopped at Allori's Judith; and I reminded my brother that the strange history of that fine work and its author had once seemed to him worthy of being related by the pen which had produced the " Fils du Titien."

It is well known that Cristofano Allori, when betrayed by his mistress, conceived the singular idea of representing her in the character of Judith, and of giving the bleeding head of Holofernes his own face. The evening that we recurred to the subject, my brother's interest in it so revived that he thought he would treat it in verse. When we separated, he continued to dream over it by himself. During the night, he arranged the plan of the work ; and the next day a few verses were already put upon paper. Unhappily, he had a painter among his friends, an accomplished man whom he often consulted. The artist was so imprudent as to say that the figure of Judith might represent Allori's mistress ; but that the face of Holofernes was not a likeness of the painter. He went so far as to say that there was no meaning in the man's head at all. Alfred was annoyed.

He felt personally injured by these doubts as to the authenticity of Allori's portrait, and the misunderstanding lasted three weeks, — one of his most protracted temper fits. Peace was signed one evening when we were discussing art; but the impressionable poet was disenchanted, and Judith and Allori were laid aside. A friend, quite innocently no doubt, was thus responsible for the failure of what promised to be a noble and interesting work. It is all the more to be regretted because the friend was wrong. The portrait of Cristofano Allori by himself in the Uffizi Gallery has precisely the same face as the head of Holofernes in the Pitti palace.[1] Here is all I have been able to find of the verses which my brother threw off when he composed the plan of the work.

CHOEUR DES PEINTRES.

Ni les sentiers battus, ni les règles antiques,
O puissant créateur, n'ont été faits pour toi.
Libre comme les vents, la loi que tu pratiques
    Est de vivre sans loi.

ROMANO.

Allori, le grand-duc forme une académie;
Il t'en nomme le chef. Les arts, en Italie,
Meurent d'une honteuse et misérable mort.

ALLORI.

Mourir avant le temps est un bienfait du sort.
Allons, nobles seigneurs, entrons chez ma maîtresse.

LE CHOEUR.

Où sont, Cristofano, les jours de la jeunesse?
Alors, on te voyait, autour les lourds arceaux,

---

[1] I verified this a second time when I was last in Florence. The number of the portrait is 263. — P. M.

Sur les murs des palais promenant tes pinceaux
Verser assidûment la couleur et la vie.
Te voilà pâle et triste.   Est-ce la jalousie
Qui t'a fait, comme un spectre, errer toute la nuit ?
Quel usage as-tu fait de ce jour qui s'enfuit ?
Prends garde au noir chagrin qui mène à la folie.
Il est un sûr remède à la mélancolie, —
Le travail, le travail !   Cesse donc de rêver:
La peinture se meurt, et tu peux la sauver.

ALLORI.

Elle est morte d'ennui, de froid et de vieillesse.
Allons, nobles seigneurs, entrons chez ma maîtresse.[1]

There is also in existence the fragment of a scene in which Allori, having obtained certain proofs of the unfaithfulness of his mistress, confides to his pupil Romano his jealousy and despair.   The author doubtless threw his useless way-marks into the fire, and only formless scraps of them have clung to my memory.

[1] *Chorus of painters.*   Beaten paths and ancient rules were not made for thee, O great master !   Thou art free as air, and the only law which thou obeyest is to live without law.

Romano.   Allori, the Grand Duke is forming an Academy, and hath appointed thee its master.   Art in Italy is dying a shameful and miserable death.

Allori.   Early death is a boon of destiny.   Come, noble sirs, let us go to my mistress.

Chorus.   Where, O Cristofano, are the days of thy youth?   Then we were wont to see thee among the low arches. wielding thy pencil over palace walls, and lavishly expending life and color.   Now thou art pale and sad. Is it jealousy that makes thee wander like a spectre all night long?   What hast thou done with the day which is flitting away so fast ?   Beware of the dark melancholy which tends to madness !   There is a sure remedy for it. Work ! work !   Dream no more !   Painting is at the point of death, and thou couldst save her !

Allori.   She is dead already of cold and weariness and old age !   Come, noble sirs, let us go to my mistress !

Our discussions of Italy were kept up all winter. This innocent pleasure was interrupted by an attack of pleurisy, which my brother caught in the most senseless manner possible, on a night-ramble in the Bois de Boulogne when the weather was fine, but the cold mortally severe. There was the same unnecessary blood-letting as before, and it protracted his convalescence. To while away the time, he wrote a novelette about the loves of two deaf-mutes which appeared in the "Constitutionnel." He also composed some lines "To my Brother on his Return from Italy," and after that he persisted in silence in spite of all manner of entreaties and offers of the most brilliant description. His friends themselves left off teasing, when they saw that it annoyed him. " I am curious to know," he said to me, "whether Petrarch had always a dozen pedagogues or policemen at his heels, forcing him at the point of the sword to write verses on Laura's blue eyes when he wanted to be quiet. This reproach of laziness is a new invention, in which one can smell the age of manufacture a league away. Why is not M. de Cambrai attacked for having written only one romance, *ad usum Delphini.* You deserve, every one of you, that I should set about writing a Latin poem, as long and as crude as Petrarch's ' Africa.' I'd like to know just how many of those who call me indolent are only repeating what they have heard somebody else say, and how many of them never read a verse in their lives, and would be at their wits' end if they were obliged to read any thing beside the ' Mysteries of Paris.' The newspaper-story is the true literature of our day."

The deterioration of public taste was one reason why he preferred to keep silence ; but there were others at once deeper and more dignified, which his modesty forbade him fully to explain, even in *tête-à-têtes* with me or his friend Tattet. The lines " Sur la Paresse " contained but half his thought. Had he completed his poem of " Judith," this negligent and scornful mood might perhaps have been illustrated in the character of Allori. The poet, as was his wont, might have endowed the hero with his own sentiments. Had an occasion and a pretext been given, he might have formulated his principles, his grievances, and the reasons of his disgust, in the language of the " Nuit de Mai," and the heart which he was determined to keep shut would have opened in spite of himself. I therefore regret the poem of " Judith " on more than one account.

There was not an hour in which this indolent man was not busy. His days were divided between reading and games of chess. He undertook to study the treatises of Philidor, Walker, &c. He had sometimes the honor of being the antagonist of Labourdonnays, and the most famous members of the chess club. Nothing could be less like laziness than this ardent study, as it were, of an abstract science. But neither reading nor chess-playing could wholly exclude *ennui.* Often did Alfred complain of the length of life, and that time the rascal did not move a step. He had withdrawn from society, and avoided his most agreeable companions. The godmother herself saw him only at long intervals.

When the notion took him to break up his usual habits and go in search of distraction, he went from one extreme to the other. He would go ten nights in succession to the Théâtre Italien, the Opéra, or the Opéra Comique ; and then some evening he would come home, satiated with music for a long while. If he joined a pleasure party, it was in the same excited frame of mind. It was all extravagant, and often injurious to his health ; but, to his dying day, he never could be restrained by reasonable precautions, or any sort of moderate *régime*. Another literary man who had once seen him intoxicated came to me one morning in the street, and, without mentioning the encounter, began to speak of the poet's long silence in a tone of hypocritical regret, amid which I detected gleams of a satisfaction which he could not wholly conceal. Jealousy, in so infinitesimal a writer, was laughable. I reassured the poet's *confrère*, about the faculties of the man of whom he was so disinterestedly fond, and I had the satisfaction of seeing his brow darken in proportion as his anxieties were relieved. About the same time, — almost on that very day, — the godmother, whom nothing escaped, told me that she had received similar expressions of condolence. She was seriously alarmed by them. " It is evident," she said, " that if envy and slander can put on the appearance of interest and compassion, they will be very much more at their ease. I have already observed an increased readiness to talk about our poet. Praise is no longer grudged him ; but people make haste to add that there is nothing more to be expected from his Muse. If you believe me, do not let a day pass before you warn him of his danger."

I replied that I should have my labor for my pains,

that our poet despised prudence, and that I had no longer any influence with him; but that the godmother herself, who was quite new to the business, might have some effect. "Ah, well!" she said bravely, "I will try."

She afterwards gave me a hint of the tone she meant to take, and the arguments she would employ; and what she said was marked by a clearness and felicity of expression that surpassed my expectations. I came away full of hope, admiring the superiority of women to ourselves in eloquence, and even in logic, when their feelings are moved. A note was dropped in the post-office containing a request that the godson would come and have a talk with his godmother, who promised to deny herself to all other visitors.

On Thursday, August 13, 1844, after dinner, Alfred accepted the invitation, and they had an interview which lasted until midnight. I was absent just then, having gone to the Vosges and Baden to meet some friends who took me with them to Switzerland, whence I went by way of Constance to Venice. Returning in the month of November, I asked the godmother about the result of her interview. "Do not speak of it," she replied with emotion. "Our dear Damis'[1] feelings were dreadfully hurt, and so were mine. I cannot repeat what he said. It would be too much for me. All is, I was beaten at every point. He is a hundred times right. His silence, his lassitude, his disdain, are only too fully justified. If he would but speak out, he would overwhelm those who have presumed to censure and pity

[1] This was one of her pet-names for her godson. — P. M.

him, and sooner or later his immense superiority will be acknowledged by all the world. Let us leave time to do its work, and not play with fire ; for we are mere children in comparison with him. After he left me, the poor boy wrote a sonnet which he sent me early the next morning, and it wrung tears from my eyes. He wanted to show me what he was capable of doing, — as if I had any doubts about that! I keep these lines among my papers, and some day perhaps they will be published, and then that dreadful thirteenth of August will not have been in vain."

I asked to see the sonnet ; but the godmother dreaded the reading of it. She would not fetch it, but spoke of something else. Thirteen years later, after my brother's death, she gave me the original. Here it is, —

"A blockhead's calumnies offend me not,[1]
Nor loud reproach of libertine and sot
From any base officious hypocrite
Whose hand I clasped in faith but yesternight.
The very glass is worthier in my sight
Which brings brief ease amid my cruel lot.
But thou, who knowest my most hidden thought
And deepest source of sorrow and despite,
Hast thou forgot whom thou didst once divine ?
And was it in thy heart to wrong me so ?
Ah, call not sorrow sin, old friend of mine !
But rather drop a tear of ruth divine
Into the cup where I would drown my woe,
In memory of thy love of long ago ! "

[1] Page 300 of the original.

XVI.

THE celebrated Liszt had a pupil named Hermann, who afterwards became a member of a religious community. Hermann often played the piano in private for the benefit of two or three friends. Alfred admired him, both as a pianist and a composer; and, while the musician improvised, the poet would devise verses adapted to the movement of the music. They composed together in this way three songs, — "Bonjour, Suzon!" "Non, Suzon, pas encore!" and "Adieu, Suzon!" Another melody by the same master, adapted to Italian words, was afterwards adopted by Steinberg for the *barcarolle*, which he sings in "Bettine." One day, in the spring of 1845, Hermann disappeared. Divine grace had suddenly touched his heart, and we heard of him later as a barefoot Carmelite in a convent in the south of France.

Just about the time that this miraculous conversion took place, I received from M. de Salvandy, minister of public instruction, a literary mission to Venice. The archives of the republic were to be searched for documents relating to the history of France. My commission was for six months, but I remained in Venice a year. Our uncle Desherbiers had held, for more than thirty years, the modest government office of sub-prefect of Mirecourt; and I proposed to my brother to pay a visit to this worthy uncle. We accordingly left Paris for Mirecourt in company, in the early days of May, 1845; and we stayed there six weeks. I then went to Epinal, whence I repaired to Venice by way of Munich, Innspruch, and Trent. Alfred remained half the summer in the Vosges, proceeding from Mirecourt to Épinal, and from Épinal to Plombières, much fêted by the good people of Lorraine, and a great favorite in the pleasant family of the department prefect.

I had been six months in Venice when, one evening in November, a clever Frenchman, named M. de Trobriant, came up to me on the square of Saint Mark, and spoke with enthusiasm of a "proverb," which he had just been reading in the " Revue des Deux Mondes." " Il faut qu'une porte soit ouverte ou fermée." I made haste to look up the number containing this proverb, and to me who had been so long absent the picture of Parisian life which it presented was delightful. Moreover, I recognized the characters. That of the count was so very like that I seemed to see my brother far away, seizing his hat at every peal of the bell, leaving the door open, and unable to decide whether to go or stay. I should have had more difficulty in identifying the lady, if the title of "marquise" had not given me a clew; but I soon learned that I had guessed correctly. The conversation had taken place almost exactly as reported in the "proverb." The termination only was fictitious. The marquise remained a widow, the poet departed, and the closed door was not opened again until the occasion of his next visit, when they adopted a new device.

It should be said, in praise of the actor Bocage, that

it was he who first pushed to the verge of achievement
the bold enterprise of having a piece of Alfred de Musset's played before a paying public. Bocage, the manager
of the Odéon, was positively determined to risk a representation of the "Caprice." Mlle. Naptal went so far
as to learn the part of Mme. Léry. The author, mind-
ful of the "Nuit Vénitienne," anticipated a second
failure, attended none of the rehearsals, and gave Bocage
carte blanche. I never knew why this project was
abandoned, but probably on account of some one of the
thousand accidents which are always happening in the
theatre; such as the engagement of Mlle. Naptal at
the Comédie Française, or the offer of some piece which
seemed to contain surer guarantees of success than the
"Caprice." When I returned from Venice, both manager and author had given up the scheme.

A piece of good fortune coming at this time occasioned great joy in our family, and a great disturbance
of our domestic arrangements. Our sister was married
and left home. She was to live in the provinces, and
her mother went with her to superintend the beginning of
her housekeeping. I stayed in Paris a while to be company for my brother, and again we talked of that beloved Italy whence I had just returned the second time.
After this, I accepted an invitation from my sister to
visit her at her own house; and, while I was away, a
young actress made her *début* at the Gymnase. Rose
Chéri found, in the part of Clarissa Harlowe,[1] an occasion for the display of talents of which she herself had

---

[1] This piece was by M. Léon Guillard, now keeper of the records at the
Comédie Française. — P. M.

hardly been conscious. Alfred de Musset was particularly fond of Richardson's fine romance, and frequently read it over. He was attracted by the title of the play, and took such a fancy to the actress, and such a liking for the piece, that he attended the performances at the Gymnase for thirty successive nights. When I returned from Anjou, I found him still under the spell of this daily pleasure, and almost as enthusiastic about Rose Chéri, as he had once been about Rachel and Pauline Garcia. The very night that I came back I had to go with him to the Gymnase. His artist's passion lasted as long as the performances of "Clarissa Harlowe" continued.

The winter of 1847 was a sad one for us : our apartment seemed half as large again as formerly. Of what use was it to make jokes at table ? There was no longer any one to laugh at them, and no more music after dinner ! Those melodies from Mozart, those *sonatas* of Beethoven, once to be had for the asking, were heard no more. The very piano had disappeared, leaving a great gap in the furniture of the drawing-room. I besought my brother to break the monotony of the winter by an excursion to Anjou or some other warm region ; but I could not tear him away from Paris, even though he complained that he knew every paving-stone in it. Not before September could I induce him to go ; but then we went together for sea-bathing to Croisic, and afterwards to our sister's house, where Alfred was so happy that I fancied him fixed for a long time. He stayed a month, and that was long for him ; but, when he returned to Paris, an incredible piece of news awaited him. The

"Caprice" was to be played at the Théâtre Français! The fortunes of this piece were truly strange.

Mme. Allan Despréaux, who had been quite forgotten by the Parisians, was in high favor at the court of Russia. Admitted to the best society, she had taken on the tone and manners of a great lady.   One day at Saint Petersburg, she was advised to go and see a piece which was being played at a small theatre, and in which there was an admirable female part, which it was thought might suit her.   They made up a party for the little theatre, and saw the piece played in Russian; and Mme. Allan Despréaux was so taken with it that she wanted it translated into French, in order that she might play it at court. Now this play was the "Caprice," and it came very near being translated into the language in which it was originally written.   The Emperor Nicholas would certainly have ordered it to be done, if a lady familiar with French literature — and there are a good many such in Russia, more even than in France — had not apprised Mme. Allan that the Russian play which she thought so meritorious was itself a translation.   The volume containing the "Caprice" was common at Saint Petersburg.   A copy was presented to Mme. Allan; and the piece was played before the court, and found great favor.

Nothing of all this was known at Paris; but when M. Buloz, administrator of the Comédie Française, was treating with Mme. Allan by letter for a return to the French stage, she expressed a wish to make her reappearance before the French public in the parts of Célimène and Mme. de Léry.   Everybody at the Comédie Française, except M. Buloz, was amazed at this selection.

Nobody knew where the little piece came from ; but the great actress, confident in her experience, persisted in her resolve. When he came back to Paris in October, Alfred de Musset found the arrangements far advanced. During one of the rehearsals of the " Caprice," he heard, from the side-scenes where he was, M. Samson, who was hidden among the shadows of the orchestra, calling out in a highly scandalized tone, — " *Rebonsoir*, my dear ? What language is that, pray ? "

This would seem to prove that, in 1847, there was still some doubt at the Comédie Française whether the author of the " Caprice" wrote in a style which one might adopt without compromising himself in the house of the correct and brilliant M. Scribe ! However, the piece was brought out on the 27th of November, and then uncertainty ceased. The success of the " Caprice " was an important dramatic event, and the extraordinary popularity of that little play did more for the author than all his other works had done. In the course of a few days, the name of Alfred de Musset had penetrated to those middle classes of the public whom books and poetry never reach. The sort of interdict which had weighed upon him was removed as if by enchantment, and not a day passed without the quotation of some of his verses.

When the thunderbolt of Feb. 24, 1848, fell upon us, Alfred de Musset saw with regret the departure of a royal family in which he had had a friend. The Revolution was destined to affect him no less than many others, but in a wholly unexpected way. The new minister of the interior held, it was said, a sort of private nocturnal council, where were elaborated those "republican bulletins" which were read by the population of Paris with amazement, and often with affright. When he saw among the names of the privy councillors that of a person who had no decent pretext for wishing him any thing but good, my brother thought that he might perhaps keep his librarian's place ; but he was mistaken. One of M. Ledru Rollin's first acts was the removal of Alfred de Musset. One journal cried out against this proceeding ; another denied the fact. Alfred then published the letter of dismissal which he had received. It was couched in terms of brutal brevity, and signed by a certain secretary-general named Cartaret. I was at that time contributing some literary articles to the "National," which was just then enjoying a popularity for which it was unprepared by its twenty years' life as an organ of the opposition. I requested one of my friends on the "National" to speak to the minister of the interior ; and he did so, but without effect.

Although he owed little to that Revolution which took away the surest part of his income, Alfred could not refrain from admiring, in one of its most sudden and energetic manifestations, that French nation — so full of life, elasticity, and unexpected resources — of which M. de Tocqueville has said that it is capable of inspiring strong love or strong hatred, but never indifference. During the sorrowful days of June, when blood ran in the streets, Alfred exposed himself freely, and spent several nights in bivouac. Amid the episodes of our civil war, the course of his dramatic triumphs was uninterrupted. As a sequel to the "Caprice," the Théâtre Français wanted to bring out the "proverb," "Il faut qu'une porte soit ouverte ou fermée," and the comedy in three acts, "Il ne faut jurer de rien," out of which MM. Provost, Brindeau, Got, and Mmes. Mante and Luther, constructed a perfect gem. This last piece was played for the first time on the twenty-second of June, 1848, at the very hour when a formidable insurrection was piling barricades all around. The Théâtre Historique gave several representations of the "Chandelier," which afterwards went back to the Comédie Française. Rachel asked the author for a part, and Mlle. Augustine Brohan displayed her wit and her coquetries for the same end. After an extremely sprightly correspondence with the poet, the queen of *soubrettes* obtained a half promise. Alfred wrote "Louison;" but some sort of misunderstanding occurred, the true story of which I never knew; and the part was given to Mlle. Anäis, and lost nothing by the transfer.

On the third of May, 1849, a musical and dramatic *matinée* was given in Pleyel's rooms for the benefit of the poor. Mlle. Rachel, Mme. Viardot, Mme. Allan, and MM. Roger, Got, and Regnier, lent their assistance; and Alfred, who had been informed of the plan some time before, wrote a "proverb" for the occasion, entitled "On ne saurait penser à tout," the insertion of which in the programme proved an attraction to a great many persons. The majority of the spectators were pretty young ladies in spring toilets, and the author met once more what he used to call *his* public of "little pink noses." The "proverb" succeeded so far as to cause a great deal of laughter; but, when it came to be produced

at the Théâtre Français, the audience of the Rue Roche-
chouart was no longer the majority, the Monday papers
were hostile, and the piece was played only ten or
twelve times.   The "Chandelier" was welcomed with a
degree of favor which repaired this slight reverse, notwithstanding it was criticised as immoral.   All Paris
went to see it ; and, when M. Léon Faucher undertook
to have it suppressed after forty performances, the author
was so much disturbed that he composed a moral ending in order to satisfy the minister.   In this new version,
Fortunio went to the wars with Clavaroche, while Jacqueline came under her old man's rod once more.   But this
alteration did not satisfy the conscience of M. Léon
Faucher, who would hear nothing of it.

In the beginning of 1850, our household was broken
up.   Our mother, attracted by her daughter to Anjou,
gave up her large apartment ; and we had to separate.
It was a cruel moment for us both, for until then we had
always lived at home.   Alfred took lodgings at first in
the Rue Rumfort ; but he found himself too far away
from me, and soon came to live in the Rue Mont Thabor,
I having taken a suite in the Rue des Pyramides.   Our
mother had found him a housekeeper capable of attending him with a devotion almost equal to that of
Sister Marcelline, whom he regretted so much in times
of illness.   The zeal and good sense of Mlle. Colin
spared my brother many anxieties, and insured him the
care which his health required.   Naturally disposed to
anxiety, it alarmed him to feel that he had only himself
to rely on for all the exigencies of life ; but, when the
first moment was over, he faced the new situation with

firmness and courage. That terrible phantom of necessity from which he had shrunk at the age of thirty, he
found himself prepared to confront by those political
catastrophes which had smitten sorely many lives beside
his own. He had done nothing since 1847, save passively
to watch the second career opened by the theatre to the
productions of his youth ; but, at the age of forty, his
taste for work suddenly revived.

That nothing may be omitted in my account of his
latest works, I will now go back a few years, and relate
one of those trifling incidents which it pleased him, with
his poetic imagination, to regard as fiats of destiny.

One day in April, 1846, Rachel had invited him to
dine with her. The other guests were men of fashion,
and all very rich. During the dinner, the left-hand
neighbor of the hostess remarked upon a very beautiful
ring which she wore. The ring was generally admired,
the skill of the goldsmith eulogized, and every guest
in turn paid some compliment to the precious jewel.

"Gentlemen," said Rachel, "since this work of art has
the honor to please you, I will put it up at auction. How
much am I offered ? "

One of the guests made a bid of five hundred francs,
another of a thousand, another of fifteen hundred. In
a moment, the ring was run up to three thousand francs.

"And you, my poet," said Rachel, "are you not going
to bid? How much will you give me ? "

"I will give you my heart," replied Alfred.

"The ring is yours."

And with the impulsiveness of a child, Rachel actually
drew off her ring and flung it into the poet's plate. When

they rose from the table, Alfred, who thought that the joke had gone far enough, wanted to give back the ring ; but Rachel refused to take it. "By Jupiter," she said, " I was entirely in earnest. You gave me your heart, and I would not give it back for a hundred thousand crowns. The bargain is closed, and there. is nothing more to be said about it."

However, despite her resistance, Alfred took her hand gently, and slipped the ring upon her finger. Rachel then drew it off again, and held it out to him with a supplicating and theatrical gesture. " Dear poet," she said, in a voice of genuine emotion, " you would not dare refuse this little present, if I should offer it to you on the morrow of the day when I shall play the famous part which you are going to write for me, and which I have been expecting all my life. Keep the ring, I beseech you, as a pledge of the promise you have made. Whenever, either owing to my fault or otherwise, you renounce for good and all the idea of writing the part I have desired so much, then bring me the ring, and I will take it back."

As she said this, she bent her knee, and displayed all the enchanting grace which nature gave her as an auxiliary of her genius. Of course, the ring had to be accepted on the conditions which she proposed. The poet came home, a good deal touched by the incident, well disposed and fully resolved this time to profit by the occasion. A few days after the scene which I have described, Rachel went to England. She had promised faithfully to write to *her poet*, but she did not keep her word ; and Alfred, who knew by experience the fitful humor of the great *tragédienne,* augured ill of her silence. It was just then that Rose Chéri was playing " Clarissa Harlowe " so successfully. Alfred had not hesitated to say before Rachel all the good which he thought of the young actress at the Gymnase, and probably Rachel thought that she discovered a purpose injurious to herself in the praise thus lavished upon another. At all events, without a word of explanation, she assumed toward the poet a harsh and scornful demeanor, to which he only replied by returning the valuable ring, which she appeared to have forgotten. She put it on again without a word of remonstrance.

Four years later, in March or April, 1851, Rachel gave a ceremonious dinner at the hotel which she had built on the Rue Trudon. Alfred was invited, and the mistress of the house took his arm when they were going in to dinner. Alfred trod on Rachel's gown, who said with her grand air, —

"When one gives a lady his arm, one should take care where he puts his feet."

"When one becomes a princess," replied the poet, " and builds a hotel, one should order of one's architect a broader staircase."

The evening began unfortunately; but after dinner there was a reconciliation. Alfred made a smiling allusion to the time when he had supped with Roxana and the covers were tin, and Rachel was amused by the reminiscence.

"Perhaps you think," she said, " when you see all my luxury and my splendid silver-plate, that I am not as amiable as I used to be; but I can prove the contrary."

" How so ? " demanded Alfred.

" I will go and see you, and entreat you once more to write me something."

And in fact she did come the next day, and talked theatre for an hour. During the days which followed, she came several times, and at last obtained the promise of a part. But Alfred was a little suspicious of that fickleness of mind of which Rachel had already given him so many proofs. He dallied. The time of leave-takings arrived, and Rachel once more left for England.

A new actress, then in the flower of her youth and beauty, had lately made her *début* at the Comédie Française. She asked for parts, and did so with the full intention of playing them. Alfred turned his thoughts in that direction, and arranged for the stage the " Caprices de Marianne." Madeline Brohan gratefully accepted the part of Marianne, which Rachel might have taken if she had understood her true interests. But in 1851, in the midst of her success, Rachel wrote from London to *her author* a pressing letter, to remind him of his engage-ment. Then, when she returned to Paris, she learned that he had lately written for Rose Chéri the part of Bettine, of which more anon ; and it may be that a touch of jealousy was blended with her fresh importu-nities for the promised *rôle*. Alfred, moved by her constancy, now arranged the plan of an entirely new drama in five acts, the scene of which was to be laid in Venice in the fifteenth century.

In the midst of these negotiations, " Bettine " was played with but moderate success ; and the ardor of Rachel seemed suddenly to cool. Alfred de Musset, offended by the silence which she maintained toward him, put the unfinished work away among his waste papers, with the remark, —

"Adieu, Rachel! It is yourself whom I have buried for ever in this drawer." [1]

All was indeed over between Rachel and him; and we shall have nothing more to say of that highly gifted actress whom nature seemed to have created and sent into the world to act in concert with the author of "Lorenzaccio," but who could never keep on good terms with him long enough for him to complete an acting play. No doubt Alfred de Musset was quite as much to blame as she. He ought to have laughed at her humors, and pushed his work forward to its completion, thus attaining the lucrative end of public representation in spite of temporary obstacles. Many others have given him the example; but the others were not poets, and we must take poets as we find them.

To return to "Bettine." Alfred remembered Mme. Rose Chéri, and the pleasure which he had taken six months before in the performances of "Clarissa Harlowe." The part of Bettine, which he wrote expressly for her, she accepted with delight; nor have I ever yet understood why the piece should have been coldly received by the audience at the Gymnase Dramatique. It was played only twenty or thirty times, a very small number for a *genre* theatre. And yet I consider it one of the most perfect productions of the pen which wrote

---

[1] The reader can judge from the fragment of "Faustine," published among his posthumous works, how much it is to be regretted that the piece was never finished. — P. M.

the " Caprice ; " and, if it did not obtain the success which
it deserved, I think it can only have been by reason of
that very perfection.   It was owing to the poetical
quality of a style unfamiliar to the ears of that public,
to the ripeness of the author's genius, and his profound
knowledge of the human heart.   The bewildered spectators listened with extreme attention, but the beauties
of the work were above their comprehension.   The last
word has not yet been said about " Bettine," and some
time or other the world will recur to it.[1]

The story of Rachel's vagaries and the resentment of
our poet has carried me farther on than I intended.   I
must go back a year and speak of a little masterpiece,
for which we are chiefly indebted to the ingenious insist-
ence of M. Véron, and also, perhaps, to Alfred de Musset's own indignation at the sort of criticism which had
been bestowed on " Louison " and " On ne saurait
penser à tout."   In 1850, notwithstanding his desire to
remain faithful to the " Revue des Deux Mondes," Alfred
had yielded to the entreaties of M. Véron, who opened
to him the columns of the " Constitutionnel " on most
advantageous terms.   " Carmoisine " came out in the
latter journal ; and it is assuredly one of Alfred de
Musset's finest works, — to my mind, indeed, the deepest
and most moving of them all.   When I read the passage
in which Carmoisine confides her hopeless love to the
jester Minuccio, it seems to me as though the scene
had been sketched by the hand of Göthe or Shakspeare.

[1] There is a letter of Mme. Allan Despréaux inserted in the notes to
the large edition, which shows that this actress, who was very clever and had
excellent taste, was particularly fond of " Bettine."   She would have played
the part herself if she had not been too old, and already ill. — P. M.

But we will leave to others the appreciation of this poetic work.

M. Véron had absolute confidence in the powers of Alfred de Musset. Without knowing how much the MS. of "Carmoisine" would prove to be worth, he agreed in advance to pay a thousand francs an act, and to leave the author at liberty to write three or five, as he might think fit. Alfred, incapable of adding an act to a piece which, in his own opinion, required only three, felt that his work would be well paid on the prescribed conditions; but M. Véron was so charmed with the piece when he came to read it, that he wanted to pay for it as if it had had five acts. The author refused to accept so large a sum, and in the end they halved the difference. I mention this circumstance, because it affords a glimpse of two sufficiently rare characters, — a generous publisher and a disinterested author.

Alfred de Musset had fancied himself too lightly esteemed by the classicists of the French Academy to aspire to become one of their number; but, encouraged by M. Merimée, he decided to make the application, and the Academy did itself honor when it opened its arms to the poet of youth. He might have done without the Academy; but if, after his name had been proposed, he had been allowed to die before the doors of the Institute were opened to him, the Academy would have repented it, and public opinion would have condemned its course. The author of the "Nuits" cared more than I should have expected for this mark of distinction, which he regarded as an indispensable consecration of his talent. On the day when he pronounced

18

the eulogy on M. Dupaty, to whose chair he succeeded, I heard, among the elegant audience of "little pink noses," murmurs of amazement and approbation at the blonde locks and youthful air of the candidate. He might have been taken for thirty.

His election was attended with some difficulty. Among the grave personages by whom he was surrounded on that day, not more than a dozen knew his works at all, and these were acquainted with some few pages only.

M. de Lamartine himself publicly proclaimed that he had never read them. Others condemned them out of hand without wanting to know more. On the eve of the ballot, M. Ancelot, who was particularly fond of the candidate and resolved to give him his vote, said, in the garden of the Palais Royal, to the publisher Charpentier, " Poor Alfred is a lovable fellow and a charming man of society ; but, between ourselves, he never did know how to make verses, and he never will."

M. Fortoul was then minister of public instruction. He wanted to testify in some way his good-will towards our poet, and accordingly he paid him a great deal of attention, and repeatedly asked him to dinner almost *en famille.*[1] One evening the minister said he would like to give him a subject for a poem. Alfred never enjoyed working to order. His independent Muse did not readily obey the behests of any one, and the evening that this proposal was made he came home considerably alarmed. But M. Fortoul's kindness had touched his heart, and he consented to consider the

---

[1] M. Fortoul was one of the editors of the " Revue des Deux Mondes," and very fond of people of talent. — P. M.

various themes which had been suggested, and among which he was to be allowed freedom of choice. One of them struck him agreeably, and without making any definite promise he put in his pocket a sort of prospectus, and said he would think it over, and send a prompt answer if he decided to treat the subject. The next time he came, he brought his poem almost complete. It was the "Songe d'Auguste." The minister was so gratified that he was bent on a solemn representation of the piece at some court festival. Charles Gounod composed music for the choruses, the best artists were to be selected from all the theatres, and the parts of Octavia and Augustus were already assigned to Rachel and M. Bressant.

But vague murmurs of disapprobation suddenly arose, and a bucket of ice was thrown upon the flame. The minister himself seemed afraid that he had been imprudent, and said no more of the proposed performance. The next year the Eastern war broke out. Now the most important scene in the poem was a dialogue between Livia and Octavia, concerning peace and war, and the author had naturally concluded in favor of peace. After the bombardment of Sinope, the "Songe d'Auguste" was out of date; and by the time that peace was concluded, two years later, oblivion had swept over the whole thing. Moreover, M. Fortoul, who alone had been interested in the work, died suddenly, although not before he had repaired the wrong which M. Ledru Rollin had done the author. The following is the letter which he wrote to Alfred de Musset, after reading the "Songe d'Auguste."

"I have the pleasure, my dear sir, of informing you that you have been appointed librarian of the department of public instruction. This office, which you have never solicited, but which I have long wished to confer upon you, has been rendered vacant by a removal which disturbs no position already acquired. I esteem myself infinitely happy to be able partially to repair the wrong done you by our now forgotten misunderstanding. I only regret that I have so little to offer one whose talent reflects the utmost lustre upon the literature of our time.

Believe me your most devoted,

H. FORTOUL.[1]

I have already had occasion to offer proofs of the fact that poets have, at odd moments, a sort of second sight. Precisely because they are not usually occupied with public affairs, when a political event does stir them, and cause them to reflect, they understand better than the vulgar its range and signification. If inanimate objects are to them *voiceless thoughts*, if they are searching for eternal truth even when they look upon a blade of grass, they have also their hours of meditation upon the actions of men and the needs of nations. When they express what they feel, they show us what we are

---

[1] M. Fortoul's regard for Alfred de Musset dated a long way back. Incontestable proof of this may be found in the "Revue des Deux Mondes" for Sept. 1, 1834. This number contains an article very laudatory of the "Spectacle dans un Fauteuil." The author of this article, which is now very curious reading, is comparing, apropos of "Lorenzaccio," the Florentine republicans of 1536 with the French of 1830. "These merchants," he says, "let themselves be tricked out of their Republic, almost as foolishly as we have done ourselves." Farther on, M. Fortoul congratulates the author of "Lorenzaccio" on having fathomed "the plebeian desires which inflame us." It is to be observed that the minister of public instruction under the second empire had not always been in favor of a perpetual dictatorship. — P. M.

capable of feeling without being able to express it. When they take the trouble to look, they see things which our eyes do not distinguish.

The moment that Alfred de Musset learned that a Piedmontese army corps had been sent to the Crimea, he drew a host of conclusions, which led him almost immediately to the prevision of a radical change in the destinies of Italy. I told him that he was going too fast, and that Austria would never consent to a rearrangement of the map of Europe which would involve the loss of some of her wealthiest provinces. " Justice," he replied, "is not as difficult as it is supposed to be. We cannot keep the branches of the tree of life from budding; and there is a people the other side of the mountains which is determined to live. Egotists think that the world was made for them, and smile at the sufferings of a great nation; but we ought rather to smile at their political schemes. Intelligence and freedom go hand in hand. It may be that the liberty which we have looked for so long is not far off, for it travels by ways which we know not."

Probably there was no connection whatever between the arrival of Mme. Ristori at Paris and the secret schemes of M. Cavour; but Alfred de Musset liked to look upon the visit of that great artist as presaging the intimate union thenceforth to subsist between France and Italy. His attendance on the performance of " Mirra " and " Marie Stuart" was so constant that he never missed one unless he were absolutely ill in bed. The bust of Mme. Ristori by the Italian sculptor Lanzirotti was placed in his little museum, on a tall pedestal constructed for the purpose ; and he liked to play upon the name by calling the noble figure the "Italia ristorata." Poetry also was to have been invoked to pay tribute to the great foreign *tragédienne;* and Alfred began some verses, which unfortunately he never even committed to paper. Illness prevented him from completing them.[1] The performances of "Mirra" were destined to be his last pleasure, and admiration for Ristori his last enthusiasm.

[1] The irregular fragment of these stanzas which M. Paul de Musset quotes from memory cannot well be translated, and seems hardly worthy even of transcription. — TR.

XVII.

THE health of Alfred de Musset had seemed for a long time to be declining. The organic affection whose first symptoms I had observed in 1842, and which had developed stealthily, made rapid progress during the winter of 1856. I do not know why the physician, who understood the nature of it perfectly, should have thought fit to keep it a secret. It was an affection of the valves of the aorta. I began to observe the well-known indications of heart disease ; but these alarming symptoms would sometimes disappear altogether, and give place to that air of health and vigor which we associate with his age. He would never submit to any curative treatment, except when he was confined to his bed ; and, therefore, I took the paroxysms of his malady for so many fresh accidents. One day I found him stretched in a *chaise longue* which he had recently bought ; and, as he showed off his acquisition, he said, " I hoped I should have died young ; but, if it is God's will that I should stay some time longer in this weariful world, I must be resigned. And this is the article of furniture in which I propose to grow old."

Severe cold and extreme heat were alike injurious to him ; and, despite his repugnance to quitting Paris, Alfred went for three years in succession to the seaside ; not to try bathing, which would have aggravated his complaints, but to breathe the fresh and tonic air.

In 1854, he visited Croisic, whence he went to our sister's at Angers, where he stayed a month. The two following years he spent his vacation at Havre. During his last journey, while living at the Hôtel Frascati, he became very intimate with an English family, the head of which was a man of note, and also of a most simple and kindly character. The daughters of M. Lyster, who were both at the fascinating age between childhood and maidenhood, became very fond of the invalid poet, and showed their affection by the most assiduous attentions. Alfred, on his part, became a child again; entered into the games of the two sisters, and devised others to amuse them. He was particularly successful in making them talk, for he always had the faculty of lending his own wit to people whom he fancied. As I have said before, he loved and venerated, above every thing else, youth, innocence, and ingenuousness. Only those who knew him well can understand the delight he took in the society of these pleasant girls.

One evening he stayed out later than was prudent upon the mole at Hâvre, and had a feverish attack in consequence. He did not come down to breakfast the next morning, and the little English girls were uneasy and sent their father to make inquiries. The idea of passing a day without seeing their new friend was intolerable. I do not know whether his room was on the ground floor, or whether its windows opened upon some sort of verandah; but the children brought their chairs to his open window and established themselves there, and the invalid from his bed took part in their games and their conversation. He enjoyed it so much that the fever

subsided, and the time flew fast in this delightful intimacy. Everybody was dismayed when the day of parting came. Alfred said his farewells, and mounted into
the omnibus which was to take him to the railway.
There his trunk was not to be found. He called for
it angrily, but no one knew what had become of it. It
was impossible to return to Paris without this important piece of luggage, so he mounted the omnibus once
more and went back to the Hôtel Frascati. At the
door of the house, he was met by loud applause : the two
little maidens were lying in wait for him. They clapped
their hands, and showed him his trunk, which they had
themselves dragged aside amid the confusion of the
departure. He could not go now for several hours, and
their joy was such that he remained in Hâvre two or
three more days.

One evening in the autumn he found, when he went
home, the card of M. Lyster. He was enchanted, and
set out the next day to visit his Hâvre friends. They
were lodging at the Champs Elysées, and the fine weather
and warm sunshine tempted him to walk. As he paced
the long avenue, he reflected on the different manners
prevailing in town and at the seaside. There would not
be in Paris the delightful ease and freedom which had
constituted the charm of their former intercourse. They
would fancy that they had a thousand things to say, but
when they came to revert to their common memories
and pleasures, they would find that they scarcely knew
each other. " My maidens will have other friends about
them," mused the poet, slackening his steps, "fellow-
countrymen perhaps. One of them may have a suitor.

I shall only be a caller like any other, and possibly a tiresome one.   Farewell, sweet familiarity and childish merriment and play!   Am I sure that I could myself recover the mirthful abandonment of the seaside?   Perhaps I shall presently be returning along this avenue, regretting a lost illusion, and the bloom of a dear memory destroyed.   It would be better not to touch the butterfly's wing."

In the midst of such reflections, he reached the door. He was divided between a longing to see the young girls again, and the fear of disturbing his cherished memories of travel.   The latter scruple prevailed.   Instead of pulling the bell, he retraced his steps.   He went home, and never saw his Hâvre friends again.

One winter evening, a regular poet's fancy seized him for making a retrospective and nocturnal visit to Italy and the age of the Renaissance.   He begged Horace de Viel Castel, who lodged in the Louvre, to open the picture gallery for him at night.   He was accordingly admitted, at ten o'clock in the evening, into the gallery of the Italian school, with a portable lamp of the kind used in torchlight processions.   He stayed there a long while, lost in thought, and came out well pleased, saying that he had lived with the old masters that night, and that there were two for whom he would cheerfully have mixed colors and cut pencils, — Raphael and Leonardo da Vinci.

In the month of March, 1857, M. Émile Augier was proposed at the Academy.   Alfred de Musset, who was very fond of him, took a keen interest in his success. On the night before the ballot, he was seriously ill ; and

M. Augier, fearing that he would not be able to be present, besought me to use all my efforts to induce him to
attend the meeting.   When the time arrived, I found my
brother resolved to go, in spite of the incessant palpita-
tion of the heart which incommoded him extremely.
He sent for a carriage, but there was none to be found.
The rain was falling in torrents, and the hour of the
ballot was about to strike.   Alfred took my arm and
started, notwithstanding the storm.   He walked slowly
along the Rue Rivoli, obliged at every twenty steps to
stop and take breath.   Finally, on the corner of the
Rue des Pyramides, I succeeded in stopping a passing
carriage.   He entered it, and arrived just in time to
vote.   Revived by the out-of-door air and his satisfaction at having voted, and exulting also in the success of
his candidate, Alfred went and dined at a restaurant
and thence to the play.   His housekeeper scolded him
for his imprudence.   "Never you mind!" he said,
"Very likely it is the last time.   My friend Tattet is
calling me, and I think I shall rejoin him before long."

Tattet, who was just as old as he, had died not long
before, from an attack of gout.

·M. Empis, of the Academy, struck by the change in
his colleague's appearance, inquired of me about his
health, and asked if he were following any course of
treatment.   I replied that he was unwilling to do so;
but that he had an excellent physician who gave him
directions and advice informally.   "We will force
him to take care of himself," said M. Empis, "and
this is the way we will manage."   I will get him invited to Saint Cloud; and, when there, he will have to

obey the physician of the house. M. R—— will cure
him.

I thought this little conspiracy might possibly succeed.
Once at Saint Cloud, Alfred would submit to guidance ;
but, while waiting the return of warm weather for the
accomplishment of this project, I made a trip of a few
days to Augers. While I was away, Alfred received an
invitation to dine at the Palais Royal with Prince Napoleon. He was very ill, but he was determined to go.
Dressing fatigued him so much that he was late, and
when he arrived the company was already at table.
After dinner, wishing to efface the unfavorable impression made by his late arrival, he drew near the Prince
and engaged in the conversation, which he soon controlled, and rendered it grave and gay by turns, but
always interesting. It is not so long ago but that many
of the persons present still remember that evening, and
they have told me that Alfred de Musset never seemed
to them more animated and pleasing. It was his last
evening out. When he went home, he took his bed, and
never rose from it again.

I was still at Augers, when I received on the 26th of
April, a letter from Alfred's housekeeper, begging me to
return. I brought forward some pretext of business and
set out for Paris. When I arrived, I found my brother
in bed ; but quiet, and without fever. The fainting fits
which had now become habitual with him recurred from
time to time ; but in the intervals he did not suffer. He
could listen to reading or talk tranquilly. The housekeeper whom I had always thought an excellent judge
of his condition, appeared less alarmed than she had

been, and I took courage. The improvement lasted until April 29th. On the 30th, I thought the doctor anxious during the day ; and his anxiety infected me as soon as I heard him pronounce the terrible word *consultation.* At seven o'clock in the morning of May 1st, M. Morel-Lavallée had an interview with the accomplished M. Rostan, whom I had summoned. Each of them told me separately that there was no immediate danger, and that they would come again the next day at the same hour. The day was not a bad one. Our invalid had obeyed all the instructions implicitly, and he experienced decided relief. He congratulated himself in the evening on his docility. "Tranquillity is a fine thing," he said. "It is a great mistake for us to be so afraid of death, which is only extreme exhaustion."

He was in an admirable frame of mind. He made plans, — one, among others, for going back to Hâvre ; but, since he must always have some subject of anxiety, he regretted not having accepted the proposition of his publisher, who had wanted him to surrender all pecuniary interest in his works, in consideration of a yearly payment of twenty-four hundred francs during his life. I had no difficulty in showing him that he need not regret the conclusion of this affair. He then made the most minute inquiries about my occupations, and afterwards asked in succession after every one of the persons whom he loved, as if he were holding a review of his personal attachments. His questions multiplied. The angelic face of Sister Marcelline came back to his memory and smiled upon him. We talked, still in the most peaceful fashion, until an hour after midnight, when he suddenly started up and pressed his hand upon his heart as though he felt some extraordinary disturbance there. His face took on a strange expression of surprise and concentrated attention. His eyes opened to their utmost width. I asked him if he suffered. He shook his head, and to my other questions replied only by these words, as he lay back upon his pillows, — "Sleep! At last I am going to sleep."

Sleeplessness had always been his most implacable enemy, and I took this for a favorable crisis in his disease. It was death. He closed his eyes, and opened them no more. His calm and regular breathing died gradually away. His last sigh was unaccompanied by a single convulsive or agonized movement. Death, for which he had wished so often, had come to him as a friend, in the guise of slumber. A congestion of the heart was the immediate cause. Was he conscious that he was dying? I do not know. Perhaps he desired to spare me the anguish of a last farewell. Perhaps his weariness with life, his sense of deliverance, and the gentle mastery of slumber, left him no strength to utter any supreme good-by.

When the first rays of dawn fell on his face, a super-natural beauty was diffused over it, as though the great thoughts to which his genius had imparted an imperishable form were shining round him like an aureole. The attendants who took care of him could not believe in this unexpected departure. "It is impossible," they said. "He is asleep. He will wake."

I touched my lips to his forehead, but it was already cold as marble.

XVIII.

IT cannot be denied that nature sometimes imprisons a beautiful soul in a deformed or uncomely frame; but usually she is pleased to bestow upon poets the gift of fine looks. When we consider the portraits of Molière, Racine, Tasso, and Byron, we are glad to see in their features a style of beauty corresponding with the character of their genius.

In his whole personal appearance, Alfred de Musset displayed the symmetry and harmony which constitute perfection. His figure of medium height (five feet four inches) remained slender and elegant so long as he preserved his health. When he was a young man, he looked but a boy, and in mature life he was often taken for a very young man. At twenty he was the perfect type of the graceful page of old-time courts, and he very often wore the costume of one at fancy balls. His face was impressive from uniting two kinds of beauty, — regularity of feature and vivacity of expression. His blue eyes were full of fire. His delicate and slightly aquiline nose recalled the portraits of Van Dyck; and his friends frequently noticed the likeness between the two. His mouth was rather large, and his lips somewhat too full, — less so than La Fontaine's, however; but they lent themselves with extreme mobility to the expression of his feelings, and betrayed all the keen susceptibility of his heart. Under the influence of the softer emotions, like pity or compassion, they quivered imperceptibly. You saw at once that that mouth could become eloquent with passion, or smile with easy irony in conversation. But his finest feature of all was his forehead, of which the shading suggested all the bumps which phrenology has designated as the seats of the most precious faculties. Whether that science be genuine or chimerical, it is certain that it attributed to the author of the " Nights " (although not invented specially for him) poetic sensibility, reflective power, perspicacity, ardor of mind, and an instinctive appreciation of all the arts.

There are but two portraits of Alfred de Musset which give a just idea of him,— the medallion of David d'Angers, and the crayon by Charles Landelle.   Unlike as the faces are, it should be remembered that they are separated by a long interval of time, — the one likeness having been taken in 1831, the other in 1854.   Landelle was mistaken in giving his sketch a dreamy aspect.   Alfred himself used to complain that the artist had made him look as if he were asleep, whereas his usual expression was very spirited.   This appears in David's medallion to a remarkable degree.   Were it not for this trifling defect, the work of Landelle would be perfect.   It has, moreover, the advantage over bronze or plaster of reproducing faithfully the beautiful color of the original, and the fine tint of his fair hair ; for Alfred de Musset had not a single gray hair when he died.

The other portraits, whatever the talent of their authors, can but bewilder the recollections of the poet's friends, and give a false and inadequate idea to those who never saw him.   I would except, however, the marble bust, made by M. Mezzara for the Théâtre Français. It was executed long after the poet's death ; and not only was that difficulty surmounted, but it is even remarkable for the correctness of the likeness.

No description whatever can take the place of the sculptor's chisel or the painter's brush in the representation of a man's physical semblance. As for the soul of the poet, if I have not failed in my task, it will be found the same in the story of his life as in his works, where he has himself depicted it with evident sincerity. A few traits of character will now suffice for the completion of his moral portrait.

1 think that there were but two men of genius, before Alfred de Musset, who ever carried so far the courage of perfect frankness ; and they were Jean Jaques Rousseau and Lord Byron. It cost them both dear. When the philosopher of Geneva laid bare his soul, he fancied that the revelation of his faults would win them pardon. He was mistaken, for the reason that those faults were enormous, and some of them were unpardonable. The English poet would seem to have gone yet farther than Jean Jacques. He is thought to have yielded to the insensate desire of seeming worse than he really was. It was giving a wide scope to calumny, which profited by the fact so far that posterity is now obliged to defend the poet against himself. The defence will be successful, but not easily so. The French poet has likened himself, not without reason, to the priest who offers his own heart in sacrifice. He offered it naked, for he had nothing to fear from the truth. The well meaning men who think themselves qualified to reprove him, have

not known Alfred de Musset aright. As for those who do not highly regard the poetry of the heart, and call it *personal poetry*, their prejudices can only harm themselves, and nothing that we can say would remove them. They do not succumb to the charm of the poetry in question, because they lack the heart in which it might awake an echo. It is an unfailing touchstone: "Tell me what poets you love and do not love, and I will tell you what you are."

Alfred de Musset was not satisfied with being sincere. He swore uncompromising hostility to falsehood in every guise. Whenever he encountered it, — and, unhappily, he saw it often and near at hand, — he struck it in the face. He could excuse all, pardon all, except deceit. He never awarded to rhymers without talent who submitted to him their verses that species of good-natured flattery which hurries young aspirants into that dangerous path at the end of which lie the mortifications of a mistaken calling. If he had ever done that cruel deed which others commit without scruple, it would have been for him a source of deep remorse. Liars had made him suspicious ; and although he called mistrust "an evil genius, introduced into his nature, but not born there," experience had cultivated the feeling. He despised the human race, yet he who had spoken to him but twice might call him friend. No man was more readily beguiled than he ; no heart opened more easily than his. A few advances, a few marks of sympathy, sufficed to obtain from him all that was desired. He was at the mercy of the impressions of the moment, especially in a *tête-à-tête,* and wholly carried away by the charms of conversation.

The Marquis of Manzo, the biographer of Tasso, makes the same remark in the precious notice of the great poet which he has left us. "These beings endowed with excessive sensibility pour out," he says, "involuntarily the treasures of their souls before the first person who presents himself. Animated by the desire to please, they confide their thoughts and feelings to whoever will listen, and even to indifferent persons."

Lord Byron carried this confiding spirit beyond the verge of imprudence. "The first person," says Thomas Moore, "with whom chance brought him in contact became the whole world to him, and might, if he pleased, know all Byron's secrets." And Moore adds, that this is a trait which we find in all times and all countries among those who have received the fatal gift of poesy.

This was the natural disposition of Alfred de Musset; but let his suspicions be ever so slightly roused, and he became the most impenetrable person in the world. He had an extreme distrust of journalists, anecdote-mongers, indiscreet story-tellers, and, above all, of editors, who peddle out to one writer what they have gathered from another. Felix Bonnaire came to see him at least once a week for fifteen years, and was no farther advanced in his intimacy at the end than at the beginning. With M. Charpentier, who repeated to him what he heard elsewhere, Alfred played, for the sixteen years during which they had business relations, a comedy at which we have more than once laughed together. This comedy consisted in the demonstration by every manner of proof of the fact that his works would not survive, but would be forgotten after his death.

A few great poets have been exceptions to the rule stated by the Marquis de Manzo and Thomas Moore. Göthe, among others, was resolved to become master of himself, and succeeded so well that he has even been reproached for his reticence. Who knows but the greatest mind of Germany, so often accused of insensibility, understood that he could escape the poet's malady only by subjugating his own heart? Tasso, assuredly, would never have been confined in his dungeon, if he had been master of himself as Göthe was; and Göthe himself — who, by the way, wrote a drama of Torquato Tasso — might have run the risk of being thought mad, and confined like his hero, had he not imposed silence upon his own heart amid the pleasures of the court at Weimar.

Even if he had tried, Alfred de Musset could never have assumed the impassible front of Göthe; but he did not carry his rashness to the same length as Byron. To judge of the keenness of his sensibilities, one needs but to open a volume of his poems. One can see by the sonnet to M. Régnier how his intellect received its impulses from his heart. He was passing one evening through the vestibule of the Théâtre Français. A strip of paper pasted on the bill, announced a change in the play. M. Régnier's daughter had died that very day. Alfred was barely acquainted with that excellent comedian, whose talent, however, he admired. The death of a child whom he had never seen, the sorrow of the poor father, smote and saddened him. A great many people passed through that vestibule, and some of them no doubt were conscious of a similar pang ; but he alone was unable to banish the sorrowful impression. He must needs relieve his feelings, and send to the bereaved father some expression of his sympathy. Hence the beautiful sonnet to M. Régnier. There could not be a better illustration of the poetic organization *par excellence.*

Few men have ever been as susceptible to the sentiment of pity as the author of these verses. The sight of a case of suffering, a sorrow confided to his ear, would agitate him to the extent of haunting his dreams. One evening he came home very late from the Théâtre Français, where he went so often. It was a cold, snowy winter night. Wrapped to his eyes in his cloak, and with his hands in his pockets, he had passed an old beggar playing a hand-organ on the bridge of the Saints Pères. The persistence with which the old man turned his crank, in the hope of obtaining a few *sous,* touched him vaguely ; but the roaring wind and falling snow, and the slippery footway which he was obliged to heed distracted his attention. Arrived at the door of his house on the Quai Voltaire, he still heard far away the plaintive wail of that organ ; and, instead of pulling the bell, he looked at his watch and saw that it was past midnight. "That poor devil," he said to himself, " would have gone home perhaps, if I had given him something. I shall be the cause of his getting an illness in this pestiferous weather."

His imagination pictured the miserable wretch dying of neglect in some garret, and the notion took such hold

of him that he could not advance another step.   He
went straight back to the beggar on the bridge, and
tossed him a five-franc piece.   "There," he said, "that
is probably more than you will get if you stay there
until morning.   For God's sake go home to bed!   I'll
give you the money only on that condition."

The beggar, who had not looked for such a windfall,
gathered up his luggage and decamped.   I represented
to my brother the next day that his alms had been
rather magnificent.   "It is impossible," he replied, "to
pay too high for sleep; and, if I had come home without
stopping that d—d music, I should not have slept for
the night."

The pitying horror with which he regarded suffering,
and his desire to relieve it, did not stop with human
beings.   Even beasts felt the effects of it.   His housekeeper one day apprised him of the critical circumstances
of a puppy about to be thrown into the river.   He
solemnly stayed the execution, and took the condemned
creature home.   So he was provided with a dog.

The cat's turn came next.   Alfred requested that he
might have one of the young ones of the first cat who
had kittens, not being able to take charge of the entire
family.   They sent him a frightful little beast, — shaggy,
and of a dirty gray color.   "I am not very fortunate,"
he said, contemplating his boarders.   "I like only beautiful things, and here I am encumbered with an ugly pug
and a regular area cat.   But what's to be done?   I did
not select them, and I cannot help respecting and admiring in these poor beasts — ugly as they are — the phenomenon of life and the work of mysterious nature."

The benefactor had no reason to repent his generosity. By dint of grace and amiability, the kitten won pardon for the homeliness of her garb, and the dog proved to be endowed with all the canine virtues and remarkably intelligent. In fact, the celebrated Marzo was the admiration of all the servant-maids in the neighborhood, and even made himself useful by going alone every evening to the newspaper stand with three *sous* in an envelope, and bringing back the " Presse " in his teeth. Without the assistance of language, he could get the house-door opened, and conclude a business transaction successfully. I shall not praise his love for his master : it would be an insult. Marzo did not consider gratitude a merit, nor devotion a virtue. He will for ever remain ignorant of the fact, that, among the breed of human beings, there are those who are envious and ingrate. Even now, in decrepit old age, he remembers him who is no more ; and when the housekeeper, his·last faithful friend, speaks to him of his master, he pricks up his ears, and shows that he is thinking of the one he loves, and whose return he is always expecting.[1]

Tattet who had less respect for the *phenomenon of life* got rid of an old dog who was in his way by having him killed. Alfred de Musset, indignant at such cruelty, overwhelmed his friend with reproaches, and treated him

---

[1] Marzo died of old age Aug. 28, 1864, cared for to the last, and deeply mourned by his old friend. Mme. Martelet, unwilling that his body should be flung into the rubbish cart, charged her husband to bury it. He set out early with Marzo's remains wrapped up in a newspaper. Arrived at Auteuil, he found some men at work digging, and asked permission to put the body in a load of earth which they were about to remove. Marzo was buried in a heap of dirt, under a new street which afterwards received the name of the Rue de Musset. — P. M.

with coolness for some time.   Before he could be forgiven, Tattet had to own that he was wrong, and say
that he was sorry.

But if the affection of a dog proves nothing, — since
these virtuous animals often attach themselves to very
objectionable persons, — the master of poor Marzo was
able to inspire the same sentiment of tender devotion in
others, less easy to win.   In the various houses where
he lived, and the haunts which he regularly frequented,
he was loved with a species of adoration; and it was
not always for the sake of his poems and his fame, for
some of his friends did not even know how to read.
There were those who would have gone through the fire
for him.   Their zeal and their demonstrations of interest
reminded him of that boy in the *café* of the Porte Maillot
who was so smitten with J. J. Rousseau, and took care
of him and served him with so marked a preference,
without dreaming that his friend was an author and a
philosopher.   Alfred de Musset set great store by these
spontaneous attachments, and often returned them by
rendering real service to these good people and interesting himself in their affairs.

At the chess club and the Café de la Régence, he
was keenly regretted.   But the fondest and truest of his
friends was his uncle Desherbiers.   There was no sacrifice which this good man would not have made for his
nephew.   He was comrade and father in one.   Alfred
loved him with filial devotion, and neither could do without the other.   On some points their opinions differed.
In literature, politics, and philosophy, they did not
always agree.   At chess or piquet, they occasionally

quarrelled, and parted in dudgeon. But the next morning Alfred would write a note of apology ; and in the evening they would meet, and make no allusion to the differences of the night before. Often, at the very instant when the letter of excuses was being despatched, the good uncle would arrive under the impression that it was he who had been in the wrong. They were like Henry IV. and D'Aubigné, whose tiffs and reconciliations, says Sully, were like those of a lover and his mistress. This impassioned friendship lasted as long as they lived.

In the address delivered at his reception by the Academy, Alfred de Musset said, " I have never quarrelled with any one but myself." A grudge was an impossibility to him. When literary differences had alienated him from the " Cénacle," and he felt that there was a coolness between Victor Hugo and himself, it was a real grief of mind to him. One day, in the spring of 1843, the two poets met at a breakfast at M. Guettinguer's. They came forward to greet each other with outstretched hands, and conversed as gaily as though they had parted only the evening before ; and Alfred was so moved by his cordial welcome that he wrote the fine sonnet which has made the memory of it immortal, " Il faut dans ce bas monde aimer beaucoup de choses."

Among the ladies of Paris most distinguished for wit, elegance, beauty, and good taste, I could cite a score who gave him proof of sincere friendship. Those to whom he has addressed verses, and whom he has designated by their initials, — Mme. T., Mme. O., Mme. G., — are easily recognizable by people in society. Now that Mme. Menessier Nodier has been named by the poet, there can be no harm in saying that the sonnet, " Je vous ai vue, enfant," and the two following ones, were composed for her. The *rondeau*, " Il est aisé de plaire à qui veut plaire," was addressed to the wife of a minister. But there are no verses in his collected poems addressed to one person whom I wish and ought to name. Mme. Ancelot was very fond of Alfred de Musset. Her support was of great use to him, when he was a candidate for the Academy, in the way of winning over M. Ancelot, and saying good things of him with that constant premeditation of which kindly women alone are capable. Moreover, he always spoke of her with gratitude and respect, and freely owned his obligations to her. Those who represent Alfred de Musset as prone to sarcasm and slander show that they had no real knowledge of him. He never slandered any one. He never sacrificed the absent to the pleasure of turning a witticism. He was even unwilling to listen to the slander of others, for fear of becoming accessory by the mere hearing. No one with the slightest regard for truth will refuse to believe that many of the ill-natured *bon-mots* which have been ascribed to him are due to those who pretend to have heard them from his lips, and take this course to gratify their private grudges. Whenever any one ventured to insult him to his face, Alfred de Musset showed a prompt and terrible power of repartee, but it never occurred to him to commence hostilities. Sometimes it was only upon reflection that he took the sense of an injurious remark, so hard was it for him to credit a malevolent intention.

Not only did he never make an unfair use of his intellectual superiority, but, in conversation, he put himself on a level with his interlocutors, as much through modesty as politeness; so that they left him as well satisfied with themselves as with him. This amenity did not prevent his maintaining his own opinion with entire frankness; but the attention which he paid to the views of other people, and the form of courtesy which he knew so well how to preserve, rendered discussion with him easy and interesting. It was a pleasure to differ from him. Few people have the courage of their opinions in the presence of men of authority; and the everlasting assent with which their remarks are received must be an exceedingly wearisome thing to princes. Alfred de Musset pleased them, because he ventured to express opinions contrary to theirs, and did it with as much tact as independence.

In the same manner, he liked to have people hold their own against himself. He liked them to defend their cause while they had a reason to give, or an argument to adduce, and especially he liked them to express their thoughts clearly. In his earliest years, he showed his antipathy for hesitation. One evening in 1828, our father took us both to the house of General Caux, at the war department, to listen to a eulogy on the late Duc de Rivière by M. Alissan de Chazet. The audience consisted of royalists, tried and true. Before we entered the minister's drawing-room, our father charged us to be careful not to wound the self-esteem of the author. M. Alissan de Chazet read his panegyric somewhat tamely; and, when he had finished, the admirers of the Duke

congratulated him.   By way of showing that he was not
intoxicated by the nectar of compliment, the author
requested criticism.   He even insisted upon it, remarking
that this was the time to point out his faults before his
MS. went to the printer.   Alfred immediately spoke up,
and said that he had a criticism to make.   The company
gathered around the little blond, who was entirely unknown, while our father knitted his brows in some
anxiety.   " Monsieur," said the lad, " in the piece which
you have read to us, every time you make a comparison,
or illustrate your thought by an image, you seem to ask
the reader's pardon by saying, ' so to speak,' or ' if I
may venture to say so.'   Now I think that one should
dare say things as he feels them, and I should advise
you to suppress those rhetorical precautions.   I prefer
too great boldness to an appearance of timidity."

The assurance of the fair-haired boy was highly amusing to the company, and his strictures did not displease
the panegyrist of M. de Rivière   Two years later, the
critic published poems, against which no one could prefer
the charge of timidity.

Yet, when circumstances required them, Musset did not
despise " rhetorical precautions."   At the house of the
Duchesse de Castries, much frequented by the old Duc
de Fitz-James, who was very fond of anecdotes of French
character, and told them wonderfully well ; at the godmother's, where fashion never excluded gayety; when
visiting other women of the world, nay even in the *salon*
of a prude, — Alfred had the art of saying things so as
not to wound the most fastidious ears.

The fact that he never neglected the opportunity of

making a joke when one came in his way shows that
there was a great fund of good-humor in the man. Yet
his jests were always innocent, and had no end save that
of amusement, for he detested mystifications. One evening Princess Belgiojoso, whose friendship for him was
very sincere, had some sort of grievance against him.
When the time came to take leave, the princess said
with some severity that she owed him a grudge. He
went home resolved to write a submissive letter and ask
her pardon, and the first sheet of paper that he took up
was a stamped one. He determined to use it, and accordingly composed a letter full of whimsical apologies,
which he wound up by saying that the official sheet
would attest the solemnity of his asseverations and the
profundity of his repentance. The next time he saw the
offended lady, she held out her hands, laughing so heartily
that the other persons present were amazed at her welcome, and demanded an explanation of it, which was
given.

Even among entirely congenial people, there are moments in the country, and in summer, when the time
seems long. At such times, Alfred de Musset delighted
in giving a new impulse to conversation. When he foresaw these hours of languor and weariness, his inventive
mind had a thousand resources. One morning, in a certain *château*, the numerous guests had abandoned themselves to the *far niente*. The *châtelain* had thrown up
his duties as proprietor ; the men were reading the newspapers, or smoking on the outside steps : the need of
some kind of diversion was universally felt. Some of
the ladies took their work, and one sat down at the

piano and played a mazourka.   Alfred thought that he
detected a melancholy meaning in the first phrase of the
air, and a gayer thought in the second, and he traced
the same contradiction through all the developments of
the theme.   He said so to the lady at the piano, and
illustrated the difference of sentiment which he had detected, by singing to the melody of the *ritornello*, —

> "Alas ! Alas !
> What sorrow in the world !
> Aha ! Aha !
> What pleasure here below !"

To show that she understood him, the lady sang it in
her turn, and then asked for more words.   "Come,"
she said, still playing, "give me two sad verses and two
gay ones."

It was not easy, for the music required alternate lines
of five and seven syllables ; but the poet gave his mind
to the task, although at that time he had never practised
with Father Hermann.   When the musician had sung a
couplet, she went back to the *ritornello*, while the *improv-
visatore* produced the succeeding couplet.   He composed
in this way as many as were wanted, all in the twofold
mood indicated in the programme.   It was a complete
little poem in the form of a plaint, but I am no longer
able to say what it was about.   Here are two or three
of the couplets, which by the merest chance I find in
the depths of my memory, —

> "I will carry my despair
> To a foreign shore :
> Italy, the ever fair,
> I will see once more !

> Now my lady-love is gone
>   From my longing view,
> 'Hither,' cries the dulcet tone
>   Of my hostess new.
>
> Listen to a lover's woe,
>   Pity all my pain !
> And, O bright-eyed maid, do thou
>   Fill my glass again ! "

The reason why I remember these three couplets is that, all day long, the ladies whom the complaint amused kept singing them over and over, so that the whole castle resounded with the refrain of the mazourka, — "What sorrow in the world! What pleasure here below!" I offer them to the reader as a specimen of those relics in forgotten drawers, which the poet of the " December Night " calls the " *débris* of happier days."

Here is another such relic, which must be classed among the improvisations. Alfred de Musset, who could sing the grace and beauty even of a staircase at Versailles, was naturally yet more disposed to pay homage to these qualities when he met them in a woman. One evening there came to the godmother's a bewitching young lady who brought the mistress of the house a little present. It was a needle-case of black shell ornamented with silver. Alfred took it into his head to have this box himself. It was a mad enterprise. The godmother could not give him what had just been given her, and her young friend declared that the box was no longer hers to give. He was very obstinate, however, and returned to the charge again and again, but without success; and so the evening wore away until near midnight.   In the dressing-room, before going home, the young lady wrapped herself up in a white *capuchon*, marvellously becoming to her rosy complexion.   Alfred said jestingly that she looked like a monk, and they parted. Early the next morning, our groom, who was well used to such errands, was traversing the streets of Paris, carrying a big envelope containing the following six-line stanzas : —

" Fairy friar in orders white,
Lo, a beggar starving quite !
Winsome friar with tints of rose,
Drop a trifle ere he goes :
Freely gives who gives aright,
Fairy friar in orders white.

Winsome friar with tints of rose,
All my hopes on thee repose !
Fairy friar in orders white.
Hopes deceive, — a saying trite :
Dare I then my suit disclose,
Winsome friar with tints of rose ?

Fairy friar in orders white,
If I say the truth outright,
Winsome friar with tints of rose,
I invoke a world of foes :
How should I their wrath invite,
Fairy friar in orders white ?

Winsome friar with tints of rose,
Evil elves their rest oppose,
Fairy friar in orders white,
Who have bidden thee, Good-night :
What's the reason ? Tell, who knows,
Winsome friar with tints of rose !

Fairy friar in orders white,
When thy glance on me did light,
Winsome friar with tints of rose,
I became as one of those, —
I who use to snore at night,
Fairy friar in orders white.

Winsome friar with tints of rose,
Men propose, but gods dispose ;
Fairy friar in orders white,
Proverbs tell the truth aright:
Listen, then, what I propose,
Winsome friar with tints of rose.

Fairy friar in orders white,
Give and take, — receive, requite, —
Winsome friar in tints of rose,
There's a bargain one may close :
'Tis our very case I cite,
Fairy friar in orders white.

Winsome friar with tints of rose,
Gavest thou the gift I chose,
Fairy friar in orders white, —
Ebon case with silver bright, —
I should pay thee, I suppose,
Winsome friar with tints of rose.

Fairy friar in orders white,
I should pay thee mite by mite,
Winsome friar with tints of rose.
All my verse and all my prose
Could devise of most polite,
Fairy friar in orders white.

Winsome friar with tints of rose,
Ne'er a virgin flower that blows,
Fairy friar in orders white,
Won such praise as I'd indite,

> Tribute stately and verbose,
> Winsome friar with tints of rose.
>
> Naughty friar in orders white,
> Say me nay, and in despite,
> Naughty friar with tints of rose,
> I'll beset thee with such woes
> Thou shalt dearly rue thy plight,
> Naughty friar in orders white.
>
> Ah, my friar with tints of rose,
> Holds my heart her secret close?
> Ah, my friar in orders white,
> I *would* tell it if I might! —
> Nay; but why the tale expose?
> Ah, my friar with tints of rose!"

Although young, the lady had already received a good many compliments, but seldom of this quality. This *impromptu*, written in haste between bedtime and the hour of rising, was a charming surprise for her; and she replied by sending the author a little sandal-wood box, containing not needles, but a pen, which afterwards achieved much writing. both in prose and verse. I could not tell the number of graceful tributes which the letter-post or the early groom has thus distributed over Paris, — how many flowers that lavish Muse scattered by the way-side. As for the long talks. now light, now serious, — but always poetical, original, and full of curious observations, — which used to detain us in the godmother's drawing-room till the small hours, they must be allowed to perish, with their occasions and the circumstances which suggested them, for lack of a paid stenographer who should give his days and nights to recording them in a folio.

This prodigality was not confined to things of the

mind. It was rooted in the very nature of the man. Rich or poor, he could only live *en grand seigneur.* If he gave his last five-franc piece to relieve some case of need, he did it as freely as though his pocket had been full. At Croisic, on the sea-side, he saw one day, before the hut of a poor salt-maker, a ragged little girl asleep in the sun with her head on a handful of straw. He drew near, and softly put a *louis d'or* between her lips, and then stole away on tiptoe, exulting in the trick, and in the pleasure which awaited the child when she should wake. I have read in the memoirs of Lord Byron, so sadly mutilated by Thomas Moore, that when the agents of the noble lord had sold his estate of Newstead, and wrote to him to ask what they should do with the proceeds of the sale, Byron replied, — "You need not trouble yourself to invest the money. I will use it for my pleasure." An enormous amount was in question, — some hundred thousand pounds sterling. Alfred de Musset was perfectly capable of making the same reply. He only needed to feel the touch of the two million and a half francs. In default of the domain of Newstead, we sold, in 1846, a small family property belonging to our father's inheritance. Alfred received one morning, as his share of the first payment, five thousand francs in silver money. He had never possessed so large a sum before. I advised him to put it in the funds; but he replied, looking admiringly at the little bags ranged along his table, — "What! change these beautiful coins into scraps of paper! I am not such a fool. It is not in the funds that I will put this money, but in my own closet."

He actually arranged the bags in a cupboard; and as
though distrustful of himself, and willing to offer proof
of his wisdom and prudence, he gave me the key to keep,
·saying that I might give it back to him mornings, but not
evenings, in the perilous hours of dissipation and play.

I agreed, put the key in my pocket, and departed. In
our dining-room, I met General de Berthois, one of our
oldest friends, and went with him to the drawing-room.
I had hardly sat down by the general's side, when I felt
myself pulled by the sleeve of my coat. I turned round,
and saw my brother, who was close behind me, and wore
a grave and preoccupied air. He stooped, and whispered in my ear, — "The key! Give me the key!"

I gave it up, and never saw it again. That fine pre-
cautionary arrangement had lasted a little less than
a minute. The five thousand francs were not invested
in the funds. Alfred de Musset never held in his hands
a receipt for rent or a railway bond. On this head, he
would take no advice. Moreover, he was, in all respects,
the most independent man alive; governed by impressions, and the fancy of the moment. He was for ever
setting out with the intention of going to some particular
place, and changing his purpose when half-way there.
From the Quai Voltaire, where he lived in 1840, the
distance was not great, by way of the Rue des Beaux
Arts, to the office of the "Revue des Deux Mondes."
One evening he was to dine there with some of his associates, and had accepted the invitation with pleasure.
As he went downstairs, he asked who the guests were to
be, and whom he was to sit next. There was one
person whom he would like very well for a neighbor.

Would he have him? Such another one, he said, would bore him. Lerminier would perhaps turn the conversation upon politics. The talk would be all, — " discussion of the address," and " attitude of the ministry." At this notion, he took fright. He changed his course, and dined alone at the Palais Royal, whence he sent a messenger with a note of apology.

Engagements of any kind annoyed him; but none alarmed him so much as engagements to perform a given amount of work. All that he has said in his story of the " Lost Poet " he felt so bitterly, that I consider that period of his life one of more cruel trial and of greater peril than he ever encountered at any other time. And yet the poet who so dreaded the lightest bond allowed himself constantly to be entangled by enthusiasm, by weakness in the presence of importunity, by imprudence, and maladministration of his affairs. He gave his signature only too many times, and often to people less obliging than the manager of the " Revue." His self-styled friends occasioned him more than one sleepless night.

All characters abound in contradictions. When Musset consented to have a housekeeper to manage his bachelor establishment, he told her that he should not keep her three months; but she stayed with him as long as he lived. Scarcely was he installed in his rooms on the Rue Mont Thabor, and still in debt for his furniture, when there was offered him a fine copy by Carle Vanloo of a Giorgione in the Louvre, — " Le Concert Champêtre." The picture was not dear, and the opportunity was precious. He took it on a four months' credit, brought it home in triumph, and hung it on his dining-room wall, saying to his housekeeper, who was by no means delighted with the acquisition, — "Put my plate opposite that picture, and take one dish off my bill of fare. I shall always like my dinner well enough."

The Duchesse de Castries twice wished him to marry. The person whom she selected first was a very fine woman ; but Alfred was then much too young and showed little zeal in the matter. The second *parti* pleased him immensely ; but he was brave enough to surmount his inclinations, and to raise objections which were found just and reasonable. Once again, — I do not know in what year, — Chenevard said to him carelessly, between two games of chess, —

"If, by chance, you should want a wife, come to me. I can point one out who will suit you."

"With all my heart," said Alfred. "Who is she?"

" I have lately," replied Chenevard, "become acquainted with M. Mélesville. This morning I called there, and was shown into the drawing-room. A most charming young girl invited me to sit down until her father should come. I had never seen her before, and I was smitten with her beauty and her pleasing and intelligent air. She is a brunette with large black eyes. Her father is the best man alive. They are a family of intellect and taste. It occurred to me at once that she would be an excellent match for you, and I resolved that I would mention it. There is my proposition. You can think it over."

They discussed the matter as they sat, and to such good purpose that the two arrived at a fixed intention of marriage. Alfred was particularly fond of large black eyes and brunette beauties. He had had but little inter-course with M. Mélesville since the days of our stay at Auteuil; but that little had been friendly and based upon mutual esteem. He remembered having seen this young girl play a part with great spirit in a little society comedy, and he knew that she was full of talent and perfectly well bred. His poet's imagination instantly took fire. Chenevard, in whom he had confidence, reit-erated that M. Mélesville was the best and simplest-hearted man in the world, with patriarchal manners, who owed his own fortune to his own talent, and would be sure to rate talent above wealth. One would like to marry just for the sake of having such a father-in-law. All possible advantages seemed to be united, and it only remained to decide what steps to take. Alfred, already devoured by impatience, sought a pretext for renewing his acquaintance with M. Mélesville and calling at the house; since he would hardly be believed if he said that he was in love with the young lady without knowing her, and he did not wish to plunge like a notary directly into the question of figures. Chenevard soon found the wished-for excuse. "You will go," he said, "to M. Méles-ville, and propose to co-operate with him about a play. It will not be hard for you to think out the plot of a comedy. Armed with this plot, you will introduce yourself: you will work with the father; you will chat with the daugh-ter. When you have had time to discover her wit and her graces, you will appoint me your ambassador. I shall be the bearer of proposals. They will be favorably received, and you will make a regular comic-opera marriage."

Alfred was enchanted with the project, and immediately adopted it. The subject which he thought of for his drama was the Arabian tale of the magnanimous Noureddin, which he proposed to weave into a comic opera. Mlle. Mélesville's name was Laure, and she had an album of drawings. Chenevard, who also was full of dreams about the projected marriage, thought he would offer the maiden a pencil-sketch. He took his subject from Petrarch's sonnets, and represented the first meeting between the great poet and Laura de Novès, giving the features of Petrarch and Laura some resemblance to those of Alfred de Musset and Mlle. de Mélesville. When the sketch was finished, he employed the suitor to add to it a French translation of the four lines which had suggested its subject. Alfred, accordingly, wrote underneath the drawing the following quatrain imitated from the twelfth sonnet of Petrarch, —

> " Bénis soient le moment, et l'heure, et la journée,
> Et le temps et les lieux, et le mois de l'année,
> Et la place chérie où dans mon triste cœur
> Pénétra de ses yeux la charmante douceur ! " [1]

This done, Chenevard proceeded to M. Mélesville's in the character of a scout, to reconnoitre the ground, and offer his drawing enriched by an autograph. At the first mention of the young girl's name, he was informed that she was promised to M. Vander Vleet, and that the marriage would soon take place. Thus ended the little intrigue. Alfred did not renounce it without regret.

[1] " Blessed be the moment, the hour, the day, the season, the place, the month of the year, and the beloved spot where the charming sweetness of her eyes penetrated my sorrowful heart."

Serious folk may smile at so very slight an outline of a romance; but I cannot help thinking that, if the scheme had been successful, the poet might have been living now. Once brought under the omnipotent influence of a beautiful and clever woman whom he loved, and who was worthy of his love, Alfred would have been the truest, happiest, and most correct of husbands. He had a reverence for plighted faith, and his independent spirit could have been made perfectly to conform to duties in whose performance lay the security for his happiness. A congenial marriage would have saved him.

Years and experience had no power to chill the heart of Alfred de Musset. On the contrary, his susceptibilities continued to grow keener as long as he lived. He was a prey to agitations, anxieties, and perpetual emotion. He felt an incessant need of free and confidential communication, either with his brother or his uncle Desherbiers. He detained us by his fireside, and we could no more resolve to tear ourselves away than he could suffer us to go. When he was in one of his feverish moods, one had to enter into all his feelings, and become dubious, dejected, wrathful, and tender by turns. This violent spiritual exercise, these contradictory emotions of a soul singularly sensitive and mobile, were sometimes fatiguing to those about him; but there blended with such fatigue an indescribable charm. Passion and exaggeration are contagious. We were carried away in spite of ourselves, — tormented, exalted! And we came back again and again, as to an indulgence from which we could not refrain, to be tormented and exalted anew. Who will give me back that agitated life, — those hours of delicious anguish? Ah, well! — for forty years at least, I revelled in the intimate knowledge of that great mind, and the riches of that sincere affection.

It is said that there are geniuses who do not know that they are such. I do not believe it. Correggio himself, simple-hearted as he was, did not long remain in that state of ignorance. Alfred de Musset, the most modest of poets, knew better than any one else the strength and weakness of each of his own works, and he judged them as soundly as if they had been another's. Those of his writings which he rated highest are the second volume of poems, the " Fils du Titien," " Lorenzaccio," and " Carmoisine."

It is to be regretted that, in France, poetical gifts cannot be a source of fortune. The " Caprice " alone was worth more to the author in money than all his other works put together. Stendhal, who was very fond of Alfred de Musset, amused himself one day with computing how much Alfred's poetry brought him by the line. He took the number of the " Revue " which contained " Rolla," and the result of their calculations was the modest sum of sixty centimes. Stendhal then opened the poems of Lord Byron, and taking for a point of comparison " Tasso's Lament," for which Mr. Murray payed three hundred guineas, he found that the English publisher had given his author more than a guinea and a half a line. Stendhal exclaimed upon the difference as scandalous and disgraceful to France.

" But, before you fly into a rage," said Alfred, " you had better consider whether there is not a corresponding difference in the quality of Lord Byron's verses and mine. Perhaps they paid me enough."

" I will never allow that," replied Stendhal.

If Lord Byron, with his well-known character, had not been a peer of England ; but if, instead, he had been no richer than the French poet, and had received but five hundred francs for his poems where he did receive five thousand, — life would have been impossible to him upon such conditions.

As he said himself in his lines to Mme. Ristori, Alfred de Musset had a heart ever prompt to answer the appeal of genius. We know the immortal homage which he paid to M. de Lamartine. He also admired Béranger, but could not understand why a gifted poet should voluntarily restrict himself to the narrow limits of the song. He blamed him for having weighted himself with the often painful shackles of a refrain, and for having dragged about his whole life long the ball of the *faridondaine.*[1] But he was not one of those who have excused themselves from doing justice to the noble character of Béranger by calling his disinterestedness coquetry.

It was not by accident that the author of the " Pensées de Raphael " spoke of Shakspeare and Racine meeting upon the table. He professed an equal admiration for these two so diverse geniuses. In the fervor of youth, he preferred the former ; but ripe reflection taught him the full value of the second. When he found in Racine a strong and impassioned expression, he ex-

[1] Say the "ding-dong bell;" any merely sonorous and unmeaning burden. — TR.

claimed that it was as fine as Shakspeare; and if he found, in the English poet, a great thought clothed in a pure and irreproachable form, he compared it to the poetry of Racine. One of the things which he liked best was a certain exclamation of Phedra's, which illustrates by its very grotesqueness the bewilderment of one sick at heart, —

"Ariane, ma sœur! de quel amour blessée,
Vous mourûtes aux bords où vous fûtes laissée?" [1]

When Rachel breathed out that strange and unlooked-for lament, Alfred buried his face in his hands pale with emotion.

I will not say that naturalness was the quality which charmed him most: but, rather, that it was for him an indispensable quality; and if its presence could not save a book from being mediocre, or even bad, no conceivable beauty could atone for its absence. For this reason the letters of Mme. de Sévigné did not please him. He detected in them at times a something artificial and affected, — a suspicion that they would be shown to other persons beside her to whom they were addressed.

The abuse of adjectives, upon which he had animadverted so comically in his letters from Ferté sous Jouarre, continued to be one of his pet antipathies. One day in 1833, a beautiful romance — of which all the world was talking, and which contained a new revelation of genius — fell into his hands before he had made the acquaintance of the author. He enjoyed the book, but found things

---

[1] "O! my sister Ariadne, by what love wounded didst thou die on the shore where thou wast abandoned?"

in it to criticise. Struck with its abuse of adjectives, he took a pencil and erased as he read, all the useless epithets, parasitic clauses, and other superfluities. The first chapter of the novel thus chastened and corrected, is infinitely more natural and pleasanter to read than the original, and the reading of it conveys an excellent lesson.[1]

In none of his works either in prose or verse, not even in his critical articles, did Alfred de Musset ever employ the first person plural. This manner of speaking, which is supposed to be modest, seemed to him, on the contrary, pretentious. Except in newspapers, where the writer who wields the pen may be considered as expressing the views of the other editors along with his own, he never liked any one to say *we* in place of *I*, and when he encountered that hackneyed idiom, he would say laughingly, — " I did not know before that the author was king of France and Navarre."

The poet of " Namouna," and the " Spanish Tales," often smiled at the futile attempts of his copyists, for never was poetry more imitated than his. " The rash creatures do not know," he used to say, " how much good-sense one needs in order to dispense with common-sense. But good-sense, tact, wit, and imagination are all in vain, if one have not especially and above all a great deal of heart. Fancy is the most perilous of all marks of talent. The ablest are led astray by it like school-boys, if they make it a matter of the head alone. Those who feel truly and keenly may give themselves up to the dangerous delight of letting their thought run

[1] I still possess this curious copy of " Indiana." — P. M.

wild, knowing that the heart will follow it step by step. But people who lack heart are invariably swamped by their fancy, if they have any. Once launched on their voyage, they can anchor to nothing, because they have no fixed point in their own souls."

Up to his latest day, Alfred de Musset read all that appeared, and wanted to know and appreciate all. He paused, well pleased, over a new idea, however trivial. His memory retained a pleasing verse, a passage containing a just sentiment, an ingenious reflection, or an original expression ; and, caring little whether the author had a reputation or no, he quoted freely what struck him as unusual. He suspected books made out of other books, and preferred himself to apply at the original sources of information rather than trust to interpretations.

But I see that I am being carried away beyond the proper limits of my subject. If I were to collect the literary judgments and opinions of Alfred de Musset on the men and things of this and previous ages, I should have to make another book. It is time to pause, in spite of the recollections which come crowding into my mind. May it but seem to the passionate admirers of the poet that I have attained the end proposed, — that of making the man known. To them alone is this notice dedicated. I have written with no other purpose than the desire to be exact, with no guide save my regrets, with no *fixed point in my soul* save my love for the brother whose untimely death has left a void in my life which nothing can fill.

THE END.

Printed in the United States
127275LV00004B/175/A

9 781417 955169

THE ORPHAN
NEXT DOOR

A SINGLE DADDY NEXT DOOR ROMANCE

ALISHA STAR

HOT AND STEAMY ROMANCE

CONTENTS

Blurb   v

1. Emily   1
2. Grant   6
3. Emily   15
4. Emily   20
5. Grant   27
6. Emily   39
7. Emily   44
8. Emily   50
9. Grant   55

Made in "The United States" by:

Michelle Love & Alisha Star

© Copyright 2021

ISBN: 978-1-64808-727-1

❀ Created with Vellum

BLURB

Emily is too young for me, but I can't shake how much I want her. I want to rescue her from her isolation. I certainly want to rescue her from that gold-digging little creep James.

I want to love her and be loved by her, and wake up to her face every morning. And of course, I'd love to make her mine. Even if our age difference didn't make me hesitate, James is doing his best to get and stay in the way, even after Emily throws him out of her life. He's stalking her; he's stalking us. And he's way too interested in my little girl for comfort. I'm determined to have Emily in my arms, safe from him and from the world's other predators. And when I finally get what I want, it's paradise. For a while, I don't think twice about that little brat and his complaining. But James isn't done. And as Emily and I work toward our first of what we hope is many Christmases to come, he's going to take his revenge. *I'm a patient man. But when he endangers my lover and my little girl, it is time for a reckoning.*

After living a life of extreme poverty, knowing nothing but neglect and loneliness, young Emily Dawn has won the New York State Lottery and become a multi-millionaire. Having moved into the most modest house she can find in Woodstock, New York, she quickly develops a crush on her next door neighbor: self-made billionaire and single dad Grant Norton. They become fast friends, especially when his cute daughter, Molly, takes a liking to Emily.

But Emily has a problem. She's been dating the charming James Parrish: a handsome and age-appropriate young man from the neighborhood who's doing his best to seduce her and make her fall in love. Grant senses that something is wrong with the smarmy young man, but doesn't know if it's just his jealousy getting the better of him —as much as he tries to fight it, he can't help his attraction to the kind-hearted Emily. Determined to break Parrish's spell on her, Grant steps in—and the attraction between them ends up catching fire.

As their affair intensifies, they must figure out how to tell Grant's daughter, especially when Parrish starts to harass all three of them. Bent on revenge, the thwarted con artist finally resorts to trying to kidnap Molly. The lovers must join forces against him to protect the young girl, and sort out what is going on between them.

1

EMILY

As I stare out the window of my new mansion as a handsome man kisses my neck, the only thought in my head is that I wish he would stop distracting me. The thought shocks me as soon as it crosses my mind—James Parrish is beautiful, blond, and dashing—but it's true. There's something about his hands on me, his lips pressing softly and wetly on my pulse, which leaves me feeling soiled—like he's leaving behind some sticky residue wherever he touches.

He's trying harder than usual to be seductive, but after everything that's happened it's all I can do not to flinch away.

I have to hide my discomfort. Last time I begged off from having sex with him he demanded to know what was wrong with me. All normal girls want to fuck him once he puts the moves on them, or so he claimed.

I had to tell him that it must be the trauma from being on the streets, and the fact that I'm not used to being touched. But afterward I felt so much worse about myself that I've since made sure to never let on that I don't want him again. It's ridiculous that I have to work so hard to spare his feelings when we've only been together for a little while—and when he's never spared mine.

So I continue to let him kiss me and play with my tits through my sweater while I distract myself. I stare out past the drops of rain clinging to the glass and down the long, grassy hillside to my neighbor's back yard. Grant Norton is out there in the rain letting his two Golden Retrievers, Pogo and Mike, run. I smile to see him, a warmth running through me that James can't evoke any more.

The trick works; James chuckles, thinking my smile is meant for him, and pulls me closer, nuzzling my cheek as I hold him limply in my arms. He thinks I'm a slow starter when it comes to romance—and I am, having no real experience with sex or affection. But if I stay cold and still and don't smile, he'll get insulted again and sulk, and kick up drama.

So I look at Grant to get my heart racing—and since I can't have him, I turn around and settle for James.

"Aw, come on, Red, what's so interesting out there?" he wheedles, tugging at one of my strawberry blonde curls.

I look back at him and smile. "Everything."

It's true. After a life filled with institutional halls and filthy alleyways, my house in Woodstock is paradise. Looking out the window at all that green, gold, and crimson would soothe my soul even if Grant wasn't out there.

I drink him in with my gaze as I lie across the bottle-green velvet couch that dominates my living room. His tall, broad-shouldered form stands under a black umbrella as he tosses neon orange squeaky balls up the slope so the dogs can race after them. His dark hair ripples in the breeze along with his black overcoat; his strong face is a tanned blur at this distance, but I can picture his strong features in my mind.

Grant is the best part of living in Woodstock—besides being able to afford it, that is. After spending a chilly spring on the streets of Brooklyn, an amazing stroke of luck six months ago changed everything in my life. Now, I have a big house in the woods, a hot neighbor, a fridge full of food and a life to look forward to...once I recover from what I went through before it took a turn for the better.

Grant—watching him in his yard, talking to him, having lunch with him and his adorable daughter Molly—makes me happy to get up in the morning. His existence in my life reminds me of all I now have to be grateful for—and all I still wish I could have. His pale green eyes, so startling against his tanned skin, are full of kindness, and his smile is contagious. A few minutes of conversation with him helps my mood no matter how bad things get.

"Hey, are you listening, baby?" James whines, and I look back up into his blank blue eyes and force a smile.

"I'm sorry, I didn't really sleep. What did you say?"

He rolls his eyes, the corner of his mouth turning up. James is almost ethereally beautiful, with smooth skin and the face of a marble angel. I used to find that babyish look cute, but I'm starting to get tired of it—along with his whiny tone when he wants something. "I said, baby, order us up some pizza! I'm getting the munchies, and I know you haven't eaten all day."

He's right about that last part. I'm still getting used to the idea that I can fill my belly whenever I want, and have a bad habit of neglecting that need. It's almost as disorienting as looking at my account statements and wondering at all those zeros. It all still seems so...foreign...to be able to satisfy my hunger whenever I need to.

"Okay, okay." I dig in my pocket to see what cash I have: none. I usually don't carry much cash around. It's an old habit too, but this one's too smart to leave behind. "I can make the order but I have no cash on me. Can you get the tip?"

It's a simple request—it's only five dollars. But the petulant look on his face deepens, making my heart sink immediately. "Oh, come on, baby, you know I'm broke until my app rolls out. It's just another few weeks. And I know you're good for it." He gives a charming smile, and my stomach clenches with the sudden urge to tell him to *go away for good*. I know I have more options in the romance department than James wants me to think.

But no matter how many options I may have, none of them are the one I want. None of them are Grant, who is a widower twice my age with a little daughter, and who, as far as I can tell, does not date.

I've had a crush on him since I moved in here, well before James got in my face two months ago and refused to leave.

James tells me that he's crazy in love with me. He tells me that there's never been anyone like me before, and that he wants to spend the rest of his life with me. Then he comes over and plants himself on my couch for hours, pushing for sex, expecting to be fed, and always asking for money.

I don't know what love is supposed to feel like, exactly, but I'm pretty sure it's not meant to feel like this. I think it's supposed to be more like how I feel when I'm around Grant, or when I see him with his daughter. All warm inside—with no reservations.

Right now, there's a chill deepening in my womb as I sit up, using it as an excuse to pull away from him. "Fine," I sigh. "What kind of pizza do you want?"

"Hawaiian, you know what I like." He waves his beer at me like he's ordering from a servant, and I shake my head as I pull out my phone. Pineapple doesn't belong on pizza.

I order a medium chicken pesto with mushrooms and olives for myself and a medium Hawaiian for him. I have stocked the fridge with beer, though I barely touch the stuff myself. I'm kind of hoping he'll get whiskey dick tonight and leave me alone.

I know deep down that these are not the sort of things that a girl should be thinking about with her first official boyfriend. But even though I'm nineteen and he's in his twenties, James is definitely the less mature one in our relationship. He's very charming when he wants to be, but right now it's clear to me what he thinks. He thinks he's won me and that he doesn't have to put in any effort at all to keep me.

But is he wrong? *Why am I still putting up with this?*

I already know. I don't like thinking about it. Part of it is that horrible, empty ache of loneliness that will yawn inside of me like a canyon the moment he leaves. The other is a deeper worry, but one that has nagged at me more and more—*what if he won't leave when I tell him to?*

I place the pizza order and put the tip on my card along with everything else. By the time I look back outside again, Grant is gone.

"So, baby doll, how much time do we have to...play...before our food gets here?" James drapes his hand over my shoulder and reaches down to cup my breast through my pale pink sweater. He gives it a squeeze that he thinks is friendly, and while it doesn't hurt, I have to force myself not to squirm.

"Twenty minutes," I make up, knowing it's more like forty, and he grunts in disgust.

"That's too little time," he grumbles.

"Hey, you were the one who wanted pizza," I remind him, and he finally shrugs and nods.

"Okay, fine. I'll just fuck you twice later." He offers a sleazy grin, and it's all I can do to force an answering smile.

2

GRANT

"Is Emily coming over to trick or treat with us?" Molly wrinkles her nose as I dab on her grease paint. She decided to go as a cat burglar this year, which, to her nine-year-old mind means a fuzzy white and cream kitty outfit with a robber's mask across her eyes.

"I'm going to ask her, though I don't know if she's had time to come up with a costume. Hold still, sweetie, I'm trying to get your kitty nose straight." Her whiskers were hard enough. Molly is incredibly energetic; even channeling it into martial arts training hasn't cured her of the wiggles.

But squirminess won't stop me. I'm determined to do daddy-daughter costumes justice. And thus, I am going trick-or-treating with Molly as Macavity from *Old Possum's Book of Practical Cats,* one of her favorites.

It took some planning behind her back, but it turned out well, and Molly squealed when she saw it. A cosplayer friend made it for me. I'm dressed in a black Victorian evening suit, with a stripy orange tail hanging out between its coattails, a top hat with kitty ears, another robber mask, and white gloves. I drew the line at face paint.

Woodstock is tiny, its houses scattered; anyone who wants a real trick-or-treat haul in the eastern Catskills has to be willing to drive from town to town. That is more than fine with me—I love to drive, and I am hoping to take my sweet neighbor Emily with us.

Emily is beautiful and kind, but she has no one. She's modest and hard-working as well, and Molly loves her. As for me...I'm starting to as well. If it wasn't for our huge age difference, I would love to pursue more than friendship with her.

But that's not why I want to take her along tonight. It's a lot more complicated than that, actually. I want her with me because I'm trying to pry loose a giant, smarmy blond leech that has attached himself to her.

Emily is young and big-hearted, but clearly traumatized and new to having money and a place to stay. The new boyfriend, James somebody, has circled in on her like a shark smelling blood in the water. He's local and a little notorious—a slacker with half a job delivering bread on his bike three seasons and shoveling driveways one. Like a lot of the spoiled sons of rich Woodstock residents, he lives on other people's money, and only works so his mother doesn't know how much weed he's buying.

Woodstock is big on gossip, especially when there's dirt to sling around. James is the son of a Hollywood producer and his trophy wife—his rich dad stashes him here with his mom to keep them out of the spotlight. James, who lives with his mother (with whom he shares a forgettable last name) between girlfriends, looks to be trying to make himself into a trophy husband.

I hate gold diggers of either sex. It's one of the reasons I have never remarried. Molly deserves to have two parents, but at least my wealth allows me to stay at home for her—except when one of my businesses has an important meeting, of course. And now, thanks to Emily, I don't even have to worry about vetting a stranger to babysit Molly while I'm gone.

I wish I could shake my growing desire to keep her.

As easy as it would be to place the blame on anyone else, I can't say it's entirely Molly's fault that I started becoming attracted to my nineteen-year-old neighbor. She didn't mean to put the idea in my head when she told me I should marry Emily so she could stay and take care of both of us. She just likes Emily and wants to keep her too.

Molly does not remember her mother, and I'm very glad of that. When we separated, Alicia said that going through with giving me a daughter was what had ruined our relationship. I don't fully understand her reasoning, but she complained that having a baby made her feel "too old."

I urged her to get counseling. I suspect to this day that it was postpartum depression. She simply wasn't like that before—wasn't like that when I fell in love with her. But Alicia was stubborn, and too proud. She refused to acknowledge that she had a problem.

I still remember the night she broke down and started shouting at me while Molly wailed in her bassinet, still too tiny to have any idea what was going on. She hated me, she hated Molly, she hated being sore and having stretch marks, and she hated her life with us most of all. I demanded that she seek treatment before her behavior started endangering herself and our baby, and she just laughed at me.

I ended up doing all the caring for Molly while Alicia refused to bond with her. Three months later she simply...drifted out of our lives. I woke up, she was gone, her things were gone, and our joint account had been cleaned out.

I went a little crazy trying to find her; her family wasn't cooperative, and the private investigators I hired turned up nothing. I had a newborn and felt, at the beginning, that Molly needed her mother. But Alicia vanished for an entire year before resurfacing again—in an obituary.

Persistence and a few bribes had gotten me the full police and coroner's reports. Molly's mother, whom I had loved for half my adult life, had been found semi-nude on a beach in Majorca. She had died out on the beach that lovely night, of what may have been a deliberate overdose on uncut cocaine and medical-grade morphine.

Further investigation indicated that she had spent the year and our money jet-setting around Europe pursuing every pleasure she could get her hands on—unaccompanied by anyone regularly, and contacting no one from her old life. She had been hospitalized for two previous suicide attempts: one in London and one in Amsterdam.

I've always shielded Molly from the truth about her mother. She only knows that her mother is dead. Not that she abandoned us and destroyed herself. And certainly not that I half blame myself for not taking steps to get Alicia into inpatient treatment before she disappeared.

Since then I've left off dating, focusing on two things: raising my daughter, and getting my head back together after learning the truth about Alicia. I don't rattle easy, but that genuinely haunts me. I didn't want to go into a new relationship dragging a lot of baggage, so I haven't even thought about it until recently.

Then along came Emily. And now I think about it all the time. Seeing Emily bond with Molly in a way that Alicia never could makes it even harder not to imagine her as a permanent part of my life—of our lives.

But Woodstock loves gossip, and I know what would happen if I actually made Emily that kind of offer. The idea of a rich billionaire marrying a girl half his age, who also happens to be his babysitter, would be tasty gossip-fodder. I don't care what the local biddies think of me, but Emily and Molly would have to live with any fallout as well. To spare them, I've forced myself to avoid even the semblance of flirting.

But I do care for Emily, and I do really want her. She's a good person, and she deserves to have people around her who care about her. Instead, she's sticking with that leech James, who is taking advantage of her inexperience and loneliness.

It's the one thing about her that frustrates me, and I can't blame her for it. Her heart is too big, and she expects too little from others. Far less than I would give her if I had the chance.

I rarely want to punch a guy in the face on first meeting, but this James guy gets to me. I've had a close encounter with someone like him before. Just thinking of James pawing at Emily in public makes my back teeth ache.

Emily may not be mine, but someone has to look after her. That may mean stepping in where James is concerned, so I'm always watchful. I don't want to get in her business unless invited, but I'll chuck all decorum out the window if he hurts her.

I step back and look at Molly, whose cream stripes and little pink nose are all even now. "There we go. Go have a look." I point at the full-length mirror across the bright bathroom, and she hurries over to it and squeals.

I lose the fight against grinning. "So did I do good?"

"Definitely an A+ job, Daddy. Now are we gonna pick up Emily?" She rocks on her heels, and my smile fades. I'm a little worried that Emily's too caught up in James's web and will let him keep her home.

"Let me call her and find out when." I don't want to presume and end up putting both Emily and Molly at the center of a tense and awkward scene. I punch in Emily's number as we walk out of the bathroom toward the rambling Victorian mansion's giant living room.

Both our Goldens sprawl out on the couch. I spent two good hours wearing them out by throwing balls and letting them run up and down the grassy slope that separates Emily's house from my own. Neither of them raises their head as we come in, but both start thumping their tails against the couch cushions. Molly goes over to pet them while I wait for Emily to pick up.

It takes three rings. As I wait, I feel my blood pressure going up as I imagine her with James, trying to answer the phone. James pulling the phone out of her hands and going back to whatever inept sex act he's imposing on her.

I have seen her discomfort at the way he paws at her in public. If there was ever a rosy glow of new love between them, he must have spoiled it quickly with all his ass-grabbing antics. My sister Catherine is still on permanent vacation in Majorca, recovering from the scars that her own version of James left her with. As for my brother—he's always been a version of James.

When Emily picks up finally, all the air whooshes out of me in relief. "Whoo. Hey. Uh, it's Grant. Molly wants to know if you'll come trick-or-treating with us."

"Oh...oh hi!" Her voice perks up at once, and suddenly I'm calm again, feeling a mix of warm fuzzies in my chest area and a tightening in my groin. "Um, well, I—" she starts, and I hear the sudden, worried hesitation in her voice. "I'd like to."

I hear rustling in the background—and then a door opens. "Who is it, babe?" says a young man's voice, and my eyes narrow in annoyance.

"My neighbor needs a hand taking his little girl trick or treating," she replies in a voice that sounds a touch too cheery. My smile goes lopsided at her small display of cunning. I never said anything about *needing* her help with Molly, but if anybody asks me I'll back her story in a second.

"What? Aw, come *on*, baby, you have a boyfriend now. You've gotta stay home and take care of me!" His deep voice wheedles like a kid's.

"Take care of you? You're a grown—" she sighs and I hear her stop to take a deep breath before going on. *Just go ahead and yell at him, honey, he deserves every bit of it.*

But she doesn't, instead answering him with frustrating patience. "Look, James. We already talked about this. You're going to your mom's tonight." She speaks slowly and carefully, as if to a child with a volatile temper, and my heart sinks.

"Fuck my mom. I want the—" he starts, laughing off her concerns, trying to sound charming. He's the kind of guy who is used to letting his pretty face get him what he wants, just like his mother. "She'll be drunk by three in the afternoon anyway, she'll pass out before the servants bring out dinner. It doesn't matter."

"James, I sat there and listened to you promise her," she urges, but he just laughs some more. I hear rustling again and a small sound of discomfort from her, and a hot flush of rage runs through me.

Let her go, you son of a bitch. I want to say it aloud, but yelling through a phone is pointless. Should I go up the hill and rescue her from Mr. Won't-Take-No-For-An-Answer's grubby paws? I hesitate, my fist clenched, wanting to do just that.

Then, a small hand tugs at my pant leg. I look down and see Molly gazing up at me solemnly. She holds her hand out for the phone. I shake my head, but she stamps her foot insistently. "I've got a plan, Dad."

I pause, wondering what my imp is up to, and then hand her the phone.

Molly listens for a moment, frowns tremendously, sticks her finger in her ear and yells *"I wanna talk to Emily right now!"*

The argument over the phone stops at once, and I'm suddenly grinning again. I should be telling her that that's not an inside voice. I don't.

She smiles. "Hi Emily! We're dressed as kitties and we need you to come help us trick-or-treat. So tell your stupid boyfriend to go back to his mommy! You've got other friends and he's just being selfish!"

My grin fades and I stare. My daughter surprises me regularly these days, but this one's a big one. *How are you nine?*

On the other end of the phone, Emily is laughing, and I hear James go "aw shit" almost sheepishly. Cute plus angry can be a potent combination. "Duty calls, sweetie. We've already got plans for tomorrow anyway, and you're out of clothes."

"Now that wouldn't happen if you let me leave some stuff here," he complains, but she cuts him off gently.

"James, I haven't even gotten used to living indoors yet, give me time before I give up my privacy entirely, okay?" Her voice is tender and patient...and is the exact same voice she uses with my nine-year-old.

Unfortunately, James is less reasonable than even Molly at her angriest and most overtired. "Oh come on, don't be a coward. I love you! We should be together. All the time."

You mean,"Your money and I should be together all the time," you damned parasite. My back teeth are still grinding together, and I hold myself still as Molly hands me the phone. *Don't do it Emily* I mouth, but if he hears me he'll make even more trouble for her.

"You shouldn't call me names," she says quietly. It's something Molly says to mean kids on the playground, but in Emily's mouth it is grave and edged with tension. James starts to stammer an answer, but she simply raises the phone back to her ear. "I need to get changed. You're doing cats?"

"Uh...yes, cat burglars, actually."

She laughs a little. "That's cute. Pick me up in fifteen minutes?"

I give Molly a thumbs-up, and snort as she bounces in place. "Sounds good. See you then."

She hangs up, cutting off James in the middle of a protest, and I tuck my phone away, chuckling. *James zero, Emily and people who actually care about her, one.*

"So when do we pick her up?" Molly asks, eyes bright with anticipation.

"We leave in ten minutes," I announce cheerfully.

"Yay!" She hugs me around my waist, and we sit down on the couch to pet the dogs as we wait.

Twelve minutes later, we pull up to the curb outside Emily's house. It's one of the other huge old Victorians dotting the woods around Woodstock. She's having the old house refurbished bit by bit while she lives in it. They're not going to finish by winter, but all rooms are livable, and some are already gorgeously restored.

She told me once that the house was like her; falling apart in some places, but becoming new and lively again. No wonder James keeps trying to move in there, while she struggles to keep him out.

When I first found out that a New York State Lottery winner was moving in next door, I expected some brash, newly rich kid. Someone a little bit like James. Instead I got Emily—endlessly grateful for every bit of her new life.

She's told me only a little of the nightmares she's gone through, but I can see a lot of it in her eyes still. She has the haunted expression of someone who's spent most of her life so isolated and starved for love that even crappy, fake, fast-food romance like the kind James is offering feels good to her.

The door bangs open seconds after I pull up, and I see James come stomping out. He doesn't seem to notice my white SUV, which has darkened windows. Hands shoved deep in his pockets, he turns the corner and walks quickly down the street, shoulders hunched against the deepening cold.

I watch him, fighting the urge to laugh at him as he retreats back to his mother's house where he belongs. He disappears around the corner at the end of the street, and I sigh with relief. *Well, that's one problem out of the way. Temporarily, anyway.*

Then the door opens again, and I look up, my heart lifting. Emily comes out, her strawberry blonde curls shining in the dying sunlight, a pink puffy overcoat not quite concealing her slim curves. She's not in costume, but as her soft sea-blue eyes settle on my SUV and light up, I see she has a sparkly-tipped cat teaser toy in her hand.

3

EMILY

I know I shouldn't let myself feel guilty about leaving James behind to fend for himself this Halloween. It's not my fault he changed his plans the moment he discovered I had some that didn't involve him. If I ever do anything he dislikes, he makes it seem like I've committed a crime against him.

When we first got together, I was so starved for love that I was desperate to please James. Any dissatisfaction he showed was my signal to scramble to make things better so he would stay, so he would still love me. But soon, I noticed that all that attention, work, and support I was giving went only one way. He never gave anything back.

I've started getting stomach aches whenever I think of James. He is still beautiful, he can still coax a smile from me, and he has tons of friends around town that he promises to one day introduce me to. But after months together, I keep looking at what he says he'll do, and what he actually does, and I'm finally seeing the huge differences between the two.

The problem is, the man I really want is too good for me. But right now, sitting next to him in his car as we drive around Ulster

County looking for houses with welcoming lights, I can pretend that's not true. I can pretend that this is my family.

"All right, Daddy, don't forget to turn up the road ahead. If we don't get the big house at the top of the hill you won't get your booze cordials!" Molly is using a pen light to peer at a makeshift trick or treating map on the clipboard in front of her.

Grant chuckles. "Wouldn't want that." He sounds just a touch embarrassed, and I smile in the safe, warm dimness of the seat beside him.

James doesn't understand that there's a difference between someone who has never been loved and one who has never loved. I might scramble after affection like a starving dog, but that doesn't mean I'm not wary of being poisoned. In the end, like the dog, I have to make a choice: take the risk, or spend another night hungry.

Without Grant around, I might have been desperate enough to cling to James. But right now, when no one is making demands on me aside from company and a bit of babysitting and car-watching, I have something to hang onto besides him. Not just Grant, but the very idea of family, of closeness, of spending time out with people you love—and of holidays that mean something.

I can't help but think back on all those desolate years in the group home, with not a single card on Christmas, and only dirty snow clinging to the windows and turkey loaf for dinner. I could never understand why nobody wanted me, but even foster parents would not take me. Instead I was stuck trying to live peacefully in a place where the rejects go to live.

But instead of being a violent kid, or disabled, or too defiant to survive anywhere like a lot of the other kids at the home, I was just...shy and ordinary. I meant no harm to anyone. Yet even the craziest bullies left me alone once they found out about my past—found out that I used to be called Ebony Christchurch.

As horrible as it is, I actually wish I had known about my parents' lurid murder-suicide before I grew up. That whole time, I had no idea why nobody wanted to adopt or even foster me. Now I know they were just afraid I would turn out like John and Ellen Christchurch—the biological parents I can't remember.

One of the things I like most about Grant is that he knows, but he doesn't care. He's told me more than once that it doesn't matter who my parents were; it only matters who I am. I have always tried to be kind, gentle, thoughtful—not like my father. And not a worm, like my mother, either.

"So, what's the haul look like so far?" I ask Molly cheerfully, forcing my attention away from thoughts of my past.

"Two and a half bags, including four full-sized Snickers!" Molly declares proudly, and I hear Grant chuckle beside me. "Definitely an improvement from last year, except that Mrs. Exeter is now doing fun-sized M&Ms, down from full-sized last year. Gonna have to downgrade her house." From her tone, she believes this to be a real pity. Then she flips back a few pages on her clipboard and actually marks a checklist.

It's all I can do not to giggle when Molly gets going. She's precocious, smart, cute, and sometimes a bit of a pain in the butt—but she's nine after all, and it's never that big of a problem. Grant has done a good job with her.

Sometimes, when Molly begs me to stay longer, I wonder if she wouldn't do even better with a mother figure around. *But I'm not her mom, I'm her babysitter. I've never had a mom myself, how could I possibly know how to be one anyway?*

"You're very quiet," Grant says speculatively as we pull up at the next house. It's James's mom's mini-mansion near the hilltop. My throat tightens.

"That's James's house," I start, and then go quiet as I realize I have no idea at all how to explain why I don't want us going near it. "I'm not sure his mother is giving out candy."

"Might as well try!" Molly chirps, and opens the door, bounding out before Grant can follow.

"Hey, hey hold up!" He looks back at me. "Stay in the car where it's warm, I'll take care of this."

I nod and he shuts the door, shutting out the chilly air. I sit back against the cushioned seat, sighing out all my air, and watch through the tinted window as he trots after his speedy daughter.

She's knocking before he's halfway up the walk, and the door opens. James's tall, blonde mother, face so taut with plastic surgery that it looks stretched over a frame, appears with a pumpkin-colored bowl of candy. She smiles down at Molly—and then something happens that startles me so badly I don't know how to react.

James pushes the door wide open and all but shoves his mother out of the way as he grabs the candy bowl. He crouches down to address Molly, with a strangely determined look on his face. And he starts asking her questions.

I can't tell what he's asking exactly, but between his expression and the quick way she takes a step back from him, I'm suspecting it's pretty aggressive. His mother puts a hand on his shoulder and pleads half-audibly. He shrugs her off and keeps hammering Molly with questions as she backs up another step.

Oh fuck. She's a kid—what the hell is he doing? Horrified, I reach for the door—but Grant gets there before I can step outside.

James looks up as Grant says something and his eyes widen. He scuttles backwards through the door as if Grant took a swing at him. Molly points at him and laughs. His mother shoves him out of sight and comes forward with the candy bowl and an apologetic look.

I sit back in the seat and close my eyes, sick to my stomach. My face is burning; being associated with James in any way mortifies me right now, and I don't even know what he's said. *Oh God, what did he do?*

As they return to the car, James's mom stands at her door with her hands over her face. Molly is still giggling and Grant is seething. For a moment, used to being the scapegoat, I expect him to start yelling at me. Instead, as Molly snickers and buckles her seatbelt, he sighs.

"I should have listened when you tried to warn us about this house. Has James been jealous this whole time?" He's speaking in as calm a voice as he can manage, but I hear the edge to it that his giggling daughter misses.

"Jealous?" *Oh no. Not this again.* "He's jealous of everyone I spend time with who isn't him, if that is what you mean."

"Not that kind of jealous." He turns a tight smile on me. "He just interrogated Molly about the nature of our relationship."

My heart pounds even harder. I'm blushing so hard it hurts. Am I allowed to hate James for this, when he's the only one who has ever loved me to any degree?

"I'm sorry. I should have been more clear."

"Don't be sorry. It's just that times like this make me wonder why you're with him." He sounds far more worried than annoyed, and I have to fight back tears.

"It's times like this that make me wonder why I am, too." Admitting it eases some of my confusion.

"We should talk about this. But not right now." He touches my arm, and my lips tremble as I squeeze my eyes shut.

Molly snorts as she goes back to sorting her loot. "He's dumb. He kept asking me the same question over and over. I don't think he listens too well."

"No, he doesn't," I admit slowly. "Really, he seems a little...out of it sometimes." It's all the pot and cheap alcohol, mixed with the crazy hours he keeps. I'm almost sure of it.

Molly giggles again. "He wanted to know if you were sleeping with Daddy."

My mouth closes suddenly. *Oh God.*

Grant nods, his jaw set. "That's not the word he used, either."

I go very cold inside. "What did he say?"

4

EMILY

"You repeatedly asked my neighbor's nine-year-old daughter if I was fucking him? Are you completely crazy?"

WE'RE ON MY NARROW, covered front porch. I've shut the door behind me to keep the heat in—and James out. I'm in my fluffy rose-colored robe over a flannel nightie, and the icy wind cuts through both.

MY VOICE ECHOES down the street and off the hills. Two doors down, one of my neighbors turns off his music to listen. I don't care.

I'M NOT GOING INSIDE until James is well away from the porch. He's not coming in tonight. If he keeps this up, he's not coming in any night.

"Calm down, baby," James replies casually with a little smirk on his face, as if he's amused by how upset I am. "That can't be the first time she's heard the word 'fucking' before." He uncurls his hand and shrugs a shoulder. "The little slut's nine, not five."

He called Molly a—!

He rambles on, oblivious to my reaction and smirking with his eyes half-closed from all the pot, while I turn to ice and stone inside. I can't even understand the noises coming out of his annoying mouth any more, and when I walk toward him he doesn't seem to notice. I don't know what I'm going to do until my palm slams against the side of his face hard enough that it goes numb.

He lets out a squawk as he loses his balance on the railing, his once casual stance turning to flailing as he launches off the short stairway. He lands on his ass on the walkway below with his smirk crumbling into a confused look.

Somewhere down the street I hear howls of laughter. I ignore the laughing and walk slowly down the stairs toward James, all hell and fury in a pink fluffy robe.

He blinks and looks around, as if trying to figure out if he tripped, and then the blood returns to his cheek and he claps a hand over it. "Ow!"

I stand over him while the wind plays with my hair, my whole body feeling like it's burning inside. "Don't you ever talk about that little girl that way again."

. . .

His eyes widen as it dawns on him what the hell just happened, and he fixes me with an astonished look. He outweighs me by half, and I'm usually all that is timid and retiring, but suddenly he's on the ground and my tiny ass is hovering menacingly over him. I wonder if he thinks he's gone crazy.

Finally, he stammers, "You...you fucking slapped me!"

"Yeah, I did. And there's more where that came from." I move closer to him, and he actually scoots back away from me as I approach. *Good.* "You do not call any girl a little slut, let alone one who is a literal child. If you *ever* say or do anything inappropriate to or about Molly or any other child in this town, I will track you down. I will beat your ass, and then drag what's left of you down the hill to the police station." My fists clench and my voice trembles, and it takes everything I have not to bend down and hit him again.

All he is doing is staring at me, blinking. He isn't making a single bit of effort to get up. "Are you on bath salts?" he finally mumbles.

I guess he never realized the volcano of anger I've been fighting down inside me for so many years. He seems terrified of it now, and is still trying to rationalize my rage.

I laugh bitterly. "Whatever gets you off my lawn and out of my life, you can feel free to believe. But you really fucked up tonight, and since you can't even figure that out, it's time for you to go."

I ignore the deep panic welling inside of me and just point down the walk. "Let your mother deal with your creepy ass from now on. I'm done."

· · ·

"You're breaking up with me?" That finally gets him to his feet. His smile wavers back onto his face and he lets out an incredulous laugh. "You're kidding me. Over a kid?"

"No, not over a kid. Over your being so fucking inappropriate with the little girl that I babysit that I will never allow you around her again. And God help you when her father finds out about this!" I take a step towards him. He smirks and stands his ground...and when I don't hesitate, he scuttles back like he did from Grant earlier.

"Look, okay, I get it," he says as he backs up with his hands spread in front of him. "You're obviously upset about something. You're not explaining it well because you're upset, and I don't know, maybe you're premenstrual."

I glare at him, and his smile crumbles the rest of the way. "I'll come by tomorrow and see if you're feeling better," he mumbles in a rush, and turns to hurry off down the street.

"Don't bother!" I call after him, but inside my guts are already curdling as I feel the connection between us start to fray. Loneliness yawns like a chasm in my future, and for a split second a wave of terror overwhelms my anger.

There will never be anyone once this one is gone, whispers the fear in the back of my head. The cold starts seeping into my bones and I almost slip as I hurry back inside and lock the door, tears already streaming down my face.

. . .

I CAN'T GET warm even though I know the heat is on full blast. I huddle in my gown and robe on my couch and feel the chill like a patch of ice deep inside me.

BUT DESPITE MY PANIC, and despite my pain, I don't call James. He's spent months making me realize that sometimes the loneliness I fear is safer than being with the wrong person. And James isn't just wrong for me—he's wrong for the other people in my life, few though they may be.

If he was just a danger to me, or to my wallet, that would be one thing. But he showed no consideration for that poor child, and didn't even seem to be aware that he was doing anything wrong. *Or maybe he just doesn't care.*

ONE OF THE things I learned during all those lonely nights of my childhood was to force myself to stop dwelling on how unfair it was I had no one to care for me. Self-pity has only ever brought me down.

BUT RIGHT NOW, it is so hard not to fall into a depression that I feel like I'm being haunted. Every room in my huge house yawns around me like the vacuum of space, deepening the chill inside of me.

IN MY MIND I'm not here, safe in my home any more.

I'M ON THE STREET, sleeping beside a dumpster now that I've aged out of the group home I grew up in, scratching bedbug bites that leave scars on my skin for almost a year. I'm starving, having lost twenty pounds in two months—not a pound of which I can spare. I'm outside with another group of street kids, nearly getting stabbed over a dry refrigerator box in a rainstorm.

I'm SITTING through Christmas morning on my bunk, watching a dozen other kids tear open gifts from distant relatives and charities. My hands are empty.

I'm IN THE LIBRARY, reading old news articles on the computer as I linger there to stay warm, and coming across the story about my parents, and how they died.

THEN MY PHONE is ringing in the pocket of my robe, and I'm back in the present again, heart pounding as I pull it out.

"Hello?" I mumble, my lips still numb. The feelings from my past recede enough that I can think and talk, even with my face streaked with tears.

"HI THERE." Not James—*thank God*—but Grant, sounding concerned. "I heard yelling. Are you all right?"

MY THROAT TIGHTENS and I squeeze my eyelids shut. I don't want his pity. I don't want to look like a basket case. I don't want to scare him off by seeming needy—I can't risk having one of the only people I actually feel good being around walk out of my life right after James.

"EMILY. SWEETHEART." His voice chides me very gently, and I shiver and swallow hard. "No lies now. Do you need me to come over?"

. . .

I SNIFFLE, and then start sobbing quietly. "Yes," I finally admit. "I'm on my way."

5

GRANT

I can't leave my little girl alone, any more than I can leave Emily alone, so I go to Emily's to pick her up and bring her back to my home. The moment I walk into her house and see the lost look in her eyes, I know I'm doing the right thing. Within five minutes, I'm ushering her in my door, having wrapped her in a down coat over her robe and helped her into proper shoes.

"MOLLY'S SLEEPING," I warn in a hushed voice as I shut the door behind us. She swallows and nods, and I lead her into the house and take her coat. My house is a bit smaller than hers, but it's fully decorated, mostly in warm wood tones, cream, and touches of blue. The dogs have woken up and come padding down the stairs to greet us, feathery gold tails wagging hard as they see Emily.

"Hi guys," she says in a weepy voice as she crouches down to hug them and get some doggie kisses. She's breathing raggedly, fighting a fit of tears with all her remaining strength. I don't know exactly what's wrong, but I can guess that it has to do with James's supremely creepy antics earlier.

. . .

I GOT in earshot of him within a few seconds of seeing that little creep crouch down to confront Molly. Just that one same question, over and over again. "Hi honey. If you want candy, I gotta get you to answer something...Is he fucking her? No, no, tell me first, then candy. That's the deal. Is. He. Fucking. Her?"

IT WAS ALL I could do not to lay him out at his mother's feet with one punch for exposing Molly to that. And now, it seemed, I have to clean up the rest of his mess.

AT LEAST IT is Emily that needs caring for. That is hardly a chore. As I lead her over to the couch with the dogs trailing after, I can feel her shaking. I do my best to keep calm and keep my voice low as I help her sit down, and then sit down beside her.

"CAN I GET YOU ANYTHING, SWEETHEART?" I ask, covering one of her hands with my own. The dogs flop down at our feet and watch us, both doing the worried eyebrow-wiggle dogs do when they sense tension.

SHE SMILES SADLY. "In a little. Right now I probably won't be able to keep anything down."

"EMILY, this isn't good. This guy..." I hesitate, seeing her lips start to tremble. "Okay, look. How about you talk, and I listen?" I drag a box of tissues closer.

HER SMILE IS thin and wobbly, ready to go away with the slightest hint of additional pain. But I'm not giving it to her. It's why I'm not sitting there bitching about the asshole who has latched onto her. Pressuring her to kick James to the curb wouldn't work anyway; too easy for her to view it as criticism of her for being victimized.

"I CONFRONTED him about what he did to Molly when he tried to come over. He wasn't even supposed to come over that late. But he didn't care. He started complaining about his mom "smothering" him, but I know he basically wanted a booty call." The corner of her mouth tugs up a little bit, as if she's taking bitter satisfaction in what happened next.

I SMILE AT HER ENCOURAGINGLY. "So you gave him hell, huh? Thanks for that. I'm afraid if I did it he'd end up in the hospital and me behind bars. I'm not lying when I say that the guy deserves it."

"YOU'RE PROBABLY RIGHT...HE tried to say that it was fine to talk like that to a nine-year-old. Then he insulted her and I..." She trails off, going from pale to red and then back again. "Sort of...might have...committed assault against him."

I STARE. "YOU PUNCHED HIM?"

"SLAPPED." She's red again, but fighting down a tiny, naughty, maybe even proud smile. "I um...knocked him off the porch. He didn't want to come too close to me after that."

HOLY SHIT. She should have dressed as Wonder Woman tonight. I blink at her several times, not sure what to say—and then I have to stifle a laugh behind my hand before I wake up Molly. "You're kidding me!"

"Um, no, not at all. He actually was very surprised. But he wouldn't stop no matter what I told him, and he wanted to get into my house when I had already decided not to let him in tonight." She runs a hand back through her tangled curls, which have all but escaped her ponytail.

"Is this his usual kind of behavior? I thought that you were pretty serious with him." I can't keep the concern out of my voice.

"He's never been this bad. I think that for a while he was on his best behavior until he could take a guess at how much bullshit I would put up with. But he was wrong." She wipes a tear away with her fingers and I hand her the Kleenex box.

"You seem pretty upset for someone who just dropped about a hundred and seventy pounds of dead weight, honey." I can't help but move closer and slip an arm around her. She shivers, and for a moment I hesitate and almost pull away—but then she moves closer and throws an arm around my chest.

It takes everything I have to ignore my body's immediate response to her warm softness pressed against me. I haven't had a lover in over six months, and I'm suddenly remembering how much I miss it. I force myself to just sit there, enjoying her sweet smell and her shining hair spilling onto my shoulder as she lays her cheek against me.

. . .

"HE's the only one who's ever loved me," she mumbles, and I go cold.

I HESITATE. If I say "that wasn't love" it could throw her deeper into despair. I could confess my own feelings for her, and hope that she trusts it. I have to step carefully, because as loving and thoughtful as Emily is, she is also inexperienced as hell—and scarred.

SHE's CONFIDED some about her lack of a family—and I've done the research on her biological parents. The newspaper articles, the morgue reports on her father's victims, the murder-suicide. I have always hoped that maybe she hasn't actually read all those things, but I know it's a vain hope. It's her personal history, after all.

"SWEETHEART, I'm sorry, but you're wrong," I say finally, reaching over to stroke her hair as she clings to me. "He's not the only person to love you. He's just the first person, and he isn't very good at it. He doesn't treat you well, or the people you care about. And anyone who can't be trusted around a kid probably can't be trusted with your heart or body either."

SHE PRESSES her lips together and those sea-blue eyes get bright again, and I just want to cuddle her until this all goes away. But I can't, can I? I'm too old for her.

"YOU DON'T SEE me as a kid?" she asks softly.

"HUH? Oh. No, no, I don't. I never have. You're younger than me, but you're far from a child. Have I...treated you like you are?" My cock is throbbing inside of my jeans, pushing at the fabric, as her heartbeat picks up against my chest.

She thinks about it a moment. "I don't have much experience," she admits quietly. "Not with people treating me like I'm...not just grown, but...acceptable."

A sudden, ugly suspicion fills my head, and she looks at me in alarm as I tense up. "It's okay," I mumble, and start stroking her hair again. "I just need to ask you some things about James."

If it turns out that that bastard has been playing on her insecurities to get his way, I may just beat the hell out of him, grieving mother or no grieving mother. I don't even care if she sues me.

She raises her head from my shoulder, her eyes bleary and confused. "What is it?"

"Does James know about your past?" I ask her softly. I'm praying that I'm wrong about all this, and he's just another dumb, horny kid with no self-discipline or social skills.

"I...told him I was an orphan and grew up in a group home. He knows I'm here because I won the lottery and that I was on the streets for a while before that." She still sounds confused. "Why?"

"Did you tell him anything about your real name or your parents? Like you told me?" I am keeping my tone as gentle as possible. I can't just tell her that this prick is bad for her and expect it to stick, or expect her to feel strong and supported enough to act on it.

I CAN ALREADY TELL that James isn't going to let this lie. Not after today's drama. He's a dumb, arrogant kid with an attitude problem— he won't know when to let something like this go.

MORE THAN THAT, he's a parasite, and he'll be reluctant to give up someone he's using. He was spoiled as a kid and learned to bank on his looks and manipulation to get everything he ever wanted. He won't believe for a second that, slap or no slap, Emily actually meant it when she dumped him tonight.

HER COPPERY BROWS DRAW TOGETHER. "No, I didn't. I mean, I almost told him my old name, since I don't think he even knows how to do a Google search. But I never told him that part of my life. Not one bit of it."

A HUGE WAVE of relief runs through me. To someone like James, a secret like Emily's murderous parents would only be ammunition. If he ever finds out the whole story, I know it will be all over Woodstock in a matter of days...and poor Emily will suffer because of it. "So you trusted me with that information, but not him? Why?"

AGAIN, that puzzled look—as if she hasn't given much thought to it before. "Instinct," she says quietly. "That and...I'm taking care of your kid. If you found out I was hiding something like that, you might not trust me anymore."

. . .

I GIVE HER A SUPPORTIVE SMILE. "I want to think that I would understand better than you think, sweetheart, but that wasn't my point." I rub my chin. "Let me put this another way then. Would you ever trust James with that information?"

"No," she says immediately, and then pauses. I can see her mind chewing all this over, and she doesn't seem very happy with the conclusion she's drawing. "He's used the homeless and orphan part against me in arguments and when he's wanted something. Telling him my parents went on a killing spree and then finished each other off before the police could catch them would...he..."

HER EYES WIDEN, and even though I feel bad I have to put her through this turmoil to bring her to these realizations, most of what I feel is relief. She's getting there.

"LOOK, sweetheart, I know it's your life, and I admit I have some ulterior motives, but the bottom line is, I care about you. I don't want to see you hurt by this guy or anyone else." We're cuddling again, and her eyes are dry now as she gazes up at me. She has relaxed a little bit.

"I TOLD HIM TO GO AWAY," she murmurs, and I nod at her. "But...is that...good enough?"

"No, no. I'm sorry, but chances are, no. Chances are, he's going to show up with flowers, or bud, or some gift that might actually be thoughtful, and he's going to try every day until he wins you back." I feel terrible telling her all this.

·   ·   ·

"So he's devoted...but only because he wants something from me. Money. Sex." She laughs sadly and has to reach for another tissue.

"I'm sorry, sweetheart. It's part of why I keep saying that you deserve better. Because you really, really do. You deserve to be with someone who will make you happy." *Someone like me.* It's on the tip of my damn tongue, but I can only imagine the emotional whiplash that would cause.

"How do you know so much about what James will do?" She doesn't sound suspicious—just surprised. "You don't seem like the kind of person who would end up treating a girl like that, even when you were James's age."

I've got about a decade on James, which of course is a lot of time for growing up, but something in her tone catches my attention. "How...old did James tell you he is?"

"Three years older than me. Twenty-two." She gives me a blank look as my heart sinks. "Why?"

"Sweetie, he's almost thirty." Her eyes widen in horror, and I sigh, suddenly wishing I had a joint. I don't keep any in the house with Molly around, though.

"What?"

. . .

MY HEART SINKS at the horror in her tone. *She really doesn't like older guys,* I think with a mix of disappointment and self-disgust.

"LOOK, I know you have lived in Woodstock for a lot of years, but...I...." Her eyes track back and forth in shock and horror.

"YEAH, well, he's a local kid, and he's always pissing somebody off, so word gets around. He's a bad case of arrested development."

A VERY BAD CASE. Always in denim and hoodies or skater wear, dressing like a teenager, acting like one, too. Working shitty low-level jobs because he has no focus. Hanging out with younger kids and pretending to be one, because he can't keep friends long and the new crop will think he's cool because he brings the weed.

WOODSTOCK HAS ALWAYS BEEN full of people like James, male and female, never wanting to grow up or support themselves—or anyone else. I love my town, but it's got problems—and James is absolutely one of them.

"OH GOD, how...I mean...how can someone get to be almost thirty and be that...childish?" she says in shocked disgust. "I understand him maybe being spoiled as a kid, and I know people my age don't always make the best decisions, but he's..."

SHE TRAILS OFF, hands over her face, and I pet her hair and wait for her. Finally, she lifts her head, still looking a bit sniffly and red-eyed. "You never answered my question. How do you know so much about guys like James, anyway?"

. . .

I HESITATE. I don't want to bring up my idiot younger brother Evan unless I have to. Not yet. "I...I've seen guys like James before. I went to Yale with a ton of them. They don't have money of their own since they won't actually work, but they're really used to living lavishly off other people's money. So once their parents get sick of them, they latch onto someone else."

I GESTURE FOR A MOMENT, trying to come up with the best way of saying this. "You are new to being wealthy, you are very young, and you have very little social and romantic experience. You also tend to withdraw from people."

I SAY this as kindly as I can, but she still looks a little embarrassed and has to wipe her eyes again. "James is a predator and an opportunist. He probably thought you would be an easy target. I'm just really glad he was wrong."

"ME TOO." She takes a shivery breath. "Love shouldn't hurt this much. I don't know much about it, but I do know that much."

"No, no, it never should. Something is wrong if it does." I wish I could have found her before James, so I could have helped her build up her sense of self-respect before he had a chance to pounce. I don't know if he conned her into sex yet, but I know he must have made a pest of himself trying.

"I'M...SO glad I never said yes to him moving in," she murmured in breathless horror. "Maybe I should take a break from dating. I've even thought about just giving up and being that spinster lady with a million pets," she mumbles.

THE AMOUNT of alarm I feel as she states this is almost ridiculous. "Uh, please don't do that. At least not the spinster part." I laugh awkwardly, and she blinks. I speak hastily. "Every unmarried man in the state of New York would be disappointed if you did that, including me."

NOW SHE REALLY IS STARING AT me, because I really did just put my foot in it in a gigantic way. I just gave away everything. I feel like a horny, awkward idiot. She just broke up with someone. Even if I wasn't twice her age—!

SHE DARTS FORWARD SUDDENLY, and I feel her soft little lips caress my own. I freeze in place, absolutely astonished, and stare down at her, blinking. My whole body is thrumming with the urge to return the kiss...and do a whole lot more. But instead, I hold still, my arms still around her, but letting her call the play.

"I'LL KEEP that in mind for when I'm over this mess," she says softly, and I feel my heart leap with relieved amazement.

6

EMILY

I'm sleeping in my bed, but somehow I'm also back in Grant's living room, curled in his arms with the dogs at our feet, kissing him. Everything is hazy and sweet, but underneath all that is my hunger to feel more of him. His mouth...his hands...his body.

What I feel for Grant is far more real than what I felt for James, because there's nothing forced or uncomfortable about it. James's attention lured my starving heart—lured me all the way into bed with him. It's not that I didn't feel any desire for him—he is handsome, and I did want him at first. But in spite of my initial desire for him, what happened after I joined him in bed killed my desire and left me frustrated and unfulfilled.

Not to mention sore, sticky, disgusted, and in need of a shower.

Love isn't supposed to be like that, Grant reassured me on that weepy night I broke up with James, and more than once in the week since. I believe him. And after his admission—and that kiss—I'm starting to understand what it might feel like, with the right man.

He's twice my age. People will talk. I don't know if I could ever be a good mom to Molly. But still, here I am on the couch with him again, for the third night this week.

We kiss like we're starved for each other, our hands working under each other's clothes, and I remember again that beautiful, delirious hunger I felt my first time—before James ruined everything. But this time it's far stronger, and far more pure—with no misgivings, no fear.

The lights go out. The feeling of his hands on me grows vague as my dreaming mind gropes for tender sensations...and finds no memory to pin these feelings on. Instead, we kiss and kiss endlessly, until I feel his weight sink down over me, and my desire and bliss grow so sharp and strong they wake me up.

I sit up, gasping in the dark with my whole body trembling, nipples painfully hard, cunt aching with so much need that it alarms me. The fact that it's a dream disappoints me deeply...but I know it's for the best. Grant is interested, and so am I...but I have healing to do.

"Grant and Molly have invited me to Thanksgiving and Christmas," I tell my financial advisor, Ora Northman, during our monthly check in a week and a half later. "It's my first time, um, celebrating."

Ora is in her forties and built like a fertility goddess, with long jet-black micro-braids, bronze skin, generous features and intense, dark eyes that stare at me shrewdly. "Emily, the more you tell me about that group home you grew up in, the more I think they were crazy to put you there. How does that place still have its license?"

"I don't know. Grant sometimes talks about suing them. But I'm wondering if exposing them wouldn't do more. I have enough money, now." I don't know what I would do if I had the kind of money Grant has—I can hardly figure out what to do with my millions, never mind a couple billion. I know he's invested heavily in many charity and community programs, and that he has a huge trust fund for Molly, but my eighteen million after taxes is more than enough for me.

Especially with Ora guiding me in how to manage it.

"That's an interesting idea, but you have to do it in a way that won't lead to them suing. Though provoking them to make the first move legally might actually be shrewd, if you're planning to see them in court anyway." She winks, and I fight a smile.

"Maybe. Right now I have some more immediate problems, and I...well..." I squirm in my plush velvet seat as I sit across the desk from her. The chairs are done up in rosewood and deep burgundy, and the velvet hisses slightly against the back of my forest green wool dress.

"Emily, you know I told you to come to me with anything. I know you're kind of short on friends right now, since you're out on your own for the first time. It hasn't been that long. I'm just glad to hear Grant and Molly are stepping up. Now, what's this about that boy James?"

"I broke up with him," I say, and she cracks a smile.

"Well it's about time! We'll have to celebrate." Her eyes twinkle, and I know what that means—sugar-loaded cappuccinos at the coffee shop on the corner. Her office in Poughkeepsie is home to a lot of cafes, being right near the college campus.

"Sounds good. Grant doesn't need me for Molly until late morning tomorrow, so I don't mind a late drive back." I'm proud of myself for getting so used to driving. I have gotten good at it with Grant and Ora's careful help.

"Good!" She checks the figures on her laptop. "Well, we're seeing the same kind of slow but steady growth on your mixed investments. Precious metals will be up all through this half of the year thanks to the holidays and end-of-year investments, so you'll see a bonus here. On a conservative estimate with your mixed portfolio, you'll be seeing roughly one million a year after taxes. How much that grows will depend on how much you reinvest."

I nod, struggling to follow along, as my head is still full of gossip about James and Grant. It's a staggering amount. I can't even imagine how I could spend a million a year. "Probably at least half of it."

"That's wise." She types a few notes as I sit there thinking.

And then it comes to me. The mess that James has left me with leaves my head altogether for one amazing moment of clarity. "I've got it."

"You've got what?" Ora raises an eyebrow and her hands drift toward her keyboard.

"Buy it."

She blinks once, and then both her eyebrows go up. "Buy Cranburg House? The group home where you grew up?"

"If I sue them that place will collapse completely, and the kids still stuck there will have nowhere to go through no fault of their own. If I buy the owner out, fire any of the staff who are part of the problem, and take over..."

Ora's face brightens "Now this sounds like an actual plan for your future besides 'recover from everything in my new house' like you've been doing so far." She leans forward, fingers steepling. "Tell me more."

By the time we leave for the coffee house, we have the basic outline of a plan to approach the absentee owner of Cranburg House about selling. We both order peppermint mochas with ridiculous amounts of whipped cream and a pair of cannolis that threaten both my outfit and my waistline, but at the moment, I barely care.

Even with the mess of my breakup, I have things to look forward to now. The gentle heat that's growing between me and Grant. My growing investments. My developing life goals. The list of good things coming my way keeps getting longer. And as for my past...well, it will be a great help knowing that the place that stole my childhood won't have a chance to do that to anyone else.

Maybe I really can handle this whole "adulting" thing after all, and maybe I'm more than just a lucky lottery winner. Maybe it will all be okay...if I can get rid of James for good.

"So, I know we didn't have time for it during your hour, but I was wondering what happened with your now ex-boyfriend. Have you seen him since you threw him out?" Ora slices the tip off one of the cannolis with the edge of her fork and scoops it into her mouth.

"Every single night around midnight, he gets drunk and tries to come by to 'make up.' The neighbors have called the cops on him twice." I sigh and take a sip of my drink, then wipe cream off the end of my nose.

"So you've never let him in?"

I shake my head. I have managed to stay strong, mostly because of Grant and Molly. Molly needs to be as far away from James as possible, just like me. As for Grant...unlike James, who half-assed everything, Grant's actions, his words—*that kiss*—all tell me that he is offering the real thing.

I am tired of living on emotional scraps. I want this. I don't want James. "No. Once I found out he's twenty-eight and has been scamming rich women for a decade, I was done."

"He's twenty-eight?" Her perfectly lined brows go up before crumpling in disgust. "Ew."

I suddenly find myself rushing to defend...something. "It's not his age. I would actually prefer someone more mature than me, but...James lied. He's also...less mature than me, by a lot."

"Yeah, I'm getting that impression. So what about this guy Grant? You're spending the holidays with him. I know he's a little old for you, but have you ever thought...?" Ora props her chin on her hand and gives me a thoughtful little half-smile. "I mean, it sounds like you're already becoming a part of his life."

I take a deep breath, and come out with it. Ora is very observant and doesn't like her intelligence being insulted. "I love him. And I know he likes me. He's even attracted to me. I just don't know..." I chew my lip, and then distract myself with a few bites of my cannoli.

"You don't know what, honey?" Ora sits back, an amused look in her eyes. "It sounds pretty straightforward to me. You love the guy, and he sounds good for you. As for James, well, his mom can take care of him, since she's the one who spoiled him."

A weight lifts off my heart at her words, but the apprehension behind it doesn't quite go away. "I haven't ever been in love before. What if I mess things up?"

She gazes at me with those shrewd eyes and I feel a little foolish, but she's still smiling. "Then you apologize, learn from it, and try again. Relationships don't usually die on one screw-up, honey, they die from people's refusal to grow and learn to do better by each other."

7

EMILY

I'm still thinking about Ora's advice as I pull into my driveway. I drove happily the whole way home. Under the bright moonlight and the glare from the highway lights, I listened to soundtracks from some of my favorite movies so lyrics didn't distract me from the road. My heart was full of optimism thanks to my time with Ora, and that feeling lasts up until the moment my headlights splash across James lounging against my garage door.

FOR A MOMENT, I fantasize about hitting the gas instead of the brakes and sending him flying through the heavy wood door. I can afford a really good lawyer now, after all. But then I force myself to stop, and calm down as best I can. *I'm not like my father.*

STILL, I'm good and angry when I finish locking my car and turn to go up the walk.

· · ·

I WALK RIGHT PAST JAMES, ignoring him as he tries to talk to me, and only hesitate when I reach the edge of my porch. It's even colder than the night we broke up, my breath misting and a few flakes of snow drifting down.

"HEY," he calls after me, sounding shocked and outraged. His hand grabs my shoulder, and my skin crawls as I immediately struggle to shake him off. "Come on, Emily! You won't even talk to me!"

I SPIN AROUND, breaking his grip, my eyes flashing. "Do not put your hands on me. You've lost that privilege for good."

HIS HANDS GO UP as his eyes widen. "Holy fuck, don't hit me again!"

I put my hands on my hips to keep them from going around his throat. "You are pushing thirty, James. Do not pull this scared little boy shit with me. And don't play stupid, either. You know why I have a problem with you right now. So get the hell off my land!"

I DON'T KNOW how I keep my voice down, but apparently the look on my face is enough to unnerve him. But he still stupidly stands his ground. "This isn't fair, Emily. So I lied about my age and wasn't polite to some stupid kid you're babysitting. Fuck that brat and her dad, it's not like you need the paycheck!"

"FEAR OF CONSEQUENCES is not the only reason to be a decent person, James. But if that's the only thing that will work for you, then fine. I'll get a restraining order." Ora seconded Grant's opinion that I should get one, and after this, I'm sold.

. . .

"A RESTRAINING ORDER?" The incredulous laugh in his voice makes me sick. "That's completely crazy, Emily! Come on, baby, don't be like this. Don't do this. I love you."

"No, you don't, okay? Stop it, James. You want my money, and my body. You don't want me. And you don't even need any of that, because if your mother will keep putting up with you after you accost a child right in front of her, she is *never* going to cut you loose." How am I keeping my voice so even?

"WRONG. JESUS, YOU ARE SO WRONG." The laugh in his voice sounds more nervous than mocking now. "Of course I want you. Your money and your booty are all just part of the package! And I like the package." He gives me a sleazy smile, and my stomach lurches.

"BUT YOU DON'T GIVE a fuck about what's inside," I mumble. I turn to walk away—and he tries to grab me again.

Neither of us have raised our voices. Neither one of us has knocked anything over. Yet somehow, someone has noticed us.

I DISCOVER that Grant has let his dogs off their leash mid-walk when two big, barrel-chested streaks dart up the walk and skid to a stop right beside me. Pogo and Mike stand at each of my flanks, and one of them—Mike, I think—lets out a deep growl.

JAMES SKITTERS BACKWARD AGAIN, and I glare at him. "Look. You had several chances. You fucked up, you lied, and you keep doing both. You never learn. I cannot deal with that in my life. Go back to your mother and let her take care of you. I need to take care of myself."

. . .

His mouth works, but he hears Grant's heavy tread coming fast through the dark, and looks down into the snarling faces of two very protective dogs. And finally, he backs off, shooting me a petulant glare.

"You know, I get it. You're gonna be a bitch to me for a while because you like kids and I don't. That's fine. I'll find a way back in."

"Hey!" Grant shouts, his voice as growly as those of his dogs, and James darts off into the night like a scared boy half his age. There's a pause—and then, to my shock, Grant runs right past my gate and after James.

Oh shit. Everything seizes up inside of me, and I worry for a moment that this is going to end very badly. Grabbing both dogs' leashes, I let them tug me to the end of the walk, but no further. "Heel!" Thank God they both agree.

I can't see the pair on the dim street beyond my front yard, but I can hear their hushed, harsh conversation. "Look, man, what is your problem?" James whines.

"Stop stalking that girl," comes Grant's cold reply. "Leave her alone. Do not bother her again, or I'll make sure you do a lot more than sit in the drunk tank until Mommy picks you up."

"What the fuck—hey, that's my girlfriend! We're just going through a rough patch." Mock indignation replaces James's wheedling tone. "It's none of your business."

. . .

"It is my business. She's my neighbor, my daughter's caretaker, and my friend. She dumped you weeks ago. Now lay off with this stalker crap and go home."

"Hey, fuck you, man! Her ass is mine! You're not moving in—" The sudden sound of a scuffle cuts off his voice for a few moments. "Ow! Man, what the fuck?"

"You're the idiot who accosted my daughter with inappropriate questions and then doubled down by calling her a 'little slut.' She is *nine*. I have already described the incident to the local cops. Believe me, they are watching your every move now, and if they don't get you...I will." There's so much danger and rage in Grant's voice that it even scares me. Yet somehow, most of what I feel is...gratitude.

"Look, I was drunk."

"That's no fucking excuse. Get out of here, and stay off this street."

I hear James's footsteps scrambling off down the damp sidewalk. My heart is beating so hard that I can't move. I realize that their conversation waded into violent territory, and it scares me.

Then Grant walks into sight and comes toward me with worry in his eyes. "You okay?"

. . .

I SHAKE MY HEAD. "I'm so tired of this. I never know when he's going to pop up outside my house."

HE TAKES me into his arms and hugs me tight, his down coat rustling under my cheek like a pillow. "I'm sorry, sweetheart. I'm glad I was outside when he started this. The cold makes voices carry."

I CLING TO HIM, closing my eyes. "I don't want to be alone tonight," I whisper.

HE FREEZES FOR A MOMENT, and then draws in a long, shuddering breath. Then he leans back to look down at me. "Okay then. Let's pack you a few things. You're staying at my place tonight, and in the morning I'll drive you to the police station to file that restraining order."

"THANK YOU," I mumble into his chest as the dogs mill around our legs.

8

EMILY

Grant insists on being a gentleman. He gets me and my clothes bundled into one of his guest rooms, has a drink with me, and tenderly kisses me goodnight. Then drives me up the wall by *leaving* and going down the hall to climb into his own bed.

Both dogs are in with Molly. I lie there in my bed in the cute, mint green silk nightie I packed, horny and hopeful, and wonder if I dare go down that hall as well. I lie there trying to sleep for several long minutes...but the heat between my thighs that started with Grant's kiss won't go away.

Finally, I get up, trembling in anticipation as much as with nerves, and creep down the hall. His door is ajar. I listen at it for a moment, and then slip inside, closing it quietly behind me.

His bedroom is enormous, dominated by a huge sleigh-frame bed with elaborate carvings and a nest of down comforters. He breathes softly in its embrace, and I move to his side, staring down at his sleeping face. I hope I'm not overstepping myself, but...*maybe he's been waiting for me to make a move this entire time.*

I slip in under the covers and he stirs against me, rolling toward me with a grunt. Too late, I realize that he's almost completely naked, except for a pair of loose drawstring shorts. The heat of his skin sinks into me through the thin silk of my nightie, and I nestle in beside him, already filling with a drowsy delight at his closeness.

He stays asleep; he must be exhausted. One arm slides limply around me, and he buries his face in my hair. My whole body tingles, and without any real knowledge of how to go about these things, I twine one leg around his thigh and rub my body softly against his side.

This time he lets out a little rumble and pulls me closer, and I feel his cock stir against my belly. It feels enormous—thick, hefty, and quickly going from soft brushes against me to a hard push. My belly flutters, and I feel my cunt tighten with the urge to feel him inside me.

I would never have been this bold with James. But I'm realizing now that James never really did much to attract my attention or my desire. He just got in my face with what he wanted, and expected me to deliver. And I did, for a while.

I don't want to push Grant away, ever. I want to draw closer to him, until his warmth sinks all the way in and drives away the chill from deep in my bones. I want to wake up next to him, not some snoring mouth-breather who drinks himself to sleep every night.

Grant's eyes still haven't stirred. I grow braver, climbing atop him as he lies on his back. I draw the quilts around us as I go, so our skin doesn't get chilled.

I am settling in when his eyes finally open, and he smiles.

I freeze for a moment, feeling a little guilty, but unbelievably turned on as well. The corner of his mouth tugs up, and he licks his lips. "I was hoping you'd come visit."

"Oh," I murmur, swallowing hard as chills and waves of heat running through me in turns. "Good."

His hands grip my hips as I straddle his thighs, and he leans up to kiss me, his cock trapped between us. His grip shifts to my ass and he squeezes gently, then more firmly as I rock back against his hands. We kiss, and this time it starts out tender, but catches fire fast as he pulls me closer.

He's careful with his strength, until his kisses and the slow sweep of his hands over my arms and back leave me trembling and feverish. My shyness is ebbing away as everything outside of these new sensations and emotions starts to fade into the background.

My skin feels like it's on fire even in the light, sleeveless silk. His thick fingertips slide under the delicate straps; he can cup a shoulder in each of his big hands. He could break me, if he wanted—he's far stronger than James ever was. But he's also far gentler.

The combination soothes and arouses me even further. It feels like I'm sinking into a hot bath. His kisses intensify and turn lingering and sensual. He darts his tongue into my mouth even as his fingers run over the silk at the sides of my breasts.

He tastes of mint gum and brandy, and I'm almost disappointed when his kiss trails away from my mouth. But then he starts kissing my neck, and his hands slide around to stroke my breasts through the silk, and I whimper, having to grab his shoulder to keep upright. My head falls back into the cup of his palm and he brings his knees up as he lifts his hips under me.

His cock slides against me through two thin layers of cloth, throbbing and jumping a little with each heartbeat. His hands push the straps of the nightgown off my shoulders and tug the thin sheath of cloth downward. I slip my arms free and shimmy slightly, wiggling out of the confining silk until my breasts bounce free and my nipples tighten in the cool air.

He groans and cups them both, pushing them together and leaning forward to bury his face between them. I cradle him, hands buried in his hair, and whimper as his tongue traces over my skin. His breath blows hot over one of my nipples—and then he runs his tongue over it and I almost squirm away from the intensity.

He grips me harder and I struggle a little on reflex as he suckles firmly at my breast in long, slow pulls, filling me with greater pleasure than I have ever experienced. I squirm and whimper as my mind and body try to figure out what to do with all this sensation.

I bite back the urge to moan aloud as he seizes the other nipple with his mouth and sucks it roughly. I whimper, and my body goes rigid and slowly grinds against him. He chuckles against my skin...and then one of his hands lets go of my breast and slips under the nightgown puddled on the tops of my thighs.

I feel his fingertips slide over the outer lips of my cunt and gasp aloud as he starts exploring me. Just the outside at first, stroking softly, before firmly kneading in time to his suckling. The doubled sensation makes it almost impossible to cry out—I'm panting so heavily I can't get my breath.

I rock back and forth on his hard thighs as he kneads and strokes my pussy, then dips his fingers into my aching slit and starts to stroke them up and down. I squirm and he focuses in more and more on my clit, circling two fingertips over it carefully, then more firmly.

I pant, my breath so harsh it burns my throat, but the rest of my body is so feverish with pleasure that even the pain is laced with it. "Oh, oh, oh..." I gasp, feeling my body start to shake uncontrollably, and even the soft vocalizations feel good as they leave my throat.

I want to scream. My head falls back—and his big hand covers my mouth. I whimper through his fingers, mixed with desperate, muffled pleas begging him not to stop.

My hips pump against his thighs as he strokes my clit. I feel him slide down underneath me so that I'm grinding against the thick, hot shaft of his cock, now freed from his briefs. I hear him groan, even as the urge to scream grows in my throat along with the pressure mounting between my hips.

My back arches, my thighs strain, and I lift up on my knees—and he guides me, curling his hips under me to settle me onto his cock inch by inch. He's thick, stretching me, intensifying the sensations as he goes back to pleasuring me.

His attention makes me squirm rhythmically, faster and faster, dancing over and around his cock while he grunts and bucks his head back, a strained look growing on his face. "Yeah! Yeah..." he pants, and starts raising his hips to meet mine.

He sinks deep, filling me as his fingers work their magic—and then he tightens his hand over my mouth again as I explode around him.

My body goes wild, muscles rippling around his shaft as I wail against his hand. It's so *good,* and I squirm wildly against him as spasm after spasm rolls through my body, bringing ecstasy and then deep relief.

When my mind is my own again I look down to see Grant stretched under me, sweat gleaming on his skin, every muscle taut as his hips roll reflexively. Fascinated, I force my tired hips to roll against him, milking his trembling cock.

"Oh, yeah, baby. Yeah, just like that...just there...yeah...." he whispers, clutching my hips as his own move sensually under me. It excites me so much to see him like that that my flesh tightens around him again, and I work my hips harder.

His eyes squeeze closed and his lips part as he lets out a primal shout of pleasure—and then I muffle his groans with my mouth. He lifts his hips hard against me and freezes, and I grind against him with everything I have left.

His grip on me is almost painful as his growling cries vibrate in his throat. Inside of me, his cock pulses hard, and then he slowly goes limp. I'm tired, sore, sweaty, but completely relaxed and feeling strangely...triumphant.

Panting, he draws me down to his chest, smiling into my hair. "I love you, sweetheart," he whispers. "I'm not letting you go after this."

"Don't," I murmur against his throat, tears pricking my eyes. "Don't ever let me go."

GRANT

I didn't let Emily go. James still can't be persuaded to leave her alone—but since he has not actually been violent we couldn't get her an emergency restraining order, and the regular process was delayed by the holidays. So as a solution, Emily came to stay at my home full time.

She's staying in her own room while we try to figure out what to tell Molly. Emily has moved many of her clothes and her laptop in, though she never actually sleeps in that guest bed except to take naps. She sleeps with me...well, eventually she sleeps.

We ate Thanksgiving dinner together and talked about what we wanted to do for Christmas. Emily looks after Molly while I go to meetings—and when I scramble around looking for a proper Christmas gift for the woman I hope to propose to soon.

I don't want to rush her. But every time I wake up to her face, I know that Emily is my second chance at a real love match, and someone who could love my daughter as much as I do. And she seems so much happier with us—she's even stopped having nightmares.

No thanks to James, though.

I hear him banging on the door downstairs and open an eye,

checking my watch. Two fifteen—exactly fifteen minutes after the last bar in Woodstock closes for the night. Emily stirs and I kiss her temple, whispering in her ear, "Shh, I'll take care of it."

James is blocked on Emily's cell phone and her house phone now. We have two of my security guys from the city looking after her house in case that idiot decides to throw another rock through her window. I personally deliver Molly to and from play dates, doctor appointments, and school, and every time that idiot James tries to tail us anywhere I swing right past the police department and he scurries off.

The police are getting as tired of his crap as we are, and every time I call them on him his mother ends up crying on the phone to me about having to bail him out again. I'm losing patience with her as well. Nobody should ever have this big of a blind spot about their offspring. I just pray I can do a lot better by Molly.

I'm in flannel pajama pants with my robe hanging open when I show up downstairs and look out the spyhole. James is out there, eyes bleary, face red and hair mussed. He's forgotten his coat and his breath is misting. He steps forward to bang again—and I open the door and step outside in my slippers, ignoring the chill.

"Get off my porch," I instruct James in a low, cold voice. He stares at me angrily and I see he's drawn a dick in the snow on my SUV windshield. "Leave, James," I sigh—and he spits at me.

I duck aside and it strikes the door, and I take a half-step forward. He scrambles backward away from me, his face screwing up petulantly. "You stole my girl, you piece of shit!"

"Nobody stole anything from you. You drove Emily away and now you're stalking her. I didn't steal her, I'm protecting her. From you." I stare into his eyes—but there's no recognition there. He can't even see that what he's doing is wrong.

"No, no, you're tricking her, and you're keeping her from me." He stabs a finger in my direction, spit spraying from his lips. "And you better give her back before I take away someone of yours!"

I go cold and feel my fists clench hard enough that my knuckles crack. "One, she's a person, not an object, and you're the one who drove her away. Two, if you *ever* threaten me or mine again, the police will be picking you up from the hospital."

He stares back at me defiantly, his chest heaving—and I take another step in his direction. The little coward darts away, leaving me standing there shivering more with anger than with cold.

We don't hear from him again for weeks after that, as the year rolls on toward its close. Christmas decorations go up and we get a live tree like we always do, which we'll plant among its fellows on one side of my yard. I make sure to make the yard ablaze with light from Christmas decorations, leaving as few shadows as possible that James could hide in.

I don't trust his silence, even though it means Emily gets some relief for a while.

It's the first week of December when she belatedly gives me the best idea for a Christmas present. "Would you mind if we visited Cranburg House over Christmas?" she asks softly. "Some of those kids won't get gifts this year."

"We should bring them Christmas too, since you came from there," Molly agrees firmly, and I laugh and nod my concession, outnumbered.

"I'll make some calls," I promise.

Locked in my office, I phone up the director of Cranburg, who is...on vacation. Most of the staff, too. The skeleton crew left includes Marcie, a new caretaker who sounds younger than Emily and a little baffled. It takes her some persuading—including some compensation for her time—but finally she agrees to make the arrangements.

We all go into a whirlwind of buying and preparing as we grab everything ten kids will need for a good Christmas: food, gifts, a tree, games and all. Their dinner will be on the twenty-second, which is the closest day to Christmas where we can get enough staff to take a shift to help us pull it off.

Late that morning the three of us busy ourselves running back and forth to the SUV, packing it full of everything we need to roll up to Cranburg bringing the party with us. We're about halfway through —the dogs are locked in the basement playroom to keep them from getting underfoot, and I'm lugging a stack of boxes out the door when Emily says suddenly, in a high, nervous voice, "Where's Molly?"

For a moment my train of thought derails and I feel a chill roll down my spine. *She's probably in the bathroom,* I try to tell myself, but I know Emily's instincts for danger are keener than mine. "Molly?" I call out from the porch, at the top of my lungs.

Silence.

My world seems to freeze around me—and then a surge of white-hot adrenaline roars through me, thawing me in an instant. "Molly!"

"Stay here," I order Emily, in case Molly wanders up while I'm running around like a madman. I start looking around everywhere—the house, the yard, the neighbor's yard. Nothing. And slowly, my mind comes to the only conclusion it can: *James.*

His threat rings in my head as I race around the side yard back toward Emily. "It's James, he must have grabbed her," I growl, pulling out my cell to call the police. I then notice she already has hers out. "What are you doing?"

"We didn't hear a car, so he's on foot. It's been under five minutes and I've been watching the street. You would have seen him if he tried to cut through the yard, and both your neighbors have dogs. So he must be hiding with her nearby."

That just angers me more. "Molly!" I call, and listen hard for an answer. *I'm gonna kill this guy.* "Are you calling the cops?"

"No," she says with a grim tone." I'm unblocking James and calling him."

"He can't be stupid enough to not mute his phone—" I start, and then remember who I'm talking about and suddenly feel a bit better about my daughter's odds.

A few seconds later, "Twerk It" blares out loudly from a nearby neighbor's bushes.

I cross the street in about two long steps and dive into the mass of branches. James is there, crouched with his hand over Molly's mouth and staring at me in wide-eyed panic.

"I'll hurt her!" he warns—and then yells in pain as Molly bites his hand. I yank his arm from around her and she bolts out of the bushes, running for Emily with a high-pitched scream. Still holding his arm, I use it to yank him all the way out of the bushes and into the middle of the street.

He sprawls on the blacktop, then scrambles up, looking between me and Emily with growing worry. His jaw sets and he takes a step toward my girls, as if planning to try and take a hostage again.

My fist crashes into the side of his head before he's halfway there. He wobbles completely around, stumbles, pitches forward, and lands in a heap at Emily's feet. He looks up at her blearily—and Molly steps forward and kicks him between the eyes. "Jerk. You smell, too. And you're stupid."

James just lies there, probably playing dead so no one will hit him again. I pull Molly back into a tight hug, and she wiggles a bit before relaxing. She's still more furious than scared, and I'm proud of her, just as I am of Emily.

It's a bad lesson to have to teach Molly; violence doesn't solve anything, unless it's something like a complete idiot trying to kidnap you from your family. Then violence is often what's needed—and deserved.

I just wish she could have been a little older before she had to learn that.

Emily hurries to my side. I grab her with my other arm and hug my girls tight. "Sorry, sweetheart, we're gonna be a little late bringing dinner. I gotta drop this guy off with the cops first."

She nods, sighing tiredly. "That's fine. I know we'll get there."

We get there at seven and order massive amounts of pizza so the kids aren't waiting for us to roast the turkey. There are ten of them—all ages, all kinds, most disabled in one way or another. Some of them can't stop fighting, even during dinner, and eye us suspiciously when we bring gifts.

None of them remember Emily, and the staff has turned over so much that nobody there that night was working there when this was her home. But several of the kids do seem happier for our visit, and that's good. They're going to be seeing a lot of us, soon.

Three days later, I wake up around dawn curled around Emily

from behind, and look out the window to see snow falling past the panes in thick, feathery flakes. Molly hasn't stirred yet; I know because as soon as she's fully awake she'll be in here like a shot demanding presents, with two rambunctious dogs on her heels.

I smile and settle back in, burying my nose in Emily's hair. She stirs and rolls over, opening her eyes blearily, and I kiss her on the nose. "Good morning," I murmur.

Emily smiles. "Good morning."

It's been a rough three days. We're pressing charges against James for his kidnapping attempt, but his mother's being a pest about it and will likely hire him a very good lawyer. It will be something of a long haul to get rid of him for good—but that's fine. I'm willing to fight for my new family.

"Mmm," she murmurs as I cup her breast and pull her closer. "How much time do we have before we deal with Christmas morning stuff?"

"Enough, I'm sure," I reply, my cock stirring against her belly as I lean over to kiss her.

As if on cue, from outside my door we hear, "Daaaaad! It's Christmaaaaas!"

Emily bursts into giggles as I back off and grin sheepishly. "Or not."

The End

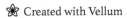 Created with Vellum

CPSIA information can be obtained
at www.ICGtesting.com
Printed in the USA
BVHW041444040221
599006BV00069B/2276

BEST
PUB WALKS
ON
TYNESIDE

Lydia Speakman &
Richard Baker

Published by Sigma Leisure – an imprint of
Sigma Press, 1 South Oak Lane, Wilmslow, Cheshire SK9 6AR, England.

British Library Cataloguing in Publication Data
A CIP record for this book is available from the British Library.

ISBN: 1-85058-461-3

Typesetting and Design by: Sigma Press, Wilmslow, Cheshire.

Cover photograph: The Tyne Bridge

Maps: Morag Perrott

Photographs: the authors

Printed by: MFP Design & Print

Disclaimer: the information in this book is given in good faith and is believed to be correct at the time of publication. No responsibility is accepted by either the author or publisher for errors or omissions, or for any loss or injury howsoever caused. Only you can judge your own fitness, competence and experience.

Contents

Introduction

Walking and discovering Tyneside   **1**
   Tyneside   **2**
   Tyneside beers, pubs and breweries   **6**
   Practical points   **10**

The Walks

1. Newcastle Town Trail   **12**

Distance: 2 miles, 3km

2. Jesmond Dene   **22**

Distance: 5 miles, 8km

3. The Newcastle Moors   **30**

Distance: 5 miles, 8km

4. Rising Sun Country Park and The Coxlodge Waggonway   **35**

Distance: 7 miles, 11km

5. Earsdon Village   **40**

Distance: 6 miles, 9.5km

6. The Avenue Branch Line **44**

Distance: 9 miles, 14km

7. Holywell Dene **50**

Distance: 8½ miles, 13km

8. Big Water **54**

Distance: 10½ miles, 17km

**9. The Wallbottle Waggonway
– a walk from Lemington to Ponteland** **60**

Distance: 6½ miles, 10km

10. The Upper Tyne **65**

Distance: 9 miles, 14.5km

11. A Wylam Circular – on the track of the railways **72**

Distance: 10 miles, 16km

12. The Shields Ferry **79**

Distance: 8 miles, 12km

13. Marsden Rock Circular **85**

Distance: 5 miles, 8km

14. Under the Tyne on the trail of The Venerable Bede **91**

Distance: 3 miles, 4.5km

15. A Jarrow March **96**

Distance: 12 miles, 19km

16. Derwent Valley Circular   **104**

Distance: 13 miles, 21km or 10 miles, 16km

17. The Bowes Railway   **110**

Distance: 13 miles, 21km

18. Chopwell Woods Circular   **117**

Distance: 10 miles, 16km

19. The South Bank of the Tyne   **124**

Distance: 5½ miles, 8km

20. Blaydon Burn Circular   **129**

Distance: 9½ miles, 15km

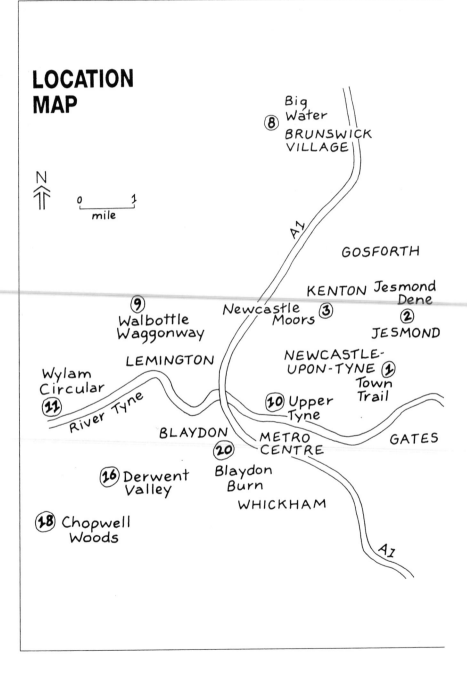

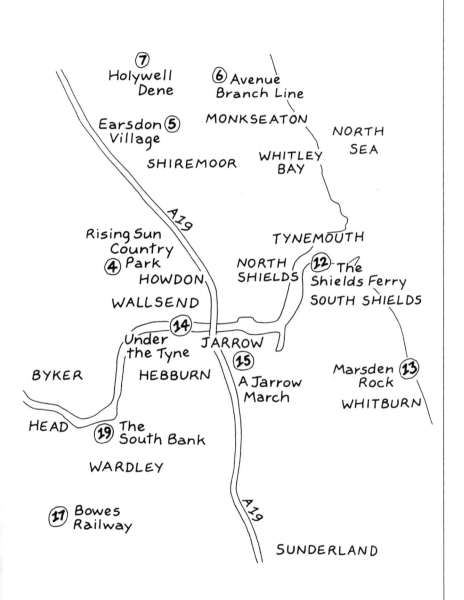

To our son, Keir, born a true Geordie

Walking and discovering Tyneside

Most regular walkers would agree that a good walk and a good pub either at lunch time or at the end of a day's walk, are what a day out in the fresh air is all about. This book is an attempt to formalise that relationship, by designing a series of walks featuring a good pub. However, this is neither a good pub nor a good beer guide. While many of the pubs are CAMRA listed, the book has been written to help walkers explore the countryside in and around Tyneside.

Tyneside is not an area normally associated with country rambles and yet, with its network of old waggonways and coastal paths, it offers urban fringe walking at its best. It is an area rich in industrial heritage, and this collection of twenty walks not only offers the opportunity to explore attractive leafy paths along the River Tyne and stunning views from surrounding hills, but also provides a chance to discover the history of old Tyneside.

Cities like Manchester, Birmingham and Leeds have their networks of canal towpaths and their mill chimneys. Tyneside has its river and its network of old waggonways and railways woven through a landscape which has remained surprisingly rural in character. The River Tyne, just as it was critical to the development of Tyneside itself, is central to this book. The river and its banks are visible from the majority of the walks, with routes along its banks, over its many bridges and using the Shields Ferry and the Tyne pedestrian tunnel to get both over and under the Tyne.

All the walks in this book have been designed to be accessible by public transport, and indeed many are linear. This is not only because the existing network of footpaths does not always enable the development of circular routes, but the excellent Tyne & Wear Metro, means that there is no reason to rely on the car. The Metro enables walkers to escape the umbilical chord mentality of a parked car and walk to a destination with a purpose.

Though a relatively small area, Tyneside has within its bounds a host of landscape contrasts on the doorstep of a major urban centre: deep rural countryside, open fields, dramatic coast line, attractive riverside walks, old industrial districts and the brave architecture of 1990s regeneration. We hope this book inspires you, as it did us in its preparation, to get out and discover what Tyneside has to offer to those prepared to look for it.

Tyneside

There is no doubt that Tyneside is unique. It has its own special identity which is difficult to quantify, but is wrapped up in its history and its people – the Geordies. There has been much debate about where the name Geordie derives from. Some suggest the name was given to supporters of the Hanoverians in the 1745 Jacobite Rising, most of whom lived south of the river. Others argue it was the name given to coal miners, derived from the pit safety lamp originally designed by George Stephenson. Others say it was a name given to those with a Tyneside accent, which was first used in Parliament when George Stephenson, a Tynesider, gave evidence to a Parliamentary Inquiry in 1826. Whatever its origins, most people would accept it is a title that those born four miles either side of the banks of the Tyne between Shields and Hexham are entitled to claim. Its a title to be worn with pride, going beyond the mere description of an accent, to embrace a state of mind and a shared culture which articulates itself in a certain sense of humour, a warmth of spirit and keen sense of loyalty to the region, expressed by many in a fanatical support for the 'Toon Army', Newcastle United.

Geography has shaped Tyneside and its people. The River Tyne was for many centuries an important border marking firstly the division between the Brigantes and Votadini (a neighbouring Celtic tribe) and then the edge of the civilised Roman Empire and the untamed Celts to the north. In later years the Tyne lay at the heart of the area dominated by the Border Wars between Scotland and England, resulting in centuries of tension, which was only finally resolved by the end of the 18th century. That feeling of being at the edge of England, 200 miles from London still seeps into the culture of the region, with an interesting mixture of ambivalence and hostility to national government.

Equally the River Tyne has been key to the area's industrial development and with it the shape of its urban settlements and its subsequent character. The river provided the cheap water transport to enable the coal reserves which lay beneath the region to be properly exploited. Indeed coal mining has been far and away the most dominant influence over the last 400 years. In the early days coal would have been moved from the shallow drift mines by horse and cart to waiting boats along the riverside. However, in the 17th century experiments began with simple waggonways. Wooden rails were constructed out of timber, enabling horses to pull laden wagons much more efficiently and quickly. The earliest documented waggonway in North East England was near Blyth in Northumberland, which was probably opened in 1609 to carry coal from mines near Bedlington to the River Blyth. This particular venture was not a success and it closed down in 1614, but the advantage of running wagons on rails, primitive as they were, had been demonstrated and by the start of the 18th century an extensive network of waggonways had been built throughout Tyneside. Waggonways were built on the north bank of the Tyne from Heddon, Holywell Main, Montague and from Wylam. The region's largest and most important waggonway network was, however, on the south bank of the Tyne.

The expansion of the waggonways paralleled the increased demand for coal as industrialisation began to spread. It led to the development of a patchwork of small mining communities each centred around its pithead and linked to a growing network of waggonways and plate inclines.

By 1820 the North East provided 95% of London coal's supply. Indeed, Newcastle's supremacy, until the mid 19th century, in coal markets at home and abroad remained entirely due to its cheap water transport, and the City's control of the river traffic. During that period the river would have been full of keel boats taking the coal down stream to sea going colliers anchored at the mouth of the Tyne. This trade encouraged the development of a range of subsidiary industries concerned with the building of ships, and the manufacture of anchors, ropes, sails and tackle, as well as the chemical industry to produce the tar for caulking and paint.

Elsewhere on Tyneside a salt making industry had developed in South Shields using sea water and coal. Coal was also an important factor in helping the development of glass and paper industries, the former becoming particularly important in Gateshead, South Shields and Sunderland

The importance of such Tyneside pioneers as Timothy Hackworth and George and Robert Stephenson to the development of the railways in Britain, is well documented. As in other parts of Britain, the contribution made by the railways to the development of industrialisation and the growth of towns and cities, was crucial to the shaping of modern Tyneside. In particular, the coming of the railways enabled the coal industry to expand and develop further. By 1910 the Northumberland and Durham coal fields were producing more than 50 million tonnes a year of which 19 million were exported mostly via the Tyne to London and abroad. The growth of the region's coal industry continued until the mid 1920s by which time around two thirds of the region's output was being exported to the continent and further afield, and more than a quarter of the area's working population was employed in the industry.

The first industry to rival the importance of coal was metals, first iron and then steel. In the mid-19th century iron began to replace wood as the main construction material for coal trucks, rails and iron plate for ships. But it was shipbuilding and the associated heavy engineering industries which were to dominate the fortunes of many Tynesiders.

The Tyne has had a ship building tradition going back to medieval times. Early ships were small, but the demands of the coal trade soon led to the building of bigger sea going colliers, which were too big to be used on the then undredged and difficult to navigate Tyne. Lighter keels were therefore used to carry coal from the mines and staithes up river above Newcastle, to colliers lying along the coast. These Tyne keels were oval, flat bottomed, square sailed and propelled by two long oars.

In the 1850s the Tyne Improvement Commission, oversaw improvements to the River Tyne, removing sand banks and dredging the main river channel to make it accessible to larger ships. It coincided with the beginnings of a ship building industry, first based on iron plate and later steel. One of the first iron ships launched on the Tyne was at Walker in 1840, the paddle steamer Prince Albert. In 1852 Charles and George Palmer built the John Bowes, the first screw propelled collier, capable of carrying 650 tons of coal to London in 48 hours.

By the 1880s shipyards on the Tyne and Wear rivers were producing more than a quarter of the world's ships. With the birth of Armstrong's armaments works at Elswick, the last quarter of the 19th century saw the Tyneside shipyards move into warship construction. By then most ship building was concentrated along the 5 miles between Bill Point and Albert Dock with repairers and fitters nearer the river mouth.

During the First World War and its immediate aftermath, naval contracts kept Tyneside shipyards busy, but by the late 1920s the industry was in decline. The National Shipbuilders Securities Company in 1930 set about rationalising the industry and dismantling some of the less profitable yards. Palmers' Jarrow shipyard was one of them causing 60% unemployment in the town and considerable hardship.

There was a short lived revival in the ship building industry's fortunes during the Second World War, and the closure of the Suez Canal in the 1950s, led to a demand for 'Super Tankers' and the great ship yards of companies like Swan Hunter's flourished. But today, the ship yards have all but disappeared, leaving a few smaller companies specialising in repairs and fitting, whilst the last shipbuilder on the Tyne, Swan Hunters hangs on by the edge of its fingertips. It has been a rapid and sudden decline in the heavy engineering industries, the impact of which still resonates throughout Tyneside. In 1980, 30% of the workforce was involved in heavy engineering; in 1995 it was just 1%. This has coincided with a similar decline in smaller industries such as glass, soap, salt, paper and textiles.

Coal mining has virtually disappeared from the region, with the exception of a few open cast mines. The decline began in the 1960s, when there was a worldwide switch to oil and later gas. Between 1957 and 1974 the North East lost 100,000 jobs in mining from a total of 150,000. The last two pits in the North East closed in 1992, ensuring that the phrase 'sending coal to Newcastle' was finally made redundant.

Some of the jobs have been replaced by the service sector which now employs 80% of Newcastle's work force. It is a shift in employment which is perhaps best symbolised by the new MetroCentre on the southern banks of the Tyne, a complex of 360 retail outlets under one roof. On the banks of the Tyne, the river frontage is beginning to change out of all recognition. Gone are the ships, the cranes, the redundant plant and the coal waggons, and in their place new industrial parks, new hi-tech companies, marina villages and attractive bollard-lined walkways which thread their way through new green corridors.

Yet for all the changes of the late twentieth century, the essential character of the Tyneside landscape and its people remain the same. The famous Tyne bridges still survive and it is still possible to trace the routes of the 18th and 19th century waggonways and railways, in places where urban expansion, new roads or opencasting have not disturbed the landscape. The River and the familiar landmarks and the hills which surround it are as they were, giving Tyneside an identity and quality which remains essentially its own.

Tyneside beers, pubs and breweries

To outsiders, the North East has long been associated with the famous bottles of Newcastle Brown Ale –'broon' or 'dog' as it is sometimes colloquially known. 'Newcastle Brown' has enjoyed phenomenal success throughout the world, with over one million barrels brewed in Tyneside every year, producing 15 bottles a second. Its sponsorship of the city's football team has also ensured the continual exposure of its famous five point star trademark. Newcastle Brown was launched in 1927, when it was advertised for sale as "Entirely new.... a good Brown Ale with a rich mature flavour, recalling the famous "audit ales of bygone days", priced at 9d a bottle. The following year it won a prestigious award at the Brewers Exhibition in London, and its success was guaranteed. Adverts quickly appeared with the slogan "Try a bottle of this hefty, honest beer today- add your preference to the approval of the experts". Since that period Newcastle Brown has been promoted as 'The one and only....'

Newcastle Brown Ale is brewed by the huge brewers Scottish and Newcastle, who dominate much of the beer market, owning five huge breweries of which the Tyne brewery in Gallowgate is just one. This was once the home of Newcastle Breweries which was founded in 1890, and a conglomeration of five smaller breweries. The famous blue star appeared in the 1920s and became an official trademark in 1932, together with the simple scarlet lettering that spelled out the name of the pub. It is an identity that, despite the merger in 1960 with Scottish Brewers, has largely remained. Scottish and Newcastle continue to be the largest pub group in the North East, and their recent merger with the Chef and Brewer group placed a total of 3,500 houses under their control. The recent changes governing pub ownership have meant that all Scottish & Newcastle tenants and landlords are now free to offer a range of guest beers of their choice. This has greatly improved the range of real ales now available in pubs throughout the North East.

Alongside the cask-conditioned beer Newcastle Exhibition, also produced by Scottish & Newcastle, it is not widely known that the Theakston range of beers is brewed in the North East. Theakston is part of the S&N Group and its famous range of beers are no longer produced in Masham in North Yorkshire, but are now brewed in Newcastle including Theakston's XB and Old Peculier.

The other two big brewers which dominate the North East pub scene are Federation and Vaux. Federation is a cooperative originally founded in 1919 to overcome the post war beer shortages, and which later expanded to supply pubs and clubs through its own depots and wholesalers. Their brewery is still run by 501 member clubs which elect the board and share its profits. From its humble beginnings, Federation now produces 1490 million pints per annum of 18 different products, including 14 different ales from its new base in Dunston alongside the Gateshead MetroCentre. Its LCL Pils lager won the world's best bottled ale in 1987 and more recently the brewery has decided to reintroduce cask conditioned ales with the Buchanan range of beers in 1991- Buchanan Best, Special and Original.

Vaux of Sunderland was established in 1837 by Cuthbert Vaux. The firm was one of the first to recognise the potential demand for bottled ales and stouts. In the mid 19th century it began producing Indian pale ale, Vaux's Nourishing stout and Maxim ale, enabling the company to grow rapidly, amalgamating with other breweries and establishing bottling plants as far afield as Wallsend, Spenny-moor, Broughton, Middlesbrough, Leeds and Glasgow. These depots received their beer in hogsheads transported by train from Sunder-land for bottling. Vaux is now one of the region's largest brewers, and it also owns Wards of Sheffield, which increasingly makes its appearance in Tyneside pubs. Vaux's range includes its bitter, Samson and the smooth brown Double Maxim ale. The latter was given its name to mark the home coming of the maxim gun detach-ment which was attached to the Northumberland Hussars and commanded by Major Ernest Vaux in the Boar War. Maxim ale was one of the first brown ales sold in bottles, and its name was changed to Double Maxim in 1938.

For real ale connoisseurs, look out for the beers of some of the smaller Tyneside breweries, in particular Big Lamp and Hadrian. Big Lamp was set up in 1982 and supplies one tied house and a growing number of free trade outlets with its bitter and Prince Bishop ale. Look out for Summerhill Stout, a malty ale with a rich roast aroma and ESB, a distinctive beer with a hoppy taste and a delightful background fruitiness.

Hadrian Brewery started with a five barrel plant in 1987 using traditional brewing methods, but grew steadily forcing it to move to new premises. Its Gladiator ale is a fresh tasting premium beer, the Centurion Best a nicely balanced beer, and the Emperor ale, which as the name would suggest, has a pleasant rich hoppy flavour with an attractive dry after taste. Emperor Ale was voted the best strong ale in Britain in the Great British Beer Festival at Olympia, London in 1994.

There are also a number of excellent real ales, brewed around Tyneside which are well worth sampling. These include Butterknowle Conciliation, a strong hoppy bitter brewed in County Durham. Camerons of Hartlepool's Bitter and Strong Arm, and Castle Eden brewed near Hartlepool, but available nationwide as part of the Whitbread group. It is also possible to find Cumbrian Jennings, as well as Timothy Taylor's Landlord and the ubiquitous Marston's Pedigree and Boddington's, which seem to make an appearance in most good real ale pubs.

As you might expect from an area closely associated with coal mining, and ship building, there are no shortages of pubs in Tyneside. However, their character varies enormously. Some remain essentially working men's clubs, offering acres of Formica and smoke filled rooms, while others cater solely for the Sunday lunch brigade luxuriating in Axminster carpets and the smells of roast beef. Neither variety are particularly friendly to walkers. However, there are many, many more which are not only friendly but offer an excellent range of beers, and often a good bar menu as well. One area of Tyneside that has to stand out for special mention is North Shields, which offers a superb range of pubs each with a distinctive atmosphere, many of which have escaped refitting and retain many of the original features. There are also some excellent pubs tucked away within Newcastle City Centre of which two, the excellent Crown Posada and Bridge Hotel, belong to the Fitzgerald group, which own over thirty pubs throughout the North East, all of which offer a superb selection of real ales. The other North East pub group worth looking out for in Tyneside is the T & J Bernard group of pubs, owned by Scottish & Newcastle. The pubs specialise in witty chalk written signs and offer a good range of ales and bottled foreign beers, as well as a selection of sandwiches. The Victory (Walk 2), Brandling Arms (Walk 3) and The Seven Stars (Walk 9) are all members of this group.

In our research we have been greatly helped by the CAMRA Beer

Guide, which has to be the bible for all real ale lovers. Where possible we have mentioned CAMRA listed pubs, though occasionally we have found some real gems of our own, which we hope you enjoy as much as we did.

Practical points

Each of the twenty walks begins with a brief introduction and an indication of its length. The routes are then described as they appear on the ground at the time the walks were researched. It should be noted that the sketch maps have been designed to give walkers a broad guidance only and are not a substitute for carrying the relevant Ordnance Survey maps. It is recommended that walkers use a map in conjunction with the route description, if only to reassure themselves that they are on the correct route if certain landmarks such as barns, fences or trees are demolished or felled. It should also be added that in Tyneside signposts have a nasty habit of disappearing or being turned round to face the opposite direction.

One Ordnance Survey 1:50,000 series Landranger map covers all of Tyneside. This is Map no.88 – Tyneside and Durham. For those wanting more detail, we recommended the excellent 1:25,000 Pathfinder series. The majority of the walks are covered by maps no. 549 (Newcastle Upon Tyne), 536 (Whitley Bay), 548 (Blaydon & Prudhoe). The following maps are also used to a lesser extent: 535 (Ponteland), 550 (Sunderland &Whitburn), 562 (Washington), 561 (Consett). The relevant maps are listed in the introduction to each walk.

With the exception of the Newcastle town trail and the walk along Jesmond Dene (walk 2), it is recommended that boots or stout footwear are worn for all the walks. It is just as easy to twist an ankle on a field path on the outskirts of a city as it is in the high moorlands. Some of the paths can be quite muddy and slippy, especially in winter and autumn, and on some of the routes care is needed.

Even for the shorter walks pack a jumper and waterproofs. At any time of year, but especially in the winter months, good protective clothing is essential. It is recommended that walkers take a windproof anorak and rainwear including over-trousers. Some of the walks along the coast can be very exposed if the weather turns nasty and it is amazing how wet and cold you can get within half an hour.

It is also well worth packing some emergency food and drink, despite this being a book of pub walks. Even those pubs which do serve meals, don't always do so on Sundays or decide to have an unexpected holiday. During the research for this book the authors were several times forced to lunch on crisps and peanuts!

Many of the walks use the Tyne and Wear Metro. For those unfamiliar with the Metro system, most of the stations have some parking available close by. Tickets can be purchased at self service ticket machines on the stations. While the machines do not accept notes, they do give change. Depending on your journey it may be worth buying a day ticket, which provides unlimited off-peak travel (after 9.30am weekdays and all day in the weekends) on the entire Metro network, including the Shields Ferry. The ticket is currently priced at £2.20.

In addition to the Metro fares, Transfare tickets are also available allowing passengers to use the metro and bus for their journey. Maps at the Metro station indicate your destination's zone, which is then typed into the self service ticket machines. Transfare tickets are also available from bus drivers. A Day Rover ticket is also available, valid on all buses and trains (including the Metro) within Tyne and Wear, and priced £3.00. The Day Rover can be bought at Travel Centres.

A few of the walks also use the local bus network, and the relevant bus numbers and the frequency of service are provided in the text. For up to date information prior to your journey, telephone the Tyne & Wear PTE Traveline on 0191 232 5325. For up to date information on the Tyne Valley line between Newcastle and Carlisle featured in walks 10 and 11, telephone Regional Railways North East on 0191 232 6262.

1. Newcastle Town Trail

The Romans were the first to establish a settlement at Newcastle with the construction of a bridge and a fort, Pons Aelius, to guard it. It was chosen because the site was the lowest bridging point of the Tyne. The River Tyne remains central to Newcastle's history and was to dominate the city's future development as a regional centre for commerce and consumption within the region. The importance of the river to Newcastle began in Medieval times. The city was able to gain control of all traffic and trade along the river. By the mid 17th century 550,000 tonnes of coal were being ferried down the Tyne by the Keelman. The coming of the railways and the dredging of the Tyne in the 19th century were to further increase Newcastle's importance as a major industrial centre. This walk explores some of the more historic parts of this great trading city, including the Castle from which the city derives its name, the old city walls, the Cathedral and the narrow streets around the quayside.

Distance: 2 miles, 3km

Map: Newcastle upon Tyne A-Z

Start and Finish: Central Railway station, Newcastle

The Pubs

The Duke of Wellington, High Bridge. A busy city centre pub with a huge central bar serving a good range of beers including Tetleys, Taylor's Landlord, Marston's Pedigree, Ind Coope Burton Ale and guest beers. The pub is decorated with photographs of old Newcastle, with the requisite horse brasses and wooden fittings.

The Crown Posada, The Side. Owned by the Fitzgerald group this is one of the city's finest pubs with elaborate ceilings and two magnificent 18th century stained glass windows. The range of beers available is always exceptional and usually includes Butterknowle Conciliation, Hadrian's Gladiator, Theakston's, Boddingtons, draught Bass, as well as guest beers; as a consequence its narrow bar is often packed. The pub reputably gets its name from a Spanish nobleman who kept his mistress here. 'Posada' is Spanish for tavern!

The Walk

Newcastle Railway station, with its huge glass canopies, is still a magnificent example of Victorian railway architecture and is a fitting introduction to the city. It was designed by John Dobson and was opened by Queen Victoria in 1850. The portico was added later in 1863.

Opposite the railway station, on the right-hand side is a statue to George Stephenson, a tribute to one of the North East's greatest railway pioneers. The statute is by a local sculptor, John Lough, and was erected in 1862.

From the railway station, cross the road using the pedestrian crossing, and turn left and then immediately right up a narrow cobbled street, Pink Lane. Pink Lane is part of a road which ran along the inside of the old town walls between Gunner and Pink towers. Where the lane meets Clayton Street, cross the road at the traffic lights, by an ornate gold clock on the side of a jewellery shop, and continue up Westgate. At the next set of traffic lights, cross the road and turn right down Bath Lane towards a section of the city's walls.

The western walls are the best preserved remains of the late 13th century walls which once encircled the city. In the 16th century, the Walls were described by John Leland, as 'surpassing all the walls of the cities of England and most of the towns of Europe'. The walls were over two miles long and extended right to the waterfront. They measured 7-10 feet wide and 14-25 feet high and were surrounded by a dry ditch for most of their length. At the time of their construction the upper parts of the town were then virtually unpopulated, with the majority of the residents being packed into a dense mass of narrow streets and passage-ways between All Saints Church and the Quay. By the 1760s, the city had expanded beyond its Walls, and they were increasingly seen as an obstruction to trade along the quayside and then to traffic along Newgate and Pilgrim Street. So the Walls began to be demolished piecemeal. It is, however, still possible to trace the blocked battlements, bastions, wall turrets, ditch and rampart walks among the remains. The western section also includes three towers: Morden, Heber and Ever.

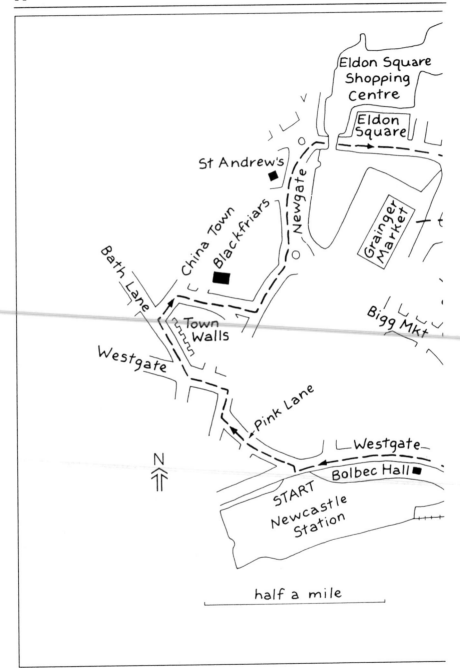

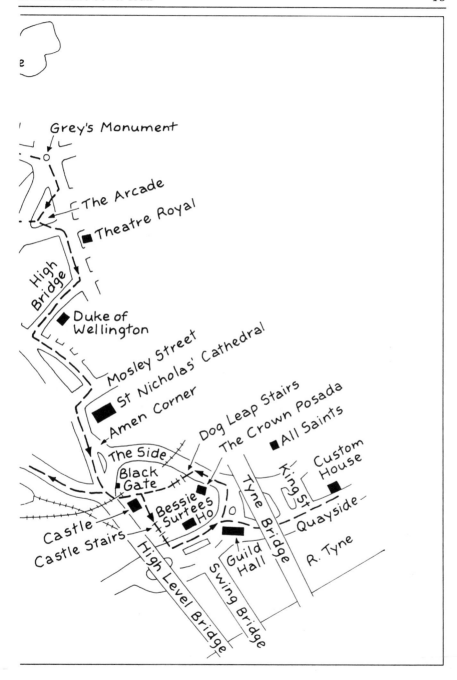

Follow the line of the Wall to a small wooden bridge crossing over the ditch, from where there is an excellent view of Newcastle United's famous and recently transformed football ground St James' Park. Look for a small doorway in the walls and go through it to enter Stowell Street and the heart of China Town. While a little drab in the cold light of day, at night this is transformed by brightly coloured lanterns, neon signs and tantalising smells from the many restaurants crowded along the street. There are also some excellent shops selling various Chinese delicacies, and as well as the obligatory themed BT telephone box.

Rather than walk along Stowell Street, continue in the same direction, along Friars Street to a Medieval building, Blackfriars. This was once a Dominican friary founded in the 13th century and the largest of the religious houses in the town. Only the foundations of the actual chapel remain, but the buildings around the cloister did survive the dissolution of the monastery in the 15th century. These were acquired by the Corporation and leased to the Guilds as meeting places. These buildings have since been restored and include craft workshops and a restaurant.

Having visited Blackfriars, continue in the same direction and go through an arch into Low Friar Street. Turn left past the huge mural on the right showing the different processes involved in the production of leather. Low Friars Street emerges at a mini roundabout on Newgate. This was once the site of the town's former market cross, 'the white cross'. Now a busy modern street, Newgate is one of the city's most ancient thoroughfares. In past centuries, it led to the north gate of the city's walls and the town's prison.

Continue in the same direction past St Andrew's church. This is the oldest of Newcastle's subsidiary churches and still has its Norman chancel and nave arches, but little of the original church remains, since St Andrews was badly damaged by Scottish cannon fire in 1644. Part of the Walls can be seen in the church yard. When the town walls were originally built they were extended to ensure that St Andrew's church was included within the city boundary. Special dispensation had to be granted to enable the Walls to be built through the cemetery.

Just past St Andrew's church, cross Newgate using the pedestrian crossing. Continue for a short distance and then turn right into Blackett Street, under the concrete arches of Eldon Square shopping centre. The street soon opens out into old Eldon Square. Only the east side of the Georgian square remains, which was originally designed by Thomas Oliver and John Dobson between 1825-31. The north and west sides of the Square were demolished in 1961, causing a huge public outcry, when the modern Eldon Square shopping complex was built. At the time of its completion Eldon Square was the largest shopping centre in Europe.

Continue past the City's War Memorial, and head for the 133-foot-high Grey's Monument. This Greek column, surmounted by a statue of Earl Grey of Howick, was built in 1838 to commemorate the passing of the 1832 Reform Act under his leadership. This Act was the first legislation passed by Parliament to extend the right to vote beyond the privileged few. The statue's head is a replacement, as the original was dislodged in a thunderstorm in 1941. An internal staircase of 164 steps within the column leads to the base of the statue from where there are panoramic views of the City. The staircase is open to the public on Saturdays and Bank Holidays between Easter and October.

Grey's Monument is the centre-piece of the early 19th century streetscape which was the brain-child of the entrepreneur and builder Richard Grainger, who in partnership with the designers John Dobson, Thomas Oliver and Town Clerk John Clayton, set about redeveloping a large area of Newcastle. Not all of their schemes were implemented, but their work has left Newcastle with a legacy of fine late Georgian buildings, built in honey coloured sandstone at the heart of its city centre. They include the Theatre Royal, Lloyds Bank and Grey Street itself with it's elegant curve sweeping from the Monument towards St Nicholas' Cathedral.

Continue down Grey Street, and then turn right to walk through the Central Arcade with its tiled walls in elegant tobacco brown, and mosaic floor below a glass vaulted ceiling. The Arcade was designed by J. Oswald and Sons and was built in 1905 when it was inserted into the facade of an older building by Grainger which had been damaged by fire.

The Arcade emerges on Market Street. To visit Grainger Market turn right. As its name suggests this too was part of Grainger's redevelopment and was designed by John Dobson in 1835, on the site of the former medieval Benedictine nunnery. The market is a Grade One listed building and one of the finest covered markets in the country. It was originally built as a meat market and amidst its grid iron of alleys, many of its stalls are still butchers shops, but it also includes a Marks and Spencers Penny Bazaar, and in the more open section fresh fruit and vegetable stalls. When the market was originally opened in October 1835, a grand dinner was held to celebrate its completion, attended by nearly 2,000 people. To continue the trail from the Central Arcade, turn left back on to Grey Street to the Theatre Royal designed by Benjamin Green in the 1830s.

Just beyond the theatre, turn right along High Bridge, a narrow street which derives its name from one of two bridges which crossed Lort Burn at this point; Upper Dene bridge and Nether Dean bridge. By the 19th century Lort Burn posed such a health risk that it had to be covered over. The Duke of Wellington pub is on the left-hand side.

High Bridge leads into Bigg market, which derives its name from a kind of barley. There is a still a regular market here, which dates back to the 13th century. Today Bigg Market earns its reputation as the centre of Newcastle night-life. In the evening the entire square is filled with young people enjoying its many pubs. Ironically, in the centre is a drinking fountain erected in 1894 by the Band of Hope Union in 1894, containing the inscription 'Water is Best'. It is a monument to John H Rutherford, the educational pioneer and a founder of the temperance festival on Town Moor, which has since been transformed into the annual June 'Hoppings'.

Turn left down Cloth Market on to Mosley Street. Straight ahead is St Nicholas' Cathedral. The original church of 1091 was burned in 1216, and the present building evolved subsequently as a parish church and it became a Cathedral in 1882. Its most distinctive feature is the remarkable 193 feet high, lantern tower borne on diagonal arches dating from the 15th century, said to be one of the most beautiful of its kind in the country. Legend has it that the Scots threatened to blow up St Nicholas during the 1644 siege, but were persuaded against it when the Mayor of Newcastle placed Scottish prisoners in the famous lantern tower. Inside, there are various monuments of interest, including one to Admiral Collingwood, who succeeded Nelson at the Battle of Trafalgar. There is also an early 15th century font, with a fine canopy, which owes its survival to being hidden from the Scots after the battle of Newburn in 1640. The 19th century wooden chancel screen is also very fine and intricately carved.

From St Nicholas' turn left passing Amen Corner and the top of the Side. This steep narrow street was once the main road between the bridge and the town before the Lort Valley was culverted in the 1780s to create Dean Street. Continue down St Nicholas' Street to the Black Gate.

Black Gate derives its name from its 17th century resident, Patrick Black, but originally it was the north gate of the Castle's barbican. The lower portions, including the archway, are mostly 13th century when the gateway was complete with portcullis and drawbridge. The gateway later underwent several alterations, principally in the 17th century.

Go over the wooden bridge and through the gateway, following a walk-way over some excavated buildings which are the remains of the castle's curtain wall. Continue through the railway arch ahead to the Castle Keep.

The Normans were not the first to appreciate the strategic importance of Newcastle, since the Romans had already established a military camp and fort on this site, but the continual threat of the Scots created a new urgency to improve England's northern defences. Within fifteen years of invading Britain, Robert Curthose, son of William the Conqueror, built a motte and bailey of earth and timber here and gave the city its name of 'new castle'. This early castle was later rebuilt in the 12th and 13th centuries by King Henry II and King John.

The stone Castle Keep was built by the same person who designed and built King Henry's mighty keep at Dover castle, and the Keep remained in royal ownership to the last century. It remains a substantial building with walls up to 18 feet thick, a massive square tower which houses a fine Norman chapel and a Great Hall. It is possible to climb to the top of the keep and on to its 19th century roof and battlements from where there are excellent views of the lower part of the City.

From Castle Keep go down Castle Stairs towards the river. This was once a clog making area, but little is left of any of the buildings. The stairs emerge at the Close. Turn left here. Prior to the industrial developments of the City, the Close was once the most fashionable place to live in Newcastle, and was the home of rich merchants and country noblemen. Few houses still survive, but Bessie Surtees' House, which once belonged to Aubone Surtees is now in the care of English Heritage. The house contains a fine Elizabethan staircase and fireplace. The house derives its present name from Bessie, Aubone Surtees' daughter who eloped in 1772 with Jack Scott, the son of a coal exporter. The couple were soon reconciled with Bessie's father and Jack Scott prospered and became Lord Eldon, who with his brother Lord Stowell, held two of the most important positions in the country.

From Bessie Surtees House, cross the road by the pedestrian crossing to the large building opposite. This is the Guildhall, traditionally the centre of power in Newcastle. It was originally erected in the 1650s, but was substantially altered between 1796-1826 after riots in the 1740s. A later fire also caused substantial damage to the building. The rioters were mostly keel men, who were provoked by corn merchants who withheld cheap grain supplied to them to relieve hunger after a bitter winter and spring had created a food shortage. The Guildhall contains several fine rooms, most of which are classical in style. The exception is the magnificent 17th century timber roofed guild hall.

From the Guildhall turn left to continue along the riverside to pass King Street from where there is a fine view of All Saints church. This can be reached via a flight of steps leading from King Street. The church was built in 1796 to replace a medieval building, in an elegant classical style by David Stephenson. It is one of the country's rare elliptical churches. Its classical porch and vestibule stand below its elegant tower. The church is no longer used as a place of worship but has been deconsecrated and is now used as a musical and educational centre.

Just beyond King Street is the Customs House, a dignified classical building with a fine royal coat of arms above its door. It was originally built in 1766, but remodelled in the 19th century. Newcastle used to have the only Customs House on the river and fought to keep things that way as it helped the City maintain control of river borne trade. However, Customs Houses were eventually built in both North and South Shields.

From the Customs House retrace your steps along the Quayside. On Sundays this is the site of a large open air market. It is also one of the best places to see Newcastle's three famous bridges: Armstrong's Swing Bridge (1868-78), Stephen's High Level bridge (1845-9) and the famous Tyne bridge (1925-8). (See walks 2 for 10 for the history of these bridges).

At the Swing Bridge turn right up the Side, towards the massive railway arch of the East Coast main line which dominates the street. Continue up the Side, to the Crown Posada. Just beyond the Crown Posada look for a flight of steps on the left, Dog Leap stairs, which leads to the Castle Keep. Go up the steps and continue in the same direction to the top of the High Level Bridge. Cross the road and take the first left, Westgate. Continue up Westgate past the Literary and Phil. building (1811) and the Bolbec and Wood Memorial Hall. Look out for the line of Hadrian's Wall marked in the concrete alongside the building. Continue past the Royal Station Hotel, designed by John Dobson and later extended in 1890 to include a glass canopy, to the end of the walk at the Central Station.

2. Jesmond Dene

One of the most famous walks in Newcastle and a great favourite with local people. The walk begins at South Gosforth Metro station and follows the Ouseburn as it meanders down the beautiful wooded Jesmond Dene to emerge at the banks of the River Tyne. The walk finishes with superb views of the Tyne bridge.

Distance: 5 miles, 8km

Maps: Landranger 88 Tyneside & Durham, Pathfinder 549 Newcastle Upon Tyne

Start: South Gosforth Metro Station

Finish: Central Metro Station

Access: Use the Tyne and Wear Metro.

The Pubs

The Ship, Byker – Small, basic but cosy traditional Tyneside pub nestling under Byker bridge serving a range of real ales including Castle Eden, Flowers Original and Boddingtons. Often busy at weekends, thanks to its proximity to the Byker City Farm, there are outside tables for those wanting to enjoy the view across the farm to the Ouseburn.

The Bridge Hotel, Newcastle – Priding itself on its range of real ales and guest beers, the Bridge Hotel is situated on the end of the High Level Bridge. A very popular pub, with warm atmosphere and an elaborately carved bar and ornate mirror above a large fireplace. The Bridge serves Bass Worthington Best Bitter, Theakston's XB and Best Bitter, Butterknowle Conciliation and Boddington's.

The Walk

Leave South Gosforth Metro station and join the road. Turn right and walk down the hill to a roundabout. Use the pedestrian crossing

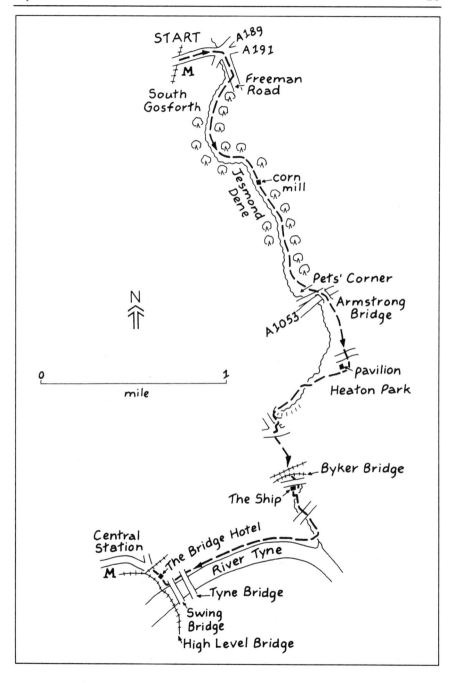

on the right-hand side to cross the road. Continue in the same direction up the hill and then turn right along Freeman Road, signed for Heaton and the Freeman Hospital. Continue for a short distance up the hill before turning right along a signed footpath through some trees.

Follow the footpath, which descends through attractive woodland, and then under the road via a tunnel which will delight adults and children alike. Just after the tunnel take the set of steps on the right which descend down to a lower path alongside the Ouseburn.

This is the beginning of the area known as Jesmond Dene, and though it might look at first glance a natural wooded valley, it has in fact been extensively landscaped to create a network of paths, bridges and attractive waterfalls. In late spring the Dene is a riot of colour from the Rhododendrons and, in amongst them, are many unusual trees such as the Turkey Oak, Spanish Chestnut and Atlantic Cedar. The Dene is also a haven for wildlife with bats, nuthatches and even kingfishers regularly seen along the banks of the Ouseburn. Jesmond Dene owes its appearance to William George Armstrong, later Lord Armstrong, the wealthy armaments manufacturer and local benefactor, who acquired the Dene in 1850. In 1883 Lord Armstrong presented the Dene to the Corporation of Newcastle for the enjoyment of local people.

The next bridge is the first of those forming part of the Dene given to the City by Armstrong and just below is a series of stepping stones. A little further ahead is a magnificent waterfall and attractive bridge which is one of the many features introduced by Armstrong to create a more picturesque landscape. Close by is the old Jesmond water mill which served as a corn mill and later a flint mill. Some gearing and foundations of an adjacent cottage survive and the water wheel has recently being replaced.

Continue past the mill, the next waterfall and the grand rococo bridge to a pair of bridges side by side where the Dene broadens out. The first bridge bore Armstong's carriageway while the second gave public access up the valley.

Continue further down the Ouseburn valley passing the exclusive

Fisherman's Lodge restaurant on the left. The next bridge provides access, via a series of steps to John Dobson's Banqueting Hall. Now in ruins, this was once a magnificent Italianate building complete with a hydraulic organ. For those wishing to make a detour to St Mary's Chapel cross the bridge and then take the next turn left to reach a road. Turn left and cross the road to a small wooden gate into a small copse and dene, Moor Crook Letch, and head up the hill to the ruins of St Mary's Chapel.

The medieval chapel dates back at least to the 13th century and is the oldest church or chapel in Newcastle. The Chapel has been a place of pilgrimages for centuries and is reputed to be linked to various miracles which have taken place among the sick who attended the Chapel and the neighbouring Holy Well. The Holy Well is just a few yards west of the Chapel (reached via The Grove,) and is marked by a headstone inscribed with the words 'Gratia'. The full inscription is said to have read 'Ave Maria Gratia Plena' (Hail Mary Full of Grace). The well was at one time reputed to be a warm spring and in cold weather steam could be seen rising from the waters. Today, however, the waters are decidedly cold!

From St Mary's Chapel return to the bridge and continue along Jesmond Dene to the Pets Corner, a collection of rabbits, ducks, goats and other animals, which is very popular with local children. Opposite is the Mill House Visitor Centre and Coffee shop which includes a display about the history and wildlife of the Dene.

Continue straight ahead towards Armstrong Bridge. Where the path forks take the left-hand fork to climb steeply up the hill to reach the top of the bridge. The 552ft long bridge was built by W.G. Armstrong & Co between 1876-8 to link Heaton and Jesmond and provides a view over the Dene. The large grassed area, immediately below now includes a pets cemetery and an attractive area of shrubs, but until the War it was an old goose field used for fattening geese for the festive season. Pedestrianised in 1960, the bridge is now host to a Sunday arts and craft market of mostly amateur crafts people selling a range of work including paintings, pottery, and leather-ware.

Do not cross Armstrong bridge, but turn left to a second smaller iron bridge crossing the busy main road. Go over this bridge into Armstrong Park, an area of dense Rhododendron bushes and wide tarmac paths. Just off the main path through the park is King John's Well complete with an inscription "Ye olde well of King John" which is in fact a little piece of Victorian embellishment and of no historic validity. The King John connection is further developed at the ruins of a fortified house, known locally as King John's Palace, which dates back to 1255 (40 years after John's reign). The house was in fact the home of Adam of Jesmond, once High Sheriff of Northumberland and a staunch supporter of Henry III and with a reputation for embezzlement.

Continue straight ahead crossing a small bridge to reach the road. Cross the road (King's John's Palace is on the left) and enter Heaton Park. At the pavilion, a reconstruction of an old aviary which once stood there, turn right alongside the attractive formal gardens and then take the path towards a children's playground and descend slowly down the hill to finally emerge at a gateway in a large stone wall. Go through the gateway on to a road and then turn left for a short distance to Blue Bell Bridge.

Cross the bridge and then look for a path alongside the Ouseburn, just before the Northern Sinfonia rehearsal rooms. This is an attractive narrow pathway which skirts along the edge of the Ouseburn to the entrance of a large culvert. Constructed between 1907 and 1912, the culvert was built to carry the Ouseburn through an area of land fill which had been designed to provided an easy level route between the city centre and Byker and Heaton, avoiding the necessity of having to cross the steep sided Ouseburn valley. The culvert measures 2,150 feet long, 30 feet wide and 20 feet high and was used during the Second World War as an air raid shelter.

Climb up the bank and, at the top, turn left onto a road. At the road turn right to a main road and then cross the road and head straight ahead across a large area of recreational land keeping a children's playing area to the left. Continue straight ahead towards Byker bridge and the huge viaduct carrying the East Coast main line railway to Edinburgh. Look for a path leading down the embankment and under the bridges carrying the railway, road and the Metro.

The Byker Bridges

The Metro is the newest of the three bridges, an impressive 2,649 feet long concrete viaduct, built in the early 1980s. The original railway viaduct was constructed in timber and was later reconstructed in wrought iron in 1869. The Byker road bridge dates from 1878 to provide access to the developing eastern suburbs, and improve access to the river mouth and coastal area. A toll was charged on the bridge until 1895.

Walk down the embankment ignoring the first fork on the right and continue to the bottom of the hill and under the bridges to a small stone bridge. Cross the bridge and turn right towards the Ship Inn. Close by is a truncated, but free standing chimney, which was once part of the adjacent 19th century steam powered flax mill. The flax mill is now divided into various units and used by artists and crafts people.

From the Ship Inn take the path through Byker City farm, a charming collection of various farm animals, murals and sculpture to a footbridge crossing the Ouseburn to join a walk-way above the burn which lies in a steep cut. At this point the Ouseburn is tidal and is used as club moorings, with a variety of pleasure craft moored here. The walk-way emerges at a flight of steps and a road.

Cross the road and turn left and then take the first right. Continue for a short while and then turn right down Malling St towards the banks of the River Tyne. At the Tyne turn right over a bridge crossing the Ouseburn and continue along the waterfront towards the Tyne bridge and Newcastle City Centre.

The section of the waterfront between the Ouseburn and the Tyne bridges is known as the Quayside and has undergone extensive refurbishment as part of the work of the Tyne and Wear Development Corporation. The new developments will include offices, shops, pubs, restaurants and leisure facilities. Already many of existing buildings on the waterfront have been restored, new retaining walls have been constructed and a promenade has been built.

From here there are excellent views to the new Tyne bridge, built in 1925-28 and the largest single span bridge in Britain at its time of opening, and the earlier Swing Bridge, built in 1868-76 by W.G.

Armstrong & Co. Until 1959 the swing bridge was driven by hydraulic pumps and in 1959 small electric pumps were fitted. Though rarely opened now, it is estimated that over half a million ships have passed through since the swing bridge was opened. Cross under the Tyne bridge and at the Swing Bridge go up the steps and turn right to join the main road. Turn left for a short distance and then go up to a flight of stone steps, Castle Stairs, which lead to the Castle Keep and the Bridge Hotel. From the Bridge Hotel cross the main road and then turn right, and then first left, along Westgate to the Central Station and the Metro.

3. The Newcastle Moors

This is an interesting urban walk beginning on the fringe of Newcastle's northern housing estates and emerging at Newcastle's famous Town Moor in the heart of the city, an extensive area of undeveloped grazing land.

Distance: 5 miles, 8km

Maps: Landranger 88 Tyneside & Durham, Pathfinder 549 Newcastle Upon Tyne

Start: Bank Foot Metro Station

Finish: Jesmond Metro Station

Access: Use the Tyne and Wear Metro

The Pub

The Brandling Arms, Jesmond is tucked into a quite corner of Jesmond in Brandling village with its dress and antique shops. A popular pub, part of the T&J Bernard group, with a warm and friendly atmosphere and with a good range of real ales including Speckled Hen, Theakston's, Youngers No. 3 as well as a good selection of continental bottled beers.

The Walk

Begin on the airport bound platform of Bank Foot Metro Station and walk down to the road and Metro bridge. Look for a small tarmac path marked by lamp posts on the right running parallel to the Metro line. Follow the path to where it emerges at a large open green space at the edge of a modern estate. Continue straight ahead, following Newbiggin Dene, ignoring the two left-hand forks to reach a subway under the Woolsington by-pass.

Just past the subway leave the tarmac path to follow a muddy path on the left along the edge of a field fringed by sparse hedgerow. Ignore the path on the right which continues along the bottom of

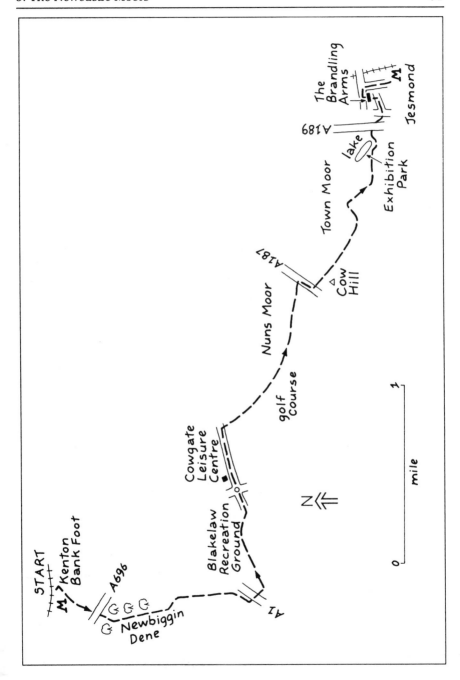

Newbiggin Dene, to continue straight ahead following the line of the
Dene. At a cross roads of paths, by a big tree, turn left up a slope to
follow a field path for a short distance to reach a metal barrier on
the right. From here there are some magnificent views back across
the fields into Northumberland. Go through the gap in the metal
barrier along a stony path to meet another path. Keep straight ahead
and go through another metal barrier. Follow the path, passing some
allotments on the right-hand side, to emerge at a road opposite a
small row of shops. At the shops turn right along the road to a small
roundabout and a main road.

Cross the road and go through a gap in the metal fence in the
left-hand corner of a large open recreation ground. Continue in the
same direction as before, following the metal fence to a road and a
turning circle and a footbridge over the western by-pass. Cross the
footbridge and then turn left to follow a path, before turning right
along Yatesbury Avenue. At the main road cross the road and
continue straight ahead through Blakelaw recreation ground. Just
after the children's play area, keep in the same direction through a
group of trees to join a gravel path which emerges onto the road.
Turn left past the Coopers Forge public house to a roundabout. Cross
the main road via the pedestrian crossing and walk straight ahead
along Harehills Avenue past the Cowgate Leisure Centre.

Just beyond the Leisure Centre, set amidst Council houses, is a
large area of open grassland, Nuns Moor. Walk towards a metal fence
and look for a gap leading on to Nuns Moor. This area took is name
from the Benedictine nunnery, the Priory of St Bartholomew, which
used to be situated between Granger Street and Clayton Street in the
City centre and who owned the land. Around 1650 Nuns Moor was
bought by the Corporation from Charles Brandling who had acquired the land and Nuns Moor became part of Town Moor.

Walk up the hill veering very slightly left to join a wooden fence
straight ahead which marks the boundary of the Newcastle United
golf course. Alongside the fence is a green track. Follow the track to
Grandstand road. This was once the site of an old cattle and horse
market, hence its name Cow Hill. The fair used to meet on October
29th for the sale of cattle, horse and swine and was said in 1800 to

be one of the largest in Northern England. Cow Hill was also used as a meeting point in 1819 for demonstrations against the Peterloo Massacre in Manchester and again in 1832 for 50,000 demonstrators protesting against the defeat of Lord Grey's Bill to reform Parliament and the electoral system

Cross the road and look for a stile straight ahead and a narrow path leading to the top of the hill through beech trees. This hill owes its existence, at least in part, to the building of the Tyne and Wear Metro, when material excavated from tunnelling was deposited here, with material from an adjacent motorway. The hill is a favourite spot for skiing and tobogganing in winter and it offers magnificent views across the city and to Town Moor below. Town Moor dates back to medieval times when it was granted to the city by Edward II. Freemen of the city still have the right to graze their animals there and this right has been fiercely defended, ensuring its protection from development. Town Moor is also the scene for various public events from public hangings, the last being in 1844, to the more recent 'Hoppings'. This is one of the largest travelling fairs in Europe which is held every June with rides, fortune tellers and various stalls covering a huge area of land. The Hoppings were a 19th century introduction and were originally designed as a temperance festival replacing the annual horse races which were moved to Gosforth Park in 1882.

At the top of the hill go through the gate and turn right to follow the ridge. Continue along the ridge and then descend down to a tarmac path. At the tarmac path turn left and where it reaches a cross roads of paths turn right. Follow the path for a short distance and where it forks, follow the left-hand fork along a grassy path into Exhibition Park, emerging at a large boating lake and the Military Vehicle museum. The park was originally created in 1878-80 and was known as Bull Park. It was used for the 1887 Jubilee Exhibition and 42 years later for the North East Coast Exhibition. Adjacent to the museum is the Turbina, Charles Pearson's experimental steam turbine craft.

Walk round the Lake and then, opposite the museum, turn right along a path to reach a bandstand. From the bandstand head left towards the road, aiming for a footbridge over the road, but use the subway under the road leading to Brandling Park.

From the subway walk straight ahead and cross the park to the top of Lambton Road. Walk down the footpath on its left-hand side until you pass an arch under one of the terraced houses leading directly to Brandling village and the Brandling Arms. From the Brandling Arms turn right onto Clayton Road and then right onto Eskdale Road passing the Girls Central High School and the Royal Boys Grammar School on your right. Turn left to Jesmond Metro Station

4. Rising Sun Country Park and The Coxlodge Waggonway

This is an excellent family walk along easy tracks. Part of the route follows the old Coxlodge Waggonway which linked the pits around East Kenton, Gosforth and Fawdon to the River Tyne. The views from the hill at Rising Sun Country Park offer some outstanding views across Tyneside, and beyond to the North Pennines and the edge of the Northumberland hills.

Distance: 7 miles, 11km

Maps: Landranger 88 Tyneside and Durham, Pathfinder 549 Newcastle

Start: Hadrian's Road Metro station

Finish: South Gosforth Metro Station

Access: Use the Metro

The Pubs

Newton Park, Longbenton A large typical 1930s Whitbread's pub whose main business is food. A favourite of families for Sunday lunch, which despite appearances is happy to welcome walkers. Look out for the mint imperial dispensing machine!

The Victory, South Gosforth A cosy pub with a series of small snugs, the Victory is tucked just out of sight of the South Gosforth round-about. The pub serves an excellent selection of real ales including Theakston's, Younger's No. 3, Speckled Hen, Exhibition and an excellent range of Continental bottled beers. Just opposite is the equally excellent **Brandling Villa**, a Scottish and Newcastle house serving McEwans 80/-, Theakston's Best Bitter and XB, as well as guest beers.

The Walk

Leave the Metro station on the Tynemouth bound platform and walk straight ahead along South Terrace, parallel to the Metro line. Take

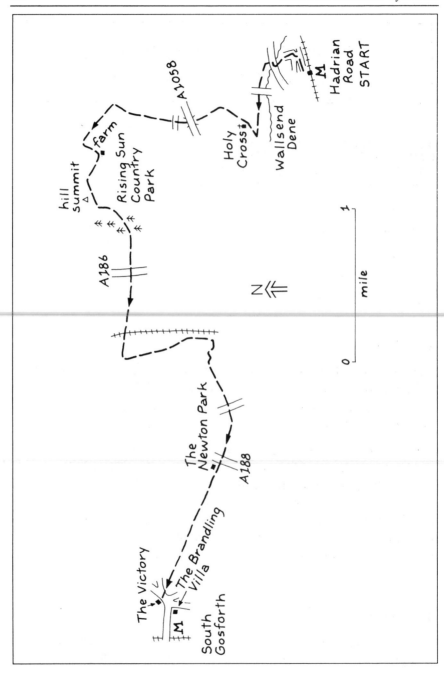

the second turning on the left and then turn right. Cross the road and turn left down Roland road, passing a Cemetery on the left. At the bottom of the road continue along a path through trees which drops down to a road. Cross the road and then turn left along a wide tarmac path running alongside a stream known as Willington Gut.

Follow the path under a concrete road bridge to where the valley narrows and the stream becomes Wallsend Burn. Now an attractive green valley, Wallsend Dene was once heavily industrialised. Where the path reaches a clearing look for the low standing ruins of a building on the right and a metal hand rail and steps. Head for the steps and go up the path to emerge at the ruins of a Norman chapel,

Holy Cross, surrounded by red railings. Holy Cross was built about 1150 to serve the parishes of Wallsend, Howden and Willington, and was linked to Jarrow Priory. The Chapel fell into disrepair at the end of the 18th century when it was no longer in regular use. With increased deterioration it was decided in 1909 to consolidate the ruin and protect it from further damage by erecting railings.

From Holy Cross cut across the grass aiming for the end house in the far right corner. From here

Holy Cross Chapel

follow a lane for a few yards behind the houses and then a clear path which soon forks. Ignore the right-hand fork into the cemetery, and follow the left fork along the edge of the valley. This is a lovely path, with a tendency to become slightly overgrown in summer with brambles and elder trees. At the top of the valley go up a few steps onto the main road.

Turn left past the bus shelter to a subway under the main A1058 road. At the other side of the subway turn immediately right to join a tarmac path cutting across the grass to a group of modern houses. The path bends alongside the houses and continues to another road. Cross the road and continue straight ahead to some trees and a narrow path down to a broad grassy valley between houses. Continue in the same direction under the footbridge to emerge at a set of red bollards and the edge of the Rising Sun Country Park, 400 acres of woodland and grassland, surrounding a marshy lake, which is now a nature reserve.

This is the site of the former Rising Sun Colliery which was opened in 1908 when a shaft was sunk to the Bensham seam. A second shaft was sunk in 1915. The colliery finally closed in 1969. It was the last colliery on the north bank of the Tyne. Since the colliery's closure the area has been extensively landscaped to create a country park for local recreation.

Walk straight ahead along a clear path. Where it divides take the left-hand fork to a red kissing gate. Turn left along a sandy cycle path, the former Killingworth waggonway where George Stephenson first experimented with fixed locomotives. Then take the next left to Rising Sun Farm. Walk past the stables and then turn right along a broad track. Continue along the broad track and then turn left through a wooden gap stile to join a path leading to a small bridge and the summit of the hill looking down on the Country Park. This was once an old slag heap. From here there are outstanding views down to the cranes on the River Tyne, and north to the Northumberland hills.

From the summit continue in the same direction towards a small conifer plantation and then follow the edge of the plantation to join a broad track. Turn right down the track towards a housing estate crossing a small footbridge over a stream and continuing straight ahead along a footpath with the housing estate on the left and open fields to the right.

The footpath emerges at a road. Continue in the same direction along an attractive hedgerow lined track, passing East Benton Farm on the left and a little further on a group of cottages by a railway bridge. Go over the railway bridge crossing the East Coat main line between Newcastle and Edinburgh and continue along a track to a lane. Ignore the first turning on the left towards a government building, but take the second turning, passing playing fields on the left-hand side. A little further on it is possible to see the main government buildings, a vision of white and glass. The track gradually veers towards the railway running parallel for a short distance until reaching a railway bridge. Do not cross the bridge but turn right along a track.

Continue along the track which bends right and soon joins a road. Cross the road and continue along a gravel track. This is all that remains of the Coxlodge waggonway which was used to carry coal from the Jubilee and Regent pits at Gosforth to the River Tyne. Previously coal had been carried in carts by road to the quayside. The line was constructed between 1806-1809 by the owners of Kenton colliery to Walker on the riverside. Although west of South Gosforth, the actual route of the railway changed several times to accommodate different pits, during its period of operation. A native of Walker, John Blenkinsop, helped pioneer a rack and pinion engine on Hunslet Moor in Leeds, and in 1813 this system was adapted for the Kenton-Coxlodge waggonway.

The waggonway emerges at a road, Benton Road. Opposite is the Newton Park pub. Cross the road and walk straight ahead along a lane keeping the Newton Park on the right. Keep in the same direction, and where the houses end, a group of bollards mark the beginning of a long clear tarmac path leading through trees to finally emerge at a series of steps and a main road. Cross the road towards the Victory and then turn left crossing a second road and passing the Brandling Villa on the left. Continue up the hill to South Gosforth Metro station.

5. Earsdon Village

Urban fringe walking at its best, tracing a network of field paths and tracks around the historic village of Earsdon. The village of Earsdon derives its name from 'Erdesdun' or 'Earls Hill', a reference to its position upon a sandstone outcrop which ensures that its church dominates the skyline for much of this walk.

Distance: 6 miles, 9.5km

Maps: Landranger 88 Tyneside and Durham, Pathfinder 536 Whitley Bay

Start: Shiremoor Metro Station

Finish: West Monkseaton Metro Station

Access: Use the Tyne and Wear Metro

The Pubs

The Cannon, Earsdon is tucked neatly into a corner on the main street through the village. The Cannon offers a very friendly local atmosphere in a pleasant setting and well kept Tetleys, Stones and Cameron's.

Also worth a visit is the **Robin Hood in Murton**, a timber framed building with some unusual wooden carvings and fine plaster ceilings. Just off the walk route, it has been extended at the back to include a pleasant beer garden. Offering Tetleys, Burton Ale and Newcastle Exhibition.

The Walk

From Shiremoor Metro Station join the road and turn left, passing a row of houses, Bridge Terrace, and some playing fields on the left. At the T-junction, cross the road and join the public footpath opposite the Grey Horse pub, which is signposted to Earsdon and East Holywell.

When the track begins to bend right take the left fork keeping

Earsdon church to the right in the distance. At a road turn left, and after a short distance join a signposted public footpath which splits almost immediately. Take the right-hand track.

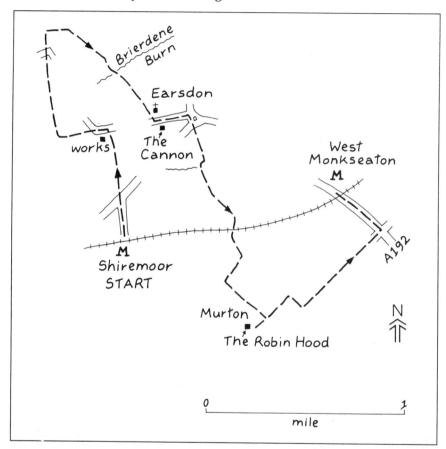

Follow this track to a junction with a dismantled railway, which is in fact the Old East Holywell Waggonway, which once connected the East Holywell 'C' pit with coal staithes on the River Tyne. Take the small path which is the second exit and which leads under two telegraph poles. Follow this path between fields to a road.

Across the road and to the right, take a public footpath signed to Holywell Grange Farm and follow a gravel road. After a short distance go through a wooden gateway to the right, and follow a track which narrows and continues between hedgerows until it reaches the entrance to fields.

At the fields take the right-hand field path keeping the imposing shape of St Alban's church directly ahead. This footpath was once the route used by miners walking to work from Earsdon village to the Fenwick pit which closed in 1973. The path skirts the edge of the pit heap now rapidly greening over with young saplings and a wide variety of plants. The approach to the church crosses a small footbridge over Brierdene Burn, and then, on the outskirts of Earsdon passes the entrance to the churchyard. Walk up the small road and turn left to the entrance of the church.

The soaring spire of St Alban's church is the focal point of the village. The church was built in 1837 on the site of the original 13th century chapel which preceded it. In the graveyard is the Hartley memorial which commemorates one of the worst disasters in coal mining history in 1862 at Hester pit at Hartley colliery. Part of an

Earsdon church

iron engine beam crashed down the only shaft and was swiftly followed by tons of debris making rescue impossible for the 204 miners who were trapped down the mine and left to die. The Memorial commemorates the names and ages of all the victims, many of whom were only ten and eleven years of age.

From the church turn left to follow the lane into Earsdon, an attractive linear village complete with a village green, on which the old plough in front of the Cannon pub lays testament to the importance of agriculture to the community.

From the Cannon, continue through the village down towards a main road. At the road look for a view of the sea and St Mary's lighthouse ahead in the distance. Turn right alongside the walls of the Red Lion Hotel and cross the road ahead. Go through a gap in the hedge on to a field path and continue along this path, through another hedge and, keeping to the right of a school playing field, head for a path in the far corner. This path continues between hedges and into a further field before entering the outskirts of a housing estate. Walk straight ahead to a small cut between house number 44 and 46. Take this cut and enter the field through a small gate. Head for another gate in the right-hand corner of the field and follow a signpost to Murton village.

Go through the gate and, taking care for trains, cross the railway and follow the field path towards Murton. Continue through two fields to a junction of paths. Turn right here, keeping the hedge to the left and at a gap in the hedge, turn left towards a row of houses on the outskirts of Murton. At the row of houses go through a cut on to the road which heads down to Murton Lane.

The Robin Hood pub is a short distance to the right on Murton Lane. Otherwise, turn left to follow the public footpath sign to West Monkseaton. The track turns right, and then left in front of a green barn before emerging into West Monkseaton on Caldwell Avenue. Walk down Caldwell Avenue to the junction with the main Earsdon Road before turning left to West Monkseaton Metro station.

---

6. The Avenue Branch Line

An attractive walk from the outskirts of Whitley Bay along the old Blyth railway to Holywell Dene and on to the edge of the Northumberland Coast. The walk includes a visit to the St Mary's Island and its lighthouse and ends with an attractive walk along the coast into Whitley Bay.

Distance: 9 miles, 14 km

Maps: Landranger No. 88 Tyneside and Durham; Pathfinder Whitley Bay No. 536

Start: Monkseaton Metro Station

Finish: Whitley Bay Metro Station

Access: Use the Metro or park your car in Whitley Bay and either catch the Metro or walk (1 km) to Monkseaton Station

The Pub

King Arm's, Seaton Sluice Perching on a rocky outcrop on the edge of a cliff, with views up the coast towards Blyth, the King's Head is a warm and friendly pub with low wooden beamed ceilings and a large stone fireplace. Decorated with the usual maritime views, you can always be assured of a well kept pint of Theakston's or Exhibition, and generous portions of food.

The Walk

From Monkseaton Station turn left on to the road. Cross the road at the T-junction. Rather than follow the road ahead look for a stony path in the corner of the grassy triangle leading into woodland. This path soon joins the line of the old railway line which used to run from Monkseaton to Blyth and is now an attractive corridor lined with broom, brambles and sycamore and is used by walkers and cyclists alike.

The Blyth and Tyne railway was constructed between 1845-7 as

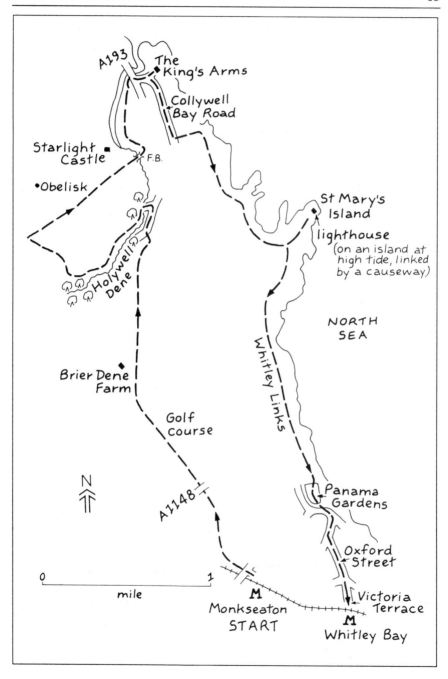

a colliery railway linked to the Seghill railway near Seaton Deleval. It was designed to form a link between the rivers Blyth and Tyne. The railway was developed and extended in the following decades to become one of the Seaton Burn colliery's main railway arteries with a coal handling staithe in Northumberland Dock, Howden, as well as becoming an important passenger line which was incorporated into the NER network in 1874. The section between Monkseaton and Hartley was known as the Avenue branch line and was constructed in 1860 on the route of the former Whitley waggonway. It earned its name from an avenue of trees close to Seaton Deleval Hall. Originally there had been plans to extend the line beyond Hartley to Seaton Sluice. Indeed work was begun, but when war broke out in 1914, the rails were removed and were never restored.

Follow the old railway under a road tunnel and along the edge of a large modern housing estate to Whitley Bay golf course. Just past the end of the golf course look for a wooden stile on the right and go over the stile to head for a second stile. Continue over the second stile and follow the path over a stream and straight ahead to another stile.

Go over this stile and then immediately over the next adjacent stile on the right into the next field. Cross this field, diagonally right, looking for a gap in the hedge. Go through the gap and continue straight ahead and then right into the field corner to a gate and the road.

Turn right along the road and just before the sign to Seaton Sluice village turn sharp left into a lane and the entrance to Holywell Farm. Follow the lane down to the bridge and then continue part way up the hill before taking a path on the left. Follow this wooded path along the side of Holywell Dene. Holywell Dene is part of the ancient woodland that once covered this part of Tyneside. In spring the woodland is carpeted with wild flowers including bluebells and wood anemones.

At a white gate turn right over a stile to follow field paths to a clear track. Straight ahead is an obelisk, part of the Seaton Hall Estate. A little further along the farm track Seaton Delaval Hall itself comes into view. Designed by Vanburgh and completed in 1728, the Hall was gutted by fire in 1822 and remained semi-derelict until the 1960s.

The path continues to a gate and into a field. Walk straight ahead, and look out for a series of steep steps on the left going down to the stream. Go down the steps and go under a large pipe and over a footbridge. Turn left and continue along a sandy path. To the left are the ruins of a folly called 'Starlight Castle' which is said to have been built in 24 hours by Sir Francis Delaval as a 100 guinea wager in the 1750s. Continue to a large road bridge and take the path up to the road. Cross the road and turn right and then first left along Colleywell Bay Road to the Kings Arms.

Seaton Sluice was once a thriving coal port and industrial centre, of which only the harbour remains as a reminder. The coal trade began in 1660 when Sir Ralph Delaval built a pier and wharves with the intention of establishing Seaton Sluice as a port for shipping locally produced salt. To overcome the silting up of the narrow Seaton Burn channel, huge sluice gates were built, just upstream of the current road bridge. At high tide the gates were closed damming a lake which stretched a mile up the valley, which is now an area of attractive marsh land. At low tide the sluices were opened to let the force of the water scour the Channel. In the 1860s the harbour proved to be too small for the number of ships using it, so Thomas Deleval cut a new entrance, with a wharf along the north side. The cut which has been restored in recent years is 900 feet long, 30 feet wide and 52 feet deep from the cliff top.

From the Kings Arms, there is a footpath on the left to a small bridge over 'the Cut' to Rocky Island and the Coastguard look out which is worth a quick visit. Otherwise turn right along Collywell Bay road past the village green. Continue along the road to a wooden gate and coastal footpath to St Mary's Island. The footpath continues along the coast passing Crag Point to a small car park which marks the boundary of North Tyneside District. Continue along the coastal path heading towards the lighthouse. Look out for the three high oblong ridges which were old rifle butts built in World War One. This section of the coast is a site of special scientific interest and in early summer is covered in wild orchids, yellow birdsfoot trefoil, white scurvy grass and pink thrift. It is also a favourite place for waders including redshanks, turnstones and gulls, as well as cormorants, kittiwakes and fulmars.

As you approach Curry's point, you will see a concrete causeway leading to St Mary's island and the light house. Curry's Point is named after a murderer whose body was hung in chains here, after being executed in Newcastle in 1739. The island is accessible three hours either side of low tide when there is an interesting walk across the causeway across an area of small rock pools hidden amongst the seaweed containing crabs, sea anemones and other creatures. At the end of the causeway a series of steps lead up to the 126-feet-high lighthouse, which stands on a huge sandstone plateau.

The current lighthouse was erected in 1897-8, but the history of the lighthouse goes back to medieval times. There was previously a chapel on the site, established by the monks of Tynemouth Priory, in which a light was kept burning continuously in the sanctuary to warn mariners of dangers. The Chapel was dedicated to St Helen, but all guiding lights for sailors were traditionally in the care of St Mary. In the mid 19th century an inn was built called 'The Square and Compass', which thanks to its location away from disturbance by the law, quickly became a popular drinking den, until the tenant landlord fell out with a local farmer resulting in his eviction. The inn lost its license and was converted into a Temperance hotel in 1895, coinciding with the decision to build the lighthouse. The lighthouse was finally decommissioned in 1984 when North Tyneside Council launched an appeal to save it for the public's benefit. The lighthouse now contains a small exhibition and shop. It is well worth the walk to St Mary's for the views north beyond Blyth to Newbiggin church, and south to Tynemouth and as far as Souter lighthouse on the cliffs at Marsden.

From the lighthouse causeway follow the road to the start of a coastal path along the edge of the cliff tops. The path is quite eroded in places so take care and avoid walking too near the cliff edge. Just past Whitley Links municipal golf course, the path descends to Brier Dene, which is currently being re-landscaped by Northumbria Water and which is due for completion in 1996. The path leads

The King's Arms, Seaton Sluice

directly on to North Promenade, testament to Whitley Bay's once enormous popularity as a seaside resort. In previous decades the entire Promenade would be full of families and couples enjoying the sea air. Whitley Bay is still a popular seaside destination for Tynesiders, but the focus of activity these days is concentrated among the pubs and amusement centres which throng the seafront and the enormous Dome of Spanish City which dominates the sky line.

Continue along the Promenade to a set of steps leading up to the formal Panama Gardens and the War Memorial. Turn right on the main road to a road junction and island. Cross the road, and then go up Park Avenue and then left up Oxford Road. Continue straight ahead over a Zebra crossing and then continue up Victoria Terrace to Whitley Bay Metro station.

---

7. Holywell Dene

A walk through the attractive arable land around Holywell dene, the last surviving pieces of ancient woodland in North Tyneside. The walk finishes with a stroll along the sand dunes north of Seaton Sluice

Distance: 8 ½ miles, 13km

Maps: Landranger 88 Tyneside and Durham; Pathfinder 536 Whitley Bay

Start: Shiremoor Metro Station

Finish: Seaton Sluice

Access: Use the Metro to the start of the walk. There are regular buses (no. 308) from Seaton Sluice, every 15 minutes (30 minutes on Sundays) to Whitley Bay and Newcastle

---

The Pub

Ye Olde Fat Ox, Holywell. This was once an old 16th century coaching inn on the main thoroughfare between Newcastle and the north. It is now a Bass pub serving Boddingtons, with a pleasant cosy atmosphere.

The Walk

Turn left out of Shiremoor Metro Station (Tynemouth bound platform), passing Bridge Terrace on the left. Just past the end of the terrace turn left along a public footpath which follows a wire fence between a school and playing fields. The path bends sharply right and then joins a road. Turn left past some shops and then cross the road to turn down Moor Edge road, passing a 1930s Masonic Hall

The lane soon becomes a track between fields, but just past a farm house, turn right on to a small road, the end of which is blocked by bollards. Continue straight ahead along a track which is muddy in places. Go past two large boulders on the road and then go over a small bridge crossing a stream and join a road. Continue straight

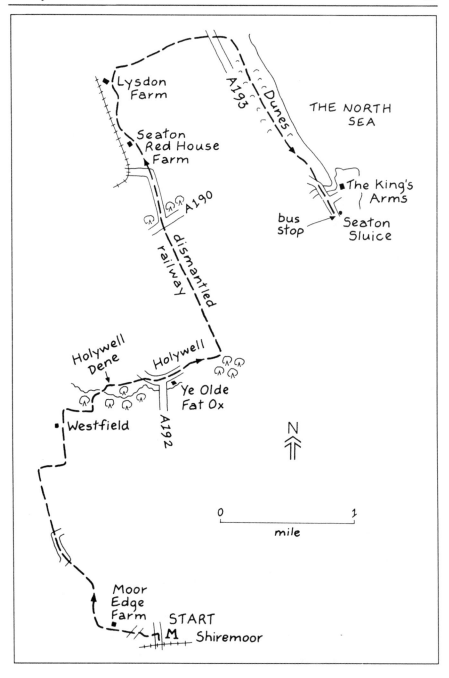

ahead through a gate passing some farm houses and kennels on the right. Where the road bends sharply to the right turn left along a farm track signed Holywell Dene and walk through open fields. Ignore the footpath sign to Holywell Grange Farm on the right, but continue straight ahead to where the path bends right and then left towards Westfield Farm. Continue past the farm and where the path appears to end at a small group of Hawthorn trees, turn right along the edge of the field. Where the path meets a track, cross a stream and a few metres on turn left and head down a path towards Holywell Dene.

Today, Holywell Dene is a relatively quiet nature reserve with a rich variety of spring flowers and bird life. In the 19th century, however, Holywell Dene was a popular countryside destination for the people of North Shields who used to travel out here in great numbers to picnic and enjoy the bluebell woods.

Follow the wooded path down to a footbridge. Cross the footbridge and follow the steam down Holywell Dene. The path emerges at some steps which lead on to the road. Continue straight ahead to join the main road and the main street running through Holywell village. Holywell village gets its name from the well that stands at the furthest end of this essentially linear settlement. At the far end of the village was a monastery and it was said that the waters could help cure blindness. There was also meant to be a secret passage from the monastery to Deleval Hall. A Manor house was later built on the site of the Monastery, where Mary Queen of Scots once stayed the night.

Continue along the main street passing Ye Olde Fat Ox on the right-hand side to the marble fountain at the end of the main street. Then take the road on the left-hand side to continue in the same direction. The road soon becomes an attractive track. Where the track crosses the dismantled Monkseaton-Blyth railway line look for steps on the right down to the former railway and turn left to follow the old railway path through attractive lined gorse cuttings to emerge into open grassland with views towards the Seaton Deleval monuments, erected in the 18th century when the Hall was built.

At the road, cross and take the road on the right which continues in the same direction. From this point there are some magnificent views towards the Blyth wind turbines. Where the road bends sharply left to cross the goods line, follow the footpath to the farm houses straight ahead. Go through the farm yard around the edge of the barn to a metal gate. Continue through the gate and then straight ahead along a green track to a wooden gate. Through the gate turn right along a hedge and at the field corner turn left towards the farm house ahead. Follow the lane to a second farm house towards a barn with bright red doors. Just before the barn turn right along a track to cross a small stream. At a gate cross the field aiming towards a white painted cottage ahead.

The path emerges at a main road. Cross the road and turn right towards a parking area and brick toilet block. Just past the toilet block turn right to follow a coastal path through sand dunes into Seaton Sluice. The dunes are particularly attractive in the spring and summer when in amongst the lyme and chuck grasses they are covered in flowers attracting moths and butterflies. Along the stretch of coast it is often possible to see cormorants, fulmars, gannets and waders. Look out too for small pieces of glass which are sometimes washed up along the shore and are testament to the days when Seaton Sluice had a glass bottle making industry.

Seaton Sluice was also once a thriving port used for shipping coal and salt when it was known as Hartley Pans (for further details see walk 6) but it is now a rather attractive sleepy village, with a village green and several excellent pubs. Cross over the cut by the road bridge and continue to the bus stop a little further along the road for regular buses into Tyneside.

8. Big Water

A walk along field paths to the Big Water Nature Reserve, a large man made lake and a haven for wildlife. The walk continues past Burradon Tower to Killingworth village, an attractive village that was once the home of George Stephenson.

Distance: 10 ½ miles, 17km

Maps: Landranger 88 Tyneside & Durham, Pathfinder 549 Newcastle Upon Tyne and Pathfinder 536 Whitley Bay

Start: Wansbeck Road Metro Station

Finish: Palmersville Metro Station

Access: Use the Tyne and Wear Metro

The Pub

Killingworth Arms, Killingworth village A typical country village pub bedecked with flowers with a friendly atmosphere. Inside there is a large bar area, as well as space to sit out at the front and enjoy a pint of Wards, Vaux's Samson or Thornes Bitter in the summer months

The Walk

From Wansbeck Road Metro station turn right along the road towards a roundabout. At the roundabout turn left and then cross the main road to the entrance of some playing fields, marked by black metal bollards. Turn left and walk along the edge of the playing fields along a small informal path used by local people as a dog walk, towards some houses and a lane. Follow the lane into a modern housing estate and at a road junction turn right and continue in the same direction to reach an area of open grassland. Look for a tarmac path on the right signed to Ouseburn.

Continue along the path which swings right to follow a stream emerging at a large area of open farm land and a small metal foot bridge, with the A1 in the far distance. Due to the recent construction of the A1 Western By-pass the footpath has been diverted, so at the footbridge turn left to follow a fenced path around the edge of the field towards a large tunnel under the new road, passing en route the remains of an old railway bridge. This is all that remains of the Burradon and Coxlodge Coal Company waggonway built in 1892 and which closed in 1956. The waggonway linked Hazelrigg colliery with the Kenton and Coxlodge waggonway to South Gosforth where it joined the North East railway.

Go under the road tunnel to a stile and then turn right to follow a footpath alongside the road. Ignore the first path on the left marked by a red metal gate, but take the second field path on the left to leave the roar of traffic behind and head towards a farm and lane. At the gate turn left along the lane, passing a group of attractive 19th century cottages with evocative names which rekindle another age – Woodbine, Myrtle, Rose and Ivy. At the next group of houses on the left turn right down a muddy tack signed Hazelrigg to a gateway. Go through the gateway and continue along the track which soon becomes an attractive grassy path leading to a stile and woodland.

Once over the stile, take the path on the right ignoring the path to the left and walk through woods to a gate. Continue straight ahead around the back of terraced housing to a road. Cross the road and, keeping in the same direction, follow a stony track skirting around the edge of Hazelrigg. The track soon becomes a grassy verge with allotments on the left and terraced housing on the right. At a group of wooden bollards on the left, take a tarmac path passing a children's play area on the left and modern housing on the right. Hazelrigg is very close to Newcastle Airport and there is a constant procession of planes landing and taking off.

The tarmac path emerges on to a road and into a housing estate. Continue straight ahead towards a road junction and the main road. At the main road turn left towards a Emmerson's Hotel and public house. Just past the pub turn right along a lane towards the Big Water Nature Reserve. The lane ends at a small car park. Head for the gate ahead and continue straight ahead into the Nature Reserve.

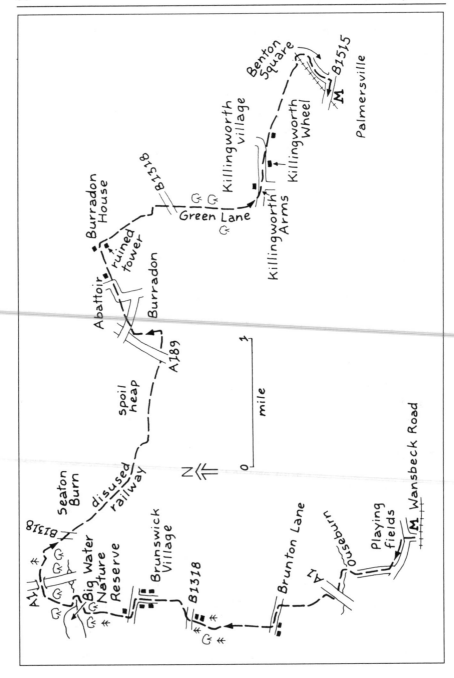

Big Water is actually a man made construction formed by subsidence from deep mining. This caused the land surface to collapse and a huge lake or flash was created. The flash is the biggest in South East Northumberland and was once twice the size, but has since been filled in with colliery waste. The site is now managed by the Northumberland Wildlife Trust and has become a haven for birds including the grasshopper warbler, willow warbler, great crested grebe and reed bunting as well as being an important wintering site for arctic birds. The Nature Reserve is rich with marsh plants and in June it is covered with yellow flax iris and early purple orchids.

Follow the path around the edge of Big Water before turning right to a bridge crossing Seaton Burn. Cross the bridge and turn left, and then look for a path on the right through willow trees leading to a wooden kissing gate and a track. At the track, turn right to go over a footbridge crossing the A1. From the footbridge follow a gravel path to the edge of a small area of trees and a stream, Brenkley Burn, which is filled with bulrushes and water plantain. Turn left to go over a footbridge over the stream and walk up the hill towards a road and row of terraced housing.

Turn right through a wooden kissing gate to follow the line of a disused railway, now converted into a cycle path by North Tyneside Council. This was once the route of the Seaton Burn railway, a branch of the Brunton Shields railway. Opened in 1837 it used fixed engines and ropes to haul waggons along the line to the junction at Burradon.

The track leads to a road, with the exit onto the road marked by a set of red bollards. Cross the road and continue straight ahead along a clear path through open wasteland. The path crosses a track. Keep straight ahead ignoring the fork on the right but continue onto an elevated section of the old track bed keeping to the main path which emerges at a large area of waste ground dominated by a large spoil heap. Skirt around the edge of the spoil heap to join a clear track and then veer slightly right to join a concrete lane leading to a road.

Cross the road and turn right and then take the track on the left heading towards a road tunnel. At the tunnel go through the left-hand arch of the tunnel to join a clear path which was once the former track bed of the railway. Straight ahead is a large industrial plant belching out steam and on the left open fields. Follow the track straight ahead and then look for a path on the left by some wooden sleepers. Follow this path across the fields past a hawthorn bush aiming for a telegraph pole ahead. The footpath emerges at a busy main road. To avoid crossing this to a very overgrown footpath, turn right along the road and scramble up the embankment by the bridge on to a road.

Cross the road and turn right. Just past the second lamp post look for a footpath on the left marked by a gap in some hawthorn bushes. The path continues across fields to emerge further up the road. Cross the road and continue in the same direction passing the entrance to a modern housing estate, Cheviot Grange on the right. Take the next road on the right at a sharp bend in the road, passing Whitley Bay Meat Supplies on the left. The lane leads to Burradon House farm. Continue past the farm buildings and follow the lane as it bends to the right passing the remains of Burradon tower, built in 1552 by Bertram Anderson.

Continue in the same direction with fields either side and with the path gradually ascending until it becomes a grassy path which finally reaches a road. Cross the road and continue straight ahead, ignoring the lane which continues to the left. This path is known as Green Lane and skirts along the edge of Killingworth as an attractive tree lined corridor. The lane continues under two underpasses and finally emerges at a small park. Follow the path which swings to the left and then aim for a set of large ornate metal gates, once the entrance to Killingworth House, and go down some stone steps to a road.

At the road turn left through Killingworth village, passing the Killingworth Arms on the left. Just past the Killingworth Arms is a road junction. Continue straight ahead along the pavement. Continue for a short distance looking out for a large metal wheel on the right-hand side. This marks the site of Killingworth High Pit, part of the West Moor Colliery sunk in 1810. It is here that George Stephenson first showed his engineering capabilities by rebuilding the pumping engine in the space of three days enabling the flooded shaft to be drained and worked. From here a waggonway ran south to Willington via Wallsend where Stephenson later experimented with fixed engines and set the waggonway gauge at the famous width of 4 foot 8 inches.

Continue along the road past the wheel to a lane on the right-hand side. From the lane, head down to a bungalow and go through the stile beside a gate. Continue straight ahead to the corner of the field and continue in the same direction towards a barbed wire fence. Follow the barbed wire fence to the Metro line embankment. Turn left to a stile and then, taking great care, cross the Metro line.

From the Metro line go along a ginnel to a road and then turn right to join another road. Follow the road round continuing in the same direction through Benton Square industrial estate to reach the main road. Turn right along the road to Palmersville Metro station.

9. The Wallbottle Waggonway – a walk from Lemington to Ponteland

A walk across the gentle undulating countryside west of Newcastle, through the attractive village of Walbottle and hamlets south of Ponteland, following for much of its route the Walbottle waggonway which brought coal from the Duke of Northumberland's collieries at Walbottle to the waterside coal staithes at Lemington on the banks of the River Tyne.

Distance: 6 ½ miles, 10km

Maps: Landranger 88 Tyneside & Durham, Pathfinder 548 Blaydon and Prudoe, 535 Ponteland

Start: Lemington Post office

Finish: Ponteland High Street

Access: Very regular buses from Newcastle Central Station and Market Street (No. 21/22) every 10 minutes Monday to Saturday, every 20 minutes on Sunday to Lemington; and buses from Ponteland back into Newcastle City Centre about every 15 minutes Monday to Saturday, hourly on Sunday.

The Pubs

The Original Masons, Walbottle. A pleasant Scottish and Newcastle pub with a warm and friendly atmosphere selling Marston's, Theakston's and Newcastle Exhibition on tap. Its real delight is its food menu with some interesting dishes including a 72 oz rump steak and a 48 oz burger which are provided on the house to those who can eat them within the hour.

There is also a good choice of pubs in Ponteland at the end of the walk: The **Seven Stars** pub is the oldest pub in the town with wooden floors and chalk written signs promoting an excellent selection of real ales and foreign bottled beer. The **Blackbird Inn** was originally a 17th century manor house, built onto a 14th century pele tower. It stands on the site of a peace treaty signed between the

Scots and the English in the 13th century. An underground tunnel links the pub with St Mary's church which stands opposite.

The Walk

The walk begins outside Lemington Post Office. Turn right towards the bridge, but just before the bridge take the path by the electrical sub station down to the old railway line. On the left is the 120-feet-high Lemington Glass Cone which is the only reminder of the Northumberland Glass Company, established in 1787. There were originally four large glass cones which produced flat glass, but in 1906 the site was purchased by GEC who expanded the works to produce bulbs and tubing for all types of electrical lamps. The surviving glass cone was cleaned and repaired in 1993.

Turn right along the old railway line and head under a bridge. Where the path forks ignore the left fork and continue straight ahead to a wooden gap stile. Go through the stile and follow a tarmac path uphill along the edge of a housing estate to a second wooden gap stile and an attractive path lined with young saplings and other hedgerow plants. The path leads to a road. Cross the road and follow the path straight ahead to the next road, a narrow country lane. Cross the road and walk up a set of shallow wooden steps to a path which provides magnificent views down to the River Tyne and on a clear day across to the Durham Dales and the North Pennines.

This path emerges at a clear cross roads of paths, just before a group of houses. On the right-hand side, where there is now rough grassland stood Milecastle 9, part of the Hadrian's Wall fortifications. As their name suggests, milecastles were constructed one Roman mile (1,620 yards) apart all along the Wall and would have housed a garrison of around 12 men.

At the cross roads turn left along a stony track running between fields towards a group of trees and the walled gardens of Walbottle Hall. The house's castellations are just visible over the wall, but a better view is afforded as the path bends round the front of the house.

Where the track meets a road turn left towards Walbottle village green. At the green continue straight ahead past a brightly painted

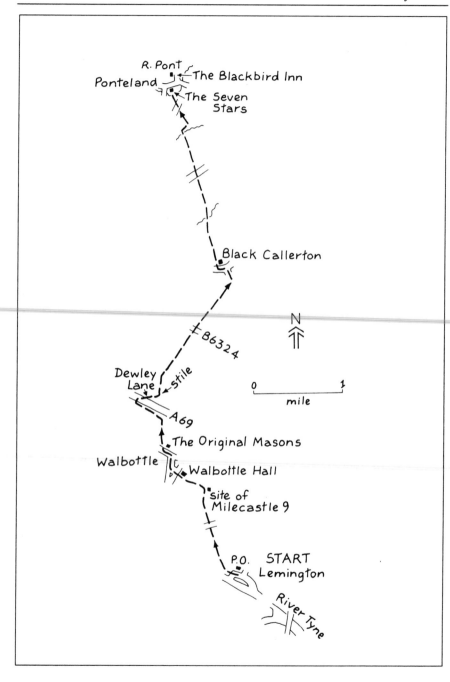

relic of a bygone agricultural age and a Victorian bath tub adorned with flowers and a plaque announcing its identity to interested passers by! At the road turn right past the local primary school and onto the main road. Cross the road with care and turn left to the Original Masons.

Immediately past the Original Masons look for a narrow lane marked with a footpath signed for Stamfordham Rd. This is the line of the Walbottle Moors Waggonway, a late 18th century horse drawn waggonway system, on which George Stephenson was employed when a boy to keep livestock clear of the tracks. Continue up the lane and through two gates, passing a school on the right. The lane soon becomes a narrow footpath which descends down a slope to a busy main road, the A69. To avoid crossing the A69 turn left to follow a footpath running parallel to the road to a underpass which leads under the road.

From the underpass follow the lane, Dewley Road, which climbs gradually between attractive fields. Look for a small wooden stile on the left in a clearing between bushes and go over the stile into a field. From here the Walbottle waggonway had three or four branches and the route follows one of them across an area of shallow pit workings.

Go over the stile and cross the field heading diagonally right towards the fence and three knee high metal poles. At the fence turn left and follow the line of the fence along a clear path aiming for a strip of hedgerow ahead. Continue straight ahead to the next stile, the path then continues between gorse bushes towards a line of telegraph poles and a stile. Walk straight ahead towards the lane

At the lane continue straight ahead over a stile signed to Black Callerton, and follow the footpath along the edge of the field to a second stile. Continue in the same direction over another field towards a metal gate and tree ahead. At the gate continue into the next field and head towards the right of a small hillock crowned with trees, aiming for the left-hand corner of the field and a stile. The stile leads over a small bridge crossing a stream and a second stile. Follow a bush lined path into a field and continue straight ahead towards a gap in the hedge. At the next field, head for a gate and a lane.

At the lane turn left to a group of farm buildings known as 'Black Callerton' where a plaque commemorates the fact that George Stephenson once worked near here at Dollypit. He was involved in developing the first locomotives to replace the horses that used to haul the waggons of coal along the wooden rails. A footpath sign points the way to Ponteland through the farm court yard under a magnificent arch and gateway. Black Callerton is very close to Newcastle airport and it provides a close up view of planes taking off from the runway. At the second gate turn right at the sign post to Hold House. Head for a stile and a small footbridge over a stream and then take a second stile. Continue straight ahead towards a group of trees and fence to a stile and gate. Go over the stile to a cross roads of paths.

Continue straight ahead following the line of the signpost marked 'Ponteland 1¼ miles', following the edge of a field down to a new road. Cross the road with care and continue straight ahead towards school playing fields to a footbridge. Turn right to follow the stream to a disused railway track which was once the Ponteland branch line railway from the Blyth and Tyne railway, which was closed to passengers in 1929. Part of the line has since been incorporated into the Tyne and Wear Metro airport branch. Follow the track to the road, and then cross the road into Ponteland park. At the footbridge over the River Pont turn right over the river and head towards Ponteland High Street, where there is a choice of excellent pubs. Buses for Newcastle leave from the bus shelter opposite the Seven Stars pub. Next to the bus stop in the grounds of the District Offices is the remains of a pele tower, known as the Vicar's Pele.

10. The Upper Tyne

A fascinating walk along the banks of the River Tyne from the heart of Newcastle city centre to the village of Wylam, exploring the industrial archaeology of the River Tyne.

Distance: 9 miles, 14.5km

Maps: Landranger 88 Tyneside and Durham area; Pathfinder Newcastle and Blaydon & Prudhoe 548

Start: Newcastle Central Station

Finish: Wylam Station

Access: Regular trains from Wylam station back to Newcastle, hourly Monday-Saturday and two hourly on Sundays.

The Pubs

The Boat House, Newburn is located in a picturesque setting on the banks of the River Tyne overlooking open fields. A friendly Bass pub with an attractive cosy interior and a small sitting out area. Don't forget to look for the 1771 flood mark on the outside wall.

The Boat House, Wylam An excellent pub to finish the walk, conveniently placed next to Wylam station. The Boat House offers a wide range of real ales including Conciliation, Theakston's, Timothy Taylor's Landlord, Pedigree and Youngers No. 3.

The Walk

From Newcastle Central Station turn right past the Royal Station Hotel and continue down Westgate Road passing Bolbeck Hall on the right. Westgate Road skirts around the edge of a railway viaduct and emerges at a road junction opposite Castle Keep. Cross the road and continue along a wooden walk-way under the old gateway. Continue straight ahead to a series of stone steps, Castle Stairs and go down to the riverside. At the road, cross with care and head to

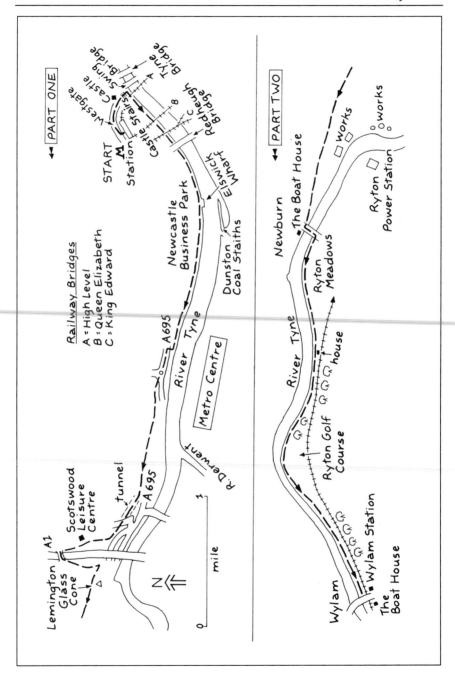

the banks of the River Tyne and an attractive lamp lined walk-way. Turn right to head up stream and go under the High Level Bridge.

The High Level bridge was constructed by Robert Stephenson and T.E. Harrison between 1845-9 to link the Darlington to Gateshead railway to the Newcastle to Berwick railway. It is a two tier bridge on which the railway runs below and the road above, and it is now a grade one listed structure.

The riverside walk-way has been extensively landscaped as part of the Tyne and Wear Development Corporation's attempt to regenerate the city of Newcastle. The first 2 miles of the walk follow this walk-way, much of which has been attractively planted, and which includes some interesting sculpture and a series of interpretative panels detailing the story of the Tyne and its industries.

The story of the Tyne is closely linked to the story of the bridges crossing its waters. The first bridge was thought to date back to the Roman Emperor Hadrian in the second century AD. It was thought to be somewhere near the swing bridge. This was replaced in the 12th century by an elegant twelve arched bridge in which the division between Northumberland and the Palatine of Durham was

Tyne bridges

marked by a blue stone. This bridge survived until 1771 when it was destroyed in a huge flood and needed to be replaced. However, by the mid 19th century, the replacement bridge was increasingly seen as an obstruction to further development higher up the Tyne and it was finally replaced by a temporary wooden structure and then by Armstrong's Swing Bridge (see walk 2).

The construction of the Swing bridge coincided with the dredging of the Tyne to be make it accessible for larger boats. Until the mid 19th century the Tyne was virtually unnavigable and filled with sand banks. The only way through was with flat bottomed barges known as 'keels' propelled and rowed along the Tyne by skilled keelmen with cargos of coal to meet sea-going vessels at the mouth of the River. The dredging of the Tyne opened the river to larger ships, and created Northumberland Dock and Albert Edward Dock, but it was to prove the death knell for the long tradition of the Tyne keelmen.

From the High Level Bridge continue past the timber framed Quayside pub dating back to the 15th century, which was a working cooperage until fairly recently. It stands in stark contrast to the newly constructed Bridge Court a few yards further on. In between the gaps of buildings on the right-hand side are glimpses of land-scaped gardens set into the cliff face.

The walk-way continues under the 1981 Queen Elizabeth II Metro Bridge, the 1906 King Edward VII rail bridge and the 1983 Redheugh road bridge. Just beyond the last bridge the walk-way continues along the parallel road for a few yards to pass a derelict building before rejoining the riverside. This area of Tyneside is known as Elswick and was once a thriving industrial sector with a tannery, gas works and lead works, all of which have long since disappeared.

A little further on is the truncated remains of Elswick Wharf, a timber wharf which was constructed in the 19th century for loading and unloading cargo, and was once 200 metres in length. The Wharf now provides excellent views of the river between Edward VII and Scotswood bridges and over the water to Dunston Staithes.

Dunston Staithes were built by the North Eastern Railway in two stages. The first staithes with three berths were opened in 1893. A second similar staith was opened in 1903. It was designed to load sea and ocean going vessels with coal, fed by a series of hoppers from coal waggons which were shunted along the upper deck of the structure. In their heyday the Dunston staithes could load six ships at once. Part of the structure was dismantled in the 1970s and 80s but the rest has been restored as a tribute to the last working timber staithes on the Tyne.

A little further on is the newly constructed Newcastle Business Park, a series of post-modernist buildings and attractive landscaped gardens complete with various spherical sculptures. This was once the site of the Elswick ship yards, founded in 1847 by W.G. Armstrong, to develop his work on hydraulic technology, to build cranes and other lifting gear and later field guns. During the Crimean War Armstrong worked closely with C.W. Mitchell of Walker on a gunboat for the Admiralty and in 1882 the two companies amalgamated, with the Walker yard specialising in merchant ships and the Elswick yard in gun boats. The Company went on to build gunboats with armaments for the Royal Navy and the navies of other nations, particularly Japan. In 1913 much of this work was transferred down stream to Walker, although guns and later tanks continued to be made at Elswick until the company merged with Vickers of Barrow in 1928.

Continue along the walk-way through the Business Park passing a small wooden jetty decorated with a stone mosaic. Opposite this was once the island of Kings Meadow, large enough to host races and athletic events. It was complete with its own public house, the 'Countess Of Coventry'. The island was removed when the River Tyne was dredged in the 19th century.

At the end of the Newcastle Business Park the riverside footpath continues up hill to join the main road. At the main road, cross and turn left past a roundabout and then take the path on the right to join the line of a disused railway line. This is the Scotswood, Newburn and Wylam railway built in 1876 and which operated until 1968. This stretch of the walk-way is currently an area of derelict land, but is gradually being improved since it is now on the line of the newly proposed Hadrian's Wall National Trail running from Wallsend to Bowness on Solway. On the left-hand side are the huge Vickers workshops, heirs to Armstrong's armaments company.

Continue through a tunnel, which has recently been breached to create more light for pedestrians and cyclists and emerge at a fenced tarmac path leading up a hill to an area of open grass. Continue along the tarmac path towards Scotswood Leisure Centre. Just before the Leisure Centre take a left fork over the footbridge crossing the Western By-pass. Over the bridge drop down to the left and then turn right along the road and then take the first right to rejoin the old railway line. This becomes an attractive route passing over the wooded Sugley Dene and then into Lemington past the Lemington glass cone on the left (see walk 9). Continue straight ahead under the road bridge, ignoring the path forking on the right to walk past Ryton power station and the tantalising smells of the huge Warburtons' bakery. The section of the old railway between Lemington and Wylam was once the line of the Wylam waggonway built in 1748 to transport coal from Wylam colliery to the staithes at Lemington. The waggonway closed in 1867 when mining ceased at Wylam and part

The Boat House, Newburn

of the track-bed was then used for the Scotswood, Newburn and Wylam railway.

The track emerges close to a bridge over the Tyne. Straight ahead is the Boat House public house. A plaque commemorates the fact that George Stephenson worked near here between 1798 and 1801. He was in charge of Robert Hawthorn's new pumping engine at Water Row Pit, where George's father Robert was fireman.

Cross Newburn Bridge over the River Tyne and look for a flight of steps on the right-hand side which joins a footpath along the riverside known as the Keelman's Way, named after the men who used to navigate the Keels up and down the River Tyne. This is a very attractive footpath which runs through an area known as Ryton Meadows, a nature reserve fringed with gorse bushes and home to a variety of birds.

At a small group of houses the footpath continues to a gate and then runs parallel to the Newcastle-Carlisle railway line. Take a path on the right down to an attractive wooded riverside walk, which emerges at Ryton golf course. Continue straight ahead along the river on a clear path, with Wylam bridge gradually coming into view. The path ends in a small car park adjacent to Wylam Railway Station The second 'Boat House' pub is straight ahead next to the railway station.

11. A Wylam Circular – on the track of the railways

This is a circular walk through attractive countryside on the western edge of Tyneside starting in the Upper Tyne Valley just within Northumberland. The walk begins and ends at Wylam, an important landmark in the development of Britain's railway network, but climbs up to Heddon-on the Wall, to one of the finest stretches of the Roman Wall outside the Northumberland National Park.

Distance: 10 miles, 16km

Maps: Landranger 88 Tyneside and Durham, Pathfinder 548 Blaydon & Prudoe

Start and Finish: Wylam Railway station

Access: Regular trains from Newcastle hourly Monday-Saturday and two hourly on Sundays. Car parking is available at the railway station and at the start of the Wylam waggonway, signed off the main road through Wylam.

The Pubs

The Three Tuns, Heddon-on-the-Wall is very much a local pub with a traditional atmosphere and offers Theakston's Bitter and XB, Marston's Pedigree, McEwans Scotch Bitter and Newcastle Exhibition. It also offers a weekday and Saturday bar menu and a Sunday dinner between 12.00 and 2.30.

The Boathouse, Wylam, opposite the station, is a free house offering a range of real ales including Theakstons XB, Timothy Taylor's Landlord, Butterknowle Conciliation, Boddingtons, Draught Bass, Younger's No. 3 as well as guest beers and a lunchtime food menu (weekends only in winter). A warm cosy atmosphere, this is an excellent pub to relax in after the walk while awaiting the train back to Newcastle.

The Walk

The walk begins at Wylam station on the Newcastle to Carlisle line which was opened in 1838. It is one of the oldest stations in Britain still in regular use and nearby is one of the more interesting features of this line, a signal box straddling the line. A plaque, on the side of the station building commemorates the South Yorkshire born engineer, ironmaster and colliery owner, Benjamin Thompson (1779-1867).

Leave the station car park and turn right across the bridge, heading into Wylam. At the end of the bridge turn right by the war memorial following signs for George Stephenson's Cottage, and the start of the Wylam waggonway.

Those interested in railway history should visit the Wylam Railway Museum on Falcon Terrace just north of the car park. The museum illustrates Wylam's remarkable place in the development of the railways as the birth place of three important railway pioneers, George Stephenson, (1781-1848), Timothy Hackworth (1786-1850) and Nicholas Wood (1795-1865). Wylam was also where William

Wylam Station

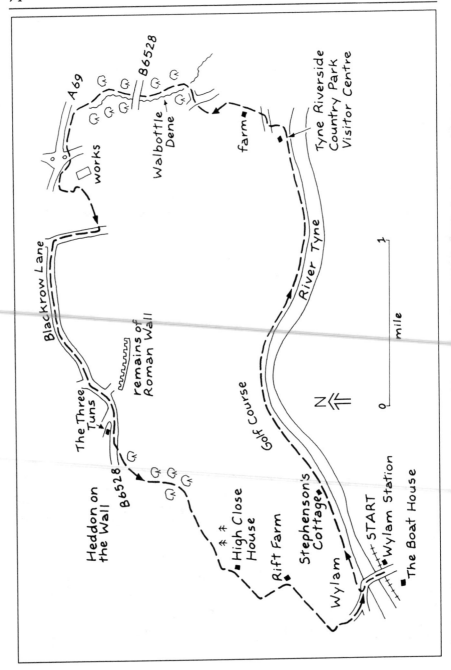

Hedley built his experimental steam locomotives, "Puffing Billy" and "Wylam Dilly".

At the car park turn right along the waggonway following a tarmac path across a small road and into woodland. The Wylam waggonway was built around 1748 to transport coal from Wylam colliery to Lemington where the river was deep enough to enable keels or barges to transport the coal to the coast. The waggonway was later part of the North Wylam line laid in 1876 and used until it closed in 1968.

The route continues on past the cottage where George Stephenson was born in 1781 and was once the home of four families, one to each room. The Stephenson family room has been restored and is the only room open to the public. This was an ideal place to stimulate the interest of a boy who was to become one of the world's greatest engineering pioneers. Stephenson would have grown up surrounded by machines and coal mine workings and would have watched the horse drawn waggons trundling along the waggonway. The cottage is now in the care of the National Trust and is open to the public on Thursday, Saturday and Sunday afternoons between 13.00 and 17.00, during the summer between April and October.

After passing the cottage continue along the old waggonway, past Wylam golf course on the left. Opposite a five bar gate and kissing gate on to the golf course, take a small gate to the right on to a small track next to the river which heads through trees.

The track stays parallel with the waggonway for a short distance before diverging to the right as it follows the line of the river. The path offers good views of the huge Ryton power station in the distance. Watch out for the stone post, dated 1785 and featuring the coat of arms of Newcastle Upon Tyne which marks the tidal limit of the Tyne.

At Ryton Island, the riverside path rejoins the waggonway and continues parallel to the river. On the outskirts of Newburn the path opens into a picnic area and children's playground which offers views over the mudflats and shingles of the Tyne. By the Newburn slipway is the Newburn Country Park Visitor Centre. Inside there are interesting photographs of old Newburn, information about the old Isabella Colliery at Throckley, the Wylam Waggonway and the flora and fauna of the Country park.

After the Visitor Centre continue along the path at the far side of the slipway for a short distance, before crossing a small footbridge. Take a left turning between the fence surrounding a sports ground and Reigh Burn. Look out for the old Newburn railway station on the left, now disused, which closed in 1968.

The path emerges on to a road. Turn right here and in front of the Newburn Leisure Centre, cross the road and head up a small lane towards a farm on the brow of a hill. Follow the lane past the right-hand side of the farm, and past a disused barn. The path narrows and enters a small wood.

The wooded path soon turns left and heads uphill towards Walbottle. It passes behind a row of houses to the end of a cul-de-sac. Turn left along the cul-de-sac and then right again on to Hallow Drive. At the top of the road cross the A6085 on to Briar Lane opposite, and at the end of Briar Lane turn left around a slight bend. After 50 yards cross the road, and go through a kissing gate into Walbottle Dene.

Take the right-hand path which drops gently into the Dene, turn left at the bottom, cross a small footbridge and follow the path on right-hand side of New Burn through an attractive wooded valley. The path rises steadily and emerges on to a road on the outskirts of Throckley. Cross the road and head back down into the Dene through a wooden gate system.

The path winds its way through the Dene. It stays on the right-hand side of the Burn and eventually bends around to the left. It eventually emerges from the trees, and turns to the right. Another path joins from the left. Head up towards the A69, and just before a right turn up to a tunnel, turn left down a small lane past some corrugated iron enclosures. This emerges on to a small road parallel to the A69. Follow this around the edge of an industrial estate.

After a turn to the left, head up to the road, cross and follow the fence opposite towards the right. Walk across the front of the entrance to the brickworks and follow a road which skirts around the right-hand side of the complex.

At a junction the road heads left towards a farm house. Head through the farmyard, and follow the road through a number of farm buildings as it turns left and then bends right, before heading away from the brickworks through fields. The road ends at a junction with Drove Lane. At this junction head right along Drove Lane and head towards another farm. At the farm take a left turn along a road between the farm and a stone house. Follow this road for some distance.

The road eventually joins another road which heads left up to Heddon-On-The-Wall. To visit the Roman remains, turn left and then first right to a section of wall which is a small part of the 73 mile long Hadrian's wall, built during the reign of Emperor Hadrian (AD 117-138). The Wall once stretched from Wallsend on the Tyne to Bowness on Solway. This section is built to the original specification of 10 Roman feet thick. Further west the Wall was later narrowed during construction to 8 feet or less, presumably to speed up the process of building.

From the Wall, walk up the hill past the village green to rejoin the B6528 opposite the white walled Three Tuns pub. From the Three Tuns turn right along the B6528. Just before the end of Heddon on the left-hand side is a metal gate and public footpath sign to Hill Head and Heddon Low Farm. Follow this path through a small wood and a clearing and into more woods behind houses. Keep on the path nearest the houses until the brow of a hill offering excellent views across the Tyne Valley.

The path begins to head downhill and bears right into a silver birch wood. Almost immediately the path intercepts the main path through the woods. Turn left on the main path and head downhill. The path swings to the right under electricity cables and emerges from the woods on to a public bridleway beneath a pylon. Turn right along a stony lane and climb over a stone stile into a field.

The path veers slightly to the left to a wooden stile in the next fence and then again across the next field. In the third field head for the bottom corner to a five bar and a kissing gate. Go through the kissing gate and join a road. Turn right here. Walk along the road for a short distance to the drive of High Close House. Follow the public footpath up the drive to the end of a beech hedge. At the end of the hedge and just before the main gate to the house turn right and follow a wall.

At the end of the wall the path goes over a wooden stile, and then left over a further stile into a small copse. Bear right through the copse, and leave over a stile into a field. Keep to the hedge at the end of the field and walk straight ahead.

Leave the field over a stile into a lane. Almost immediately there is a public footpath sign to the left, heading to Stephenson's Cottage and Wylam. Take this path towards Rift Farm. Just before Rift Farm use the wooden stile over a fence to the right, and at the end of the fence go left over another stile. Cut diagonally across a small field to a wooden stile at the bottom, and follow the steps into a wood. Go over a small footbridge and ascend the other side of the valley over two other small bridges. Enter a field through a kissing gate. Slightly to the right is a small path which gently bears left to a ladder stile into the outskirts of Wylam. Continue straight on a gravel path behind houses.

At the road turn left on to Dene Road and take the cut directly across. Head straight on to the junction and take a right fork towards the rear of shops and then turn left on to Jackson Road. At the end of Jackson Road turn right on to Hedley Road and then left on to The Dene. At the bottom of The Dene, turn left in front of a school and then immediately on the right, head back to the car park. Head out of the car park, and back over the bridge to the Railway Station and the Boathouse.

12. The Shields Ferry

Beginning with dramatic cliff views, this walk explores the coast between Marsden and South Shields and continues around the mouth of the Tyne to the riverside shipyards and docks. The walk uses the Metro ferry to cross the Tyne and finishes at Tynemouth by the historic ruins of Tynemouth Castle and Priory.

Distance: 8 miles, 12km

Maps: Landranger 88 Tyneside and Durham, Pathfinder 549 Newcastle upon Tyne

Start: Grotto Public house at Marsden, Grid Reference 399649

Finish: Tynemouth Metro station,

Access: Regular buses from South Shields (on the metro) to Marsden Grotto, no E1 every 20 minutes. Use the Metro from Tynemouth Metro station

The Pubs

This route offers a wide range of excellent pubs. There is no lack of choice, and it is very difficult to make recommendations. However, two which are well worth visiting stand opposite each other on either side of the Tyne. **The Alum House, South Shields** is a lively pub which serves a wide range of real ales. On our visit these included Everards Beacon, Shepherd Neame's Bishops Finger, Marstons' Pedigree, Camerons' Strongarm and Banks' Bitter. It is located by the South Shields ferry platform and is an ideal place to await a ferry.

On the other side of the river, just around the corner from the North Shields platform is **The Chainlocker, North Shields**, a small cosy pub with a real fire in winter and a range of ales including Tetley Bitter, Pilgrim Progress and Crusader, Burton Ale, Timothy Taylor's Landlord, and Bass, as well as its excellent Chainlocker Ale brewed at Marston Moor. The Chainlocker also serves Addlestones cider and a superb menu with some excellent fish dishes. Also well worth a mention en route is the **Port Hole**, close to the Chainlocker offering a more maritime atmosphere with an equally good selection of real ales.

The Walk

From the Marsden Grotto pub, head north along the coast into the National Trust Leas Nature Reserve. Follow the path, which offers stunning coastal views towards Tynemouth Priory in the far distance. At a number of points along this path there are interesting interpretative panels detailing the history of the coastline, and identifying some of the most interesting flora and fauna.

Look out for the unusual small twin-humped island known as Velvet Beds or Camel Island which still retains the remains of an old roman quay which was used by Gypsy parties in the 18th and 19th centuries. The walk continues alongside Frenchman's Bay. Frenchman's Bay is the site of an old gun battery which was so-named to mark the site of an old ship which foundered in these waters. In the past a set of wooden steps from the beach to the top of the cliff made the bay an ideal haunt for smugglers. These bays are the homes for many interesting birds at different times of the year including the fulmar petrel in spring and summer and the turnstone in winter.

Just after Frenchman's Bay the path divides. Take the path which heads down hill to Trow Point and Graham Sand. Walk along the tarmac path, noting the interesting stacks and sandstone platforms. At the end of the coastal footpath descend on to the beach in front of the Waters Edge pub.

Continue along the beach until a small lifeguards hut, and leave by a small tarmac path between the sand dunes. Head for the large Sundial pub. Pass this and head to the road. Cross the road and enter the South Marina park with its attractive boating lake. Keeping to the right side of the lake walk towards the end of the park, being ever vigilant for the small gauge miniature steam trains of the lake-side railroad!!

Cross the railway track and walk along the side of the lake and at

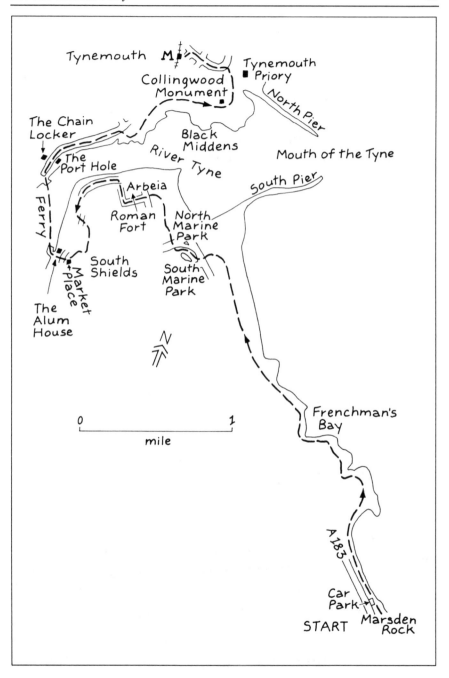

the far end turn right over the railway and up to a gateway on to a road. Cross the road and walk past a preserved life boat, the Tyne, over two hundred years old and one of the first to be built. A panel explains in detail the dispute between its two alleged inventors, William Wouldhave and Henry Greathead both of whom claim credit for the design.

From the life boat turn right into North Marina park, an attractive park with some Japanese style gardens and a magnificent children's play area with a mock up wooden ship. Following signs to the Arbeia Roman fort, head up the hill through the park to a beacon overlooking the harbour. The beacon was erected in 1988 to mark the four-hundredth anniversary of the defeat of the Spanish Armada. From here there are superb views of the two piers guarding the mouth of the River Tyne.

Follow the path to large signs welcoming visitors to the Roman Fort at Arbeia. Cross the road and continue down Fort Street which runs alongside the excavated fort. Arbeia was once a major supply base for the Roman campaigns in Scotland and was later used by garrisons stationed along Hadrian's Wall. The Fort is the only known permanent stone-built supply base of the Roman Empire. The excavations are quiet extensive and remain on-going. There is also a reconstruction of the fort's gateway and a museum containing an exhibition containing many of the finds found during recent excavations and is well worth a visit. After passing the fort turn right on to Baring Street past the visitor entrance to Arbeia and then turn left towards the Turks Head pub. From here there are good views over to North Shields and some of the docks and warehouses along the Tyne.

At the pub, cross the road and walk along a footpath which follows the line of the riverside below. As the footpath bends, the yellow Tyne Metro ferry can often be seen crossing the river. On the other side of the river is the old High Light lighthouse and a mural of two fish carved into the hillside. A little further on is a statue of Dolly Peel, a well known South Shields fishwife by day and smuggler by night. She lived between 1782 and 1857 and was famous for her protection of fugitives from the press gang, and her wartime nursing activities which preceded Florence Nightingale by some 50 years. At the bridge ahead, take the steps down to Wapping Street, turn left and follow the footpath beneath the bridge.

The path runs parallel to the Metro line sidings, before emerging at Salem Street, where the route head towards South Shields Town Centre. The walk can be terminated here by turning left and heading to South Shields Metro station, but to do so would be to miss out on the walks two excellent pubs which are just around the corner!

Turn right and head towards the market cross and through the market to a gap between buildings. Continue down the hill towards the South Shields ferry platform and the Alum House pub which stands adjacent.

The ferry runs approximately every 30 minutes and the short crossing takes about seven minutes. The trip across the Tyne provides an interesting waterside view of the large ships moored along docks either side of the river bank.

On leaving the ferry head up the jetty, and turn right on to dry land. Immediately ahead is the Chainlocker. From the Chainlocker turn right and walk past the Port Hole pub towards the Fish Docks. This area has recently been extensively refurbished with attractive benches and various sculptures. North Shields is still an active fishing port as the number of fishing boats and nets testify. Fresh fish can be bought at shops along the quayside and it is well worth stopping off for a bag of fish and chips. At the end of the quay, just past the fishing sheds, turn right at the New Dolphin pub. Head through an area of small warehouses used to store the freshly caught fish and then towards the harbour mouth.

On reaching the riverside turn left following public footpath signs to Tynemouth Priory and Castle along the promenade. Take the second path on the left up to the large monument on the hill to Admiral Collingwood, Nelson's second in command at the battle of Trafalgar in 1805. From the Collingwood monument descend down a grassy slope to a track and road and then continue up the road to Tynemouth Priory and Castle.

Now in the care of English Heritage, Tynemouth Priory was the site of one of the earliest Christian monasteries in 7th century Northumbria and was the burial place for St Oswin, formerly King of Deira. The monastery was attacked and destroyed by the Vikings in 800 and was only refounded as a Benedictine priory after the Norman Conquest. It was heavily fortified with a continuous wall with towers around the headland. Following the dissolution of the monasteries in 1539 the site became part of Henry VIII's national defences and the fortifications were extended across both headlands. Tynemouth Priory was to remain an important military site until 1960 and today visitors can not only see the remains of the medieval monastery, but also a twentieth century battery used in both World Wars which has now been restored to show the guns, ammunition stores and shell hoists.

At the castle there is a magnificent view across the harbour back to South Shields and Marsden Rock. Turn left by the clock tower into Tynemouth, with its elegant High Street. Cross Alexandra Place and continue straight on to the left of a small park until reaching Huntington Place. Turn left here and head down the road to Tynemouth Metro station.

13. Marsden Rock Circular

A walk of outstanding views from the Cleadon Hills across the South Shields coast. The walk passes some of the region's finest coastline between the famous Marsden Rock and the dramatic cliffs around Souter lighthouse, and for those interested in wildlife, it is well worth bringing binoculars, as the cliffs are important nesting grounds for a wide variety of sea birds.

Distance: 5 miles, 8km

Maps: Landranger 88 Tyneside and Durham; Pathfinder 549 Newcastle Upon Tyne

Start and Finish: Marsden Grotto Pub

Access: Regular bus services from South Shields E1 every 20 minutes; large public car park near the Marsden Grotto pub.

The Pub

The Marsden Grotto, Marsden is an unusual pub housed in a grotto at the bottom of the cliff face reached only by lift (small charge) or by a staircase winding down the rock face. In good coastal tradition this grotto was once used by smugglers, but was carved out as a house by Jack the Blaster during the 1780s while working at Marsden quarry. The Grotto became an inn in 1828 and is now a Vaux pub. While often full of day-trippers enjoying the view out to sea and the small sandy cove around the foot of the Marsden Rock, the Grotto is well worth a visit if only to admire the rooms cut into the rock.

The Walk

From the Marsden Grotto pub cross the road and turn left towards a caravan park and then take the footpath up the hill alongside the outer edge of the caravan park to a road. Almost opposite are the remains of Old Marsden Quarry, now a local nature reserve, and a bridleway, signed Cleadon Park. Follow a stony path which climbs slowly around the edge of the quarry, past Marsden Hall, a much restored building resplendent with castellations. From here there are some superb views down to the Marsden sands and on a clear day across South Shields to Tynemouth Priory.

Continue straight ahead around the edge of South Shields golf course along a path fringed with gorse. Where the path forks take the left fork to a stile in the wall. The route continues over the golf course following a clear grassy path aiming for the red brick tower ahead. This splendid Italianate tower is part of the Cleadon Hill water pumping station and is over 100 feet tall. Opened in 1863, the station pumps 1 million gallons of water a day to South Shields.

The path continues through a gap between the wall and a fence,

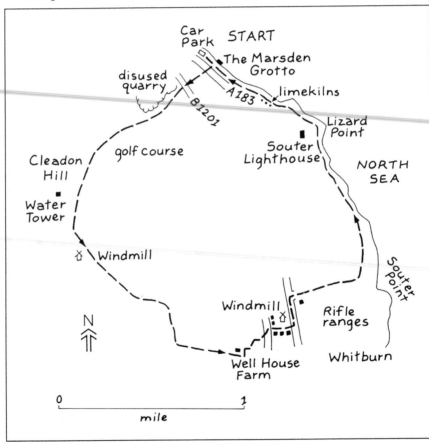

to follow the line of a dry stone wall towards the ruins of a windmill. This is Cleadon windmill. The current building dates back to the 1820s, but there has been a windmill on this site since medieval times. The windmill was used as an artillery base in World War One and as a observation post in World War Two for enemy aircraft in the North Sea.

From the wind mill continue in the same direction, and where the path forks take the left fork heading up the hill over a wooden stile to a stony outcrop of magnesian limestone. From here there are views over the fields towards Cleadon and Sunderland and, on a clear day, to the Cleveland hills to the South and the Simonside hills to the North. Follow the path along the edge of the field to a second stile and walk around the edge of the field to another stile and enclosed path leading to a stile. Turn left and continue through the farm yard to a road.

At the road turn left towards a caravan site and then right along a public footpath emerging at Cedar Grove and a second windmill, Whitburn Windmill which stands amidst modern housing on a grassy square. Originally built in 1796, the current windmill dates

Whitburn Windmill

from the middle of the 19th century, but was derelict until its recent restoration when the roof and sails were renewed.

From the windmill continue down to the road, turn left and just past a bus stop take the footpath on the right towards the coast and turn left to follow the coastal path. On those occasions when a red flag is flying, this section of the coast is closed due to firing on the Territorial Army military ranges. Continue for a short while past the bus stop and then turn right down Marsden Avenue to join the coastal path a little further along.

The section of the coast to Souter lighthouse is known as the Whitburn coast and is an area of attractive bays, rock arches and rock pools from limestone rock over 245 million years old. The area is also an important bird nesting ground attracting kittiwakes, fulmars, cormorants, razorbills, gulls and ornithologists! Just beyond the Military ranges is a nature reserve and bird observatory managed by Durham Bird Club. This is located on the site of the former Whitburn Colliery which has now been landscaped as a coastal park.

Dominating the skyline ahead is the 75-feet-high white tower of Souter Lighthouse, now owned by the National Trust. The lighthouse actually stands on Lizard Point, but to avoid confusion with the Lizard lighthouse in Cornwall, it is named after Souter point one mile south. Built in 1871 by Sir James Douglas this was the first lighthouse designed to be powered by electrical illumination.

Continue along the coastal path passing the Marsden limekilns on the left. The kilns were built around 1870 from brick and used to burn limestone to produce slaked lime for cement, limewashing and for scattering on fields. The kilns were coal burning using coal from Whitburn colliery and limestone from nearby Marsden quarry.

Around the next headland is a stretch of coast owned by the National Trust and known as the Leas. Designated a site of special scientific interest on account of its rich flora and fauna in summer, this area of large open grassland is covered in rock roses, spotted orchids, wild thyme, and harebells. Just ahead is the famous Marsden Rock a once huge craggy arch, carved out of the cliffs by the sea,

Marsden Rock

it has recently collapsed. It is still a major landmark visible all along the Tyneside coast. The rock is now host to several bird colonies including kittiwakes, fulmars and a favourite roosting site for cormorants. From Marsden Rock continue for a short distance along the coast to the Grotto and the end of the walk.

14. Under the Tyne on the trail of The Venerable Bede

At three miles this is the shortest walk in the book, and is ideal for a pleasant afternoon stroll. However, for those interested in medieval heritage, this walk can be the basis for a whole day out exploring a fascinating period in the history of the North East. Starting on the north bank of the River Tyne, to give walkers the chance to use the pedestrian Tyne Tunnel under the River Tyne, the walk emerges to the north of Jarrow close to one of the oldest religious buildings in the United Kingdom, dating back to 681 AD, and Bede's World, a newly extended museum exploring the history of early medieval Northumbria.

Distance: 3 miles, 4.5km

Maps: Landranger 88 Tyneside and Durham, Pathfinder 549 Newcastle upon Tyne

Start: Howden Metro station

Finish: Jarrow Metro station

Access: Use the Tyne & Wear Metro

The Pub

The Gas Light pub, Jarrow, is situated close by the southern end of the pedestrian Tyne Tunnel, set among an attractively landscaped area on the river-bank. A Victorian pub with a relaxed atmosphere and comfortably furnished with many of the original fittings, the Gas Light sells the beers produced by the famous Vaux brewery from Sunderland including Double Maxim Ale, Samson and Lorimers Best Scotch. Its Bar meals menu also caters for vegetarians.

The Walk

Leave Howden Metro and walk down Howden Lane, heading towards the Tyne. Pass a park and industrial buildings and turn left on to Norman Terrace. Where the road turns into an industrial estate

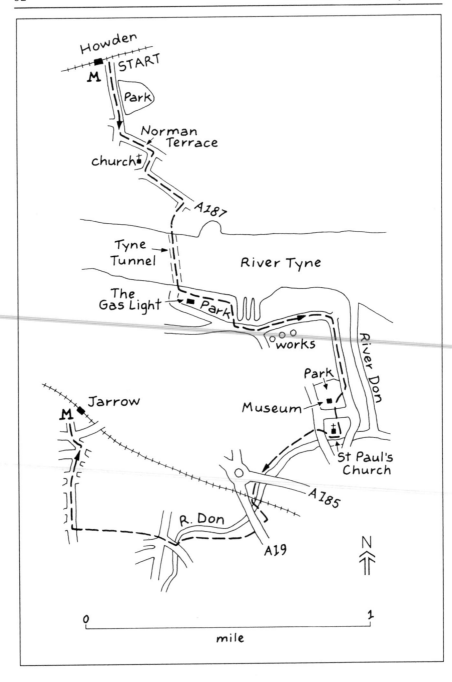

St Paul's church, Jarrow

continue straight on, passing the ornate porch on house no. 55. Just past St Paul's church turn right between some bollards and emerge at a main road.

Turn left and, following a sign, turn right across the road and head towards the Tyne Tunnel pedestrian entrance. Ahead is a lift down to the pedestrian tunnel. Close by the head of the lift is the site of a steam powered winding engine which was built in 1802. George Stephenson was the engine's brakeman for a short time, and he lived in a cottage close by where his son, the equally famous Robert Stephenson, was born.

Take the escalator which descends below the river. It drops some 180 feet. The pedestrian and cycle tunnels were begun in June 1947. The building work was difficult because of the presence of the abandoned workings of the Jarrow and Howden collieries some 760 feet below the Tunnel which were sunk in 1801 and 1804. It was further complicated when the miners were confronted by an ancient river channel filled with alluvial deposits rather than the expected rock, which caused a 40 ft wide crater to appear on the river bed. This had to be plugged with extra material before the work could be completed, ready for the opening in 1951. The pedestrian and cycle tunnels are each 900 feet long and are 10 feet 6 inches and 12 feet in diameter respectively. While walking through the tunnel observe the tiles reminiscent of the London underground, and look out for the border between the old counties of Northumberland and Durham half way along. The tunnel takes about 10 minutes to walk through and is well lit. Video cameras are also in use along the tunnel for additional security.

After leaving the tunnel turn left and follow a cycle path into a landscaped area. To the left is a statue of Charles Mark Palmer, founder of both the Palmer works and the town of Jarrow. Palmer was the first Mayor of the Town in 1875 and an MP from 1874, firstly for North Durham and then for Jarrow. To the right is "The Gaslight" pub.

From the Palmer statue turn right on a footpath by the river which winds up a small road behind a gasometer to a larger road. Turn left, and then take a lane on the left between walls, keeping a large storage cylinder to the right. Follow the road down to the River Don. Turn right and walk upstream by the river.

Just before a small parking area, take a set of steps on the right leading to a landscaped garden in front of the Bede's World, a museum housed in the late 18th century Jarrow Hall. The museum is mainly concerned with the story of the Anglo-Saxon Jarrow monastery which was home to the Venerable Bede, famous as author of one of the earliest written histories of Britain. The museum houses the oldest piece of Anglo-Saxon stained glass and a collection of intricately carved Anglo-Saxon stones, together with various objects found during excavations of the monastery. The museum is gradually being extended to include reconstructions of medieval timber buildings as well as authentic species of animals and crops farmed during that period. The museum has a small cafe and shop.

From the museum, head across the gardens towards St Paul's church. The church dates back to 681AD when it was part of the Jarrow monastery. The 685 AD dedication stone still survives above the church's chancel, part of the original Saxon church. Throughout the 8th century the Monastery was an important centre of northern learning until it was ravaged by the Vikings sixty years after Bede's death. The current ruins surrounding the church are of a later monastery which dates from the 11th century. Inside the church are some Saxon carvings including a magnificent Saxon cross and glass dating from the 7th century.

After leaving the church head back down towards the river and turn right on to the River Don footpath and follow it around behind the church into an avenue of trees. From the path there are excellent views of the ruins of the 11th century monastery.

At a fork, head to the right and walk up to a road. Cross the road outside the main gates of the church and follow a gravel footpath which winds its way between trees and the river. Where the track forks take the left-hand fork and follow a tarmac path which stays by the river and heads under the A19. The path bends to the right and then heads under the railway.

Turn left following the River Don footpath and then turn right to head under a road. Follow the path around to the left and then to the right, passing a churchyard. At a road turn right and emerge at a signpost to the Hill Farm Estate. Cross the road to steps opposite and take a path overlooking allotments. When the path meets a road turn right and head into Jarrow. Cross the main road at a pelican crossing and head along Railway Street to Jarrow Metro station.

15. A Jarrow March

In 1936 207 unemployed men carrying two banners emblazoned with the words 'Jarrow Crusade' left Jarrow led by the local Member of Parliament Ellen Wilkinson. They headed for the House of Commons carrying a 11,572 name petition calling for Government assistance to provide work for the people of Jarrow. Although not following the route of the original march, the walk begins at the Metro station and a memorial to the marchers and then follows a series of green corridors to join the banks of the River Wear outside Sunderland.

Distance: 12 miles, 19km

Maps: Landranger 88 Tyneside and Durham, Pathfinder 549 Newcastle Upon Tyne, Pathfinder 562 Washington

Start: Jarrow Metro station

Finish: Sunderland Railway station.

Access: Use Tyne & Wear Metro to the start of the walk at Jarrow. There are regular trains between Newcastle and Sunderland every 15 minutes Monday-Saturday, half hourly on Sunday.

The Pubs

The Black Horse Inn, West Boldon is in the corner of an attractive square close to the entrance of the Parish Church. It combines the best in local atmospheres with a wide range of Real Ales and a good food menu every day but Sunday. The choice of beers is comprehensive featuring Burtonwood's Top Hat, Morlands' Old Speckled Hen, Boddingtons', Flowers' Original, Timothy Taylor's landlord, Bentleys', Whitbread Winter Royal, Castle Eden and Stones!

The Saltgrass, Sunderland was voted the best pub in the North East by CAMRA in 1993 and very much merits this accolade. A traditional pub with relatively low ceilings and very popular, the Saltgrass offers a range of beers which include Thornes Bitter, Wards Bitter, handpulled Vaux Samson, Extra Special and Double Maxim and Waggle Dance Honey Beer. It also features an interesting selection of whiskies.

The Walk

Leave Jarrow Metro station on the southern side and head down Railway Street. Cross the A185 at traffic lights, turn right along the pavement and then left on to Park Road. At the end of the road enter the Park and take the path on the left.

Leave the park at the left-hand corner and cross Wansbeck Road. Head down the small road ahead and cross on to a recreational ground. Go through a black iron gate and walk straight ahead following a tarmac path, keeping the allotments to the right.

The path leads down wooden steps to the main road. Cross the road and head right. Take a tarmac path heading downhill by trees, and cross a wooden footbridge over the River Don. Follow the path alongside the river.

At a second wooden bridge re-cross the river and turn left. Keep to the low path running parallel to the river. After a short while the walk passes the Mill Dene Town Farm, where there is usually a selection of farm animals to be seen including donkeys, pigs and goats. A little further on to the right is the Primrose Nature Reserve, at which an area of wetland has been recreated along the banks of the River Don and which is now the home to a wide variety of plants and wildlife.

The path ends at a road. Cross the road and head under Primrose Bridge. As the road begins to bend left take a tarmac path on the right which heads straight on, again keeping the River Don to the left. The path emerges at a farm cottage by a road. Turn right here and head uphill. The road bends to the left. At the top cross on to Hawthorn Drive and take the footpath to the left of the Greyhound Pub. Continue between fences and follow the path round as it bends behind houses, and then to the right into open land. Follow the sandy path as it gently inclines. The path forks on to two grassy paths. Take the right-hand fork uphill and take steps downhill by the railway bridge.

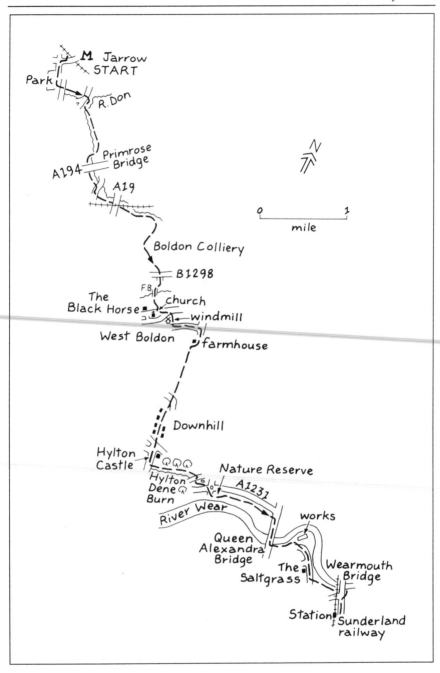

Following the public footpath sign to Hedworth cross the A19 with care. For those not wishing to cross the road directly, it is possible to walk a few hundred yards to the left and take the footbridge over the road, and rejoin the right of way on the opposite side.

Ascend the embankment and follow the sign for the River Don footpath, keeping the railway to the left. The path bends to the right around a housing estate. As it straightens turn left and cross the road to rejoin the River Don footpath downhill into a valley. As the path rejoins the river, look out for the remains of an old water corn mill. The headrace is still visible and some of the stone work has recently been consolidated.

The tarmac ends at a stone bridge with iron rails. Turn right here and head uphill keeping the housing estate to the right. Straight ahead are the remains of Boldon Colliery which closed in 1982. It is now a huge area of waste land, some of which is being open cast. When the path turns sharply right go ahead through a wooden gate which takes the footpath just to right of trees, and moves away from the estate. Follow this path to a road opposite a small industrial estate. Turn left and cross in front of an installation by a mini-round-about. Turn left again on to a muddy track which skirts the edge of a quarry, turning right after a short distance to keep to the edge of a sports field. At the start of a wooden fence on the right, turn left and cross a field diagonally.

At the road, turn right and then cross and head along New Road, which then changes to become Ernest Street. As the road becomes Wilfred Street, take a cut between numbers 61 and 59, and turn right to follow the path. Cross a footbridge over a stream. Head straight uphill between houses and continue up Hillside. Turn right along Boldon Drive and left up Prospect Gardens. Turn right along a cut and head left uphill using the church spire as a guide. Go back on to a road and cut through by No. 6, St Nicholas View to emerge by St Nicholas church with its medieval spire. Turn right along a narrow lane to emerge at a small square in the centre of Boldon. The Black Horse Inn is on the right-hand side.

Boldon is famous for the Boldon Book, known as the Domesday

Book of the North. The original Domesday book of 1086 excluded
Northumbria and Durham. But in 1183, on the orders of Hugh Du
Puiset, a survey was undertaken of the extensive See of St Cuthbert
of Durham to assess the land's worth, its annual rents and confirm
any tenures.

After leaving the pub, walk back in front of the church and then
continue on past. Emerge at the main road and cross the road. Just
before the turning on to Aviemore Road take a tarmac path to the
right. Look out on the right, near the entrance to Mansfield Court,
for an interesting feature – the remains of an old windmill now
converted into a house standing strangely amidst a modern housing
estate.

Continue on and follow the road around to the left. Almost
immediately on the right cut through a break in the fence by a white
building to join a smaller road. Turn left and walk round in front of
the Boldon Golf Club, and follow the road as it bears left and right.
At the next turn left, turn right down a bridle path and head down
a lane.

At the end of the lane continue to the right, ignoring the marked
footpath. The lane then bears to the left to enter a field. Go straight
ahead and skirt the fence around the Golf Course. At the top of the
rise, take a look to the left for a view of the sea. At the end of the
fence, look ahead for a view of the Penshaw Monument built to
commemorate the death of the Earl of Durham in 1840 on the
summit of Penshaw Hill.

Head down through the field and leave it at the bottom right-hand
corner, and turn left down a track to meet the road at a black gate.
Turn right and then left on to a paved path between houses. Turn
right to go around the edge of a school and then follow the path left.
Cross a turning circle heading diagonally right and cut up Kidd
Square and Kingsclere Avenue. Cross Kidderminster Road and
climb a small flight of steps to join a paved path. Turn right and then
left on to a muddy track. To the right is a view of the huge Nissan
car plant at Washington.

Follow the path as it descends. Ignore a path which crosses it and

Hylton Castle

a right-hand fork and head for Hylton Castle straight ahead. Cross the main road and head down in front of the castle. All that remains of Hylton Castle is the tower house which was built about 1400 by William de Hilton. It is reputedly haunted by "The Cauld Lad of Hylton", the shivering ghost of a stable lad murdered by one of de Hilton's descendants, Baron Robert Hilton. A Chapel, probably built in the 15th century also survives, standing a little distance from the Castle. Both are in the care of English Heritage.

Turn left between iron railings into Hylton Burn Dene, and follow a path through trees overlooking the valley. Just before the path leaves the woods and begins to wind uphill, turn right downhill into the valley and at the bottom, turn left on to a path by the stream. The path winds its way down the valley. At the embankment head up to the left to a black metal gate. Cross the road and join a small path to the right of a red brick building.

The path winds to the right and then to the left to join a track. Turn left and head downhill and to the right around a pond into a wooded area, The path rises up to the road. Cross a wooden stile and walk left along the pavement.

Before the roundabout cross the road and head down Timber Beach Road. Turn left at a mini-roundabout and join a footpath on the right heading down towards the river, and which circles behind an office facility.

The path winds back up to the road. By the Hylton Riverside Nature Reserve turn right and head along a road. Cross on to the other side and head along a gravel path parallel to the dual carriageway. At the time of writing this area was still being developed and this path may well become a pleasant green route through the industrial area.

By a blue painted bridge take the left fork and walk along a gravel path which goes through an underpass. Just before a second underpass turn right on to a footpath which bisects the gravel path. Head down to the Alexandra Bridge and cross the road carefully before crossing the bridge. The Alexandra Bridge was opened in 1909, and originally had two separate levels. It was the heaviest bridge in Britain on its completion and took four and a half years to complete and used 2600 tons of steel. The upper deck was designed to carry coal trains but was only in use for 12 years.

At the end of the bridge turn left and head down towards the river to join the River Wear Trail. Go down steps to the road, turn left to head downhill and take a path on the left, before turning right to head down to the Ropery pub, which is the oldest industrial building in Sunderland and, as its name suggests, was used for rope making.

Walk past the front of the pub and join a paved path. Turn right at a tarmac path and join a road in front of a factory. Leave through the gates. Turn left at the road and head for the Saltgrass.

From the Saltgrass head up Hanover Place past the Winston and then turn left in front of the Kings Arms. Follow the road round, and then turn left on to a gravel path to rejoin the River Wear trail through an attractive landscaped garden. The path heads down steps between beds of miniature roses, and bends right to walk overlooking the river and heading towards the Wearmouth Bridge, built in 1929, and the Hog Back Iron Railway Bridge built in 1878. The path emerges at a landscaped garden. Continue through the gardens towards the bridges from where there are views down the river.

Pass under the bridges by the foot of their right side leg, and turn right to walk up a cobbled walk-way. At the top turn right on to Panns Bank, the commercial heart of old Sunderland, and walk up to the road by the bridge. Turn left and take the underpass under the road junction, and leave the underpass to the right. Return to ground level and walk straight ahead along Fawcett Street into the town centre, before turning second right, following Tourist Information signs to arrive at Sunderland Railway Station.

16. Derwent Valley Circular

A circular walk, part of which follows the old Derwent Valley railway, which is now the heart of a very well managed Country Park, and an important wildlife corridor. Having climbed up to the pretty village of Burnopfield, just over the County Durham border, the walk follows a series of attractive paths offering superb views over the Derwent valley and the surrounding hills.

Distance: 13 miles, 21km (it is easy to reduce this to 10 miles/16km by beginning and ending the walk at the Swalwell Visitor Centre at Grid Reference (197619)

Maps: Landranger 88 Tyneside and Durham, Pathfinders 548 Blaydon & Prudhoe, 549 Newcastle, 561 Consett, 562 Washington

Start and finish: Gateshead MetroCentre Bus Station, or for the shorter walk Swalwell Visitor Centre.

Access: Excellent bus and train links to Gateshead MetroCentre, where there is also ample parking. For Swalwell Visitor Centre catch buses 608, 611, 642, 644, 745 from Newcastle and 608, 648, 649 from Gateshead. There is also a car park at the Visitor Centre.

The Pub

The Burton House in Burnopfield. This is a Free House and is very much part of the local community, with a warm and friendly atmosphere. Burton House sits at the top of a row of shops on a quiet road, hidden from the main road and remains slightly off the beaten track. Its beers include Boddington's, Pedigree and Flowers Original.

The Walk

The walk begins at the MetroCentre Bus Station. Cross the road which orbits the MetroCentre and walk beneath the overpass towards the MetroCentre railway station over a grassy space.

Join a gravel path and turn left, walking parallel to the railway line. The path heads under a road bridge, before gently bending to

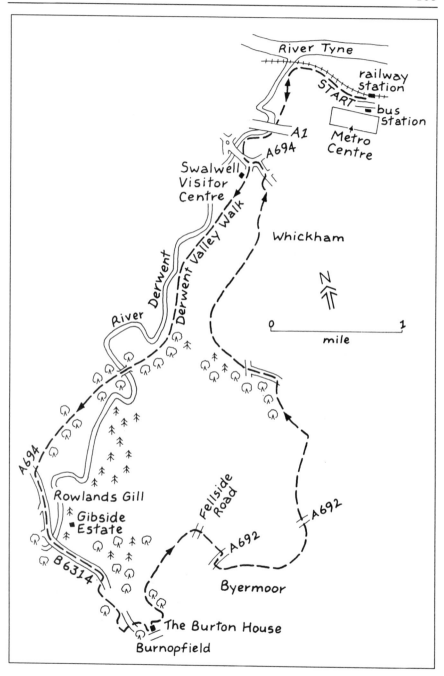

the left and crossing a small footbridge. Walk beside the railway in sight of the River Tyne to an iron bridge which crosses the River Derwent. This area is known as Derwenthaugh Marina and has now been attractively landscaped with trees and pedestrian walk-ways. It was once an important coal and shipping point with its own staithe and was used to transport coal from the collieries at Chopwell and Garesfield.

The path turns left before the bridge over the Derwent and heads upstream, and under a road bridge. Take a right fork and walk along a gravel path by the River which gently bends right and then sharply left before passing a weir. It then follows the line of the River through parkland and under the A1 bridge.

Ignore forks to the left and follow the path as it bends to the right along the river bank. The path passes a blue iron bridge and then heads underneath an arch in a stone bridge. It emerges on a lane by the entrance to the Swalwell Cricket Ground. Turn left and walk up to the road opposite Blaydon Rugby Ground. Taking care, cross the road and turn left, and then right, following signs for the Derwent Walk Country Park and the South Tyne Cycleway. The entrance is marked by an impressive mural on the truncated end of the railway bridge showing the front of a steam engine surrounded by some of the plants and animals to be found along the Derwent Walk.

At a wooden gate on the left head gently uphill to the start of the Derwent Walk. This is the beginning of the walk from the Swalwell Visitor Centre. A path leads from the Visitor Centre up a grassy slope to join the Derwent walk a little further on.

The Derwent Walk Country Park is one of the largest in the North East. The main thoroughfare is the route of the old Derwent Valley railway which, at its peak transported over 500 000 people per year with six stations along its route. It was also an important freight line with regular goods traffic including timber, bricks and coal into Newcastle and iron ore to Consett. The railway was opened in 1867 and took three years to build. Zigzagging its way up the Derwent Valley, the railway crosses the river four times over four impressive viaducts. The railway closed in 1962. The walk which traces its route was opened in 1972 for walkers and cyclists.

The path is a straight route between an avenue of birch and other deciduous trees which are particularly attractive in spring and autumn. There are plenty of smaller trails and view points sign-posted along the route. Follow the path to the Nine Arches Viaduct which offers views across the river valley to Snipes Dene Wood and the 140-feet-high Column of Liberty erected in 1757 on part of the Gibside estate. Look out also for the ruins of Holinside Manor, a 13th century Manor House.

The path finally emerges on the outskirts of Rowlands Gill. Exit through a kissing gate and turn left to walk along the road. Turn left on to the B6314 towards Burnopfield and continue past the Derwent Caravan Park. Follow the road as it bends to the left and crosses the River Derwent over a road bridge. Pass in front of the entrance to the Gibside estate and continue as the road ascends. Now a National Trust property, the Gibside Estate was landscaped in the 18th century and though the 17th century Hall is now in ruins, there are attractive walks through the parkland to a Mausoleum Chapel and the Banqueting Hall.

Leave the road at a public bridleway on the right-hand side and head uphill into a wood. The path bends to the left. Take a left fork following a public footpath sign and climb parallel to the edge of a field to the right. The path levels out as the rooftops of Burnopfield begin to be visible through the trees.

Ignore turnings to the left and keep to the main path as it descends through the trees. Just before it reaches the road, take a fork to the right which climbs into the woods and continue up wooden steps to a wall at the top of the valley, before turning left to join a road. Turn left down the road to a commemorative fountain, and cross over to a marked public footpath opposite, which heads downhill over a footbridge across a pretty valley.

At the end of the footbridge turn left and then immediately fork right to head up a cut between a house and a fence. Turn right up another cut which bends and heads uphill until it emerges at a road. Head straight down the road, Derwent Terrace, to the bottom, and turn right the few yards uphill to the Burton House pub.

After leaving the pub head back down to Derwent Terrace. This time turn right along Raglan Place. At the end of the road, turn left at a footpath sign and cross a green space towards newer houses opposite. At the road take a cut next to number 46, which heads up to a wooden stile. Cross the stile and turn left behind the houses. The path passes a number of other stiles on the left before crossing over one straight ahead to join a fenced path through fields. As another path merges from the left, continue straight on to a kissing gate in the corner of the field, enjoying the views of Rowlands Gill and Chopwell Woods across the valley.

Through the kissing gate, turn right and then left around the field. Cross a stile and head across the field, slightly to the right, using the farm buildings ahead as a guide. Cross a further stile and then turn right, over a further stile by an iron gate on to a track. Follow the track up to the farm and to the road.

Cross the road and take the footpath signposted to Byermoor, going through two gates and into a field. Head for a further gate in the top right-hand corner of the field and having crossed into a further field, head up to another road. Cross the road, and turn left by a public footpath sign. Skirt around a children's play area and head straight on over waste ground to a rough road. Turn left here and join a road behind red brick houses, which leads to a stile by a gate. Cross the stile and head into a field.

At the end of this field cross a rough road and enter the field opposite. Cross a stile and then go through a kissing gate, and head across a field diagonally to the left around the edge of farm buildings to another stile. Cross this stile and turn left to head up a farm road to a major road. Cross the road and take a footpath signposted to Sunniside.

Keeping to the field boundary, cross the field, take a stile and cross a further field, heading for a kissing gate diagonally to the right. Go through the kissing gate, and walk by the fence through a further kissing gate. At the end of this field join a farm road, and turn left up to farm buildings. After the buildings take a marked footpath, over a stile and head diagonally to the left to join the line of the fence.

Follow the fence as it turns right, then left and then right again before heading downhill, past gorse bushes to a stile by a white gate. Cross this stile, and then another, and then turn left down a rough road. At a junction with a major road, cross and head straight ahead. Take a track to the right.

The track skirts the edge of Whickham as it offers views across the Derwent Valley, and also the tree lined route of the old railway which formed the early part of the walk. Follow this track for some distance, ignoring paths on the left.

When the path finally forks, with the right-hand fork heading into a housing estate, take the left fork which heads behind houses and begins to descend gently. The path emerges on to a quiet cul-de-sac. Continue heading down hill, and join a rough road ahead, which bends to the right, and heads down to a major road.

Turn left and head down towards the Poacher public house. Cross the road at the bottom and turn left, back towards the Blaydon Rugby Club. For those who shortened the walk, this is the end of the route. The Swalwell Visitor Centre lies behind the Rugby club. For those continuing to the MetroCentre, follow the road as it bends to the right, and then take the small lane which heads back to the entrance to Swalwell Cricket Club.

Follow the footpath sign to the Hurrocks on the right, and work back to the River and follow the path on its banks. This time, just after the A1 road bridge, turn right along a track to a road, and then turn left. Head for the public footpath straight ahead. Take this path until it merges with the path by the river, cross under the road bridge and head back to the MetroCentre Bus Station following the original path.

17. The Bowes Railway

The Bowes Railway was one of the oldest and longest of the major colliery railways in the Great Northern coalfield. Opened in 1826, the line was extended to 15 miles, including seven rope-hauled inclines and three loco-worked sections. This walk follows the Bowes railway for much of its route, through the southern edge of Gateshead District and through some surprisingly lovely countryside offering spectacular views across into Durham and north to the River Tyne. One of the longest walks in the book, it is also one of the most scenic and for those interested in railway history there is an opportunity to visit the world's only preserved standard gauge rope hauled railway and one of the world's oldest surviving railways, the Tanfield railway.

Distance: 13 miles, 21km

Maps: Landranger 88 Tyneside and Durham, Pathfinders 549 Newcastle upon Tyne and 562 Washington

Start: Pelaw Metro Station

Finish: Gateshead MetroCentre Transport Interchange

Access: Use the Tyne and Wear Metro

The Pubs

Adjacent to the Pelaw Main waggonway, the aptly named **The Wagon Inn, Eighton Banks** is a large, attractive and lively free house which features Grays Landlord Bitter and Theakstons XB. Its food menu is extensive and includes some vegetarian choices, and there is a small beer garden, offering views of the surrounding countryside. The pub is very busy on Sunday lunch times when it serves a Sunday lunch menu only.

The Lambton Arms, though very close, has a different feel to the Wagon Inn. Small and cosy, it is ideal for a quieter drink. It has a good range of real ales including Flowers Original, Boddingtons and Marstons' Pedigree and it also serves meals. The tables in the bar at the front have an excellent view of the Bowes railway descending down the hillside towards Kibblesworth.

The Rose Inn Sunniside, is a friendly, local Bass pub which features regularly changing guest ales alongside its standard range of beers.

The Walk

Turn right out of Pelaw Metro station and then turn left to follow a fence alongside the railway to join a tarmac track. At a rough road turn right and walk alongside a housing estate.

At a road turn left, cross and walk along the pavement. Walk alongside a sports ground by a beech hedge. Turn right through a green gate and cross the sports ground diagonally. At a junction turn left and then right across a gravel area to join a muddy track by allotments. This emerges at the disused Bowes Railway, originally known as the Monkton line, which carried coal from the Springwell colliery to the coal staithes at Jarrow. The line was later extended to the collieries at Kibblesworth and Marley Hill. It became known as the Bowes Railway in 1932, after the owners of the Gibside Estate, who acquired the railway in the mid-19th century.

Turn right and continue onwards looking out almost immediately for evidence of the old railway including the pedestrian underpass beneath the track and old railway sleepers which remain in the ground along the route.

Cross over a road and then immediately under the A184 before following the railway as it gradually works its way out into the countryside through housing estates and crossing a series of minor roads. The last of these roads before leaving the housing estates, is an old Roman Road, the Wrakendike.

Continue to follow the route of the old railway. Look out for distant views of the Penshaw Monument near Washington to the left. Looking back there are views back into Tyneside and the coast.

By allotments, go through some green gates and past large black gates to walk by the site of an old marshalling yard which serviced the old Springwell Colliery, which was worked between 1826 and 1932 for its coal. This is now the site of the Bowes Railway Centre

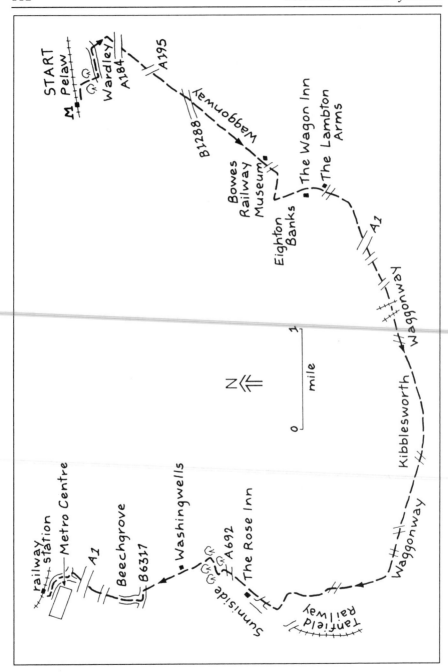

where there is an exhibition and steam hauled passenger trains, as well as the rope hauled railway designed by George Stephenson.

Follow a track running around the outside of the Bowes Railway Centre to emerge at a road. Turn left here, and then right down a waymarked public footpath towards the edge of Springwell Colliery. Then turn diagonally right across a field towards the village of Eighton Banks, heading towards a works site and large incinerator. Turn left to walk alongside a disused railway line, the Pelaw Main waggonway, which joins a gravel bridleway and cycle path. Cross the railway at the Wagon Inn.

Rejoin the bridleway and walk past the pub car park over a wooden stile. The path offers excellent views of the surrounding countryside. At a fork take the higher path which bends to the right and heads to the walk's second pub, the Lambton Arms.

From the Lambton Arms cross the road and take a footpath opposite. Take the right-hand path and descend, and then bend to the left, before turning right to rejoin the route of the Bowes railway by the old Mount Colliery reservoir.

Turn right and follow the line down hill, passing beneath the A69 through underpasses. The path is bordered by hedgerows on either side and passes through attractive countryside. The walk eventually emerges from under a railway underpass and the village of Kibblesworth comes into view. Cross Rowletch Burn on an old railway bridge and walk between fields heading for the village.

Cross a road and begin to ascend gradually. Where the rough road turns left at the edge of a works site, continue straight ahead behind houses to skirt the village. At the far end of the village cross a small lane and continue straight on.

At this point, look out for some unusual features. At intermittent points are carved tree trunks, the result of an Arts and Countryside initiative in which an artist in residence was based in the village of Kibblesworth for several months. The sculptures, used as footpath way-markers, were designed to help raise awareness of the local countryside and are based on local themes including one of the Bowes railway itself. Continue upwards, crossing another small road and follow the bridleway. This stretch of the walk is quite sensational offering superb views across the Team Valley and the southern edge of deeply rural Gateshead District. The path crosses further roads by a stone sculpture and a farm.

After about ten minutes the path ascends very sharply to the right out of a railway embankment. This is a very easy turning to miss as it is poorly marked and involves a scramble up through a cleared area between gorse bushes. The clue is to look out for two fences diagonally opposite at the top of the embankment which are the marking of the route. Reaching a concreted area indicates that you have gone too far. Turn round and return to the turning.

At the top of the embankment follow the path diagonally ahead, keeping to the right-hand side of the fence. Cross a wooden stile in the field corner, and cross a further field and head straight ahead towards a further stile and a group of footpath signposts.

Cross the stile and turn left down the road. Just after a disused building take a stile to the right and follow a public footpath. The whole of Tyneside is spread out ahead. Cross the field, heading for another stile. Take this and immediately take another to the left. Head across the field, slightly to the right using a tree ahead as a guide. Cross a wooden gate-stile and head downhill between gorse bushes to another stile at the far side of the field.

Cross the field diagonally to the left to another stile to join the disused railway on the outskirts of Sunniside. This is the route of the Tanfield railway, one of the world's oldest railways which originally opened as a waggonway in 1725 between Blackburn Fell and Dunston staithes on the Tyne. The waggonway was later extended to Tanfield, Beamish and South Moor. Part of the line includes the famous Causey Arch thought to be one of the oldest surviving railway bridges built in 1725 over Causey Burn At its height, the Tanfield Railway was carrying almost one third of the total output of the Great Northern Coalfield. For those interested in visiting the Tanfield Railway, turn left along the railway route to reach a road. Continue in the same direction and follow signs. A passenger service is operated along a section of line from the Marley

Unusual carved footpath sign at Kibblesworth

Hill engine shed to Sunniside and there is a small exhibition of locomotives, carriages and stationary engines.

To continue the walk, turn right along the disused railway and gently descend crossing a minor road. Shortly after joining the railway look out on the left for the third pub, The Rose. From the Rose continue along the track along a section of the railway which was once rope hauled and which was used to operate a passenger service on Saturdays only between Tanfield Lea and Gateshead. Cross under an old footbridge and head down between an avenue of hawthorns to emerge at a road. Cross carefully and follow a footpath signposted to Broom Lane. Follow a nature trail down hill into a wood. Cross Black Burn on a footbridge and head uphill. At a fork almost immediately, head right along a marked trail by the burn.

Turn left before another footbridge and wind up steps to the right and then to the left. At a fork turn right, keeping a fence to the right, go over a wooden stile and walk across a field towards farm buildings. Go through a kissing gate and head up a lane past the farm, At a road by Wishing Well Cottage turn left and head uphill. Cross the road just after the police station and head down Duckpool Lane.

Where the lane bends to the left go down a cul-de-sac taking a footpath to Market Lane. Cross the road by the Crowley Hotel and follow a sunken lane downhill. Cross under the A1 and, passing the Federation Brewery to the right, head towards the Transport Interchange at the Gateshead MetroCentre.

18. Chopwell Woods Circular

This walk is a circular route taking in attractive woodland walking close to the Gateshead/Durham border. The walk begins at Rowlands Gill, along a tree lined stretch of the Derwent Walk, a disused railway which is now the heart of the Derwent Walk Country Park. From Chopwell Woods, the walk continues through gentle undulating fields, before dropping back into Rowlands Gill following Spen Burn.

Distance: 10 miles, 16km

Maps: Landranger 88 Tyneside and Durham' Pathfinders 548 Blaydon and Prudhoe and 561 Consett

Start and Finish: St Barnabas church, Rowlands Gill.

Access: Regular buses from Gateshead and Newcastle alight outside Tesco's. Parking available on various side streets surrounding St Barnabas church.

The Pub

The Fox and Hounds, Coalburns a Vaux pub with a very much local village atmosphere reminiscent of an earlier age. It is located by a small village green and is an attractive location to break a walk. Its beers include Samson Bitter and Lorimers Scotch.

The Walk

Walk away from the main road down the side street by St Barnabas church past a row of Retired Mineworkers cottages, and follow the road as it bends to the left. Turn right into a car park and join the Derwent Walk over an old railway viaduct, which follows the now disused route of the railway which brought coal and steel from Consett to Tyneside between 1867-1962 (see walk 16 for further details). The Durham-Gateshead border follows the line of the river Derwent and the first part of the walk is actually in County Durham.

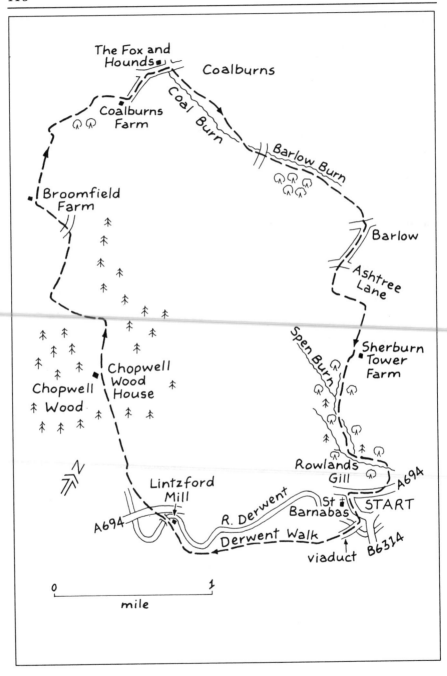

The Fox and Hounds

Coalburns

Coalburns Farm

Coal Burn

Barlow Burn

Broomfield Farm

Barlow

Ashtree Lane

Chopwell Wood House

Spen Burn

Sherburn Tower Farm

Chopwell Wood

Rowlands Gill

A694

Lintzford Mill

R. Derwent

St Barnabas

START

A694

Derwent Walk

viaduct

B6314

N

0   ½   1
mile

At the far side of the viaduct look out on the right-hand side for the remains of the 12th century Friarside Chapel

Continue straight ahead along the woodland walk through Silver Birch trees. Go under a bridge and then, just after a wooden stile at the end of a route to the left, take a steep waymarked path down hill into the woods to the right.

At the bottom of the hill cross a small brook, and then take a left fork to follow the line of a fence. To the right there are views of the River Derwent as it meanders through the hamlet of Lintzford Mill. Look out for the old mill and weir.

At a rough track turn right and head downhill towards buildings and then left over a stone bridge. Turn left at the road, cross carefully and take a waymarked footpath to the right. After a short distance the path goes through a gate and ascends into Chopwell Woods, a mainly coniferous forest managed by Forest Enterprise.

The path bends to the right and then heads sharply uphill and to the left. At a fork by a bench and viewpoint continue straight ahead ignoring a red arrow to the left. After the path bends gently to the left, another major track joins from the right. Continue straight ahead on what is now the major track through the woods and emerge by a group of houses. Take the road between the houses and follow it as it bends to the right.

At a T-junction turn left heading towards Carr House and then immediately right going past a white iron barrier. The path gently winds to the right until it meets a junction of a number of footpaths. Go left on the second darker path, marked by a blue arrow. This is the route of a old railway which ran from Chopwell colliery to the coal staithes at Derwenthaugh on the River Tyne.

The path gently bends to the right. and continues to the edge of the woodland. Just before the end of the woods, turn right along a path which bends backwards and then immediately left over a wooden stile into a field. Walk through the field to the left of a row of hawthorn, gorse and trees. Head for another stile straight ahead. From here look back to enjoy outstanding views of the Durham

Dales/North Pennines over the rooftops of the old pit village of Chopwell.

Cross over the stile and head uphill. Half way across the field take another stile and continue between two rows of trees on a muddy track over two further stiles to go past Heavygate Farm.

Cross a road and take the footpath signed to Leadgate. Cross a stile in the field corner to join a gravel road up to Broomfield Farm. Just before entering the farmyard turn right up a rough road between enclosures and walk up on a track into a field. Continue ahead keeping the hedge to the left through two fields. The top of a hill is a good viewpoint across Tyneside.

At a wooden stile slightly to the right of the corner of the second field, cross, and continue, keeping the fence to the right. Ahead are views into the Northumberland hills. At the corner of the field turn left along a farm track. Almost immediately, at the end of a copse of trees, turn right to skirt the edge of the copse. Just through the trees head for a wooden stile. Continue next to some conifer trees and then into a wood to follow an obvious path.

Cross a stile into a field and head left under electricity pylons. Walk by the hedge to the left and turn right at the next fence and follow the hedge towards Colbrookes Farm. Take a stile over the hedge to the left and follow the fence, keeping the farm to the right. Cross a stile into the farmyard and head down in front of the house to the road. At the road turn left and then right on to a road heading towards the Fox and Hounds pub in Coalburns.

From the Fox and Hounds continue along the road. Turn right over a wooden stile opposite Coalburns cottages, following a sign to Spen Lane and Barlow. Keep to the edge of the first field by the Coal Burn. Cross through a gap in the hedge into the next field and cross straight ahead to a stile. Head across the next field to an iron gate. Go through the gate and follow the track across the field to another gate. Head to the right and walk alongside Coal Burn to a stile in a corner which leads to stepping stones across the stream. Cross into a field and skirt around the edge to emerge at a road.

Cross the road and, using a stile, follow a public footpath to

Barlow over a further stile in the corner of the field. After the stile turn right along the stream and cross over a wooden footbridge and then left over a stile. To the left ascend into a field up wooden steps and walk along the left edge of a field by the stream. At the edge of the field go through a hedge of hawthorn to walk by large clumps of gorse and down into a wooded avenue by the stream. Go up wooden steps and then wind in and out between more gorse. Go over a stile to join a delightful path overlooking a stream and then join a path heading up hill through gorse.

When the path emerges into a field head directly uphill over a stile and head for a five bar gate. Cross a stile and head up a farm track to the road. Turn right and head for farm buildings. Cross the road at the farm and take a waymarked public footpath which skirts a field, keeping a hedge to the right, to another stile in the right-hand corner which leads to another road. Turn left along the road and then, opposite a road junction, turn right over a wooden stile into a field.

Walk ahead keeping the field boundary to the left and at the end of the field follow a track which bends to the left along the brow of the Derwent valley. Keep to the track, part of the dismantled Chopwell railway, as it bends to the right over a stile by an iron gate and descends to go past Sherburn Tower farm.

At the end of the track take a path straight ahead through a five bar gate into a wood which overlooks a small brook. The track joins a rough road running by Spen Burn. Turn left and cross the stream and follow the track as it rises and then descends.

At the end of the track, take a footpath to the right through the trees which descends sharply to a stream. Cross the stream fork to the left and join a path on the left bank which winds through the woods, which in spring is thick with wood anemones and bluebells. At two forks keep to the higher path and at a third shortly afterwards, take the right fork. This path joins another. Keep to this path as it works down to the river. Cross a small tributary which runs into the main Spen Burn and follow a path which winds uphill to the left to emerge by houses and a large grass area by a major road.

Strolling along the Derwent Valley

Walk to the right around the edge of the wood and then take a gravel path behind the Towneley Arms Hotel to emerge at a public footpath sign on the main road through Rowlands Gill. Turn right and head up the road to return to St Barnabas church.

19. The South Bank of the Tyne

This easy to follow walk is great for a summer evening, following the cycleways and footpaths on the southern side of the river. It offers excellent views of the industrial landmarks on the north bank, before entering Gateshead town centre on a route through the industrial buildings beneath the Tyne Bridge, the most well known of the bridges in the series which dominate the Tyneside landscape.

Distance: 5½ miles, 8km

Maps: Landranger 88 Tyneside and Durham, Pathfinder 549 Newcastle upon Tyne

Start: Hebburn Metro Station

Finish: Gateshead Metro Station

Access: Use the Tyne and Wear Metro

The Pub

The Albion Inn, Bill Quay, is about half way along the walk and offers a friendly out of town atmosphere and a good choice of beers. As a Scottish and Newcastle House it includes Newcastle Brown and Exhibition, McEwans Scotch and Export, and Theakston's Brews. It also has guest beers including Ridleys Bitter and Four Seasons.

The pub makes the most of its riverside location and on display there are various photographs and bric-a-brac linked to the sea, the river and sailing – look out for the interesting boat doorway. The Albion's beer garden is an ideal place to watch the river go by, and to take in views both up and downstream on a quiet summer evening.

There are several excellent pubs in Gateshead, **the Station Hotel** on Hills Street on the southern end of the High Level Bridge is a small basic pub serving Jennings, Ruddles and various guest beers, with a small adjoining room to the main bar, known locally as the coffin, thanks to its collection of replica skulls.

The Walk

Leave Hebburn Metro and head towards the River. Head along Prince Consort Road to the County pub. Opposite the County turn left on to St Aloysios View and take the track to the right which leads behind a housing estate. Where the track bends to the left continue straight on along a gravel path and head downhill towards the River over a playing field. To the right, the forest of cranes stand as testament to Tyneside's enduring links with shipbuilding and include those of the famous Swan Hunter ship yard, builders of the HMS Ark Royal. The yard's long term future is still uncertain.

Join the tarmac path at the bottom of the hill and turn left, walking parallel to the River. The path ascends gently and then levels out as it heads through an attractively landscaped riverside. At a bollarded junction go straight ahead as the path continues to climb gently and head to the left. Just above a bend in the river fork to the right on to Keelman's Way and head between trees. The Keelman's Way derives its name from the keelmen who used to steer low keeled barges from

The River Tyne at Hebburn

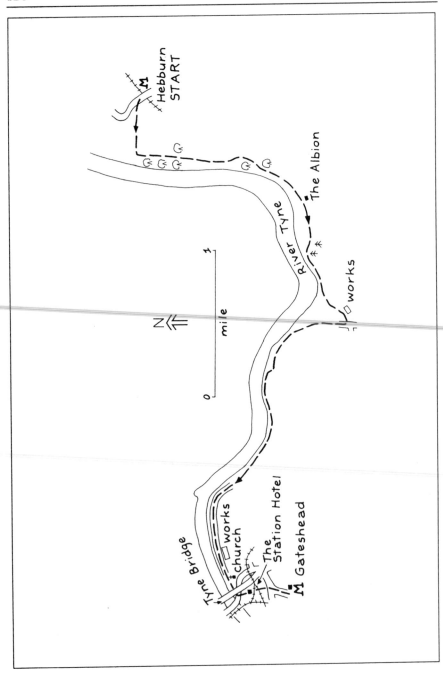

the many coal staithes along the Tyne to sea going colliery ships, in the days before the Tyne was dredged.

Just after a hedgerow begins look out for a narrow path on the right-hand side, signposted as walk 16. Head down this path which emerges at the Albion Inn. After leaving the Albion, head uphill to the right, cross a road and rejoin Keelman's Way, along Jonadab Road. The track works its way between buildings and then emerges by the river. A sharp bend in the River enables views across to the north bank and directly into Newcastle Upon Tyne. Look out for the distinctive shape of the Newcastle Civic Centre.

Just behind white industrial buildings the path heads uphill to the left, across a small road and between an enclosure and red brick buildings, before turning right behind houses and around a fenced establishment. The path emerges at a road. Turn right along the pavement, continuing to follow the Keelmans Way markings.

At the end of Abbotsford Road, turn right and head back down towards the River. At factory gates at the end of the road turn left, following the road around. Almost immediately a cut on the right heads down to the river.

The path heads left, looking down over the Tyne and progressively becomes wilder as it heads through privets and sycamore. It finally emerges opposite a small marina. This is St Peter's Basin village which has been developed by the Tyne and Wear Development Corporation from an area of derelict land which was once the site of a small shipyard and whaling station and now contains over 300 homes. Look out for the stone on the right commemorating the Friars Goose Footpath restoration in 1981.

Head right towards the Riverside Lodge and then left by the river. The path turns uphill and then sharply right keeping the river to the right. When the path meets a car park, cross the entry road and continue along Keelmans Way through the bollards. At the road continue ahead behind factory buildings keeping the flats ahead in the distance.

At the end of the road turn right following Keelmans Way and then left in front of a gravel plant and follow the road past warehouses and workshops. At a slight turn to the left, there is an excellent view of the Tyne Bridge between buildings. Walk in front of J. Rank Ltd, the famous producer of Hovis products.

On the approach to the Tyne Bridge watch out for stone steps on the left. Just after these steps take a steep cobbled lane which bends up to the left and opens up an excellent view across to the North bank of the Tyne and Newcastle.

At the top cut right in front of the church. This is St Mary's church, a medieval church and a 18th century tower. Look out for the carved stone on the left commemorating the occasion in October 1854 when an explosion sent massive stones and timber beams on to the church roof. From the church there are superb views down to the Swing Bridge, the High Level Bridge (see walks 2 and 10 for further details of the bridges) and down to the cruise ship 'Casino Royale' which is permanently moored here and is a night club famous for its cocktails.

At the end of the path turn left and take steps down to the road, cross and go under the bridge. Then turn left up the hill to follow an attractive path through a landscaped area to join a road, the unusually named Bottle Bank, which leads to the top of the High Level Bridge. Turn right along Hills Street under a railway bridge past the Station Hotel to emerge at a very busy main road. Cross the road with care, and continue up the hill crossing another road to a magnificent ornate clock. This clock is often used in Gateshead publicity and was presented to Gateshead by its Mayor in 1898. Continue up the hill, passing a marble fountain on the left and a huge concrete sculpture on the right. This is 'Sports Day' by Mike Winshore which was erected in 1986. It consists of a figure in a large sack to represent the sack race, and a tortoise, hare and fox from Aesop's fable, in which the tortoise is cleverly used as the egg, for the egg and spoon race.

Just past the 'Sports Day' sculpture, turn right down a pedestrian subway marked by two yellow bollards to Gateshead Metro station.

20. Blaydon Burn Circular

A superb walk through the varied countryside around the town of Blaydon offering views across the northern banks of the River Tyne and the city of Newcastle. The walk passes various industrial archaeology sites which provide another fascinating insight into the history of Tyneside.

Distance: 9½ miles, 15km

Maps: Landranger 88 Tyneside and Durham, Pathfinder 548 Blaydon and Prudhoe

Start and Finish: Blaydon Bus Station,

Access: There are regular buses to Blaydon from Newcastle Eldon Square bus Concourse, every 5-10 minutes Monday-Saturday, and every 20 minutes on Sunday (nos. 602, 604, 605, 606, 610). Car parking is available by Blaydon Library.

The Pub

The Black Horse at Barlow is perched on the hills overlooking the picturesque valley of Barlow Burn. It serves the full range of Jennings beers including the interesting "Sneck Lifter" premium ale, the excellent Cumberland Ale and Jennings stout, Dark Mild and Bitter. It also features a range of Guest Beers which often include Hook Norton's "Old Hooky", Ruddles County, Bellhaven's "Sandy Hunter Traditional". It has a lunch menu and a restaurant which serves mostly traditional dishes, but also includes provision for vegetarians.

The Walk

From Blaydon bus station cross the road and turn right to join a raised footpath around the traffic island. Follow the pavement along the A695 out of town. When the pavement ends, cross the road carefully and cross a small grassy area diagonally, heading down hill to go through a line of small trees. Turn left along a small ridge,

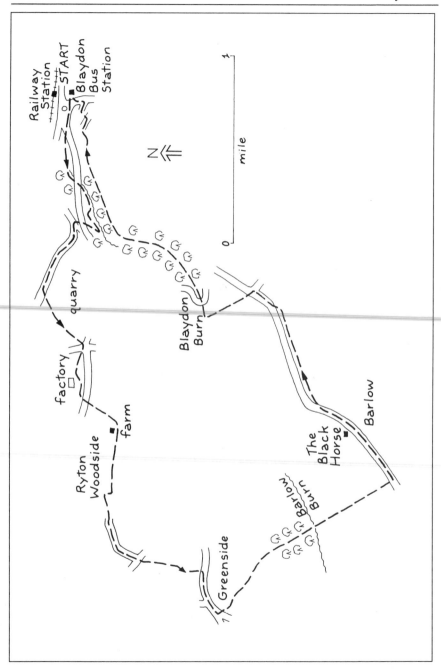

and follow the path right as it crosses a small stream. Turn left at a track and walk gently up hill. These earthworks and remains of buildings are all that remains of the water powered Blaydon foundry which was in operation until the 1890s using water stored in a large horseshoe-shaped dam.

As the track develops, it turns left, heads beneath a road bridge and enters a delightful wooded valley known as Blaydon Burn. This was once an important industrial area, especially in the early years of the 20th century, when it became involved in the coal and coke industry. Further along there are a set of coke ovens which were built along the waggonway which passed along the valley, and the remains of a coking platform. These are passed towards the end of the walk. These ovens were superseded by the more modern Priestman Ottovale Coke and Tar works, the first in the world to produce petrol from coal. This product was known as Blaydon Benzole and later National Benzole. These works closed in the 1970s.

When the track emerges at a rough road turn sharply right and head up to a main road. Just before a metal gate, take a small track leading through bushes to emerge at the side of the road. Cross carefully, and join a path which leads right to a road by a small terrace of houses.

At the end of the terrace, turn left down the Hexham Old Road past a deserted farm house. The road bends uphill and to the right. Ignore public footpath signs leading from the road to the right. Shortly after the small junction with Stella Lane, take steps to the left uphill, cross a small bridge and ascend, taking care to keep to the footpath as it is close to deep earthworks. The view back across the River Tyne includes an interesting cone shaped furnace, the Lemington Glass furnace which dates back to the 18th century (see walk 9 for further details).

The path rises and turns gently to the left. The allotments to the right are on the outskirts of Ryton and Stargate. As the path begins to descend into gorse bushes, it intercepts a path. Turn left along the new path, walking parallel to electricity cables, past the edge of the quarry and follow it as it bends right underneath the cables, before heading left and downwards, through a kissing gate, to the road.

Turn right and cross the road which enters Stargate and take the track between wooden fences directly opposite and go through a gate. Follow a small footpath ahead up to a wire fence and turn right alongside the fence around an industrial estate and through trees and bushes. The path heads through a small gap between the wire fence and a wooden fence before emerging at the front entrance of the industrial estate.

The right of way heads directly through the industrial estate. Take the main thoroughfare and follow it straight through ignoring the public footpath sign which heads off to the right. At the far end of the industrial estate, take a wooden stile into a small wood, which emerges at a wooden gate by a road.

Cross the road and use the wooden kissing gate directly ahead to enter a field. Follow the track which turns right and then left and heads up to Stephens Hall North Farm. Look out for the interesting fortifications on the farm's barn. Just after the farmhouse turn right next to a bungalow, following the public footpath sign to Folly Lane. Go through a gate into a field ahead. Cross the field and directly ahead take a small wooden stile on the right-hand side of a fence. Continue ahead keeping the fence to the left, ignoring a road to the left until the fence turns right and then left. Follow the line of the fence and head for houses at Ryton Woodside. At a wall follow around to the right and then left and head over a stone stile.

Go between houses on to a road, walk slightly to the left and ahead which begins to descend and curves to the right. At the foot of the hill turn left on to Gingler Lane which rises gently to a road. Cross the road and follow the public footpath sign opposite into fields, keeping the hedge to your right.

At the end of the field, cross into the next, this time keeping the hedge to the left and follow its line as it bends right and heads down hill. At the foot of the hill, turn left into a field keeping the wall to your right. Just after a row of cottages is a wooden stile to the right. Take this path, walking between gardens to emerge at the main road through the small town of Greenside. Turn right and follow the road. Cross Woodside Lane opposite the Community Centre which, built in 1925, used to be the Old Colliery Welfare Hall. Just before the junction where the road divides for Chopwell and Rowlands Gill, cross the road and pass by the left-hand side of the public toilets, to follow a track past a sports field.

Follow the public footpath sign to Barlow on the left over a stile, and follow a path between a hedge and gorse bushes. The path keeps to the left-hand side of the hedge, over a wooden stile and heads diagonally across a field to another stile. After this stile keep next to the hedge and head to the bottom right-hand corner of the field. Cross another stile and then immediately take another to the left, and then turn right, through a gate, into a lane between hedges following way markings. This heads downhill to a gate and a stile.

Cross the stile and head diagonally towards an electricity pylon. At a line of hawthorn bushes walk straight ahead following the hedge to a gate and stile. Cross the stile and turn right, keeping the hedge to your right-hand side. Ascend gently a take a path between the hedge and gorse bushes, which overlooks fields. Hidden in the corner of the field is another wooden stile and gate. Cross here and walk directly ahead keeping to the right of the fence. Ignore the wooden stile to the left and head into a small copse, walking by the fence on the left. Head downwards, cross a stile at the bottom of the hill and cross pretty Barlow Burn using a small footbridge.

From the footbridge, begin to ascend to the left taking a stepped footpath, which winds uphill through rambling gorse bushes. The path emerges at a stile into a field. Cross this and head straight ahead across the field to another stile and gate. Cross here into a lane and head up to a quiet road. Turn left and head downhill along Barlow Road, until you arrive at "The Black Horse".

From the Black Horse continue down the hill through Barlow alongside the road. Just after the last house on the right, follow the public footpath sign into a field, signed 'Winlaton and Knobby Ends' and follow the path by the wall over a number of fields and stiles. At the end of the third field, exit by a white gate to the left, turn right and walk along to a footpath sign on the left.

Take this stile and walk down hill next to the wall. At a line of hawthorn bushes take another stile into an adjoining field and

Barlow Burn – winter scene

descend, keeping the wall to the right. At the bottom corner of the field the path heads down a track behind a corrugated iron enclosure, and turns right on to a rough lane before emerging at a road by Blaydon Burn House.

Cross the road into a wood and follow the path. At a fork turn left and join a more substantial track. Keep to the track as it winds through the woods, passing the remains of the coking ovens. Follow the track as it ascends to the right out of the woods and walk above Blaydon Burn from where there are superb views across the Tyne valley.

At an electricity sub-station continue straight on, keeping the sub-station to the right, on to common land. Go through a gap in the hedge and take the path across the next field.

Go through a second hedge of Hawthorn and take the left fork immediately which heads down hill. The path goes past garages before emerging on to Delacour Road. At the end of Delacour Road, turn left down hill and using the church tower as a guide, head back to the Bus Station.

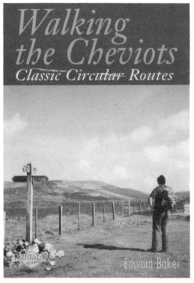

WALKING THE CHEVIOTS: Classic Circular Routes

This book provides an excellent introduction to this solitary, wild countryside. Everyone is catered for – from weekend family walkers to the experienced hill walker with all the walks personally checked and trod by the author. Each route contains details of the natural history, geology and archaeology of the area descriptively written by Edward Baker who has lived his whole life in the region. For ease of reference, the book is in two sections, covering the northern and southern Cheviots - distinct areas with their own unique character. In all, there are almost 50 walks - by far the most comprehensive collection published for the Cheviots. *£7.95*

Here are some selected titles from our 'Pub Walks' series: all written by experienced authors with personal knowledge of the best walks and, of course, the best pubs: ones that welcome walkers and serve real ale!

BEST PUB WALKS IN NORTHUMBRIA

Stephen Rickerby   £6.95

BEST PUB WALKS IN THE YORKSHIRE DALES

Clive Price   £6.95

PUB WALKS IN THE YORKSHIRE WOLDS

Tony Whittaker   £6.95

PUB WALKS ON THE NORTH YORK MOORS AND COAST

Stephen Rickerby   £6.95

BEST PUB WALKS IN & AROUND SHEFFIELD

Clive Price   £6.95

BEST PUB WALKS IN & AROUND LEEDS

Colin Speakman   £6.95

All of our books are available from your local bookshop. In case of difficulty, or to obtain our complete catalogue, please contact:

Sigma Leisure, 1 South Oak Lane, Wilmslow, Cheshire SK9 6AR
Phone: 01625 – 531035
Fax: 01625 – 536800
E-mail: sigma.press@zetnet.co.uk

ACCESS and VISA orders welcome – call our friendly sales staff or use our 24 hour Answerphone service! Most orders are despatched on the day we receive your order – you could be enjoying our books in just a couple of days. Please add £2 p&p to all orders.